THE FLETCHER JONES FOUNDATION
HUMANITIES IMPRINT

The Fletcher Jones Foundation has endowed this imprint to foster innovative and enduring scholarship in the humanities.

The publisher gratefully acknowledges the generous support of the Fletcher Jones Foundation Humanities Endowment Fund of the University of California Press Foundation.

CINEMA'S MILITARY
INDUSTRIAL COMPLEX

CINEMA'S MILITARY INDUSTRIAL COMPLEX

Edited by

Haidee Wasson and
Lee Grieveson

UNIVERSITY OF CALIFORNIA PRESS

University of California Press, one of the most distinguished university presses in the United States, enriches lives around the world by advancing scholarship in the humanities, social sciences, and natural sciences. Its activities are supported by the UC Press Foundation and by philanthropic contributions from individuals and institutions. For more information, visit www.ucpress.edu.

University of California Press
Oakland, California

Library of Congress Cataloging-in-Publication Data

Names: Wasson, Haidee, 1970– editor. | Grieveson, Lee, 1969– editor.
Title: Cinema's military industrial complex / edited by Haidee Wasson and Lee Grieveson.
Description: Oakland, California : University of California Press, [2018] | Includes bibliographical references and index. |
Identifiers: LCCN 2017036815 (print) | LCCN 2017041870 (ebook) | ISBN 9780520965263 (Ebook) | ISBN 9780520291508 (cloth : alk. paper) | ISBN 9780520291515 (pbk. : alk. paper)
Subjects: LCSH: Motion picture industry—Military aspects—United States. | War films—United States—History and criticism. | Military cinematography—United States.
Classification: LCC PN1993.5.U6 (ebook) | LCC PN1993.5.U6 C5285 2018 (print) | DDC 384.80973—dc23
LC record available at https://lccn.loc.gov/2017036815

Manufactured in the United States of America

26 25 24 23 22 21 20 19 18
10 9 8 7 6 5 4 3 2 1

For Ava, Cooper, Lauren, Riley, and Stella

CONTENTS

ILLUSTRATIONS

ACKNOWLEDGMENTS

Our thanks, first, go to Mary Francis at the University of California Press for her initial support for this book and, second, to Raina Polivka for continuing that support and confidently ushering the book into production. Both Mary and Raina solicited smart reports that have greatly improved this book, and we thank the three anonymous readers and in particular Gregory Waller, who provided characteristically precise, tireless, and thoughtful comments on the entire manuscript. Zuha Khan has been a helpful and efficient editorial assistant at the press. *Considerable* thanks are due also to our own editorial assistants, Kaia Scott and especially Matthew Ogonoski, who have played a crucial role in keeping the editing and production process going and in getting this book finished. Philipp Dominik Keidl helped in the early stages, and Natalie Greenberg helped at the very late stages as well. Their assistance was made possible by a grant from the Social Sciences and Humanities Research Council (Canada), Le Fond pour la Formation de Chercheurs et l'Aide à la Recherche (Quebec) and Concordia University, Montreal.

Our contributors have stuck with us through the long process of conceiving, planning, researching, writing, and rewriting this book. We owe all of them a debt of gratitude. The strength of the book is a consequence of their work and gracious acceptance of numerous editorial interventions. In addition, Charles Acland has been, as always, an indispensable sounding board and source of sage advice as we have navigated through the complexities of these issues and pulled this book together. He is a model of professionalism and scholarly integrity.

Lee Grieveson would like to thank also Lora Brill for her unstinting support, help, and for the myriad acts of daily generosity that have made it possible for him to work intensively on this book; and for the ideals that make it necessary. Plus comrades and fellow travelers Peter Krämer, Kay Dickinson, Mark Betz, Tom Rice, Colin MacCabe, Francis Gooding, Stephanie Bird, Jon Lewis, Priya Jaikumar, and Noah Angell. Big thanks to all of them for being smart, challenging, interesting, and fun to be around. Cooper, Lauren, and Riley (as well as Lora) supply the sustaining fun and love outside of work that makes work possible. Thanks are due also to the students at UCL who have heard parts of this research rehearsed in class—particularly in my class Political Media—and have contributed to its development. Parts of this have been rehearsed elsewhere, too, perhaps most notably at The Political Screen conference organized by Shakuntala Banaji and myself as a coproduction of LSE and UCL under the aegis of the Screen Studies group at the University of London. But most of all thanks are due to Haidee for being—as always—brilliant, funny, hardworking, and committed to the highest standards of scholarship. I signed up to the hard work of coediting this book because I believed in the project that we developed together; but equally—simply—because of the chance to work again with Haidee.

As all sustained scholarly projects, this book has complex interconnections to other ongoing research activities that don't necessarily manifest here. That said, this book has been shaped by many conversations with scholars and archivists who helped to make its frequently daunting premise worthwhile and also manageable. Haidee would like to especially thank Dino Everett, Michael Cowan, Jonathan Kahana, Alice Lovejoy, Barbara Miller, Dana Polan, Greg Waller, and Chuck Wolfe for supportive and stimulating conversations. My Concordia colleagues are a continuing source of inspiration. Thanks especially to Luca Caminati, Kay Dickinson, Martin Lefebvre, Josh Neves, Elena Razlagova, Katie Russell, Masha Salazkina, Marc Steinberg, Jeremy Stolow, Darren Wershler, and Peter van Wyck for their daily provocations and commitment to making the university a better and more ethical place to work. Carrie Rentschler and Jonathan Sterne remain exemplars of intellectual energy and engagement. Special thanks go to Jen Holt for her end-of-project, supernatural can-do consultation sessions. Brian Real helped to speedily navigate the US National Archives and Records Administration in Maryland. This project has also benefitted from presenting parts of its overall rationale at several venues, including the Chicago Film Seminar, Northwestern University, Harvard University, the University of Southern California, the University of California Santa Barbara, the University of California Berkeley, and, closer to home, Concordia University, McGill University, and the University of Toronto. On a more personal note, thanks to Charles, Stella, and Ava for providing "designs for living" that make everything, all of it, better. Lastly, thanks to Lee for copiloting. I can hardly wait for our next project.

THE MILITARY'S CINEMA COMPLEX

Lee Grieveson and Haidee Wasson

The American military is a singularly powerful institution. Born with the nation itself, in revolutionary war, the military transformed into a professionalized and technologically advanced force in the latter years of the nineteenth century in conjunction with US imperial expansion and the complex global conflict of 1898.[1] The growth of the US military mirrored the rise of the United States to a position of global centrality, and hegemony, that began first with the late-nineteenth-century wars of imperialism but was more fully realized in World War II and its aftermath. In 1947 the National Security Act (alongside a series of amendments in 1949) created the US Air Force, the Department of Defense, the secretary of defense, the Joint Chiefs of Staff, the National Security Council (NSC), and the Central Intelligence Agency (CIA), reorganizing and strengthening military and intelligence organizations and activities that existed before.[2] By this legislation the basic structure of the contemporary military was established—splitting the air force from the army, maintaining a large navy and advanced marine force—and affirming its civilian governance in the new Department of Defense. From this point onward, the American military became a distinctly powerful *global* institution, significantly larger in terms of personnel, budget, reach, destructive capabilities, and "preponderant power" than any other military in the world.[3]

Cinema's Military Industrial Complex thus explores the ways in which this uniquely powerful globe-spanning institution began to use "cinema" as industry, technology, media practice, form, and space to service its needs and further its varied interests. Collectively these essays ask: What are the ways in which cinema has been useful to the military? How did this usefulness develop and transform across history? What institutions emerged within and in close relation to the

armed forces to make, circulate, and exhibit military films? What kinds of technologies were developed? What are the distinct forms of knowledge that have been
fostered by military film use? What cinema cultures took shape among the enlisted
during or after service? How have the differences between a military at war and at
relative peace affected these dynamics? What role have the state and other cognate
institutions played in bolstering relations between the military and cinema? How
has the world's largest and most powerful film industry—"Hollywood"—been
implicated in these dynamics? The answers that emerge across the essays in this
volume are, as they must be, empirical, detailed, and precise. But this precision is
in service of a fuller reckoning with both how and why one of the most significant
and powerful institutions in the world began to use cinema to further its goals.

One example here at the outset can illustrate some of the often surprising, widespread, and varied uses. Consider it a form of orientation. In 1954, in the aftermath
of the 1947 National Security Act, the US military commissioned the Motion Picture Association of America (MPAA), the official and most powerful American
film trade and corporate lobbying organization, to examine the film and photography operations of its various branches.[4] The study sought to identify efficiencies in
current activities across the military and—among other things—to explore the
advisability of fuller, deeper collaborations between the military and Hollywood.
The report detailed a remarkable range of film activity—none of it guided by the
profit-generating, commercial logics of Hollywood. Yet production, distribution,
and exhibition systems were vast and highly developed, with, for instance, over one
thousand film libraries housing tens of thousands of film prints. Hollywood and
other American industries supplied some of these films, but many more were made
by a kind of tributary system constituted by hundreds of internal military production units. Orientation, training, and morale films—a small few of which were
made by known Hollywood directors—constituted an estimated 15 percent of military film use. Some 75 percent of film and photography use was "strictly of a strategic nature."[5] In other words, the majority of films were devoted to applied military
functions, including ordnance testing, aerial and underwater reconnaissance and
mapping, operating manuals, tactical support to combat missions, immersive gunnery training, battle-front briefs, research and development, munitions testing, and
data recording and analysis. Vectors of film use were frequently directed inward to
military personnel and intraorganizational needs. Cinema performed predictable
tasks such as entertaining war-weary soldiers, as well as helping to build efficient
bureaucratic systems where films served as office memos, as operational updates,
and as content for a partly automated educational and training playback system.
But this production system also maintained strong vectors outward, with footage
regularly supplied to commercial and noncommercial film circuits, as well as to the
television industry. For instance, military-made footage, and sometimes complete
films, were widely available, servicing often overlapping goals to entertain, educate,

and promulgate the virtues of the military and its activities. Public relations and propaganda were intertwined. By midcentury, then, Americans could frequently and regularly see such moving images and hear their sounds on televisions in their living rooms and on film screens in movie theaters, classrooms, libraries, veterans' organizations, factory floors, boardrooms, and countless other private and public forums. Military films were a common element of American media ecosystems. Such films also became integral to international campaigns to ensure the "American way," efforts that grew especially after World War II.

Cinema's Military Industrial Complex contributes to the growing interest in thinking about cinema less as an art or as commercial entertainment and more as a *deployment* of particular technologies, forms, practices, and spaces that have coalesced as "cinema" to forward particular social, economic, and political objectives. This approach to film has recently been dubbed "useful cinema."[6] Building on this term, this book explores what cinema's utility might mean within the context of a specific but also vast and uniquely powerful institution. Our authors build on recent work devoted to assessing the role of film as adaptable technological assemblage, used across entertainment, industrial, scientific, educational, and governmental entities to influence the movement of resources, the instrumentalization of new forms of knowledge, and the promulgation of preferred behaviors.[7] It is our hope that detailed historical work on how this military used cinema to further what the most recent US Department of Defense budget simply calls "our interests" can connect to—build alliances with, if you will—significant scholarly work on other media and other militaries.[8] Ultimately, we hope to contribute to the increasingly urgent necessity of understanding the place of media in facilitating and sustaining the asymmetries of power, resources, and interests that structure the modern world.

· · ·

What were those American military and state interests? What are the structures, policies, and practices they have enabled? The sketch here cannot be definitive, of course, but it can offer a broad context from which to read the essays that follow. The US military grew markedly in the late nineteenth century, with the imperial agenda to fashion new global trade routes and sustain strategic interests, with particular emphasis on parts of Latin America, Asia, and the Pacific.[9] The spurt of US territorial imperialism that started with the Spanish-American War and included the annexation of Guam, Hawaii, and the Philippines was fueled also by the interests of the large corporations emerging in this period that sought access to materials, labor, and markets.[10] Global expansion, driven by a fusion of state and economic interests, required that military innovations paralleled or directly drew from industrial practices and procedures. The technological and organizational might of this new military was quickly subject to the gaze of another of the powerful technologies of the second-stage industrial revolution: moving-picture cameras. Documentary film footage, particularly of the technology of gunships, was widely circulated in 1898–99 as a visible and mobile signifier of imperial state strength and was significant to the burgeoning popularity of film in the United States.[11] Cinema, we might say, functioned as an earlier form of "shock and awe," symbolic of the technological modernity most brutally manifested in the mechanization of warfare that enabled the imperial expansion integral to globalization. Both cinema and the military grew rapidly thereafter.

Naval, army, marine, and security forces were subsequently further deployed in Latin American nations in the early twentieth century to protect the property rights of US corporations, securing materials central to industrial development. Military actions in Colombia (1903, 1919), Nicaragua (1909), and Mexico (1914–17), among others, demonstrate the fusion of state and economic interests that have undergirded US foreign policy, and that have driven the expansion and deployment of the military. Broadly speaking, one can discern *logics* here—of state and capital—that have been enacted in specific, contingent circumstances and that frame an imperialism that begins with territorial expansion but mutates quite quickly in the early twentieth century mostly into new forms of "economic imperialism."[12] These new practices began to be called by critics "dollar imperialism" in the 1920s, when the US state worked in conjunction with private banks and transnational corporations to exercise significant control over crucial resources.[13] Oil was (and is) particularly significant. Dollar imperialism became the default position of state/capital interests thereafter, backed up frequently with military force and "regime change" when necessary for economic and/or strategic interests.[14]

Despite its role in numerous actions in the first third of the twentieth century, the military experienced only spasmodic growth in the period before World War II. Its expansion was constrained both by the long-standing republican distrust of the potential of standing armies to serve authoritarian governance and by the isolationism (indeed, at times pacifism) that followed participation in the European imperial war of 1914–18. Yet, the rearmament required for World War II, beginning in the late 1930s, effectively ended the Great Depression and made clear the economic utility of an expanded military and advanced technological arms industries to the political economy of the nation.[15] New regimes of accumulation were henceforth closely tied to militarism. The massive expansion of the military in the early Cold War—mutating into both arms and space races—was a primary engine in economic growth during the postwar years up until at least the early 1970s. Cold War exigencies and an expanding ideology of national security motivated the massive growth and global deployment of standing military and security forces. American national security was inextricably bound to shoring up the borders of the "free world" and facilitating the economic circulation and expansion integral to the capitalist system.[16] By the mid-1940s, safeguarding that circulatory system became the cornerstone of American foreign policy.[17] New international financial and security agencies, like the International Monetary Fund and elements of the United Nations, both established in 1945, were important to this. So was the State Department's 1948 Marshall Plan to rebuild capitalist Europe and Japan. Military alliances like those enshrined in the 1949 North Atlantic Treaty Organization furthered the proliferation of US military bases in Europe, the Middle East, and Asia in particular. These treaties and organizations sanctioned a range of interventions that fostered regimes favorable to American strategic and economic interests. The clear role of military force employed to secure resources essential to a booming US economy is plainly illustrated by the case of Iran. In 1954, during the early Cold War, British and US military and security forces allied to overthrow a democratically elected leader threatening to nationalize oil resources. The unelected replacement was favorable to the combined interests of the British and US state and their oil producers; less so to the interests of the Iranian population.[18]

Our list of similar interventions in the Middle East and Latin America could be a lot longer.[19] But here it is enough to observe that American entry into the war in 1941 initiated rapid expansion of the military and related arms industries, spurring industrial and economic growth, all of which continued well beyond that particular conflict. Deep military entanglements with research institutions—including initiatives undertaken at universities and large corporations—also took hold during this same period. Research and development in chemistry, physics, and aerospace, among other areas, served military exigencies, making all manner of things lighter, stronger, faster, more effective—and destructive—on a mass scale.[20] The alliance among the military, research, and innovation shaped new technologies across the twentieth and now twenty-first centuries, including a number of media technologies. For example, even before these sizable realignments, radio developed with significant military and state investment in the 1910s.[21] The technological complex that eventually formed the basis of the Internet grew from here as well several decades later.[22] Both radio and the Internet developed in part from logistical needs central to the military's globe-spanning operations, some of which were banal and bureaucratic and some others more conventionally strategic.[23] Cinema, it turns out, shares some of this history.

By the early 1940s, then, new and consequential relationships began to be established among the so-called iron triangle of state, military, and advanced industry, which significantly shaped policy and the continued expansion and deployment of the military.[24] In his prescient televised 1961 farewell address to the nation, President Dwight D. Eisenhower sharply denounced the logics of this complex:

> The conjunction of an immense military establishment and a large arms industry is new in the American experience. . . . The total influence—economic, political, even spiritual—is felt in every city, every statehouse, every office of the federal government. . . . In the councils of government, we must guard against the acquisition of unwarranted influence, whether sought or unsought, by the military-industrial complex. The potential for the disastrous rise of misplaced power exists and will persist.[25]

Eisenhower had been a five-star general, and leader of the US forces in Europe during World War II, before serving as president. By the time he left office he had become deeply frustrated by his inability to control the Cold War military buildup, and his speech carefully described how the mutual interests among the military and its industrial suppliers had distorted the political process and further entrenched the symbiotic growth of the military and related industrial sectors.[26]

At our point, some fifty-five or so years later, we can simply state that the reality of the "disastrous rise of misplaced power" clearly exists. Conflicts in Vietnam, Iraq, Afghanistan, and oil-rich Iraq again, among others, have clearly been driven (as many have observed) by a fusion of political and economic interests.[27] The recent expanded global "War on Terror" has furthered the close ties among state, military, and high-tech industry, and has motivated "exceptional" military practices, including torture and extrajudicial killing, that have had devastating consequences on many people and populations. In the process the United States became the only state to have explicitly authorized contravention of the Geneva Conventions governing the practice of warfare.[28] New techniques of battle, such as drones and cyberwar, have also grown alongside these new forms of exceptional state and military power.[29] Quite clearly the long arc of military growth, from the wars of imperialism of the late nineteenth century to the current "era of permanent war," has significantly shaped both US domestic and foreign policies and the current world order.[30] Media technologies have played a role throughout.

. . .

What roles has cinema, specifically, played in this expanding, mutating military? What did the American military want from cinema? Building on patient archival and critical methods, this book addresses the military's cinema across a history that stretches principally from World War I to the ongoing counterinsurgency campaigns in Iraq. Contributors explore the military's direct development and sponsorship of new forms of cinema technology; its use of cinema to recruit, train, entertain, comfort, and heal soldiers; its direct deployment of cinema to test new technologies and techniques of warfare; the viewing of films to learn about the enemy, about foreign cultures, and more generally about military activities. Our authors also examine the use of film to foster civilian support for military engagement and for related state policies domestically and internationally. This book includes histories threaded through particular conflicts (in Europe, but extending also to Korea, Vietnam, and Iraq), and also histories situated within broader geopolitical objectives and tensions (notably the Cold War and the War on Terror). Our authors also explore the ways in which the military was ambitiously experimental with film use, calling for not only technological innovation but also new methods of film viewing and analysis. Chapters demonstrate the ways in which cinema was a mode of work, a set of skills, and a creative outlet for the thousands who labored to make, circulate, and show films while enlisted. Plus, as the existence of the MPAA's 1954 report for the military makes clear, the military sustained regular and occasionally deep ties to the commercial American film industry, using its technical expertise, infrastructures, and talent to help achieve military goals. Essays here chart and consider those links, many of them previously unexamined.

Together these essays show us that the military embraced cinema as an iterative apparatus with multiple capacities and functions, some of which were intraorganizational and some of which extended beyond immediate military function. Propaganda was significant to this, as other scholars have rightly emphasized.[31] Similarly, elements of the military and the CIA have worked hard to shape commercial cinema, too, by establishing "liaison officers" and exchanging military technology—like ships and airplanes—after vetting Hollywood scripts to ensure they favorably represent the military and its endeavors.[32] Our book seeks to add to and expand this significant work on propaganda and the interfaces of hard and soft power by focusing on the military's direct use of cinema and its technologies. Doing so necessitates expanding our conception of "film" beyond the terrain of specific propaganda institutions or the commercial and mostly fictional forms that have been central to much previous work on cinema and the military. This book does not focus on Hollywood films and their representations of the military, its personnel, or key events in military history. Rather, chapters address the military's use and transformation of cinematic technologies, forms, and practices, some of which have shaped commercial cinema. Take, for example, the development of wide movie screens in the 1950s, commonly regarded as Hollywood's response to television. The immediate predecessor to Cinerama and its subsequent widescreen imitators was in fact a device developed during World War II under military direction to mimic aerial battle to train plane gunners. Nuances of narrative, character psychology, editing, mise-en-scène, and cinematography were largely incidental to the capacity of projectors and screens to yield images of rapid airplane movement across a wide field of vision.

The military's cinema was elastic, stretched at particular instances to exploit one among many of its qualities, addressing tasks and servicing distinct institutional needs. Consider another example: celluloid's capacity to record moving objects at high film speed, allowing the rendering of images that would be otherwise unobservable by the human eye alone. Celluloid provided significant visual detail of ordnance explosions and machines in operation, which made tracking, testing, and measuring change possible in new ways. Doing so transformed moving images into analyzable data, serving as tools of nuclear physicists, aerospace engineers, and chemists alike.[33] In still other circumstances it was the mechanical reproducibility of film and its mobility that was significant to the military. The capacity to circulate these films from place to place, predicated on a new international infrastructure for portable film projectors, enabled a global network of select content, targeted at particular audiences in specific settings. The repeatability and adaptability of projecting prerecorded, standardized, and carefully designed films was thought to enable efficiencies in recruitment, orientation, education, and reeducation, as well as in getting soldiers back to work. The languages of cinema and the distinct aesthetic conventions that evolved in films made and shown by the military became rhetorically complex and highly specific in pedagogic, psychiatric, and propagandistic forms, but much differently so in the realms of data analysis, flight simulation, and munitions testing. Although broadly deployed, and seen regularly by millions, the military's cinema was rarely designed simply as a mass medium, but rather as a highly strategic one, encompassing specific groups of varying sizes and of many disciplines and skills, with clear institutional procedures and desired outcomes. Exploring this history challenges many of our received categories for understanding cinema's institutions.

Quite clearly the military was a creative force when it came to the development and use of film. New technologies, forms, and practices emerged. The innovation of more-sensitive film stock, powerful lenses, and flashes, for example, facilitated aerial surveillance and munitions testing. More-rugged portable projectors ensured reliable film performance in all climates and theaters of operation. The military was also an innovator of nonfiction films, crafting raw footage into standardized operational updates, tactical reports, and procedure manuals as well as regularly repurposing footage in recombinatory processes from one public-information film to another educational short. The military also used film to make extensive records of its activities, developing detailed labeling and categorization systems and modes of storage and retrieval. New viewing scenarios were forged, including impromptu cinemas, immersive galleries, console viewers, frame-by-frame lab analysis, and multimedia war rooms. The dynamics of spectatorship were distinct from commercial entertainment. Enlisted soldiers were frequently instructed on how to watch, with particular rules and procedures in place to help ensure a sanctioned range of responses. But we also know that soldiers were often rowdy and frequently rejected the authority of the screen when it was permitted, and it was.[34] Spectatorship itself must be understood here as frequently though not always highly codified, with many screenings required, compelled, or occurring under duress. Many watched in pursuit of a pressing goal or performance of a task, including the strategic function of planned recreation: effective leisure helped make better soldiers. Last, disciplines that exist beyond the parameters of the military proper each had a role in shaping its cinema, including among them anthropology, psychiatry, psychology, education, mass communications, industrial efficiency, information design, governance and statecraft, economics, physics, and chemistry. The technologically advanced and global military force was enthusiastically interdisciplinary. Our contributors attend to these varied innovations, practices, and interdisciplinary entanglements in the essays that follow.

Our imperative in this book has been to combine multiple vectors of analysis in order to keep both the specific uses of cinema and the broad logics and dynamics of the role and function of the military in play together. By doing this we hope to contribute to work by media scholars on the military's use of other media forms and technologies, like the aforementioned example of radio and the Internet, but also to such scholars' work on photography, magnetic tape, television, satellites, GPS, and drones.[35] Writing on cinema and the military has so far tended to eschew the detailed material analysis visible in work on other media. Broadly speaking, there have been two primary dynamics at play in film scholarship. On the one hand, the brief and sketchy remarks by Paul Virilio on the violence of cinema's representational abstractions and by Friedrich Kittler on the connections between military and media machines have too often stood as shorthand for the seeming violence inherent in cinema. Such approaches frequently obscure the complex historical relations that have long operated at multiple scales, and that require patient and detailed explication.[36] On the other hand, there is a body of scholarship on Hollywood's fiction films, particularly those representing war, and on documentary films made by famous directors during wartime.[37] Both of these latter tendencies are consistent with a discipline—film studies—that has historically focused on these two categories (fiction and documentary) to the exclusion of other forms of nontheatrical, nonfictional, and useful cinema. Recent work has started to expand this remit, including some scholarship on various militaries and their institutionalization of cinema.[38] Building on such efforts, our contributors tend to the many ways in which the American military made, showed, watched, and used films, sometimes in collaboration with state and civilian organizations, industries, and individuals. Rather than focusing on one particular conflict or one particular aspect of military cinema, this book surveys a range of topics across the twentieth century, providing additional, original, and comparative points of entry into this complex history. The result is an overview of the long, deep, and persistent investment by the American military in cinema broadly defined.

· · ·

To facilitate this overview, the essays in this book are gathered into four sections that explore crucial dynamics in the military's deployment of cinema. Each of these sections is organized chronologically. Our first section examines film technologies and viewing infrastructures; the second is devoted to film watching and analysis; the third addresses, directly, military filmmaking; and the fourth gathers chapters that assess agencies, organizations, and institutions whose activities were supportive of and inextricably linked to the military. Various methodologies are deployed throughout the book to explicate different dynamics and historical developments. Some chapters start with close, detailed historical analysis and expand to include reflection on the specific praxis that operated to make cinema such a significant military asset. Others examine the broader logics in which the military's cinema operated and that helped to sustain the hegemony of the United States and the global order of the twentieth and twenty-first centuries.

Our first section, "The Military's Cinema Apparatus," gathers essays that primarily address cinema's technological and exhibitionary apparatus, from small and nimble projection machines to massive, architectural screens. Essays in this section explore a full range of ways in which military films were shown and seen, and consider the broader impact of the innovations mapped. Haidee Wasson and Andrea Kelley focus on small screens and portable devices, while Rebecca Prime and Ross Melnick examine large-screen and theatrical infrastructures. Together they provide a portrait of a diversified viewing system, each with particular links to different elements of the film industry. Wasson charts a range of military experiments with film projection. She shows that the military aggressively called for innovations in film equipment that favored portability, ease of use, adaptability, and ruggedness. These qualities were crucial for cameras but equally so for projectors. The film industry answered the military's call. Her essay also addresses highly specialized devices designed to expand the human sensorium, and also to record and display information, placing the film projector into histories of data processing and nonlinear storage and retrieval. Under military direction, film projection was frequently disarticulated from theatrical architecture and rearticulated to a number of institutional imperatives that happened in meeting rooms and laboratories, on battlefronts, and in offices. Wasson contends that some of these experiments proved paradigmatic: the ideals of easy, reliable, rugged film projectors became a practical reality after the war, with such machines far outnumbering movie theaters from the 1950s onward.

One of these now largely forgotten devices was a form of console cinema, housed in furniture units and working through a system of rear projection. Before World War II these were known as Panorams, and they resembled domestic radios and early televisions in their design. Andrea Kelley traces the multiple uses for this so-called daylight cinema on airfields and in recreation rooms, officers' quarters, hospitals, and government offices. As a popular amusement, the Panoram developed first to feature music more than movies, and was akin to the coin-operated jukebox and the vending machine. But its history illustrates the ways in which small cinema consoles were quickly enlisted to serve a diverse set of purposes during World War II, putting popular quotidian entertainments in dialogue with military utility. Both Wasson and Kelley demonstrate the ways in which expanded film technologies had deep links to the consumer-electronics industry, and both help further our understanding of the intermediality of the military's cinema, with plain connections to sound technologies (microphones, amplification devices), automatic self-operated machines, and popular music, among others. The smallness of the screens was also crucial, as were small audiences and short films. Equally important was the normalization of a playback device for moving images and sounds that could function independently of purpose-built spaces, enabling an expanded utility and increased use across the military institution and beyond.

In stark contrast to small, adaptable, and self-operated film projection stands the monumental and high-tech Cinerama, commonly associated with the film industry's efforts to differentiate itself from the emergence of television with its small screens in the 1950s. This ultra-wide-screen format, which used three 35mm projectors and a curved 146-degree screen, led the way at midcentury in novel theatrical technologies and ultimately ushered in the enduring reshaping of the film screen toward not just a larger size but a different shape, emphasizing a more horizontal plane. Rebecca Prime shows us that the military played an integral role in the development, making, and circulation of this technology and its films. Prime also examines the figure of Merian C. Cooper, who was both a key player in Cinerama's commercialization and a producer and director of its debut film, *This Is Cinerama!* (1952). Cooper maintained and exploited a network of long-held military contacts while developing and promoting Cinerama. Prime maps these links and also examines the recurring and extensive use of aerial photography in key Cinerama titles, documenting the use of air force and navy equipment to secure its "thrilling" and "immersive" footage. In doing so her essay provides a compelling portrait of the military ideologies and material supports inseparable from Cinerama's mass spectacle and big-screen technological might. Connecting to the chapters in the final section of this book, Prime also charts the screening of select Cinerama films by the State Department as it deployed American culture internationally as part of its Cold War strategy. By midcentury, mass technological and patriotic spectacle was inextricably and concretely linked to the American military.

The military explored the small and the big of film technologies, yet it also fully embraced one of the mainstays of Hollywood's industrial model: the movie theater. Ross Melnick surveys the army's theater circuit, showing that movie theaters were for the better part of the twentieth century considered integral to army operations, understood as crucial for maintaining the morale and welfare of the enlisted. During World War II, domestically, the army circuit was second in size only to Paramount's theater chain. Some army bases held as many as eleven theaters onsite. Three decades later, the US Army operated the largest theater chain in the world, with 1,328 theaters in sixty countries—more than double the size of the largest domestic chain. Army theaters were also multiuse venues, with a complex sociality, which included the injustices of segregation. Concurrent to Wasson and Kelley's documenting of the drive towards portability and adaptability, Melnick shows that movie theaters remained an enduring element of the American military's infrastructure, alongside the growth of other media forms, and well after civilian movie theaters began to decline. The military pursued all manner of screen size, accommodating models of film performance that were diminutive and utilitarian as well as grand and excessive.

Building on these insights, the authors in our next section, "Strategies of Viewing," zero in on military efforts, and undertakings by related ancillary organizations, to institutionalize and regularize film watching. Our focus here shifts from technology and its transformation toward evolving forms of knowledge and disciplinary practice that shaped the meaning of the encounter with projected moving images and sounds. Tom Rice discusses the role of veterans' organizations and the ways in which they promoted and programmed commercial films in the 1910s and 1920s as but one element of the broader cultural project to fuse militaristic, patriotic, and nationalistic sentiments. Cinema has long played an indirect role in ideas of national belonging and national difference, as countless scholars have observed. But here paramilitary institutions like the American Legion took an activist role in orchestrating particularly conservative forms of ethnic nationalism, largely through film programming. Rice analyzes how particular institutions utilized cinema and media for goals that were simultaneously local—for example, to form group identity—and assimilated to the broader dynamics of racist nationalism that have so frequently accompanied war. The formerly enlisted members of the American Legion understood themselves to be continuing their service long after official actions had ended.

Kaia Scott shifts our focus to active-duty rather than retired soldiers by examining the relatively new area of military psychiatry, which during World War II began to experiment with film in order to understand and heal the damaged minds of frontline personnel. Scott analyzes these experiments, some fleeting and some enduring, wherein military psychiatrists developed new forms of treatment for wounded and traumatized soldiers, as much to heal them as to get them back to work. In therapeutic settings, films were shown to individuals and integrated into ongoing and related treatment practices, while others were shown to groups in the spirit of efficiency. Repetition was a foundational principle; films were shown over and over, used alongside therapists and often aided by psychopharmaceuticals to expedite healing. The rapidly expanding profession of psychiatry, embraced by the American military during World War II and thereafter, also made use of film to expand its own disciplinary apparatus. Scott examines the role of media in transforming therapeutic, professional, and public-relations practices that affected millions of enlisted soldiers and ultimately helped shape a boom in postwar civilian psychiatric practices.

Turning from the soldier's psychiatry to national psychology, Nathaniel Brennan examines ways in which the military struggled to understand the enemy. During World War II, military personnel and others working for the war effort began to use seized German nonfiction films, reasoning that such films might yield valuable information. This included simple procedures such as identifying the physical properties of enemy aircraft. Yet, German entertainment films were thought to aid in analyzing and assessing inimical national psychologies as well. Focusing on anthropologist Gregory Bateson, Brennan examines the construction of cinema as a form of cultural intelligence. Bateson and his team worked with civilian organizations, laboring under the premise that commercial cinema was emblematic of culture's standardization, a medium by and for the industrial masses. As such, films could be useful tools for identifying frameworks that reflected aggregate behaviors and "national character." Individual foreign films, then, were studied but also recontextualized, used to teach soldiers efficiently about cultural difference. Elements of the military expressed interest and supported Bateson's efforts. The specifics of this project were ultimately short-lived, but migrated to other educational fields, including indeed film studies and the emerging field of communication studies.

Vinzenz Hediger takes a different approach to the procedures of analysis, beginning with one particular film screening in the Pentagon in the fall of 2003 when military and political personnel watched and discussed the classic *Battle of Algiers* (Gillo Pontecorvo, 1966). What did the world's most powerful military want from a film that dramatized anticolonial resistance in the late 1950s and the brutal French response to it? Building on a long history of the film's use as a tool of warfare in theaters of operation across the globe, Hediger uses *Battle* as a way to diagnose more-fundamental aspects of American military strategy in the wake of the chaotic aftermath to the invasion of Iraq in 2003. By doing so Hediger shows that the nuanced lessons of Pontecorvo's film were no match for ascendant practices within the military—namely, the determined and sanctioned use of torture in contravention of international law. Hediger examines a canonical political film and its repurposing, and considers how the military's strategies of viewing can help us to understand the evolution of tactics and strategies by the Department of Defense and the State Department in the ongoing "War on Terror."

Distinct from these practices of viewing, the military also made movies. Indeed, it made a lot of movies. The authors in our third section, "Military-Made Movies," address different approaches to filmmaking as it operated at specific historical moments, within distinct elements of the larger military institution, and as it was articulated to specific audiences and purposes. Florian Hoof and Noah Tsika each discuss training films, among other things. Hoof examines an early link between industrial efficiency efforts and military ones through the figure of Frank B. Gilbreth, best known in film and media history for his efforts, along with those of Lillian Gilbreth, to merge cinema with the new industrial science of time-motion study. Hoof situates Frank Gilbreth within a particular moment in military history—one in which mechanization, automation, and machine efficiencies were forging new links between industrial innovation and military might. The brutal results of this during World War I are well known. Gilbreth considered military needs as contiguous with those of his industrial clients; both sought to improve human–machine interfaces. This essay documents Gilbreth's efforts to sell film as a modern training tool, and his brief working relationship with the US military.

Gilbreth was an outsider to the military but worked his way in, seeking contracts with both the German and US military. By contrast, Tsika looks at filmmaking as it was enacted at a later and more developed phase—from World War II onward—when making and also circulating films was a highly regularized component internal to the military. Building on the institutional imperative to train and to communicate effectively with a rapidly expanding number of enlisted men, Tsika maps the unique mode of film production that developed within the army during World War II and into the television era. He shows that military nonfiction films were highly dynamic forms, frequently assembled from a range of recorded materials secured across numerous contexts, and then frequently reassembled again and again. In other words, military films, including training films, can be understood as an assemblage of highly flexible materials, remade continually with an eye to actively circulating military material widely across the military, and through civilian film and television circuits as well. Tsika addresses the institutional imperatives that produced these texts, which often blurred the divisions between training, education, and public relations. In doing so, his essay inserts a voluminous body of nonfiction filmmaking into the history of documentary cinema.

Military filmmaking took place within dedicated units that existed across the distinct arms of the military, and took different forms within its vast operations. Camera crews might have existed within particular units, or might have been embedded by a more centralized office into a local unit, resulting in mismatched mandates. Some units were relatively autonomous, while others were highly specialized and worked under strict orders. Reflecting these variations, three very different kinds of filmmaking receive the focus of the remaining essays in this section. Susan Courtney examines the specialized processes developed to record and ultimately test atomic bombs. Essentially a film studio that was also a military base, Lookout Mountain Air Force Station (located in Laurel Canyon, near Los Angeles) served as the primary location for making top-secret atomic-test films. The facility was staffed by both military and civilian personnel recruited from nearby film studios. The base housed a remarkable production apparatus. Reportedly as many as six hundred cameras might be used to document a single detonation, of which there were hundreds. The resulting footage allowed for precise analysis of single frames or sequences of frames, yielding data about otherwise immeasurable phenomena like cloud expansion and particle fall. Test films were also frequently made widely available to commercial, civilian filmmakers and distribution outlets for public release, to inform but also to demonstrate and declare the military's ominous power. Because of these military films, images of atomic explosions became ordinary—a prominent element of American media vernacular, constituting a crucial element of the Cold War's mass culture. Courtney addresses what had become highly visible within the visual culture of "the bomb," thereby examining the role of test films in promulgating and naturalizing American military power.

Sueyoung Park-Primiano focuses on military filmmaking during the American occupation of South Korea in the aftermath of World War II. She examines principally the interregnum between the end of that conflict and the official start of the Korean War in 1950, assessing American efforts to use film as part of its occupation efforts. Examining the ubiquitous informational and educational films, she explores the ways in which these films were used to promote the "American system of life." Educational films made and circulated by the military included reports on its activities, as well as films that illustrated modern medical techniques, strategies for improving public health, and lessons in how to use technologies like telephones and automobiles. Approved films, including Hollywood titles, were shown free of charge in movie theaters and traveling educational units that used trains to reach and propagandize rural areas. Park-Primiano provides a careful view into a set of ideological practices wherein commercial and military films worked together to persuade a population as to the virtues of ostensibly benevolent "modernization." Many kinds of films were instruments in these early days of the Cold War, used as part of a complex geopolitical apparatus to secure the American position in Asia.

Efforts to secure that position led in time to the debacle in Vietnam, after the United States had first attempted to prop up the crumbling French empire in Indo-China. The military used cinema in various ways to sustain these efforts. James Paasche focuses on one example of that, exploring the development and operations of the Department of the Army Special Photographic Office (DASPO) and its activities across the Vietnam conflict in the 1960s and 1970s. DASPO was less a propaganda, training, or public-relations effort and more an internal film unit tasked with documenting the work *of* the army *for* the army, as well as creating footage for a stock library, to be used for undefined and unknown purposes in the future. Film was primarily understood to service the production of a voluminous and disinterested record of army activity and the everyday life of its soldiers. Paasche explores the work of DASPO members and the particular dynamics of intraorganizational image making that they worked under. He also examines what happened to the voluminous footage afterward, most of it never seen by the units that created it, or possibly by anyone else. Documenting a unique mode of work, Paasche raises compelling questions about the tension between creative autonomy, the military's institutional bureaucracy, and its questionable military objectives.

Last, DASPO grew directly from intramilitary conflicts (in this case, between the army and the air force), reminding us again that the military was and is a complex bureaucracy with sometimes differing agendas among constituents.

Together our contributors in this section demonstrate that filmmaking came to be seen as important to military operations, playing a small role beginning notably around World War I, expanding considerably through World War II, and continuing through the Cold War and the proxy wars in Korea and Vietnam. The military developed unique modes of production that focused heavily on editing, reassembly, and other elements of what is usually termed postproduction, balancing the · usual emphasis on preshoot scriptwriting or strong directorial oversight. Chains of command that shaped a final film product were frequently impersonal and hierarchical. While many military films were scripted and made with a high degree of deliberation, many others grew from vast stores of unscripted footage that was regularly repurposed according to changing institutional and political needs. Filmmaking was also attenuated to particular audiences within an expanding global arena. These essays help us to understand better precisely what modes of production were forged by this *institution,* and the larger contexts and constraints in which that filmmaking took place. The military's cinema demonstrates a complex geography operating often in contexts of frequently profound asymmetry.

The final section of the book pursues some of the state logics that have definitively shaped military actions and agendas. "The Military and Its Collaborators" includes essays brought together by their mutual focus on institutions and practices that exist in close, sometimes indistinguishable, and often constitutive relation to the military and its activities. Some authors focus on civilian organizations such as the Committee on Public Information (CPI), and others discuss organizations based in the film industry such as the War Activities Committee. Still others examine organizations and strategies that evolved out of war and the military into state praxis. Lee Grieveson's essay frames this section by charting the ways in which exceptional state practices during wartime led to new methods of producing, managing, and controlling communication and media that endured beyond particular conflicts. Focusing on the years during and just after World War I, Grieveson charts the formation and rise of the CPI, whose mandate was to shape public opinion about the European conflict and to communicate strategic state goals. Grieveson explores the ties forged between state and media institutions to produce new forms of persuasion (journalism, public speeches, film) and the political and economic logics that underpinned these developments. Propaganda and the making of media content paired with new forms of exceptional regulation and constraint upon dissident opinion. Grieveson argues that these new practices of media production and regulation, although instituted during wartime, had close ties with broader political and economic logics and expanded thereafter, particularly during the long Cold War and the ongoing "War on Terror."

Beginning also with the CPI, Sue Collins examines the emergence of the use of Hollywood stars during wartime that began first in World War I but grew afterward, notably during World War II. Collins documents the governmental use of media and the figurations (i.e., stars) that it was spawning. In doing so she reframes Hollywood stars as military consorts, pondering the logics that enabled this. Both Collins and Grieveson discuss the deep historical interconnections among war, the military, and American media industries, providing a piece of the wider context in which cinema and its related techniques and capacities were mobilized to support military engagement.

Moving from largely domestic organizations and operations of state, Alice Lovejoy and Katerina Loukopoulou in their essays consider those who worked beyond American borders. Loukopoulou specifically examines the films circulated in conjunction with the Marshall Plan (1948–52). She focuses on Greece, the only European country where the US military intervened after World War II as part of the American containment foreign policy to prevent Western European countries from falling under USSR influence. The Marshall Plan was a sizable and complex set of policies that, along with extensive diplomatic efforts, provided American capital, goods, and services to devastated countries. Loukopoulou provides a nuanced examination of the ways in which American-sponsored films were a regularized element of a steady and broad social, economic, and geopolitical project to rebuild Europe in ways friendly to, and dependent upon, American resources. Marshall Plan films worked alongside military action, crucial in Greece in the aftermath of a civil war that the US military had helped to end. Complementing this, Lovejoy focuses on the parallel but distinct circulation of mostly Hollywood-made films immediately after the war to select European nations. Lovejoy pays special attention to Czechoslovakia, on the borders of "the free world." Here the corporate American film industry also looms large, as it readily participated with and indeed requested assistance from military and transitional organizations in the postwar environment to aid in reestablishing its strategic position in European markets. Corporate and state goals intertwined.

· · ·

Looking at the military as a powerful institution of cinema requires us to think about a global production, distribution, and exhibition infrastructure—one whose effectiveness was built on aggressive expansion, technological innovation, and geopolitical might; one that by most measures and at certain points far exceeded the powers and positioning of Hollywood. The military created a vast production and distribution infrastructure, at midcentury likely the most expansive in the world, spanning the globe and indicating a considerable elasticity in its ability to adapt and serve. Technologies of cinema were widely institutionalized; new techniques for making films as well as watching them were innovated. Considerable traffic in talent and expertise across the film industry and military can be discerned. New and close ties between state, military, and media were established, with consequential effects for all of those components and indeed for the world more broadly. Equally important is that our authors frequently show that film's history is closely intertwined with that of other media forms. The role of radio, music, print, and television appears across many of the essays in this volume. This is a history, we contend, that matters to those concerned with understanding cinema broadly and as fully imbricated in the mediated social, cultural, and political present.

Cinema's Military Industrial Complex can, of course, be read differently, and more clearly, as a history. Readers who prefer chronological pathways might start with Grieveson, Rice, Hoof, and then Collins, who all address World War I; Wasson, Kelley, Brennan, Tsika, and Scott document activities during World War II; Prime, Courtney, Park-Primiano, Lovejoy, and Loukopoulou all address the postwar and Cold War periods; Paasche and Hediger deal with Vietnam and the more recent War on Terror; Melnick's essay spans all of these conflicts. Following essays chronologically demonstrates the plain yet gradual institutionalization of film during World War I into practices of training, recruitment, and money raising (war bonds), as well as discourses of ethnic nationalism and security. Focusing on World War II maps the diversification and spread of film use into an increasing range of operations and on an unprecedented scale. And, at midcentury, our authors chart the ongoing normalization of filmmaking and also especially notable efforts to circulate films nationally and internationally through expanded film and television circuits. The continuities here register longstanding practices by states and other political organizations well beyond American borders to direct the powers of cinema toward desired sociopolitical ends. Our book contributes to the necessity to explicate those practices. Regardless of how you choose to navigate this book, together these essays make a rich and telling contribution to our understanding of the American military's cinema complex, mapping developments of significant consequence and of enduring influence.

Our book started with the statement that the American military is a singularly powerful institution. And it is. But we must also recognize that the military is a heterogeneous, internally divided, bureaucratic institution that changed quite dramatically across history. Likewise, some of the chapters in this book document experiments with film or practices of cinema that were brief, or relatively insignificant to a thesis of immanent military expansion, even as they migrated to other cultural and institutional venues. We do not contend that the histories here chart a univocal or simple set of phenomena. Chapters operate at different scales, with distinct methodologies and unique bodies of evidence. Some of our authors use previously classified materials, and others use widely available newspapers or industry publications. Together our authors and their range of resources have begun to document and discuss key aspects of the relationship between the American military and cinema, beginning from the early twentieth century and stretching into the early twenty-first. Inevitably, there are gaps. The broad sweep of this at times requires scampering over details. Our hope is that the book will be useful for future work exploring the histories of the militarized use of cinema and media both in the United States and beyond.

NOTES

1. The professionalization of the military forces in the United States is outlined in Paul A. C. Koistinen, *Mobilizing for Modern War: The Political Economy of American Warfare, 1865–1919* (Lawrence: University Press of Kansas, 1997). See also Robert P. Saldin, *War, the American State, and Politics since 1898* (Cambridge: Cambridge University Press, 2011), 12–13, 32–33. The political and economic logics of the Spanish-American War, and conflicts in the Philippines, China, and East Asia in 1898, are explicated in Thomas Schoonover, *Uncle Sam's War of 1898 and the Origins of Globalization* (Lexington: University Press of Kentucky, 2013). Writes Schoonover: "The conflux of rapid technological change, an aggressive and expansive US political economy, and resistant traditional states in Spain and China ended in conflict. . . . The War of 1898 and its aftermath transferred the leadership (unwillingly on the part of Spain, most of Europe, and Japan) in [the] quest for wealth in Asia and the Pacific to the United States" (2).

2. Melvyn P. Leffler, *A Preponderance of Power: National Security, the Truman Administration, and the Cold War* (Stanford, CA: Stanford University Press, 1992), 141–81; Adrian R. Lewis, *The American Culture of War: The History of US Military Force from World II to Operation Iraqi Freedom* (London: Routledge, 2007), esp. 169–200.

3. The establishment of a network of global military bases began first in the 1930s but expanded in particular in the postwar period, from the mid-1940s. See Kent E. Calder, *Embattled Garrisons: Comparative Base Politics and American Globalism* (Princeton, NJ: Princeton University Press, 2007), esp. 4–35. For an account of the comparative size of the US military, see, for example, Paul A. C. Koistinen, *State of War: The Political Economy of American Warfare, 1945–2011* (Lawrence: University Press of Kansas, 2012). The United States currently spends more on its military than the next eight largest militaries combined.

4. Motion Picture Association of America, "Report of the Film Survey Committee," July 5, 1954, Binger Collection, American Museum of the Moving Image.

5. Ibid., 5.

6. Charles Acland and Haidee Wasson, eds., *Useful Cinema* (Durham, NC: Duke University Press, 2011).

7. See, for example, Vinzenz Hediger and Patrick Vonderau, eds., *Films That Work: Industrial Film and the Productivity of Media* (Amsterdam: Amsterdam University Press, 2009); Lee Grieveson and Colin MacCabe, eds., *Empire and Film* (London: Palgrave Macmillan, 2011); Lee Grieveson and Colin MacCabe, eds., *Film and the End of Empire* (London: Palgrave Macmillan, 2011); Devin Orgeron, Marsha Orgeron, and Dan Streible, eds., *Learning with the Lights Off: Educational Film in the United States* (Oxford: Oxford University Press, 2012); Oliver Gaycken, *Devices of Curiosity: Early Cinema and Popular Science* (Oxford: Oxford University Press, 2015); and Scott Curtis, *The Shape of Spectatorship: Art, Science, and Early Cinema in Germany* (New York: Columbia University Press, 2015).

8. "Department of Defense (DoD) Releases Fiscal Year 2017 President's Budget Proposal," release no. NR-046–16, February 9, 2016, accessed August 22, 2016, www.defense.gov/News/News-Releases/News-Release-View/Article/652687/department-of-defense-dod-releases-fiscal-year-2017-

presidents-budget-proposal. The US military's budget exceeds the total government expenditure in countries such as Spain, Australia, the Netherlands, Mexico, Sweden, and India, among many others.

9. Thomas J. McCormick, *China Market: America's Quest for Informal Empire, 1893–1901* (Chicago: Quadrangle Books, 1967); Walter LeFeber, *The American Search for Opportunity, 1865–1913*, vol. 2 of *The Cambridge History of American Foreign Relations* (Cambridge: Cambridge University Press, 1993); Schoonover, *Uncle Sam's War of 1898*.

10. Emily S. Rosenberg, *Spreading the American Dream: American Economic and Cultural Expansion, 1890–1945* (New York: Hill and Wang, 1982). The history of key aspects of this imperialism, beginning with intervention in Cuba partly to defend sugar interests, but expanding to include the annexation of Hawaii, Puerto Rico, Guam, and the Philippines, is voluminous. See, for example, Philip S. Foner, *The Spanish-Cuban-American War and the Birth of American Imperialism, 1895–1902*, 2 vols. (New York: Monthly Review Press, 1972); Paul A. Kramer, *The Blood of Government: Race, Empire, the United States, and the Philippines* (Chapel Hill: University of North Carolina Press, 2006); Thomas D. Schoonover, *The United States in Central America, 1860–1911: Episodes of Social Imperialism and Imperial Rivalry in the World System* (Durham, NC: Duke University Press, 1991); and David J. Silbey, *A War of Frontier and Empire: The Philippine-American War, 1898–1902* (New York: Hill and Wang, 2008).

11. Charles Musser, *The Emergence of Cinema: The American Screen to 1907* (New York: Scribner's, 1990), 225–62; Kristen Whissel, *Picturing American Modernity: Traffic, Technology, and the Silent Cinema* (Durham, NC: Duke University Press, 2008), esp. 58–60, 216–19.

12. David Harvey draws a useful distinction between a "territorial logic of power" pursued by state actors "whose power is based on command of a territory" and the "capitalist logics of power," which "flows across and through continuous space, toward or away from territorial entities." David Harvey, *The New Imperialism* (Oxford: Oxford University Press, 2003), 26–27.

13. Scott Nearing and Joseph Freeman, *Dollar Diplomacy: A Study in American Imperialism* (New York: Allen and Unwin, 1925); Emily Rosenberg, *Financial Missionaries to the World: The Politics and Culture of Dollar Diplomacy, 1900–1930* (Cambridge, MA: Harvard University Press, 1999); Cyrus Veeser, *A World Safe for Capitalism: Dollar Diplomacy and America's Rise to Global Power* (New York: Columbia University Press, 2002).

14. The broad sweep of US foreign policy and imperialism in the second half of the twentieth century is brilliantly explicated in Perry Anderson, "Imperium," *New Left Review* 81 (May–June 2013): 5–111. See also Harvey, *New Imperialism*.

15. Giovanni Arrighi, *The Long Twentieth Century: Money, Power, and the Origins of Our Times* (London: Verso, 1994), 274–76.

16. Odd Arne Westad, *The Global Cold War: Third World Interventions and the Making of Our Times* (New York: Cambridge University Press, 2005); Deborah Cowen, *The Deadly Life of Logistics: Mapping Violence in Global Trade* (Minneapolis: University of Minnesota Press, 2014).

17. Anderson, "Imperium," 11–67.

18. Stephen Kinzer, *All the Shah's Men: An American Coup and the Roots of Middle East Terror* (Hoboken, NJ: John Wiley, 2008). The story is told in the first ninety seconds of the commercial film *Argo* (Warner Bros., 2012), before the story shifts to the heroic derring-do of the CIA in rescuing hostages taken after the unelected shah of Iran was deposed in 1979.

19. John Coatsworth, for example, estimates that the United States played a role in the overthrow of twenty-four governments in Latin America during the Cold War alone. John Coatsworth, "The Cold War in Central America, 1975–1991," in *Cambridge History of the Cold War*, vol. 3, ed. Melvyn P. Leffler and Odd Arne Westad (Cambridge: Cambridge University Press, 2012), 220–21. See also William Blum, *Killing Hope: US Military and CIA Interventions since WWII* (New York: Zed Books, 2003); and Tim Weiner, *Legacy of Ashes: The History of the CIA* (London: Penguin, 2008).

20. See, for example, David Hounshell, "The Evolution of Industrial Research in the United States," in *Engines of Innovation: U.S. Industrial Research at the End of an Era*, ed. Richard S. Rosenbloom and

William J. Spencer (Boston: Harvard Business School Press, 1996), 13–85; John Kenly Smith Jr., "World War II and the Transformation of the American Chemical Industry," in *Science, Technology and the Military*, ed. Everett Mendelsohn, Merritt Roe Smith, and Peter Weingart (Dordrecht, Netherlands: Kulwer Academic Publishers, 1988), 307–22; Henry Etzkowitz, "The Making of an Entrepreneurial University: The Traffic among MIT, Industry and the Military, 1860–1960," in Mendelsohn, Smith, and Weingart, *Science, Technology and the Military*, 515–40; and Stuart W. Leslie, *The Cold War and American Science: The Military-Industrial-Academic Complex at MIT and Stanford* (New York: Columbia University Press, 1994).

21. Daniel R. Headrick, *The Invisible Weapon: Telecommunications and International Politics, 1851–1945* (New York: Oxford University Press, 1991), esp. 139–48; Rosenberg, *Spreading the American Dream*, 87–107; Susan J. Douglas, *Inventing American Broadcasting, 1899–1922* (Baltimore: John Hopkins University Press, 1987), esp. 102–43.

22. Parts of that history are told in Manuel Castells, *The Rise of Network Society*, 2nd ed. (Oxford: Blackwell, 2000), esp. 40–47.

23. Cowen, *Deadly Life of Logistics*.

24. Michael Hogan, *A Cross of Iron: Harry S. Truman and the Origins of the National Security State, 1945–1954* (Cambridge: Cambridge University Press, 1998).

25. Cited in James Kurth, "Military-Industrial Complex," in *The Oxford Companion to American Military History*, ed. John Whiteclay Chambers II (Oxford: Oxford University Press, 1999), 440–42.

26. James Ledbetter, *Unwarranted Influence: Dwight D. Eisenhower and the Military-Industrial Complex* (New Haven, CT: Yale University Press, 2011). Rebecca Thorpe has shown clearly how developments in the 1940s, expanding in the Cold War, created a number of congressional districts that were economically dependent on the military-industrial complex. By doing this the process effectively entrenched the interests of that complex in the political system. Rebecca Thorpe, *The American Warfare State: The Domestic Politics of Military Spending* (Chicago: University of Chicago Press, 2014).

27. See, again, Harvey, *New Imperialism*; Anderson, "Imperium"; and, for example, Michael Mann, *Incoherent Empire* (London: Verso, 2005).

28. The scholarship on the post-9/11 period is, rightly, voluminous, but for an extraordinarily detailed and precise account of the legal expansion of exceptional practices delegating sovereign power to the president, see Jane Mayer, *The Dark Side: The Inside Story of How the War on Terror Turned into a War on American Ideals* (New York: Anchor Books, 2009).

29. Giorgio Agamben, *State of Exception*, trans. Kevin Attell (Chicago: University of Chicago Press, 2005). The development of drone warfare is explored in Medea Benjamin, *Drone Warfare: Killing by Remote Control* (New York: OR Books, 2012). For one compelling account of the deployment of cyber-warfare, see the documentary *Zero Days* (Alex Gibney, 2016) on the "stuxnet" computer virus developed by the United States in conjunction with Israel and recently deployed in Iran in an attempt to destroy its nuclear program.

30. Gary Gerstle, "A State Both Strong and Weak," *American Historical Review* 115, no. 3 (June 2010): 781.

31. E.g., J. Michael Sproule, *Propaganda and Democracy: The American Experience of Media and Mass Persuasion* (Cambridge: Cambridge University Press, 1997); Gary S. Messinger, *The Battle for the Mind: War and Peace in the Era of Mass Communication* (Amherst: University of Massachusetts Press, 2011); David Culbert, ed., *Film and Propaganda: A Documentary History*, vols. 1–4 (Westport, CT: Greenwood Press, 1990); and Laura Belmonte, *Selling the American Way: US Propaganda and the Cold War* (Philadelphia: University of Pennsylvania Press, 2008).

32. Tricia Jenkins, "How the Central intelligence Agency Works with Hollywood: An Interview with Paul Barry, the CIA's New Entertainment Industry Liaison," *Media, Culture, and Society* 31, no. 3 (2009): 489–95; Tricia Jenkins, *The CIA in Hollywood: How the Agency Shapes Film and Television* (Austin: University of Texas Press, 2012); David L. Robb, *Operation Hollywood: How the Pentagon*

Shapes and Censors the Movies (New York: Prometheus Books, 2004); Matthew Alford, "The Political Impact of the Department of Defense on Hollywood Cinema," *Quarterly Review of Film and Video* 33, no. 4 (2016): 332–47.

33. For more on the development of high-speed film and photography, see Ned O'Gorman and Kevin Hamilton, "EG&G and the Deep Media of Timing, Firing, and Exposing," *Journal of War and Culture Studies* 9, no. 2 (May 2016): 182–201. See also James Elkins, "Harold Edgerton's Rapatronic Photographs of Atomic Tests," *History of Photography* 28, no. 1 (Spring 2004): 74–81.

34. For a look at film viewing in the military, see William Friedman Fagelson, "Fighting Films: The Everyday Tactics of World War II Soldiers," *Cinema Journal* 40, no. 3 (Spring 2001): 94–112.

35. Including, for example, Gerd Horten, *Radio Goes to War: The Cultural Politics of Propaganda during World War II* (Berkeley: University of California Press, 2003); James Schwoch, *Global TV: New Media and the Cold War, 1946–69* (Chicago: University of Illinois Press, 2009); James Der Derian, *Virtuous War: Mapping the Military-Industrial-Media-Entertainment Network* (Boulder, CO: Westview Press, 2001); Des Freedman and Daya Kishan Thussu, *Media and Terrorism: Global Perspectives* (London: Sage, 2012); Toby Miller, "The Media-Military Industrial Complex," in *The Global Industrial Complex: Systems of Domination,* ed. Steven Best, Richard Kahn, Anthony J. Nocella II, and Peter McLaren (Lanham, MD: Lexington Books, 2011), 97–116; and Caren Kaplan, "Precision Targets: GPS and the Militarization of US Consumer Identity," *American Quarterly* 58, no. 3 (2006): 693–713.

36. Paul Virilio, *War and Cinema: The Logistics of Perception* (London and New York: Verso, 1989); Friedrich A. Kittler, *Gramophone, Film, Typewriter,* trans. Geoffrey Winthrop-Young and Michael Wutz (Stanford, CA: Stanford University Press, 1999).

37. For a representative sample, see Jeanine Basinger, *The World War II Combat Film: Anatomy of a Genre* (Middletown, CT: Wesleyan University Press, 2003); Thomas Doherty, *Projections of War: Hollywood, American Culture, and World War II,* rev. ed. (New York: Columbia University Press, 1999); Clayton R. Koppes and Gregory D. Black, *Hollywood Goes to War: How Politics, Profits and Propaganda Shaped World War II Movies* (Berkeley: University of California Press, 1990); Peter C. Rollins, "Frank Capra's *Why We Fight* Film Series and Our American Dream," *Journal of American Culture* 19, no. 4 (1996): 81–86; and Gregory D. Black and Clayton R. Koppes, "OWI Goes to the Movies: The Bureau of Intelligence's Criticism of Hollywood, 1942–43," *Prologue* 6, no. 1 (1974): 44–59. More recently, see Douglas A. Cunningham and John C Nelson, eds., *A Companion to the War Film* (Chichester, UK: John Wiley & Sons, 2016).

38. Recent works that expressly focus on intramilitary filmmaking and film activities both in the United States and in other national contexts include Alice Lovejoy, *Army Film and the Avant Garde: Cinema and Experimental Film in the Czechoslovak Military* (Bloomington: Indiana University Press, 2015); Peter Lester, "'Four Cents to Sea': 16mm, the Royal Canadian Naval Film Society and the Mobilization of Entertainment," *Film History* 25, no. 4 (2013): 62–81; Douglas Cunningham, "Imaging/Imagining Air Force Identity: 'Hap' Arnold, Warner Bros., and the Formation of the USAAF First Motion Picture Unit," *Moving Image* 5, no. 1 (Spring 2005): 95–124; and Kevin Hamilton and Ned O'Gorman, "Filming a Nuclear State: The USAF's Lookout Mountain Laboratory," in *A Companion to the War Film,* ed. Douglas A. Cunningham and John C. Nelson (Chichester, UK: John Wiley & Sons, 2016), 129–49. Recent dissertations also lend significant depth to our understanding of military filmmaking; see, for example, Douglas Cunningham, "Imagining Air Force Identity: Masculinity, Aeriality, and the Films of the US Army Air Forces First Motion Picture Unit" (PhD diss., University of California, Berkeley, 2009); and Noah Tsika, "The Soldier's Circle: The Social Documentary and the American Military, 1940–1945" (PhD diss., New York University, 2012).

PART ONE

THE MILITARY'S CINEMA APPARATUS

2

EXPERIMENTAL VIEWING PROTOCOLS

Film Projection and the American Military

Haidee Wasson

During World War II the American military integrated and normalized filmmaking, film projection, and film viewing into its operations. Driven by the imperatives of war, new cinema technologies developed and were used across the military throughout the 1940s and beyond. The devices associated with these technologies, along with the viewing scenarios they engendered, addressed the needs of a rapidly and dramatically expanded military. Film technologies helped to recruit, orient, train, and entertain soldiers. Yet, they also served a considerable range of other institutional needs, including intraorganizational communication, tactical analysis, and research and development. With regard specifically to film performance and viewing, many of the new scenarios bore little resemblance to the beloved movie theater upon which Hollywood had built its fortunes. It is true that the army had an elaborate chain of movie theaters, and also held regular film shows for enlisted men. Nevertheless, it also boldly dissembled cinema's settled routines and structures, rearticulating film projection as but one integral element of a growing institution with highly complex needs.

These new ideas about and practices of film viewing did not develop as a rebuke to Hollywood. Rather, they evolved in full cooperation with it. In particular, companies that provided the technological infrastructure for the American studios—cameras, film stock, lighting, lenses, projectors—played a key role. This included entities such as Eastman Kodak, Bell and Howell, and Radio Corporation of America (RCA). It also included the Society for Motion Picture Engineers (SMPE, now called SMPTE), the official professional organization for the film industry's technical wing, which gathered electrical and sound engineers, chemists, physicists, and theatrical technicians, as well as celluloid and equipment manufacturers, among others. Together SMPE members worked to establish technological standards and to address evolving needs, maintaining stability and catalyzing innovation across all segments of the film industry. During the war, they did the same for the military, authoring design protocols for film equipment based on industry expertise addressed to emerging military demands. These same companies then made and sold their products to the military, helping to ensure not just the place of cinema as a tool of military operations, but also that their own interests would thrive during the war and beyond.

This chapter surveys a range of military experiments with film projection during and after World War II. "Projection" here is understood broadly to mean the performance and display of images—and sometimes sounds—recorded on and delivered by celluloid, normally shown on a screen. The use of the term "projection" is not confined to familiar ideas about a "film show" or "film exhibition." These terms predominantly refer to a particular ideal of cinema, developed most powerfully to support the performance of professional films in a dedicated, highly commercial and controlled space, usually known as a movie theater. Rather, this chapter explores the many ways in which the American military eagerly expanded what it meant to show and to watch films. These experiments involved a range of screen sizes and viewing configurations, and were integral to the making and use of a surprising assortment of films serving diverse purposes. This expansion of film technology, form, and function was in part facilitated by the regular military practice of tethering film projectors to a range of other media devices not conventionally considered cinematic: microphones, consoles, electromagnetic interfaces, data machines, and multimedia war rooms. The military's cinema was highly elastic, disavowing any interest in medium purity or specificity; its parts were eagerly disassembled and reassembled into new and often provisional wholes. As such, the term "cinema" here, then, is not used to designate a group of film texts but more to delineate a mode of institutionalized visualization and viewing, one that entailed a family of technologies, spaces, discourses, and practices.

This chapter charts military experiments with, and institutional practices of, film projection, contextualizing these within the broader uses of cinema by the military during World War II. The military's relations with the American film industry and its adjacent industries provide a telling backdrop. This chapter concludes by discussing some of the implications of the military's expanded viewing apparatus for thinking about what cinema has been, and how it has operated, historically. In other words, in looking at the military's cinema, one finds rather quickly that received ideas about a coherent and unchanging cinema apparatus provide little help in mapping the ways in which film and its technologies were imagined and instrumentalized. What follows demonstrates that the American military's cinema can help us to understand the broader relations among film and other media, as well as the ways in which such technologies and their aesthetic forms have been shaped by notably powerful military and industrial entities.[1]

To begin, some broader contextual information is helpful. There are several prominent and well-documented fronts on which the film industry (Hollywood) worked to support the American war effort during World War II. In the years before the American entry into the war, the studios were regularly making military training films.[2] Upon America's entry into the conflict, these relations expanded. For instance, Hollywood's War Activities Committee (WAC) undertook an active relationship with the Office of War Information (OWI), technically a civilian or government and not a military agency. The OWI's Bureau of Motion Pictures (BMP) worked to exert influence over the content of Hollywood films during the war. The BMP also secured the assistance of the WAC, distributing government-made war films to the extensive circuit of commercial movie theaters throughout the United States. In addition, during this period, "war movies" became a prominent production cycle, with war-related themes appearing regularly in other genres as well. Enlisted Hollywood talent included marquee directors, key among them Frank Capra, who made the iconic film series *Why We Fight,* shown to the millions of military personnel who had been put into service. In addition, stars helped to raise money for the war effort, and also entertained soldiers. Studios supplied film prints reduced to the substandard 16mm size, which circulated to the military's overseas units, providing recreation and morale boosting to soldiers. In return, various elements within the armed services supplied footage and support to film production by providing access to military bases and equipment.[3]

Beyond this sketch of the important established relations between Hollywood and the American military, there is much more to tell about the many ways in which this newly global and rapidly expanded industrial-bureaucratic organization made use not just of Hollywood but of cinema more broadly. For now, let me turn to focus on a specific subset of this larger story: film technology. During the 1940s, the tools of photography and filmmaking were widely militarized. Cameras became integrated into military planes, articulated to weapons mounts, and outright shaped like guns. Film and photography equipment was finished in army green or navy blue. Projectors, like movie cameras, became standard operating equipment, encouraging a series of innovations that included materials that were lighter in weight, more durable, and resistant to environmental factors (hot, cold, wet, dry) that caused corrosion, mold, or inoperable parts. New protective cases helped to preserve this equipment as it was transported across all manner of terrain. Simplified control knobs and inner mechanisms helped to expedite operation and repairs.[4] Camera and projector innovations also responded to the needs generated by rapidly expanding aerospace and munitions fields—growth areas that demanded specialized recording and display equipment. During the 1930s, film recording and analysis had become but one among many tools of an ascendant industrial research and development culture. This led to faster shutter speeds, powerful electronic flashes, more-sensitive film emulsions, and more-powerful lenses—all of which ushered in military and industrial applications of high-speed photography to machine analysis, ordnance testing, aerial surveillance and reconnaissance, and flight-instrumentation assessment, to name but a few. During the war, a growing fleet of cameras also recorded footage used for intraorganizational communication, which included new film genres such as "field reports," which might illustrate troop movement, document conditions in POW camps, or provide battle updates: movies served as sometimes gruesome and sometimes banal illustrated operations updates and intraoffice communiqués. Film technologies also entered into the design of new information environments, comprising film projection, three-dimensional terrain models, epidiascopes (opaque projectors), and other devices aimed at new modes of visualizing data and generating strategic analysis in multiple dimensions using multimedia displays.[5] Celluloid and projectors also served as elements within new conceptualizations of information storage, retrieval, and analysis. Vannevar Bush's much-heralded "memex," essential to what became the computer, included film projections that served as flexible data interfaces.[6] Film's distinct and multiple technical capacities—to record, store, access, project, display, and be moved from place to place—made moving images and their projection useful to the military in various ways. This includes the use of film technologies in the development of other technologies—a phenomenon that continued to grow throughout the postwar period with strong military support.

Many of these aspects of cinema's utility to (and transformation by) the military were regularly reported to key segments of the film industry. Film technology and other matters related to military film use appeared regularly in the pages of the *Journal of the Society for Motion Picture Engineers* before, during, and after the war.[7] Membership of the SMPE included engineers (electrical and chemical), designers, and manufacturers representing all of Hollywood's technical branches, many of which were also part of larger businesses with significant holdings and interests beyond Hollywood's immediate purview. This includes, for instance, the chemical industry and the electrical conglomerates, themselves often with significant military contracts. During the war, SMPE meetings regularly included participants active in the military. Captains, lieutenants, majors, and corporals alike gave presentations on military activities.[8] Crucially, a joint military-SMPE committee formed, along with members of the American Standards Association, to advise on and establish technical standards for military film equipment across relevant arms of service. Members of the signal corps, the army, and the navy participated. First reporting in 1944, this committee focused in particular on 16mm systems—a smaller gauge than the industry-sanctioned 35mm, and increasingly used by the military (especially for overseas use) for its portability, reduced cost, and lighter weight.[9] War had accelerated and amplified the relationship between the military and the technical constituents of the broader film industry. This active collaboration and consultation continued on during the 1950s. A 1954 report, commissioned by the military but conducted by members of the film industry, confirmed that the military had plainly institutionalized the broad use of photography and film technologies, used variously, to support "practically every activity of the Armed Forces."[10] The relationships were by this point secure and deep.

Further affirming the sheer volume of film activity during the war, the military built a major studio and postproduction facility in Queens, New York, operational from 1942 until 1970. Richard Koszarski has declared this studio the single busiest motion-picture production center in the world during the war, with forty-five editing rooms and twenty-four screening rooms.[11] In addition, the American military built a dispersed and expansive film production system, with all major bases housing smaller and more-basic filmmaking facilities.[12] Beyond the tactical and research-based uses named above, these films in their broadest sense served many purposes. In addition to providing entertainment, soldier morale, and public information, the films recruited, documented, charted and mapped, propagated, trained, taught, prepared, healed, recruited, reported, ministered spiritual aid, fund-raised, distracted, and served themselves as a mode of work. Indeed, thousands of soldiers contributed to image production during the war and after. Given this wide use of film and the many genres and subgenres these uses spawned, many questions remain. But the question I would like to focus on here is, How did all of these films get seen? Or, more precisely, How were they shown?

During World War II the military innovated an unprecedented global viewing platform composed mostly though not exclusively of 16mm projectors. This platform initially grew in tandem with but quickly exceeded the sizable chain of purpose-built military theaters, which operated domestically using 35mm equipment. Like cameras, projectors were institutionalized as elements of standard operating procedure, making soldiers into film spectators, linking remote bases with homefront stories, and turning frontline encampments into ad hoc screening spaces. I now turn to describe the workaday projector designed by and for the military to service the bulk of this expansive new viewing platform. Yet, I will also tend to some of the more experimental military viewing devices to make a case that collectively this portrait indicates the relatively elastic way in which moving-image technologies were being both imagined and realized, designed and used by the American military.

A key element of the American military's global viewing system was a projector detailed in the design protocol referred to as the JAN P-49, frequently just called the JAN.[13] Its letters were an acronym for "joint army navy," and the *P* stood for "protocol." The JAN was as much an abstraction as a thing—a fifty-eight-page, highly technical list constituting an ideal film projector, delineating qualities and performance standards desired by the military.[14] The protocol was authored by the joint committee named above: that is, the JAN protocol was crafted by both the military and the film industry's technical organizations working together. The JAN

FIGURE 2.1. With its elaborate metal casings and recessed lamp, the JAN projector was designed to be rugged and reliable in everyday and extreme performance scenarios. Its handle signaled the device's portability: the JAN was designed to be carried by a single soldier. (Photo by Haidee Wasson; JAN from the Herbert E. Farmer Motion Picture Technology Collection at the University of California Hugh M. Hefner Moving Image Archive.)

constituted a whole projection system, intended to operate independently of any particular space. It came with an amplifier and a screen that roughly emulated the Academy ratio—that is, the 1.37:1 aspect ratio standard of the Academy of Motion Picture Arts and Sciences—and that ranged in width from five and a half to seven feet. The protocol was both a product of—and a callout to—American industry, amplified by military exigency: make this for us and we will buy it. It should also be said that in practical terms, there was no single JAN. The protocol resulted in a family of projectors, manufactured by a number of large and small American corporations. Yet, examining the JAN protocol allows us to answer a reasonably important question: What did the American military want from a film projector? How did the military want films to appear?[15] Big, loud and bright? Small, quiet and dim?

The JAN protocol, first published in 1944, represented an enduring idealization of the military's film display and performance needs: it favored such qualities as ease of operation, maintenance, and repair; amplified sound; continuous operation; portability; and adaptability to varied spaces and environments.[16] It featured modestly sized collapsible screens that could be easily carried and then erected again and again. Like other industrialized military equipment such as tanks, guns, and jeeps, the JAN was also meant above all to be reliable and rugged, with the design protocol stating that the projector should operate at full capacity even after being dropped from a height of eighteen inches ten times onto a concrete floor![17] The imperative to make the JAN easy to use in part responded to the need for untrained or quickly trained soldiers to work and fix the machine, moving away from the highly specialized skills of commercial projection and toward a form of film performance that could be accomplished with minimal experience and relatively unskilled hands. The nonflammable acetate base for 16mm film stock eliminated previous concerns about fire and hence the need for fireproof booths that had previously weighed upon portable projection scenarios. The call for lightness of weight is also made more meaningful when one considers that the JANs manufactured and sold under this protocol often weighed as much as seventy pounds. Portability is clearly a highly relative concept. Anecdotally it seems that, while the JAN, with its handle articulated to a single human hand, was intended to be moved by one carrier, soldiers frequently threaded a stick through its handle so that two could share its load. The handle and the rugged case further indicate that the JAN was made to be moved, and frequently, by human and all other manner of transport: plane, ship, truck, and mule. The JAN protocol also stipulated high performance under heavy, near-constant use in all theaters of operation (arctic, tropical, desert)—a kind of all-weather, all-terrain device. It was designed to run all of the time, anywhere.

Yet, it should be made clear that the JAN was also dirty, heavy, and frequently broken. It was the product of a highly bureaucratic structure, replete with operation and repair manuals, forms for ordering parts, and procedures for use. A global system of film libraries and procurement processes further shaped its capacities. While the JAN answered, it seems, many of the military's needs, it is clear that the projectors made in service of the protocol were far from the sleek, speedy "abstraction devices" imagined by Paul Virilio. Likewise, these same devices operated quite differently from the machine-enhanced, horrific powers of the projector's distant mechanical machine-gun cousin, as speculated upon by Friedrich Kittler.[18] More important was the fact that the JAN's relative portability and adaptability enabled an expansive utility; it enlarged and amplified a sizable body of audiovisual content that could be played for audiences of varied sizes, configurations, and purposes. But it was still a film projector and worked by throwing light from one point to another, with no intrinsic ability to ensure that all of that light reached the screen, or could even be seen by those gathered to watch. At peak operating performance, the JAN threw light at roughly three hundred lumens, whereas most movie theaters today operate at thirty-three thousand lumens and are thus

1000 percent brighter. The bulk of its images were rarely larger than between seven and ten feet high. Soldiers regularly complained that its sounds were inaudible. By contemporary standards, the JAN's images were small and dim, and its sounds frequently distorted and faint.

The JAN nonetheless became the backbone of the military's film display system during this period. It played film outdoors on airstrips as well as in remote tents, strategy rooms, soldiers' barracks, submarines, hospitals, classrooms, and mess halls and from the backs of jeeps at bases and encampments large and small.[19] Growing from rather insignificant numbers before the war to a fiftyfold or 5000 percent increase, there were at least 16,000 projectors at war's end.[20] This makes the military's international circuit of projectors almost as numerous as civilian movie theaters in the United States at the time. But these diminutive projectors serviced the roughly 10 percent of the American population that had enlisted, indicating a significantly higher per capita concentration of military projection capabilities than in civilian sectors. It is worth noting that this increased density of portable projectors became a civilian reality after the war, with their numbers increasing into the millions by the end of the decade. Movie theaters notably declined in number.[21]

The JAN was not singularly responsible for this proliferation of portable projectors. But the protocol did set a performance standard that influenced military and civilian projectors for decades, facilitating the transformation of film projection into an ordinary institutionalized fact within and beyond the military. After the war, private and public film performance grew rapidly in homes, schools, factories, unions, clubs, and governmental and policing organizations, as well as corporate offices. Film projection also became a standard element of new international organizations such as the United Nations and its suborganizations like UNESCO. After the JAN, portable projection replaced the movie theater as the most common site for encounters with moving images in the United States, and likely internationally. Its design principles echo plainly in immediate postwar industry predictions and plans for a consumer mass market in which film projectors took their place alongside phonographs, radios, and televisions as part of a postwar media environment. Simplification of technical capacities, ease of use, durability, and reliability of operation continued as dominant design principles throughout the 1950s and 1960s.[22]

The JAN normalized and standardized projection ideals and thus enabled the subsequent spread of projection practices more broadly. Yet, there were many other versions of projection devices elaborated within the remit of the military during these years. Among them was a modified JAN, designed to facilitate not conventional film projection—from one side of an open, darkened space to another—but what is commonly called "rear projection." While the JAN P-49, discussed above, was the most common form of military cinema—rugged, designed like a tank, and operated like a blunt playback device—the JAN P-229 detailed a rear-projection protocol, issued one year after the paradigm-setting JAN P-49. It

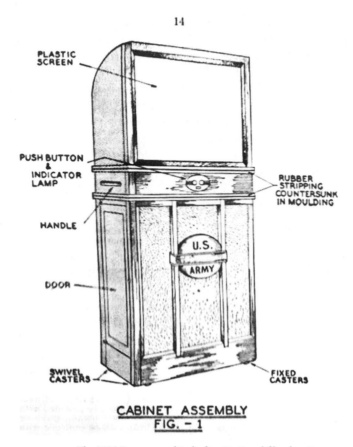

14

PLASTIC
SCREEN

PUSH BUTTON
&
INDICATOR
LAMP

RUBBER
STRIPPING
COUNTERSUNK
IN MOULDING

HANDLE

U.S.

ARMY

DOOR

SWIVEL
CASTERS

FIXED
CASTERS

CABINET ASSEMBLY
FIG. - 1

FIGURE 2.2. The JAN P-229 was a kind of institutional film furniture. It was designed to be movable from room to room, with casters at its base. Controls were positioned at the front of the unit, with a microphone jack in the rear. The projector was housed inside the unit; the image rear-projected onto the industry standard 1.37:1, slightly rectangular film screen—the official Academy of Motion Picture Arts and Sciences screen ratio. ("JAN P-229: Projection Equipment, Sound Motion Picture, 16-mm, Continuous," June 27, 1945, p. 14, National Archive Records Administration.)

called for a console film projector, one that looked like a piece of furniture and that operated on principles of continuous rear projection. The JAN P-229 embodied a rather different screening scenario and a distinct mode of watching.[23]

Like the P-49, the P-229 evinced continual operation and high use. It was also fitted with a looping mechanism for situations in which it was desirable to play the same film repeatedly. The projector itself was entirely housed in a cabinet, with castors at its base to facilitate what was likely limited movement. The rear-projection setup worked to better control the effects of environmental light typical of standard projection scenarios. As such, the projector was secured in a fixed relation to the screen's rear, all of which was encased in furniture, creating a dark box that better contained light from the projector and also kept ambient light away. From the front, the film console looked much like early radios and televisions. The screen measured twenty-nine by twenty-one inches, emitting rather than reflecting light, and emulating Academy ratio of 1.37:1. The console was also to be built with movable panels and a movable projection mount in order to allow for ceiling projections, likely articulated to soldiers lying on their back—recovering from battle wounds or psychological traumas.[24] The console featured a pushbutton interface on the front, which allowed a technician, teacher, lecturer, or therapist to control the film, pausing it to allow live interjections, to facilitate a discussion, or just to stop it. Military teachers and trainers were expressly directed not to let films play but to actively animate them, suspend the show, augment the images, edit them, turn the sound up and down, show only relevant parts, or talk over them.[25] This helps explain why a microphone jack was integrated into the console. Film sound switched to microphone sound with the simple flip of a toggle. Many such portable projection devices (including the JAN P-49) were also designed to operate as stand-alone public-address systems as well. In other words, portable film projectors were multiuse media machines, here transformable into a sound machine, amplifying and augmenting sounds and thus transforming how we hear as much as how we see.

So, in a sense this projector was a piece of institutional furniture. It was designed to move but with limited range. As a playback device, the JAN P-229 could facilitate endless loops; it could be used for everyday screenings or more-event-oriented performances, but only in front of small audiences. It allowed casual illustrative uses in classrooms, and invited live interjections and accompaniments through its microphone toggle and its accessible volume controls. Yet, because of its looping capacity, the JAN P-229 also enabled a kind of "ambient cinema," akin to what Anna McCarthy has called "ambient television"; that is, it was a cinema machine that was designed to just keep playing, to always be on. All in all, its design principles allowed for a highly scheduled, intentionally performative or casually "running in the background" kind of use.[26]

This device likely served several purposes. In this volume, Andrea Kelley writes that during this period rear-projection machines entertained soldiers and civilians, primarily by way of their use as a "film jukebox." These devices were frequently placed in leisure and transport zones in major American cities.[27] Before the war, the Empire Marketing Board (UK) used similar devices in train stations to show its films. And, in venues such as industrial fairs, expositions, and retail outlets, such machines displayed product films and advertisements.[28] In the context of American military operations, these devices were also used on airfields for pilot training and in officers' recreation rooms. They were also part of the military's training programs, compensating when needed for the shortfalls of the more common JAN P-49. Largely, it seems the P-229 was designed as a form of daylight cinema, in part to respond to the need for displaying images in venues that could not be sufficiently darkened, or where darkness was a kind of liability to full effectiveness. Some military studies indicated that standard projection scenarios led to soldiers falling asleep or becoming drowsy during film screenings when projection was designed to do precisely the opposite: make the learner more alert. Moreover, the disjuncture between the educational imperative to write things down (requiring light) and the need to see what's on the screen clearly (requiring dark) persisted. Military officials determined to make cinema an effective teaching tool—or to move resources elsewhere (which they also did). So in addition to studies of effective content, using cinema for diversified military applications also entailed multiple studies of some basic things. Exploring the limits of legibility, these officials asked, How bright does the image need to be to ensure attention? Or, How dim can movies be before they become illegible? Conversely, How bright or dark the room? Results indicated that a half-bright room was deemed the best balance, with frequent instructor intervention also recommended.[29] Compulsory watching in the military was constituted by specific presentation techniques and protocols.

Still another rear-projection device, developed after the war with research support from the air force, resembled more what we now think of as a microfilm reader, using 35mm film.[30] Tactical, equipment-operation, and surveillance films resulted in millions of feet of moving images reconceived more as reels of data than as raw film footage per se. This entailed a particular mode of viewing: to watch film images that were recorded continuously but that yielded relevant or useful information only periodically, or perhaps rarely. Watching became necessarily something that resembled both the observance of a steady, speedy blur paired with a selective, sustained focus; its controls were intended to allow an analyst to efficiently procure highly specific and precise data from reels upon reels of continuous celluloid.[31] The device offered full control over film speed, such that an analyst could search efficiently through what could amount to thousands of feet of irrelevant data, and then spend focused time on the single frame that held significant data. Speed changed by way of a foot pedal, like on a sewing machine or an automobile. A viewer-analyst searched images of airplane instrumentation, scenes of atrocity, aerial dogfights, undersea mapping, and all manner of munitions test films. Surveillance films likely figured as well. Heat-absorbing glass, mirrors, a smaller image size, and the close proximity of projector and viewer to screen maximized legibility and required less-powerful lamps. Intense bulb heat, which regularly damaged film prints—especially those slowed down for closer viewing—had long plagued the enduring impulse to control the speed and achieve the stasis of projected moving images. Like similar viewing machines (microfilm readers and film-editing tables such as the industry-standard Steenbeck), the military innovated film devices that rendered image movement and film watching more controllable, and indeed answerable to the longstanding efforts to constrain it, transforming the kinds of information it might yield and the ways in which film viewers might examine it.

Before moving to a conclusion, there are two other projection devices developed during World War II worth mentioning—one that contributed to a widely influential form of popular, commercial film in the postwar years, and another that remained highly specialized. The Waller Flexible Gunnery Trainer, developed to prepare pilots in the United States and in the United Kingdom, began being used experimentally early in the war, and grew directly out of recent industrial display imperatives to create wondrous all-encompassing environments embodying corporate ideals. Fred Waller, one of the trainer's lead inventors, presented the trainer to the SMPE, with an article appearing in the organization's journal in July 1946.[32] Waller himself evinced a fascination less with size or immersion and more with peripheral vision.[33] The Waller Flexible Gunnery Trainer used five 35mm projectors, though 16mm equipment was used in early stages of development. The trainer's screens curved around two centrally positioned trainees, who responded to footage of enemy planes in flight. Sitting side by side behind gun-like mechanisms, two pilots directed electromagnetic beams at images of planes as they moved across the screen. This elaborate device assisted in familiarizing pilots not only with recognizing enemy planes but also with hitting them as they moved at varying speeds and at varying angles within and just beyond the trainees' normal range of vision, exercising the eye to attain greater acuity at expanded angles and increased speeds. A direct strike registered sonically to the shooters through headphones. An instructor oversaw the sessions, and sat perched above an electrical control panel that scored performances, registering pilot accuracy. The gunnery trainer was not just an oddball experiment but a successful one in military terms. Seventy-five Waller training systems were built and in near constant use, sometimes working round the clock during the war, used by the US Army, the US Navy, and the Royal Air Force. Enthusiasts claimed that it trained more than a million pilots.[34] Film technologies here engaged the whole seated body, employing recent innovations in electromagnetic sensing, individualized address, and simulations of aerial attacks.

After the war, the wide-screen element of the trainer was augmented by sizable movie theaters, stereophonic sound, rich Technicolor processes, large audiences, and Hollywood showmanship; it became Cinerama. More-economical widescreen formats followed and were gradually adopted broadly by commercial theaters. The size and shape of the commercial film screen was substantially changed thereafter.[35] As discussed by Rebecca Prime in this volume, many of the Cinerama films continued a relationship with the military via personnel, consultants, shared equipment, and mutual interests in American world centrality. Though it should be added that although the place of the gunnery trainer in the history of large-screen theatrical cinema is clear and plain, its use of movable seating, electromagnetic beams, head phones, and control panels also situates film technologies within a longer lineage of innovations not generally categorized as cinematic, including weaponry, teaching machines, electroacoustics, and all manner of sensing machines, gaming systems, and flight simulations, as well as so-called immersive environments.

Lesser known than the Waller trainer was a similar projector system developed specifically for the US Navy's aviation training program. This system relied on an unusual variable projector, using a curved 360-degree screen.[36] The impetus was to design a system that not only could project images that appeared as if seen from a fully maneuvering aircraft but that also could respond dynamically to individualized training scenarios. This prototype used the image of a relatively stationary battleship at sea as its primary material, and worked to animate that prerecorded image to make it appear as if it could "wander all around the horizon," emulating the view from a cockpit. A relatively static image became larger and smaller, farther and closer, level and at odds with the horizon once it passed through the projector. To achieve this, a 16mm projector with variable speed, and also variable magnification, sat on a rotating mount that could pivot on three planes. The device thus projected images that could turn on multiple axes, which allowed the projection of images that moved around the seated observer. These images appeared to move toward and away from the pilot, creating altered angles of approach to the target. Researchers claimed that this device could essentially project an image that could move around its own axis. The projector used a combination of lenses, mirrors, and prisms that transformed a looped film of a target ship into a multiply articulated, shifting, dynamic flight simulation. The ship was not quite animated, but once projected, it changed in size, speed, and angle of viewing. A skilled teacher-trainer became a performer of images, requiring mastery of the various capacities of the device, actively spinning knobs and moving levers. Here projector manipulation worked to replace effects that would normally be achieved by camera movement or an animator's hand, confirming the productive place of this projector in the creation of content, and not simply as a blunt playback device. From reports to the SMPE, this experimental projector was built as a prototype and used in navy training centers.[37]

The degree to which other elements of cinema's technologies were used and transformed by the war during this period are known. For instance, the earlier German invention of magnetic tape was taken up internationally, including in the United States, and forever changed the way that film sound was recorded, edited, and mixed. Devices such as the portable magnetic Nagra recorder facilitated new film movements such as Direct Cinema, allowing for on-the-fly synchronized sound recording and other observational styles of cinema. Insofar as film is an art constituted by innovations in chemistry, we can also look to the many improvements, in color and in film for low-lighting scenarios, that grew after the war from innovations made by chemical giants such as Dow, Dupont, and Agfa (whose parent company is the notorious German-based IG Farben), each of which had deeply troubling relations to the development of particularly gruesome war weapons.[38] The material discussed above inserts innovations in projection into this much larger history.

This survey provides a glimpse of one organization—albeit a powerful and large one—that exercised an ambitious, diversified, experimental campaign to put cinema technologies to work and to war. The result was a military cinema, one that was big and small, dim and bright, slow and fast, highly abstract and didactic. In other words, cinema was clearly within the confines of this one institution and during this period a multiply articulated or iterative technology, one whose malleability rendered it integral to experiments in utility conducted by institutions of national and international significance, and of uncommon power. The experimentation charted predates the period in film history when "expanded cinema," "structural film," and other modes of formal experimentation coalesced into what we commonly think of as "experimental," "avant-garde" and "underground" cinema— a body of films and artistic movements devoted to exploring formal principles and aesthetic experimentation free from the imperatives of big budgets and commercial logics, coalescing in the late 1950s and 1960s. The American military's experiments also precede the American iterations of what Fred Turner has termed the "democratic surround," wherein film and other media were part of an intentional experiment to create through expanded media experiences resilient, technologically adequate democratic citizens.[39] While the military's cinema diverges from such undertakings with its highly instrumental and here war-driven goals, each of these developments disrupted and reorganized classical Hollywood's seemingly coherent apparatus. Innovative, immersive, abstract, and expanded viewing scenarios worked under the rubric of experiment to support innovation. Yet, the military's was a particular and highly diversified form of experimentation, operationalized less to free the cinema or to further a devoted cinephilia or to free the democratic mind than to conscript film and its technologies to the workings of industry, the state, and the demands of war.[40] This was a form of experimentation that unfolded in tandem with the state and industry to defeat fascism but also to reaffirm a continued American geopolitical power, which was not only about defeating fascism and later communism through propaganda but also about improving bureaucracy, organizational efficiency, expedient training methods and establishing superiority on the frontiers of technological innovation.

Fueled by the exigencies of World War II and then the subsequent Cold War, the military used techniques of abstraction, distortion, immersion, dissonant sounds, looping, and direct address. And it showed Hollywood films. It also envisioned and built new kinds of spaces, hybrid technologies, and normalized extreme perform-ance expectations for moving images and sounds, arriving upon protocols that influenced commercial, consumer, everyday, educational, politicized, and even subversive media for decades. These experiments serviced vast and ostensibly pressing needs. In some instances, these new languages and techniques embodied attempts to heal soldiers and comfort distressed men and women, to teach about foreign cultures, and to rebuild communities.[41] In other instances, these technolo-gies and their uses were indissociable from other blunt instruments of military power, the tools of war, and the imperatives of an aspiring state. Last, it should be pointed out that a key element of cinema's utility was its agility and flexibility in responding to institutional needs, helping to facilitate a degree of coordination across dispersed geographies and ideologies.

With regard specifically to film projection, a range of new or adapted viewing devices and techniques emerged, which included new portable projectors but also small consoles articulated to stationary, standing individuals. Some of these pro-jection devices worked with sizable and notably wide screens that tested the limits of human vision and bodily reaction times. Spectatorship thus involved training the sensorium through dynamic gunnery-training techniques but also adapting that same sensorium to the mundane work of data analysis. Through the JAN, the American military made projecting moving images ordinary, accessible, adapta-ble, and far more nimble than had any civilian organization before it. Through the broader rubric of projection, this essay demonstrates that the American military from World War II onward institutionalized a highly complex relationship with cinema, considerably expanding our idea of what celluloid and its projection was for, and what it would become, during war and well beyond it. This is a story not only about militarizing or democratizing a particular piece of the apparatus but also about how institutional imperatives beyond Hollywood have long trans-formed that apparatus, its images, and its sounds. Portable projectors provide a point of entry into cinema's history that charts a complex expansion of film's itera-tive forms and functions. This expansion invites us to further consider the kinds of films we think about, the variety of institutions, industries, and spaces that are relevant, and also film's deep links to other technologies and media forms.

Portability and projectability help us to think through the negotiated materialities of showing movies, and the persistent rearticulations of cinema's aesthetics. The size, brightness, speed, volume, and density of film performance and display are here appropriated as a technology dynamic to be used within an expansive institutional remit. Thinking about the whole of this institution thus entails tending to the half-bright, the small, the still, and the moving, the quiet and the loud, the live and the recorded. With the case of the military we also have to think about cinema as a technology of observation, storage, retrieval, and display, wherein projectors enlarged, amplified, and made audible the images and sounds stored on celluloid in miniaturized, otherwise illegible form. The American military embraced these qualities of the technology and put them to work.

Entering cinema history through the point of projection invites us to denaturalize the false coherence and partiality of how we have thought about what cinema has been. That includes the movie theater as a space but also more generally things like the dialectics of light and dark, the dynamics of expanded spaces, and the ways in which modulated looking and listening are each a part of cinema's improvisational histories but also its institutionalized ones. The case of the American military complicates the idea of experiment (technological and aesthetic) and encourages us to explore the ways in which not just an expanded film industry but all manner of industry came to instrumentalize film. We will also need to continue our openness to a range of other disciplinary knowledge and expertise: design, psychology, industry, the military, physics, chemistry, and beyond.[42] Moreover, this research demonstrates the ways in which the American film industry's technical apparatus—broadly defined—was like other American industries: quick to support, shape, and ultimately benefit from the growing might of the expanding military and its increasingly permanent place in the world. The military–industry link operated in the form of protocols, materials innovations, and widespread applications of cameras, projectors, and celluloid, which continued to develop long after.

NOTES

1. See, for instance, the classic and highly influential version of this: Jean-Louis Baudry, "Ideological Effects of the Basic Cinematographic Apparatus," in *Narrative, Apparatus, Ideology*, ed. Phil Rosen (New York: Columbia University Press, 1986), 286–98.

2. Clayton R. Koppes and Gregory D. Black, *Hollywood Goes to War: How Politics, Profits, and Propaganda Shaped World War II Movies* (Berkeley: University of California Press, 1990).

3. For a concise summary of Hollywood's war activities, see Thomas Schatz, "The Motion Picture Industry during World War II," in *Boom and Bust: American Cinema in the 1940s* (Berkeley: University of California Press, 1997), 131–68; Thomas Schatz, "Wartime Stars, Genres, and Production Trends," in *Boom and Bust*, 203–61, esp. 239–61; and Clayton R. Koppes, "Regulating the Screen: The Office of War Information and the Production Code Administration," in *Boom and Bust*, 62–81.

4. For a brief overview of military influence on cameras, see H. Mario Raimondo-Souto, *Motion Picture Photography: A History, 1891–1960* (Jefferson, NC: McFarland and Company, 2007), esp. 293–96.

5. For a fascinating discussion about the Office of Strategic Services, an American intelligence organization active during World War II and predecessor of the Central Intelligence Agency, and its enlisting of key industrial designers to design and build new command centers and war rooms, see Barry Katz, "'Visual Presentation' and National Intelligence," *Design Issues* 12, no. 2 (Summer 1996): 3–21.

6. Microfilm and projectors were essential elements to the "memex," a speculative machine that presaged the modern computer. See, for instance, Vannevar Bush, "As We May Think," *Atlantic Monthly*, July 1945, 101–8. Bush headed the Office of Scientific Research and Development during World War II, responsible for harnessing research in science to military research and development. He is widely understood as a crucial inspiration for the emerging first generation of computer scientists.

7. See, for instance, M. E. Gillette, "The Use of Films in the US Army," *Journal of the Society of Motion Picture Engineers* (hereafter *SMPE*) 26, no. 2 (February 1936): 173–82; William R. McGee, "Cinematography Goes to War," *SMPE* 42, no. 2 (February 1944): 102–12; C. II. Woodward, "The Motion Picture Program of the Industrial Incentive Division, U.S. Navy," *SMPE* 42, no. 2 (February 1944): 113–16; George W. Reutell Jr., "The Standardized 16mm JAN Projector," *SMPE* 68, no. 12 (December 1959): 828–31; and Max Kosarin, "Preparation of Foreign-Language Version of US Army Films" *SMPE* 62, no. 6 (June 1954): 419–22.

8. For a list of presentations, see "Program of the Fifty-Third Semi-Annual Meeting," *SMPE* 40, no. 6 (June 1943): 391.

9. D. E. Hyndman, "Report of the Engineering Vice-President on Standardization," *SMPE* 43, no. 1 (July 1944): 1–4. Hyndman was the vice-president of the SMPE and presented this published report at the April 19, 1944, meeting of the society's Technical Conference. Members of the SMPE worked with the American Standards Association's War Standards Committee on Photography and Cinematography, and with the War Production Board. This larger committee acted partly as a centralized source for requests from distinct wings of military institutions, including the US Army Signal Corps, the US Army Air Forces, the US Army Corp of Engineers, the Bureau of Aeronautics, the US Navy, and the US Marine Corps. The SMPE also had a standards committee, and subcommittees that specifically addressed 16mm cinematography, sound, projection, and laboratory practices, representatives of which served on this joint committee.

10. Motion Picture Association of America, "Report of the Film Survey Committee," July 5, 1954, Binger Collection, American Museum of the Moving Image, 17.

11. Richard Koszarski, "Subway Commandos: Hollywood Filmmakers at the Signal Corps Photographic Center," *Film History* 14, nos. 3/4 (2002): 305.

12. For more details on the military's filmmaking infrastructure, see Motion Picture Association of America, "Report of the Film Survey Committee."

13. Haidee Wasson, "Protocols of Portability," *Film History: An International Journal* 25, nos. 1–2 (2013): 236–47.

14. See "JAN-P-49," May 31, 1944, Joint Army Navy Specification: Projection Equipment, Sound Motion Picture, 16-mm, Class I, National Archives Records Administration (NARA).

15. The document outlining the JAN protocol was not issued until May 31, 1944. The first projectors issuing from the protocol were not ready to use until the war ended. For a succinct overview of its development, see James A. Moses, "Trends of 16mm Projector Equipment in the Army," *SMPE* 55, no. 5 (1950): 525–35.

16. For an easily accessible description of this protocol and its evolution over the years, see George W. Reutell Jr., "The Standardization of the JAN Projector," *SMPE* 68, no. 12 (December 1959): 828–31. See also Philip M. Cowett, "Department of Defense Photographic Standardization Plans," *SMPE* 66, no. 9 (September 1957): 535–37. Reutell reports that the Jan-P-49 specifications were first agreed upon in 1943, but my findings indicate that the work of the joint committee was not completed until spring 1944, with the protocol published May 31, 1944.

17. Raymond Spottiswoode, *Film and Its Techniques* (Berkeley: University of California Press, 1951), 260. An interesting side note, some military "cultural technologies" were less designed for sturdiness than for planned degeneration. During World War II, augmenting the military's well-developed book-lending service, the American publishing industry issued 122 million copies of 1,322 paperback titles in an unusual disposable printing format. The books were designed for portability: they were foldable and to be carried in a soldier's pocket or slipped into a pack, but also were to decompose after a certain number of readings. Christopher P. Loss, "Reading between Enemy Lines: Armed Services Editions and World War II," *Journal of Military History* 67, no. 3 (July 2003): 811–34.

18. For frequently invoked ideas about the uncanny relations between cinema and abstraction, see Paul Virilio, *War and Cinema: The Logistics of Perception,* trans. Patrick Camiller (London and New

York: Verso, 1989). For another recurring set of speculations that postulates a deep connection between the machinelike regularity of cinema and that of the machine gun, see Friedrich A. Kittler, *Gramophone, Film, Typewriter* (Stanford, CA: Stanford University Press, 1989).

19. For an overview of film use and types of films used, see Robert A. Kissack, "Army Film Distribution and Exhibition," *SMPE* 46, no. 1 (January 1946): 26–29.

20. James A. Moses reports that by the end of the war, the signal corps alone had procured more than sixteen thousand projectors from several commercial manufacturers. Moses, "Trends of 16mm Projector Equipment," 525–35. Moses also reports hundreds of thousands of 16mm training films—a figure that far overshadows the mere thousands of Hollywood entertainment films shipped overseas (527).

21. These statistics include 8mm and 16mm projectors and were published regularly in the annual reports entitled *The Wolfman Report on the Photographic Industry in the United States*, compiled by Augustus Wolfman, using statistics from the US Bureau of the Census as well as published studies issued by elements of the audio-visual industry.

22. See Percival Case, "Some Engineering Aspects of Amateur Projection for the Mass Market," *SMPE* 49, no. 2 (August 1947): 139–45. Manufacturers continued well after the war to meet the performance ideals laid out in the protocol. See, for instance, a representative of Eastman Kodak, Edwin C. Fritts, declaring definitive progress toward JAN protocols in 1950 in "A Heavy-Duty 16mm Sound Projector," *SMPE* 55, no. 4 (October 1950): 425–38.

23. "Jan-P-229: Projection Equipment, Sound Motion Picture, 16-mm, Continuous," June 27, 1945, NARA: 20130606100356024.

24. See Kaia Scott's chapter in this volume.

25. See James J. Gibson, ed. *Motion Picture Testing and Research*, Army Air Forces Aviation Psychology Research Reports, Report no. 7 (Washington, DC: Government Printing Office, 1947); see, in particular, "The Instructional Techniques Peculiar to Motion Pictures," 241–60. These reports explored all manner of variables, including illumination of room and brightness of screen, angle of viewing, size of image, disrupting the film, talking over the film, size of audience, position of student in room, position of student in relation to screen, air flow in room, and the role of accompanying pedagogical techniques and devices (teachers, other illustrations, notebooks and note taking, textbooks).

26. Anna McCarthy, *Ambient Television* (Durham, NC: Duke University Press, 2001).

27. Andrea Kelley notes thirty-five hundred machines at their peak from 1941 to 1947. See Andrea Kelley, "'A Revolution in the Atmosphere': The Dynamics of Site and Screen in 1940s Soundies," *Cinema Journal* 54 no. 2 (Winter 2015): 72–93.

28. See Lee Grieveson, "The Cinema and the (Common) Wealth of Nations," in *Empire and Film*, ed. Lee Grieveson and Colin MacCabe (London: British Film Institute, 2011), 73–114; Haidee Wasson, "The Other Small Screen: Moving Images at New York's World Fair, 1939," *Canadian Journal of Film Studies* 21 no. 1 (Spring 2012): 81–103; and Michael Cowan, "From the Astonished Spectator to the Spectator in Movement: Exhibition Advertisements in 1920s Germany and Austria," *Canadian Journal of Film Studies* 23, no. 1 (2014): 2–29.

29. For more information on working to make films that were sufficiently engaging that they could stand alone and rely less on instructor intervention, see Charles F. Hoban (Lt. Colonel) and James A. Moses (Army Pictorial Service), "Cameo Film Production Technique," *SMPE* 59, no. 3 (September 1952): 195–204.

30. Walter M. Clark and Lee R. Richardson, "Film Reader for Data Analysis," *SMPE* 57, no. 6 (December 1951): 574–79.

31. Ibid, 574.

32. Fred Waller, "The Waller Flexible Gunnery Trainer," *SMPE* 47, no. 1 (July 1946): 73–87.

33. Giles Taylor, "A Military Use of Widescreen Cinema: Training the Body through Immersive Media," *Velvet Light Trap* 72 (Fall 2013): 17–32.

34. Ibid., 17.

35. For the standard history of wide-screen film, see John Belton, *Widescreen Cinema* (Cambridge, MA: Harvard University Press, 1992).

36. F. G. Back, "Nonintermittent Motion Picture Projector with Variable Magnification," *SMPE* 47, no. 3 (September 1946): 248–53.

37. Ibid., 253. The air force used many methods to help pilots improve their sense of sight while in flight. Identifying enemy aircraft was of particular importance. This led to many visual techniques including films and flashcards, but also the use of 3-D View-Masters. See Mary Ann Sell and Wolfgang Sell, "View-Master in WWII: Military Training Reels," in *View-Master Memories,* ed. Mary Ann Sell, Wolfgang Sell, and Charley van Pelt, 2nd printing (Maineville, OH: Mary Ann Sell and Wolfgang Sell, 2007 [2000]), 229–31.

38. John Kenly Smith Jr., "World War II and the Transformation of the American Chemical Industry," in *Science, Technology and the Military,* ed. Everett Mendelsohn, Merritt Roe Smith, and Peter Weingart (Dordrecht, Netherlands: Kluwer Academic Publishers, 1988), 12:307–22. Barry Salt addresses both the influence of magnetic technologies and chemical innovations vis-à-vis color in *Film Style and Technology* (London: Starword, 1992).

39. See, for instance, P. Adams Sitney, *Visionary Film* (New York: Oxford University Press, 1974); Gene Youngblood, *Expanded Cinema* (New York: E. P. Dutton & Co., 1970); and David James, ed., *To Free the Cinema: Jonas Mekas and the New York Underground* (Princeton, NJ: Princeton University Press, 1992). For more recent work on these experimental films, technologies, and contexts, see, for instance, Tess Takahashi, "Experimental Screens in the 1960s and 1970s: The Site of Community," *Cinema Journal* 51, no. 2 (Winter 2012): 162–67; and Michelle Pierson, David E. James, and Paul Arthur, eds., *Optic Antics: The Cinema of Ken Jacobs* (Oxford and New York: Oxford University Press, 2011).

40. See Fred Turner, *The Democratic Surround: Multimedia and American Liberalism from World War II to the Psychedelic Sixties* (Chicago: University of Chicago Press, 2013), which links the history of multimedia and technological immersion to its intricate history with artists, designers, and state institutions.

41. A compelling example of formal experimentation in educational media can be seen in Hoban and Moses, "Cameo Film Production Technique." Using direct address, offscreen voices, call-and-response techniques, and repetition to ensure effective teaching, the film discussed in this article attempts to show military personnel how to operate a film projector.

42. See Scott Curtis, *The Shape of Spectatorship: Art, Science, and Early Cinema in Germany* (New York: Columbia University Press, 2015); Michael Cowan, *Walter Ruttman and the Cinema of Multiplicity: Avant Garde, Advertising, Modernity* (Amsterdam: Amsterdam University Press, 2014); and Justus Nieland, *Happiness by Design: Modernism, Film, and Media in the Eames Era* (Minneapolis: University of Minnesota Press, forthcoming).

3

MOBILIZING THE MOVING IMAGE

Movie Machines at US Military Bases and
Veterans' Hospitals during World War II

Andrea Kelley

Film exhibitions at US military bases during World War II evoke images of large, makeshift screens set up in mess halls or outdoor amphitheaters, where soldiers, enjoying an evening's entertainment, watch a Frank Capra film or a Mickey Mouse cartoon. Emphasizing the displacement of the soldier and the longing for home, popular accounts frame military film exhibitions as familiar and social practices that strove to replicate the theatrical film-viewing experience in unlikely, provisional venues. Such nightly screenings of Hollywood fare were a central part of soldiers' experiences on base—"an integral diversion," as Peter Lester explains, "necessary for the maintenance of troop morale."[1] Though vital and significant in its own right, this kind of screen practice represents only one aspect of soldiers' encounters with film during their military service. As recent historical film scholarship on small-gauge projectors by Gregory Waller and Haidee Wasson has shown, the US military's profuse mobilization of 16mm film technologies evidences a deep institutional commitment to the integration of film into military settings during World War II and illuminates the highly developed state of film use well beyond the screening of Hollywood films and their theatrical modes of exhibition.[2]

Circulating among these small-gauge film projectors on US military bases and camps was the Mills Novelty Panoram, a self-operating, 16mm, jukebox-style movie machine. Originally designed to play musical shorts called Soundies, the Panoram typically circulated in commercial locales like bars, nightclubs, and restaurants. Its migration to military spaces during World War II, as this chapter will show, modified its function as a novelty amusement machine and patterned new ways for interacting with small-screen technologies that would extend well beyond the Panoram's brief cultural life in the 1940s. Mills Novelty Company, a Chicago-based manufacturer of vending machines, first premiered the Panoram as a coin-operated amusement novelty in September 1940 in conjunction with Soundies Distribution Corporation of America (SDC), an independent short-film distribution company. At their height of popularity in the early 1940s, almost five thousand Panorams were in circulation throughout the United States. The Panoram itself comprised a 16mm projector encased in an Art Deco–style walnut cabinet that stood over six and a half feet tall and featured mechanisms that allowed for the automatic looping of film for repeatable playback. Its seventeen-by-twenty-two -inch glass screen displayed flashing lights when not in use to attract viewers, and a scrolling marquee listed the song titles and artist names from the particular reel in play. A dime would play one short from the eight-film reel. Individual films could not be selected from the self-looping reel, so customers had to enjoy their random selection or continue to insert coins to get to a particular film. Because the machine was large, its cabinet was mounted on wheels so that, if needed, it could be moved throughout its screening locale. Its volume was also adjustable so that it could accommodate and adapt to the acoustics of its various environs.

Captain James "Jimmy" Roosevelt, FDR's eldest son, was the first producer of Soundies films and the company's first president, which helped Soundies gain a lot of attention during the business's initial commercial launch.[3] In the fall of 1940, Jimmy Roosevelt hosted several premiere parties for Panoram Soundies at swank locales including the Hawaiian Blossom Room at the Roosevelt Hotel in Los Angeles and the Starlight Roof of the Waldorf Astoria in New York.[4] Just before the bombing of Pearl Harbor and the United States' entry into World War II, Jimmy Roosevelt stepped down from his position as president of SDC and reported for duty as a captain in the US Marines. Once he was in service, Roosevelt maintained corporate affiliation as "unsalaried" vice president of SDC, chairman of the board, and "a heavy stockholder."[5] Although the war imposed production and material restrictions on the manufacture of amusement and vending machines like music jukeboxes, Mills Novelty Company, manufacturer of "Captain Jimmy's Jukes," applied for priority grants since its machines were already in army camps. According to Mills president Fred Mills, "government departments want the machine for educational purposes."[6] Although Mills and SDC hoped to gain manufacturing priority by capitalizing on the "business" of troop morale and training, they ultimately were stymied by the aluminum ban and had to halt the production of new Panoram machines in February 1942.[7]

As the war effort grew on the US home front, Panorams increasingly migrated from commercial locales to institutional spaces, like government buildings, where they were implemented in more-official capacities as displays for war-bond sales and for military recruitment. Presenting a balanced program of Soundies musical shorts alongside public service announcements produced by the Office of War Information, the Panoram often was used as an enticement, luring in passersby with the promise of a free movie if they would buy a bond or enlist in service. By 1943, about fifteen hundred Panorams were located in schools and war plants.[8] Though a fringe film novelty machine, almost half of all Panorams were repurposed for "war work" during their six-year cultural life.[9] During this time, the Panoram was used by the military in training facilities at domestic military bases, veterans' hospitals, government buildings, and sites specifically designed for servicemen during their recreational hours.

The Panoram's implementation by the military provides an expanded portrait of military film use during the 1940s beyond both the morale-boosting experiences of the nightly Hollywood screening and the more frequently employed portable projection equipment. As the above description indicates, the Panoram is not the typical, military-issue projector like the 16mm JAN, which was standard equipment for all overseas film operations and designed for maximum portability.[10] With its bulky, and rather deluxe, walnut cabinetry, the Mills Novelty Panoram hardly seems amenable to the makeshift setups required by military protocols. The Panoram's differentiation from conventional 16mm projectors begs certain questions about what this adapted film jukebox could and in fact did offer in military contexts. Its all-in-one screen-projection unit and automated features provided convenience and efficiency of setup and use. Although it was not portable in a hand-held sense, the Panoram's large cabinet was on casters, so it could boast a degree of mobility in that it could be pushed from room to room like a deluxe audiovisual cart. Best for accommodating single or small-group viewings, the Panoram's small, self-operating vending mechanisms enabled modes of film display that were small or even individualized, where screenings could be repeated ad nauseam in rooms that did not require darkness or a film projectionist. Seemingly counter to the military's goals of collective instruction and information deployment, the Panoram's features of automation, repetition, and spatial adaptability transformed militarized practices in film projection to an expanding set of multisited small-screen encounters.

This chapter examines the military's adaptation of this commercial film technology by surveying internal military accounts of the Panoram alongside trade coverage of the Panoram in military settings in magazines like *Business Screen* and *Billboard*. Couched in militarized discourses ranging from combat to rehabilitation, these accounts of the US military's deployment of the commercial Panoram effectively recast the role of the small film screen as a necessary instrument of war while consequently bolstering consumer-oriented screen technologies within institutional spaces. The final part of this chapter turns to advertisements for the Panoram and its follow-up model, called the Sono-Vision, as these machines transitioned from military practices to commercial endeavors. As the military's uses for the Panoram subsided after the war, these advertisements retained the Panoram's residual ties to its military protocols in order to secure and extend consumer desire for adaptable and automatic small-screen technologies in the postwar market.

KEEPING THE SOLDIER OCCUPIED: RECREATIONAL SCREEN ENCOUNTERS

Soldiers most frequently encountered Panorams in recreational sites like the post exchanges (PXs) on military bases or servicemen's recreation centers located just off base. Situated within or located near to camp, these sites served as liminal spaces where institutional and civilian life melded together, where soldiers sought diversion from work and reminders of home while in service. As microcommunities activating their own social practices and regulations, PXs and military recreation centers offered spaces where soldiers received their mail, bought cigarettes and gum, and drank diluted beer with a 3 percent alcohol content. In these at once official and unofficial places of temporary sojourn, soldiers could encounter an array of activities that helped to keep them occupied and from wandering to less-regulated establishments for (undiluted) liquor and prostitution.

According to an anonymous account from a woman who served as an army service-club director at Camp Kilmer, New Jersey, during the war, Panorams were installed at "three service clubs, one officer's club and three or four PXs in spite of a regulation forbidding vending machines and forbidding payment for entertainment."[11] Even though Panorams were technically not allowed, club directors regularly ignored commands to remove them, and GIs willingly paid money to see Soundies. Since Camp Kilmer was large enough to function as its own "small city," such on-base indiscretions were probably the norm as long as soldiers remained within the parameters of rules governing camp or spaces designed for military recreation.[12]

In, appropriately, a former department store converted into a servicemen's center in Fort Lauderdale, the Panoram was located on the main floor alongside a dance floor with a few musical instruments, indicating that this was not a space for quiet viewing but for the music and the screen to be enjoyed communally in "a wholesome place of recreation for those men in the armed forces in their off-duty hours."[13] With facilities offering jukeboxes, table tennis, swimming pools, pianos, free ice cream, and cards (but "no gambling"[14]), soldiers gathered around the Panoram, where, according to one *Billboard* account of a Chicago servicemen's lounge, they "get a kick out of seeing the machine in action."[15] Within this atmosphere of contained leisure time, the Panoram playing a Soundie provided a brief burst of entertainment. Since Soundies often evoked touristic places like Hawaii or employed Latin-themed music and dances, they could offer a potentially transportive experience for the soldier. For instance, Soundies like *Heaven Help a Sailor* (1941) and *My Little Grass Shack* (1941) cultivated GI fantasies of exoticism by featuring sailors singing to "island girls" of the South Pacific.[16] These screenings, so often justified as necessary and utilitarian in maintaining and managing troop morale, figured heavily in providing the illusion of mobility while the soldiers bided their time and awaited deployment.

Unlike the spaces on base that might host a nightly film screening, places where Panorams were available offered other diversions; there, screen viewing was decentralized in a room full of other activities. Amenable to spaces that were well lit, busy, and noisy, the Panoram provided a momentary attraction; but, most likely, its screen was ambient, with soldiers freely circulating and socializing throughout the facilities as Soundies played.[17] Though the Panoram was a novelty amusement, its placement normalized the presence of the screen as a diversionary activity for those in service. As a specific iteration of extratheatrical film practices, these recreational accounts of the militarized Panoram incorporate commercial entertainment as a mundane experience, akin to listening to the radio, within these institutional spaces and practices.

"FILM IS A WEAPON"

A 1942 *Chicago Tribune* article reported that Mills Novelty Company would no longer produce coin-operated machines like the Panoram during wartime. It stated: "The machinery which manufactured the vending robots that told your weight, released a candy bar, handed you a cold drink, or ran off a quick movie while you drank a beer, is now shaping cold steel into projectiles and other war implements which bear an obituary for axis soldiers."[18] Like a vast number of American industries with highly developed manufacturing facilities, the Mills Novelty Company was undergoing a transformation from a manufacturer of automatic vending movie machines to a producer of "machined articles of death and destruction"—a change that evidences a quite literal repurposing of the Panoram's industrial materials into weapons and its former factory into an armory. As Raymond Williams states, "New technology is itself a product of a particular social system . . . but . . . contradictory factors . . . may make it possible to use some or all . . . for purposes quite different."[19] Although the Panoram functioned primarily as commercial screen entertainment during moments of leisure, such accounts of material repurposing remind us of the "quite different" possibilities for such machinery. Foregrounding wartime priorities of weapon manufacturing supplanting civilian amusements, the above account situates entertainment technologies firmly within the discourse of war and signals the shared industrial base of both.

Business Screen's coverage of educational and industrial film's role in militarized settings touts the idea that "film is a weapon" and "pictures are bullets."[20] Stressing the importance of film for military education and training, trade discourse from the war era evidences both the centrality of training films for the military and the rampant expansion of the military's exhibition practices. As Colonel Emmanuel Cohen, executive producer for the Signal Corps Photographic Center (SCPC), recounted at the war's conclusion in 1946, "What had started out to be a simple training film program had now become a vast, complex medium of information, education, military planning, advanced training and entertainment."[21] Utilizing claims from military personnel to bolster film's status from supplemental to essential, "as important to the men as rations," these trade accounts move beyond patriotic boosterism to seamlessly meld the interests of the various film industries (encompassing the commercial and industrial) with those of the US military.[22]

Within this milieu, the integration of the Panoram proves particularly apt for meeting the needs of military instruction. One of the primary concerns of relying on films for military training was gauging the efficacy of instruction, particularly when "films can be shown only in darkened projection rooms . . . if the G.I. audience slept through the picture, valuable training time was lost."[23] The Panoram redresses this issue of "considerable dozing" with its rear-screen projection design for viewing in well-lit environments. An ad for the Panoram as an instructional device for the army and navy emphasizes that a "darkened room [is] unnecessary."[24] Recasting the Panoram as an instructional tool rather than a coin-operated Soundies machine, the ad shows a full-page picture of the Panoram projecting an image of an airplane, with its marquee announcing "Educational Sound Films." (See figure 3.1.) The ad also claims that these machines were made available "by special government authorization" and a "push button switch" replaced their coin operation. Although this ad clearly illustrates its militaristic film content and emphasizes the Panoram's capacity for projecting training films, it still gestures toward the Panoram's commercial function and versatility by recommending the play of "musical and news shorts" alongside training films.[25] Whether the military actually programmed the Panoram as such remains inconclusive, but the ad suggests that the seamless integration of educational content with entertainment would not be unusual.

A 1945 article from the *Washington Post*, lamenting the current state of public education in the United States, noted the "incredible effects of the specialized training given to Army and Navy personnel" by taking "advantage of up-to-date aids: viz. films, records, models."[26] In addition to shifting away from "learning with the lights off" film instructional models to creating an atmosphere conducive to alertness and brightness, the US military's integration of the Panoram evidences its institutional commitment to creating effective, visually engaging learning environments where screens were used purposefully alongside other forms of instruction. For instance, a training center called the War Room, at the Army Air Force Pilot School at Shaw Field Air Force Base near Sumter, South Carolina, comprised an intelligence library with an adjoining room featuring an eight-by-twelve-foot world map, a six-by-eight-foot relief map, wall panels that were updated daily with

FIGURE 3.1. A Mills Novelty Company ad recasting its Panoram-style projector as a useful machine for military training.

FIGURE 3.2. Photo showing a solider watching a military training film on a Panoram at the Shaw Field "War Room." (Photo from The Digest article "Dayroom Information Centers Feature Shaw Field Program," *Digest*, May 1944, 5.)

pertinent war information from the press, and sandboxes with models of sea and land formations.[27]

Among other visual instructional materials, including a table filled with both View-Masters and stereoscopes, the Panoram was stationed to play a twenty-eight-minute film program on identification and military intelligence subjects that was changed weekly. As seen in figure 3.2, a single soldier stands in front of a Panoram that is projecting an image of a military airplane. In this didactic image of individualized film viewing of military content befitting the instructional environ of the "intelligence library," the Panoram evokes a stately presence within the multimedia military library. However, as is somewhat evident from the photo, the Panoram itself is still marked by its original commercial function, with its rotating banner announcing, "We Proudly Present Panoram Soundies: America's Latest Form of Musical Entertainment." Since its programming banner could have been removed (the banners were designed to be exchangeable to advertise specific film programs), this Panoram machine offers a residual reminder of its commercial functions and gestures toward other possibilities for small-screen encounters. Although classified military reading materials and popular magazines (*Time, Life,* etc.) were available for browsing, the Shaw Field War Room is marked as a place less for reading than for viewing, with flags and insignia covering every wall of the library, including the ceilings. Placed alongside other solo viewing apparatuses in a room festooned with maps and visual aids, the Panoram machine exemplifies the military's approach to visually rich multimedia instruction.

Frequent screen encounters were the norm at Shaw Field, with programming also including a regular Sunday screening of "newsreels and sports features" for groups of two hundred accompanied by a quiz program in which soldiers could win prizes for accurately answering orientation questions.[28] With both small- and large-screen viewing experiences couched within and alongside other orientation activities, the military situated the screen as a necessary wartime technology and sought to innovate its uses in emergent capacities. For instance, the Panoram was used as part of an outdoor training installation designed to orient soldiers to other cultures. Comparable to an educational kiosk in a museum space, the Panoram screened films about indigenous fruits, vegetables, and animals of the South Pacific within a simulated hut environ. To assess the soldiers' comprehension of the film, a converted pinball machine called an "automatic rater" would quiz the soldiers on the content and give them a score.[29] The dual placement of these repurposed amusement machines in this training setting suggests that they may have provided some level of entertainment while offering instruction—a scenario not so different from the implementation of interactive video games into more-contemporary military training settings. Like the aforementioned use of the Panoram in the War Room, this outdoor installation also marks this militarized space as an interactive and modern educational site.

In addition to allowing for bright spaces (including daylight) for alert and interactive viewing activities, this kind of mechanized and assessed learning experience evidences the importance of efficiency and effectiveness in militarized instruction. With war-era ads for projectors boasting "more learning in less time,"[30] recurrent accounts from reports conducted by the US military tout the efficacy of film in military training in similar terms of efficiency. Cohen states: "Any lingering doubts about the value of film, not only in routine training courses, but also in spreading information quickly and in attacking specific morale problems, were completely dissipated."[31] Not only is it presumed that film content in general was easier and faster for soldiers to absorb (certainly more so than reading training manuals or listening to lectures without visuals), but the Panoram machine itself further models these ideals of efficiency and speed with its automatic features and its short, self-looping film content, making the overall instructional screen experience user-friendly and befitting the training goals of the military. Since the Panoram did not require a trained projectionist, the soldier-student could learn directly from the automatic screen without the additional need for an instructor. With the ideals of efficient learning through film becoming a dominant discourse in late 1940s learning environments,[32] the military's mass deployment of and outspoken support for these visual instruction strategies augmented the legitimacy of (and market for) instructional screens for postwar classrooms.

"FILMS AS MEDICINE"

If films were deemed vital in preparing soldiers to engage in military combat, they played an equally restorative role in aiding the GI's recovery from the tribulations of battle. In what *Business Screen* refers to as "celluloid therapy," "films fill tremendous needs at the hospitals . . . where battle casualties march the road back to health."[33] From instructional films on coping with disability ("the fears of the amputee are met by motion pictures") to entertainment for those suffering from "the traumatic boredom of hospital existence," films for recovering veterans "teach new skills or talk of sports or raise a laugh when it is needed most."[34] The film content at hospital screenings is described as ameliorative and instructive by specifically accommodating and adapting to the particular needs of the wounded veterans.

Among these regular hospital screenings, the Panoram's use at a military hospital in Chicago garnered special mention for its military service. On July 14, 1944, Soundies Distribution Corporation even received a government commendation for "entertaining and rehabilitating the hospitalized veterans" at Gardiner General Hospital in Chicago.[35] In contrast to the aforementioned account of the Panoram's raw materials being used to craft weaponry, the Panoram, it seems, had more benign functions in the war effort as well. Inextricably linking rehabilitation with film's ability to entertain, a heading in a *Billboard* article claims that the Panoram "Has Health Value."[36] This account explains that the Panoram was brought to the hospital and played Soundies programs every other Tuesday. Reportedly, screenings were a preferred activity at hospitals, "taking top place even over the 'personal appearances' of stars of stage and screen."[37]

These Panoram programs were tailored specifically to avoid associations with wartime trauma and official military duties. Retaining their prior associations as novelty amusement machines, Panorams played only Soundies, and anything having to do with the military was "eliminated from the reels."[38] Such Soundies programs comprised musical shorts, like "top band and girl acts," providing "entertainment for wounded servicemen" in this institutional setting.[39] Other popular Soundies genres for hospitalized veterans mentioned are "comedy, western and hillbilly" musical shorts.[40] "Aside from the entertainment value" and "boost they give to the morale," Soundies are described as being "therapeutic" in that the musical content of the films acts as a kind of physical therapy. The films "unconsciously and automatically" cause the patients to wiggle their fingers and toes to the music, "thereby getting much needed exercise."[41] According to *Billboard*'s enthusiastic account, soldiers responded to Soundies with "whoops and yells . . . stamping and the whistling," which the hospital staff takes as "an indication that the boys are doing fine."[42]

In addition to the films themselves being seen as therapeutic through their entertainment value for the individual soldier, the circulation of films, their exhibition, and their technological integration in military hospital environments also figured in medical discourse that positions film as central to wartime recovery, rehabilitation, and transition. For instance, the structure of a Soundies program in veterans' hospitals tended to be of a shorter duration (about thirty minutes) so that the same program could be repeated throughout all the wards. This notion of increased film circulation put the Panoram operators on a rotation comparable to that of a medical staff, allowing for maximum distribution of services. In order for these film programs to circulate throughout an entire hospital, the projection equipment had to be portable: "Wherever possible . . . the use of portable equipment carts . . . is encouraged to facilitate in-the-ward film showings."[43] This emphasis on the portability of the projection technology directly complements medical discourse of patient accessibility and mobility.[44]

The wheeled Panoram satisfied the need for mobile film projection while also encouraging further mobility from the patients: "[S]ome of the boys . . . go from one ward to another right along with the unit, seeing the films over and over again."[45] In addition to the Panoram's adaptivity to the hospital environment, with its automatic projection and the ease of program repetition owing to its self-looping mechanism, the Panoram's emphasized mobility seems to directly extend from the screen's possible rehabilitative functions. According to *Billboard,* the Panoram is "wheeled from room to room since many of the men are unable to get out of bed to the main auditorium or some assembly point."[46] Here the film machine not only provides good entertainment; its mobility reframes the Panoram as an assistive medical device, where small, individualized film screens accommodate those not able to participate in collective, auditorium-style viewings. Figure 3.3 also documents a GI in his hospital bed, with three uniformed servicemen at his side. The Panoram machine stands in the background in play, with only one man vaguely looking toward the screen, which also indicates that these screens were becoming commonplace in the busy hospital environment.

The Panoram's attributes announce its modernity through mechanized patterns of automation and mobility, while the film content, with its purported therapeutic effects, is readily integrated into the institutional viewing context. Framed as an adaptable adjunct to a range of medical activities, the Panoram, according to one account, provides "treatment [that] can be continued while the show is going on: backs can be rubbed, temperatures taken, medications administered thru the entire program while the boys comfortably enjoy the movies from their beds or wheel chairs."[47] These details offer an unexpected and lively portrait of film exhibition—where screen viewing occurs alongside a host of other therapies. In these militarized, medical surrounds, the discourses of film and its technologies are repeatedly interwoven with the hospital's own therapeutic endeavors. From their adaptable film programs purportedly aiding veterans in their healing to the Panoram's design protocols allowing for increased accessibility to film viewing, institutional Panorams, by these accounts, helped to mobilize the screen into postwar civilian practices. Since many civilians initially were called to action by the Panoram at war rallies at the war's inception, the Panoram's placement at the veterans' hospital effectively bookends the soldiers' wartime service.

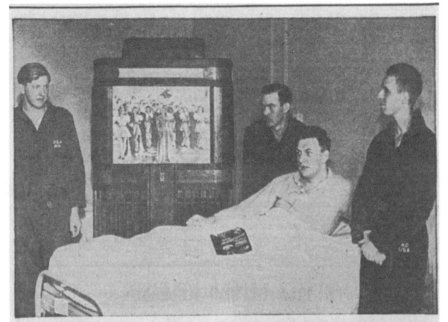

MOVIE MACHINE PROVES GREAT help to wounded veterans. Left to right, Privates C. Bailey, W. Bailey, R. Bauer and J. K. Williams have a Soundie in one of the wards of Gardiner General Hospital, Chicago.

FIGURE 3.3. Photo from the *Billboard* article "Movie Machines' Public Service." (*Billboard*, June 16, 1945, 65.)

FROM SERVICE TO SALES

The US military's use of the Panoram positioned small-screen technologies into expansive spaces and practices, both institutional and otherwise, for military personnel during the war. By the war's end, the soldiers' familiarity with these small-screen technologies would prove amenable to their reentry into postwar society. With government incentive programs like the GI Bill designed to assist their reconversion to civilian life, the returning veteran (especially the white male) was met with ample opportunities to participate in the recovering postwar economy.[48] Recognizing a valuable business opportunity, Soundies Distribution Corporation announced a franchise opportunity designed exclusively for veterans seeking employment upon their return from service.[49] SDC proposed offering rent-to-own discounts for vets who were interested in owning and operating Panorams. In addition to offering fiscal incentives, SDC also planned to offer veterans a "serviceman school" where they could learn "standard operating policy" for a Soundies franchise. SDC proposed teaching the operators about the machines through training films that would be played, naturally, on the Panoram.[50]

The SDC plan for veterans maps a direct and clear transition from soldier to salesman in which the Panoram is still used as a training device for veterans who are familiar with this mode of filmic instruction, while they are being coached on the possibilities of the Panoram as "a powerful advertising medium." Recognizing a rich opportunity to fill the "idle time" between Soundies on the Panoram with advertising films and slides, the general manager for SDC anticipated that a "constant flow of commercial films and announcements . . . will not only provide an important, new source of revenue to operators, but will serve to increase the cash collections from movie machines."[51] Similarly to the military's use of Panorams at recreation centers or hospitals to fill idle time for soldiers with moving images and music, the industry envisioned the postwar Panoram providing a "constant flow" of commercial images. While evoking what would become the future magazine format for advertising on US television, the postwar Panoram differed from SDC's prewar commercial model, where the Panoram screen only flashed lights while awaiting the next costumer to drop a dime into the machine. Patterning the military's protocols of efficient, automatic playback, the lag time in awaiting coin operation is made more efficient in these aggressive marketing plans and offers a new modality for screens being in perpetual play. Although no new Panoram machines were manufactured after the war, ultimately rendering these veteran business opportunities moot, the Panoram's varied military exhibitions helped to cultivate new ways of thinking about small-screen exhibition practices, the machines' "flow" of images, and the potential functions of self-contained projection units.

In a series of Mills projector ads that ran in *Business Screen* from 1943 to 1946, the marketing of the Panoram and the company's revamped model, the push-button Sono-Vision, touts the machines' convergence with military affairs while using their military functions as a catalyst for further postwar opportunities. Both the US Navy and US Army topped the list of users featured in Mills ads for the Panoram and Sono-Vision, which frequently featured military subjects on the machines' screen displays. For example, a Sono-Vision ad from 1945 shows servicemen loading military cargo onto a plane.[52] Although the image clearly marks the projector as a utilitarian machine for military training, the language within the ad mingles wartime service with sales. The heading reads, "to train and sell!"[53] With emphasis on the machine being "time-saving," "mobile," "self-contained," and requiring "no darkened room," the ad clearly addresses the aforementioned training protocols of the military while also looking toward peacetime by making mention of "your post-war sales and training plans." Building their commercial integrity on the institutional legitimization of the US military, Mills Novelty charts a seamless transition between the machine's functions for training and sales. The ad beckons the current serviceman as it defines and shapes the soon-to-be salesman in the postwar market. While planting this seed for commercial enterprise, the ad also acknowledges the current production constraints on the "release of critical materials." Once these materials are available, which, "we sincerely hope, will be soon," Mills urges buyers to place their order, since supplies "for the first 12 months will be limited."[54] Although the claims are tempered, the ad focuses on the future availability of the machine more than its present-day function, ultimately serving as little more than a wartime placeholder in the projector market.

Although subsequent marketing efforts quickly removed the self-contained projectors from their military training capacities soon after the war, residual aspects of their military discourse continued to circulate around the promotion of these projectors through 1946. A surreal Sono-Vision ad boasting "three-dimensional selling" depicts a projector encased in a transparent globe with a free-floating ear and eye hovering in the background.[55] The projector's screen displays a nondescript image of a man doing a demonstration, but the language of the ad is decidedly militaristic: "You enlist each of the three dimensions in your sales task force." In addition to this notion of recruitment, the ad calls the projector one of the "most persuasive sales and advertising weapons you have ever used."[56] Recalling the military's integration of film technologies as essential armaments, this ad now situates the projector as a "weapon" of consumer culture, mobilizing sales through the power of the automatic screen.

Drawing upon their manifold screen encounters during their military service, GIs, now returning to the civilian workforce with not just exposure to, but also specific training in, this kind of screen technology, could identify with this notion of the mobilized moving-image screen. Acclimated to the integration of moving-image technologies, the returning soldier is then rendered the target demographic for buying into this tech-savvy dream of a postwar America.[57] Having been trained, entertained, and sustained by film screens during military service, the (upwardly) mobile private emerges from military service acclimated to a burgeoning consumer culture where moving-image screens, ranging from televisions to home projectors, take precedence as the foregone conclusion of wartime.

CONCLUSION: THE MOBILIZATION OF THE MOVING IMAGE

From these various iterations of the Panoram's circulation beyond its initial commercial capacities to expanded institutional environs, the enduring protocols that frame the Panoram's implementation throughout these military contexts underscore the importance of automation, screen integration, and mobility. By retaining its commercial function as an automatic film-vending technology, the Panoram's individual, small-screen viewing repeatedly is marked by notions of user control (at the push of a button) and programming repetition, with its self-looping projector. By placing the automatic film machine into institutional military spaces, these individualized and user-friendly screen encounters transcended their prewar novelty and commercial functions, positioning the screen as integral to a range of military training practices and helping to expand institutional screening spaces.

As an amusement machine in servicemen's recreational centers, as a therapeutic machine in veterans' hospitals, and as instructional devices at military training sites, the Panoram, with its manifold military functions, evidences broader desires for both screen technologies and moving-image content that can be scaled to and integrated with its surroundings. From the positioning of films as weapons of war to therapeutic remedies, the diverse discourse of military film exhibition frames site-specific screens like the Panoram as always functional to a particular viewing context. By rendering these screens as ordinary, utilitarian fixtures in often bright, multipurpose environs (from hospital wards to outdoor training facilities), the military's innovative implementation of cinematic technologies made the screen a naturalized part of daily life.

Rather than the war era putting a halt to the development and expansion of moving-image technologies (as is often recounted in the histories of US television, e.g.), the US military's mobilization of the Panoram evidences an innovative time of screen adoption and adaptation. The military's implementation of the automatic, small-screen Panoram reframed the display of film from movie viewings in darkened rooms to individualized and integrative small-screen engagements. Because the Panoram represents just one of the many film and moving-image screen technologies employed by the US military during World War II, such institutional appropriations of consumer-oriented screen technologies reveal emerging screen protocols that extend well beyond the practices of war. In their training of the mobile private in automatic and integrated film technologies, the US military helped to precipitate the "mobile privatization" of postwar screen culture.

NOTES

1. Peter Lester, "'Sweet Sixteen' Goes to War: Hollywood, the NAAF and 16mm Film Exhibition in Canada during World War II," *Canadian Journal of Film Studies* 19, no. 1 (Spring 2010): 2.

2. For in-depth analyses of the advertising and industrial discourses on 16mm film projectors during the 1930s and 1940s, see Gregory Waller, "Projecting the Promise of 16mm, 1935–45," in *Useful Cinema,* ed. Charles Acland and Haidee Wasson (Durham, NC: Duke University Press, 2011), 125–48; and Haidee Wasson, "Protocols of Portability," *Film History: An International Journal* 25, no. 1–2 (2013): 236–47.

3. The company was initially called Mills-Globe Company after Jimmy Roosevelt's Globe Productions and Fred Mills of the Mills Novelty Company. See Wally Hose, *Soundies* (St. Louis: Wally's Multimedia LLC, 2007), 7. Additional details on the in-flux organization of the Soundies and Mills business

structure are available in Scott MacGillivary and Ted Okuda, *The Soundies Book: A Revised and Expanded Guide to the "Music Videos" of the 1940s* (New York: iUniverse, 2007).

4. Several accounts of these premiere parties describe them as lavish, three-day affairs and also emphasize the atmosphere of racial inclusion for African American entrepreneurs and artists. See "Mills Novelty and Jas. Roosevelt's Classy N.Y. Preem for 'Soundies,'" *Variety*, October 23, 1940, 16; and "Hollywood," *New York Amsterdam News*, September 21, 1940, 13.

5. "Expect Priority to Build Capt. Jimmy's Jukes," *Chicago Daily Tribune*, August 31, 1941, 1.

6. Ibid.

7. Ibid.

8. "Movie Juke Boxes . . . What about Them?" *The Billboard 1943 Music Yearbook* (1943), 73.

9. "Equipment Field Notes," *Film Daily*, September 10, 1943, 1.

10. Wasson, "Protocols of Portability."

11. Quoted in Westbrook Pegler, "James Roosevelt as a Partner: Manufactures of 'One-Arm Bandits' Welcomed Him in Gala Party Brochure," *San Diego Union*, September 19, 1950, 20.

12. As one of the largest bases in the United States, Camp Kilmer contained expansive recreational facilities including 20 softball diamonds, 30 volleyball courts, and 160 horseshoe courts. The camp also had its own band, orchestra, and football team. "National Archives at New York City, Camp Kilmer," U.S. National Archives and Records Administration, accessed March 6, 2015, www.archives.gov/nyc /exhibit/camp-kilmer.

13. Mary Jane Medlin, "A Community Project in Service Men's Recreation," *Journal of Health and Physical Education* 14 (1943): 364, 402.

14. Ibid., 364

15. "Industry Mentions," *Billboard*, October 30, 1943, 71.

16. For a detailed discussion of this GI fantasy, see Susan Courtney, *Hollywood Fantasies of Miscegenation: Spectacular Narratives of Gender and Race* (Princeton, NJ: Princeton University Press, 2005).

17. In using the term "ambient," I am evoking Anna McCarthy's *Ambient Television* (Durham, NC: Duke University Press, 2001), in which she provides a conceptual framework for, and historical overview of, the ways in which nondomestic television screens were integrated into various public spaces in the United States.

18. Lloyd Norman, "Penny-in-Slot Devices Now Pay Death—to Axis," *Chicago Daily Tribune*, August 9, 1942, A10.

19. Raymond Williams, *Television: Technology and Cultural Form* (London and New York: Routledge, 1974), 140.

20. Col. Emmanuel Cohen, "Film Is a Weapon," *Business Screen: Army Pictorial Issue*, no. 1 (1946): 43, 72, 74; Howard L. Luray, "Pictures Are Bullets," *Business Screen* 6, no. 5 (1945): 72.

21. Cohen, "Film Is a Weapon," 43.

22. *Business Screen: Army Pictorial Issue*, no. 1 (1946): 59.

23. Cohen, "Film Is a Weapon," 43.

24. Mills Novelty Company ad, *Business Screen* 5, no. 1 (1943): 31.

25. Ibid.

26. Roger W. Babson, "Preparing for Jobs," *Washington Post*, April 2, 1945, 12.

27. "Dayroom Information Centers Feature Shaw Field Program," *Digest*, May 1944, 4–5.

28. Ibid, 5.

29. Lt. Claude A. Eggertsen, "Education Home from the Wars," *Educational Administration & Supervision* 31 (1945): 492.

30. General Electric ad, *Business Screen* 7, no. 6 (1945): 10. This ad for a GE projector contains a photo of GIs gathered for a screening in an outdoor amphitheater.

31. Cohen, "Film Is a Weapon," 43.

32. For more on efficient learning in postwar instructional-film discourse, see Charles Acland, "Curtains, Carts and the Mobile Screen" *Screen* 50, no. 1 (2009): 148–66.

33. "Films as Medicine," *Business Screen: Army Pictorial Issue*, no. 1 (1946): 46.

34. Ibid.

35. "Movie Machines' Public Service," *Billboard*, June 16, 1945, 65.

36. Ibid.

37. Ibid.

38. "Soundies Fetes Wounded Vets," *Billboard*, May 13, 1944, 76.

39. Ibid.

40. "Movie Machines' Public Service," *Billboard*, June 16, 1945, 65.

41. Ibid.

42. Ibid.

43. "Films as Medicine," *Business Screen: Army Pictorial Issue*, no. 1 (1946): 46.

44. For an analysis of our contemporary fascination with notions of "portability" and "screen mobility" within 1940s instructional film materials, see Acland, "Curtains, Carts and the Mobile Screen."

45. "Movie Machines' Public Service."

46. "Soundies Fetes Wounded Vets."

47. "Movie Machines' Public Service."

48. For an exceptionally detailed history of the United States' socioeconomic transition from World War II to postwar prosperity, see Lizabeth Cohen, *A Consumer's Republic* (New York: Vintage Books, 2003). For Cohen's discussion on GI incentives and favoritism, see esp. chap. 3, "Reconversion," 112–65.

49. "Vet's Plan, Better Pix, Service School and Venue from Ads Spotlight Soundies Post-War Plans," *Billboard*, April 22, 1944, 64. See also "Soundies for Vets," *Tide*, July 1, 1944, 72–73.

50. "Vet's Plan."

51. Ibid.

52. Sono-Vision ad, *Business Screen* 6, no. 5 (1945): 87.

53. Ibid.

54. Ibid.

55. Sono-Vision ad, *Business Screen* 7, no. 2 (1946): 7.

56. Ibid.

57. For further cultural analysis of the war's role in supporting a future-thinking ideology based upon notions of technological progress, see Alan Brinkley, "World War II and American Liberalism," in *The War in American Culture: Society and Consciousness during World War II*, ed. Lewis A. Erenberg and Susan E. Hirsch (Chicago: University of Chicago Press, 1996), 313–30.

4

___

THROUGH AMERICA'S EYES

Cinerama and the Cold War

Rebecca Prime

In the tense days of the Cuban Missile Crisis in October 1962, Brigadier General Merian C. Cooper convened a secret meeting at the Forum theater in Los Angeles with members of the US Air Force.[1] Cooper, whose impressive Hollywood career as a director, producer, and studio executive was equally matched by his wartime service in military aviation, had arranged a screening of low-level aerial footage of Havana shot during the making of *Seven Wonders of the World* (Tay Garnett et al., 1956), one of the two Cinerama films he had coproduced.[2] Convinced that the United States would be at war with the Soviet Union within forty-eight hours, Cooper pointed out key government buildings and other landmarks during the screening to assist air force pilots in selecting their targets.[3]

This anecdote encapsulates the practical and ideological imbrication of cinema and military technology during the twentieth century and specifically, the military's use of aerial photography and cinematography—with its the dehumanizing, omniscient perspective—as a tool of war.[4] It also highlights a little-known but significant aspect of Cinerama's history: its close ties with the US government and its active role in the cultural Cold War. Standard histories of American cinema in the 1950s present Cinerama—a type of wide-screen cinema that uses three synchronized projectors and a supersized curved screen to create an intensely immersive cinematic experience—as another technological gimmick (much like 3-D) intended to help wage the battle against television.[5] While this characterization is not inaccurate, it overlooks entirely Cinerama's political and ideological dimensions, which form the subject of this chapter.[6] Beginning with Fred Waller's invention of the Waller Flexible Gunnery Trainer, a wartime antecedent of Cinerama, this study charts the relationship between Cinerama, the US military, and the State

Department during the 1950s and early 1960s. In their production, Cinerama films relied on cooperation from the US military, and they returned the favor through their patriotic narratives and celebration of American military and industrial power. *This Is Cinerama* (Merian C. Cooper et al., 1952) was among the US Information Agency's (USIA) preferred tools of cultural diplomacy thanks to its hugely successful appearances at trade fairs in key strategic nations such as Syria and Thailand.

The history of Cinerama that emerges from the archival documents drawn upon in this chapter vividly illustrates the unofficial partnership that existed among the government, the military, and the film industry during the postwar era. That their interests converged in the *technology* of Cinerama reflects both the emphasis on technological competition that was a defining characteristic of the Cold War and Hollywood's focus on the technological transformation of the industry. Indeed, in constructing a promotional campaign for their new motion-picture process, Cinerama's producers were adamant that the technology itself be the story, that Cinerama was the "hero."[7] Yet because this "new kind of hero" evoked a "new kind of emotional experience" in audiences, one that addressed the spectators' bodies as much as their minds, it is important to consider the ways in which the content of these films worked in concert with their aesthetics when thinking about their function as propaganda.[8]

In relation to the historical epic that often made use of wide-screen technologies including Cinerama, Vivian Sobchack observes that the "formal excessiveness" of the genre is fundamental to its ability to allow the spectator to "experience—not think—that particular mode of temporality which constituted him or her as a historical subject in capitalist society before the late 1960s."[9] In a similar vein, this chapter considers how the Cinerama films of the 1950s, along with the discursive field in which they participated, contributed to the construction of Cold War political subjects. Finally, I will discuss the ideological implications of Cinerama's extensive use of aerial cinematography and how they inform the dynamics of wide-screen spectatorship. Considering the ways in which the aesthetics of Cinerama converged with Cold War–era concerns thus contributes to our understanding of the role not only of film, but of the film *experience,* in the cultural Cold War.

TRAINING AN AUDIENCE

As has been documented elsewhere, Cinerama's technological origins date to World War II and its successful use as a virtual-reality training simulator by the US military.[10] In the mid-1930s, Fred Waller, an inventor and former head of special effects for Paramount's Astoria studios, began developing a new motion-picture process that would create the illusion of depth by engaging the viewer's peripheral vision. At the war's onset, Henry Baker, an old friend of Waller's and a ballistics expert, suggested that the technology could be adapted for military training purposes. By August 1940, Waller had built a model trainer.

To approximate the field of human vision, the Waller Flexible Gunnery Trainer used a photographic unit of five cameras as well as five projectors. Since the films projected had to mimic the gunner's point of view, it was imperative that the camera unit be small enough to fit in the nose, tail, or some other small space on bomber airplanes usually occupied by antiaircraft machinery. The planes on which the cameras were mounted flew at speeds of over two hundred miles per hour. The aerial footage recorded in these conditions was then projected over the five panels of the trainer's wide-screen dome, with flight paths crossing unpredictably and sometimes making directly for the screen. By engaging the gunner's central and peripheral vision simultaneously, the trainer provided an intense, full-body experience that makes the thrills recounted by later Cinerama audiences seem like child's play.

Over the course of the war, Waller's company, Vitarama, produced about seventy-five trainers, with impressive results. The navy reported vastly improved hit rates, and the air force estimated that 250,000 casualties had been averted due to the trainer.[11] In addition to proving highly effective from a military perspective, the Waller Flexible Gunnery Trainer also furthered Waller's interest in developing three-dimensional cinema for commercial purposes. Not only did the experience allow him to work through a number of technical glitches, but it proved important in creating an audience for a new kind of cinematic experience. As Waller explains: "With Trainers all over the country, in Hawaii and England, many running 24 hours a day, seven days a week, this new kind of moving picture experience was seen by thousands and thousands of men. I began to hear more and more frequently, 'When are we going to see regular pictures like this?' Indeed, I received well over a thousand such requests from G.I.s alone."[12] Because of its specific military function, the Waller trainer made films that followed strict formal guidelines; the films needed to provide an "accurate visual representation of aerial experience and to force viewers to identify with the subjective image frame," as Giles Taylor notes.[13] As we will see, this emphasis on the aerial shot framed by the latest in American military technology—and the ideological perspective it implies—would be integral to the aesthetics and politics of the Cinerama experience.

CINERAMA'S MILITARY PRODUCTION

The relationship established between Vitarama and the US military during the war exerted a distinct influence on the new motion-picture process's postwar development. When Hollywood proved reluctant to take a chance on Cinerama—as Vitarama was rechristened in 1946—the company decided to try to sell the Department of Defense on the technology's utility. As the centerpiece of his sales pitch, Cinerama president (and pioneering sound engineer) Hazard Reeves commissioned a hardcover book, entitled *In America*, in which the context of the Cold War and the atomic age is strongly invoked to argue for Cinerama's vital military relevance.[14] Fred Waller presented Cinerama to various armed services groups and by 1950 was working on another military trainer. And although it was ultimately not the military, but the showmen Lowell Thomas and Mike Todd, who would secure the financing for Cinerama's first production—*This Is Cinerama* (1952)— the Cinerama Corporation maintained close ties with the Department of Defense throughout the 1950s.

In March 1949, two years before *This Is Cinerama* began filming, a Cinerama executive wrote to the US Army Air Force Public Information Office in Dayton, Ohio, requesting permission to shoot footage at the US Military Academy at West Point of an aircraft landing on a navy carrier at sea, and of a "six motored bomber with jet assist, if such is possible."[15] Although his query was met with interest by Donald Baruch, chief of the Motion Picture Section (MPS) of the Department of Defense's Office of Public Information, these sequences were either never filmed or at least not included in *This Is Cinerama*.[16] Subsequent Cinerama productions, however, did make direct use of military assistance. The jet bomber footage requested in 1949 makes an appearance in *Cinerama Holiday* (Robert L. Bendick and Philippe De Lacy, 1955), for which the US Navy permitted the Cinerama crew to film on the USS *Lake Champlain* aircraft carrier, as well as from the nose of a jet.[17] *Seven Wonders of the World,* the round-the-world travelogue Lowell Thomas and Merian Cooper devised as their follow-up to *This Is Cinerama*, relied on support from high-ranking officials in the State Department—including Secretary of State John Foster Dulles—to facilitate access to over twenty-one countries where they wished to film.[18] That Thomas and Cooper were both Republicans, staunchly anticommunist, and had powerful connections in Washington (where Cooper had been stationed during World War II) undoubtedly assuaged any qualms the government may have had in offering assistance in matters of foreign relations.[19]

For the fourth Cinerama production, the military came out from behind the scenes to play a starring role. While sticking to the Cinerama formula of the loosely structured travelogue, *Search for Paradise* (Otto Lang, 1957) incorporates two characters, an air force major and a sergeant, who accompany Lowell Thomas on his trek through "the lands of Marco Polo" en route to the 1956 coronation of King Mahendra of Nepal. Although the major and the sergeant are played by amateur actors, the air force fully cooperated with the production, which opens and concludes at Eglin Air Force Base in Florida and showcases the latest in aviation technology. The film derives its loose structure from the contrast between scenes of what Thomas calls "the machine age, push button era" with those showcasing the "traditional Oriental magnificence" soon to be lost to modernity. Returning home, the major and the sergeant conclude that their "search for paradise" ends where it started: in the cockpit of a plane. As supersonic jets fly in formation toward the blue horizon, the narration makes explicit the chauvinistic perspective that informed Cinerama's explorations of the world and encouraged the association among America's military might, industrial technology, and modernity: "In the world of the Himalayas, they saw the past, but in the realm of modern science, there lies the future."

The fifth and final Cinerama travelogue, *South Seas Adventure* (Carl Dudley, Richard Goldstone, et al., 1958), likewise involved extensive cooperation from the US military. Originally titled *Battlefields Revisited* and intended to retrace the US armed forces' Pacific campaign, coproducers Carl Dudley and Richard Goldstone plotted an itinerary that included major strategic sites such as Iwo Jima, Guadalcanal, and Pearl Harbor. Their engagement with Cold War geopolitics is evident in their desire to make "graphic reference to the nuclear experiments which have been periodically conducted there to insure the maintenance of peace in a Free World" and to shoot footage in locales such as Formosa (Taiwan) in order to "dramatize the current situation at this Western-most bastion, here where the conflicting philosophies of the two worlds face each other across the narrow Formosan Straits."[20] Donald Baruch of the Motion Picture Section offered his full support for the project, for which the air force and navy provided assistance.[21] The fictionalized vignettes that make up the story, however, bear little resemblance to the producers' original vision for the project.

Dudley and Goldstone's notion that filming the nuclear-test sites in the Pacific would demonstrate America's efforts to ensure a meaningful peace reflects the influence of President Eisenhower's Atoms for Peace campaign (see figure 4.1), launched in December 1953 to reassure the public of the "constructive aspects, not destructive" intent of the government's atomic energy program."[22] Cinerama's most direct involvement with this program, however, was never completed. In September 1955, Cinerama president Hazard Reeves announced plans for the production of a film dramatizing the peacetime uses of atomic energy, to be made with the technical assistance of the Atomic Energy Commission.[23] Grant Leenhouts, a vice-president at Cinerama since 1951 and former head of planning and production for the US Navy Motion Picture Division, was put in charge of the production. His correspondence with Donald Baruch of the MPS suggests a two-way exchange, with Baruch facilitating military cooperation for Cinerama productions in return for his story ideas receiving serious consideration. In a letter from December 1955, Leenhouts writes that he has been able to generate great enthusiasm for Baruch's proposal for a Cinerama film "pertaining to continental defense and total fire power of the US," which he sees as an ideal follow-up to the atomic-energy project, now entitled *The Eighth Day*.[24] Over the course of 1956, Leenhouts asked Baruch for assistance with tasks ranging from obtaining stock footage of

FIGURE 4.1. "Atoms for Peace." (Records of the Office of the
Secretary of Defense 1921–2008, RG 330, Box 3, National Archives
College Park, MD.)

atomic blasts for a montage sequence to filming a simulated atomic explosion at
Georgia's Fort Benning.[25] To ensure scientific accuracy (and further strengthen
Washington's hand in the project), Robert LeBaron, former deputy to the secretary
of defense for atomic energy, was hired as a consultant.

The production proceeded in fits and starts, however, due to disputes between
Cinerama Inc. and Stanley Warner, who had acquired the production and exhibition rights to Cinerama's films in 1954.[26] Ultimately, only about one hour's worth of
material was shot, including footage of the launch of the nuclear submarine *Sea-
wolf* and the hydrogen bomb tests at Bikini Atoll. While this footage no longer
exists, the production storyboards reveal that the film approached the subject of
atomic energy from a religious framework that perhaps was meant to be comfort-
ing, but that from a contemporary perspective seems like a straight precursor to
Dr. Strangelove. The film's title is meant to evoke the Book of Genesis, with the
"eighth day" representing "the dawn of the atomic age."[27] By presenting the atomic
age as further proof of God's bounty, the script seeks to reconfigure the association
between the atomic bomb and destruction and to obscure the memory of Hiroshima and Nagasaki. Perhaps this is why those involved in the project thought that
images of atomic blasts experienced with the full force of Cinerama would prove
something other than horrifying to audiences.

Much like the Atoms for Peace program itself, *The Eighth Day* was a wolf in
sheep's clothing, intended to shore up public support for the government's nuclear-
arms program while distracting it from the implications of these expenditures.

The producers' commitment to promoting the government's Cold War agenda by presenting military technology as indispensable to national security is evident in a letter from Leenhouts to Donald Baruch:

> After THE EIGHTH DAY is launched into production this fall, we would like to begin research on the total fire power subject with the idea of developing a concept, a format, and a story that would carry forward the policies of our government, and at the same time show the people of the United States and the world the military strength of our armed forces. I cannot help but feel that such a picture would go a long way in showing the great contributions made by the armed forces to the technological developments of this country, as well as to the building of better citizens of the young men and women who are, or have been, associated with the armed forces.[28]

This perspective, put forth by a vice-president of Cinerama Inc., helps explain why the US armed forces were so willing to collaborate with Cinerama on its various projects over the course of the 1950s. Perhaps the more interesting question is why Cinerama continually courted the military during these years. Was it some formal quality of the technology that determined this orientation, or rather the background, experience, and politics of the men involved? The limitations imposed by the Cinerama technology (such as the challenges of filming at a variety of camera distances) made it difficult to apply traditional editing techniques and encouraged the nonnarrative structure and panoramic compositions best suited to the travelogue. With regard to subject matter, the decision to train Cinerama's three lenses on the Western world and its sphere of influence seems predictable given Thomas's and Cooper's anticommunist, neoimperialist worldview and the geographic limits of the military assistance upon which they relied. That the films promoted "American nationalist globalism"—a belief in American national greatness, global responsibility, and containment of communism that some historians consider fundamental to early Cold War ideology—is confirmed by another chapter in Cinerama's history: *This Is Cinerama*'s service as the State Department's secret weapon for winning hearts and minds overseas.[29]

THIS IS CINERAMA: AMERICA'S GOODWILL AMBASSADOR

In its celebration of the wonders of the "Free World," from European high culture to American popular culture, *This Is Cinerama* seems tailor-made for America's Cold War propaganda program. It is structured as a stage show with an intermission. The first act, directed by Mike Todd, presents the sights and sounds of Western Europe, from the canals of Venice to the Vienna Boys' Choir. However, it was in *This Is Cinerama*'s second portion, directed by Merian Cooper, that the technology achieved its aesthetic and political potential. Cooper's use of Cinerama makes good on cinema's etymological promise of writing in movement. From the rush of the Jet Skis in a theme-park aquacade to the whoosh of a B-52 jet as it dives into the Grand Canyon, Cooper's footage is all about sensation and spectacle, about cinema as pure experience. With regard to content, Cooper employs Thomas's voice-of-God narration to offer a paean to the spirit of American enterprise and youthful vitality. A sequence shot in Florida's Cypress Gardens theme park advertises a 1950s vision of a sanitized, sunny, and homogenous American way of life, while the subsequent "America the beautiful" sequence recapitulates the country's manifest destiny in its westward movement. We begin on the East Coast with shots of Manhattan's skyscrapers and the Pentagon, "famous for its size, headquarters of the vast military power of the US," according to the narration. We then move west, across the "fertile farmland" and vigorous cities of the Midwest, "where the song is one of modern industry." As we fly over the wheat fields of America's heartland, we hear the Mormon Tabernacle Choir begin to sing "America, the Beautiful." The song segues into "The Battle Hymn of the Republic" as we cross the Rockies and enter the dramatic landscapes of the American southwest before the returning to "America the Beautiful" for the film's concluding ascent to the clouds.

What John Belton calls the sequence's "fetishizing of the American landscape" did prove highly affecting, as domestic audience response would attest.[30] However, in addition to showcasing America's natural beauty, the images in *This Is Cinerama* celebrate America's economic vitality and willingness to reward success, whether in the form of a Florida swamp transformed into a popular theme park or the thriving industrial cities of the Midwest. While the novelty of Cinerama's form was largely responsible for its appeal to audiences both at home and abroad, the immersive, sensory experience it offered provided an effective (and affective) vehicle for capitalist ideology.

This Is Cinerama's commercial and critical success was such that it is hardly surprising it would come to the attention of the US government, which understood motion pictures as a powerful means of shaping spectators into ideal political subjects.[31] Cinerama's entry into the arena of Cold War propaganda came via the international trade fair—a form of cultural display that quickly assumed a prominence in government policy after the Soviets took first place at the 1953 Bangkok Constitution Fair, in which America had not even participated.[32] Anxious to prevent a repeat of Bangkok, the USIA arranged to bring Cinerama to the 1954 Damascus Fair despite the complex logistics involved. (The US Air Force delivered thirty-five tons of equipment: four projectors, seventy-two speakers, and a 62,000-watt generator.)[33] The exhibit immediately attracted capacity crowds of four thousand for the twice-nightly screenings of *This Is Cinerama*. (See figure 4.2.) A week later, the local USIA office cabled Washington: "Streets rife with rumor that Communists will attempt stop CINERAMA by sabotage. Communists only line thus far is that CINERAMA is 'unfair competition.'"[34] A report submitted by

FIGURE 4.2. Syrian President Hashem Atassi and other guests at
the Damascus International Fair in 1954. The USIA arranged to
bring Cinerama to the fair. (Records of the USIA 1900–2006, RG
306, Box 5, National Archives College Park, MD.)

the USIA office in Beirut concerning the "psychological impact" of the Damascus
Fair specifically credits *This Is Cinerama* with the fair's positive effect, concluding
that "'This is Cinerama' in itself carries an effective message of goodwill and
Americana."[35]

This Is Cinerama's triumph in Damascus led to a deluge of requests from other
USIA bureaus for similar exhibitions.[36] It was the "big show-stopper" of the US
exhibit at the Bangkok Fair in December 1954, packing a two-thousand-seat open-
air theater twice nightly.[37] Demand for the screenings was such that US ambassador John Peurifoy cabled USIA director Theodore Streibert to request that
Cinerama's run be extended, warning that "unless extended there is danger USIS
will make as many enemies among the thousands denied admissions as it will
achieve friends among those who do see it."[38] Peurifoy's report gives a dramatic
picture of Cinerama's appeal overseas and its efficacy as a goodwill ambassador.[39]

But what exactly were these overseas audiences responding to? As Robert Haddow observes, the international trade fairs and world's fairs of the 1950s were
"pavilions of plenty" in which America's commitment to "peace, comfort and
human progress—not war," according to Eisenhower's stated policy, was translated
into lavish displays of material goods.[40] *This Is Cinerama* corresponded perfectly
with the image of American abundance (and excess) the fairs wished to convey.
Most reviews of the Damascus presentation of the film in the Syrian, Lebanese,
and Jordanian press discuss Cinerama as a "miracle" of technological progress.
One journalist explicitly, if unconsciously, connects the wonder of Cinerama to

America's military power, writing that "[t]hose who were the first to explode the atom bomb, those who have subjugated hydrogen power to the will of human beings, today strive to entertain the world."[41] Another asserts that *This Is Cinerama* contains "no propaganda for America; it is simply beautiful scenes shot from certain places in America, Italy, Spain, Austria, and other places."[42] The excerpts cited in the State Department dispatches are, of course, partial, which may explain why they emphasize Cinerama's content over its experiential qualities.

However, if we can extrapolate from the US response to *This Is Cinerama*, which placed almost exclusive emphasis on the immersive experience offered by the new technology, it seems probable that overseas audiences were likewise primarily enticed by Cinerama's novel aesthetics.[43] As James H. Krukones notes in his discussion of the Cold War rivalry between Cinerama and its Soviet counterpart, Kinopanorama, Cinerama's underlying ideology was either too subtle or too in sync with the contemporary cultural current to be picked up by most American reviewers, who let the tag line "Cinerama puts you in the picture" shape their critical approach.[44] What is fascinating is how readily this emphasis on audience *participation* slips toward *submission*. As Ariel Rogers notes in her astute analysis of the public discourse surrounding wide-screen cinema in the 1950s, "the idea that widescreen subjected viewers to an overpowering experience was central to the format's appeal."[45] While for most viewers, the tactile and kinesthetic assault rendered by Cinerama was experienced as a thrill—in other words, as a form of cinematic pleasure—some, such as the playwright and screenwriter Robert Sherwood, observed that the wide screen's ability to "submit the audience to any experience we want to give them, and what is more, condition them for that experience," was "almost frightening."[46]

Based on an extensive survey of primary, contemporaneous responses to Cinerama, viewers, both at home and abroad, walked away from screenings most impressed by the physical sensations they experienced (or submitted to). Yet, how did this help promote America's Cold War agenda? Vivian Sobchack has suggested that "the era of the Hollywood historical epic . . . can be characterized as informed by those cultural values identified with . . . bourgeois patriarchy, with colonialism and imperialism, and with entrepreneurial and corporate capitalism."[47] The degree to which Cinerama was shaped by these same cultural values is evident in its shared history with the US military and government. Cinerama's visual excess is also a *politics of excess,* drawing spectators into an experience that is not only physical but also political in its depiction of material and aesthetic excess: of America's physical beauty, thriving industry, and resplendent youth in the case of *This Is Cinerama,* of lavish stage shows and thrilling winter sports in *Cinerama Holiday,* of the marvels of the Western world and its sphere of influence in the final three Cinerama travelogues.

Cinerama's Cold War ideology was also embedded in its formal perspective, particularly its use of aerial cinematography.[48] In a penetrating analysis of *This Is*

Cinerama, Chris Marker argues that the European footage presents the world "as Americans imagine it from afar and see it when they are near." The second part of the film presents America from the point of view of a "*Bon Dieu touriste*" who has blessed the country by his divine providence. "This hierarchy of perspectives, which makes us see America through God's eyes and the rest of the world through America's eyes, is no doubt unconscious. But the subconscious . . ."[49] The distinction Marker observes can be practically explained by Mike Todd's and Merian Cooper's different approaches to the Cinerama process. However, the aerial shots taken from the cockpit of a military jet, which have their origins in the Waller Flexible Gunnery Trainer and were first on display in *This Is Cinerama,* became a hallmark of subsequent Cinerama productions. As Cooper explained to MGM production chief Sol Siegel, he and Lowell Thomas decided to have "the last 24 minutes of THIS IS CINERAMA consist solely of aerial shots of the United States . . . for one—and only one—purpose—to arouse the innate patriotism of the people of the United States."[50] Although Cooper doesn't elaborate, he implies that the visual excess provided by aerial shots of America's dramatically beautiful landscapes and experienced through Cinerama's immersive screen triggers a specific and prescribed emotional response on the part of the audience. By aligning audiences with a perspective that foregrounds and celebrates America's military technology, Cinerama's extensive use of aerial cinematography contributed to America's Cold War battle for hearts and minds.

NOTES

1. The Forum theater was purchased by Cinerama Inc. in the mid-1950s and used as a test facility for Cinerama film stock. See William Gabel and Ken Roe, "Forum Theatre," accessed March 9, 2015, http://cinematreasures.org/theaters/492.

2. The other film was *This Is Cinerama,* on which he was also a director (1952). Cooper would also coproduce *Best of Cinerama* (1963).

3. With thanks to Kevin Brownlow and David Strohmaier for sharing this footage shot for inclusion in the documentary *Cinerama Adventure,* directed by David Strohmaier (2002).

4. See Paul Virilio's seminal exploration of the codevelopment of industrialized warfare, aviation, and cinema, *War and Cinema: The Logistics of Perception* (London and New York: Verso, 1989).

5. Peter Lev, *The Fifties: Transforming the Screen, 1950–1959* (Berkeley: University of California Press, 2003), 112–15; Robert Sklar, *Movie-Made America: A Cultural History of American Movies* (New York: Vintage Books, 1994), 282–85: Kristin Thompson and David Bordwell, *Film History: An Introduction,* 3rd ed. (McGraw-Hill, 2010), 300–302.

6. An exception is John Belton, who, in his comprehensive history of wide-screen processes, notes the significance the US government placed on Cinerama's propaganda value overseas and concludes that "large-screen cinema, as an index of technological prowess, became an unlikely participant in the Cold War." John Belton, *Widescreen Cinema* (Cambridge, MA: Harvard University Press, 1992), 90.

7. Lowell Thomas, "A New Kind of Hero," *This Is Cinerama* program, 1952, Cinerama Corporation collection, box 1, Billy Rose Theatre Division, New York Public Library.

8. *This Is Cinerama* promotional brochure, 1952, Cinerama Corporation collection, box 1, Billy Rose Theatre Division, New York Public Library.

9. Vivian Sobchack, "'Surge and Splendor': A Phenomenology of the Hollywood Historical Epic," *Representations*, no. 29 (Winter 1990): 24–49.

10. Giles Taylor, "A Military Use for Widescreen Cinema: Training the Body through Immersive Media," *Velvet Light Trap* 72 (Fall 2013): 17–32; Fred Waller, "The Archaeology of Cinerama," *Film History: An International Journal* 5 (1993): 289–97; Fred Waller, "Cinerama Goes to War," in *New Screen Techniques*, ed. Martin Quigley (Groton, MA: Quigley Publishing Company, 1953), 125; see also Belton, *Widescreen Cinema*, 101–3.

11. Waller, "Cinerama Goes to War," 125.

12. Ibid.

13. Taylor, "Military Use for Widescreen Cinema," 24.

14. The authorship of the book is unknown. Robert Weisberger, an engineer who worked for Reeves in the 1960s, observes that Reeves was "very well connected with the New York advertising agencies as they were all customers of his . . . sound studio. He most likely hired an . . . agency as the . . . book was not a 'home brew' project." Robert Weisberger, phone interview with author, January 9, 2015. Reeves also had many contacts in the Department of Defense, since he had built his company's fortunes during the war through military contracts. "Hazard Reeves Gives Sound Advice," press release, Cinerama Corporation collection, box 1, Billy Rose Theatre Division, New York Public Library.

15. Alfred Treder, Cinerama Corporation, to US Army Air Force, Public Information Office, Wright Field, Dayton, OH, March 9, 1949, Department of Defense Film Collection 1, box 15, folder 3, Georgetown University Special Collections.

16. Donald Baruch (Chief, Motion Picture Section, Pictorial Branch, Air Information Division) to Alfred Treder, Cinerama Corp., April 5, 1949, Department of Defense Film Collection 1, box 15, folder 3, Georgetown University Special Collections.

17. *Cinerama Holiday* promotional brochure, 1955, box 8, Cinerama Corporation collection, Billy Rose Theatre Division, New York Public Library.

18. John Foster Dulles to Lowell Thomas, 30 August 1954, entry no. A1 1011: "Program and Media Studies; 1956–1962," record group 0306, container no. 1, US National Archives, College Park, MD.

19. The vision for the film Cooper outlines in a memo to Lowell Thomas underscores the degree to which Cold War geopolitics informed the structure of *Seven Wonders*. He writes: "I wanted each and every person in the audience to feel that he had seen the world and all the wonders thereof this side of the Iron Curtain—and I was going to slam down the Iron Curtain at least two or three times . . . to lend drama and excitement to the odyssey." Cooper concludes by asserting his belief that the picture "will do great good for the country." Merian Cooper to Lowell Thomas, 26 August 1954, box 12, folder 8, Merian Cooper Papers, L. Tom Perry Special Collections, Harold B. Lee Library, Brigham Young University, Provo, Utah.

20. Richard Goldstone to Carl Dudley, interoffice memo, Dudley Pictures Corporation, October 15, 1956, Department of Defense Film Collection 1, box 18, folder 17, Georgetown University Special Collections.

21. Donald Baruch to Nathan Lapkin, Stanley Warner Corporation, April 15, 1957, Department of Defense Film Collection 1, box 18, folder 17, Georgetown University Special Collections.

22. President Dwight Eisenhower, address to UN General Assembly, December 8, 1953, accessed August 7, 2016, https://www.iaea.org/about/history/atoms-for-peace-speech.

23. "Cinerama to Make Atomic Energy Film," *New York Times*, September 8, 1955.

24. Grant Leenhouts to Donald Baruch, December 6, 1955, entry no. A1 1006, record group 330, National Archives, College Park, MD.

25. Grant Leenhouts, correspondence, January–August 1956, entry no. A1 1006, record group 330, National Archives, College Park, MD.

26. When Warner's license expired in 1959, Reeves secured a $12 million loan from Prudential Insurance, which then declared that MGM would be Cinerama's partner on all future productions. Convinced that MGM did not properly understand or value how the Cinerama process differed from

conventional filmmaking, Reeves sold his interest in the corporation, and work on *The Eighth Day* ceased. "Prudential Backs Hazard Reeves; Cinerama Entering Fresh Story Era," *Variety*, February 25, 1959.

27. Box 1, Robert Le Baron Papers, 1946–1983, Hoover Institution Archives.

28. Grant Leenhouts to Donald Baruch, August 3, 1956, entry no. A1 1006, record group 330, National Archives, College Park, MD.

29. John Fousek, *To Lead the Free World: American Nationalism and the Cultural Roots of the Cold War* (Chapel Hill: University of North Carolina Press, 2000).

30. Belton, *Widescreen Cinema*, 90. The *New York Times* reported that President Eisenhower sang along to music. "President at Cinerama: Sees Private Film Screening at Washington Theatre," *New York Times*, July 6, 1955.

31. In addition to advising on both the production and distribution of Hollywood films, the Motion Picture Service of the US Information Agency (the centralized information service created by President Eisenhower in 1953) acted as a producer, assigning directors to projects that articulated "the objectives which the United States is interested in obtaining" and that were most likely to reach "the predetermined audience that we as a motion picture medium must *condition*." Turner Shelton, Motion Picture Service, to Cecil B. DeMille, May 11, 1953, cited in Frances Stoner Saunders, *The Cultural Cold War: The CIA and the World of Arts and Letters* (New York: New Press, 1999), 289. (My italics.) For more on the "informal system of cooperation" that the State Department maintained with Hollywood during the postwar years, see Nicholas Cull, *The Cold War and the United States Information Agency: American Propaganda and Public Diplomacy, 1945–1989* (New York and London: Cambridge University Press, 2008), 84, 185.

32. Sarah Nilsen, *Projecting America, 1958: Film and Cultural Diplomacy at the Brussels World's Fair* (Jefferson, NC: McFarland & Company, 2011), 56.

33. "Going to the Fairs," *Time*, September 13, 1954, 33.

34. USIS-Damascus to USIA, September 9, 1954, Cinerama 1953–1954 (IAN), RG 306 National Archives College Park, MD.

35. USIS-Beirut to USIA, October 21, 1954, Cinerama 1953–1954 (IAN), RG 306, National Archives College Park, MD.

36. USIS-Cairo to USIA, October 4, 1954. *This Is Cinerama* was also considered for exhibition at the Pakistan International Industries Fair in March 1955. Cinerama 1953–1954 (IAN), RG 306, National Archives College Park, MD.

37. "America Triumphs at Bangkok Fair," *Life*, January 31, 1955. The US exhibit was awarded first prize at the fair.

38. Ambassador John Peurifoy to Theodore Streibert, undated telegram, folder labeled "1950–1986," Cinerama Corporation collection, box 3, Billy Rose Theatre Division, New York Public Library.

39. Cinerama was officially recognized in the Congressional Record for its "notable contributions to United States foreign policy." "Cinerama Scores Diplomatic Victories in Near East: Extension of Remarks of Hon. Frances P. Bolton of Ohio," *Congressional Record*, March 30, 1955.

40. USIA to Karachi, 5 November 1954, Cinerama 1953–1954 (IAN), RG 306, National Archives, College Park, MD. See Robert H. Haddow, *Pavilions of Plenty: Exhibiting American Culture Abroad in the 1950s* (Washington and London: Smithsonian Institution Press, 1997).

41. *Al Ahrar*, USIS-Beirut to USIA, 21 October 1954, Cinerama 1953–1954 (IAN), RG 306, National Archives College Park, MD.

42. *Falustin*, USIS-Amman to USIA, 22 September 1954, Cinerama 1953–1954 (IAN), RG 306, National Archives College Park, MD.

43. The clippings file on *This Is Cinerama* contains extensive domestic reviews along with summaries of the overseas press compiled by Cinerama's international division. A constant theme of these reviews, whether domestic or international, is that "Cinerama Puts Spectators in the Act," to cite a

headline from the *Detroit Times* (March 24, 1953), box 1, Cinerama Corporation collection, Billy Rose Theatre Division, New York Public Library.

44. As the Cinerama franchise wore on, reviewers focused their critique on the derivativeness of the Cinerama formula. James H. Krukones, "Peacefully Coexisting on a Wide Screen: Kinopanorama vs. Cinerama, 1952–1966," *Studies in Russian and Soviet Cinema* 4, no. 3 (2010): 287.

45. Ariel Rogers, "'Smothered in Baked Alaska': The Anxious Appeal of Widescreen Cinema," *Cinema Journal* 51, no. 3 (Spring 2012): 74–96.

46. Cited in Rogers, "Smothered in Baked Alaska," 82.

47. Sobchack, "Surge and Splendor," 41.

48. The correlation with the prominence of aerial landscapes in the fascist cinema of Mussolini and Stalin merits further exploration. See Noa Steimatsky, *Italian Locations: Reinhabiting the Past in Postwar Cinema* (Minneapolis: University of Minnesota Press, 2008), 14–30; and Emma Waddis, "'One Foot in the Air?' Landscape in the Soviet and Russian Road Movie," *Cinema and Landscape,* ed. Graeme Harper and Jonathan Rayner (Bristol, UK, and Chicago: Intellect, 2010), 73–88.

49. Chris Marker, "And Now This Is Cinerama," in *Cinéma 53 à travers le monde,* ed. Andre Bazin, Jacques Doniol-Valcroze, Gavin Lambert, Chris Marker, Jean Queval, and Jean-Louis Tallenay (Paris: Les Editions du Cerf, 1954), 19 (my translation).

50. Merian Cooper to Sol Siegel, June 14, 1960, box 23, folder 5, Merian Cooper Papers, L. Tom Perry Special Collections, Harold B. Lee Library, Brigham Young University, Provo, Utah.

5

AN ARMY OF THEATERS

Military, Technological, and Industrial Change in US Army Motion-Picture Exhibition

Ross Melnick

Without movies we'd go nuts.
—UNNAMED GI, *TIME*, JULY 31, 1944

For nearly a century, motion-picture theaters have provided diversion and military training as well as operational spaces for US servicemen and servicewomen during wartime and peacetime. Venues for film exhibition for the US Army, Navy, Air Force, and Marine Corps have primarily served as central community and recreation centers on the home front and overseas in outdoor, makeshift, retrofitted, or purpose-built cinemas as well as in slightly less voluminous spaces on vessels above or below sea level. Of these four branches, the relationship between the US Army and motion-picture exhibition has had an especially integrated and complex history. Two decades after their inception in 1921, permanent and makeshift movie theaters became integral both to army operations and to the maintenance of morale, welfare, and recreation as the Army Motion Picture Service (AMPS) grew into one of the largest motion-picture exhibition circuits in the world—a reflection of the army's sprawling yet tightly managed bureaucracy. Although these theaters have been principally dedicated to the exhibition of motion pictures, they have also served as critical daytime and wartime spaces for training, planning, operations, community organizing, and many other on-base functions.

The base theater became a locus of US Army life during the mid–twentieth century as nighttime for servicemen and women was often spent in one of five locations: the mess hall, officers' and other social clubs, the gym (and other recreational facilities), the barracks, or the movie house. The attachment to moviegoing was due in part to the relative lack of competing venues for recreation as well as the remarkable stability of military movie theaters in the face of industrial and social changes occurring in off-base commercial cinemas. During the 1960s and 1970s, American cities and towns began losing their single-screen cinemas; other movie houses were converted into twins and triplexes; multiplexes were built; and some older cinemas began offering art-house, foreign, adult, and other films. Army-base theaters, by contrast, typically maintained their classical Hollywood exhibition strategies: three program changes per week, Saturday matinees, Hollywood releases, single-screen architecture, and an intimate relationship between theater managers and their patrons. Longer than most commercial theaters, army theaters offered the vanishing small-town moviegoing experience without fear of real-estate developers, local competition, lack of parking, or crime causing the base's cinema or cinemas to close. Lack of competition and immediate proximity to patrons created a simulacrum of small-town/urban neighborhood life in which the movie house became a focal point for the base's ever-rotating but also constant sense of community. Before video games, home video, and other late-twentieth- and early-twenty-first-century competitors, the army theater occupied a key space and played an important role for soldiers and their families: to provide distraction, entertainment, and a sense of community far from home. Through its classical exhibition practices, the base theater generated familiarity among its patrons, provided escape from toil and ennui during peacetime, and reinforced the importance of the home front during wartime.

Although never part of the army's Morale, Welfare, and Recreation (MWR) unit, films and theaters were, for decades, key to the maintenance of all three. Thus, the movies and the movie house were not provided solely to occupy a soldier's time. Through the curated exhibition of American films and its part in the simulation of American life on domestic and overseas bases, the army theater served a key role in maintaining mental health for the homesick, the war weary, and the battle hardened, as well as for the growing number of Army families that shifted from one base to another, where the spare, no-frills architecture of the base theater and the huddled masses of similarly contingent souls fostered a calming familiarity and congruity with other base theaters. As families increasingly moved onto military bases throughout the twentieth century, army posts became self-sustaining villages that crafted their own intimacies and "small town" life. These cinemas, which were often homogenous from one base to another due to the army's standardization of both size and aesthetics, sold patrons a simulacrum and a simulation; with the lights off and the projector whirring, moviegoers were transported to a highly familiar place.

This chapter captures the rust, boom, and bust cycle of three key periods in the history of US Army film exhibition: its exceedingly humble beginnings from 1919 to 1926, its rapid growth during World War II, and finally the period between 2011 and 2015 when waning capital and military support doomed half of the army's remaining theaters and altered the future of film exhibition on global bases. This chapter further analyzes how the financial and organizational structures of the

AMPS, the Army and Air Force Motion Picture Service (AAFMPS), and its current operator, the Army and Air Force Exchange Service (AAFES), have strongly influenced the origins, development, and current status of the army's movie houses and their operations over the past century. In so doing, this essay broadens our understanding of Hollywood's multilayered relationship with the US military and reflects the changing nature of the army, domestic and global army bases, and the leisure practices thereon. In short, this chapter charts the ways in which a Hollywood institution like the movie theater became integral to (and then largely faded from) army operations.

ORIGINS OF THE US ARMY MOTION PICTURE SERVICE (AMPS)

Upon the United States' entry into World War I in April 1917, the War Department's Commission on Training Camp Activities (CTCA) built Liberty theaters at army camps around the country to entertain and educate American soldiers by presenting vaudeville, legitimate productions, and motion pictures. Delays in the construction of fireproof projection booths and a preference for booking legitimate and vaudeville productions instead of film reduced the availability of motion pictures in these venues, which totaled just seventeen theaters by April 1918.[1] Sue Collins writes that "Hollywood's efforts to aid the war mobilization movement were circumscribed from the start of US intervention." The Committee on Public Information's Division of Film, for instance, was purposely devoid of motion-picture industry leaders, and even at this early stage, the US Army refused to book films directly and instead relied on "a noncommercial agency," part of a deliberate plan to allow self-appointed elites interested in social uplift and morality to book films for American soldiers.[2] After a change in CTCA management in July 1918, however, motion-picture programming steadily rose, and by war's end there were forty-two Liberty theaters across the country.[3]

After the war, when the CTCA relinquished control of the remaining Liberty theaters to the US Army in September 1919, film and vaudeville became the only two forms of entertainment.[4] By then, the postwar Liberty theaters were so badly financed and mismanaged that their New York office was unable to book any vaudeville acts, and by December 1919, the army had to rely almost entirely on motion pictures.[5] One year later, with a singular focus on creating a sustainable chain of army-post movie theaters, a new office for the "War Department Theaters of the US Army Motion Picture Service" (AMPS) was opened in New York to work directly with the film industry.[6]

While the Navy Motion Picture Service (NMPS, founded in 1919) became a lynchpin of the navy's effort to boost morale and relieve tension, the beginning of the AMPS was disorganized and scarcely funded.[7] The AMPS was officially born on

January 1, 1921, without a congressional appropriation to operate any of the remaining War Department theaters and newly opened exchanges in the (then) forty-eight states along with Washington, DC, Alaska, Newfoundland, Bermuda, and the Trinidad sector of the Caribbean Defense Command. (Post theaters in Hawaii and Puerto Rico were at that time operated by another organization.)[8] "Those of us who were present at its birth will never forget how puny was the infant or how dismal was its outlook," Raymond B. Murray, AMPS director from 1922 to 1945, later wrote. "Its foster-father was a well-wishing but skeptical War Department and its foster-mother an unsuccessful commercial concern. Its only assets were a woefully small sum of money with a discouraging official title of 'Loss on Motion Picture Fund'; a few buildings which were theaters in name only; about enough World War I projectors to permit one to a theater; and some devoted nurses who seemed to think the infant had latent possibilities."[9] These meager beginnings, and the for-profit mandate given to the management of the AMPS, would ultimately shape the structure of the organization and the army's interest in theatrical film exhibition for a century.

Charles Welpley, AMPS architect, observed that by 1923 the growing circuit of 110 theaters, to continue Murray's metaphor, was still an orphanage of abandoned "service clubs, mess halls, hangars, etc., whose only claim to the title 'theater' was that they were officially so designated."[10] Theater seats comprised "anything that could be gathered up around the post, such as mess stools or benches." Instead of building cinemas, its first five years were largely focused on "financial survival."[11] *Variety* noted that if it were not for the major distributors' decision to supply these theaters with films at a "much reduced charge . . . the service could not be continued."[12] In addition to the film industry's own interest in publicizing its support of the armed services, industry trade journals also covered this area of the nontheatrical business.[13]

By 1926, the AMPS had finally received enough Hollywood support, military accolades, local ticket sales, and net revenue to remodel two existing buildings (at Fort Sheridan, Illinois, and Fort Russell, Wyoming) into proper theaters.[14] Still operating under a tightly controlled budget, the AMPS was allowed renovations including sloped floors and insulated walls. Lighting renovations, Welpley recalled, were similarly humble, "exemplified by attractive indirect lighting fixtures constructed from salvaged helmets and water-closet pull-chains."[15] The *Los Angeles Times* reported that the organization's 150 theaters were "entirely self-supporting, the profits of the best patronized theaters going to maintain motion-picture programs at small, remote camps."[16] Revenue from the 4.5 million tickets sold also enabled the AMPS to outfit its first theater with air conditioning in May 1926 and then furnish an additional twenty-one units to its theaters by 1927.[17] Having, at last, demonstrated to army brass that the AMPS could be a lean operation and that theater remodeling improved operations, the division was granted the opportunity to launch a "limited" theater construction program in 1928. This continued frugality was not for show: the AMPS was still operating within a statute that required any army-post building costing more than $20,000 to receive direct authorization from Congress.[18]

AMPS OPERATIONS

With the exception of occasional one-time funding packages, the AMPS operated for much of its history without appropriated funds from Congress or army operating budgets and instead survived, like commercial theaters, through revenue generated from ticket and concession sales. "The decision to operate on a self-sustaining basis," and effectively construct a private/public partnership between Hollywood distribution and Army exhibition, was built, Raymond Murray noted, on the idea that "the avoidance of an operational loss provides the incentive for efficiency in the management of the enterprise" and assures "the successful accomplishment of its mission." Rather than funding these theaters through army MWR appropriations, as the navy did with its own theaters, if soldiers wanted to go to the movies and/or operate these theaters as a second job, they would need to support these theaters as ticket buyers and aid their efficiency as employees.[19]

The AMPS designed, planned, built, and equipped each post theater and booked its films, but each base cinema was managed by a commissioned officer selected by the post commander to fulfill all of the duties of a commercial theater manager, but on a part-time basis during the officer's free time. For their work, theater managers were paid up to fifty-two dollars per month by 1942 in addition to their military pay. Below the manager were the usual (part-time and paid) positions of assistant manager, cashier, ticket taker, chief projectionist, assistant projectionist, relief projectionist, and janitor.[20] AMPS bookers off the base, like their civilian counterparts, negotiated terms with distributors on a percentage basis for feature films, on a flat rental for short films, and "on an age basis" for newsreels. Feature films were distributed to AMPS theaters "within thirty days of their national release," whether their showing competed with nearby civilian theaters or not—a policy that would spur considerable upset with nearby commercial theaters, which demanded clearances from the studios. While all army bookings were later centralized out of the Washington headquarters, district and branch managers could request changes or direct certain films to specific posts based on feedback from managers or due to regional proclivities. AMPS officials were adamantly opposed to censoring films, except, however, in the case of "those pictures that portray[ed] US Army life and activities."[21]

These and other military theaters, therefore, challenge a simplistic binary between what constitutes theatrical and nontheatrical distribution and exhibition. Theatrical exhibition refers to conventional commercial exhibition sites (first- and second-run cinemas, art houses, drive-ins, etc.) that sell tickets to patrons. Nontheatrical exhibition, in film-industry jargon, is a larger, amorphous categorization

FIGURE 5.1. War Department Theater Auditorium, Hamilton Army Air Field, Novato, California. (Courtesy of Library of Congress Prints and Photographs Division, www.loc.gov /pictures/item/ca2669.photos.327108p/.)

that generally refers to venues that exist outside of the commercial release system and may include schools, museums, libraries, houses of worship, public transportation (planes, buses, etc.), and other nontraditional spaces that may or may not charge a fee for entry/viewing. Army theaters, however, challenge these tidy classifications: They sell tickets like conventional theaters, follow standardized release patterns akin to commercial second-run theaters, and market their screenings through display advertisements. Yet, like many exhibition venues that operate at a degree of remove from the film industry, army theaters are not open to the public, are administered by a government entity and not a for-profit company, and are classified by the film industry itself as a "nontheatrical" venue (with bookings handled by distribution executives who specialize in this area). Thus, the history of army movie theaters follows the contours—the hills and valleys—of US theatrical exhibition in terms of technology, audience attendance, and typology of films but is more closely aligned with other nontheatrical exhibition sites as classified by the film industry and by these theaters' longstanding multiuse functionality as military and recreational venues and by their importance in maintaining a sense of community on the base. It should also be noted that all wings of the American military have elaborated display systems designed specifically to be adaptable to spaces that are/ were notably untheatrical; over the past century, these venues have also serviced a diverse range of functions in a wide-ranging set of spaces.[22] Finally, while the Navy Motion Picture Service has remained a vital, well-funded unit of its own MWR operations since its inception in 1919, the model established by the army and the AMPS in the 1920s forced base theaters to operate as if they were part of a second-run, for-profit theater circuit, with many of the challenges of a commercial theater but with all of the additional complexities of military protocols and mandates.

During the 1930s, once the nontheatrical infrastructure of the AMPS was fully operational with positive cash flow, new theaters were constructed through open bids to builders, with work supplied by the Works Progress Administration.[23] In 1932, the AMPS also received a one-time gift of $640,000 of unappropriated War Department funds that General Douglas MacArthur, then chief of staff, had earmarked for new theaters. Thirty-one new army-post theaters were built during the nadir of the Great Depression between 1932 and 1934, the latter benefiting from a new ruling by the judge advocate general of the army that rescinded the $20,000 building restriction that had stymied the creation of more-elaborate theaters. More new base theaters were also built over the next six years, as peacetime slowly came to a close.[24]

PROJECTING TROUBLE AHEAD, 1941-1945

In June 1940, with just eighty army-post theaters still extant,[25] the army began preparing new military camps (and airfields) to house "the first peacetime compulsory military service in the history of this country." The AMPS was conscripted into this effort and charged with designing and building an enormous new fleet of theaters within six months. Movie theaters, for the first time, were now considered integral to the expansion of the rapidly growing army.[26] Following the attack on Pearl Harbor, existing AMPS theaters were transformed overnight, repurposed into spaces used "primarily to provide a means of training our men in the methods of war, and only secondarily to provide recreation."[27] New AMPS theaters were also constructed following three highly standardized plans for base cinemas seating *exactly* 308, 422, or 900 patrons.[28] The new and repurposed AMPS theaters served multiple uses during the war: as training centers for soldiers, lecture halls for troop education, community centers aimed at boosting morale and camaraderie, and places to instill patriotism and military fervor. Training films, newsreels, official war releases, and military briefings became central to the day-to-day programming in these army cinemas. Nighttime screenings followed, with Hollywood films and more war-themed content.

After their early period of scraping and scrapping, AMPS theaters had now become central to every base, especially with the need for an unprecedented number of conscripted recruits to watch training and other war-related films and to gather together for briefings as well as evening recreational screenings. "To the men," Major General Fred H. Osborn, director of the Morale Services division of the US Army, noted at the time, "movies mean home—familiar streets, familiar people." General Dwight Eisenhower declared: "Let's have more motion pictures."[29] In 1942 alone, 118 million admissions were recorded at base theaters,[30] and by the beginning of 1943, the number of AMPS theaters had skyrocketed from less than one hundred before the war to seven hundred in operation, with an estimated nightly seating capacity of over a half million.[31] The AMPS became the second-largest domestic-theater circuit for Hollywood films. (Paramount still operated more than twelve hundred domestic theaters during the early 1940s.)[32] By the middle of 1943, there were 1,041 AMPS venues in the United States, Alaska, Newfoundland, and Bermuda—more than a tenfold increase in a year and a half. Some of the largest bases now had up to eleven movie houses on site.[33] The speed with which these theaters could be built reduced from 182 days for construction in October 1940 to less than 60 days by November 1942.[34] Some of the newly built theaters were "quite elaborate," according to *The Film Daily*,[35] while others were conceived as rudimentary, temporary spaces in rough environments.[36] All of these outlets translated to almost $9 million per year in film rental, making the AMPS another revenue-generating outlet for Hollywood distributors.[37] While ticket prices were markedly lower than in commercial theaters, the volume of attendance provided enough funds to maintain the growing circuit.

Access to these venues was not always uniform, however, because African-American soldiers were often the victims of theater discrimination. A black sergeant, for example, wrote to the *Pittsburgh Post* about an Alabama base theater that forced him and other officers to leave because there was not enough room for white soldiers to sit.[38] At Fort Custer, Michigan, a separate, smaller theater was built solely for "negro troops."[39] In Colorado, another soldier decried the ongoing discrimination at a base theater at the La Junta army airfield: "Negroes have been jim-crowed at this theater ever since I came here in 1942," he wrote.[40] Another black soldier reported that he was allowed to attend only one out of five theaters on his base—an open-air theater that closed whenever there was inclement weather.[41] Despite a recommendation by members of the War Department's Advisory Committee on Negro Troop Policies to abolish segregation in army movie theaters—which the Special Service Division that controlled AMPS backed—committee chairman and Assistant Secretary of War John J. McCloy vetoed the proposal, and the racial divide continued unabated.[42] These policies mimicked other separate but unequal facilities at service clubs, medical offices, and guesthouses for white and black army troops during this period, and also separate times for shared training, administrative, and social spaces.[43] Despite a later, March 10, 1943, directive from the War Department to desegregate camp facilities, many commanders simply ignored these orders and split white and black troops up by units under army regulations. (Black and white troops formed distinct units and could therefore be easily separated.) *Army Service Forces Manual M-5 (Leadership and the Negro Soldier)*, published in October 1944, noted that despite its national integrationist policies, "[t]he Army has no authority or intention to participate in social reform" and thus did not interfere in this persistent segregation.[44]

World War II also put a new focus on projection technology and aesthetic innovation. As basic as some of these new AMPS theaters may have been on the home front, they were luxurious compared with the temporary/mobile exhibition spaces at home and abroad. Makeshift training and battlefront locations outfitted with portable projectors and a billowy screen required creativity and the training of hundreds of men for projecting positions in some of the toughest settings. Overseas, in combat locations, mobility, enemy fire, weather, lack of resources, and other challenges made moviegoing far more problematic. Here, the Overseas Motion Picture Service (OMPS)—under the command of the army's Special Service division, and created in part by the AMPS, of which it served as a model—shipped 16mm films around the world to soldiers on the front. The major distributors provided short and feature films without charge to the OMPS, and those makeshift spaces abroad, in turn, did not charge soldiers.[45]

Many of these temporary and mobile exhibition spaces were set up quickly and inexpensively thanks in part to the development of the JAN P-49 (commonly known as the JAN), a portable 16mm projector whose acronym stood for "joint army navy protocol-49."[46] (For more on portable projectors, see Haidee Wasson's chapter in this volume.) William Fagelson argues that these OMPS-serviced "beachhead bijous" offered a radically different viewing experience from AMPS theaters at home. Machine-gun fire and other explosions regularly broke up frontline screenings. One soldier described these "jungle theaters" as "a roof with coconut fronds, a floor of mud, packing box seats, and airconditioned [*sic*] by pounding rains." War and weather were not the only problems; the projectors, despite their nimble technology, were singular in number, thus requiring breaks between reel changes.[47] (All hard-top AMPS theaters, by contrast, had at least two projectors for changeovers.[48]) Breakage due to the projectors, the environment, and/or the wear and tear of aging prints in harsh conditions led to even more show stoppages.[49]

POSTWAR BLUES

Well before the war's end, in 1944, the US Army had already begun to reduce the number of personnel on its US bases, causing the number of AMPS theaters to decline. From a peak of 1,176 theaters in 1944, still second only to Paramount's national circuit, that number dropped to 964 by May 1945.[50] Those numbers dwindled to 377 in 1946 and fell to 290 by June 1947.[51] In the ensuing years after the war, the AMPS took on the responsibility of managing film distribution and exhibition at air force bases when that branch of the service was established independent of the army in 1948. The AMPS was subsequently renamed the Army and Air Force Motion Picture Service (AAFMPS) and managed movie theaters on army and air force bases for the next three decades, including a highly expanded role beginning in 1956 when the AAFMPS absorbed all of the army and air force's overseas theaters as well. During the late 1950s through the mid-1970s, the global circuit of the AAFMPS remained an integral part of a soldier's social life on domestic and overseas army and air force bases. With continued program changes up to three times per week and perennially low ticket prices, AAFMPS theaters were a throwback to a fading age of classical Hollywood exhibition.[52]

Here, once again, movie theaters on army and air force bases served as simulacra of home, an imitative space that recalled the pleasures and experiences of one's hometown while blending disparate soldiers and their families together to form a contingent yet increasingly bonded community. In its spare construction and adornment, the postwar base theater absorbed all of the color and energy on and off the screen to repurpose, for a few hours, a multiuse venue into a lively neighborhood theater for enlisted men and women and their families. Base theaters placed their focus on the screen, with little ornamentation on the walls or in the lobby to distract or call attention to the differences between this theater and the rural or urban jewel box a soldier had left behind. Meanwhile, overseas, the emotional connections and longing for home, coupled with the new bonds forged at base theaters during the watching of American movies, no doubt drew on a powerful sense of national and local community, recalling and reinforcing the home front for those huddled together in these movie houses.

By 1975, the AAFMPS, with its immense global circuit, had grown to become the world's largest exhibitor, with 1,328 venues in sixty countries, and with more than 1,150 sites on domestic bases. This figure represented roughly 13 percent of the total count of US theaters at the time and was more than double the size of the nation's largest commercial theatrical circuits (General Cinema and United Artists). The circuit of the AAFMPS also included exhibition sites on foreign posts, venues for military attachés, and urban and rural installations for military-assistance advisory groups (which were used extensively before, during, and after the Vietnam War to train local forces and advise on combat operations). In June 1975, right at the peak of its size, the operations of the AAFMPS and its 2,700 part-time theater employees and 247 full-time workers were absorbed by the larger Army and Air Force Exchange Service (AAFES), a nonappropriated unit created by the War Department and carried forward by the Department of Defense, which operates restaurants, stores, and numerous other retail and service businesses on bases around the world.[53] The AAFES, which partners with both the army and the air force's MWR programs, was given direction over the "worldwide operation, management, and supervision of motion picture activities, personnel, properties, and funds," and, in 1977, local exchange managers of the AAFES took over the duties and responsibilities once granted to local base-theater officers. Thus, the AAFES turned the global AAFMPS circuit of locally managed theaters into a centralized chain where decision-making power was now held in AAFES offices, far from local bases.[54]

The consolidation of the AAFMPS under the AAFES, and the centralization of what had been locally managed theaters and regions, mimics the economic logic of media corporations of the era. In the 1970s, studios like Paramount became part of Gulf & Western, and exhibitors such as Loews Theaters became a small part of the larger Loews Corporation, which had developed highly profitable hotel, cigarette, and insurance divisions. Carol A. Habgood and Marcia Skaer write that the absorption of the AAFMPS by the AAFES was "a logical action to achieve economies by eliminating overlapping functions"—and, thus, overlapping people and office space.[55] The army was also changing in 1975 as the end of the Vietnam War led to a reappraisal by the Ford administration of defense budgets and the need for cost cutting. Secretary of Defense James Schlesinger's "turnaround defense budget" expressly called for comparatively higher appropriations to the navy versus the rest of the armed services, "with the Army descending into last place."[56] The absorption of the AAFMPS by the AAFES reflected the army's decreased funding and enabled it to transfer all film responsibilities to the AAFES at a time of significant belt tightening.

REEL TIME THEATERS

In the intervening years between 1977 and 1994, as moviegoing declined in civilian theaters, that downward trend was also felt at AAFES theaters, now part of the "Reel Time Theaters"–branded circuit. The rise of cable television, home video, and pay-per-view, along with outdated theatrical exhibition equipment and nonsensical policies that delayed film releases to AAFES theaters by up to eighteen months, all played a hand in the closing of theaters on army and air force bases around the world.[57] The end of the Cold War also led to the closure of numerous bases and with it their on-site movie theaters. By 1994, AAFES/Reel Time had lost more than half of its inventory—from 1,328 theaters in 1975 to roughly 600 cinemas in 1994, "of which," Habgood and Skaer write, "more than 60 percent" were nontraditional, free movie sites operated by AAFES in often shared spaces for training and recreation, typically in more remote locations.[58]

A decade later, the remaining 160 AAFES/Reel Time theaters faced a host of new challenges,[59] including changes in movie-theater technology and design standards, increased competition from civilian megaplexes, congressional and military budget cuts, lifestyle changes, and a desire to leave the base when off-duty. Competition

FIGURE 5.2. Exterior view in 2006 of Reel Time's Vicenza Theater at Camp Ederle in Vicenza, Italy. The single-screen theater is still open Wednesday through Sunday to provide military personnel "with a small taste of home." The Vicenza advertises its ability to show "First Run Movies." (Courtesy of US Army Africa. Flickr, Creative Commons, www.flickr.com/photos /usarmyafrica/3800350443/.)

from other forms of media display and leisure activities also factored. "Historically, base theaters have played the movie theater role because of limited mobility and limited off-base entertainment options for airmen," a 1995 Air Combat Command Morale Welfare Recreation and Services manual had noted. "Now, however, airmen and their families have much more mobility. Many base locations that were once rural or remote have become urbanized and afford the base community a wider range of options for spending their leisure time and extra money. The result is a decline in the use of base theaters as movie theaters since patrons go off base for their recreational needs." With their declining attendance, AAFES movie houses became increasingly utilized for military education, in-processing (first day of arrival for new recruits) and administrative briefings, continuing-education lectures, award and retirement ceremonies, town meetings for military-family housing residents, and commander's calls (mandatory meetings between commanders and those under their command), while still showing movies from three to seven days per week depending on location.[60]

In the early 2010s, struck by the rapid industry changeover to digital projection and a growing audience desire for large-format theaters and 3-D screenings, AAFES executives were forced to decide whether to convert all AAFES theaters to digital projection or select for conversion only those that could eventually recoup the investment. Unlike the fully funded Navy Motion Picture Service, which converted all of its theaters for digital projection,[61] the AAFES model forced decision makers to put revenue generation ahead of the theaters' importance for base morale and recreation. AAFES spokesman Judd Anstey argued that "[i]t's just not cost effective for the exchange service to invest the $120,000 per theater needed to convert from 35 millimeter film to the new format at the theaters that are being closed," adding that the delayed AAFES exhibition calendar had become increasingly problematic due to off-base competition from deluxe theaters as well as collapsing windows between theatrical release and streaming-service availability.[62]

In the end, the AAFES ceased operating half of the more than 120 Reel Time Theaters remaining around the globe, with only 26 US-based theaters and 34 overseas locations converted for digital projection. The AAFES relinquished its management of the others.[63] Colonel Mark Weatherington, the Twenty-eighth Bomb Wing commander at Ellsworth Air Force Base in South Dakota, deflected criticism away from his command over the base's theater closure, for instance, noting that this "was not a base decision" but "a business decision by AAFES."[64] While many of the decommissioned theaters would now be converted for community and training purposes, others would no longer have revenues from the AAFES to maintain their condition, equipment, and viability.

Navy Motion Picture Service theaters, meanwhile, financed entirely by the navy's MWR division under Navy Installations Command, received new digital projectors and servers.[65] In 2013, the AAFES generated $8.3 billion in gross revenue, $332 million in net earnings, and was therefore able to commit $208 million in "dividends" to "soldiers, airmen and their families," including $116.4 million to the army and $69.4 million to the air force. The AAFES did not, however, spend the $7.4 million needed to upgrade and keep open its other sixty theaters.[66] Instead, while the AAFES continued to sell Blu-rays, DVDs, and streaming media devices through its exchange, theatrical exhibition became a declining priority.

Another reason the AAFES may have turned away from a full digital conversion of its circuit is that the army was already looking to the future instead of the past. With social clubs and AAFES movie theaters dwindling in attendance and importance, the army's own MWR division began opening new "high-tech concept" centers, called "Warrior Zones," "to engage young soldiers on base during down time" and tap into the current generation's interest in physical activity and interactivity versus moviegoing, which was deemed more passive. These structures were commissioned after the army's MWR unit conducted focus groups "to help us develop a new vision of what a military entertainment center should be."[67]

The Warrior Zone at Joint Base Lewis-McChord (JBLM), near Tacoma, Washington—completed after the first Warrior Zone opened at Fort Riley, Kansas, in 2011—offered "16 game stations with 55-inch high-definition monitors for Xbox and PS3 video games, computers with high-speed Internet access, more than 50 high-definition 52-inch televisions equipped with DirecTV, and 32 Alienware custom gaming computers." The $11 million Warrior Zone also featured pool tables, a restaurant and bar, and a "home theater" space for watching movies—but not a traditional movie theater.[68] "We tried to ferret out activities that the single soldier of today would want and we thought that would include bowling alleys and movie theaters," Adam Wyden, the design project manager, commented upon the JBLM Warrior Zone's opening in 2012. "But that wasn't really what they wanted." Wyden, echoing the base theater's once-central role in connecting soldiers back to their civilian life, added that online video games, social media, and interconnectivity enable soldiers to compete and ultimately connect "with their best friends from back home."[69] Additional Warrior Zones have since opened at army and navy bases in the United States and overseas. The decline of traditional base theaters and their replacement by gaming, social media, streaming video platforms, and other interactivity reflects the broader conditions in which civilian and military film exhibitors operate: the new generation of moviegoers (and soldiers) has become oriented to very different kinds of leisure activities and technology.

CONCLUSION

The army's lack of institutional support for motion-picture exhibition at the conception of the AMPS in 1921 ultimately foretold its precarious future. Today, after serving the US Army for nearly a century, the army's remaining theaters at home and abroad are still at risk as the recreations of the moment—video games, fitness centers, mobile media, and other contemporary diversions—continue to rise in popularity. From over thirteen hundred cinemas in 1975, the AAFES now manages just over sixty Reel Time Theaters around the world. (This precipitous decline is further evidence of the toll digital conversion has had upon independent, second-run, and nontheatrical venues like army-base theaters.) With numerous army cinemas no longer showing motion pictures, what was once a vital community center has diminished at many bases and vanished from others.

The history of army motion-picture exhibition—whether through the CTCA, AMPS, AAFMPS, or AAFES—provides military and media historians with an opportunity to examine the ways in which army (and air force) base movie theaters have provided a venue for morale, welfare, and recreation and for a wide range of official military activities. This research also contributes to a growing body of scholarship on nontheatrical distribution and exhibition by challenging academic and industrial definitions of that enterprise, underscoring how army theaters, while often functioning more like theatrical exhibition sites, remain "nontheatrical" by definition in that they are closed to the public, have alternate interstitial programming, and work with nontheatrical-film distribution personnel and companies. As the AAFMPS took over the army's global chain of theaters, developed by the OMPS during World War II, the US government also became one of the largest operators of motion-picture theaters outside the United States. It is in these gray areas, between theatrical and nontheatrical, domestic and global, that research on army theaters provides us with a window into the changing nature of military life, movie-going, and public amusements, and the ways that Hollywood films have supported, formally and informally, the US armed forces over the past century.

ACKNOWLEDGMENTS

Thank you to Danny Grinberg for his invaluable research assistance.

NOTES

Works frequently cited are identified by the following abbreviations:

LAT	Los Angeles Times
MPN	Motion Picture News
TFD	The Film Daily

Epigraph: "G.I.s and Movies," Time, July 31, 1944, 52.

1. Weldon Durham, Liberty Theatres of the United States Army, 1917–1919 (Jefferson, NC: McFarland & Company, 2006), 1–4, 138–45; "Liberty Theatre Circuit," Variety, April 12, 1918, 20.

2. Sue Collins, "Film, Cultural Policy, and World War I Training Camps: Send Your Soldier to the Show with Smileage," Film History: An International Journal 26, no. 1 (2014): 5.

3. Ibid., 1.

4. Durham, Liberty Theatres, 1–4, 138–45.

5. "Army Booking Office Closed," Variety, December 5, 1919, 32.

6. "Films in Army Posts," Wid's Daily, December 24, 1920, 1.

7. Logan E. Ruggles, "Circle Globe with Pictures: Navy Builds Up Huge Film Exchange," LAT, March 26, 1922, III35. By 1929, with floating cinemas, ashore theaters, and navy film exchanges around the world, the Washington Post noted, the NMPS had become "the greatest motion-picture distributor in the world." John L. Coontz, "Films aboard Ship Joy to Sea Fighter," Washington Post, April 28, 1929, M7.

8. R. B. Murray, "Administration of U.S. Army Motion Picture Service," Journal of the Society of Motion Picture Engineers 11 (January 1943): 61.

9. Ibid., 54.

10. "Pictures and People," MPN, April 7, 1923, 1656; "War Dept.'s Theatre Circuit May Reach 25 Playing Weeks," Variety, June 21, 1923, 6; Charles Welpley, "Construction of War Department Theaters," Journal of the Society of Motion Picture Engineers 11 (January 1943): 4.

11. "Army Theaters Pay, Report Says Film Shows Also Give Profits to Men," LAT, April 10, 1926, 4.

12. "94 Army Post Theatres Supported by Film Industry," Variety, October 20, 1926, 58.

13. This was due in part to the financial remuneration Hollywood received from their deals with the army, navy, and other military theaters and because film-industry leaders—many of whom were immigrants—were eager to demonstrate their patriotism and the motion picture's centrality to American cultural, social, and military life.

14. "94 Army Post Theatres."

15. Welpley, "Construction of War Department Theaters," 4.

16. "Credit Granted Film Patrons: Soldiers Merely Say 'Charge It' to Enter Army Cine," *LAT,* November 10, 1926, PS-11.

17. "Millions Served by M.P. Service," *MPN,* November 6, 1926, 1758c; Arctic Nu-Air Corp. advertisement, *MPN,* April 29, 1927, 1574.

18. Welpley, "Construction of War Department Theaters," 5.

19. Murray, "Army Motion Picture Service," 55.

20. Murray, "Army Motion Picture Service," 57; "Role of Projectionists in the US Army," *International Projectionist,* December 1942, 10.

21. Murray, "Army Motion Picture Service," 59, 60.

22. See Haidee Wasson's and Andrea Kelley's chapters in this volume.

23. "Plan Army Theater," *TFD,* June 14, 1932, 7; Karen DeMasters, "On the Map: New Life for a Theater Where War-Bound Officers Caught a Movie," *New York Times,* January 30, 2000, NJ3.

24. Welpley, "Construction of War Department Theaters," 12.

25. "Army Post Cinemas Expected to Double Present 400G Rentals," *Variety,* September 11, 1940, 16.

26. "Army's Post-War Size to Rule Equip. Disposition," *TFD,* August 2, 1943, 7.

27. Welpley, "Construction of War Department Theaters," 23.

28. Ibid., 20.

29. "Movies Go to War Front," *Salt Lake Tribune,* September 17, 1944, 5.

30. "Acting Awards to James Cagney," *TFD,* March 5, 1943, 6.

31. Murray, "Army Motion Picture Service," 62.

32. "US Army Now Has World's Largest 'Theatre Circuit,'" *International Projectionist,* November 1942, 17; "Army Film Service Grows Apace," *Variety,* June 24, 1942, 20; "Army Circuit 2D to Par," *Variety,* September 2, 1942, 27; United States Temporary National Economic Committee, "The Motion Picture Industry: A Pattern of Control," *Investigation of Concentration of Economic Power* (Washington, DC: Government Printing Office, 1941), 10, 11.

33. "Army's Post-War Size," 7; "US Army Post Theaters," in *The 1945 Film Daily Year Book of Motion Pictures,* ed. Jack Alicoate (New York: Film Daily, 1945), 773.

34. Murray, "Army Motion Picture Service," 62.

35. "Army's Post-War Size," 7.

36. Murray, "Army Motion Picture Service," 63.

37. "Pix Rentals from US Camp Theatres Now Nearly $9,000,000 per Annum," *Variety,* January 13, 1943, 1.

38. Sgt. Jesse L. Wilkins, "Five Seats for Colored Boys," *Pittsburgh Courier,* November 29, 1944, n.p., reprinted in *Taps for a Jim Crow Army,* ed. Benjamin Quarles and Bernard Nally (Lexington: University Press of Kentucky, 1993), 200, 201.

39. "More Army Theatres," *Variety,* February 26, 1941, 21.

40. A Negro Soldier to NAACP, "Negroes Will Naturally Sit with One Another," March 19, 1945, reprinted in Quarles and Nally, *Taps for a Jim Crow Army,* 179.

41. Bert B. Babero to Truman K. Gibson, "A Figure Head," February 13, 1944, reprinted in Quarles and Nally, *Taps for a Jim Crow Army,* 50.

42. Daniel Kryder, *Divided Arsenal: Race and the American State during World War II* (New York: Cambridge University Press, 2000), 144.

43. Raymond R. Weyeneth, "The Architecture of Racial Segregation: The Challenges of Preserving the Problematical Past," *Public Historian* 27, no. 4 (Fall 2005): 18, 32.

44. Jonathan B. Sutherland, *African Americans at War: An Encyclopedia,* (Santa Barbara, CA: ABC-CLIO, 2004), 1:550.

45. Murray, "Army Motion Picture Service,"61. "Army Film Service Grows Apace," 20; "Army to Have 1,000 Theaters in Camps," *TFD*, November 20, 1942, 8; "Movies Go to War Front," 5.

46. Haidee Wasson, "Protocols of Portability," *Film History: An International Journal* 25, nos. 1–2 (2013): 236–47.

47. William Friedman Fagelson, "Fighting Films: The Everyday Tactics of World War II," *Cinema Journal* 40, no. 3 (Spring 2001): 99, 100.

48. "Army's Post-War Size," 7.

49. Fagelson, "Fighting Films," 101.

50. "Cut in Army Camps Affects Theater Biz," *TFD*, May 7, 1945, 1, 6.

51. "Million 'GI's' See Films in 500 Houses," *Motion Picture Daily*, June 6, 1947, 4. While the AMPS was closing down a large percentage of its domestic and international theaters after the war, the War Activities Committee began setting up 150 new 35mm-equipped theaters for American troops stationed in Europe beginning in April 1945, using film-industry executives and AMPS officials as advisers. The number of those cinemas would grow to 250 by April 1947. "250 Army Theaters Operating Overseas," *TFD*, April 21, 1947, 2; "Army Theaters Drop from 1,188 to 410," *TFD*, July 16, 1946, 1.

52. Carol A. Habgood and Marcia Skaer, *One Hundred Years of Service: A History of the Army and Air Force Exchange Service, 1895 to 1995* (Dallas: Army & Air Force Exchange Service, 1994), 146.

53. Richard Albarino, "How Many Film Sites Are There?" *Variety*, January 8, 1975, 7; Walt Trott, "Army & Air Force's 1,300 Global Theatres May Get New Operator," *Variety*, April 16, 1975, 32; "1,300 GI Theatres Worldwide Merged into Exchange System," *Variety*, July 30, 1975, 35; Habgood and Skaer, *One Hundred Years of Service*, 147.

54. Habgood and Skaer, *One Hundred Years of Service*, 147; "Army & Air Force's 1,300 Global Theatres" 32.

55. Habgood and Skaer, *One Hundred Years of Service*, 146.

56. Leslie H. Gelb, "The Defense Budget: More, More, More," *New York Times*, June 15, 1975, E2.

57. "GI Cinemas in Europe Pick Up Attendance after 5-Year Decline," *Variety*, June 10, 1987, 26.

58. Habgood and Skaer, *One Hundred Years of Service*, 147; "Attendance Down at GI Houses in Europe; Poor Equipment Cited," *Variety*, April 4, 1984, 43; "1,300 GI Theatres Worldwide," 35.

59. Bob Tourtellotte, "Movie Distributors, U.S. Army Begin Fight over 'Fahrenheit 9/11,'" *Houston Chronicle*, August 16, 2004, accessed August 23, 2017, www.chron.com/entertainment/movies/article/Movie-distributors-U-S-Army-begin-fight-over-1520215.php.its.

60. Air Combat Command: Morale Welfare Recreation and Services, "Base Theater Design Standards," *Morale, Welfare, Recreation and Services, Langley Air Force Base*, ca. 1995, 4, accessed August 23, 2017, www.wbdg.org/FFC/AF/AFDG/basetheater.pdf.

61. Trevor Andersen, "3-D Upgrades Made at Three Navy Theaters in Japan," *Stars and Stripes*, August 17, 2012, accessed June 11, 2015, www.stripes.com/news/3-d-upgrades-made-at-three-Navy-theaters-in-japan-1.186001.

62. Dirk Lammers, "Digital Age Prompting Closing of Base Theaters" *Military Times*, January 20, 2013, accessed June 11, 2015, http://archive.militarytimes.com/article/20130120/BENEFITS07/301200308/Digital-age-prompting-closure-base-theaters.

63. Ibid.

64. Jennifer H. Svan, "Some AAFES Theaters Going Digital, but Others Shuttering," *Stars and Stripes*, February 14, 2013, accessed June 11, 2015, www.stripes.com/military-life/some-aafes-theaters-going-digital-but-others-shuttering-1.207965; "3-D Upgrades Made at Three Navy Theaters in Japan."

65. Svan, "Some AAFES Theaters Going Digital."

66. "Army & Air Force Exchange by the Numbers," AAFES, accessed June 12, 2015, www.aafes.com/about-exchange/exchange-by-the-numbers/.

67. D. Craig MacCormack, "US Army Goes Back to the Future with Warrior Zone Club," *Commercial Integrator,* June 21, 2013. www.commercialintegrator.com/article/us_army_goes_back_to_the_future_with_warrior_zone_club.

68. Mollie Miller, "Fort Riley Opens Army's 1st Warrior Zone," *US Army Public Affairs,* September 8, 2011, https://www.army.mil/article/65191/Fort_Riley_opens_Army_s_1st_Warrior_Zone; "Warrior Zone," Joint Base Lewis-McChord Morale Welfare & Recreation. www.jblmmwr.com/warrior_zone/index.html.

69. Dwyn Taylor, "Military Architecture Goes Modern," *Military Engineer,* n.d., accessed June 11, 2015, http://themilitaryengineer.com/index.php/item/184-military-architecture-goes-modern.

PART TWO

STRATEGIES OF VIEWING

6

WAR IN PEACE

The American Legion and the Continuing Service of Film

Tom Rice

The 1920 Fox Film Corporation picture *The Face at Your Window* confronts the contemporary issue of labor agitation in a modern industrial town and features as its hero Frank Maxwell, the head of the local American Legion post. Maxwell works in his father's factory mill and, after he falls for Ruth, the "pretty daughter of an immigrant worker," is stabbed in the back by Ivan, another immigrant worker jealous of their relationship and critical of his family's "humane" treatment of the workers. The personal confrontation between American employer (Frank's father) and foreign employee (Ivan) is magnified by the arrival of Comrade Kelvin, "a tall foreign looking stranger" who intends to mobilize the workers. In response, Frank summons the American Legion, which races to protect the American city from this foreign invasion.[1]

The American Legion emerged in the immediate aftermath of World War I in March 1919—a point at which the focus of conservative discourse and government policy shifted from overseas campaigns to domestic threats, from military to political targets. This shift is often indexed by the Red Scare of 1919, which historians have now recognized as a crucial starting point for the Cold War. Within this context, the American Legion became one of the most prominent and influential conservative forces in America, championing the rights and causes of veterans and remolding military citizens within an emerging "state of exception."[2] We see this process in *The Face at Your Window*, which imagines an important role for the American Legion in contemporary America. The film identifies a need and outlet for a militaristic response and helps to orchestrate a form of conservative nationalism ("Americanism") that was fostered during the war but that was soon after aligned with escalating fears of immigration and that segued into anti-unionism.

The Legion featured on-screen in other modern contexts—for example, fighting a Japanese enemy in California in *Shadows of the West* (1920), which like *The Face at Your Window* helped to foreground the American Legion within a year of its formation as the legitimate, government-supported response to foreign "terror" threats.

The Legion's heroic appearance in *The Face at Your Window* further indicates the group's imbrication with the political mainstream as it expanded and appropriated military activities and imperatives into peacetime America. The film was endorsed by the Congress-approved Americanism Committee of the Motion Picture Industry (ACMPI), which had been set up in January 1920 to educate "immigrants in the ideals of America."[3] By this time, barely nine months after its formation, the Legion claimed almost a million members and was increasingly looking to use media and the emerging field of public relations as tools for its expanding remit. Its newspaper, the *American Legion Weekly,* launched on July 4, 1919, with a print run of twelve thousand, but by November it had a circulation of three hundred thousand.[4] From the outset, the Legion turned to film not only to define and promote its own role within postwar America but also to represent and challenge new enemies that emerged out of the European conflict. As early as October 1919, Legion officials were offering their "hearty cooperation in every way possible" to support the widespread exhibition of *Everybody's Business,* a film that they believed would do much "to enlighten the public on the methods pursued by the Bolsheviks in their efforts to create lawlessness, disorder and unrest amongst the working classes."[5] Samuel Goldwyn, president of Goldwyn Pictures Corporation, also wrote to the Legion offering his company's services in producing or distributing the Legion's stories. "You stand on the threshold of a new epoch in American Life. You, yourselves, are to be the builders of that epoch," Goldwyn wrote. "The message of which you are the bearers is full of dramatic possibilities; it is vibrant with the color and magnetism of a new patriotism."[6] Aside from using contemporary films and potentially producing its own patriotic films, the Legion also repurposed existing war films. Before the end of 1919 the government offered the Legion the use of its patriotic war films, and in its general media operations the Legion learned from the Committee on Public Information (CPI) and from the government's quite extensive use of film during World War I.[7]

The Legion's increasingly prominent position in a country that was now preoccupied with questions around immigration, unionism, and, more broadly, population management is borne out by its escalating influence within the Americanism Committee. Colonel Arthur Woods, who served as chairman of the Legion's own National Americanism Commission (NAC), was asked to join the ACMPI in April 1920 and then in November succeeded former secretary of the interior Franklin K. Lane as its head.[8] Woods had previously served as assistant to the secretary for war in charge of reemployment and had asked producers and exhibitors for their help in finding jobs for returning soldiers. Through his ongoing work with the NAC, Woods sought to promote and define "100% Americanism" and looked toward film to achieve this.[9] On assuming the leadership of the ACMPI in 1920, Woods determined that "there should be injected into every picture some ideas that would make better Americans."[10] Indeed it was the then-head of the ACMPI, Franklin K. Lane, who requested the production of *The Face at Your Window* and approved its scenario. "It was intended to depict the ever present danger of malcontents and traitors within the country," the film's producer, William Fox, explained, "and to give timely warning to the nation to assert to its fullest extent the American patriotism that predominates in this country."[11] By the time it was released, Woods was acting chairman of the ACMPI and urged that the film be "exhibited in every city, town and hamlet in the United States."[12]

For all of Woods's attempts to define Americanism, the concept remains elusive and malleable, reworked across the nation, depending in part on differing migratory patterns, and across time, as we see in twenty-first-century America with the onrush of new threats and popular anxieties. From the outset this concept would motivate the Legion's work (one of the founding aims of the American Legion was to "foster and perpetuate a one hundred per cent Americanism") and so warrants brief exposition here. At its initial convention, when the Legion established its National Americanism Commission, it outlined its "duty" to realize "one hundred per cent Americanism" through education. It listed five goals that partly indicate the ways in which this term would be used to justify the management and shaping of populations, transforming immigrants and "alien residents" into productive citizens and inculcating them with what it defined as American ideals. In particular, it foregrounded language training and the teaching of Americanism in schools as keystones to this Americanization campaign. Yet, the concept of Americanism is, by its nature, exclusionary, defined as much by what is not "American." This is apparent in the first listed goal, which promised to "combat all anti-American tendencies, activities and propaganda."[13] The subjects chosen for the commission's annual essay-writing contest also attest to this more regressive attempt to "combat" particular practices. While the 1922 contest asked schoolchildren to expound on the theme "How the American Legion Can Best Serve the Nation," in 1923 the topic was "Why America Should Ban Immigration for Five Years," and in 1924, "Why Communism is a Menace to Americanism."[14] By this stage, the concept of Americanism would be widely adopted and adapted by all manner of organizations and political figures, including the Ku Klux Klan, which defined 100 percent Americanism in racial and religious terms. Writing in 1928, the chairman of the NAC, Frank Pinola, stated, "We of the Americanism Commission have come to the conclusion that it is a subjective term; it means just what you choose it to mean."[15]

The links between the American Legion and the US military permeate the Legion's film operations, as it looks to film—in various forms and spaces—

to continue service long after fighting has ceased, to support veterans' rights and treatment, to shape public policy, but also to promote a pervading, and enduring, conservative ideology ("Americanism") that aligns militaristic and nationalist sentiment. Writing in *Visual Education* in 1923, the national commander of the Legion stated, "[W]e cannot admit more immigrants until we Americanize those already here."[16] Such language positions the Legion as a successor to the work of the CPI, which had used film and accompanying talks to mobilize and inculcate immigrant audiences within the cinema space. The Legion would now look to extend this use of film, exhibiting within local cinemas, Legion buildings, and nontheatrical sites, and using advertisements, endorsements, and competitions to circulate its messages beyond the screening venue. The Legion's multifarious use of film contributes to recent scholarship on what Charles Acland and Haidee Wasson have termed "useful" cinema.[17] Indeed the Legion's active role in recognizing, and organizing around, film as a key site for shaping public life in the 1920s further highlights that those groups using film as a platform for a cultural politic went well beyond the widely acknowledged women's and religious groups. My own work on the Ku Klux Klan provides one such example, while Lee Grieveson has recently shown how Henry Ford's Motion Picture Department produced films during the Red Scare.[18] By 1919 Ford imagined film not only as a means of instructing modern workers in industry and work but also, as Grieveson noted, as one of "visualizing citizenship" for young working-class and immigrant audiences.

The American Legion emerged at this precise moment and recognized these possibilities. Earle A. Meyer, the director of the American Legion Film Service, argued that "[t]here is no activity through which the American Legion can accomplish more good than that of community movies. Our interpretation of community movies," he continued, "is the utilization of moving pictures in advancing through visual entertainment and education a better appreciation of good citizenship and clean living."[19] Meyer's comments attest both to the prominent, though historically overlooked, role of film in the American Legion and also to the particular ways in which film was imagined at the height of anxieties around immigration—which reached their apex with the introduction of the Immigration Act of 1924—as a means of defining and creating model American citizens. These anxieties were closely aligned with criticisms of the "movies." Indeed, Meyer's reference to "clean living" may be construed as a critique of Hollywood, at a moment when the nascent industry was enveloped in scandal. By 1923 the Legion was a significant voice in film reform, prominently featured in Will Hays's Committee on Public Relations and, in the words of Meyer, running a campaign "for cleaner and more truly American films."[20] What follows examines the myriad ways in which the American Legion used film at this critical juncture in American social and political history. In short, whether appropriating wartime government films, partaking in film reform, or, after the establishment of a designated film service in

1921, producing, distributing, and exhibiting movies, the Legion would look to champion the rights of veterans, project its own model of citizenship, and, in the process, extend and reimagine state intervention through its quasi-military veterans' organization.

"HOUSES BUILT ON CELLULOID ARE AS SOLID AS HOUSES BUILT ON ROCK": DISTRIBUTING AMERICANISM

The American Legion Film Service began in 1921 as one of four agencies within the Legion's publicity division, alongside the *American Legion Weekly*, the American Legion News Service, and the National Speakers' Bureau—collectively tasked with keeping members and the public informed of Legion activities and, moreover, of maintaining a "favorable attitude of public opinion toward the Legion."[21] The Legion emerged at the precise moment when the very idea of "public opinion" was being articulated, and then measured, within America. It partly developed this idea from the state—again the CPI, which embraced the ideas of PR pioneers like Walter Lipmann, is an important precursor here—adapting wartime exigencies for an organization that represented the military in peacetime. Writing in 1924, the *American Legion Weekly* stated, "Public Opinion is the force which rules the world, or comes mighty close to." The "Legion has grown great because public opinion has informed the Legion," and this has happened "by design and not by accident."[22]

So what role was imagined for film within the publicity division? For figures like Woods, film was intended to promote and disseminate the Legion's notion of "Americanism," but it also provided a means of "increasing interest and attendance at post meetings"—effectively drawing people into the Legion—and of linking the local Legion posts to the wider community through public film shows.[23] The plans for the establishment of the Film Service in August 1921 certainly suggest a strong economic motivation. The annual conference of the Indiana department of the American Legion addressed the "pressing problem" of the "empty treasury" and the challenge of finding a "legitimate and dignified means for the department to raise money," while the *American Legion Weekly* subsequently recognized a primary function of the service as being a "revenue producer for posts and units."[24] One advertisement in the *American Legion Weekly* for the Film Service was headlined "Easy Money," with the subheadings "There Is No Better Way to Earn Money" and "It's Dead Easy." (See figure 6.1.) Years later the Legion labeled its official booklet, listing all the films available through the service, "Here's Money for Your Post." The booklet recognized the *value* of film to the Legion—in extending its message and attracting Legion members, and also more directly in economic terms, explaining that "every legionnaire owes it to his post to investigate this dignified and highly successful method of raising funds."[25] In this way, the Legion recognized an important way to

Easy Money

There Is No Better Way to Earn Money

IT'S DEAD EASY

Every Legionnaire Should Be Interested

WE'LL SHOW YOUR POST HOW

MAIL COUPON TODAY

The American Legion Film Service
Dept. A, Indianapolis, Ind.

Name _____

Street _____

City _____

State _____

Post _____

FIGURE 6.1. A coupon that appeared on page 16 of the *American Legion Weekly*'s issue of December 19, 1924, emphasizing the money-making potential of film for Legion posts.

commercialize its Americanization efforts as, through film, the process of constructing postwar citizens became a commercially lucrative Legion activity.

In initially outlining exactly how this financial model would work, the Indiana
conference determined that the "most satisfactory way" of running a film show
involved local posts contacting the department headquarters to book "a film
drama especially suited for Americanization purposes." The first film offered
through this scheme, which was appositely described as a "joint Americanizing
and financing movement," was the 1918 Arnold Daly film *My Own United States*.[26]

Although *My Own United States* played extensively across Indiana in 1921, it
was in early 1923 that the Film Service secured exclusive distribution and exhibition rights for the film, which it now promoted—using the title of its source material—as *The Man without a Country*. In February, coupons appeared in the
American Legion Weekly, with a tagline "If your post is looking for a way to make
money," which invited commanders of Legion posts to send their details to the
Film Service in Indianapolis. The coupon read, "Please tell me how my post can
increase its prestige and add to its treasury by showing the Legion's motion picture
film, 'The Man without a Country.'"[27] (See figure 6.2.) Over the next few months,
the *American Legion Weekly* encouraged further bookings by reporting on succes-
ful screenings, including an eight-day run at one of the largest cinemas in Louisville, Kentucky, which brought a net profit of seventeen hundred dollars. While the
Film Service was responsible for the technical details, the local post was tasked
with publicizing and bringing a crowd to the event. In Louisville, this involved a
beauty contest run through a local paper, six airplanes dropping leaflets and tickets
over the city, a parade of schoolchildren, and a chain telephone message through
which each Legion member would contact ten friends to pass on details of the
film. The governor also attended a screening and gave an opening address.[28]

Reports emphasised the usefulness of the film as a pedagogical tool: "If the
American Legion had spent thousands of dollars in launching a program teaching
the ideals of Americanism, through lectures and meetings, it could not have had
the 'creeping under the skin' effect" of *The Man without a Country*—but the impact
stretched beyond those that had attended the film.[29] The screening was used to
define and promote the Legion within the community, since the newspaper coverage, advertisements, and promotional events helped position the Legion as an
established, legitimate, pedagogical force within America. The Legion often organized special matinees of its films with reduced admission prices for children (or
free for those pupils "too poor to pay"), and arranged writing contests with subjects such as "The Most Useful American" and "The Ten Greatest Americans."[30]
Prizes were given to the children that sold the most tickets for shows, Boy Scouts
were used to publicize films, and, for example, when a local Legion post presented
The Man without a Country at a high school auditorium in Waukesha, Wisconsin,
a suburb of Milwaukee, it donated the profits back to the school.[31] In Anderson,

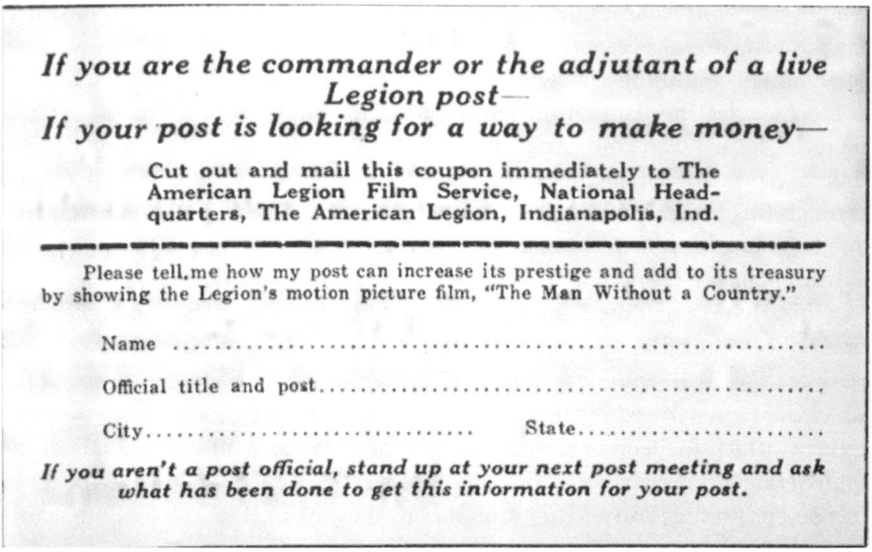

If you are the commander or the adjutant of a live Legion post—
If your post is looking for a way to make money—

> Cut out and mail this coupon immediately to The American Legion Film Service, National Headquarters, The American Legion, Indianapolis, Ind.

Please tell me how my post can increase its prestige and add to its treasury by showing the Legion's motion picture film, "The Man Without a Country."

Name ....

Official title and post...

City.............................   State.......................

If you aren't a post official, stand up at your next post meeting and ask what has been done to get this information for your post.

FIGURE 6.2. A coupon that appeared on page 18 of the *American Legion Weekly*'s issue of February 16, 1923, for Legion posts interested in screening *The Man without a Country*.

Indiana, alongside the newspaper campaigns, automobile stickers, and essay contests, the Legion arranged a private screening of *The Man without a Country* for the ministers and school officials of the city, "which resulted in the ministers announcing the film favorably from the pulpit."[32] The James E. Ryan Post, in West Alexandria, Virginia, which initially showed films in the local school auditorium, produced a twelve-page program for each screening, filled with advertisements from local businesses, and would generate further goodwill each month by offering prizes to the boy and girl with the best school record. In this instance, the post even established its own censor board—involving the mayor, a minister, and the superintendent of schools—who not only approved the pictures but, by extension, offered their support for the work of the local Legion.[33] Such endorsements served to promote the Legion and, more particularly, illustrated the group's attempts to extend and repurpose a form of nationalism that had previously been fostered during the war. The wartime challenges of constructing a nation of migrant workers and of defining a common fighting unit were now taken up in peacetime by the Legion and other religious, conservative groups, through their use of film.

Advertisements for other Legion-distributed films reveal similar practices. *Flashes of Action,* an official War Department film taken by signal corps photographers, was widely advertised as a film that "EVERY RED BLOODED AMERICAN" should see, with further taglines claiming, "It will make you a better

ANNOUNCEMENT EXTRAORDINARY!

THE PICTURE THAT MADE THE KAISER SAY

"IT'S GOING TO BE A LONG, TOUGH WAR!"

"Flashes of Action"

THE MOST AUTHENTIC WAR-PICTURE YET RELEASED.
A PICTURE EVERYBODY MUST SEE!
THE LATE WAR BROUGHT TO IRONWOOD IN ITS ORIGINALITY.
NO POSED WAR SCENES!   NO IMITATION BATTLES!

SEE THE LANDING AT BREST
GERMAN SHELLS BURSTING IN RAMBUCOURT

SEE THE VICTOR, RAYMOND VAMIER, FRENCH AVIATOR
GERMAN HEADQUARTERS SHELLED BY OUR BOYS

SEE THE FAMOUS "75's" IN ACTION
"GERMANY AT LAST"—OUR BOYS IN GERMANY

SEE Captain "Eddie" Rickenbacker

SEE General Pershing's Farewell to France

SEE General Pershing's Reception Home.

EVERY RED BLOODED AMERICAN

Should see "Flashes Of Action.". It will make you a better American. This picture will be presented under the auspices of American Legion Post No. 5, at the

Rex Theater Wednesday and Thursday May 17-18

MATINEES DAILY—2 SHOWS NIGHTLY

SPECIAL PERFORMANCES ARE BEING ARRANGED FOR CHILDREN

Prices Children, 25c
Adults, 50c

SPECIAL MUSIC
Added Attraction—"Watkins"

TICKETS MAY BE PURCHASED FROM ANY LEGION BOY

FIGURE 6.3. Advertising *Flashes of Action* in Ironwood, Michigan. *Ironwood (MI) Daily Globe,* May 16, 1922, 5.

American." (See figure 6.3.) Such publicity attributed a transformative power to the movie. This official war film, depicting American soldiers predominantly in France, was now used to create and mold postwar American citizens, while also seeking to define (and perhaps distinguish) its audience as "red blooded" Americans. The national commander of the Legion, John R. Quinn, noted the "priceless publicity" generated from these screenings, bolstering the Legion's role and identity within the local community.[34]

The Film Service sought to disseminate not only its films and projectors, but also its exhibition practices, since the *American Legion Weekly* regularly published accounts of film shows on its letters page. The "Step Keeper" who moderated the correspondence suggested that if he printed all the letters outlining how posts exhibit films, "this space would have to run over about eight pages" and jokingly added that he had now gathered enough material to "back Marcus Loew and a few prominent exhibitors off the map."[35] The paper published pictures of theaters—for example, sandbags adding a "realistic touch" outside a theater showing *Flashes of Action*—while the Film Service offered a twenty-five-dollar prize for the post with the best exploitation stunt.[36] In the one-year span of August 1923–24, Legion posts put on 2,076 shows using films distributed by the Film Service, and a reported five million people "went to the movies and read a Legion message on screen." Although these screenings brought in $33,000 to the national headquarters, the estimated take for local posts was considerably higher.[37]

The infrastructure of the Legion—as a national organization comprising local posts, often with their own buildings and supported by a chain of state, regional, and local officers—provided a network for the distribution of films. Through this network of local chapters the Legion was able to disseminate its propaganda about American national identity across the nation, so that it was not an ideological fantasy but a concept supported and promoted, often through the use of film, within disparate local communities. James E. Darst emphasized from the outset that the Film Service would also provide projecting machines, ensuring that these films could be circulated around the Legion's network of eleven thousand posts. These films could thus play at Legion halls but also at cinemas, schools, or even church buildings, hired out by the Legion to present its messages of Americanism—and indeed itself—within the local community.

This distribution-and-exhibition model counters much received wisdom about the American film industry. The Legion continued to distribute and monetize films long beyond their traditional life expectancy. In October 1924, the director of the Film Service wrote to Jason Joy in the Hays Office, inquiring whether the office could extend the Film Service's distribution rights for *The Man without a Country*. At the time, the Legion held rights only in cities with a population of up to forty-five thousand, but six years after the film's initial release, the Legion saw value in presenting it within major urban centers.[38] Its appropriation of war films transformed them for contemporary audiences, recirculating and reimagining them within small towns, in nontheatrical spaces and through sponsored shows. As early as 1922, members of the Film Service, buoyed by the distribution not only of films but also of projectors, claimed that 90 percent of Legion posts had "given some kind of movie show" and hoped that by midsummer the Legion would "have in circulation the largest non-theatrical library in the United States."[39] The films not only showed publicly in theatrical spaces, but also increasingly after 1923—when rental prices were further reduced—as free, "good entertainment features for regular meetings."[40] In circulating films made for the war long after the end of the conflict, the Legion operated on a different temporality, now expanding the practices and values of wartime and, with it, transporting a form of conservative nationalism into a fresh social context.

Through its distribution and, by extension, appropriation of war films, the Legion not only projected its vision of "Americanism" but also supported specific campaigns for veterans. For example, it used *Flashes of Action* to promote state campaigns for adjusted compensation, and this proved particularly successful in Illinois and Kansas, where the film was exhibited in more than 150 towns and cities. The Film Service director concluded, "There is no stronger argument in favor of adjusted compensation than the camera's story of the war."[41] With fifteen prints in circulation, the film was shown by Legion posts in every community in Pennsylvania in advance of a vote on state-adjusted compensation in November 1923. After the film was shown, text appeared on-screen asking, "Voters of Pennsylvania: You have seen what the boys did in 1917–18. What are you going to do November 7th?" In addition, the Legion's speakers' bureau prepared an explanatory lecture, which was delivered during screenings.[42] In this way, the Legion was formalizing its appropriation of these historical war pictures so that they were not only positioned as American Legion films, but also, as the Legion pushed for legislative reform, now directly related to contemporary politics.[43] The Legion's methods here—in finding a fresh use and context for war films—matched its broader goal to reposition soldiers as valued and productive citizens after the completion of the war.

In this way, the Legion used film to organize around and advocate for the rights of veterans. *Lest We Forget,* made for the Legion by Storey Pictures in 1921, depicted the efforts of the Legion to obtain justice and employment for disabled veterans.[44] *The Whipping Boss* (1924) fictionalized the recent, well-publicized case of Martin Tabert, a North Dakotan war veteran who was flogged to death in a convict lumber camp in Florida in 1923. The Legion had demanded an investigation into Tabert's death, which led to the conviction of his whipping boss and the abolition of the convict leasing system in Florida. The film celebrates and foregrounds the Legion's role within the narrative—the film's hero is a young Legion commander, and it features Legion meetings—and positions the Legion at the center of a nationwide campaign to end the convict lease system. With a degree of dramatic license, the Legion manages to save the victim from death in *The Whipping Boss,* appearing, in the words of *Photoplay,* as "the St. George that slays the dragon of viciousness."[45] In handling the picture, the Legion sought to champion veterans' rights and, moreover, to celebrate its position as a champion of veterans' rights. John R. Quinn, the Legion's national commander, wrote to Legionnaires explaining the decision to handle the picture. "I believe pictures leave a deeper impression upon the average mind than the spoken or printed word," he wrote, adding that the picture presented the Legion as a "community and national asset." Beyond this, Quinn saw the representation of veterans as an indication of the Legion's work in extending wartime demands within peacetime America. "The film graphically proves that the Legion is an organization carrying on now as it did in war," Quinn concluded, "for humanity and righteousness."[46]

The struggles facing returning veterans also interested leading producers, who recognized the dramatic and commercial possibilities of this subject. The Legion announced a deal in 1922 with Thomas Ince to produce a picture with the working title *Blood Bond*, at a cost of $200,000. The story was written by C. Gardner Sullivan and would depict the problems confronting veterans on their return from war. The director John Griffith Wray traveled to Oregon and Eureka Falls, California, in search of locations, and a competition was planned in the *American Legion Weekly* that would determine a suitable title for the film. Announcing the production, the national commander of the Legion explained that his organization was interested in producing films that would "inspire good citizenship and faith in our government and the people." The production was intended for release in time for the national American Legion convention in New Orleans in October, although there is no evidence of its release.[47] The Legion did, however, sponsor screenings of Ince's *Skin Deep* at this point, a "virile, red-blooded drama" that told of a former gangster returning from war, regenerated by his experiences. The national commander of the Legion spoke at its Chicago premiere, cinemas used Legion members to sell tickets, while Ince reportedly gave the Legion 10 percent of the profits.[48] Members of the Hollywood Legion post acted out a preamble to the film and also featured predominantly in the two-reel comedy *O Promise Me* (1922), which was filmed in and around the Legion clubhouse and was widely shown by posts.

The Legion also produced short instructional, educational, and news films, which served primarily as a way of propagating and teaching its form of Americanism.[49] For example, the 1922 national convention determined that a film should be produced to illustrate the "proper etiquette of the flag," a repeated focus of the Legion Film Service. Indeed the service described its 1929 film on flag etiquette, *Old Glory*, as an "educational classic that every American should see."[50] Alongside the educational shorts were news films, solicited by the Film Service as it provided projectors and cameras to posts. "If your post is planning to promenade down Main Street on twenty foot stilts, or to blow up the old bridge over Fall Creek as part of a sham battle (with the due permission of the authorities), tell the Film Service about it well in advance," the *American Legion Weekly* advised. "Someone will be there with a cranked box to record it." As a more specific example, the Film Service produced and distributed films showing members from every state parading in San Francisco at the 1923 convention and again in St. Paul, Minnesota, in 1924. Film served here as a way of connecting the local chapters within the national body, indicative of the ways in which the Legion stitched together a national identity (in part through military displays) and then, in turn, disseminated this across the nation.[51] These local news items, of course, remained useful for those posts depicted. The *American Legion Weekly* commented on a post in New Jersey that had recorded its own history on film, which it would add to each year. In noting that the post had played this film on three occasions and netted more than $300 for its building fund, the paper recognized the value of film in the construction—both literal and ideological—of the local post. "Houses built on celluloid," it concluded, "are as solid as houses built on rock."[52]

THE LEGION, HAYS, AND FILM REFORM

The Legion used film to promote, define, and fund itself and, moreover, to propagate a particular model of Americanism across the postwar nation. It did this not simply through the production, distribution, and exploitation of film, but also by promulgating broader political stakes through film culture, positioning itself as a prominent reformer by campaigning for what it defined as "cleaner and more truly American films."[53] From the outset, Legion posts were active in protesting against films or practices that ran counter to its ideals of Americanism. It launched protests against the production of German operas in Los Angeles in 1919 and 1920, even threatening to buy up all the opening-night tickets for one show and to take "drastic action" as soon as the first word was uttered in German.[54] In 1921, the Hollywood post of the Legion would protest—with the aid of some egg throwing—in front of Miller's Theater, where *The Cabinet of Dr. Caligari* (1920) was scheduled to appear. Typical of the placards carried by "crippled" ex-servicemen was one reading, "Why pay war tax to see German-made pictures?" as this widely publicized protest became part of a more organized campaign to introduce higher tariffs on imported films.[55] Within a week of its successful protests against *The Cabinet of Dr. Caligari*, the Hollywood post hosted a meeting that saw the establishment of a permanent organization opposed to the importation of German films. The Legion promulgated a form of cultural nationalism, which other groups soon embraced. Kerry Segrave notes that "every branch of the motion picture industry was lining up against the foreign product," with representatives from Equity, the Hollywood Board of Trade, and the Screenwriters Association among those represented and brought together by the Legion. *Variety* suggested that the Legion's protests against this "invasion" of German films were "having great sentimental weight with the politicians."[56]

The protest against *The Cabinet of Dr. Caligari* is indicative of the ways in which Legion groups would mobilize against individual films and theaters. The Hollywood post would also seek to suppress Erich von Stroheim's *Foolish Wives*, which it claimed (incorrectly) was being made by a German director with German money "as German propaganda," and in 1924 the Legion, along with other veterans' groups, forced the cancellation of screenings of *The Fifth Year*, claiming that the film's purpose was to "disseminate Soviet propaganda."[57] Yet, the establishment of a permanent organization opposed to imported films also illustrates the ways in which the Legion, as a national organization, would seek to direct public policy, often by working alongside other influential parties. This was evident in Arthur

Woods's work with the Americanism Committee and again in 1922 when Will Hays became the first president of the newly formed Motion Picture Producers and Distributors of America (MPPDA). One of Hays's first moves was to establish a Committee on Public Relations, which sought to offer a "channel of communication between the public and industry," relaying comments, criticisms, and suggestions to the industry. The committee comprised seventy-eight members from sixty-two national organizations, as Hays sought to appease and negotiate the concerns of religious, educational, labor, and fraternal groups. Among the organizations well represented was the American Legion, which had two members on the committee and one on the twenty-strong central body.[58]

The Legion's correspondence with the Hays Office testifies to its elevated position within film's powerful institutions, and those institutions' discourses, at this seminal moment for the industry. Shortly after his appointment, Hays wrote to the leader of the Legion praising a recent article, "The Movies Discover America," published in the *American Legion Weekly*. Hays endorsed this "constructive effort, which typifies in my mind the spirit of your organization," and corresponded regularly with Legion representatives, even advising on production and distribution queries.[59] For example, Earle Meyer wrote to the Hays Office in 1923 asking for help in making and distributing a film that would give the soldier's perspective on the adjusted-compensation appeal, while Jason Joy, the director of public relations at the MPPDA, attended a conference in Washington in 1923 called by the Legion. Among those attending this conference, which involved sixty-seven national organizations, was President Harding. The conference sought to compile a "Flag Code," and Joy confirmed that the MPPDA's Committee on Public Relations would do all in its power to ensure that the flag was used in a "proper and dignified manner." He even suggested the production of a film instructing people in the "proper use of the flag." The Legion foregrounded the flag as a significant symbol of the state, and sought to rework it as a visual shorthand for its own form of nationalism.[60] Indeed we can see the fingerprints of the Legion on some of the film industry's most significant policy documents. As one example, the MPPDA's "Don'ts and be Carefuls" from 1927 lists "The use of the Flag" as its first subject to warrant "special care." Three years later, when this directive was formalized in the MPPDA's Production Code, the line reads: "The use of the Flag shall be consistently respectful."[61]

The Legion directly criticized on-screen representations that ran counter to its own values. In his role as head of the Film Service, Earle Meyer endorsed familiar criticisms, offered by a contrasting range of reforming groups from the Ku Klux Klan to the Catholic Church, when he criticized producers in 1924 for making pictures that would appeal to the "'thirteen year old' intelligence of the average motion picture audience" and spoke disparagingly of the continued presence on film of "flappers, custard pies and triangles."[62] However, the Legion also responded to very specific depictions on-screen, writing to Hays and urging "drastic meas-

Official publication of The American Legion and The American Legion Auxiliary.

Owned exclusively by The American Legion.

The AMERICAN LEGION Weekly

Published by the Legion Publishing Corporation. President, Hanford MacNider; Vice-President, James A. Drain; Treasurer, Robert H. Tyndall; Secretary, Lemuel Bolles.

EDITORIAL AND BUSINESS OFFICES: 627 West 43rd Street, New York City

OCTOBER 20, 1922   Copyright, 1922, by the Legion Publishing Corporation.   PAGE 3

What Are the Movies Up To?

Knock Them If You Must—But Remember the Bathtub, Bessemer Steel, and the Steam Cars While You Do It

By Ralph Hayes

A WEEK-OLD copy of the London *Daily Mail's* Continental Edition, torn and wrinkled, passed through many hands to mine in January, 1919, somewhere north of Baccarat. It was a badly damaged thing, but it did bring news of the States. There was, for example, a story headed "In Bone Dry America," quoting a prominent divine describing just how American was since it had taken on the Eighteenth Amendment. This was his conception of what had happened:

"The rain of tears is over. The slums will soon be only a memory. We will turn our prisons into factories and our gaols into storehouses and corncribs. Men will walk upright now; the women will smile and the children will laugh. Hell will be forever for rent."

I have no disposition to criticize prohibition—I do suggest that those of its proponents place upon it a wholly unnecessary burden who would label it a panacea for flat feet, Bolshevism and scarlet fever.

It's that way with a new thing under the sun; however sound it may be in the center, lusty-lunged extremists gather around its edges rapturously to praise or viciously to condemn it, whatever It may be.

That's been true as far back as the eye can reach.

> THE AMERICAN LEGION has a special interest in motion pictures because it is represented in the councils of Will H. Hays, former postmaster general, now head of all motion-picture activity in America. Three months ago, at the invitation of Mr. Hays, representatives of many civic, educational and welfare organizations met with him to express their views and co-operate in the improvement of the movie. Out of this meeting grew a permanent general committee which will include representatives of more than one hundred organizations. Its purpose, among others, is "to establish and maintain the highest possible moral and artistic standards in motion-picture productions and to develop the educational value as well as the entertainment value" of moving pictures. The central body of this general committee is a Committee of Twenty, and The American Legion has the distinction of being represented on this committee in the person of National Commander MacNider. Ralph Hayes, author of the accompanying article, is a former assistant to Secretary of War Newton D. Baker and is now assistant to Will H. Hays. They are not related.

A sizable Christmas party was given at Cincinnati in 1842; the Big Idea was to show the guests a contraption recently made by the host—a bathtub, probably the first in the country. The next day the Cincinnati newspapers right roundly denounced this pretentious, undemocratic vanity. Other cities took up the anti-bathtub crusade. In the Philadelphia town council there was serious consideration of an ordinance making bathing unlawful between the first of November and the middle of March. Boston debated a municipal regulation prohibiting bathing except when prescribed by a physician, and Virginia taxed the tubs $30 a year.

Unoffending things like railways, too, took some stiff wallops from Antonio Vox Populi while on their way to respectability. At a meeting of the school board of Lancaster, Ohio, in 1826, the business before the house

FIGURE 6.4. *American Legion Weekly* article by Ralph Hayes, an assistant to Will Hays, about the work of the Hays office.

ures" to "stamp out" instances that ridiculed or disrespected the US service uniform. Whenever a director wished to make a scene "look tough, obscene and rough" or to show men under the influence of liquor, the Legion wrote, "all that needs to be done is to place a few hard boiled extras in the uniform" of the armed services. The complaint was motivated by the Pathé film *Dynamite Smith* (1924). Hays responded by promising to get in touch at once with the distributor, to look more closely at the picture, and to see "what can be done about eliminations."[63] The correspondence reveals Hays's role in liaising between the Legion and the industry and also a desire to support and placate a group that was increasingly influential in determining the values and policies of postwar America. The relationship between Hays and the Legion was largely positive and mutually beneficial, and through this the Legion helped frame a nationalistic film discourse that was broadly consistent with a model of "Americanism" and with formations of citizenship that emerged out of the war.

CONCLUSION

The American Legion represents an early, prominent example of a conservative organization that looked to film to mold American citizens and to determine the values of a rapidly changing nation. The Legion was born out of war and appropriated both the films and values of wartime America for the postwar nation. The varied practices it adopted—whether using films to support specific campaigns, exhibiting films in schools and churches, profitably distributing war pictures to small-town theaters, or filming and exhibiting its own activities—served to highlight the needs of veterans and, beyond this, as the Legion became an influential and respected voice in film and political discourse, foregrounded a military agenda in the construction of this postwar nation. Through film, these veterans promoted and funded the Legion's place in America, fanning the memory of war while finding fresh battles and confronting new threats that would serve to define what it means to be "American."

The story, of course, does not finish here. The Legion would exercise an even greater influence on film thirty years later, once more in the aftermath of war, as it stirred up anticommunist hysteria and enforced and extended the Hollywood blacklist against apparent communist sympathizers. It listed associations, named names, boycotted and picketed films, and visited studios, ultimately acting as judge on those with "suspect" affiliations.[64] The Legion's initial uses of film as it established itself across America after 1919 presage this more familiar history of the McCarthy era, of an industry—and a nation—challenged and torn apart by anxieties around immigration, by foreign threats, and by a wider battle over American national identity. It suggests a continuity between the periods and reveals a conservative group of veterans using film to define and project a form of "Americanism" that simultaneously challenges the "Bolshevism" and "Un-American" practices attributed to the Hollywood industry. The success of the Legion—evidenced and enacted through film—reveals a nation defined, then as now, by conflict and a military discourse. In these ways, this chapter presents not only a study of the American Legion or even the uses of film by social and political groups but also an example of the ways in which film would help to perpetuate a military agenda and culture beyond the dates of armistice. While the media forms may change and the face at the window may look different today, these practices remain as relevant as ever in twenty-first-century America.

ACKNOWLEDGMENTS

I am very grateful to Joseph J. Hovish for his help in accessing materials at the American Legion Library, Indianapolis. I would also like to thank Haidee Wasson and Lee Grieveson for their very helpful feedback on this chapter.

NOTES

1. Advertisement for *The Face at Your Window*, directed by Richard Stanton, *Augusta Chronicle*, August 26, 1921, 5.

2. Giorgio Agamben, *State of Exception*, trans. Kevin Attell (Chicago: University of Chicago Press, 2005). For further consideration of the extension of "police power" after the war, see Lee Grieveson's chapter in this volume.

3. "Woods Accepts Chairmanship of Americanism Committee and Will Work out Plan of Co-operation," *Moving Picture World*, December 11, 1920, 704.

4. Thomas A. Rumer, *The American Legion: An Official History, 1919–1989* (New York: M. Evans & Company, 1990), 75; *American Legion Weekly* (hereafter cited as *ALW*), November 28, 1919, 6, 7, 12.

5. "Unique Drive on W.H. Feature Picture," *Motion Picture News*, October 4, 1919, 2821.

6. Advertisement, *ALW*, December 19, 1919, 26.

7. The CPI was set up almost immediately after the declaration of war and, as Lee Grieveson shows in his chapter in this volume, adopted numerous strategies to convince immigrant audiences of the merits of American participation in a European war.

8. The committee's first production, *The Land of Opportunity*, had received a full-page advertisement in *American Legion Weekly*, where it was described as a "two-reel superfeature that embodies the spirit of Lincoln—the spirit of America." "Announcing the Initial Americanization Production," *ALW*, February 6, 1920, 36. For more on the work of the Americanism Committee of the Motion Picture Industry, see Steven J. Ross, *Working-Class Hollywood: Silent Film and the Shaping of Class in America* (Princeton, NJ: Princeton University Press, 1998), 129–30.

9. "Asks Help to Employ Soldiers," *Film Daily*, August 20, 1919, 4; "What Is Americanism?" *ALW*, February 13, 1920, 18. Woods presented a report on the Americanism efforts of the industry in Washington in December 1921, outlining the continued efforts to make the screen "a strong influence for right things in America." "Americanism via Screen," *Exhibitors Herald*, December 24, 1921, 143.

10. "Woods Accepts Chairmanship," 704.

11. William Fox to NAACP, September 23, 1921, Records of the NAACP, box 1, C 312, Library of Congress, Washington, DC.

12. "Fox's Production, 'The Face at Your Window,'" Proves a Big Success throughout Country," *Exhibitors Trade Review*, November 27, 1920. Woods's call would prove somewhat problematic. Fox's defensive explanation of *The Face at Your Window* came in the form of a letter to the NAACP, after it had complained to Fox that the film was being widely used as propaganda for a reemergent Ku Klux Klan. The Klan's exploitation of the film challenged the Legion's own use. In St. Augustine, Florida, where it was screened to raise funds for the local Legion post, a letter complained that "the Klan is glorified and everyone goes away with the impression that the Legion and the Klan are affiliated." The Klan's attempts to reappropriate *The Face at your Window* for its own cause mirrors the Legion's more

approved use of government film throughout this period. Correspondence between Fox and the NAACP is in Records of the NAACP, box 1, C 312, Library of Congress, Washington, DC; "Klan Membership Peddlers Tried to Connect Masonry and American Legion with Ku Kluxism to Gain Recruits," *Fort Wayne (IN) News-Sentinel,* September 23, 1921, 5. For more on the ways in which the Klan used film during this period, see Tom Rice, *White Robes, Silver Screens: Movies and the Making of the Ku Klux Klan* (Bloomington: Indiana University Press, 2015).

13. "Putting the Three R's 'to Work," *ALW,* January 16, 1920, 5–7, 26.

14. Joel Spring, *Educating the Consumer Citizen: A History of the Marriage of Schools, Advertising and Media* (Mahwah, NJ: Lawrence Erlbaum Associates, 2003); "These Youngsters Show the Way," *ALW,* February 9, 1923, 7; "Youth Speaks to America," *ALW,* July 4, 1924, 13; "Puncturing the Windy Bag of Communism," *ALW,* May 22, 1925, 14.

15. Rumer, *American Legion,* 181.

16. Alvin Owsley, "What Constitutes American Citizenship," *Visual Education,* September 1923, 218.

17. For recent work in this field, see Charles R. Acland and Haidee Wasson, eds., *Useful Cinema* (Durham, NC: Duke University Press, 2011); Devin Orgeron, Marsha Orgeron, and Dan Streible, eds., *Learning with the Lights Off: Educational Film in the United States* (New York: Oxford University Press, 2012); Lee Grieveson and Colin MacCabe, eds., *Empire and Film* (London: Palgrave Macmillan, 2011); and Lee Grieveson and Colin MacCabe eds., *Film and the End of Empire* (London: Palgrave Macmillan, 2011).

18. Rice, *White Robes;* Lee Grieveson, "The Work of Film in the Age of Ford Mechanization," *Cinema Journal* 51, no. 3 (Spring 2012): 25–51.

19. "Americanization Work," *Visual Education,* "Why We Use Movies" section, January 1923, 16. The "Why We Use Movies" section had a few months earlier featured the American Legion's national chaplain, who credited the movies with "rapidly diminishing" religious prejudice. Somewhat speculatively, he suggested that Christ would likely embrace the movies—that he "probably would write scenarios, direct His own pictures and even go so far as to act for the camera"—because he would recognize the "possibilities of the screen in reaching multiplied audiences." "Churches and Sunday-schools," *Visual Education,* "Why We Use Movies" section, October–November 1922, 351–52. Lemuel Bolles, the national adjunct of the Legion, further argued in this section that film "can inspire a finer appreciation of our government and of the country we are privileged to call our own than any other medium of teaching." "What Constitutes American Citizenship," *Visual Education,* "Why We Use Movies" section, April 1923, 125.

20. "Film Service Gets Generous Approval," *Pinedale (WY) Roundup,* March 6, 1924.

21. "The Year's Work at the Legion's G.H.Q.," *ALW,* October 28, 1921, 35.

22. "Spending $10,000,000 to Make Good a Promise," *ALW,* August 29, 1924, 17.

23. "The Year's Work," 35.

24. L. R. Gignilliat, "Putting Punch in a State Conference," *ALW,* August 19, 1921, 15; "Crank, Crank, Crank, the Reel's-a-Winding," *ALW,* July 7, 1922, 9.

25. Advertisement, *ALW,* December 19, 1924, 16; Advertisement, *American Legion Monthly,* September 1929, 81.

26. Gignilliat, "Putting Punch in a State Conference," 15.

27. Advertisement, *ALW,* February 16, 1923, 18.

28. "Funds from Films," *ALW,* March 16, 1923, 16. *ALW* concluded that as a result of the screening, "Jefferson Post is on the map in Louiseville."

29. "Legion Post Brings Big Picture Here," *Stevens Point (WI) Daily Journal,* February 14, 1922, 1.

30. "School Contests Attest Legion's Interest in Education," *ALW,* November 16, 1923, 13; "Keeping Step with the Legion," *ALW,* August 3, 1923, 10.

31. "Crank, Crank, Crank," 9, 24–26; "Great Lesson in Americanism at School May 18," *Waukesha (WI) Daily Freeman*, May 17, 1922, 1. Further reports in *ALW* ("Going into the Movie Business," January 26, 1923, 10) noted that the film had "stirred communities deeply" whenever it had played and had offered a "great lesson in patriotism to the children of hundreds of communities."

32. "Keeping Step with the Legion," *ALW*, April 20, 1923, 20–21.

33. Ibid.

34. "Advertisement," *Ironwood (MI) Daily Globe*, May 16, 1922, 5; "Legion Will Distribute Feature Picture," *Exhibitors Trade Review*, February 16, 1924, 13.

35. "Keeping Step with the Legion," *ALW*, August 3, 1923, 10.

36. Franklin Stetson Clark, "Putting Jack in the Post Till," *ALW*, August 11, 1922, 11.

37. "Spending $10,000,000 to Make Good a Promise," *ALW*, August 29, 1924, 17.

38. Henry J. Prue to Col. Jason Joy, October 9, 1924, accessed at the American Legion Library, Indianapolis.

39. ""Crank, Crank, Crank, 9, 24–26. The article explained that a "non-theatrical library is one in which there are no films with captions like, 'And as the dawn of the new day rosed the gentle crests of the placid Berkshires, Willard and Iolanthe rode out from Chester into the golden void of the future.'"

40. "Lower Prices Make Legion Film Available to Every Community," *ALW*, September 7, 1923, 17. Rental prices were dependent on the size of the community's population. "Free Movies," *American Legion Monthly*, April 1929, 33.

41. "Keeping Step with the Legion," *ALW*, 29 December 1922, 19; "He's In Again," *ALW*, November 24, 1922, 15. Many of the films distributed by the Legion directly related to the war or contained official war footage. For example *The Lost Battalion*, which was first released in 1918 and then handled by the Legion in 1924, featured, as its actors, survivors from the Argonne. ""The Lost Battalion' in Films Now Available for Your Post," *ALW*, November 7, 1924, 17; "Advertisement," *ALW*, December 26, 1924, 20.

42. "President Meets Competition on His Alaska Tour," *ALW*, July 20, 1923, 9; "The Legion Projector," *ALW*, October 20, 1922, 17.

43. The Adjusted Compensation Act of 1924 authorized payment to veterans who had served in the war, depending on their length of service. Payments of less than fifty dollars were paid in cash, while others were awarded a certificate that, much like an insurance policy, would be redeemable in 1945.

44. "Anetha Getwell, Contest Winner, Starred in Coscarder Production" *Exhibitors Herald*, December 11, 1920, 70; "Finish American Legion Film, 'Lest We Forget,'" *Exhibitors Herald*, April 30, 1921, 59.

45. Box text, *ALW*, February 1, 1924, 23; picture caption, *ALW*, February 8, 1924, 15; "Will Depict Crime," *Edwardsville (IL) Intelligencer*, March 3, 1924, 8; "The Whipping Boss," *Photoplay*, February 1924, 90. The example deviates slightly from those already discussed; in this instance, the Legion secured the exclusive distribution of a newly released feature film with "one of the largest deals put over recently in the independent market."

46. "American Legion to Handle Monogram's 'Whipping Boss,'" *Moving Picture World*, February 23, 1924, 636; "Legion Will Distribute Feature Picture," 13.

47. "Films and Footlights," *ALW*, August 4, 1922, 28; "Amer. Legion Films," *Film Daily*, August 15, 1922, 1; "The Legion Projector," *ALW*, September 22, 1922, 20.

48. "The Legion Projector," *ALW*, October 20, 1922, 27; "Hear Legion Head at 'Skin Deep' Opening," *Exhibitors Herald*, October 7, 1922, 33; "Skin Deep," *Visual Education*, December 1922, 411.

49. The *American Legion Weekly* recognized these films as a "powerful aid in membership drives," and as an attraction that helped "get everybody out for a meeting." "He's In Again," 15; "Film Service Rights Extended," *ALW*, May 18, 1923, 27.

50. "The Fourth National Convention," *ALW*, November 10, 1922, 9; *The American Legion Presents Old Glory: An Educational Classic That Every American Should See* (American Legion Film Service, 1929).

51. Earle Meyer not only recognized film as the "most lucrative post activity," but also saw the circulation of short news films as a chance to see what other posts were doing: "They take you on a trip to France with the Legion delegation, or on a tour of the United States with Marshal Foch." "Money-Raising Campaigns," *Visual Education,* March 1923, 92.

52. "Crank, Crank, Crank," 25.

53. "Film Service Gets Generous Approval."

54. "American Legion to Fight Hammerstein German Opera," *Variety,* December 10, 1920, 10.

55. "Riot over German Feature Picture: 'Cabinet of Caligari' Egged on Coast," *Variety,* May 13, 1921, 47; "All Hollywood Now Lining Up against German Made Films," *Variety,* May 20, 1921, 1; "Public Demonstration Wins Withdrawal of Foreign Made Picture," *Exhibitors Herald,* May 21, 1921, 35; "Right Off the Grill," *Picture-Play,* August 1921, 53.

56. Kerry Segrave, *Foreign Films in America: A History* (Jefferson, NC: McFarland and Company, 2004), 22–27; "Tariff Fixers Said to Look Favorably on High Film Duty," *Variety,* June 3, 1921, 46.

57. Louis Pizzitola, *Hearst over Hollywood: Power, Passion and Propaganda in the Movies* (New York: Columbia University Press, 2002), 399; *Exhibitors Herald,* February 23 1924, 97.

58. Anne Morey, *Hollywood Outsiders: The Adaptation of the Film Industry, 1913–1934* (Minneapolis: University of Minnesota Press, 2003), 124; Ralph Hayes, "What Are the Movies Up To?" *ALW,* October 20, 1922, 3.

59. Will Hays to Commander Alvin Owsley, May 1, 1923, accessed at the American Legion Library, Indianapolis. "The Movies Discover America," by Charles Phelps Cushing, appeared in *ALW,* May 4, 1923, 3–5, 28–30. Hays's assistant, Ralph Hayes, wrote "What Are the Movies Up To?"—a lengthy piece in the *American Legion Weekly* (October 20, 1922, 3–6, 28–30), outlining the role of the committee in 1922.

60. Earle A. Meyer to Jason S. Joy, December 18, 1923, accessed at the American Legion Library, Indianapolis; Jason S. Joy, "Resume of Activities for Week Ending 16 June 1923," MPPDA Digital Archive, http://mppda.flinders.edu.au/records/85.

61. Reprinted in Jon Lewis, *Hollywood v. Hard Core: How the Struggle over Censorship Saved the Modern Film Industry* (New York: New York University Press, 2000), 301–7.

62. "Film Service Gets Generous Approval."

63. Resolution, December 10, 1924; Will Hays to General James Drain, January 22, 1925; both accessed at the American Legion Library, Indianapolis.

64. "Did the Movies Really Clean House?" *American Legion Monthly,* December 1951, 12–13, 49–56; "The Movies and the American Legion," *American Legion Monthly,* May 1953, 14–15, 39–43; Larry Ceplair, *Anti-Communism in Twentieth Century America: A Critical History* (Santa Barbara, CA: Prager, 2011); Edward Dmytryk, *Odd Man Out: A Memoir of the Hollywood Ten* (Carbondale: Southern Illinois University Press, 1996), 91–92.

REFERENCES

Archives

American Legion Library, Indianapolis
   American Legion Weekly and selected papers
MPPDA Digital Archive, Flinders University Library Special Collections, Adelaide, South Australia
   Documents from the Motion Picture Producers and Distributors of America
Library of Congress, Washington, DC
   Records of the National Association for the Advancement of Colored People

Newspapers and Periodicals

American Legion Monthly
American Legion Weekly
Augusta (GA) Chronicle
Edwardsville (IL) Intelligencer
Exhibitors Herald
Exhibitors Trade Review
Fort Wayne (IN) News Sentinel
Indianapolis News
Ironwood (MI) Daily Globe
Moving Picture World
Photoplay
Picture-Play
Pinedale (WY) Roundup
Stevens Point (WI) Daily Journal
Visual Education
Variety
Waukesha (WI) Daily Freeman

7

MANAGING THE TRAUMA OF LABOR

Military Psychiatric Cinema in World War II

Kaia Scott

Over the course of the Second World War, psychiatric discourses went from circulating among a small group of specialists and devotees to becoming one of the most influential explanatory paradigms at work in public policy, private industry, and media and communications in the United States.[1] The US military's heavy investment in psychiatry as a strategy for "conserving manpower," facilitated in part by the use of film and visual technologies, played a huge role in psychiatry's astonishing institutional growth throughout the war and into the postwar period.[2] Cinema, among other media, was an essential tool used to disseminate psychiatric ideas and practices among millions of personnel in the US military. This chapter traces two applications of film in military psychiatry that helped to accomplish this task during the Second World War. The first was the use of military-made films to destigmatize psychiatric ideas as part of an effort to make military labor more efficient by using widespread psychiatric monitoring and management techniques. The second was the use of films and other visual technologies by military psychiatrists as a tool for administering therapeutic treatment techniques to soldiers on a mass scale.

The military had an extremely well-developed filmmaking apparatus responsible for many thousands of training films and countless other films intended to make operations more efficient. These films covered an incredible range of subjects, from *The Tank Platoon in an Attack* and *The Operation of the Quartermaster Mobile Laundry* to countless reels of surveillance footage and private communiqués.[3] One military-film genre was the "mental hygiene" film, which included psychiatric training films like *Combat Fatigue: Insomnia* (1946), where a young soldier is coached to manage his own sleeping problems after being driven to distress while watching a Donald Duck cartoon parodying sleeplessness.[4] Employing a recognizable aesthetic of 1940s black-and-white dramatized documentaries, the amusingly anachronistic subject treatments, performances, and paternalistic narrators make these films look like many other comical and unsettling propaganda relics of the past. However, contextualizing their use within the expanding role of psychiatry to teach soldiers, officers, and doctors how to manage distressed minds, and alongside experimental films used in the clinical treatment of soldiers, these films give insight into the instrumental applications that psychiatry came to offer large institutions such as the military. Weaving together discourses of care with those of military labor efficiency, psychiatric training films and clinical psychiatric films tirelessly framed the human mind as something that could be put to work, managed, and treated with relative ease, even under hostile conditions.

Logistical considerations (winning wars and paying disability pensions, among others) have always given modern military institutions huge stakes in how mental health is represented and managed. From the strategic naming and renaming of terms such as "shell shock," "combat fatigue," "post-Vietnam syndrome," and "post-traumatic stress disorder" to the training of new cohorts of psychiatrists and the funding of their research, war has indelibly shaped narratives of the mind. Film histories have documented the well-known case of John Huston's *Let There Be Light,* a film commissioned by General William Menninger, head of the army's Neuropsychiatric Division, as a public-relations move to reassure the public of the normalcy of psychiatric casualties in the aftermath of the war.[5] Set within the context of the military psychiatric program's use of films throughout the war, *Let There Be Light* is revealed not as the *beginning* of a communications strategy, but as the *culmination* of a well-developed communications apparatus with films at its center.

Seeking to manage not only discourses, but the productivity of military labor as well, the use of film in military psychiatry during the Second World War set historical precedents for the contemporary use of digital imagery in military training, stress management, and therapy.[6] Despite changing parameters of interpretation and contextualization, both Second World War experiments that used films as "exposure therapy" and contemporary uses of virtual reality to treat what is now diagnosed as post-traumatic stress disorder work with the principle that moving images can produce psychiatric "habituation," or the ability to desensitize patients to the fear of particular stimuli.[7] In an attempt to manage the unruly effects of fear on the mind, psychiatric films, seen by soldiers in both training and in treatment, became twin gateways of soldier production and release: asking them to make war in one instance, and to return to peacefully productive citizens in the other.

PSYCHIATRY IN THE UNITED STATES AND
THE SECOND WORLD WAR

Prior to the Second World War, the dominant model of mental health care in America was institutionalization in asylums or mental hospitals. Almost all professional psychiatrists worked in hospitals and generally understood their patients to be long-term or lifetime wards with afflictions that were to be managed rather than cured. The beginning of a radical shift in the orientation of American psychiatry was catalyzed by a reduction in the quality of care for patients during the Great Depression, exacerbating a growing dissatisfaction with the palliative model of psychiatry. This spurred interest in what Gerald N. Grob calls "radical therapeutic innovations" that "seemed to hold out the prospect of recovery for tens of thousands of severely and chronically ill persons."[8] Curative procedures that targeted the body's functioning rather than the patient's biography, such as insulin shock, metrazol shock, electroshock, and lobotomies, were quicker to administer than ongoing psychotherapy. They also resonated with a desire to adopt more biomedical approaches to treatment as the psychiatric community rebranded itself from palliative asylum administrators to medical-science professionals.[9]

This burgeoning change in the discipline had two elements that lent themselves well to the military's uptake of psychiatry in the upcoming war: first was the expectation that experimental therapies could produce radical results and efficiency, offering a curative rather than custodial model of care (despite the fact that an empirical connection between therapies and cures was impossible to demonstrate).[10] Second, as Grob notes in his study of this historical transition, "The rapid acceptance of these therapies [in the absence of significant proof of their effectiveness] was also facilitated by the vast publicity accorded them in the popular media. Newspapers and magazines as well as radio disseminated information about these therapies and created the impression that they represented major breakthroughs."[11] Both the use of radical therapies and the ability to sell their effectiveness through media were key elements seized upon by the US military's psychiatric program, the establishment of which became the single most significant catalyst in the change of the psychiatric profession in the United States.[12]

Whereas First World War officials had built many psychiatric hospitals to treat soldiers, military administration in the early years of the Second World War hoped to avoid repeating this costly maneuver. Their initial strategy in the early years of the war was to try to prevent losses by screening new recruits and draftees through psychiatric tests and interviews. Despite this effort, the war produced vast numbers of psychiatric casualties,[13] and the dominant view that one could distinguish between "weak" and "strong" men changed to an acceptance that "everyone had their breaking point."[14] Following this, prevailing understandings of neuroses as products of "predisposition" shifted to recognize the role of contextual or experience-induced "stress," reinforcing the ongoing disciplinary shift from a palliative model of care to one that sought to use psychiatry as a tool to prevent and manage "maladaptive" behavior. These ideas were not new—Freud and others studied soldiers in World War I and wrote about the traumatic effects of war on the psyche of otherwise "normal" individuals, a view that many military psychiatrists working in World War II also subscribed to—but the ideas had remained marginal in the discipline.[15] During the Second World War, the "environmentalist" view of psychiatry came to prominence due to its ability to account for the stressors of combat, but that view was frequently tempered by coupling it with a "developmentalist" view that measured a soldier's ability to handle stress by the success or failure of his upbringing. Military psychiatry adapted multiple, competing models of psychiatric theory to generate the most institutionally functional approach to dealing with the problem of "psychiatric casualties."[16]

The institutionalization of military psychiatry during the latter part of the war greatly accelerated the ongoing shifts in the discipline's orientation, and generated a dramatic change in the makeup and professional experience of psychiatrists themselves. In 1940, the American Psychiatric Association (APA) had 2,295 total registered members, two-thirds of whom worked in psychiatric hospitals. During the war, William C. Menninger, chief of the army's Neuropsychiatric Division, assigned an *additional* 2,400 medical physicians to work as psychiatrists to meet wartime demands, doubling the number of professionals dedicated to this task, but serving a relatively small subset of the population.[17] This massive new cohort worked under a strict military imperative to get patients back to work, favoring strategies that provided quick and demonstrable successes over ongoing custodial care and psychotherapy. Beginning in 1943, integrating psychiatric practice into front-line medicine was understood as a key intervention that could limit losses from inevitable psychiatric casualties.[18] The job of this new cohort was to implement an aggressive "forward psychiatry" program to get soldiers out of beds and back to work by treating them as early and efficiently as possible.

Tackling taboos and skepticism about psychiatry's usefulness and legitimacy as a medical practice was crucial to implementing the "forward psychiatry" program—in particular, what the military termed variously "combat fatigue," "combat exhaustion," and "operational fatigue."[19] Accepting the normalness of fear and learning techniques to manage its effects became an imperative of military efficiency; this newly dubbed "preventative psychiatry" became a hopeful site for institutional modernization and was promulgated widely in books, pamphlets, and television programs; on radio; and in films.[20] Psychiatrists Lieutenant Colonel Louis L. Tureen and Major Martin Stein wrote in a US Army medical bulletin from 1949: "[D]elay in psychiatric treatment causes a preventable loss of manpower. Thus the nature of psychiatric disorders, as well as the basic task of every military medical installation—the restoration to effective duty of as many soldiers as possible—makes it imperative that psychiatric casualties be handled quickly and expertly. . . . Audio visual aids can set the stage by quickly creating a receptive emotional tone."[21] Many military psychiatrists, including Tureen and Stein, hoped that films could be enlisted to teach people to recognize, diagnose, and treat the psychological effects of war.

1. Films in Military Psychiatry's Communications Campaign

In early 1943, new policy mandated a minimum of six hours of lectures on military psychiatry for every officer, and a minimum of three hours of mental-hygiene training for enlisted men. The policy instituted that "all Army officers [should be given] some understanding of mental hygiene . . . in the hope that such knowledge would reduce the number of psychiatric casualties."[22] The hope was that soldiers would be given insight into the "psychosomatic dynamics of [their] syndrome," which could ease symptoms by way of sublimation and rationalization.[23] Films were used alongside other media to accomplish this task, and targeted, for the most part, very specific audiences. A range of films addressing either soldiers, officers, or military doctors were part of a communications campaign aimed at convincing different groups of personnel that men suffering from psychiatric distress were not simply "goldbricks" trying to get out of duty, or "psychos" who shouldn't have been in the army in the first place.[24] Surveying these films as a whole, one sees a clear hierarchy of imperatives teaching each audience how to manage fear and optimize the wartime duties of the group subordinate to it: it was the psychiatrist's job to convince doctors of the value of psychiatric interpretations of soldiers' afflictions; the medic's task to treat these symptoms as best he could and send patients back to work; the officer's duty to apply psychiatric surveillance to his troops and to intervene at warning symptoms; and finally, it fell on the soldier to recognize and sublimate his own symptoms.

The restricted *Combat Fatigue* film series produced by the navy comprised several black-and-white dramatized documentaries shown to soldiers to introduce them to the language of military neuropsychiatry. Titles in this series include *Introduction to Combat Fatigue* (1944), *Irritability* (1946), the previously mentioned *Insomnia* (1946), and *Assignment Home* (1947),[25] and feature actors playing soldiers in common scenarios of distress and frustration. A psychiatrist-narrator gives explanations, terminology, and reassurance about symptoms and techniques for their alleviation, modeling a kind of diagnostic laboratory of the mind. As Alison Winter has observed, the narrator in *Introduction to Combat Fatigue* provides his audience with a clear taxonomy of "productive and unproductive modes of fear":[26] fear that can be useful for stimulating quick responses to dangerous situations, and fear that "becomes so overwhelming that it paralyzes the subject" or "continues to affect the body after the danger has passed."[27] The films worked to create relatable characters to empathize with, including a couple of appearances by recognizable faces such as that of Gene Kelly starring as a marine suffering from repressed grief and of Donald Duck as a frustrated insomniac.[28] Portrayals of distress are mild in nature, making the protagonists' transition from "troubled" to "cured" over the course of the film relatively believable. The *Combat Fatigue* films were the most extensively screened of all the psychiatric training films, with many of them shown during soldier training and again in military hospitals to orient new patients to their conditions and to trigger empathic reactions to on-screen scenarios as part of treatment.

Films made for audiences of higher-ranking officials stressed the managerial techniques of "forward psychiatry." *Combat Psychiatry: The Battalion Medical Officer* teaches field doctors to solicit the help of combat-unit officers to treat fear reactions in soldiers, emphasizing the value of early psychiatric diagnosis in making companies efficient.[29] In one scene, a casual conversation between company officers and a doctor at a mess table plays out a common trope in which skeptical soldiers/officers/medics complain about wasting their time with "psychos" and "goldbricks" while there are "real men" with wounds that need to be worried about, leading one officer to quip sarcastically: "[L]ook out for competition, doctor, seems like we're all turning into a bunch of psychiatrists." The medical officer replies sagely, "You know that's very interesting, because if you realize it or not, you've hit it right on the head. Platoon leaders can be our biggest help in this whole problem. . . . There could be an unnoticed and unnecessary leakage of manpower if company officers [don't] understand the problem of combat anxiety in its many and varied forms."[30] Films such as this did the spade work by opening the door to a more general conversation about psychiatric language and diagnosis, while lectures, pamphlets, and other instructional materials followed up with detailed information for officers on how to diagnose and manage the mental health of their company soldiers.[31]

Combat Exhaustion (1943), a restricted professional medical film made by the US Army Signal Corps for military doctors, fills out the chorus of "why" one should adopt psychiatry with a much more detailed explanation of "how" to do so, eschewing the soft sell seen in other films for direct commands and instructions. Shot at the 312th Station Psychiatric Hospital in England, where military doctors trained in a one-week crash course in psychiatry, the film uses a combination of actual patients, doctors, and actors, and its story line follows a team of doctors visiting a psychiatric hospital to learn about "combat exhaustion."[32] In an opening scene, the hospital's head psychiatrist confronts the doctors' skepticism about the legitimacy of psychiatric conditions, repeating the trope common to all of these films. After describing a patient's case file, the psychiatrist asks the doctors how they would treat him, causing the group to erupt in protestation: "We're going to be busy out there with guys who are *really* shot up, and we won't have time to monkey around with guys like that." The psychiatrist responds firmly: "Gentlemen, you

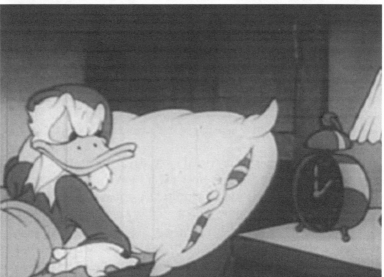

FIGURE 7.1. Gene Kelly plays a marine in group therapy in *Combat Fatigue: Irritability.*

FIGURE 7.2. A Donald Duck cartoon parodying sleeplessness triggers the frustrations of an insomniac soldier in *Combat Fatigue: Insomnia.*

are not *requested* to treat these patients, you are *directed* to do so."[33] Later in the film, another psychiatrist laments that by the time patients are sick enough to be sent to his hospital, he "can return only a very small percentage of patients to actual combat duty. Whereas *you,* out in the forward area, can, by getting at them early, send *70 to 80 percent* back to duty on the front line."[34]

This oft-repeated promise of productivity made absolutely clear the institutional directive underlying the films' call to take psychiatric casualties seriously, claiming widely that catching neuropsychiatric casualties early could "salvage" soldiers for active duty.[35] These films and others spread strategic psychiatric discourses and techniques throughout all levels of military service and administration, shifting away from earlier models of fear as a moral failing, and shaping a narrative of trauma's ordinariness, insisting that it was on some level observable, predictable, treatable, and, ultimately, under control. Films mobilized psychiatric language to build empathy for conditions afflicting millions of soldiers, but did so according to the belief that medico-psychiatric understandings of these conditions would go a long way toward eliminating the problems they presented. By aggressively labeling all manner of conditions "normal," psychiatric training films changed ideas about who was considered productive, recasting an older model of the "stoic soldier" with a new model of adaptable wartime labor that could accommodate not only "good soldiers," but also those who appeared unwilling or unable to fight. The promotion of a mass assembly model of military labor—where all workers can be good workers if managed in the right way—empathetically acknowledged the normalcy of fear in extreme conditions while simultaneously placing the focus on how best to adapt, rather than on the source of the conditions themselves. Nikolas Rose has written about the use of what he calls the "psy" sciences (psychology, psychiatry, psychotherapy, psychoanalysis) in Foucauldian structures of labor management. He writes that the "psy" sciences have generated the capacity to produce a corps of trained and credentialed persons claiming special competence in the administration of persons and interpersonal relations, and a body of techniques and procedures claiming to make possible the rational and humane management of human resources in industry, the military, and social life more generally.[36]

The psychiatric training films employed by the military in the Second World War were acting in concert with larger developments in industry and elsewhere that not only used psychiatrists and psychologists as technicians for modernizing labor, but further enlisted all levels of military personnel in the "psy" management for efficiency. In this case, the imperative to win the war provided a strong motivational rationale for doing so.

Beyond merely teaching doctors *why* they ought to administer psychiatric therapy, films such as *Combat Exhaustion* were also made to train them *how* to do so.[37] The primary method of treating conditions caused by stress and trauma was rest for milder cases and, for more aggressive ones, catharsis therapy, or "narcosynthe-sis." In this treatment, psychiatrists or doctors made vocal sounds such as gunshots or explosions and/or acted as a fellow soldier or commanding officer in order to provoke heavily sedated patients to spontaneously relive/act out traumatic memories. This method's popularity meant that audiovisual performances became a standard element of military psychiatric treatment, and the mysterious and complex damaged human mind was suddenly put on display as a relatively coherent set of audiovisual tropes (cowering, seeking cover, cries of distress, trying to flee, etc.).[38] Reinforcing the expediency of this treatment was the fact that it lent itself very well to being portrayed on film and was thus easily communicable to viewers without having to delve deeply into complex psychiatric explanations.

Combat Exhaustion's most bizarre scene demonstrates this treatment in order to teach military medics to use it themselves. In the film, the visiting group of doctors watch as a psychiatrist treats a partially paralyzed patient by injecting him with sodium pentothal to bring about "chemical hypnosis."[39] Once the patient has been drugged, a flashback scene of the same actor panicking in a foxhole signals to the audience that he is reliving his trauma, which the film equates with a virtually instantaneous purging of his obstacle to recovery. After the flashback, the psychiatrist calmly and confidently rouses the patient and coaches him to walk again. The patient marvels at the use of his legs, and the psychiatrist parades his newly cured patient for the other doctors, encouraging him to "put your shoulders back. . . . Let's see you walk like a soldier."

The use of the flashback to show doctors how the mind could be triggered to release its trauma with the help of drugs was not simply cinematic shorthand. The flashback mimicked a formalization of practices of abreaction/catharsis therapy that understood the patient's mind as able to visually project a buried memory, if triggered properly, for the therapist to see. These films and the treatments they promoted portrayed a model of the patient's mind as *cinematic in itself*—as something that could retain complete "scenes" from his or her traumatic past and be "rewound" to display its expulsion, therefore assuring doctors that their techniques were working.[40] These practices also used film and other sensory stimulation to teach patients' minds how to produce these kinds of cinematic performances by attempting to trigger abreaction on the one hand, and by modeling what was expected on the other.

2. Therapeutic Films in Military Hospitals: Visually Stimulated Catharsis in Group Therapy

The proposed outcome of teaching the language and tactics of psychiatry to military personnel was to make good on "salvaging up to 80%" of "combat exhausted" soldiers. Postwar studies have suggested that such ambitious claims may have been a PR strategy to improve morale, since even optimistic psychiatrists from forward

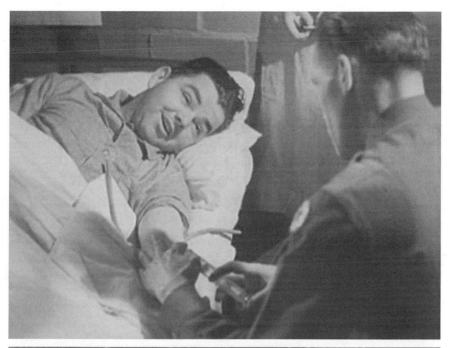

FIGURE 7.3. Administering drugs for narcosynthesis in *Combat Exhaustion*.

FIGURE 7.4. A flashback in *Combat Exhaustion* cues the audience that treatment is working.

areas claimed only a 60 percent possible return to duty.[41] The bleaker reality was that only about 2 percent of servicemen who left fighting for psychiatric reasons went back into combat, while the rest of the return percentages included soldiers transferred from combat to "noncombatant service in quiet sectors."[42] Despite forward psychiatry's goal of stemming the tide of casualties leaving their jobs and filling overcrowded and costly hospitals, huge numbers of soldiers required psychiatric treatment.[43] The official US Army review, *Neuropsychiatry in World War II*, acknowledges the massive disparity between the number of patients needing treatment and the number of trained specialists available, stating that military and veterans' hospitals often had the option of offering patients "group treatment or no treatment."[44] The same economy-of-scale tactics that used film to promote forward psychiatry were used again in hospital treatment, where a number of psychiatrists thought that films could both provide information and act as a more complex interlocutor, efficiently triggering therapeutic expressions of emotion from patients in group therapy.[45]

This latter use of film in group therapy was an extension of the kinds of catharsis therapy treatments that became common during the war. The first psychiatrists sent to work with soldiers on the battlefront, Roy Grinker and John Spiegel, formalized the "narcosynthesis" treatments described in the previous section.[46] Due to a lack of space and resources, they began treating soldiers in an open medical tent in plain view of other patients and, as a result, noted the potential of visual stimulus as an aid in group therapy. They observed that while the doctors and patients were acting out battle scenes during narcosynthesis treatment, other patients within eyeshot were liable to react with sympathetic displays of distress.[47] This observation formed the basis of experimentations with and standardizations of treatments that used visual and auditory stimulus.

The same didactic lecture films that taught inductees to rationalize symptoms during training were also used on veterans in military psychiatric hospitals, such as the *Combat Fatigue* series, which was commonly used as an aid to group therapy. Dr. Elias Katz's 1944 survey on the use of audiovisual aids in military hospitals praises these films for their ability to stimulate productive group discussion,[48] and in an article published for the US Navy in 1945, psychiatrist Dr. Howard P. Rome writes that the films were successful in "assist[ing] the patient in understanding the nature and cause of his illness" in group psychotherapy sessions.[49] In addition, some psychiatrists used these films to trigger emotional catharsis. The films often portray soldiers experiencing emotional outbursts followed by recovery and resolution, presenting not only a model for understanding how the steps of recovery should proceed, but also a performance available for mimicry.

In *Combat Fatigue: Irritability*, the main character, Lucas—a naval mechanic, played by Gene Kelly, on leave at a recovery station—erupts in anger during a group-therapy session where he is made to recount being blown out of his ship.

Lucas is eventually shown with his head in his arms, broken down in tears. There is no flashback illustrating this scene; the camera stays fixed on Lucas's face and upper body in a medium close-up as he shakes and shouts and cries. As a film for soldiers, it did not emphasize the coherence of the memory that was being expunged, as did the films made for doctors, but rather offered a model of visible/emotional performance that was expected of patients. Following his outburst, Lucas is ushered out of the room and given a sedative by the presiding psychiatrist, who returns to the rest of the participants in the group session to tell them, "[E]very one of you must go through a similar realization of what lies behind symptoms. . . . You have to face those memories, get them out in the open, exactly as Lucas has done." The film narrates, for the group *in* the film and the group *watching* the film, the expected course of therapy in a feedback loop of teaching and triggers that hoped to produce spontaneous emotional abreactions from viewers.

In his study on the use of film in military group therapy in 1945, Rome notes that subsequent to screening one of the *Combat Fatigue* films for patients in group therapy, "72% of patients showed psychosomatic reactions such as: vomiting, sweating, tremors; 52% had startle reactions to war scenes; 86% said they are vividly reminded of their own combat experience; . . . and 45% were agitated for 2 days following screening."[50] Rome praises the benefit of these triggered reactions, claiming that "this undercarriage of tension can be used readily to accomplish beneficial abreaction and constructive cathexis." He concludes that this is key to the larger healing process: "[L]ike drugs or other potent therapy, therapeutic films have the capacity for inciting response whose benefit is proportional to the skill and judgment of the therapist."[51] Rome and others encouraged the use of films that produced affective, bodily responses, echoing the rhetoric promoted in official military psychiatric texts such as the scenes in *Combat Fatigue: Irritability* and *Combat Exhaustion* discussed above: once a performance of emotional release has been solicited, the therapist can press forward with the treatment process. Despite the diversity of patients and afflictions, discourses such as these proposed a standardizable trajectory of efficient treatment and predictable outcomes.

Military psychiatrists also used more-abstract types of motion pictures to generate affective responses. Writing in 1946, Dr. Elias Katz describes Auroratone pictures as approximately thirty minutes of changing prismatic color patterns syncopated with slow, sad music. He thought that the sound track, made up of songs like "Home on the Range," sung by Bing Crosby, and "Ave Maria" produced a kind of subliminal nostalgic recognition while the changing color patterns soothed the conscious mind.[52] Katz suggests that these effects subtly evoke the painful subject of home, and observes that most patients became intensely absorbed in the films, noting that some with extremely compromised attention spans might watch with rapt attention after fifteen viewings.[53] Along with increasing attention spans, he describes results including relaxation of the body and

FIGURE 7.5. An image from the soothing, prismatic Auroratone film *When the Organ Played "Oh Promise Me,"* set to the song of the same name sung by Bing Crosby, with organ accompaniment by Lieutenant Colonel Edward Dunstedter.

nervous habits, weeping, and increased openness to discussion, claiming that these cumulative effects open up pathways to patients' "inner life" through auditory and visual channels, with "repeated exposures render[ing] them more accessible to positive psychotherapy."[54]

On the other end of the spectrum were motion pictures that used actual war footage as a form of exposure therapy. Lieutenant Commander Dr. Louis A. Schwartz writes in 1945:

> Most encouraging is the use of visio-auditory stimulation in the "deconditioning" process of combat experience. . . . Briefly, films of actual combat scenes, graded in order of intensity of stimulation[,] are shown, followed or accompanied by a record of battle sounds. The more innocuous sound films are introduced first, such as animated cartoons caricaturizing stupidity or neglect of weapons, films of ship-to-shore landings, and types of ordnance. This is followed immediately by group discussion which reactivates the traumatic event in a shielded environment. . . . [Later] actual combat films of bombings, strafings, and some captured Japanese films are shown with the battle sounds.[55]

Schwartz notes that "some [patients] actually flee from the scene, sweat, develop uncontrollable tremors, vomit, or exhibit severe vasomotor manifestations,"[56] praising these as useful abreactions that could be treated with sedation and/or talk therapy.

Describing a similar film-based exposure-therapy treatment, psychiatrists Dr. Leon J. Saul and colleagues cited techniques for training police horses to remain calm in traffic by playing audio recordings of street noise in their stables.[57] They apply this principle to treating soldiers, writing that "[a]ttempts have ... been made to decrease the startle reaction and the anxiety in men who have been incapacitated by combat fatigue, by exposing them to the mock battles used for training, and by showing them motion pictures."[58] Early stages of treatment included films with no scenes of injury or death; they took place in a room with doors open, window shades up, and no sound, gradually closing doors, pulling blinds, and giving patients the opportunity to increase the volume as they acclimated to the pictures. As the treatment extended over several sessions, the intensity of stimulus increased, and the psychiatrist would introduce films containing scenes of fighting and gruesome casualties after the less graphic ones ceased to produce startle reactions.[59]

Psychiatrist Schwartz, who writes about his experimentations with "deconditioning films" in 1945, commends them for their speed, efficiency, and cost-effectiveness. He suggests that, if taken up on a large scale, film-desensitization treatment could eliminate the need to build veterans' facilities and could be used to treat "civilian 'war neurosis,'" in which people's symptoms arise from shared trauma, building further on the foundational conviction (or at least the hope) that traumatic states were predictable and their treatment could be standardized.[60] Films had succeeded at bringing well-managed messages about psychiatry and its usefulness to vast publics of military personnel. This, combined with films' perceived capacity to produce "useful" affective responses, gave them a key role in rationalizing the ongoing expansion of the military-psychiatric apparatus throughout the war. As the large cohort of newly trained psychiatrists began to look to civilian society and postwar rehabilitation when their jobs in military service began to end, some of them continued to see film as a ready tool for breaking new professional ground.

CONCLUSION

Audiences comprising millions of soldiers, doctors, and psychiatrists, many encountering psychiatric discourses for the first time, meant that the films made and used within the military's psychiatric apparatus irrevocably changed the way that psychiatry and the distressed mind were understood, treated, talked about, and managed not only in the military, but in postwar society as well. The military's role in the expansion of psychiatric practices and discourses into daily life in the United States during and after the Second World War was vast and multifaceted. The establishment of a military psychiatry division in the Surgeon General's office with an active public-relations officer during the war established networks through which the lessons promulgated in the films examined here found their way into the explosion of popular culture and news media interested in psychiatric topics.[61]

Not only did the films themselves have aftereffects, but the substantial military psychiatric apparatus and its techniques continued to function after the declaration of victory. In the immediate postwar period, psychiatrically informed films were used to try to acclimate returning soldiers to civilian life. Newsreels and documentaries were sometimes screened for returning veterans to ease the transition home and soothe possible resentment toward civilians. An article on the treatment and rehabilitation of prisoners of war prescribes the use of documentary films followed by discussion to reorient soldiers to circumstances in their home country and encourage "psychotherapeusis"—an effect the authors attribute to watching the rehabilitation of physically injured soldiers on-screen.[62]

A similar PR-based approach to the one the military had used to sell psychiatric discourses to personnel could be seen in films made by industry and insurance companies introducing laymen and employers to "nervous conditions" they might encounter while working with returned veterans. Titles such as the Zurich Insurance Company's *Weathering These Storms* and *Keep Your Head* were intended to reduce misinformation about mental illness and demonstrate how coworkers and friends could make social adjustments to accommodate people's suffering.[63] The best-known example of these types of films is Huston's *Let There Be Light,* a documentary of veterans in a psychiatric hospital made to dispel public misconceptions about combat fatigue. The now-infamous suppression of Huston's film and its subsequent remaking in 1948 by a different director as the moralizing and mother-blaming *Shades of Gray* was likely, at least in part, in response to the fact that the former film ceased to fit within the evolving paradigm of psychotherapy that best served the military's postwar interests.[64] *Shades of Gray* reoriented the etiology of combat fatigue from a product of war trauma to one of improper child-rearing, thus subtly shifting toward a position that helped to displace some of the responsibility for distressed soldiers from the military to the Mother and suggesting that psychiatry had a postwar role to play in the therapy of the American family.

With their implementation in the final phase of military therapeutics—reintegrating veterans into civilian life—these and similar films became vehicles for promoting a nationwide program of mental hygiene.[65] A general popularization and proliferation of psychology and psychoanalysis in postwar film, radio, and television, prompted in part by the institutional legitimization the disciplines received via their war efforts, came together potently with a widespread discourse of anxiety and empathy around the return of soldiers from overseas with ominous-sounding war neuroses.[66] These media texts helped to normalize the role of newly medicalized psychiatric discourses in spaces of everyday life including the home, the school, and the workplace, and to expand the role of psychiatry and associated sciences in the adjustment of veterans to civilian life more generally.[67]

In a chapter reviewing the effects of World War II on mental-health practices in America, Grob writes that after the war, psychiatrists "maintained that their specialty possessed the knowledge and techniques to identify appropriate and environmental changes that presumably could optimize mental as well as physical health. 'Good mental health or well-being,' wrote [psychiatrist] Henry W. Brosin in spelling out the implications of the military experience for American society, 'is a commodity which *can be created* under favorable circumstances.'"[68] By 1957 only 17 percent of the APA's 10,000 members worked in psychiatric asylums, in sharp contrast to the 67 percent of the 2,295 who did so before the war. The astonishing new cohort of psychiatrists, some 8,300, largely migrated to jobs that interacted with a broad cross-section of the public. Rather than working with the severely disabled, they worked in community clinics, education, government posts, medical schools, private practices, or as consultants for industry and manufacturing.[69] The technique of mobilizing communications to change public understandings of the discipline—refined by the military psychiatric apparatus—facilitated this thorough and rapid change to the disciplinary makeup. Watershed events in this centralization were the signing of the Mental Health Act and subsequent establishment of a federal budget to support the National Institute of Mental Health in 1946, for which crucial testimony and lobbying were provided by prominent military psychiatrists.[70] Once established, the National Institute of Mental Health took charge of the Publications and Reports sector of the Military Psychiatry division that had been set up to provide PR material during the war, "disseminat[ing] information about mental illness and its prevention . . . and produc[ing] films, exhibits, study kits, catalogues and printed materials for use by the public."[71] Models carried over from the war, such as the use of media to lobby for a centralized organization and a change in national mental-health policy, solidified a shifting concern in psychiatry from the chronically ill to "all of human society" and, by extension, from the care of vulnerable communities to a purview that included the optimization of productive ones.[72]

While the wartime mobilization of mass communication allowed for the postwar expansion of psychiatric practice into realms of everyday life and labor, the more experimental technologies such as desensitization films set precedents for therapies and experimentation in hospitals and laboratories that enjoyed better postwar funding as a result of new government policy.[73] The films discussed above, used in training and in treatment, acted as gateways that prepared soldiers to work better under traumatic conditions, and again to "expel" trauma from them once they could no longer work, presaging a similar contemporary use of video games for training, stress management, and therapy. In his essay "Affectivity, Biopolitics and the Virtual Reality of War," Pasi Väliaho looks at the Virtual Iraq Therapy program used to treat soldiers returning from Iraq with PTSD. The VR images used in the program "initially recycled the graphic assets built for a tactical simulation training platform, which was also released as the commercial video game *Full Spectrum Warrior* in 2004."[74] Väliaho dubs this multiphased use of media a "closing circle . . . of warrior production," showing that researchers today speculate that digital images may act as "stress inoculation training," or desensitization tools that, through repeated exposure, disarticulate images of combat from emotional responses.[75] He observes that the use of digital war images in military psychiatry continues to expand the biomedical framing of affect and distress. VR therapy's image, sound, and vibrational immersion is intended to target "neurophysiological and sensorimotor adjustment rather than cognitive control."[76] Bypassing struggles to articulate their experience, this type of treatment uses VR to take patients back to a traumatic incident over and over again using cues including vibrations from explosions, images of dead insurgents and dying colleagues, and the sounds of AK 47s and crying babies.[77] When the effects of VR are discussed in laboratory research contexts, more so than exploring the patient's relationship with her or his experience and the social world outside the image, the intended results are focused on training the brain to stop triggering somatic fear reactions, continuing the model of mind and treatment popularized in World War II that seized on the manipulation of image-based memories to adjust personnel to the conditions of war.

This chapter does not presume to evaluate whether these kinds of programs worked with respect to the mental health and overall fighting efficiency of soldiers in the US military, nor does it constitute an indictment of military psychiatrists, who were mostly doing their best to care for patients under incredibly difficult circumstances. What is relevant here is analyzing the central place of cinema in the dissemination and rhetoric of a communications campaign and medical practice to help adapt psychiatry to the institutional mandates of the military. In the context of the unprecedented growth of psychiatry's popularity during the war, the implications are significant. The extension of the efficiency model to military labor via psychiatry found a way to accommodate a person's desperate final recourse to objecting to their job: extreme expressions of self-protection, understood variously by the military as "shell shock," "combat fatigue," or "post-traumatic stress." The formative uses of cinema in military psychiatry mapped out here left a deep mark in the role that psychiatry has continued to play in understandings of how human minds can and ought to be adjusted to the world around them, particularly in situations that might otherwise provoke emotional, cognitive, or political resistance from the subject.

NOTES

1. Sigmund Freud and other psychoanalysts studied trauma and the human mind—for example, writing about "shellshock" in soldiers emerging from the First World War—but these studies circulated among a very narrow audience. On the public obscurity of psychotherapy, Ellen Herman writes: "Before the war, psychotherapy had been associated largely with the elite office practice of psychoanalysis . . . or with a range of techniques employed by psychiatrists functioning in the institutional

context of state hospitals. . . . Psychotherapy was not relevant to ordinary people. . . . If anything, it was stigmatizing." Ellen Herman, *The Romance of American Psychology: Political Culture in the Age of Experts* (Berkeley: University of California Press, 1995), 112.

2. Many histories map the change the war brought to the prominence of the social sciences—in particular, psychiatry and psychology. Of particular interest here are Herman's *Romance of American Psychology;* Gerald N. Grob's *From Asylum to Community: Mental Health Policy in Modern America* (Princeton, NJ: Princeton University Press, 2014); and Ben Shephard's *A War of Nerves: Soldiers and Psychiatrists in the Twentieth Century* (Cambridge, MA: Harvard University Press, 2001). Fred Turner's *The Democratic Surround: Multimedia and American Liberalism* (Chicago: University of Chicago Press, 2013) highlights the relationship between media and the social sciences during this period.

3. Both films are listed in Edmund North's "The Secondary or Psychological Phase of Training Films," *Journal of the Society for Motion Picture Engineers* 42, no. 2 (February 1944): 119.

4. Listed in Dr. Elias Katz's article "A Brief Survey of the Use of Motion Pictures for the Treatment of Neuropsychiatric Patients," *Psychiatric Quarterly* 20, no. 1 (March 1946): 205.

5. Shephard, *War of Nerves*, 271. For an excellent overview of the film's role in military management of mental health discourses, see C. A. Morgan III, "From *Let There Be Light* to *Shades of Grey*: The Construction of Authoritative Knowledge about Combat Fatigue (1945–48)," in *Signs of Life: Medicine and Cinema*, ed. Graeme Harper and Andrew Moor (London: Wallflower Press, 2005), 132–52.

6. See Robert N. McLay, *At War with PTSD: Battling Post Traumatic Stress Disorder with Virtual Reality* (Baltimore, MD: Johns Hopkins University Press, 2012); and Pasi Väliaho, "Affectivity, Biopolitics and the Virtual Reality of War," *Theory, Culture & Society* 29, no. 2 (2012): 63–83.

7. McLay, *At War with PTSD*, 85.

8. Gerald N. Grob, *The Mad among Us: A History of the Care of America's Mentally Ill* (New York: Free Press, 1994), 178.

9. Gerald N. Grob, *Mental Illness and American Society, 1875–1940* (Princeton, NJ: Princeton University Press, 1983), 296.

10. Ibid., 183.

11. Ibid. (my emphasis).

12. Herman's *Romance of American Psychology* details the enormous opportunity the US military provided for the growth of specialists in mental health care during the war, writing that "[b]oth professions [psychiatry and psychology] would experience a historically unprecedented postwar growth curve, far outstripping general population growth or even the spectacular growth of the health-related professions" (20).

13. Herman notes that psychiatric casualties made up 26 to 40 percent of all medical evacuations, with numbers jumping as high as 75 percent in particularly brutal campaigns. Herman, *Romance of American Psychology*, 89.

14. The change in views is a commonly repeated refrain found in films discussed later in this essay.

15. See Sándor Ferenczi, Karl Abraham, Ernst Simmel, and Ernest Jones, *Psychoanalysis and the War Neuroses*, with an introduction by Sigmund Freud (London: International Psycho-Analytical Press, 1921).

16. The first chapter of Grob's *From Asylum to Community* gives an overview of the relative power of psychodynamic versus psychosomatic models of psychiatry during the war and in the postwar period. Both "environmental" and "developmental" psychiatry fall under psychodynamic models, and psychosomatic treatments were often employed to treat psychiatric casualties.

17. Grob, *The Mad among Us*, 196.

18. See order of operations in "Appendix II: Method of Handling Neuropsychiatric Casualties in Theatres of Operation," in "Combat Psychiatry," supplement, *Bulletin of the US Army Medical Department* 9 (1949), prepared under the direction of R. W. Bliss, Surgeon General (Washington, DC: Government Printing Office, 1949).

19. In the "Psychiatry at the Army Level," Major Alfred O. Ludwig writes of "combat exhaustion:" "This term was, frankly, a euphemism . . . however, it served to imply rapid recovery after a short period of rest. . . . It also avoided giving the impression that incurable mental illness was present." *Bulletin of the US Army Medical Department*, 92.

20. John W. Appel, "Preventative Psychiatry," in Medical Department of the United States Army in World War II, *Neuropsychiatry in World War II*, vol. 1, *Zone of the Interior* (Washington, DC: Office of the Surgeon General Department US Army, 1966), 388.

21. Louis L. Tureen and Martin Stein, "The Base Section Psychiatric Hospital," *Bulletin of the U.S. Army Medical Department* 9, suppl. (1949), 105.

22. William C. Menninger, "Education and Training," in Medical Dept. US Army WWII, *Neuropsychiatry*, 66.

23. Norman Q. Brill, "Station and Regional Hospitals," in Medical Dept. US Army WWII, *Neuropsychiatry*, 284.

24. Ludwig writes that the term "combat exhaustion" helped to displace others such as "psycho." Ludwig, "Psychiatry at the Army Level," 92. "Goldbrick" was a common slur referring to a malingering soldier who was lazy, conniving, or trying to shirk duties.

25. These films are listed in several publications, including "Therapeutic Films and Group Psychotherapy," by Howard P. Rome, *Sociometry* 8, nos. 3/4 (1945): 247–54; Menninger's "Education and Training" chapter in *Neuropsychiatry in World War II*; and *Psychiatry and Modern Warfare*, by Kenneth Appel and Edward Strecker (New York: Macmillan Company, 1945).

26. Alison Winter, "Film and the Construction of Memory in Psychoanalysis, 1940–1960," *Science in Context* 19, no. 1 (2006): 120.

27. Ibid.

28. A young Gene Kelley starred in *Combat Fatigue: Irritability*, and a screening of a Donald Duck cartoon on a military base triggers recognition in a soldier struggling with sleep difficulty in *Combat Fatigue: Insomnia*.

29. It has been difficult to date this film accurately. According to documents in its production file at the National Archives, the film was given clearance for rerelease for public circulation in 1962, and this is the date that appears in the title reel of the copies available to view. It seems likely that the film was originally made during or shortly after World War II, since it is very similar in style, tone, and rhetoric to the other psychiatric training films made in this period, and it is filed under Second World War military films at the National Archives.

30. *Combat Psychiatry: The Battalion Medical Officer*, Department of Defense (United States Army Signal Corps, 1962).

31. An outline of a standard lecture to be delivered to officers by psychiatrists, titled "Recognize Abnormal Mental States in Your Men and What to Do," appears in "Psychiatric Orientation of Military Nonmedical Personnel," by Major Samuel H. Kraines, in *Manual of Military Neuropsychiatry*, ed. Harry C. Solomon and Paul I. Yakolev (Philadelphia: W. B. Saunders Company, 1944), 488.

32. Menninger, "Education and Training," 66.

33. *Combat Exhaustion* developed in the 312th Station Hospital by Col. Lloyd J. Thompson, MC, Col. Ernest H. Parsons, MC, and Maj. Howard D. Fabing, MC, Department of Defense (US Army Signal Corps, 1945).

34. Ibid.

35. See Spafford Ackerly, "Trends in Mental Hygiene: An Interpretation," *Review of Educational Research* 13, no. 5 (1943): 416–21; and Hans Pols, "War Neurosis, Adjustment Problems in Veterans, and an Ill Nation: The Disciplinary Project of Military Psychiatry during and after World War II," in *The Self as Project: Politics and the Human Sciences*, ed. Greg Eghigian, Andreas Killen, and Christine Lauenberger (Chicago: University of Chicago Press, 2007), 72–92.

36. Nikolas Rose, *Inventing Ourselves* (Cambridge: Cambridge University Press, 1998), 11.

37. A modeling of this kind of treatment is also portrayed in films such as *Psychiatry for the Field Medical Officer* and *Psychosis and Allied States*. Menninger's "Education and Training" chapter in *Neuropsychiatry in World War II* lists several films used and made by military psychiatry, as does the "Program of Films" screened during the Twenty-sixth Annual Meeting of the Western Psychological Association as recorded by Lester F. Beck in *American Psychologist* 1, no. 10 (October 1946): 448–58.

38. There are many descriptions of this treatment and its outcomes in military psychiatric literature. See, for example, Ludwig, "Psychiatry at the Army Level," 96.

39. Sodium pentothal and sodium amytal were the most common drugs administered in military psychiatry. Electroshock therapy was also a very common method for intervening in patient behavior.

40. On cinematic metaphors that military psychiatrists used in this period to describe memory, see Alison Winter, *Memory: Fragments of a Modern History* (Chicago: University of Chicago Press, 2012), 64.

41. Edgar Jones and Simon Wessely, *Shell Shock to PTSD: Military Psychiatry from 1900 to the Gulf War*, Maudsley Monographs 47 (New York: Psychology Press, 2005), 87.

42. Roy Grinker and John Spiegel, *War Neuroses in North Africa: The Tunisian Campaign January–May 1943* (New York, 1943), 235, quoted in Jones and Wessely, *Shell Shock to PTSD*, 88

43. In some of the worst campaigns, up to 34 percent of all casualties were psychiatric in nature. See Pols, "War Neurosis," 77.

44. Brill, "Station and Regional Hospitals," 289.

45. See Howard P. Rome, "Military Group Psychotherapy," *American Journal of Psychiatry* 101, no. 4 (1945): 494–97; Francis J. Braceland, "Psychiatric Lessons from WWII," *American Journal of Psychiatry* 103, no. 5 (1947): 587–93; Fred D. Kartchner and Ija N. Korner, "Use of Hypnosis in Treatment of Acute Combat Reactions," *American Journal of Psychiatry* 103, no. 5 (1947): 630–36; Moody C. Bettis, Daniel I. Malamud, and Rachel F. Malamud, "Deepening a Group's Insight into Human Relations: A Compilation of Aids," *Journal of Clinical Psychology* 5 (1949): 114–22; Elias Katz, "Audio-Visual Aids for Mental Hygiene and Psychiatry," *Journal of Clinical Psychology* 3 (1947): 43–46; and Jacob L. Moreno, "Psychodrama and Therapeutic Motion Pictures," *Sociometry* 7 (1944): 230–44.

46. Shephard, *War of Nerves*, 214; Winter, "Construction of Memory," 116.

47. Tureen and Stein, "Base Section Psychiatric Hospital," 129.

48. Katz, "Aids for Mental Hygiene," 44.

49. Howard P. Rome, "Audio-Visual Aids in Psychiatry," *Hospital Corps Quarterly* (US Navy) 18, no. 4 (1945): 37–38.

50. Ibid.

51. Ibid.

52. Walter Forsberg's article "God Must Have Painted Those Pictures: Illuminating Auroratone's Lost History" describes the Bing Crosby Enterprise's investment in Cecil Stokes's prepsychedelic film apparatus and lists all known Auroratone films. The article appeared in *Incite!* no. 4 (Fall 2013), accessed July 23, 2015, www.incite-online.net/forsberg4.html.

53. Elias Katz and H. E. Rubin, "Auroratone Films for the Treatment of Psychotic Depressions in an Army General Hospital," *Journal of Clinical Psychology* 2 (1946): 335.

54. Ibid., 337–39. One could speculate that these mesmerizing protopsychedelic films shown to chemically sedated audiences may have piqued the interest of military psychiatrists who would go on to research the effects of LSD and other drugs on soldiers.

55. Louis A. Schwartz, "Group Psychotherapy in the War Neuroses," *American Journal of Psychiatry* 101, no. 4 (1945): 498–99.

56. Ibid., 499.

57. Leon J. Saul, Howard Rome, and Edwin Leuser, "Desensitization in Combat Fatigue Patients," *American Journal of Psychiatry* 102, no. 4 (1946): 476.

58. Ibid.

59. Ibid., 477.

60. Schwartz, "Group Psychotherapy," 500.

61. In an address to a graduating class of military-trained psychiatrists, William Menninger states that there is a "well-trodden path to our little division in the Surgeon General's Office by writers from magazines and newspapers, from radio stations and motion-picture producers . . . . Our Public Relations officer has told me that except for special drives . . . neuropsychiatry probably receives more newspaper column space, and he receives more inquiries about it than any other branch of the Surgeon General's Office." Printed as William Menninger, "Psychiatric Objectives in the Army," *American Journal of Psychiatry* 102, no. 1 (July 1945): 106.

62. Maxwell Jones and J. M. Tanner, "The Clinical Characteristics, Treatments, and Rehabilitation of Repatriated Prisoners of War with Neurosis," *Journal of Neurology, Neurosurgery, and Psychiatry* 11, no. 1 (1948): 55.

63. Katz, "Aids for Mental Hygiene," 45.

64. Morgan, "From *Let There Be Light*," 135.

65. For a discussion of the postwar expansion of military mental-hygiene infrastructure, see Grob, *From Asylum to Community*.

66. John D. M. Griffin and William Line, "Trends in Mental Hygiene," *Review of Educational Research* 16, no. 5 (1946): 397.

67. Herman, in *Romance of American Psychology*, writes about the role that psychiatrists and psychologists envisioned for themselves as postwar peacekeepers and "custodians of a vital social resource—mental health—without which economic prosperity, democratic decision making, and intergroup harmony were implausible, perhaps impossible" (121).

68. Grob, *The Mad among Us*, 195.

69. Ibid., 196, 202. The prewar statistic is from 1940. My own research suggests that many former military psychiatrists went on to advise private companies on worker-management relations.

70. Grob, *The Mad among Us*, 202.

71. Menninger, "Psychiatric Objectives in the Army," 106.

72. Grob, *From Asylum to Community*, 56.

73. The signing of the National Mental Health Act earmarked federal funds to support psychiatric research, in particular "demonstration studies dealing with prevention, diagnosis, and treatment." See Grob, *From Asylum to Community*, 53. These ideas also surface regularly in popular-culture treatments of dystopian mind control and brainwashing in such films as *The Manchurian Candidate* and *A Clockwork Orange*. See Charles Acland's book *Swift Viewing: The Popular Life of Subliminal Influence* (Durham, NC: Duke University Press, 2012).

74. Väliaho, "Affectivity," 65.

75. Ibid., 76.

76. Ibid., 68.

77. Sue Halpern, "Virtual Iraq: Using Simulation to Treat a New Generation of Traumatized Veterans," *New Yorker*, May 19, 2008, accessed August 10, 2015, www.newyorker.com/magazine/2008/05/19/virtual-iraq.

8

THE CINEMA INTELLIGENCE APPARATUS

Gregory Bateson, the Museum of Modern Art Film
Library, and the Intelligence Work of Film Studies
during World War II

Nathaniel Brennan

In October 1941 *Motion Picture Herald* carried a brief report on the proceedings of the Westinghouse Photographic Lighting Conference in Bloomfield, New Jersey. Of particular interest to the trade paper was the presentation of one Colonel M. E. Gillette of the US Army Signal Corps, who told conference attendees that the army was considering Nazi propaganda for use in its training programs. As a supplement to the signal corps's own training films, "rookie soldiers and officers alike" would be shown official Nazi propaganda films of the blitzkrieg as it moved across Western Europe. These films, "showing panzers, dive bombers and tanks in action," Gillette told his audience, "actually can give selectees and enlisted men a first hand opportunity to analyze and discuss with their instructors Nazi operations in the field." Cinema and photography—in this case, foreign-made films—he concluded, would "for the first time in history . . . play a major part in training soldiers."[1]

The use of film and its institutions by American military and government authorities during the Second World War is a well-known facet of film history. Much of this history has focused on the shaping of commercial entertainment, brokered by collaborative ventures between federal wartime agencies and the American film industry. In what is surely the best-known example, the film industry worked closely with the Office of War Information (OWI) to ensure that Hollywood films properly reflected Allied war aims and the American spirit of democracy. Similarly, in what would be a controversial practice, the Research Council of the Motion Picture Academy of Arts and Sciences handed out US Army Signal Corps training-film production contracts to the major studios.[2] The production of training films and the reinforcement of democratic ideals in entertainment films are examples of what has recently been termed "useful cinema"—a mode of cinema that "*does* something."[3] In addition to making a particular kind of useful film, the military repurposed films made by others. In this case, Nazi propaganda films were edited and became important elements of World War II orientation and training films. These films ironized the ideological nature of the German footage, either to mock the Nazis' mindless conformity and fetishism of authority or to illustrate the brutality of their tactics and worldview. In the case of Colonel Gillette's "terror-films," however, the purpose for film reuse was more practical: it was to be a tool for the visual identification of Nazi aircraft and mechanized infantry as well as Nazi field tactics. To the signal corps, these films constituted a form of intelligence.

As important as this form of intelligence was, there were yet other forms that we have yet to fully consider. Indeed, the deployment of *cinema as a source of cultural intelligence* is a missing piece in the complex history of cinema in World War II. Intelligence can be understood as the focused production of predictive strategic knowledge based on the outcome of prior experience and the active collection and interpretation of new information. Unlike the immediacy of intelligence gathered from newspapers, intercepted reports, and informants, the nature of cinematic intelligence applied to long-range strategic goals. What could popular entertainment films produced by other nations tell American policy makers and military authorities about the psychological proclivities and outlook of the peoples American soldiers would encounter in theaters of battle? For that matter, how could an analysis of Hollywood feature films illuminate unconscious trends in American morale and public opinion? These and other questions would be asked by numerous governmental and military agencies throughout the war; the difficulty was that the answers to these questions were not self-evident. Creating useful cinema (that is, making films) in aid of the war effort was one thing. Studio personnel knew how to seamlessly integrate prodemocratic messages into feature films and how to make an instructional film that clearly demonstrated the process of cleaning and assembling a rifle. Knowing what to do with stockpiles of older films, and especially those made far beyond American borders, how to store them, make them available, study them—in short, how to make them useful—was another matter entirely. For these tasks, federal and military authorities sought the help of experts from institutions seemingly far outside the purview of military necessity.

The critical and time-sensitive challenges faced by a military force during wartime will generate innovative solutions devised and adapted from sometimes nontraditional materials. For the American military, the period between the isolationist late 1930s and the conclusion of the Second World War was marked by unprecdented expansion in all corners, as well as deepening economic and even intellectual entanglement with numerous nonmilitary civilian organizations that reflected, of necessity, its willingness to experiment with unusual approaches that attempted to accelerate and retool outmoded or inefficient standard operating procedures. As the chapters of this volume attest, cinema was pressed into military service throughout the twentieth century for a variety of seemingly nontraditional purposes— that is, as innovations responsive to the demands of the moment that could just as easily be abandoned as failed or immediately outdated experiments. One such (ultimately abandoned) experiment was the analysis and adaptation of motion pictures by cultural anthropologists at the height of the war for the purposes of acclimating US servicemen to the cultures and personalities of enemy and ally alike—in other words, militarizing the formal and critical strategies of film analysis.

Critical film analysis—"thinking" with cinema—even in the 1940s was already a complicated endeavor that called for flexible, interdisciplinary approaches to cinema. That form of expertise lay beyond the scope of the many information, propaganda, and intelligence agencies established during the war. In the remainder of this chapter, I explore the use of cinema as a source of cultural intelligence by focusing on the work undertaken by the British anthropologist Gregory Bateson on the study of national character and mentality at the Museum of Modern Art Film Library, a key institution for governmental and military film programs during World War II. In order to illustrate the extent of the federal government's wartime film programs and the role that the Film Library (and, by extension, Bateson) played within them, this chapter is organized following the conceptual model of the intelligence cycle—a feedback loop of knowledge production common to all forms of academic inquiry and disciplinary formation, but central to the modern intelligence community. With each section the terms of discussion become more specific, ultimately concentrating on a single project within the Film Library—a three-way collaboration among the Film Library, the anthropologist-*cum*-film analyst Gregory Bateson, and the short-lived Army Specialized Training Program.

COLLECTION AND PROCESSING

Collecting, processing, and storing films was a perpetual problem for federal authorities throughout World War II that lasted well into the postwar era. Of all the phases in the intelligence cycle, the task of collecting intelligence—in this case, the maintenance and storage of thousands of reels of film—and making it available to intelligence producers was the most consistent and enduring. It was in this capacity that the Museum of Modern Art Film Library worked most closely with federal and military intelligence agencies.

The Film Library was established in the mid-1930s amid heightened public anxieties surrounding the undue influence of subversive, antidemocratic propaganda and the ease with which such material was disseminated through American media channels. Although the American public had been wary of mass mediated political messages since the end of the First World War, the rise of totalitarian regimes in Europe gave way to renewed fears of more-sophisticated foreign and domestic propaganda, slickly produced and engineered to push the United States into another foreign war or, conversely, to ensure that it remained neutral in world affairs.[4] To this end, propaganda and publicity offices such as the German Library of Information and the British Library of Information attempted to sway American public opinion with reams of handsomely illustrated pamphlets and newsletters, while the American branch offices of international film concerns like Amkino Corporation and Ufa Films, Inc., distributed feature films and newsreels from the Soviet Union and Nazi Germany, respectively, throughout North America.

For its part, the American film industry stridently worked to avoid anything that could be construed as political partisanship in its products and in its business practices. Having just emerged from a much publicized entanglement with American religious organizations over the contents of its films and with a renewed commitment to enforcing the Production Code, the film industry wanted nothing to do with controversial topics that might jeopardize domestic and international box-office grosses. In many ways, though, Hollywood was merely following the lead of public opinion. While the country slowly emerged from the Great Depression under the aegis of the Roosevelt administration's New Deal recovery program, the spread of totalitarianism in Europe provided congressional and public opinion enough reason to remain neutral in world affairs, lest the nation be drawn again into a foreign war for alien interests. Public suspicion of the unchecked influence of foreign propaganda made even dispassionate scholarly analysis of communications and propaganda a difficult proposition.

From the very first, the Museum of Modern Art Film Library seemed an unlikely institution to undertake propaganda analysis. Sharing its name and public mission with those of the Museum of Modern Art, the Film Library had as its mandate first and foremost to foster greater public appreciation for the cinema as an art and to collect and make available the very materials of film history for scholarly study. However, even before the Film Library was formally established in June 1935, its staff was quietly engaged in semiofficial intelligence work. The first such request came to Film Library staff in February 1935 from an unnamed Department of Agriculture official who wanted to discuss "foreign propaganda films which might be beneficially studied by the government department making propaganda films."[5] That meeting, held "in strict confidence," would exemplify the relationship between the privately funded Film Library and the federal government for the following decade. Beyond making the library's collections available to government intelligence and information agencies, Film Library staff provided something of greater value: expertise in analysis.

For Film Library staff, the necessity of professional discretion in matters pertaining to politics and propaganda was well founded. In its first years of operation the Film Library faced harsh criticism over the inclusion of Soviet and German films in its circulating programs, while "whisper campaigns" insinuating that members of its staff were Stalinist infiltrators resulted in resignations and acrimony.[6] Despite, or perhaps because of, these accusations the Film Library in its first years assembled an unparalleled collection of foreign propaganda films and related materials, particularly those from the Soviet Union and Nazi Germany. When Film Library director John Abbott and curator Iris Barry traveled through Europe in the summer of 1936 to establish contacts with other film archives and collect materials for the library, they acquired from the German film conglomerate Ufa not only prints of vital Weimar-era masterworks, but also more recent films, like the Nazi family drama *Hitlerjunge Quex* (1934), as well as a "complete file of year books and catalogues," "stills from all UFA films that have been sent [to] the [Film Library]," and "publicity on the majority of UFA's production[s]."[7] By early 1941, the library had acquired prints of other Nazi propaganda films, including *Triumph of the Will* (1935) and *Baptism of Fire* (1940).[8]

The basis for this early foray into intelligence gathering lay not with the mandates of the museum per se, but with the research imperatives of the Rockefeller Foundation's Humanities Division, which supplied the most substantial source of the Film Library's initial funding, thereby shaping the library's educational philosophy and research initiatives in ways that diverged from the larger institution with which it shared its name. On one hand, the Film Library's activities—collecting and preserving films, supporting research, curating exhibitions, packaging circulating programs—advanced the public missions of both the Museum of Modern Art and the Rockefeller Foundation's Humanities Division.[9] On the other, these same activities synchronized with the Humanities Division's nascent communications research projects that, while motivated by the public good, were carried out discreetly, particularly when these projects were linked in the late 1930s to the handful of government agencies concerned with American preparedness in case of war and protection from antidemocratic propaganda. From these connections the Film Library was brought into the orbit of various governmental agencies as the United States lurched from political isolationism and public anxiety over the influence of propaganda to full mobilization of an "arsenal of democracy" that would comprise not just war materiel, but also new forms and uses of knowledge. This relationship was complex and unprecedented—the sort of pairing produced by the exigencies of the national war emergency and a sudden need for specific kinds of expertise contingent upon the shifting demands of successfully prosecuting a war of global proportions.

The Museum of Modern Art Film Library was one of several Humanities Division projects to emerge in the latter half of the 1930s designed, in part, to facilitate the study of mass communications and their audiences. In 1939 John Marshall, assistant director of the Humanities Division, assembled a working group of media experts and social scientists, variously referred to as the Communications Group or Communications Seminar, to determine how best to consolidate the disparate strands of media and propaganda research into a useful intelligence apparatus. If the United States was to be drawn into the war, Marshall hoped that preformed overlapping research programs would assist federal authorities in coordinating their own information campaigns while establishing what Brett Gary describes as a "propaganda prophylaxis" to neutralize harmful or misleading messages emanating from foreign sources.[10] Thereafter, the Film Library was aligned with other institutions hosting projects funded by the Humanities Division, particularly the New School for Social Research and the Library of Congress. Both of these institutions housed projects engaged with a broad range of media propaganda, but the Film Library's concentration of film knowledge, professional expertise, and primary materials made it a valuable addition to the emergent intelligence apparatus envisioned by Marshall's Communications Seminar.[11]

The Film Library maintained an especially close working relationship with the Library of Congress throughout the war. And although the first suggestion of a collaborative venture between the two libraries was made only several months before the Japanese attack on Pearl Harbor, the origins of the Film Library's wartime intelligence work can be traced back to the propaganda and media analysis suggested by the Communications Seminar and initiated at the Library of Congress by the newly appointed Librarian of Congress, Archibald MacLeish, and the political scientist Harold Lasswell. As an outspoken liberal antifascist, MacLeish recognized the pressing need for sustained analysis of the content and form of mass communications. After taking office in 1939, he began reorganizing the library into a centralized intelligence resource that was to house privately funded research projects responsive to the intelligence needs of a select group of government and military agencies. Lasswell was a key contributor to the Communications Seminar and coordinated the Rockefeller Foundation–funded Experimental Division for the Study of Wartime Communications in (but not directly affiliated with) the Library of Congress.

Although the Library of Congress had been quietly collecting all kinds of propaganda materials for Lasswell's Experimental Division since 1939, it had done little to build up a comparable collection of films. Lasswell addressed this problem in June 1941 when he noted in a memorandum to Archibald MacLeish that US copyright law entitled the library to the physical deposit of newsreels and feature films, but that, due to space restrictions, this practice was not enforced. Lasswell recommended that this policy be reversed, since an up-to-date collection of recent films would be of inestimable value to the content-analysis programs undertaken in the Experimental Division. "If desired, a beginning might be made with newsreels, since this material is of special documentary importance," he wrote. If no space was available to facilitate such a collection at the Library of Congress, Lasswell suggested, "perhaps such arrangements could be worked out with the film library of the Museum of Modern Art, New York."[12] By late November the Film Library and the Library of Congress had moved forward in planning a centralized clear-inghouse for cinema intelligence, even if it was not entirely clear what sort of work that would entail, when it would be required, or who would use it. These would be recurring questions for Film Library personnel throughout the war, but in late 1941 the primary concern was to secure as much material as possible.

The number of films confiscated by the federal government grew rapidly in the first years of the war, and officials were hard-pressed to adequately manage the collection. In March 1943 a cooperative arrangement was established between the Justice Department and the Library of Congress to store, service, and index these films for the use of other federal agencies. In turn, Library of Congress staff sought additional vault space and processing work from the staff of the Museum of Modern Art Film Library in New York. However, despite the byzantine network of institutional relationships established in the months prior to December 1941, it was not immediately apparent how this accumulation of films was to be trans-formed into useful intelligence, or, for that matter, who was qualified to carry it out.

ANALYSIS

By late May 1942, the Museum of Modern Art had taken on thirteen government contracts, three of which were directly linked to the Film Library: the Library of Congress Film Project, the Latin American Motion Picture Project, and the ambiguously named Q Film Project (variously referred to as the Q Contract). The Latin America project, undertaken at the behest of Nelson Rockefeller's Office of the Coordinator of Inter-American Affairs (CIAA), entailed the production of 16mm nontheatrical educational films for distribution throughout Latin America. The mission of the Library of Congress project was ostensibly an exercise in public morale that sought "to index, screen and analyze current films submitted for copy-right," and to select for permanent inclusion in the library's collection the films most representative of the American character and experience, for permanent inclusion in the library's collection.[13] The Q Film Project, underwritten by the CIAA, involved the "purchase, review and analysis, and safekeeping of motion picture films produced by or in the Axis countries." The overall purpose of the Q Contract seems to have been to study the penetration of Nazi propaganda films into the South American market, though the analyses it produced rarely men-tioned this. Unlike the veneer of morale boosting and film-industry goodwill that accompanied the Library of Congress project, the Q Contract generated almost no publicity, sequestered away as it was in office space loaned by the War Department in Washington, DC. At $56,000, the operating budget for Q more than doubled the amount allocated to the Library of Congress Film Project.[14]

Both projects were staffed by teams of four to five analysts and overseen by the Film Library's curator, Iris Barry. Barry's role in steering the Film Library during the war, in virtually every capacity, cannot be overstated. In addition to overseeing the library's day-to-day business, she acted as de facto project director and liaison between the projects' analysts and the government officials who had commissioned their reports. Much of her time was split between New York and Washington. On the federal side of the institutional equation, Lasswell and MacLeish envisioned the work of the Film Library as an extension of the content-analysis projects undertaken in the Library of Congress's Experimental Division for the Study of Wartime Communications. Although the Library of Congress had gathered an unparalleled collection of foreign propaganda materials, the Experimental Division was primarily concerned with the analysis of print media. Similarly, unlike the serious study of radio and its audiences, much of which had been underwritten by the Rockefeller Foundation in the 1930s, cinema remained critically unexplored as a mass medium.

In a memorandum to MacLeish in late December 1941, Lasswell elaborated on the necessity of integrating film study into the ongoing intelligence work carried out elsewhere: "The purpose of the content analysis of film material is to provide information needed by policymakers. This information concerns the favorable or unfavorable presentation of American and foreign officials, groups, and institutions." He added, "The reporting practices for film analysis have been planned to integrate with the studies of press, radio and similar agencies of mass communication. . . . Thanks to this degree of coordination, the trend reports respecting films will be comparable with the trend reports about press, magazines, broadcasts, and other relevant channels of communication."[15] Lasswell envisioned a mass-media-based intelligence apparatus capable of illuminating the unspoken trends in the attitudes, outlook, and opinions of the broad public. This information would then be transmitted to policy makers, who, in turn, would utilize the same media to alleviate group tensions and provide more information to the public, essentially coaxing it into "right" thinking. That this model of technocratic discourse uncomfortably resembled the social engineering of the totalitarian media apparatus was of little concern to Lasswell, who saw mass communication as a "value-neutral tool" capable of instilling and reinforcing democratic ideals that could and *should* be used by policy makers in democratic governance.[16]

Ostensibly, the primary purpose of Lasswell's Experimental Division was to train analysts for the growing number of government agencies that required intelligence work in the prosecution of the war.[17] It seems, however, that the empirical methodology embraced in the Experimental Division did not transfer to the Film Library's humanist methodology. Iris Barry worked tirelessly to mediate the demands of government intelligence agencies and sooth the frustrations of her staff. But by the summer of 1942, Barry and MacLeish realized that it would be necessary to seek out specialists in film study that could help guide the project analysts. In addition to Barry herself, the film specialists drafted into this role included the German émigré scholar Siegfried Kracauer, who had been at work at the library studying Nazi propaganda films and newsreels under a Rockefeller grant since the previous summer; James Agee, a highly regarded journalist; Leo Rosten, author of a sociological analysis of the Hollywood filmmaking community who now worked for the Office of War Information; and the British anthropologist Gregory Bateson, engaged at the time in organizing social science research on national morale. Agee and Rosten advised MacLeish on the Film Library's reports, but did not interact directly with project staff. Kracauer briefly contributed plot summaries and content analyses to the Q Contract before turning to a new project funded by the Rockefeller Foundation on the history of pre-Nazi German cinema. It was Bateson who worked closest with Film Library staff to reform and stream-line its government-sponsored intelligence work.

Bateson was an unlikely collaborator. Compared with the other specialists asso-ciated with the content-analysis projects, his knowledge of cinema was limited. Bateson's path to the Museum of Modern Art was largely determined by the cir-cumstances of the war emergency. In 1936 and again in 1938, he and his then-wife, Margaret Mead, conducted fieldwork on the island of Bali, where they made extensive use of still and motion photography to document the behavior of the Balinese natives, with particular focus on the relationship between parents and children. When Mead and Bateson returned to the United States in 1939 they brought back with them some "25,000 photographs and 20,000 feet" of documen-tary footage depicting everyday life in Bali. Exhaustive photographic documenta-tion was virtually unknown in ethnographic fieldwork, and both Mead and Bateson understood film and photographic documentation as a "naïve check upon the observer" for recording behavior more objectively than was possible in written field notations.[18] Although they had not intended photographic documentation to be so central to their fieldwork in Bali, the experience of hashing out a documen-tary methodology for fieldwork stimulated further reflection on the usefulness of film as a communications medium and pedagogical tool.

In the fall of 1941 Mead established the Council on Intercultural Relations (CIR) on a shoestring budget out of office space provided by the American Museum of Natural History. The council's purpose was to coordinate research projects among a core group of anthropologists, sociologists, and psychologists interested in analyzing contemporary complex cultures in ways that would have applicable value to federal and military officials. Bateson described the CIR as "a clearing house for bodies of data on major European and [American] cultures— especially on contacts between these cultures," adding, "There is, I think, a pretty big field in post-war planning for the 'cultural' approach, and it is a field which is rather unlikely to [be] represented at the peace table."[19] The operative function of the CIR was therefore not necessarily just to provide and analyze wartime intelligence per se, but also to advocate for greater knowledge and deeper consideration of cultural differences that might make planning a postwar peace more sustainable than the one that had followed the First World War. After Pearl Harbor, however, Mead accepted a position in charge of the National Research Council's Food Habits Committee, which required her to spend most of her time in Washington, DC, leaving Bateson in New York to act as the council's secretary.[20]

The council's primary focus at the onset of the war was the theorization and analysis of national character structures, particularly those of the United States, Great Britain, Nazi Germany, and imperial Japan. As an abstract concept, national character went far beyond the usually localized parameters of anthropological investigation. Cultural anthropologists had typically eschewed analyzing modern cultures because they were deemed to be too fragmented and complex, preferring instead the holistic unity of so-called primitive cultures that enabled a relatively coherent, self-contained analytical framework. When confronted with the criticism that the application of anthropological methodology to complex cultures was reckless and overly simplified, Mead and Bateson argued that the "urgency of international affairs" demanded that social scientists "provide whatever simple shortcuts we can to aid in the solution to practical problems." As Bateson put it, the expediency of the war emergency required "recipes for thinking about people and cultures" that, in the absence of carefully considered research and fieldwork, would have to make do with what was available.[21] Analyzing the broad characteristics of friendly and enemy nations would, in part, provide critical intelligence for military personnel in theaters of combat and occupation. Facilitating the critical understanding of the cultures that American soldiers would encounter in the field would hypothetically help avoid intercultural misunderstandings, but also make it easier to predict and manipulate the form that this contact would take and its outcome. Still immersed in the raw footage and photographs from Bali over the course of 1941 and 1942, Bateson came to see cinema as one such "shortcut" that could stand in for the nearly complete lack of field experience in countries that were otherwise inaccessible for the war's duration.

Bateson argued that the key to understanding national character structure was to examine the means through which groups of people were inculcated with a particular worldview, or ethos. This could be done, he suggested, by studying the "context of learning" rather than "what is learned."[22] Bateson believed, as did Mead and many of the CIR participants, that the best evidence for this viewpoint lay in the examination of differences in child-rearing techniques across cultures. However, Bateson also saw cultural standardization as a process of continuous "mass learning" that, in addition to traditional sites of cultural interpolation like family, religion, and education, was supplemented by the "slick perfection of our movies and radio programs." Movies, he observed, reinforced dominant cultural ideology and outlook, thereby "standardizing" the audience "towards a passive acceptance . . . rather than towards active emotional or intellectual participation."[23] From the standpoint of research into national character, this made popular cinema a useful framework for understanding how the standardization of cultural ethos motivated or discouraged certain behaviors. Popular cinema may not have been "true" in an objective sense, but it was "true" in the sense that it reflected the social imaginaries and naturalized behaviors of the societies that produced them. Furthermore, Bateson and Mead were convinced that documentary films were unsuitable for training purposes because the documentary filmmaker's aesthetic impulse to craft a compelling narrative only undermined the "real" aspects of what had been caught on film. The potential for subversive manipulation of facts and events placed documentary perilously close to propaganda. As Mead put it in a letter to Lawrence Frank, "[W]e are pretty convinced that documentary films often have less validity than an ordinary successful commercial film—a point of view which the word *Hollywood* hardly carries."[24]

By early September 1942, news of the council's research on popular cinema and national character reached Lieutenant Colonel Hardy C. Dillard, director of instruction at the army's School of Military Government, who expressed interest in the project and its possible application in officer training. Bateson proposed to undertake a pilot study analyzing a single feature film that would then be intercut with "silent titles pointing up the significance of the various [plot] incidents" for teaching purposes. "Such a doctored moving picture would probably be an ideal teaching device," he continued. "It could show the very striking differences in the handling of basic human themes—authority, servility, pride, courtesy, etc.—in the various nations, and the lessons could be given additional point by showing that the same 'national character' could be observed in the villain and the heroine and in the young and the old."[25]

Bateson's proposal reiterated the CIR's insistence that the cultural approach be included alongside economics and public administration in the training of occupying forces and postwar civil administrators. However, he admitted that the traditional approaches adaptable to cultural training were cumbersome and time-consuming, noting on one hand the need for intensive language training and on the other a reliance on esoteric artworks and fictions that, taken together, might convey some semblance of national characteristics. In other words, because there was no time for soldier-students to be immersed in key works of art and literature, a traditional "gradual education" in the humanities would be "impractical." Likewise, the prospect of inundating students with cultural information in compressed periods of time would likely produce only "grotesquely over-simplified" generalizations.[26] Although all cultures shared the same "pan-human" behavioral building blocks, Bateson considered these terms of analysis too imprecise and "hardly appropriate as a means of giving rapid orientation in a foreign culture to people without professional and technical training in this sort of science." Using films for cultural training, however, would speed up the process of learning, circumventing both clumsy technical jargon and oversimplified explanation. As Bateson explained, "In the movie, the context is there on the screen—and the analysis could be kept to comparatively simple terms. In place of formal definition, it would only be necessary to refer to the context; and to point up the differences in national character, it would only be necessary to say: '*That* is what he does in this situation.' . . . And it would be possible to show how the same national characteristics run through the behavior of contrasting characters in the plot."[27] Bateson emphasized the high teaching value of films dealing with childhood, adolescence, and family melodrama.

Dillard was receptive to Bateson's proposal but reticent to offer any financial commitment since the project was entirely untested. Securing seed money was only one of Bateson's immediate problems; the other was access to films. Renting films from the distribution market would be prohibitively expensive for the already cash-strapped council, but Bateson had heard that the federal government was stockpiling captured enemy films "somewhere in Washington, rumor says in the Library of Congress."[28] The solution to both problems came after a series of meetings with Iris Barry at the Film Library in mid-September 1942. Barry was intrigued by Bateson's proposal and arranged for the diversion of funds from the CIAA's Q Contract budget toward the completion of the pilot study, consisting of one analyzed film and a research report. Having gained access to the Film Library's collections, Bateson immersed himself in its collection of Weimar-era and early Nazi films while reading through the reports on the captured-film collections prepared by the Q Contract analysts. He selected the 1934 film *Hitlerjunge Quex* (acquired by the library in 1936) to be the subject of his pilot study. In return for the use of its collections, Bateson contributed to and advised the Film Library's beleaguered Library of Congress and Q Contract content-analysis projects, offering suggestions as to how their analyses could be made more efficient and useful, for the purposes both of training and of the state intelligence apparatus.

In a series of memoranda to Iris Barry, Bateson elaborated a series of suggestions that would make the content-analysis reports more usable as cultural intelligence. Bateson also sympathized with the analysts' frustrations over the contradictory instructions issued to them by various intelligence and propaganda offices. Supervisors at OWI, CIAA, and the Library of Congress had demanded analyses that were fragmented and piecemeal in their approach to propaganda content, requiring analysts to focus on specific moments in each film. The analysts, however, saw their job as reflecting the individual film "as an artistic and psychological *whole*" from which "the various propagandic [*sic*] themes and bits can only properly be considered in the context of that whole."[29] The emphasis on wholeness and totality resonated with Bateson's anthropological fieldwork. Echoing the methodology of Kracauer's work-in-progress on the history of pre-Nazi German cinema, the analysts saw narrative films as valuable specifically because they presented a narrative world enmeshed in the collective ethos and cultural imaginary of the society in which they were produced.

While he praised the analysts' astute observations, Bateson made a clear distinction between the job of the analyst and that of the expert. The analyst's job was to sift through and make sense of the films provided by the Library of Congress; but it was the expert, trained with specialized knowledge, who was to convert that information into useable intelligence. Project analysts, Bateson suggested, should produce comprehensive film surveys that would aid the specialist in digesting narrative information. "[W]e ought not to expect from their work answers to the very various questions which we may want to ask of the film material," he wrote. "The analysts are not military technicians. . . . Similarly they are not psychologists and we cannot expect them to analyze or interpret the complex and characteristically German handling of human relations, guilt, parenthood etc." Thus, the relationship between analyst and expert was to be a hierarchical division of intellectual labor. Bateson continued: "Any specialist approaching the synopses is however entitled to demand that the synopsis will tell him *which* films contain material relevant to his special problem. After that, it is his job to look at the selected films with his own technically trained eyes."[30] Barry evidently agreed with Bateson's assessment of the Film Library's workflow problem and saw great potential in the psychological-anthropological approach he proposed for the analysis and application of captured enemy films.

By early November 1942 Bateson was devoting most of his time at the Film Library toward the preparation of the *Hitlerjunge Quex* test film and requested from the War Manpower Commission a three-month deferment from selective service to complete the pilot study. In a statement in support of Bateson's deferment application, Barry wrote, "I am quite certain that . . . the completion of his present plan for a model analysis of one Nazi film will contribute to the work in this field now being carried on in the various information offices and by the Army. . . . He can't be replaced, of course, there are only about twenty such people and the others are in government service."[31] A rough draft of Bateson's research findings and a new version of the first reel of *Hitlerjunge Quex* with added explanatory intertitles were completed by mid-January 1943, by which time administrators in the newly established Army Specialized Training Program had taken notice of the project.

DISSEMINATION

By aligning the Council on Intercultural Relations and the Museum of Modern Art Film Library to the purposes of military training, Gregory Bateson gained access to the federal government's wartime intelligence community. Through the Film Library he was privy to the applied film-studies projects of the Library of Congress and the CIAA and quickly gained Iris Barry's trust. Bateson's expertise in anthropology and psychology made him a useful addition to these projects, even if his knowledge of cinema was comparatively undeveloped. Bateson was a fast learner and enthusiastic about the Film Library's research program. "Also, there is a purely personal aspect of the manner," he admitted to John Abbott in February 1943. "I like films. They are the most beautiful and articulate material that I have ever tried to analyze."[32]

Bateson presented his research, as well as the first three reels of *Hitlerjunge Quex*, at a mid-January meeting of the psychology section of the New York Academy of Sciences to demonstrate how popular cinema could be made useful when traditional fieldwork and documentation were unavailable. Anthropological analysis required two things, Bateson told his audience: "the recognition of significant themes and . . . the verification that these themes are in fact characteristic of the culture that we are studying." Drawing together the separate research projects of the CIR and the Film Library, Bateson argued that popular films helped discern the former, while interviews with German émigrés provided the latter.[33] In lieu of fieldwork, the data collected from these interviews would serve as a check on the researcher's analytical interpretation of the film. With research for the *Quex* test film largely completed, Bateson now had something to show the army officials that demonstrated the value of the cultural approach in training officers and soldiers for contact with other cultures.

The sheer scale of the global conflict created unprecedented challenges for the American military. One such challenge, recognized belatedly by army officials, was that American soldiers in the field would potentially have to operate as civil administrators in the temporary void created during the transition from total warfare to occupation and liberation.[34] The purpose of the Army Specialized Training Program (ASTP) was to train soldiers in subject areas that the army itself was unable to teach. For these specialized subjects the army turned to American higher education, enlisting the facilities and faculties of approximately three hundred colleges and universities to develop and implement its curricula.

In January 1943, the army's Military Government Division began planning a conference in Chicago that would bring together teams of faculty from the likes of Harvard, Yale, Princeton, Stanford, and the universities of Wisconsin and Michigan to discuss the implementation of regional training within the ASTP curriculum. Although the CIR was not to participate directly in the conference, Mead and Bateson prepared a general statement to be circulated to conference participants highlighting "the various sorts of materials—films, cartoons, literature, living informants, etc." that could be used in accelerated cultural instruction.[35]

Pictorial and narrative materials, especially, would expedite and maximize teaching by giving students a window into foreign culture as a whole; Mead and

Bateson believed that materials such as films, comic strips, and radio broadcasts provided students with surrogate "experiences" of the culture that produced them, "essential if the men are to act appropriately and with confidence in their various regions."[36] Teaching through an appeal to experience could evoke empathy and understanding, could persuade the American occupying forces to, as Ruth Benedict suggested, "see people *as people*."[37] But surrogate experience and knowledge could also provide a critical advantage in the field. To understand the cultural logics of specific behavior was, in part, to be able to predict and manipulate it. "The student must not merely build up knowledge of his region," Bateson explained, "he must acquire a capacity to *act* in that region," and "the material should be presented in such a way that the insights which it provides would be translated in the classroom into practical experience."[38]

Bateson attended the Chicago conference in March, where the CIR memorandum met with an enthusiastic response from army officials. On returning to New York he and John Abbott drafted a proposal to set up a Wartime Regional Materials Unit within the Museum of Modern Art responsible for circulating museum pieces, graphic materials, photographs, and films to college campuses hosting the army program, and eventually to nongovernmental agencies involved in postwar reconstruction. Bateson's proposal suggested that the Wartime Regional Materials Unit would address several pressing needs. First, the unit would act as a clearinghouse for information and teaching materials organized and circulated by a single organization. This overarching institutional structure would ensure a uniform methodological approach to cultural analysis, one that was "much less standardized" than the techniques of other regional training programs, particularly language instruction. Centralization of the project, materials, and personnel would "secure the maximum give and take of ideas between the collaborators."[39] Second, in addition to standardizing the terms of analysis, the Wartime Regional Materials Unit would, like Lasswell's Experimental Division, train analysts in how to interpret information and then pass that information along to others. The unit would be staffed by a group of three or four experts in cultural analysis who would oversee "a team of from five to ten post-doctorate research assistants who would assist in the analyses while at the same time being trained to become cultural teachers."[40] Finally, Bateson promised that the unit would work swiftly, confidently predicting that it could produce comprehensive cultural analyses at the rate of "one culture a month."[41]

While materials and films were at least attainable from the Film Library's collections, funding was scarce. Bateson's proposal estimated the unit's monthly operating cost at slightly over $9,293 ($128,000 in current dollars). Making matters more complicated, Bateson insisted that the unit's materials and exhibits, while seemingly self-evident because they were primarily visual, required a specialist to guide students through them if they were to be at all effective as teaching aids. "There is a great deal to be done in this field, the work urgent and the workers few," he explained to the secretary of the Harvard Film Service. "And unless the analytic work is done there is serious risk of two types of misfortune. First, there is the likelihood that the films used will be merely thrown at the students without any serious attempt at teaching or analysis, and second, there is the likelihood that the films used will be actually misleading. . . . Such distorted material could of course be used for teaching purposes but in this case positive use should be made of the distortions. The students should be made to see how the cultural bias of the film makers has expressed itself."[42]

In mid-June Bateson was given an opportunity to demonstrate the value of foreign-language films for purposes of cultural instruction as a guest lecturer in two sessions of an ASTP course in German history at Cornell University. For the Cornell demonstrations, he brought along the "annotated" version of *Hitlerjunge Quex*, "some Balinese films," and a number of Weimar-era German films from the Film Library's circulating collection. In a follow-up letter to Charles Hyneman of the Military Government Division that he hoped would jump-start the army's enthusiasm for the project, he wrote, "I have just returned from my first 'circuit riding' expedition in which I did ten hours' teaching in two days. . . . I found both the men and the faculty enthusiastic about the sort of stuff I had to offer." But, despite an enthusiastic response from ASTP administrators, there were no promises of financial support.[43]

Bateson's two sessions at Cornell constituted the only full application of his proposed film-based teaching methodology. In August, the army informed Bateson that it would begin making and circulating the required film prints, thereby rendering the proposed Wartime Regional Materials Unit obsolete. "The Army, of course, has been very friendly throughout but was not able to finance any work on the analysis of films or any other cultural materials," he admitted in a letter to Carl E. Guthe. "So—no straw, no bricks."[44] Frustrated and disappointed by the unceremonious end of the project he had worked on for almost a year, Bateson accepted an offer to join the Office of Strategic Services (OSS), where he remained for the rest of the war. In 1944, the OSS transferred Bateson from Washington to the Far Eastern Theater in Burma, where he was tasked with overseeing psychological-warfare operations against the Japanese and producing policy papers on easing relations between Allied forces and native populations.[45] Although his work for the OSS occasionally referred back to his time at the Museum of Modern Art Film Library, Gregory Bateson's brief foray into the nascent world of American film study had come to an end.

FEEDBACK

Bateson returned to the United States in November 1945, deeply troubled by the subterfuge he had carried out in Southeast Asia under the banner of applied anthropology. His faith in anthropology shaken, Bateson gradually abandoned ethnography and moved on to the emerging fields of communication theory and cybernetics, which closely aligned with his lifelong engagement with questions of epistemology. The strain of the war years had other consequences; in the years after his return to civilian life, Bateson and Margaret Mead drifted apart and eventually divorced in 1950, by which time he had relocated to California.[46] He never returned to film research.

By all accounts, the months Bateson spent at the Museum of Modern Art Film Library constituted a footnote in a long and varied interdisciplinary career. This is not to suggest, however, that Bateson's foray into film studies was merely a curious artifact of the war emergency. Instead, the critical model Bateson (and Siegfried Kracauer, among others) developed during the war that drew a connecting line between popular, narrative cinema and national character found new life in the postwar era. While Bateson appeared to have distanced himself from his wartime film analysis, two of his articles on cinema and national character written during the war were republished in a 1948 textbook on cultural anthropology, preventing them from sinking into academic oblivion.

If Bateson gradually abandoned his work on film analysis, it was Margaret Mead who was chiefly responsible for adapting it to Cold War intelligence work. Unlike Bateson, Mead remained optimistic that the production and application of social scientific knowledge could promote respect for, and cooperation between, different cultures. In the years after the war, Mead ensconced herself in the task of co-managing, with Ruth Benedict, the Research in Contemporary Cultures (RCC) project at Columbia University. Through the RCC, Benedict hoped to maximize for the postwar period all the collaborative social scientific work that had been so successful during the war. In 1947 she secured major financial backing for the project from the Office of Naval Intelligence. Stimulated by the exigencies of wartime, in which cultural intelligence was produced without the benefit of direct fieldwork or language experience and from nontraditional sources, the RCC's overall project came to be known as the study of "culture at a distance."

Much like the aborted Wartime Regional Materials Unit proposed by Bateson and John Abbott, the projects undertaken by the RCC drew from a wide range of cultural objects and informants to generate intelligence (or rather, knowledge, since Benedict did not consider the RCC a military enterprise despite the source of its funding) about other cultures.[47] Following Benedict's death in 1948, Mead took over the project, and under her direction, the analysis of foreign films became a chief component of the "culture at a distance" approach. When the RCC's findings were published as a "manual" in 1953, Mead and her chief collaborator and coeditor, Rhoda Métraux, dedicated an entire section of the nearly five-hundred-page book to analyses of the popular cinemas of the Soviet Union, France, and China, among others. First among these essays was a condensed version of Bateson's unpublished 1943 *Quex* manuscript.[48]

The use of film as a medium of intelligence was a novel approach to wartime knowledge production, due mostly to the fortuitous circumstance that during the interwar decades the nations of the Axis had so widely disseminated the cultural materials that wartime intelligence agencies would later gather and dissect. This was a situation never to be repeated. By the time Mead's manual on the study of culture at a distance appeared in print, the national-character moment had already passed from the social sciences. The culture and personality approach that Mead and Bateson had so enthusiastically championed during the war met with increasing skepticism from other social scientists, who regarded the use of totalizing psychoanthropological models in the study of complex cultures—at the expense of fieldwork and rigorous language training—as methodologically inadequate and dangerously oversimplified in times of relative peace. Furthermore, as Peter Mandler points out, the cultural relativism espoused in Mead's approach to national character was outflanked in the 1950s by the prominence of Cold War internationalism and modernization theory in matters of American foreign policy.[49]

Given Bateson's disillusionment with applied anthropology and the disfavor to which the study of national character at a distance was subjected, it is not surprising that Bateson's work at the Film Library was all but forgotten by postwar film studies. At the same time, the work carried out at the Film Library demonstrates the refracted multidisciplinary appeal of film study that would inform numerous postwar intellectual trajectories, including anthropology, American and area studies, and, ultimately, film studies. In short, it might be productive to think of postwar film studies as a demilitarized discipline, albeit one more firmly rooted in the humanities than was its wartime iteration. In the years after the war, the projects undertaken at the Film Library were variously adapted to academic film study (Kracauer) or gradually forgotten (Bateson), signaling the discipline's turn from the social sciences to the humanities and the production of knowledge for its own sake, rather than that of intelligence.

NOTES

1. "Nazi Film Boomerang," *Motion Picture Herald*, October 11, 1941, 9.

2. Clayton R. Koppes and Gregory D. Black, *Hollywood Goes to War: How Politics, Profits, and Propaganda Shaped World War II Movies* (New York: Free Press, 1987); US Senate, Special Committee Investigating the National Defense Program, *Investigation of the National Defense Program: Part 17, Army Commissions and Military Activity of Motion Picture Personnel*, 78th Cong., 1st sess., 1943 (Washington, DC: Government Printing Office, 1943), 6879–93.

3. Haidee Wasson and Charles R. Acland, "Introduction: Utility and Cinema," in *Useful Cinema*, ed. Charles R. Acland and Haidee Wasson (Durham, NC: Duke University Press, 2011), 6.

4. For an overview of American propaganda anxiety during the interwar period, see Michael Sproule, *Propaganda and Democracy: The American Experience of Media and Mass Persuasion* (New York: Cambridge University Press, 1997), chaps. 2–4.

5. John E. Abbott to Abby Aldrich Rockefeller, 5 March 1935, folder I.12.0, box 7, Early Museum History Administrative Records, Museum of Modern Art Archives, New York (hereafter cited as Early Museum History, MoMA Archives).

6. Haidee Wasson, *Museum Movies: The Museum of Modern Art and the Birth of Art Cinema* (Berkeley: University of California Press, 2005), 117–18, 167–68.

7. John E. Abbott, "Report of the Museum of Modern Art Film Library as of November 6, 1936," folder I.14, box 8, Early Museum History, MoMA Archives.

8. Iris Barry, "Report on Film Library Activities, 1941–1942," June 19, 1942, 4, "Museum of Modern Art, 1942," box 190, Library of Congress Archives, Central File Unit Records (hereafter cited as LC Central File), Library of Congress Manuscript Division, Washington, DC (hereafter cited as LC Manuscript Division).

9. Wasson, *Museum Movies,* 121–24.

10. Brett Gary, *The Nervous Liberals: Propaganda Anxieties from World War I to the Cold War* (New York: Columbia University Press, 1999), 87–89.

11. For more on the projects assembled under the umbrella of the Communications Seminar, see ibid., 110–22.

12. Harold D. Lasswell to Archibald MacLeish, June 25, 1941, "MOPIC 4, 1939–46," box 885, LC Central File, LC Manuscript Division.

13. "Minutes of the One Hundred Second Meeting of the Board of Trustees of the Museum of Modern Art," May 21, 1942, 4, "Museum of Modern Art, 1942," box 190, LC Central File, LC Manuscript Division.

14. "Minutes of the One Hundred Second Meeting," 4. For more on the Library of Congress Film Project, see Peter Decherney, *Hollywood and the Culture Elite: How the Movies Became American* (New York: Columbia University Press, 2005), chap. 5.

15. Harold D. Lasswell to Archibald MacLeish, December 30, 1941, "MOPIC 4-2, 1941–44," box 890, LC Central File, LC Manuscript Division.

16. Gary, *Nervous Liberals,* 65–71.

17. Ibid., 171.

18. Gerald Sullivan, *Margaret Mead, Gregory Bateson, and Highland Bali: Fieldwork Photographs of Bayung Gedé, 1936–1939* (Chicago: University of Chicago Press, 1999), 11.

19. Gregory Bateson to Claude Guillebaud, February 19, 1942, folder 4, box O2, Margaret Mead Papers and the South Pacific Ethnographic Archives (hereafter cited as Margaret Mead Papers), LC Manuscript Division.

20. See Peter Mandler, *Return from the Natives: How Margaret Mead Won the Second World War and Lost the Cold War* (New Haven, CT: Yale University Press, 2013), 62–69.

21. Gregory Bateson, "Some Systematic Approaches to the Study of Culture and Personality," *Character and Personality* 11, no. 1 (1942): 76.

22. Ibid., 77.

23. Ibid., 80–81.

24. Margaret Mead to Lawrence K. Frank, September 3, 1942, folder 1, box O7, Margaret Mead Papers, LC Manuscript Division.

25. Gregory Bateson to Lt. Col. Hardy C. Dillard, September 3, 1942, folder 1, box O7, Margaret Mead Papers, LC Manuscript Division.

26. Gregory Bateson, "The Use of Moving Picture Material to Illustrate Differences in National Character," September 3, 1942, 1, folder 1, box O7, Margaret Mead Papers, LC Manuscript Division.

27. Ibid., 3–4.

28. Gregory Bateson to Lawrence K. Frank, September 8, 1942, folder 1, box O7, Margaret Mead Papers, LC Manuscript Division.

29. Gregory Bateson to Iris Barry, n.d. [late 1942], 5, folder 8, box O6, Margaret Mead Papers, LC Manuscript Division.

30. Gregory Bateson to Iris Barry, October 26, 1942, folder A-28, box 3, Archive Files, Museum of Modern Art Department of Film and Media Records (hereafter cited as DF Archive Files), Museum of Modern Art Film Study Center, New York (hereafter cited as MoMA Film Study Center).

31. Iris Barry to War Manpower Commission, November 6, 1942; Iris Barry to Capt. Leonard Spigelgass, November 6, 1942; both in folder A-28, box 3, DF Archive Files, MoMA Film Study Center.

32. Gregory Bateson to John E. Abbott, February 25, 1943, folder 1, box O7, Margaret Mead Papers, LC Manuscript Division.

33. Gregory Bateson, "Cultural and Thematic Analysis of Fictional Films," *Transactions of the New York Academy of Sciences,* 2nd ser., 5, no. 4 (February 1943): 72.

34. Harry L. Coles and Albert K. Weinberg, *Civil Affairs: Soldiers Become Governors,* United States Army in World War II (Washington, DC: Office of the Chief of Military History, Department of the Army, 1964), 4–5.

35. Margaret Mead to members of the CIR Planning Committee, January 3, 1943, folder 1, box M25, Margaret Mead Papers, LC Manuscript Division.

36. Gregory Bateson, Ruth Benedict, Margaret Mead, et al., "On Supplementing the Regional Training Curriculum by the Use of Materials on the Contemporary Peoples, Their Culture and Character," n.d. [March 1943], 1, folder 2, box M25, Margaret Mead Papers, LC Manuscript Division.

37. Ruth Benedict to Gregory Bateson, March 5, 1943, folder 1, box M25, Margaret Mead Papers, LC Manuscript Division.

38. Bateson et al., "Regional Training Curriculum," 3.

39. Gregory Bateson, "A Proposed Wartime Regional Materials Unit to Be Set Up in the Museum of Modern Art," n.d. [April 1943], 5, folder A-28, box 3, DF Archive Files, MoMA Film Study Center.

40. Ibid., 5–6.

41. Ibid., 6.

42. Gregory Bateson to Mrs. E. G. R. Free, June 4, 1943, folder 4, box O2, Margaret Mead Papers, LC Manuscript Division.

43. Gregory Bateson to C. W. de Kiewiet, June 9, 1943; Gregory Bateson to Charles Hyneman, 21 June 1943; Gregory Bateson to C. W. de Kiewiet, June 22, 1943, folder I.3.e, box 1, Early Museum History, MoMA Archives.

44. Gregory Bateson to Carl E. Guthe, August 2, 1943, folder I.3.e, box 1, Early Museum History, MoMA Archives.

45. David H. Price, "Gregory Bateson and the OSS: World War II and Bateson's Assessment of Applied Anthropology," *Human Organization* 57, no. 4 (Winter 1998): 380–82.

46. Ibid., 382.

47. Mandler, *Return from the Natives,* 191–97.

48. See Margaret Mead and Rhoda Métraux, eds., *The Study of Culture at a Distance* (Chicago: University of Chicago Press, 1953).

49. Mandler, *Return from the Natives,* 282–84.

9

EPISTEMOLOGY OF THE CHECKPOINT

Gillo Pontecorvo's *Battle of Algiers* and the Doctrine of Counterinsurgency

Vinzenz Hediger

I'll be damned if I permit the United States Army, its institutions, its doctrine, and its traditions to be destroyed just to win this lousy war.

—SENIOR US ARMY OFFICER ON THE VIETNAM WAR, QUOTED IN *LEARNING TO EAT SOUP WITH A KNIFE*, BY JOHN NAGL

A government that is losing to an insurgency is not being out-fought, it is being out-governed.

—BERNARD B. FALL

In times of crisis, the cowboy draws his gun and his instruments of torture.

—FRANTZ FANON, *YEAR V OF THE ALGERIAN REVOLUTION*

In the fall of 2003, a few months into the Iraq war, the Pentagon screened Gillo Pontecorvo's film *La battaglia di Algeri* (*The Battle of Algiers*), from 1966, for a group of senior officers. The screening of the film, a reenactment of the insurgency of the National Liberation Front (Front de Libération Nationale; hereafter FLN) against the French in Algiers in 1957, made news: "What does the Pentagon see in 'Battle of Algiers'?" asked the *New York Times*. Why indeed would the American ministry of defense be interested in an old black-and-white art-house film about a war in which the United States barely had a stake?

By the fall of 2003, for lack of a functioning power structure after the toppling of Saddam Hussein, the war in Iraq had devolved into an insurgency. US forces faced a situation of protracted asymmetrical warfare, for which they were ill prepared. Despite—or rather, as we will see, because of—the defeat in Vietnam, the US military lacked a doctrine of counterinsurgency. Far from being motivated by cinephilia or artistic considerations, the screening of Pontecorvo's film was part of a learning process that would lead to the formation of such a doctrine.

This chapter will trace how *The Battle of Algiers* served as a text of reference for counterinsurgency experts in the wake of the Iraq invasion. Simultaneously, and in a parallel, or rather parallax, reading, I will argue that the film can serve as a blueprint that helps us understand why and how the US military ultimately lost the war. Military theorists like John Nagl have pointed to the inertia of the American military's institutional culture to explain the lack of an appropriate response to the situation in Iraq in the fall of 2003. *The Battle of Algiers* formulates, in epistemological terms, the conundrum of a war against an enemy that cannot be identified. The film demonstrates that the default solution to the problem of the unknown enemy is the use of torture to obtain information about the location and identity of enemy combatants. What the film also demonstrates is that, while an enemy that cannot be defined cannot be defeated, torture defines not the enemy, but the torturer. Seemingly effective in the short run, the use of torture becomes a recruiting tool for the enemy and leads to ultimate defeat.

As I will argue, Pontecorvo's film exemplifies the problem of the unknown enemy through what we might call an epistemology of the checkpoint. At the checkpoint, the enemy becomes visible but remains unidentifiable—a paradox that reveals the impotence of the dominant force in asymmetrical warfare. In both the narrative progress of the film and the logic of the war situation, the checkpoint scene marks the threshold at which the organized violence of conventional warfare turns into the violence of torture—that is, the use of violence to rule over the body of the elusive enemy in a way that is both sovereign and, eventually, ineffectual. As such, Pontecorvo's film provides insight not only into the US military's institutional learning process, but also helps us better understand what, from an outsider's perspective (albeit that of a film scholar with a modicum of military experience), appears to be the structural inability of the world's largest military bureaucracy to adapt to a post-9/11 environment.

I

In early 2006, David Kilcullen, an Australian officer working for the US State Department, wrote an essay titled "Twenty-Eight Articles: Fundamentals of Company-Level Counterinsurgency," which was first published in the May–June edition of the *Military Review*.[1] In Australia, Kilcullen had devised an antiterror strategy called "disaggregation," which treated Al-Qaeda as a global insurgency and aimed to sever the links between the network's nodes. Kilcullen was brought to Washington by Deputy Secretary of Defense Paul Wolfowitz, one of the authors of the United States' grand strategy for the Middle East since the 1980s,[2] to work on the *Quadrennial Defense Review,* a strategy paper produced for Congress by the Pentagon every four years.[3] Referencing T. E. Lawrence's famous "Twenty-Seven Articles," from 1917,[4] Kilcullen's "Twenty-Eight Articles" drew on his own combat experience in East Timor and his 1999 dissertation on the Darul Islam conflict in western Indonesia in the 1950s to offer a set of instructions for counterinsurgency combat. Kilcullen had circulated a first draft via e-mail to counterinsurgency experts working on the US Army and US Marine Corps's *Counterinsurgency Field Manual* (originally published in October 2006 as *US Army Field Manual no. 3-24* [henceforth FM 3-24]). The draft included the disclaimer that it represented the views of the author and not those of "any department or agency of the US government or any other government."[5] The version published in the May–June edition of the *Military Review* included the feedback from Kilcullen's colleagues, but no disclaimer. Conrad Crane, the field manual's main author, together with his team later adopted Kilcullen's "suggestions" and turned them into FM 3-24's appendix A, entitled "A Guide for Action."

In a version published in a 2010 book, Kilcullen addresses the "Articles" to a company commander who already has FM 3-24 at his disposal: "Your company has been warned for deployment on counterinsurgency operations in Iraq or Afghanistan. You have read David Galula, T. E. Lawrence, and Robert Thompson. You have studied FM 3-24 and now understand the history, philosophy, and theory of counterinsurgency. You have watched *Black Hawk Down* and *The Battle of Algiers*, and you know this will be the most difficult challenge of your life. But what does all the theory mean at the company level?"

Apart from T. E. Lawrence, Kilcullen's syllabus includes the other two key theorists of counterinsurgency in the twentieth century: Robert Grainger Ker Thompson and David Galula. In his 1966 book *Defeating Communist Insurgency: Experiences in Malaya and Vietnam*, Thompson offers a firsthand account of the successful British campaign against a Maoist guerilla force in Malaya in the run-up to independence in 1957, and discusses the lessons of Malaya for Vietnam. Having witnessed Mao's rise to power and the Indochina war as a French diplomat and the Greek civil war as an UN observer, before participating in the French campaign in Algeria as a company commander from 1956 to 1958, David Galula, a Tunisian Jew, wrote two books, which together constitute the single most important reference for FM 3-24: *Pacification in Algeria* (1963) and *Counterinsurgency Warfare: Theory and Practice* (1964).

Drawing on a long history of film as teaching a tool in military training—which had never been limited to documentary or educational short films[6]—Kilcullen adds two films to his list: Ridley Scott's 2001 *Black Hawk Down*, about a failed US counterinsurgency mission in Somalia, and *The Battle of Algiers*. While *Black Hawk Down* offers a case study of military hubris in an urban littoral (i.e., coastline) theater of war, *The Battle of Algiers* was more than just a repurposed piece of cinema. It had a contentious history as a training tool even prior to the Pentagon screening.[7] In fact, the film was explicitly designed as a manual for revolutionary warfare by its authors.

II

Shortly after independence in 1962, the government of Algeria contacted a number of Italian film directors to make a film about the Algerian war of independence. The Algerians chose Italy for reasons of both spatial and political proximity. Enrico Mattei, the powerful head of ENI, Italy's government-owned oil corporation, had supported the FLN against US and French corporate interests throughout the 1950s—a story recounted in Francesco Rosi's 1972 docudrama *Il caso Mattei*.[8] Mattei even commissioned a film against the OAS (Organisation Armée Secrète), the terrorist organization formed by renegade French officers led by General Raoul Salan in the late stages of the war, for which Franco Solinas wrote a screenplay.[9] For the new film, Solinas eventually teamed up with Gillo Pontecorvo, the scion of a wealthy Jewish family from Tuscany, who ended up paying for the film largely out of his own pocket. Solinas and Pontecorvo considered a fictional story about a French paratrooper before they settled on the "battle of Algiers," in which the French used torture to break up an FLN cell in the Kasbah in 1957. Shot on location in black and white, with a haunting score by Ennio Morricone, the film models its main character on General Massu, the French officer in charge of the operation, and features Yaseef Saadi, the surviving leader of the FLN cell, who plays himself. Lauded for its gritty documentary realism, the film won the main prize at the Venice Film Festival, but remained banned in France until the mid-1970s.[10]

Avid readers of Frantz Fanon, Pontecorvo and Solinas teamed up again for *Burn!* (*Queimada*) in 1969, in which Marlon Brando cynically engineers a slave revolt in the Caribbean to prepare the British takeover of a Portuguese colony. Whereas *Burn!* was distributed by United Artists and offered a critique of colonialism for a broad audience, *The Battle of Algiers* was meant to be more than a monument to the anticolonial struggle of Algeria. When he was asked about the Pentagon screening in 2004, Pontecorvo found it "a little strange": his film, he said, could "teach how to make cinema, not war."[11] But at the time, the filmmakers intended the film as a manual for urban guerilla warfare.[12] The first groups to take this claim seriously were the Black Panthers and the IRA in the late 1960s.[13] In the New York trial of the "Panther 21," the prosecution screened the film as evidence that the Panthers were influenced by "African terrorism." The district attorney argued that the film was dangerous to the "uneducated minds" of the defendants, but one of the jurors stated that the film helped him better understand their point of view; the defendants were acquitted.[14] Elsewhere, the film was used to train counterrevolutionaries in South America in the 1960s and 1970s and Tamil Tiger insurgents in northern Sri Lanka in the 1980s.[15]

Using the film to train counterrevolutionaries may seem cynical, given its original intent. But if the coup d'état is a technique and not an ideological program, as Curzio Malaparte argues in his study of the Russian Revolution and Mussolini's march on Rome, revolutionary warfare is also primarily a technique.[16] In that sense, the Pentagon screening was remarkable not because the sole remaining military hegemon used an anticolonialist film for training purposes, but because the American military developed a serious interest in counterinsurgency at all.

Confident that the Americans would be greeted as "liberators," the Bush administration neglected postwar planning prior to the Iraq invasion and even considered it an impediment to war.[17] As a consequence, at around the time of President Bush's "Mission Accomplished" photo op in May 2003, the conflict turned into an insurgency. In August CENTCOM commander John Abizaid, the four-star general in charge of operations in Iraq, admitted that remnants of the Ba'athist regime and other insurgents were conducting "a classical guerilla-type campaign against us."[18] Yet for months, Pentagon policy was not to acknowledge the nature of the conflict. Secretary of Defense Donald Rumsfeld even banned the use of word "insurgency" in connection with Iraq.[19]

This may be read as neoconservative hubris. However, as historian Andrew Bacevich argues, the invasion was part of a larger war for the Greater Middle East, which the United States had waged since the late 1970s over access to oil.[20] As such, regime change in Iraq fit into a bipartisan pattern of American expansionism, which William Appleman Williams describes as "anti-colonial imperialism." It can be traced back to the late nineteenth century and the "open door policy," which aimed to secure unfettered market access through the promotion of liberal democracy around the world.[21] With the Third Gulf War, the United States merely reversed "the practice of exempting the Islamic world from neo-liberal standards" and chose preemptive war to bring democracy and market economics to the Middle East.[22] At the same time, the insurgency in Iraq was consistent with Williams' earlier analysis that in twentieth-century foreign affairs, "American integrated reformist and economic expansion provoked trouble," and the reaction ultimately "took the form of terror."[23] The Iraq insurgency confirmed the "inner logic" of expansionist thought, "whereby both opportunity and difficulty, good and evil are externalized."[24] Michael Bay's *Thirteen Hours,* from 2016 (set during the Obama administration and thereby confirming the bipartisan nature of the problem), provides a succinct summary of the "tragedy of American diplomacy": upon his arrival in Benghazi, the US ambassador tells Libyans, "We are here to bring you democracy and prosperity"; mayhem ensues; the ambassador dies.

However delusional, Rumsfeld's refusal to acknowledge the insurgency in Iraq resonated with his rank and file, if only because the American military was utterly unprepared for asymmetrical warfare in an urban theater. "Militaries evolve primarily through the shock of defeat," David Kilcullen reminds us.[25] In the run-up to Iraq, the American military had proven to be immune to two shocks of defeat. Both the attacks on September 11, 2001, and the "Black Hawk Down" episode in Somalia in 1993 can be described as defeats in urban littoral warfare. The first ended in withdrawal, while the second led to two conventional ground wars in remote theaters, Afghanistan and Iraq. For lack of preparation, in the fall of 2003 in Iraq, the American military was on the brink of snatching defeat from the jaws of victory. The Pentagon screening marks the point where the US military finally starts to acknowledge the insurgency in Iraq.

The story of *The Battle of Algiers,* the Pentagon, and the doctrine of counterinsurgency has the makings of a melodrama: it is the story of a military organization drawing the wrong conclusions from the shock of defeat at first, and drawing the right conclusions too late. In order to better understand the melodramatic structure of this story, a discussion of military doctrine and institutional learning is in order.

III

Military theory is a body of knowledge based on institutional memory, case studies, and previous experience, drawing on a variety of fields ranging from sociology and anthropology to game theory. Through a process of deliberation and formalization, institutional memory can be codified into doctrine—that is, a set of stated principles that guide the allocation of personnel, weaponry, and other resources in a situation of armed conflict.[26] Doctrine differs from strategy and tactics in that doctrine prescribes a default pattern for the allocation of resources, whereas strategy and tactics concern a military's actions in a given conflict. The formation of military theory is a constant and ongoing process. "Because war can be a matter of life and death to states and nations," writes David Galula, "few other fields of human activity have been so consistently, thoroughly, and actively analyzed."[27] Since doctrine is the codification of institutional memory, doctrine is a matter of organizational culture and can vary from case to case. The doctrine of the American military since the Civil War has been one of overwhelming force, aimed at the annihilation of the enemy's military capabilities. Known as the Jominian doctrine, after Antoine-Henri Jomini, a Swiss native and general for Napoleon, this doctrine has been taught at West Point since the 1850s.[28] Jominian doctrine laid the groundwork for Sherman and Grant's war-of-attrition tactics in the Civil War, and it continued to inform strategic thinking in the twentieth century. The Weinberger-Powell doctrine, which formed the basis for the first US-led Iraq war and was again invoked for the second Iraq war, is based on Jomini's principles: deploy US forces only where vital national interests are at stake and political objectives are clear, but always use overwhelming force to secure quick victory. George W. Bush, in front of the "Mission Accomplished" banner, claimed a win in the sense of the Weinberger-Powell doctrine. As it turned out, the political objectives of the operation were ill defined, and the war, though waged as a conventional war, had never been one to begin with.

Sometimes, military organizations have no doctrine, or their doctrine is unsuited to the purpose. For instance, according to Galula, the French "had no theory, no plan in the 1870–71 Franco-Prussian War. In 1940, they duplicated a World War I recipe and fought a 1918 type of war against German panzer divisions," with disastrous results in both cases.[29] Depending on the organizational culture, an institutional learning process may or may not be set in motion when the doctrine is found lacking. As John Nagl argues, colonial forces in British Malaya in the late 1940s quickly adapted to the communist insurgency through bottom-up learning, while American forces in Vietnam failed to heed the lessons of the French defeat in Dien Bien Phu or learn from their own current problems.[30] In terms of organizational culture, this difference may derive from the fact that the British were a territorial empire with a rich experience in administering occupational regimes, whereas the Americans acted as a global power that derived its strength from a deterritorialized technological superiority. As Marnia Lazreg points out, the French developed a revolutionary-war theory in Algeria in the early 1950s, but the results were scattered.[31] When David Galula became a company commander in Kabylia in 1956, there were three different approaches to counterinsurgency, only one of which worked, and even this only temporarily.[32] Against this backdrop, the Pentagon screening of *The Battle of Algiers* stands out as part of an institutional learning process in which the world's largest military bureaucracy starts to question the validity of a doctrine to which it had adhered for roughly 150 years.

In addition to doctrine, conventional warfare is governed by judicial law and something akin to laws of nature. In conventional warfare, three "laws of war" or basic rules apply: first, the strongest camp wins; second, in a situation of parity, the more resolute party wins; third, if both camps are equally resolute, the camp that seizes the initiative or manages to surprise the other wins.[33] Furthermore, conventional wars have been contained by international law since the peace treaty of Westphalia in 1648.[34] International law, as it first emerged as the "*ius publicum europaeum*," regulates war as a conflict between sovereign nation-states and stipulates rules for the opening, conduct, and termination of hostilities. Later additions include rules for the protection of civilians and the treatment of prisoners of war. Against this legal and doctrinal framework, the terms "irregular warfare" and "asymmetrical warfare" describe armed conflicts that take place not between sovereign nation-states and in which the three "laws of war" do not apply. Unconventional conflicts are "irregular" in that insurgents are not members of a regular military and usually wear no uniforms. Accordingly, they are treated as "unlawful combatants" under international law. Furthermore, in asymmetrical warfare insurgents are usually inferior in number and resources. They use tactics such as sniping, ambushes, and bomb attacks, which are usually described as terrorism and aim to undermine the enemy's hold on power rather than achieve outright military victory. Insurgents win by not losing, while their enemies lose by not winning.

The asymmetry in resources is counterbalanced by an asymmetry in motive. Irregular wars usually pit the government of a sovereign nation-state against insurgents with a revolutionary cause. The partisan, notes Carl Schmitt, is a "telluric figure"—that is, he is bound to and draws his strength from being anchored in a specific terrain. However, in the twentieth century, partisans or insurgents come in two categories: the "autochthone-defensive" insurgent, who defends his territory or fights for freedom from occupation; and the "world-revolutionary aggressive" insurgent, who chooses a terrain to fight for what he sees as a just cause, whether communist world revolution or the new caliphate.[35] In either case, insurgents have the upper hand: they believe in the "sanctity of their cause" and have "more passion," to quote Raymond Aron.[36]

Schmitt's distinction between "autochthone-defensive" and the "world-revolutionary aggressive" insurgents intersects with the concept of the "accidental guerilla" proposed by David Kilcullen. "World-revolutionary aggressive" insurgents start conflicts that "accidental guerillas" find themselves involved in by accident, forced to defend their security. Schmitt defines politics as the state's capability to distinguish between friend and enemy. For Schmitt, both the partisan and the revolutionary, as warriors with a political cause, are the enemy of the state and thus the enemy par excellence. But the notion of "accidental guerilla" indicates that the insurgent is not necessarily and always the ineluctable enemy of the state. Raymond Aron distinguishes between "occasional," "permanent," and "absolute" enemies in warfare.[37] In Aron's taxonomy, the bourgeois imperialist is the absolute enemy of the "world-revolutionary aggressive" communist, just as every nonbeliever is the absolute enemy of the Takfiri Islamist insurgent. Yet enmity remains a matter of degree. In anticolonial insurgencies, the final defeat may not even be experienced as such. Algeria is a case in point. To put it in Aron's terms, the OAS, the mutinous terrorist network led by General Raoul Salan, continued to treat the FLN as the absolute enemy even as the war was already lost.[38] Meanwhile, the French government and the mainland public had moved to a view of the FLN as an occasional enemy and eventually experienced Algerian independence as a relief (even if war and torture continued to haunt the French, as witnessed in such films as Alain Resnais's *Muriel ou le temps d'un retour* [1963], Bertrand Tavernier's *La guerre sans nom* [1992], and Michael Haneke's *Caché* [2007]). A significant number of native French went even further as they took up the cause of Algerian independence in the 1950s.[39]

Taking Mao's successful campaign to establish communist rule in China as the template, military theorists have described irregular conflicts for most of the second half of the twentieth century as "revolutionary wars." More recently, the term "small wars" has been adopted for a broader range of armed conflicts involving nonstate actors. As Frantz Fanon argues, the term "revolutionary war" is apposite because the violent confrontation of the insurgency induces social change that would otherwise not occur. One tactic of the French in Algeria, for instance, was to unveil Muslim women and to force them to wear European clothes. Ostensibly a measure to promote emancipation, unveiling was designed to undermine the authority of Muslim men. But the FLN rapidly turned unveiling into an insurgent tactic. A particularly powerful scene in *The Battle of Algiers* shows three Algerian women changing into European clothes in preparation for a bomb attack in downtown Algiers. For Fanon, unveiling as an insurgent tactic reveals the transformational force of war: once insurgent women unveiled themselves rather than being forced to do so, the congenital jealousy and mistrust of the Algerian male "just melted away at the contact with the revolution."[40]

Fanon's observation highlights another difference between conventional and irregular warfare. While wars, states the Prussian general and military theorist Carl von Clausewitz, are "merely the continuation of politics by other means,"[41] conventional wars nominally exclude the civilian population, and international law treats attacks on civilians as war crimes. Revolutionary wars, on the other hand, are fought over control not of territory, but of the population, with the ultimate goal of governing the population. In Mao's famous metaphor, the revolutionary moves in the population like a fish in water, and the tactical challenge for the counterinsurgent is to drain the water. According to Galula, if the insurgent manages "to dissociate the population from the counterinsurgent, to control it physically, to get its active support, he will win the war, because, in the final analysis, the exercise of political power depends on the tacit or explicit agreement of the population or, at worst, on its submissiveness."[42]

As political scientist Stathis N. Kalyvas argues, populations choose sides in insurgencies motivated by safety concerns and a concomitant interest in reliable governance and swift justice, rather than ideology: "Irrespective of their sympathies (and everything else being equal), most people prefer to collaborate with the political actor that best guarantees their survival."[43] Populations usually break down into two small groups of insurgents and collaborators, and a large middle ground. The fight is over the majority in the middle, and the main tactic is not violence, but rather good governance, usually facilitated by an effective use of media. In Algeria, the FLN organized access to the health-care system of the colonial government for both insurgents and civilians and used radio as an instrument of governance.[44] In Afghanistan, the Taliban created a system of mobile courts, which outperformed the existing corrupt justice system and created dependencies that allowed insurgents to operate with the population's tacit support. More recently, ISIS has used mobile courts to establish control over civilians in Iraq.[45] If irregular wars are fought over control of the population, then counterinsurgency warfare, to use David Kilcullen's terms, is applied social work based on a study of culture and backed up by a threat of violence. The theory of counterinsurgency is thus a "theory of competitive control" of the population.[46] Competitive control depends on governance and communication, or the administration of security, justice, and health plus control of the narrative. Algerian independence would have remained elusive for much longer without access to radio, and without the

FLN's capacity to frame the debate in Western notions of justice, emancipation, and self-governance, with the support of public intellectuals with political backgrounds as diverse as Jean-Paul Sartre's and Raymond Aron's.

The melodramatic structure of the Pentagon's belated interest in counterinsurgency becomes all the more apparent if we consider that most wars fought after 1945 were, in fact, partisan wars.[47] The Cold War created an equilibrium in which classical rationales no longer applied. The likely outcome of a nuclear war was not the annihilation of the enemy's military capabilities but the annihilation of the enemy population, and likely one's own population as well.[48] War could no longer be politically justified and imagined only as a catastrophic event, or in the mode of black comedy, as in Stanley Kubrick's *Dr. Strangelove or: How I Learned to Stop Worrying and Love the Bomb* (1964). Once the Soviet empire crumbled, the United States was better prepared than ever to annihilate the military capability of the enemy, but there were no conventional enemies left to fight. As late as the summer of 2001, a retired US general claimed that in the future, military operations would be limited to short, surgical peacekeeping missions from the United States and their allies.[49] Yet only two years later, the United States embarked on its two most protracted large-scale ground operations, one of which, the Iraq war, it lost after winning (i.e., after destroying, Jominian style, the military capacity of the enemy), while it continues to lose the Afghanistan war by not winning. While conventional warfare may have reached its "end of history," armed conflict continues apace, mostly as "small wars" waged by irregular forces, and increasingly in urban littoral theaters of war.[50]

The United States' confounding inability to adapt to the reality of long-term small wars is rooted in the conclusions that its armed forces drew from Vietnam. Writing about American tactics in Vietnam, John Nagl argues: "An army that saw its raison d'être as winning wars through the application of firepower and manpower to annihilate enemy forces simply could not conceive of another kind of war in which its weapons, technology, and organization not only could not destroy the enemy, but usually could not even find or identify him."[51] Rather than developing a doctrine aimed at governance and control of the population, the US focused on "search and destroy" missions—that is, the continued use of overwhelming force even where targets could not be conclusively identified. Francis Ford Coppola's *Apocalypse Now* illustrates this tactic in the scene in which a cavalry battalion on choppers, to the sound of Wagner's *Die Walküre,* destroys a Vietnamese village suspected of harboring insurgents—before celebrating its pyrrhic victory, and its institutional culture, by making time to go surfing on a nearby beach.

In Vietnam, the institutional culture, which kept the US military from developing a doctrine suited to the realities on the ground, also prevented it from drawing the right conclusions from the shock of defeat. According to Nagl, the consensus view, which emerged around a study by Col. Harry Summers, of the Army War

College, from 1982, was "not that the army was too conventional in its approach to fighting the war in Vietnam, but that it was not conventional enough":[52] that more firepower, rather than social work backed up by violence, would have solved the problem. The French in Algeria failed to develop workable counterinsurgency tactics because they were similarly entrapped in their institutional culture. "Medals were given on the basis of valor in combat," writes Galula. "If there was no combat because the local commander had succeeded in pacifying his area, too bad for him—no medal."[53] If the kill rate, rather than the degree to which the enemy is no longer able to operate, is the decisive metric, there is no incentive to develop tactics that contain violence.

Faced with insurgencies in Iraq and Afghanistan, the US military finally found a local commander who succeeded in pacifying his area, and whom they listened to. Appointed commander of an airborne division in Mosul in early 2003, David Petraeus, an avid reader of Galula and at the time a major general, always opened his morning briefings by asking, "What have we done for the population?" Petraeus pacified the city by focusing on governance and security and parlayed his success into a promotion to four-star general. In this capacity, he commanded the "surge," the first large-scale application of FM 3–24, which he was instrumental in devising. The perceived success of the "surge" in turn earned him the directorship of the CIA. Petraeus's rise was partly based on his skill in controlling the perceptions of politicians and policy makers, while producing results on the battlefield to match these perceptions.[54] For Andrew Bacevich, the "surge" was a carefully orchestrated "pseudo-event" in the sense of Daniel Boorstin—a battle staged for political gain in a war that was already lost and devoid of strategic purpose.[55] Even though Petraeus has since resigned in disgrace because of a secrecy leak and marital infidelity, he continues to wield influence in the American security establishment as a partner in KKR, an equity firm and pioneer of the leveraged buyout.[56]

Petraeus's rise remains remarkable if we consider to what extent the tactics he pioneered depart from the American military's institutional culture. For instance, a passage in the first chapter of FM 3–24, entitled "Paradoxes of Counterinsurgency," includes the following: "Sometimes, the more you protect your force, the less secure you may be"; "Sometimes doing nothing is the best reaction"; "Some of the best weapons for counterinsurgents do not shoot"; "Sometimes the more force is used the less effective it is"; and "The host nation doing something tolerably is usually better than us doing it well."[57] It is no surprise that even after Petraeus's rise, remnants of a Jominian mind-set continued to resist such restraint and gradualism. While most commanders during the "surge" tried to adhere to FM 3–24,[58] rogue officers both in Iraq and in Afghanistan disregarded counterinsurgency tactics and continued to focus on kill rates.[59] And the road to a counterinsurgency doctrine after 2003 was far from straightforward. It led, in fact, through Abu Ghraib. *The Battle of Algiers* can help us understand why: the film shows how, in the absence of a definable enemy, torture can serve as a substitute for the organized violence of conventional warfare.

IV

After the three women in *The Battle of Algiers* change into European clothes, we see them passing through checkpoints that separate the Kasbah from the European downtown. The women flirt with French soldiers to avoid being searched, carrying their explosives to their targets undisturbed. In the scene after the attacks, General Mathieu briefs senior officers with a screening of 16mm films. The films show the checkpoint as the women pass through. We recognize the women; Mathieu and his staff do not. But Mathieu is aware of his ignorance. "Here is some film taken by the police," he tells his officers. "The cameras were hidden at the Kasbah exits. They thought these films might be useful, and in fact they are useful in demonstrating the usefulness of certain methods. Or, rather, their inadequacy."

"War is the realm of uncertainty," writes Clausewitz, "and three quarters of the factors on which action in war is based are wrapped in a fog of greater or lesser uncertainty."[60] In conventional warfare, the "fog of war" problem is situational; in asymmetrical warfare, it is permanent and structural, as the failings of the checkpoint reveal. A technique to make the invisible enemy visible, the checkpoint is a kind of film set to perform a "theological understanding of sovereignty," as David Fieni argues,[61] but its practical effects are limited to random success.

Mathieu next turns to a pyramid-like structure on a drawing board, representing the FLN cell: "We must start again from scratch. The only information we have concerns the structure of the organization. And we must start from that."

For Jose Teboho Ansorge, this scene is an early example of network analysis in counterinsurgency: "The network is drawn when vision is not up to the task of seeing the foe."[62] But network analysis remains a cumbersome substitute for vision. As FM 3–24 states: "Developing knowledge and using network analytic tools requires an unusually large investment of time compared to conventional analytic problem-solving methods."[63] In particular, it involves the work of highly qualified linguists and even anthropologists.[64] And even when those resources are available, information gained from the population has limited payoffs. As Stathis Kalyvas argues, when the insurgents are in control, the population will not share information; when the occupational forces are in control, information will be abundant but of little value, since the situation is already stable.[65] The challenge of counterinsurgency is that in the absence of actionable intelligence, risk must substitute for information. As FM 3–24 states, "[S]ometimes, the more you protect your force, the less secure you may be." By moving around the population, the counterinsurgents expose themselves to attacks, but they also create a relative sense of security, which makes it difficult for insurgents to operate and helps force them into the open.

FIGURE 9.1. Flirting with the invisible enemy: The checkpoint scene in *The Battle of Algiers*.

Neither General Mathieu nor his models chose this course of action. Ultimately, they compensated for their lack of vision not with network analysis or risk, but with torture. French generals in Algeria publicly defended torture, and soldiers openly admitted to it. "I have tortured, because we had to do it," one paratrooper named Jean-Marie Le Pen told an interviewer in 1962.[66] As late as 2000, General Paul Aussaresses advocated torture in a book, and he reiterated his stance in an interview with Mike Wallace on ABC in the fall of 2002.[67] *The Battle of Algiers* acknowledges the use of torture from its opening scene. Under duress, a militant gives up the information that leads to the capture and killing of the heads of the network, and the film tells that story in a flashback, working its way back to the opening scene. The briefing scene marks the turning point in the story. For Mathieu, the failure of film as an instrument of reconnaissance creates the evidence that justifies torture: legal protection in conventional war accrues to an enemy who is both visible and identifiable; an enemy who, as the surveillance films show, may be visible but is not identifiable forgoes such protection.

American advocates of "enhanced interrogation" claim that torture works and like to cite polls suggesting—falsely—that a majority of Americans after 9/11 supported torture.[68] In the same vein, Kathryn Bigelow's *Zero Dark Thirty,* a 2013 film produced with input from CIA operatives, suggests that torture led to the capture of Osama bin Laden. Security experts, however, agree that information obtained through torture is unreliable.[69] It remains debatable whether *The Battle of Algiers* subscribes to the first position.[70] Torture may win Matthieu the battle of Algiers, but the film ends with the uprising that leads to independence. What the film shows unambiguously is that torture is not "senseless violence."[71] Joseph de Maistre, the French counterrevolutionary, justifies torture in his 1815 defense of the Spanish Inquisition by arguing that "all modern nations have used this terrible means of discovering the truth."[72] For de Maistre, the Inquisition is the Christian Spanish nation's legitimate—and legal—self-defense against its enemies—that is, Jews and Muslims. With anthropologist Nathan Wachtel, we can argue that torture in the twentieth and twenty-first centuries continues in the same tradition of physical coercion of the nation-state against its perceived enemies.[73] De Maistre, who was nothing if not lucid, defends torture by stressing its modernity.

However, as Mathieu's actions in *The Battle of Algiers* demonstrate, there is a specific military logic to torture in asymmetrical warfare. The limit of visibility— the boundary at which the enemy disappears—is also the boundary where the military's power over the enemy disintegrates. While never symbolic for those who endure it, torture symbolically restitutes that lost power. It transforms the organized violence of overwhelming force into the expressive violence of absolute domination over the body of the perceived (in the double sense of presumed and visible) enemy. As such, torture is an expression both of a will of domination and of impotence in the face of an intangible enemy.

V

In the fourth season of *Homeland*, former CIA head Saul Berenson (Mandy Patinkin) argues that the Americans make no progress in Afghanistan because they have been fighting a fourteen-year war in one-year budget cycles—which is another way of saying that global counterinsurgency is more protracted, costly, and frustrating than even a post-Jominian American military can tolerate. Even so, however, the specter of overwhelming force continues to haunt the American military. The use of drones, for instance, is a "de facto experiment in globalizing counterterrorism techniques" of the kind General Stanley McChrystal used to decimate Al-Qaeda in Iraq (McChrystal mainly employed stealth killer commandos.)[74] Considering that drones trade in technological superiority and annihilate the enemy at the price of routine civilian losses, they appear merely as the latest reiteration of the "search and destroy" tactic that failed in Vietnam. It is no surprise that counterinsurgency experts like Kilcullen are adamantly opposed to drone warfare. But in light of the ascendancy of ISIS and the resilience of the Taliban, Kilcullen now also considers "disaggregation" a failure and advocates for the buildup of conventional forces.[75]

In any case, the "War on Terror" may well have been lost before FM 3–24 was ever written. Shortly after the Pentagon screening of *The Battle of Algiers*, American soldiers photographed themselves torturing inmates in Abu Ghraib, a prison in Iraq filled to the brim with terror suspects. As Errol Morris shows in *Standard*

Operating Procedure, his 2008 film on the scandal, the torturers may not have anticipated the public outcry that the publication of the photographs would create in May 2004. But it was clearly important to them to have their picture taken with their victims.

These soldiers almost certainly had never heard of Pontecorvo's film. Yet their actions constitute a form of acting out the transformation of the functional violence of overwhelming force into the hybrid, real and symbolic, violence of torture, which the film explains in cinematic terms. As if to disprove the briefing scene's evidence that the enemy is invisible, the Abu Ghraib photographs produce the enemy as a visual spectacle. This enemy is both occasional and absolute: occasional, because, as the prison commander later admitted, 90 percent of the inmates were unlucky bystanders, and the victims were randomly chosen from the inmates. Absolute, because the visual spectacle of torture turns the random victim into a visible representation of the invisible enemy. This enemy-as-spectacle is a nobody that is anybody, a figure that oscillates between the contingent and the metaphysical but no longer provides an actionable military target.

As Andrew Bacevich argues, Abu Ghraib "represented a political setback of monumental proportions," to the point where "we may date the failure of the Third Gulf War from this point."[76] Asked about the Pentagon screening in 2004, Yacef Saadi, the film's protagonist and head of the FLN cell, said: "*The Battle of Algiers* should be able to teach people some lessons, but the Americans are bad students, like the French were, and they are making things worse."[77] As one Republican candidate for president, who went on to become commander in chief, stated in the fall of 2015, even if waterboarding "doesn't work, they deserve it anyway for what they do to us."[78] "They" in this sentence stands for anyone who happens to be on the receiving end of torture, while "us," inferring from the speaker, represents the mostly Caucasian Americans who administer the treatment. But random imaginary retribution is no tactic, just as "terror" is no enemy. The self-defeating logic that *The Battle of Algiers* explains and Abu Ghraib exemplifies is this: the transformation of the functional violence of overwhelming force into the hybrid, real and symbolic, violence of torture produces an enemy that no doctrine can defeat.[79]

NOTES

1. David Kilcullen, "Twenty-Eight Articles: Fundamentals of Company-Level Counterinsurgency," *Military Review* 83, no. 3 (May–June 2006): 103–8; David Kilcullen, *Counterinsurgency* (New York: Oxford University Press, 2010), 17–27.

2. Andrew Bacevich, *America's War for the Greater Middle East* (New York: Random House, 2016), 16.

3. David Kilcullen, *Blood Year: Islamic State and the Failure of the War on Terror* (London: Hurst, 2016), 11.

4. T. E. Lawrence, "Twenty-Seven Articles," *Arab Bulletin* 60, August 20, 1917.

5. Kilcullen, *Counterinsurgency,* 27.

6. Vinzenz Hediger, "Von Hollywood lernen heißt führen lernen," *Montage AV* 15, no. 2 (2006): 139–152.

7. Paul B. Rich, "Rossellini, Pontecorvo, and the Neorealist Cinema of Insurgency," *Small Wars and Insurgencies* 26, no. 4 (2015): 640–67.

8. Irene Bignardi, *Memorie estorte a uno smemorato: Vita di Gillo Pontecorvo* (Milan: Feltrinelli, 1999), 120.

9. The film was never finished. My source is Luca Peretti, who is currently completing a dissertation on ENI films at Yale.

10. Patricia Caillé, "The Illegitimate Legitimacy of *The Battle of Algiers* in French Film Culture," *Interventions: International Journal of Postcolonial Studies* 9, no. 3 (2007): 371–88.

11. Thomas Riegler, "Gillo Pontecorvo's 'Dictatorship of the Truth': A Legacy," *Studies in European Cinema* 6, no. 1 (2009): 55.

12. Bignardi, *Memorie estorte,* 122, 139.

13. Riegler, "Pontecorvo's 'Dictatorship of the Truth,'" 49.

14. Murray Kempton, *The Briar Patch: The Trial of the Panther 21* (New York: Da Capo, 1973), 270.

15. Stephen J. Whitfield, "*Cine Qua Non:* The Political Import and Impact of *The Battle of Algiers,*" *Révue Lisa* 10, no. 1 (2012): 249–70.

16. Curzio Malaparte, *Tecnica del colpo di stato* (Milan: Adelphi, 2011).

17. James Fallows, *Blind into Baghdad: America's War in Iraq* (New York: Vintage, 2006), 61.

18. Bacevich, *America's War,* 258.

19. Fred Kaplan, *The Insurgents: David Petraeus and the Plot to Change the American Way of War* (New York: Simon and Schuster, 2013), 58.

20. Bacevich, *America's War,* chap. 2.

21. William Appleman Williams, *The Tragedy of American Diplomacy* (New York: W. W. Norton, 2009), 57.

22. Bacevich, *America's War,* 240.

23. Williams, *Tragedy of American Diplomacy,* 66.

24. Ibid., 42

25. Kilcullen, *Counterinsurgency,* 104.

26. John A. Nagl, *Learning to Eat Soup with a Knife: Counterinsurgency Lessons from Malaya and Vietnam* (Chicago: University of Chicago Press, 2002), 7.

27. David Galula, *Counterinsurgency Warfare: Theory and Practice* (Westport, CT: Praeger, 1964), xii.

28. Nagl, *Learning to Eat Soup,* 16–19.

29. Galula, *Counterinsurgency Warfare,* xii.

30. Nagl, *Learning to Eat Soup,* 191–212.

31. Marnia Lazreg, *Torture and the Twilight of Empire: From Algiers to Baghdad* (Princeton, NJ: Princeton University Press, 2007), chap. 1.

32. David Galula, *Pacification in Algeria, 1956–1958* (Santa Monica, CA, and Arlington, VA: Rand, 2006), 64–67.

33. Galula, *Counterinsurgency Warfare,* xii.

34. Carl Schmitt, *Der Nomos der Erde im Völkerrecht des Jus Publicum Europaeum* (Berlin: Duncker & Humblot, 1950).

35. Carl Schmitt, *Theorie des Partisanen: Zwischenbemerkung zum Begriff des Politischen* (Berlin: Duncker & Humblot, 1963), 26, 39.

36. Raymond Aron, *Guerre et paix entre les nations* (Paris: Calman-Lévy, 1962), 47.

37. Ibid., 46.

38. John C. Cairns, "Algeria: The Last Ordeal," *International Journal* 17, no. 2 (1962): 87–97. See also Schmitt's discussion of Salan's defense in court in the final chapter of *Theorie des Partisanen*.

39. Frantz Fanon, *Œuvres* (Paris: La Découverte, 2011), 379–407.

40. Ibid., 295.

41. Carl von Clausewitz, *On War* (Princeton, NJ: Princeton University Press, 1976), bk. 1, chap. 1, sec. 24.

42. Galula, *Counterinsurgency Warfare*, 4.

43. Stathis N. Kalyvas, *The Logic of Violence in Civil War* (Cambridge and New York: Cambridge University Press, 2006), 12.

44. Fanon, *Œuvres*, 305–30; 355–37. See also John Mowitt, "Fanon's 'guerre des ondes': Resisting the Call of Orientalism," in *Orientalism and War*, ed. Tarak Barkawi and Keith Stanski (London: Hurst and Company, 2012), 223–44.

45. Abdel Bari Atwan, *Islamic State: The Digital Caliphate* (London: Saqi, 2015).

46. David Kilcullen, *Out of the Mountains: The Coming Age of the Urban Guerilla* (New York: Oxford University Press, 2013).

47. Schmitt, *Theorie des Partisanen*, 29.

48. Herman Kahn, *On Thermonuclear War* (Princeton, NJ: Princeton University Press, 1960).

49. David Kilcullen, *The Accidental Guerilla: Fighting Small Wars in the Midst of a Big One* (New York and Oxford: Oxford University Press, 2009), 2.

50. Kilcullen, *Out of the Mountains*, chap. 1.

51. Nagl, *Learning to Eat Soup*, 198.

52. Ibid., 207.

53. Galula, *Pacification in Algeria*, 65.

54. Bacevich, *America's War*, 171, 181–88.

55. The "surge" "bought time and kept the public from intruding into policy." Bacevich, *America's War*, 283, 285. See also Daniel Boorstin, *The Image: A Guide to Pseudo-Events in America* (New York: Atheneum, 1971).

56. Michael J. Schmidt and Matt Apuzzi, "David Petraeus Is Sentenced to Probation in Security Leak," *New York Times*, April 23, 2015; Sheryl Gay Stolberg, "After Scandal: Petraeus Stays under the Radar but Not Out of the Spotlight," *New York Times*, February 27, 2015.

57. US Army and US Marine Corps, *Counterinsurgency Field Manual* (hereafter FM) (Chicago and London: University of Chicago Press, 2007), 48–49.

58. In David Finkel's 2009 book on a ranger unit during the "surge," FM, 3–24 appears on the commander's desk in the second chapter and again in the last chapter, at the end of the nine-month deployment, covered with dust. David Finkel, *The Good Soldiers* (New York: Picador, 2009), 27.

59. Bacevich, *America's War*, 314.

60. Clausewitz, *On War*, bk. 1, chap. 3.

61. David Fieni, "Cinematic Checkpoints and Sovereign Time," *Journal of Post-Colonial Writing* 50, no. 1 (2014): 7.

62. Joseph Teboho Ansorge, "Orientalism in the Machine," in *Orientalism and War*, ed. Tarak Barkawi and Keith Stanski (London: Hurst and Company, 2012), 141.

63. FM, 3–24, 130.

64. The chapter of FM 3–24 titled "Intelligence in Counterinsurgency" was coauthored by cultural anthropologist Montgomery J. McFarlane. This prompted the American Anthropological Association to issue a resolution against the use of anthropological knowledge in torture. Cf. Roberto J. Gonzalez, "Towards Mercenary Anthropology? The New US Army Counterinsurgency Manual FM 3–24 and the Military-Anthropology Complex," *Anthropology Today* 23, no. 3 (2007): 19.

65. Kalyvas, *Logic of Violence*, 13.

66. Alan Cowell, "Le Pen Accused of Torturing Prisoners during Algerian War," *New York Times,* June 4, 2002.

67. Paul Aussaresses, *The Battle of the Casbah: Counter-Terrorism and Torture in Algeria, 1955–1957* (New York: Enigma Books, 2002), xi.

68. Paul Gronke and Darjus Rejali, "US Public Opinion on Torture, 2001–2009," *Political Science and Politics* 43, no. 3 (2010): 437–44.

69. Jean Maria Arrigo and Richard V. Wagner, "Psychologists and Military Interrogators Rethink the Psychology of Torture," *Peace and Conflict* 13, no. 4 (2007): 393–98.

70. See the excellent analysis in Murray Smith, "*The Battle of Algiers:* Colonial Struggle and Collective Allegiance," in *Terrorism, Media, Liberation,* ed. John Slocum (New Brunswick, NJ: Rutgers University Press 2005), 94–110.

71. For a critique of "senseless violence," see Kalyvas, *Logic of Violence,* chap. 2.

72. Joseph de Maistre, *Lettres à un gentilhomme russe sur l'inquisition espagnole* (Lyon: J. B. Pélagaud, 1871), letter 2.

73. Nathan Wachtel, *La logique des bûchers* (Paris: Editions du Seuil, 2009).

74. Bacevich, *America's War,* 335.

75. Kilcullen, *Blood Year,* 218.

76. Bacevich, *America's War,* 266.

77. Quoted in Riegler, "Pontecorvo's 'Dictatorship of the Truth,'" 55.

78. "Donald Trump on Waterboarding: 'Even If It Doesn't Work They Deserve It,'" *Guardian,* November 23, 2015, accessed 10 July, 2017, www.theguardian.com/us-news/2015/nov/24/donald-trump-on-waterboarding-even-if-it-doesnt-work-they-deserve-it.

79. To quote Bacevich, the failing of America's thirty-year war for the Greater Middle East is a result of "the absence of a consistent understanding of what the United States is fighting for and whom it is fighting against." Bacevich, *America's War,* 365.

PART THREE

MILITARY-MADE MOVIES

10

BETWEEN THE FRONT LINES

Military Training Films, Machine Guns,
and the Great War

Florian Hoof

Starting in 1917, Frank B. Gilbreth, the US Army Signal Corps, and the J. R. Bray Studios jointly produced training films for the US Army. These films built on earlier efforts by Gilbreth to secure consulting contracts for training films for the German army. The films and the work of Frank Gilbreth and his wife, Lillian, have become relevant to film historians as scholars have used them to show the close ties between film and rationalization. The Gilbreths' films have been analyzed as examples of scientific filmmaking, and more generally as prototypes for modern visual culture in the making.[1] Although in the context of film history the Gilbreths are commonly known for their time-motion studies and the use of cinema as a way of speeding up workers' movements in the industrial sector, they also did significant work for the military, applying to the American army the logics of biomechanical efficiency initially developed for the factory floor. I will focus on these lesser-known aspects of their work in order to analyze the relations between film and the military. The case shows some of the business strategies deployed by filmmakers to enter the military complex that cannot be accounted for only in terms of patriotism but must also be seen as part of an enduring set of mutually beneficial relations between the film industry and various military forces that formed as early as the 1910s.

The Great War, the first example of completely industrialized warfare on a global scale, was not decided solely on the battlefields but by the capacity of military management to successfully coordinate industrial mass production, logistics, and military operations. In this context, the knowledge and concepts the Gilbreths developed in the industrial sector became important to the military. Starting in 1912, they worked as consultants to several big companies—including U.S. Rubber, Eastman

Kodak, Remington Typewriter Company, and Ball Brothers—to rationalize production facilities.[2] Here, the Gilbreths used film to analyze workers' movements, to improve ergonomics, and to assist with vocational training. Based on their activities and the knowledge they gained through their work in the industrial sector, they also pioneered the use of film to train soldiers to operate machine guns, to throw grenades, and to improve their fencing skills. Existing research on military film covering this period mainly focuses on propaganda aimed toward large civilian audiences.[3] In contrast, I focus on how film was used by the military in relation to its organizational culture and practices, with some contextual discussion of the German military as well. How the Gilbreths used film in these different contexts provides an interesting case to analyze in terms of the utilization of film in the military, partly because their work evolved during the tremendous changes wrought by the rise of industrialized warfare. While in the context of factory work they reorganized the human body in an ergonomic way to function as a "human motor"[4] on the factory floor, for the military they organized efficient fighting bodies on the battlefields. What this teaches us, among other things, is that cinema was but one tool of industrial rationality, transferred in this case from industrial production to industrialized killing.

THE LOGICS OF INDUSTRIALIZED WARFARE

Nineteenth-century military logics—expressed in concepts such as those presented in Carl von Clausewitz's *Vom Kriege*[5] (*On War*)—mainly focused on decision making and strategic behavior on the battlefields and did not pay much attention to aspects of modern warfare such as supply logistics and the effective training of soldiers. But as the expedient movement of goods and skilled fighters became crucial for successful warfare, military logics began to adapt industrial concepts such as standardization and scientific management. In other words, at the beginning of the twentieth century, the exchange of ideas between the military and the industrial sector was common, since both fields were concerned with similar problems of logistics and efficiency. Consequently, interchangeable and shared concepts of how to approach and understand these issues evolved. Successful consultants such as Harrington Emerson borrowed organizational models and command structures from the military to restructure industrial enterprises,[6] while the Gilbreths used concepts of efficiency developed in the industrial sector to advise and modernize the military. This cross-sectoral traffic blurred the line between the logics of the military and those of the industrial sector and at the same time functioned as a building block for the evolving military-industrial complex.

Industrial and technological sophistication led to new weaponry such as water-cooled automatic heavy machine guns and long-range artillery. This development fundamentally altered the demands on modern combat soldiers. Duties were extended toward operating and understanding sophisticated machinery, quite similar to the duties of the modern industrial workforce on the factory floors. Soldiers in the trenches operating automatic machine guns or artillery could be characterized in some respects as machinists. This had multifold implications concerning the training of soldiers because they had to be prepared to handle complex machinery and to perform new, "scientific" forms of machine gunnery.[7] They needed the skills not only to correctly operate the devices but also to cope with jamming and other forms of technological breakdown. Infantry marching had already been analyzed by the French physiologist Etienne-Jules Marey at the end of the nineteenth century for the French army, which had contracted Marey to develop a less tiring way of marching; however, equally important skills such as riding a horse and fencing were rather complex technological issues that could not be accounted for by physical training alone.[8] Instead, a more sophisticated method of teaching was needed to allow for transferring this kind of knowledge to prospective soldiers. The high mortality rate for soldiers on the front lines meant also that it became crucial to establish a system that could replace the skilled soldiers who had fallen in duty. New skilled men that were capable of operating and maintaining complex devices such as automatic machine guns and long-range artillery also had to be ready to serve. This system of preparing a deep supply of equipment operators was only in its infancy with the onset of World War I.

Film became of particular interest to the military in this precise context. Film promised to provide a modularized, almost standardized vocational training system that would deliver consistent training quality. Films were capable of storing information about handling complex machinery that could not be compromised by potentially incompetent instructors in one of the remote military training centers that—in case of the United States—were spread all over the country. Thus, film could be used to establish a standardized and centrally mechanized procedure for education, helping to secure a continuous supply of trained soldiers for the trench war.

Focusing on early vocational training films produced for the military in the context of World War I, I describe how the army utilized films, and how producing, promoting, and selling vocational training films turned into a profitable business model for entrepreneurs such as the Gilbreths and the J. R. Bray Studios. That the military became an ever-expansionist apparatus is also a result of its ability to provide business opportunities for third parties and thus to also economically expand and integrate with civilian economies. The Gilbreths made films but also provided film-based consulting during World War I, serving as a paradigmatic case for understanding the early utilization of film in the military context.

SELLING FILM TO THE MILITARY

The Gilbreths acquired consulting jobs with the military by using approaches identical to those they had successfully applied to the economic sector. By chance, their first attempt to sell film-based consultancy to the military was directed toward the German army. When World War I started, Frank Gilbreth was working for the Berlin-based company Deutsche Gasglühlicht AG, an innovative high-tech enterprise with close ties to the military and thus itself a showcase for the evolving structures of military-industrial cooperation. In 1915, when the company started to produce supplies for the use of gas in the waging of war, it was categorized as a critical war supplier (*kriegswichtiger Betrieb*).[9] About twenty-five years later the company became a crucial part of the German nuclear-weapons program. Gilbreth's task was to restructure the company according to the principles of scientific management.[10] A long-term contract had not been secured yet, so he still needed to convince the management to invest in his methods of "film-based consulting."[11] At the same time he was trying to establish contact with the German military in the hopes of gaining contracts from the army.

To prove the modernity and superiority of his consulting method, Gilbreth specifically chose to demonstrate to Deutsche Gasglühlicht AG and German army officials his film-based motion studies in person. In 1913, he filed a patent in the United States for this procedure with the title "Method and Apparatus for the Study and Correction of Motions."[12] It basically describes the so-called cyclegraphic method, in which light bulbs are attached to the extremities of a person such as an arm. These light bulbs are then lit so that the movements of this arm can be captured on film as a clearly defined light line. The method also consists of a device that interrupts the electricity for the light bulbs on a regular basis. When it is applied, the method captures not only movement in space but also the exact amount of time needed to perform this movement by segmenting the light lines of the bulbs into dots and dashes that correspond to certain time units. From this data, then, the original movement can be analyzed, and finally synthesized into a faster and less-tiring movement for the workers.

In Berlin, Gilbreth relied on innocuous cycle-graphic motion studies of sports activities to show the diverse aspects connected to film-based consulting. "I am planning to cyclegraph a famous fencer and send the pictures to the Kaiser," he wrote in a letter to Lillian.[13] To fulfill this objective, he filmed a German and a Russian fencer who "are supposed to be the best in all Germany and are retained by the army."[14] The German guests included the two most important executives of Deutsche Gasglühlicht AG, as well as influential politicians with close ties to the German emperor and the military. All present were reportedly fascinated by the motion studies.[15]

As planned from the very beginning, Gilbreth used the fencing studies to try to secure further consulting deals. This was by no means a new practice. In the United States, he had previously used sports studies to obtain a range of contracts and to boost public awareness of his consulting firm. In May 1913 he conducted motion studies of pitching and batting activities during a baseball game of the New

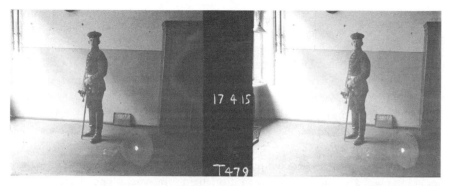

FIGURE 10.1. Stereographic photo of a German soldier taken by Frank Gilbreth on January 17, 1914, in the context of his fencing studies. (TECHNOSEUM, Landesmuseum für Technik und Arbeit, Mannheim, Nachlass Witte / Gilbreth, Nr. 2005–0872.)

York Giants against the Philadelphia Phillies. He also filmed sprinters at the track-and-field club of Brown University. Furthermore, he carried out motion studies of golfers. These films functioned as "advertising gimmicks"[16] for his recently founded consulting firm, Gilbreth Inc., based in Providence, Rhode Island. Baseball and golfing, as well as track and field, were popular leisure activities in the United States and thus attractive to a wider audience. Among others, the Gilbreth films were shown as part of newsreels in movie theaters across the country, making Frank and Lillian Gilbreth and their children, who were often included in their motion pictures, widely known role models for the efficiency movement in the progressive era. These films were also shown at trade fairs and were frequently projected for prospective customers of the company's consulting services.

In Germany, Frank Gilbreth's films used fencing, since he deemed the activity a similarly attractive and popular one, boosting the appeal of his sports motion studies in the hopes of acquiring new contracts. Fencing was an intrinsic part of the aggressive-militaristic culture in Wilhelminian Germany.[17] Fencing being a core element of the cultural identity of the military elite, Gilbreth used the studies to establish contacts with the German army and to secure a meeting with the German emperor, Wilhelm II. Gilbreth wrote to Lillian, "I'll send [the fencing studies] to the Kaiser . . . and that will pay for them other than in money."[18]

Fencing studies were specifically suitable for demonstrating Gilbreth's consulting services. They offered a direct link to German military culture, but at the same time they could also be perceived as just an interesting example of a sports-related motion study. Or to put it differently, fencing studies did not appear to be crass advertisements because they did not show the product that they actually wanted to sell—that is, consulting services to rationalize the German army. This indirect approach enabled Gilbreth to engage his potential clients in innocuous conversations about his method and the history and origins of movement and efficiency.[19] Gilbreth's utilization of media technology bears some resemblances to that of Etienne-Jules Marey, who impressed the Parisian bourgeoisie with moving pictures of athletic bodies and racehorses.[20] Like baseball, golfing, or fencing in the United States, track and field and horse racing were part of the cultural identity of, or of interest to, the French elite. While Marey used the public attention he was able to generate to secure further research funds, Gilbreth applied a similar strategy to target the executive management of private companies and the military to obtain further consulting contracts.

His ultimate goal was to convince Wilhelm II that his film-based motion-study technique was a viable path toward rationalizing the operations of the German army. He specifically thought about using cycle-graphic motion studies and their utility for helping to understand the newly introduced machine guns. "I will show him [i.e., Wilhelm II] how to load his guns faster," he told Lillian.[21] His plan was first to analyze existing methods of handling these weapons, second to come up with more-efficient ways to operate them, and finally to produce films that could be used to train the soldiers according to the new methods.[22] But in July 1915, Deutsche Gasglühlicht AG was categorized as a critical war supplier. From now on foreign employees were no longer allowed on the premises. Consequently, Gilbreth's contract was canceled. He suspended all of his plans and returned to the United States.

PRODUCING TRAINING FILMS FOR THE US ARMY

Aside from the fencing studies, Gilbreth did not produce a single film for the military up until 1917. But during World War I, film became more and more important for the US Army. As Larry Wayne Ward has stated, "By the end of the First World War, the Photographic Section in the Signal Corps had built a staff of nearly six hundred men, and Signal Corps cameramen had shot almost one million feet of film in Europe and the United States."[23] The growing importance of film for the military not only led to new film units inside the military organization but also presented promising business opportunities for external consultants and film professionals. In this context Gilbreth started to establish contact with the US Army, although it was not at all an easy start.

At the beginning he was faced with hostility when he suggested the adoption of film as a tool for military training. Until then, the military utilized film mainly for propaganda—for example, to promote war bonds—and not for military training. Confronted with a well-established work culture and the formidable bureaucratic structures of the US Army, Gilbreth strategically argued that film would offer a uniquely precise scientific method to boost efficiency.[24] He sent copies of his and Lillian's recently published *Applied Motion Study* to leading military officials.[25]

These efforts accompanied further activities. Among others things, he asked personal friends to send letters to military personnel underlining the importance of
scientific film for the military success of the army.[26] He basically argued that he
could extend the concept of industrial-production rationality—to get more surplus
value from the people—to the military: to kill people more efficiently. Finally, his
attempt to include film in military operations was successful. In December 1917,
Gilbreth started his active duty in the army reserve. He was vested as a major in the
Engineer Reserve Corps at the Infantry School of Arms, Fort Sill, Oklahoma.

That same year the US Army introduced a number of new weapons, opting for
the all-new M1917 Browning as their principle heavy machine gun. Before entering the war the army did not show much interest in machine guns, and it still
operated with an outdated model. But when the United States entered the war, the
situation changed, forcing the military to introduce a more reliable, lighter, and
quicker, water-cooled automatic heavy gun. Consequently, in a short period of
time numerous recruits had to be trained in how to properly handle new weapons.
Furthermore, a vocational training system was needed that could quickly replace
the casualties with new trained recruits. Under these specific circumstances, film
appeared to be one among many tools to assist with and to speed up the military
training necessary to expand the army from under 135,000 men in 1917 to up to
four million in 1918.[27] The US Army Signal Corps was put in charge to produce and
distribute these training films. To facilitate these efforts, the US School of Military
Cinematography was established at Columbia University in 1918. There, film
experts such as Josef von Sternberg and Victor Fleming worked on training films
and lectured to the soldiers of the signal corps on the basics of filmmaking in
training courses that lasted for six weeks.[28]

The advent of complex weapons that were more difficult to handle was also part
of a larger organizational shift inside the army. Here, the military management
started to replace big units comprising hundreds of soldiers with specialized subu-
nits.[29] Small squads of eight to twelve soldiers would, for example, operate one
M1917 machine gun. These more flexible platoon tactics and new organizational
structures also affected concepts of military training, since these soldiers needed to
be trained differently. Albeit still part of the chain of command, they needed skills
that would enable them to react more autonomously in certain combat situations.

In this context Gilbreth was "charged with preparing a set of motion pictures to
supplement field instructions for new recruits in order to reduce their training
time and get them to France more quickly."[30] He saw this as a unique opportunity
to demonstrate the superiority of film for military training. Films were meant to
serve as a means to rationalize existing training practices and to conduct the training of recruits more efficiently and more precisely. The films should standardize
existing teaching methods and provide the recruits with the ultimate "One Best
Way"[31] to do their job. The goal was to produce about "thirty reels of film on

infantry, artillery, and cavalry training, on the assembly and use of various machine guns, rifles, and hand guns, and on efficient techniques of bayonet use."[32] The films would then be distributed by the signal corps to military training camps around the country.

At Fort Sill, activities concerning military training and film had already been in place when Gilbreth arrived. Besides the internal photographic section of the signal corps, the army also gathered experts from the entertainment and film industry. Among them were Victor Fleming and ten cameramen he selected for the signal corps.[33] Furthermore, Max Fleischer and Jack Leventhal, film specialists from the technical division of the J. R. Bray Studios—a studio that specialized in animation—were supervising the production of these very first military training films for the army.[34] In 1918, they finished the films *How to Operate a Stokes Mortar, Contour Map Reading/How to Read an Army Map,* and *How to Fire the Lewis Machine Gun.* In this context, Gilbreth's task was "to critique the films that the War College had already made and edit their 'scenarios.'"[35] Among other things, he criticized the "unnecessarily small"[36] pictures and "demanded tighter framing in scenes of rifle cleaning."[37] But on a more fundamental level, he argued that the films needed to generate "interest" to be more "pleasant" to watch, since they needed to "be shown many, many, many times."[38] After observing that the present audience did not engage with the films but only endured them passively, he demanded that a psychologist work on the films to improve their quality. His overall estimation of the films that had already been produced was that they were "gloomy and monotonous."[39] *Lewis Aircraft Machine Gun,*[40] a one-reel film produced by the signal corps in 1918, consisted solely of shots showing technical details of the machine gun.

When Gilbreth started to conceptualize and shoot films, he reacted to this situation and made a couple of suggestions as to how to improve the films. One was to incorporate more-interesting scenes into the training films. Being a passionate moviegoer himself, he had ideas and concepts that directly stemmed from the emerging commercial cinematic culture. He was specifically fascinated by the innovative action scenes, camera shots, and narration techniques that D. W. Griffith used in his first feature-length film, *Judith of Bethulia.*[41] Consequently, Gilbreth began to include "motion picture-like" narrative sequences such as "horses in the pens fighting for food"[42] into his training films. Furthermore, he recommended adopting "as standard practice the insertion into each movie of motivational 'hate' footage showing enemy 'atrocities.'"[43] He also suggested showing scenes that depicted wrong methods at different speeds to make them look ridiculous and to boost the pedagogical value of film. This mixture of "entertainment" and "didactic illustration," he believed, would make film a productive tool for education. Exemplary cases are the training films *The Browning Machine Gun (First Section)* (see figure 10.2) and *The Browning Automatic Rifle (Third Section).*[44] Here

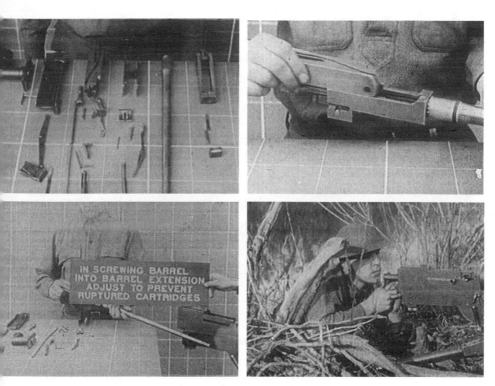

FIGURE 10.2. Stills from the film *The Browning Machine Gun (First Section)*. (Original Films of Frank B. Gilbreth. Prelinger Collection, Library of Congress.)

explanatory parts alternate with action sequences showing diverse firing positions to demonstrate how the weapons would appear in action. The latter film ends with footage showing bullets hitting a body of water. This sequence has no value for vocational training at all. Its primary purpose is to feature the cinematic spectacle of spraying water. Similarly exploiting visual appeal rather than utilitarian technical illustration, the signal corps even shot a sequence that showed not one or two but thirty M1917 machine guns in action, "the greatest number of machine guns ever fired in the United States at one time."[45] The supervising cameraman, Victor Fleming, argued that these films should give "recruits about everything there is in gunnery except the feel of hot metal and the smell of powder."[46]

In case of the film *The Browning Machine Gun*, which demonstrated the "one best way" to handle the weapon, Gilbreth included intertitles to structure the film and even used them to pose tasks to the audience, such as, "While this expert assembles the gun without lost motions, see how many parts you can name."[47] These are examples of Gilbreth working to draw more "interest" and engage trainees during the otherwise highly technical and largely unadorned films. This film also demonstrates how to unjam the weapon in action. After recruits had seen the film, they were blindfolded and asked to repeat the movements they had seen on the screen with a real weapon. This was meant to prepare them for unjamming the M1917 in night conditions and self-sufficiently, without assistance. Gilbreth had already applied the concept of "blindfolded learning" to other types of tasks—such as typewriting—in industrial organizations. It was a method that stemmed from pedagogical theories developed by Maria Montessori, an Italian educational theorist,[48] whose empirical approach to early-childhood education relied on object-based learning as the basic abstract principle for developing the potential of children.[49] Gilbreth adopted her approach for the training of soldiers and workers. Film, Gilbreth assumed, functioned as part surrogate for, and also aid to, live object lessons. This particular example also shows how closely related industrial and military machinery were. Since industrialized warfare used machinery that was similar to that on the factory floor, vocational training methods originally developed for efficient industrial production could be easily adopted for military purposes.

Film-based training of soldiers lasted only a couple of months. In 1918 filming activities at Fort Sill were suspended and partly moved to the newly established US School of Military Cinematography at Columbia University.[50] The reasons for the move remain partly unclear. First, the war came to an end. In the most basic sense, the films produced to train the operators of the M1917 machine gun and the Browning automatic rifle were no longer needed. In addition, serious supply and production issues concerning both models resulted in the fact that, contrary to original plans, the weapons were not widely used in World War I. The American expeditionary forces that were rushed to the Western Front after Germany's spring offensives from March to July 1918 were for the most part equipped and trained with British and French weapons.[51] The American Browning guns were used only in the last few weeks of the war. It was only in World War II and in later conflicts such as the Korean and Vietnam wars that the M1917 was commonly used by the army.

But, besides issues that lay beyond Gilbreth's sphere of influence, other problems also obstructed his filming activities. He was deeply shocked by the inflexibility and inefficiency of military structures and hierarchies. He even feared getting infected by their lax military standards and concluded that no private business whatsoever would survive if it was structured like the US Army.[52] Gilbreth had the impression that films were used in a dysfunctional way because of inflexible army regulations: "Army regulations required that three films be shown at each session, and the officer assigned to show the films study them carefully first. . . . These officers, however, received no instruction for using the films; the films would be shown only once, and no lecture would accompany their projection."[53] Besides utilizing film in an inappropriate way, film was in general considered by the military officials as "one of the smallest irons they have in the fire" and as a "hobby"[54] for those on the War College's training committee. To the army officials, film did not appear to be a serious tool for military training.

Nevertheless, a notable number of military training films were produced during World War I, marking them as something more than a novelty. At Fort Sill alone, the signal corps shot 1,636 feet of footage for *Horses at War,* 2,045 feet of footage for *Remount Station Ft. Sill, Oklahoma,*[55] and 4,731 feet of footage for *Firing Practice at School of Artillery Fire, Ft. Sill, Okla.*[56]. The signal corps also shot 2,734 feet of training-film footage depicting infantry field practice at Camp Meade, Maryland. This footage was used to produce the Word War I training film series *The Training of the Soldier,* which consisted of at least thirty parts, each with a duration of one film reel.[57]

The army did produce military training films during World War I, but they were not used systematically for training purposes. However, it was during this period that the army gained professional knowledge from external film specialists about film production and gathered practical experience in how to integrate training films into a military system. Word War I ended, but the army kept its acquired knowledge about film production and continued to produce training films, which helped it prepare for the industrialized wars to come. In 1937 the one-reel training film *The Employment of the Machine Guns in the Defense* is described as the twenty-ninth in a new series of training films called *Official Training Films of the War Department.*[58]

CONCLUSION

Frank B. and Lillian Gilbreth are known for their industrial work. Between 1914 and 1918 they worked to transfer their concepts for boosting industrial efficiency to the military, both in Germany and in the United States. Due to the development of industrialized warfare, concepts from their industrial work proved to be newly relevant for the military. Film addressed the problem of how to organize the transfer of complex topics in military training into a standardized and predictable method. The military invested in film for this reason. From this perspective, the utilization of film in the military can be situated in the broader context of a film history on marginal forms of films including industrial films, scientific films, educational films, and vocational training films.[59]

Furthermore, the films I discussed here are part of a more specific history of army and military films. The case shows that the introduction and adaptation of film opened up "contested terrains" inside the military.[60] At the same time that film was being used as a practical tool to conduct military training, it also became part of the organizational discourse and struggle inside the military administration. I have argued that the main reason for these tensions was the diverse demands made upon film. First, it was thought that film should provide a standardized vocational training system to secure a continuous supply of well-trained soldiers for the ongoing war. Second, it was thought that film should make training efforts more efficient. And third, officials required that film should extend vocational training from purely physical exercises to the transfer of complex knowledge to an expanding body of recruits. Specifically, the second and third aspects of film's remit conflicted with the organizational culture of the military. New ways of presenting facts, such as adding visual and dramatic interest to the films, as proposed by Gilbreth, compromised the perception of film as a proper tool for education by military officials. Gilbreth asserted that the strength of film was its capacity to blend learning and enjoyment—and that this would make training more interesting for the recruits and thus more efficient. At the same time, elements of the military administration did not welcome the new educational methods that were connected to the emerging medium of film.

Planning and production of vocational training films as well as the ambivalent reactions provoked by the film medium in military officials help us document the circumstances under which film was initially adopted by the military. The first experiments to produce military training films were halted. But the imperatives to integrate mechanized image production with military training continued, stretching to other uses in later conflicts—as examined in some of the following chapters.

NOTES

1. Research from film history includes Florian Hoof, *Engel der Effizienz: Eine Mediengeschichte der Unternehmensberatung: 1880–1930* (Konstanz, Germany: Konstanz University Press, 2015); Florian Hoof, *Angels of Efficiency: A Media History of Consulting* (New York: Oxford University Press, forthcoming); Scott Curtis, "Images of Efficiency," in *Films That Work: Industrial Film and the Productivity of Media,* ed. Vinzenz Hediger and Patrick Vonderau (Amsterdam: Amsterdam University Press, 2009), 85–99; Florian Hoof, "'The One Best Way': Bildgebende Verfahren der Ökonomie als strukturverändernder Innovationsschub der Managementtheorie ab 1860," *Montage AV* 15, no. 1 (2006): 123–38; Nicholas Sammond, "Picture This: Lillian Gilbreth's Industrial Cinema for the Home," *Camera Obscura* 21, no. 3 (2006): 103–32; and Laurel Graham, "Lillian Gilbreth and the Mental Revolution at Macy's, 1925–1928," *Journal of Management History* 6, no. 7 (2000): 285–305.

2. In business and management history, Frank and Lillian Gilbreth are perceived as predecessors of Frederick W. Taylor. See Harry Braverman, *Labor and Monopoly Capital: The Degradation of Work in the Twentieth Century* (New York: Monthly Review Press, 1974); and Horace B. Drury, *Scientific Management: A History and Criticism,* 3rd ed. (New York: Longmans, Green & Co., 1922 [1915]). Whereas Taylor used the stopwatch as an instrument to speed up production, the Gilbreths relied on film to record, analyze, and synthesize work movements in the industrial sector. Furthermore, their approach tended to the psychological and ergonomic aspects of workplace rationalization. Over time, due to the fact that they used film to raise the awareness level for their consulting firm, Frank and Lillian Gilbreth became prominent figures in American culture. Lillian, the first woman in the United States to be awarded a PhD in industrial psychology, was an equal partner in their consulting firm. But in the case of the training films for the military discussed here, Frank Gilbreth was the more active.

3. See, for example, Larry Wayne Ward, *The Motion Picture Goes to War: The U.S. Government Film Effort during World War I* (Ann Arbor, MI: UMI Research Press, 1985).

4. Anson Rabinbach, *The Human Motor: Energy, Fatigue, and the Origins of Modernity* (Berkeley: University of California Press, 1992).

5. Carl von Clausewitz, *Vom Kriege: Hinterlassenes Werk des Generals Carl von Clausewitz*, 18th ed. (Bonn: Dümmler, 1973 [1832]).

6. Hoof, *Engel der Effizienz*, 188–90.

7. Paul Cornish, "Machine Gun," in *International Encyclopedia of the First World War*, ed. Ute Daniel, Peter Gatrell, Oliver Janz, Heather Jones, Jennifer D. Keene, Alan Kramer, and Bill Nasson (Berlin: Freie Universität Berlin, 2014), accessed October 22, 2016, doi: 10.15463/ie1418.10779.

8. For more information on Marey, see Marta Braun, *Picturing Time: The Work of Etienne-Jules Marey (1830–1904)* (Chicago: University of Chicago Press, 1992), 320–48; Hoof, "'One Best Way,'" 125–26; and Rabinbach, *Human Motor*, 84–119.

9. Irene Witte to F. B. Gilbreth, August 10, 1915, Gilbreth Library of Management (hereafter cited as GLOM), Special Collections (hereafter cited as SPCOLL), NF 104/116–87, Purdue University Libraries.

10. Scientific management relies on the concept of "functional foremanship," which sharply distinguishes between hand labor and the management and planning of labor. For more information, see Frederick Taylor, *The Principles of Scientific Management* (Norwood, MA: Plimpton Press, 1911).

11. Hoof, *Engel der Effizienz*, 190–226.

12. Frank B. Gilbreth, "Method and Apparatus for the Study and Correction of Motions," US-Pat. no. 1.199.980, filed May 23, 1913, granted October, 3, 1916.

13. F. B. Gilbreth to L.M. Gilbreth, January 14, 1914, GLOM, SPCOLL, NF 91/813–6, Purdue University Libraries.

14. F. B. Gilbreth to L.M. Gilbreth, January 16, 1914, GLOM, SPCOLL, NF 91/813–6, Purdue University Libraries.

15. Ibid.

16. Jane Lancaster, *Making Time: Lillian Moller Gilbreth—A Life beyond "Cheaper by the Dozen"* (Lebanon, NH: Northeastern University Press, 2004), 144.

17. Norbert Elias, *Studien über die Deutschen: Machtkämpfe und Habitusentwicklung im 19. und 20. Jahrhundert* (Frankfurt am Main: Suhrkamp, 1989).

18. F. B. Gilbreth to L.M. Gilbreth, January 31, 1914, GLOM, SPCOLL, NF 91/813–6, Purdue University Libraries.

19. F. B. Gilbreth to L.M. Gilbreth, January 23, 1914, GLOM, SPCOLL, NF 91/813–6, Purdue University Libraries.

20. Braun, *Picturing Time;* Philipp Sarasin, "Der öffentlich sichtbare Körper: Vom Spektakel der Anatomie zu den 'Curiosités physiologiques,'" in *Physiologie und industrielle Gesellschaft*, ed. Philipp Sarasin and Jakob Tanner (Frankfurt am Main: Suhrkamp, 1998), 419–52.

21. F. B. Gilbreth to L. M. Gilbreth, January 18, 1914, GLOM, SPCOLL, NF 91/813–6, Purdue University Libraries.

22. There is evidence that, due to censorship issues or other strategic reasons, Frank Gilbreth refrained from documenting these contacts. There is also the possibility that the inventory of the Gilbreth Papers might have been altered afterward concerning this aspect.

23. Ward, *Motion Picture Goes to War*, 1.

24. For details on the distinction between scientific "film" and ordinary "movie," see Hoof, *Engel der Effizienz*, 292–96.

25. Frank Gilbreth and Lillian M. Gilbreth, *Applied Motion Study: A Collection of Papers on the Efficient Method to Industrial Preparedness* (New York: Sturgis & Walton Company, 1917).

26. Brian Price, "One Best Way: Frank and Lillian Gilbreth's Transformation of Scientific Management, 1885–1940" (PhD diss., Purdue University, 1987), 401.

27. Mark E. Grotelueschen, "Warfare 1917–1918 (USA)," in *International Encyclopedia of the First World War*, ed. Ute Daniel, Peter Gatrell, Oliver Janz, Heather Jones, Jennifer D. Keene, Alan Kramer,

and Bill Nasson (Berlin: Freie Universität Berlin, 2014), accessed October 22, 2016, doi: 10.15463/ie1418.10021.

28. "Government Will Establish Military School on Campus," *Columbia Daily Spectator* 41, no. 62 (January 9, 1918). See also Michael Sragow, *Victor Fleming: An American Movie Master* (New York: Pantheon Books, 2008), 55–64.

29. Paddy Griffith, *Battle Tactics of the Western Front: The British Army's Art of Attack, 1916–18* (New Haven, CT: Yale University Press, 1994); Jeffrey LaMonica, "Infantry," in *International Encyclopedia of the First World War*, ed. Ute Daniel, Peter Gatrell, Oliver Janz, Heather Jones, Jennifer D. Keene, Alan Kramer, and Bill Nasson (Berlin: Freie Universität Berlin, 2014), accessed October 22, 2016, doi: 10.15463/ie1418.10773.

30. Price, "One Best Way," 402.

31. Frank Gilbreth, "Applications of Motion Study: Its Use in Developing Best Methods of Work," *Management and Administration* 7, no. 9 (1924): 295.

32. Price, "One Best Way," 402.

33. Sragow, *Victor Fleming*, 56.

34. Donald Crafton, *Before Mickey: The Animated Film, 1898–1928* (Cambridge, MA: MIT Press, 1982), 158.

35. Richard Lindstrom, "Science and Management: Popular Knowledge, Work, and Authority in the Twentieth-Century United States" (PhD diss., Purdue University, 2000), 227.

36. F. B. Gilbreth to O. O. Ellis, December 31, 1917, GLOM, SPCOLL, NF 158/948–5, Purdue University Libraries.

37. Lindstrom, "Science and Management," 228.

38. F. B. Gilbreth to O. O. Ellis, January 12, 1918, GLOM, SPCOLL, NF 120/827–5, Purdue University Libraries.

39. Ibid.

40. *Examples of the Use of Motion Pictures in Military Training*, training film no. 0029, Records of the Office of the Chief Signal Officer (hereafter ROCSO), record group (hereafter RG) 111, National Archives at College Park, College Park, MD (hereafter NACP).

41. Hoof, *Engel der Effizienz*, 239–44.

42. F. B. Gilbreth to L. M. Gilbreth, February 3, 1918, GLOM, SPCOLL, NF 112/813–8, Purdue University Libraries.

43. Price, "One Best Way," 402.

44. *The Browning Automatic Rifle*, miscellaneous film no. 534, ROCSO, RG 111, NACP. The archival documentation states that this film might have been produced in 1925. But since the rifle was introduced in 1917 and the footage is partly filmed in the same setting and with the same style as the film *The Browning Machine Gun (First Section)*, it is likely that the film was produced in 1918.

45. *Field Artillery Training in the United States, 1918–1919*, production files historical film (hereafter PFHF) no. 1203, ROCSO, RG 111, NACP.

46. Quoted in Sragow, *Victor Fleming*, 57.

47. Intertitle in *The Browning Machine Gun (First Section)*, Original Films of Frank B. Gilbreth, Library of Congress, Washington, Motion Pictures, Broadcasting and Recorded Sound Division, Prelinger Collection.

48. Hoof, *Engel der Effizienz*, 245–51.

49. Maria Montessori, *The Montessori Method* (New York: Frederick A. Stokes Company, 1912).

50. Sragow, *Victor Fleming*, 57–58; Lindstrom, "Science and Management," 231.

51. *Training Activities of the 83rd Division, Camp Sherman, Ohio, 1917–1918* shows the training of the American expeditionary forces by French army officials with French weapons including the Chauchat machine gun. See *Training Activities of the 83rd Division, Camp Sherman, Ohio, 1917–1918*, PFHF no. 1210, ROCSO, RG 111, NACP.

52. Lindstrom, "Science and Management," 233.

53. Ibid., 228.

54. Ibid.

55. *Cavalry Training in the United States, 1917–1918*, PFHF no. 1201, ROCSO, RG 111, NACP.

56. *Field Artillery Training in the United States, 1918–1919*, PFHF no. 1203, ROCSO, RG 111, NACP.

57. *The Browning Automatic Rifle*, miscellaneous film no. 534, ROCSO, RG 111, NACP.

58. *The Employment of Machine Guns in the Defense;* Historical Film no. 1176, ROCSO, RG 111, NACP.

59. See Oliver Gaycken, *Devises of Curiosity: Early Cinema and Popular Science* (New York: Oxford University Press 2016); Scott Curtis, *The Shape of Spectatorship: Art, Science, and Early Cinema in Germany* (New York: Columbia University Press, 2015); Hoof, *Engel der Effizienz;* Devon Orgeron, Marsha Orgeron, and Dan Streible, eds., *Learning with the Lights Off: Educational Film in the United States* (New York: Oxford University Press, 2012); Charles R. Acland and Haidee Wasson, eds., *Useful Cinema* (Durham, NC: Duke University Press, 2011); and Vinzenz Hediger and Patrick Vonderau, eds., *Films That Work: Industrial Film and the Productivity of Media* (Amsterdam: Amsterdam University Press, 2009).

60. The concept of "contested terrains" has been deployed to understand and describe ongoing struggles and power fights between different stakeholders in an organization. See Richard Edwards, *Contested Terrain: The Transformation of the Workplace in the Twentieth Century* (New York: Basic Books, 1979).

11

FROM WARTIME INSTRUCTION TO SUPERPOWER CINEMA

Maintaining the Military-Industrial Documentary

Noah Tsika

During World War II, the United States military embraced documentary film as an especially adaptable pedagogic agent, one that could instruct both new recruits and seasoned soldiers, build institutional consensus, and assuage civilians' anxieties about the national costs of combat. Developing its film program within a distinctly intermedial economy, the military frequently combined documentary enunciation with other sources of instruction, including radio broadcasts and transcriptions, phonograph records, pamphlets, and symposia. The institution thus fused diverse forms of knowledge in order to redefine the borders between soldier and civilian, officer and infantryman, and Hollywood and the US Army Signal Corps, the latter of which produced over two thousand wartime documentaries in New York starting in 1942. From dramatic navy features to self-reflexive army shorts, and from documentaries produced "for soldiers' eyes only" to those given the widest possible distribution, these films functioned simultaneously as vehicles of practical instruction and tools of public relations, reflecting the military's multidirectional investment in "useful cinema." Such a cinema has, as Charles R. Acland and Haidee Wasson have shown, "as much to do with the maintenance and longevity of institutions seemingly unrelated to cinema as it does with cinema per se."[1]

In this chapter, I examine the military's cultivation of documentary as a form of "useful cinema," focusing on activities initiated during World War II. I argue that the military's emphasis on formal hybridity and pedagogic adaptability was a strategic part of a broader attempt to naturalize its newly massive scale and ensure its permanence. Through its wartime output, the military managed to advance an idea of nonfiction film that dramatically expanded the contours of "the documentary" even while drawing inspiration from select aspects of documentary history and theory. As apt to borrow footage from Hollywood as to tout a thoroughly original observational style, and as "at home" in a deployment center as in a private manufacturing plant, wartime military films ushered state documentary into a new aesthetic and material flexibility, a new openness to diverse and sometimes competing uses and arenas of reception. For even when the armed forces identified them as timely documents designed to catalyze an Allied victory, many military films were designed to last—to remain useful tools of the American military-industrial state, whether screened in conjunction with the public-education initiatives of local newspapers, excerpted for use in private manufacturing plants, or presented to high school students as sources of instruction and inspiration.[2] Examined in detail, they defy a certain documentary mythology—the notion that the war years represented a period of stasis for documentary cinema, during which crude patriotic mandates prevented the military film from acquiring the kind of formal and ideological features that would render it "relevant" during peacetime. In *War and Cinema,* Paul Virilio provides the plainly erroneous assertion that the military's wartime documentaries "were withdrawn from circulation" immediately following Japan's surrender—an assertion that thoroughly ignores the nontheatrical distribution networks that multiplied after 1945.[3] What I aim to do, in the space of this chapter, is begin a revisionist history of wartime military documentaries—one that not only acknowledges their status as documentaries (and thus their implications for documentary history and theory), but also considers their lasting value for institutions (the army, the navy, the marine corps, the air force, the coast guard) committed to their own permanence as well as to that of the war economy. Far from halting documentary's development, World War II marked a period of intense debate about documentary's scope and significance, setting the stage for the ideological obsolescence of the newsreel and the emergence of an adaptable model of audiovisual education—one that transcended theatrical spectatorship and transformed the immediate postwar period into what Zoë Druick has characterized in terms of "an unprecedented utilization of film for political ends, intensive and extensive, covert and explicit, educational and entertaining."[4]

The nontheatrical exhibition of nonfiction film was hardly a military invention, but it would acquire a new discursive force during and after World War II—a new legitimacy as part of the campaign first to win the war and finally to assure the ascendance of the American armed forces amid efforts to spread "freedom and democracy" around the world. The military nurtured a comprehensive view of nontheatrical-film reception, regarding this sweeping arena as containing not only future soldiers but also strategically essential manufacturers—not only those directly tied to the armed forces but also those capable of acceding to the permanence and versatility of a large-scale military. In this sense, then, the adaptability of the military documentary—its calculated capacity to infiltrate any number of nontheatrical spaces and with any number of official and tacit justifications—

mirrored that of the expansionist, increasingly interventionist institution itself. If the military could travel into previously overlooked zones in order to claim hegemony there, so could its many documentaries. Contrary to a dismissive suspicion that has, regrettably, calcified into common sense in the field of film studies, the military's nonfiction works were widely considered documentaries during World War II, and they certainly merit the label today. While the term "training film" has held sway in military circles since as early as 1940, when the army established its Training Film Production Laboratory in Fort Monmouth, New Jersey, the documentary value of the films falling under this classification should hardly be in question. The point is not to deny the significance of various subcategories (training films/"nuts and bolts" films, "film bulletins," "morale films," and so on) but to consider what the military's own nonfiction films—and especially their diverse uses—have to teach us about documentary history and theory. As Major General Dawson Olmstead, the army's chief signal officer, announced in September 1942, the military's filmmaking goal was documentary-specific—to move beyond merely "recording events for news and history" by accommodating something closer to a Griersonian conception of the "creative treatment" of actual and probable experiences.[5] This goal applied to the sizable category of "training films" as well as to many other categories of military-film production. Such films—works of nonfiction that offer basic truth claims and involve the creative, often dramatic shaping of factual material—provide a powerful case study of the extent to which "useful cinema" has often rested upon vast ambitions for documentary as an aesthetically complex vehicle not only of training but also of public relations. As Joris Ivens, himself an employee of the US Army Signal Corps, noted in 1942, "We must learn to think of documentary as requiring a wide variety of styles—all for the purpose of maximum expressiveness and conviction."[6] John Grierson himself, in his "First Principles of Documentary," may have denigrated educational, scientific, industrial, and training films as "lower categories" of filmmaking far removed from the lofty echelons of documentary proper, but there is little reason to believe that his logic was shared in military circles. In fact, an abundance of evidence points to documentary's carefully engineered adaptability within and in the service of the armed forces.[7] In this chapter, then, I presume that "training films" are a subset of the broader category of documentary. I also suggest that the category of "training films" itself can be used broadly to name not just films that prepared soldiers, but also those that prepared civilians and industrial partners alike for an enduring, naturalized, trusting relationship with the military-industrial state.

PUBLICIZING MILITARY-INDUSTRIAL TRAINING

One of the most salient features of the wartime military film was its shifting, sometimes incompatible itineraries, which reflected the military's belief that cinema could be useful as a source of instruction on both an ad hoc and an enduring basis. For instance, John Ford's signal corps documentary *Sex Hygiene* (1941), produced in collaboration with the Office of the Surgeon General and the Research Council of the Academy of Motion Picture Arts and Sciences, remained in institutional circulation for three decades. Neither disposable instruments nor treasured works of art, wartime military films are prime examples of the functionality and durability of "useful cinema"—the filmic tools through which the military advanced an institutionally convenient conception of documentary at a time of widespread mobilization. As Jonathan Kahana argues, state documentary "addresses its viewers as citizens," inviting them "to recognize that by interpreting the documentary text, or code, they take part in an ideal form of national community"[8] For its part, the military-sponsored nonfiction film—a particular type of state documentary that, for the duration of the war, became the dominant form of government film production in the United States—sought to position its spectators as diverse "war workers," situating them in terms of the following, often overlapping categories: soldiers, private arms manufacturers, and civilians capable (at the very least) of purchasing war bonds at their local movie theaters. In the 1940s, the military documentary became a means of soliciting broad spectatorial identification with the military itself—an ideological task that was hardly limited to wartime exigencies, and that troubles conventional accounts of state propaganda, which tend to reduce World War II training films to modest, temporary dimensions. Contrary to such accounts, these were, as the military itself maintained, "motion pictures of documentary importance."[9] Some were, to be sure, strictly utilitarian (such as short, step-by-step guides to lubricating machine guns), but even these were routinely reused by a range of filmmakers committed to the realist representation of the armed forces. They were also repurposed by the military itself, including on the army's public-service television program *The Big Picture*, nearly a thousand episodes of which were produced between 1951 and 1971. Wartime military documentaries remained useful as more than just B-roll material, as *The Big Picture*'s regular practice of using footage from signal corps archives attests. The military's nonfiction films, produced with the intent to train and educate, were also remediated to fulfill a number of seemingly unrelated aims. They entered union halls (such as those of the United Auto Workers) in order to foster a lasting sense of the connectedness of labor and military might. They also made their way into Rotary clubs in order to cultivate an appreciation for military intervention as a humanitarian affair.[10]

The military's film program was predicated not only on a sense of the sheer utility of documentary as a fundamentally pedagogic enterprise, but also on the genre's capacity to "honestly" promote identification with the military and its shifting goals. This included the use of footage shot to document war activities as much as to expressly teach or train. A key player in this context was the War Department's

Bureau of Public Relations (BPR), which in 1945 invited "any individual, group or local theater" to request in writing the "privilege" of screening images that allegedly could not be seen elsewhere—that exploded the boundaries of documentary as a civilized enterprise even while preserving many of the instructional and citizen-building ideals that Grierson had championed.[11] The BPR, which was founded in February 1941, maintained a direct line to the American popular press via a privately run propaganda organization known as the Writers' War Board, and it often served as an unofficial mechanism for marketing and distributing military documentaries to the general public. Toward the end of the war, the BPR was, for instance, regularly reminding prominent American publishers of the existence of footage of concentration camps, occasionally exhorting those publishers to run stories and sidebars devoted to the availability of what it termed "atrocity films"— all as part of its "strategy of truth," a manifesto of sorts (shared by the army's Information and Education Division and the Office of War Information) that identified the military's documentary praxis as a particularly honest enterprise.[12] In pursuing its goal of communicating "to the general public" the exceptionality of the wartime military documentary, the BPR did more than just wait for requests from civilian quarters. Before it was phased out in September 1945, returning to the broader functions of the War Department general staff, the BPR took an active, prescriptive approach, regularly instructing the signal corps to ship 16mm prints of allegedly "unprecedented" works to the offices of various American newspapers (including the *New York Times* and the *St. Louis Post-Dispatch*), requesting that they eventually be returned "by prepaid express."[13] At the same time, the signal corps was shipping special 35mm prints of military documentaries to various community organizations (such as the National Conference of Christians and Jews) that had rented commercial theaters for morning screenings of those nonfiction films that they took to be unique.[14]

"Atrocity films" were among the more observational of the military's wartime documentaries, simply recording in somber long takes the horrors of concentration camps as seen by members of the Ninety-ninth Infantry Division (including Hollywood filmmaker George Stevens). But such films were especially useful not only as reflections of documentary's visual and evidentiary power, but also as advertisements for the military's capacity to "liberate" and as indices of the evils against which the institution would ostensibly continue to fight. These films asked spectators to identify with the military as an ultimately humanitarian collection of institutions and with documentary as a humanizing discourse—a way of improving Americans by educating them about concentration camps and exposing them to the experiences of individual victims. On May 28, 1945, just under three weeks after VE-Day, an audience of five hundred saw the army's *German Atrocities Unexpurgated* (1945), along with Frank Capra's *Your Job in Germany* (1945), at the Museum of Modern Art.[15] In St. Louis, an estimated eighty thousand people saw these films in a number of theatrical and nontheatrical settings, in a series of screenings arranged by the *St. Louis Post-Dispatch*.[16] An additional 177 American towns and cities hosted screenings of *German Atrocities Unexpurgated* through the organizational efforts of the BPR, the Writers' War Board, and local newspapers, and by the summer of 1945, the National Conference of Christians and Jews was arranging for screenings of the film throughout New York City—including at the historic Normandie Theatre on Park Avenue and 53rd Street, and at the more modest Circle Theater in the Bronx.[17] The wide circulation of *German Atrocities Unexpurgated* was not without controversy, however, indicating that military documentaries were hardly the seamless agents of unification that the armed forces hoped they would be, however successfully they managed to tap into a national imaginary that valorized industry, martial strength, and global exploration. The *Milwaukee Deutsche Zeitung*, one of seven German-language newspapers in the United States in 1945, protested the BPR's suggestion that it arrange for public screenings of *German Atrocities Unexpurgated*. In an open letter, the newspaper's editor, who had previously doubted the authenticity of still and moving images of the horrors at Buchenwald, claimed that the suggestion to screen *German Atrocities Unexpurgated* may have been "motivated by vengefulness, or intended to stir up animosity and hatred against Germans as a race." Rather than refusing to screen the film, however, the editor of the *Milwaukee Deutsche Zeitung* simply requested that it be supplemented by a film about "the frightfully destroyed German cities and the millions of innocent women and children buried under the ruins of these once proud and flourishing cities." The military, with its vast archive of wartime documentaries, readily furnished this in the form of *The Battle of Peace* (1945), a signal corps film about the US military government in Germany that features observational footage of German ruins and outlines efforts to "rebuild and rehabilitate" them.[18] It was not a particular documentary per se that upset the newspaper's editor, then, but the genre's inflection as a tool of the military's public-relations apparatus—one that, in offering visible evidence of Germany's crimes against humanity, could only obscure the military's own role in spreading misery and destruction. The editor and staff took umbrage at the wide circulation and capacity to "mislead" of the "horrific" *German Atrocities Unexpurgated*. Nevertheless, the *Milwaukee Deutsche Zeitung* dutifully organized public screenings of the film, demonstrating that a contested military documentary could enjoy as broad and diversely functional a distribution pattern as its more agreeable counterparts.

LICENSING THE MILITARY-INDUSTRIAL DOCUMENTARY

The military had an ideological as well as material stake in circulating its films beyond its own institutional parameters. Investing in the production and active and wide circulation of nontheatrical nonfiction films helped to ensure the prosperity of the American armed forces, whether by appealing to students in the classroom, workers in the factory, congregants in the church, or patrons of the museum.[19] Even those wartime films that were initially withheld from public circulation—"classified"—received broader distribution later in the war or during the immediate postwar period. For instance, *Combat Exhaustion* (1945) was first categorized as "restricted," its exhibition limited to army officers, medical personnel, and their patients. Yet archival evidence indicates that, like John Huston's *Let There Be Light* (1946) and many others, the film was eventually screened in civilian psychiatric hospitals, and also made available as a source of stock footage for documentary films and television programs. It was also held by select libraries.[20]

Military classifications were not the only challenges to the wide circulation of World War II training films, however, since the formal hybridity of these films was often the result of complicated and prohibitive licensing arrangements. Produced in the wake of VE-Day, the signal corps documentary *G-5 in Action* (1945), which addresses "the job of military government" and outlines efforts to "de-Nazify" and "demilitarize" Europe while caring for displaced persons, was initially intended for exhibition only in military settings, pursuant to an agreement with Paramount Pictures and several other studios whose original musical scores are featured in the film. In fact, *G-5 in Action* makes use of no fewer than fifteen Hollywood scores (from such films as Jacques Tourneur's *Cat People* [1942] and Jean Renoir's *This Land Is Mine* [1943]), but it also, in a further indication of the longevity and adaptability of wartime military documentaries, features excerpts from the unpublished scores of three other army films: *Tunisian Victory* (1944), *The Negro Soldier* (1944), and *Diary of a Sergeant* (1945).[21] When, over two years after the film's completion, the War Department announced its plans to dramatically expand the circulation of *G-5 in Action,* signal corps executives were obliged to contact those who held the rights to both the sounds and the images that the film "incorporates." A 1947 letter to Paramount summarizes the initial agreement between the studio and the signal corps ("Clearance was granted . . . for military personnel showings only") before stressing that "public exhibition of this film is now desired." The letter concludes with the War Department's request that Paramount "extend the necessary clearance" in order to enable the wide distribution of *G-5 in Action,* including to schools, factories, and any number of other nontheatrical settings.[22] Three days earlier, the signal corps had sent a similar letter to Look-Ampix Productions—a collaboration between *Look* magazine and American Pictures, Inc., that had produced and distributed numerous nonfiction short films since 1940—in order to request "full commercial exhibition rights . . . to the public on a worldwide basis" for *G-5 in Action,* which features footage of a boys' marching band taken from the Look-Ampix production *Crisis.*[23] What had made wartime military films so strategically relevant—so adaptable to a range of exhibition contexts within the armed forces—was the inclusion of varied audiovisual elements and styles of argumentation adopted from a range of military and extramilitary sources. Yet this amalgamating approach also presented obstacles to a given film's broader distribution.

The military was, nevertheless, committed to surmounting these obstacles to its entangled methods of production and distribution through the signal corps and other subdivisions devoted to nonfiction film. This commitment entailed aggressive and ongoing negotiation with rights holders in order to ensure the expansive and continued circulation of the military's hybridized documentaries, largely on the assumption that formal hybridity would continue to pay diverse dividends, appealing to a vast array of spectators in a variety of theatrical and nontheatrical venues. If a rights holder withheld clearance, military technicians could simply recut the film in question, or replace its entire soundtrack. For example, when five of the eight film studios from which the signal corps had borrowed music for its 1945 documentary *The Army Nurse* withheld clearance, the film was recut, enabling it to be broadcast on network television in 1953.[24] In the case of the postwar life of *G-5 in Action,* the military hoped to continue using the film to promote its role as a global watchdog—to screen it both theatrically and nontheatrically, both commercially and on a nonprofit basis, everywhere from major American movie houses to overseas classrooms and makeshift screening spaces. This, they believed, would better ensure broad recognition of American military might and democratic efficacy during the Cold War. Thus by the early 1950s the adaptability of the military documentary was marshaled for a host of new purposes as the military sought an expanded global legitimacy that occasionally hinged on the revival of World War II training films—precisely those works that had established a language of visual education aimed at promoting military might.

The durability of wartime military films meant that they survived through long distribution cycles and diverse repurposing strategies and, in the process, transformed "from wartime propaganda to superpower propaganda."[25] Rather than disappearing into the ether, these films persisted, both militarily and well beyond the borders of the armed forces. The survival of military documentaries was not accidental—a consequence of the piecemeal circulation of "stock footage"—but was, rather, the product of the military's careful attention to various sites of spectatorship. Occasionally, the military was forced to negotiate with local censors, including those threatening to prevent *The Negro Soldier* (1944) from reaching the United Auto Workers. The union had hoped—on the army's own recommendation—to use the film to prepare for racial integration in the workplace and to improve the social experience of the assembly line. Yet its aims were complicated by local censorship boards hoping to suppress so "racially charged" a film. The military prevailed, however, and *The Negro Soldier* was eventually screened for union members, PTA members, prisoners, MoMA visitors, and audiences assembled by the American Council on Race Relations.[26] The case of *The Negro Soldier* thus attests to the tenacity with which the military often pursued screening opportunities for its wartime documentaries even long after the end of hostilities. This commitment to longevity and wide relevance can be seen in the military's repeated efforts to alter the most arcane of documentaries in order to "invite" potential spectators, and to lay the discursive groundwork for the films' inclusion in any number of possible exhibition sites.[27]

The sheer hybridity of the typical wartime military film was the essence of a multipronged effort to mobilize spectators in support of the emergent military-industrial state. The success of this documentary-specific mobilization effort can be seen in the response of the privately owned Empire Plow Company to John Huston's *Report from the Aleutians* (1943), a signal corps production that standard histories of documentary cinema tend to position as a minor, institutionally super-fluous work.[28] Focusing on US military strategy in the Aleutian Islands campaign, Huston's film was screened for both soldiers and civilians, and it so impressed executives at the Empire Plow Company that one of them, C. C. Keller, wrote to the War Activities Committee to request a print. According to Keller, since the company's patented Airplane Landing Mat (Pierced Plank Type) "is shown quite extensively" in *Report from the Aleutians,* Huston's film could serve as a "morale builder" for the men engaged in its manufacture. Recognizing the hybrid and readily adaptable style of many American military documentaries of the era, Keller outlined his company's plans to further "transform" *Report from the Aleutians,* which involved intercutting the film with original footage of the company's production line, the better to take employees "thru fabrication [of steel landing mats] on thru use [of these mats] by our Armed Forces."[29] Mimicking the military's own rhetoric for describing its wartime training-film program—rhetoric that the BPR routinely disseminated to the general public via press releases, and that often appeared on-screen in wordy opening crawls—Keller demonstrated that the utility of the military documentary extended well beyond basic training and into the realm of private industry. He eventually oversaw the transformation of Huston's film into an "in-house" advertisement for the Empire Plow Company, and his labors were made possible by the military's amenability to the remixing of its documentaries, even when this remixing was orchestrated independently of the armed forces.[30] Where "atrocity films" invited diverse spectators to identify with the military's allegedly humanitarian aims, other documentaries (in both their original and "transformed" versions) exhorted factory workers to identify the military as the recipient of their manufactured goods—the direct, globally forceful beneficiary of their labors.

INTERMEDIALITY

As formulated within the armed forces during World War II, cinema's military-industrial complex was attuned as much to the precise aims of the institution as to the discursive contours of the broader social imaginary in whose name it fought. Wartime military films not only offer insight into the general institutional utility of documentary in the 1940s; they also reveal that the military's expansive, accommodating conception of documentary legitimacy often embraced self-reflexive gestures, obviously staged sequences, and folksy asides designed to defuse concerns about the totalitarian potential of state-sponsored cinema. Such concerns— widely expressed in the popular press and in major Hollywood films—were the emotive effects of a broad cultural awareness of Axis-produced documentaries in general and of Leni Riefenstahl's *Triumph of the Will* (1935) in particular. In express opposition to the uniformly lionizing techniques that Riefenstahl employed in the service of National Socialism, a number of military filmmakers sutured facetiousness to otherwise serious institutional imperatives, injecting allegedly healthy doses of audacity—as in the ribald, scatological *Private SNAFU* series (1943–45)— into efforts to mold the minds of soldiers. In some cases, military documentaries even went so far as to poke fun at officers, and it was precisely the intermedial economy in which military films were produced that convinced officials of the permissibility of such iconoclasm. Like so-called comic-strip manuals—cartoonish step-by-step guides to executing complex military maneuvers—training films were permitted a certain flexibility precisely because their educational counterparts (such as live lectures and technical journals) were more "serious."

Consider, for instance, a 1943 training manual entitled *Your Body in Flight*, which furnishes a defense of its own comic-strip form. "Pictures are easier to remember than words!" proclaims an introductory note to the reader, which proceeds to trumpet not just the general documentary qualities but also the specific military legitimacy of cartoons—an argument that clearly reflects the institutional popularity of the defensive rhetoric surrounding *Private SNAFU*, with its irreverent pedagogy, but also the contentious, far-from-Griersonian notion that "silliness" could adequately instruct: "This book is done for fast remembering. Military training has accepted the 'thought-picture' method: it is just as scientific to present these facts in cartoon as it is to do them by diagram and chart." Rendering resistance in the figure of an aged professor who foolishly wags his finger ("Tsk! Tsk! It's all very unscientific!"), the manual provides a rebuttal in the form of a humanized, happy airplane that speaks on behalf of its pilot: "This flyer understands what he's reading!" it cheerfully announces.[31] Such gestures were doubly educative, and they extended to the military's self-reflexive documentary films: on one level, these films attempted to convey immediately useful information; on another, they sought to engage in—and end—contemporaneous debates about whether documentary, as a pedagogic category extending from typed bulletins to audiovisual media, could possibly sustain a "cartoonish," unashamedly attention-grabbing approach. So pronounced was the military's commitment to animation as a documentary device that it regularly outsourced the production of official documentary films to various animation studios. Even so serious a subject as mental illness received the Disney treatment: the army's animated *Ward Care of Psychotic Patients* (1944) was made by Walt Disney Productions under the supervision of military psychiatrists Lauren H. Smith and Olin B. Chamberlain.

In a 1939 essay, Richard Griffith endeavored to mitigate the ambiguity in which the term "documentary" had been mired since Grierson's influential 1929 definition of the genre as representing "the creative treatment of actuality," and he concluded that the cartoon form was much too "creative" for a documentary film, however factually accurate, to lay claim to it.[32] For Griffith, accessibility—the pandering implicit in the use of eye-catching animation—was the currency of advertising, not of documentary. If the military adopted a different approach, it was by promoting a certain slippage between the two categories, such that its documentary films could always be readable as advertisements for the institution itself, even long after an Allied victory. In its production of flexible, hybridized documentaries, the military was thus dismissive of the kinds of taxonomic hierarchies and bourgeois taste claims at the center of much of the era's documentary criticism, embracing an eclecticism that was deemed necessary if a film was to transcend its immediate purpose and satisfy a diversity of spectators, securing their trust in the ever-expanding armed forces. In perceiving the lasting value of institutional advocacy as a component of practical instruction, the military presciently embraced artistic license—a hybridic creativity that would serve it well in the immediate postwar period, as its films were transformed from timely instruments of training into the resourceful, broadly inspirational achievements of the recent past.

If many military documentaries (with the conspicuous exception of "atrocity films," which tended to be strictly and somberly observational) were granted a certain freedom from "stuffiness," that did not prevent them from attracting the attention of those capable of countering their occasional irreverence. In fact, the military rarely afforded training films the exclusive authority to instruct personnel, instead relying on various "in-house" experts to explain or at least echo their most salient points (due in part to the sheer, sometimes ambiguous hybridity that is the subject of this essay). As Nathaniel Brennan argues in his chapter in this volume, social scientists and cinema scholars were instrumental in convincing the military of the importance of live, embodied, "expert" testimony as a supplement to film spectatorship. The formal experimentation and discursive flexibility deemed essential to the training film's successful transition into a variety of civilian venues were precisely those factors that seemed to demand an expert presence in the military's own sites of exhibition. Military officers and other instructors routinely provided the "moral disposition" that Ronald Walter Greene sees in the "pastoral mode" of nontheatrical film exhibition in the 1920s and 1930s, extending into military settings the function of the "talking secretaries, teachers, and preachers who often lectured alongside, before, and after" screenings.[33] If, in other words, an individual training film dared undermine—or at least lightly spoof—military hierarchy, an officer would always be available (often for a postscreening question-and-answer session) to reestablish order, consolidating whatever institutional standards a cheeky documentary had, if only momentarily and fantasmatically, undone. Equally available were written documents that converged with various live performances (including simulations and step-by-step reenactments of proper combat techniques) in order to emphasize that intermediality—what Mary Simonson describes as "the articulation of a concept across media types"[34]—would inform soldiers' experiences of documentary cinema.

Wartime military films were far from uniform in their didacticism, and the strategic infusions of humor that characterize many of them were born of the military's interest in presenting its documentary enterprise as democratic and thus far removed from the purview of Axis propaganda. Formal experimentation was implicitly homologous with democratic expansiveness, the plasticity of the military documentary a symbol of the institution's departure not merely from the rigidity of typical documentary criticism but also from the fascism of Axis filmmaking. Considerably more complicated, though no less strategic, was the military's relationship to reenactment, which the institution not only recognized but also celebrated as a legitimate method in nonfiction filmmaking, the very essence of documentary artistry and authenticity. Pushing past the borders of documentary as understood by the likes of Grierson and Richard Griffith, and as practiced by the likes of Leni Riefenstahl and Fritz Hippler in the service of National Socialism, the military embraced methods more conventionally associated with fiction films, employing dramatization and reenactment to suit its own institutional imperatives. As a tool of the military-industrial state, one that extended well beyond the screen, this ethos of reenactment provided a road map for military filmmakers tasked with reproducing institutional claims.

Individual military documentaries—particularly those about the stubborn subject of combat trauma—were obsessively remade or "reimagined" throughout World War II and well into the postwar period. From 1944's *Psychiatric Procedures in the Combat Area* (an adaptation of several military documentaries about psychiatry) to 1947's *Shades of Gray* (a remake of Huston's *Let There Be Light*, among other works), these films moved almost immediately beyond institutional contexts in order to "reassure" potential employers about the viability of all veterans, even "nervously wounded" ones. By 1945, they were in heavy rotation in various manufacturing plants and were often heralded as ways to demonstrate to both employers and employees "the veteran's physical and mental coordination and his general intelligence."[35] Furthermore, manufacturers responsible for the continued supply

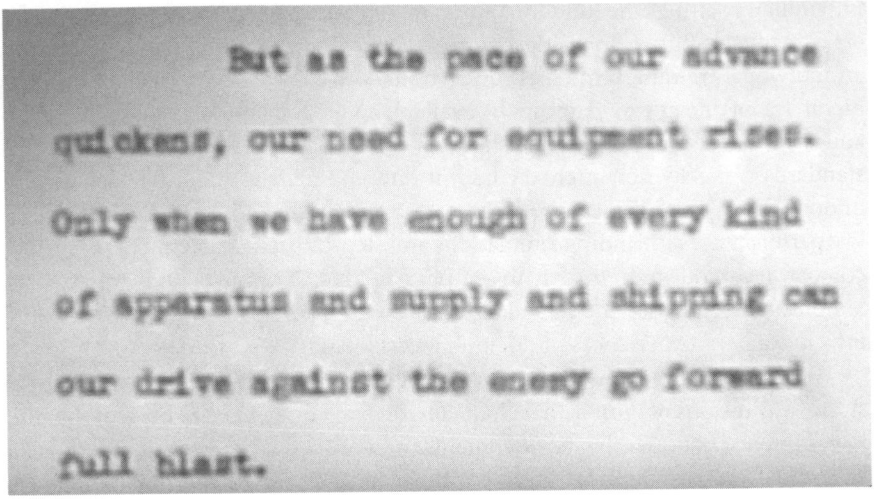

> But as the pace of our advance
>
> quickens, our need for equipment rises.
>
> Only when we have enough of every kind
>
> of apparatus and supply and shipping can
>
> our drive against the enemy go forward
>
> full blast.

FIGURE 11.1. An intertitle from the navy documentary *Return to Guam* (1944), which stresses the military's dependence on private industry for necessary materials. Such means were widely used in postwar efforts to normalize this dependency as the essence of the military-industrial state.

of armaments to the military were given frequent reminders of military needs, often in the form of films (such as those in the military's *Industrial Incentive* series) that simply restated the claims of their predecessors. The trade journal *Industrial Relations*, which began publication in 1942 and targeted "war work" (a category encompassing a range of manufacturing activities), ran advertisements for military documentaries that were readily available for use in factories and plants. A 1944 issue touted the navy film *Return to Guam* (1944), which stresses the military's increasing "need for equipment"—its commitment to gaining "enough of every kind of apparatus and supply and shipping."

The same issue features a section entitled "How to Use Films," which notes that all military documentaries "are sound films and cannot be run on silent projectors." Emphasizing the importance of screening these documentaries in various production sites, the better to cultivate worker appreciation for the military's vast needs, the journal warned manufacturers that there could be no conceivable excuse for avoiding the use of military films: "If you do not have a projector, a local film distributor can rent you excellent equipment."[36] Reminding readers that such major manufacturers as the Curtiss-Wright Corporation and the Caterpillar Tractor Company regularly exhibited the military's *Industrial Incentive* films, *Industrial Relations* presented the nontheatrical exhibition of military documentaries as a key component of management, a way of disciplining workers into respecting the scope of the new military-industrial state.

CONCLUSIONS

The military's wartime output of films both crystalized and catalyzed debates about documentary as, at once, a particular category of cinema, an adaptable teaching tool capable of accommodating other pedagogic forms, and an artistic pursuit. More specifically, wartime military films were, if not the most popular or the most profitable, then certainly the most functional and adaptable cinematic instruments of an emergent military-industrial state. As such, they bridged the gap between the social advocacy of state documentary characteristic of New Deal liberalism and the blatant institutional advocacy typical of mid-twentieth-century examples of industrial and sponsored film. In wartime military documentaries, appeals to "social progress" routinely coexist with references to industry; films that praise the wartime work of enlisted men and women simultaneously celebrate the assembly line (as in 1945's *Strictly Personal*). Such canny strategies set the stage for decades of military-sponsored theatrical and nontheatrical films that use formal experimentation and generic indeterminacy as vehicles for conveying institutional authority.

This earlier tendency has contemporary exemplars. Consider, for instance, Mike McCoy and Scott Waugh's *Act of Valor* (2012), which lies somewhere between documentary reenactment and Hollywood fiction, combining a variety of audiovisual sources and assimilating self-conscious claims to wide relevance in ways that recall the diverse strategies of wartime military films. Promoted as "a motion picture starring active-duty Navy SEALS," *Act of Valor* began as an instructional video that McCoy and Waugh produced for the navy's special warfare combatant-craft crewmen, and it embeds a commitment to recruitment, military-industrial expansion, and technological mastery in a hybrid form that it identifies as unprecedented. Like Peter Berg's *Lone Survivor* (2013), the making of which provided many military advisers with promotional materials for the institution's use—multiple ways of visualizing the operation of its equipment for active-duty soldiers and potential recruits—*Act of Valor* revived the military's earlier conception of documentary as a form of institutional advocacy with any number of sources and inexhaustible potential. Indeed, the relatively poor box-office performance of *Act of Valor* is immaterial in light of the military's multipronged and indefinite use of the film, as both a feature-length recruitment vehicle and an eminently divisible source of footage of navy equipment in need of continued manufacture. Unfolding from the visual perspectives of "real SEALS," *Act of Valor* further evokes the documentary devices of other media, especially the video-game franchise *Call of Duty*, with its "first-person shooter" aesthetic, which closely resembles simulations used in actual military exercises. The ideological success of wartime military films—the product of particular cultural and historical contingencies—may appear to have been short-lived in terms of the *longue durée* of American documentary. But if, by the early 1970s, antiwar documentaries had eclipsed military propaganda in terms of circulation and cultural impact, more-recent interventions in the form of massively successful video games suggest the rhetorical staying power of World War II films, particularly given their insistence on the intimate links between the military and private enterprise. Consider, for instance, the establishment in 2009 of the Call of Duty Endowment, a nonprofit foundation created by the company behind the titular video-game franchise, which is intended to help military veterans find employment, and which frequently relies on new forms of documentary instruction (such as YouTube videos and Facebook testimonials) in order to guide former soldiers and prepare potential employers.

There is a telling moment in Frederick Wiseman's documentary *Basic Training* (1971) that highlights the lasting pedagogic and public-relations utility of wartime military films—shorts and features wrongly believed to have fallen out of institutional use after the Allied victory. Introducing back-to-back film screenings to an auditorium full of men newly inducted into the army, a sergeant notes that this double bill combines new and old, bringing together, for instructional as well as inspirational purposes, a documentary about US policy in Southeast Asia (possibly the Defense Department's *Why Vietnam?* [1965]) and "an old one"—a World War II film that, based on the sergeant's description, is most likely the signal corps's *Hell for Leather* (1943), which explores army victories "through the ages," stressing the division's "undefeated" status. A historical docudrama, the ten-minute *Hell for Leather* was widely distributed for decades after its completion in 1943, often as part of the army's *Pride of Outfit* series, which, from World War II until as late as the 1990s, circulated among new and potential recruits in a variety of nontheatrical settings, including community centers and high school and college classrooms.[37]

As Wiseman's documentary suggests, the lasting utility of wartime military films was tied as much to their formal diversity as to their ideological adaptability. Made to facilitate Allied victory, they could later serve as advertisements for everything from limited conscription to global peacekeeping to private manufacturing. Whether produced at the Signal Corps Photographic Center or at the Training Films and Motion Picture Branch of the Bureau of Aeronautics, each wartime military documentary was, in its own way, an agent of the military-industrial state—an advertisement for a permanent large-scale military and a justification for increasing defense expenditures. Broad, nontheatrical distribution also contributed to rhetoric that positioned the military documentary as the opposite of the "mere" newsreel, which would soon obsolesce amid the disintegration of the Hollywood studio system and the rise of television broadcasting. The wartime military film was, however, not so much the anti-newsreel as the supra-newsreel—a form capable of rising above extant categories by assimilating all of them, a cannibalistic strategy of self-justification that lent the genre a broad and lasting utility.

ACKNOWLEDGMENTS

Support for this project was provided by a PSC-CUNY Award, jointly funded by the Professional Staff Congress and the City University of New York.

NOTES

1. Charles R. Acland and Haidee Wasson, "Introduction: Utility and Cinema," in *Useful Cinema,* ed. Charles R. Acland and Haidee Wasson (Durham, NC: Duke University Press, 2011), 4.

2. A key example of these public-education initiatives was that sponsored by the *St. Louis Post-Dispatch,* which arranged public screenings of two military documentaries—*German Atrocities Unexpurgated* (1945) and Frank Capra's *Your Job in Germany* (1945)—that cultivated a total audience of over eighty thousand civilians in the summer of 1945. See the Writers' War Board Monthly Report for July 1945 (no. 27, p. 1), in record group 111, Records of the Office of the Chief Signal Officer, 1860–1985, 111-M-1241 (hereafter cited as RG 111), box 10, folder labeled "Concentration Camp Atrocities," National Archives and Records Administration, College Park, MD (hereafter cited as NARA). An example of military documentaries being excerpted for use in private industry can be seen in the case of the Empire Plow Company, which endeavored to make extensive, "inspiring" use of John Huston's army film *Report from the Aleutians* (1943). See C. C. Keller to War Activities Committee, October 18, 1943, RG 111, box 3, NARA. Initially reserved for coast guard use, the navy's *The Inside Story of Seaman Jones* (1945), which dramatizes a young man's psychosomatic symptoms and their psychiatric treatment, was acquired in 1948 by the Nassau County School District for mandatory use in health-education classes throughout the county. "Yule Seal Sales Net $28,000 First Week," *Freeport (NY) Leader,* December 2, 1948, 7.

3. Paul Virilio, *War and Cinema: The Logistics of Perception,* trans. Patrick Camiller (London: Verso, 1989), 13.

4. Zoë Druick, "UNESCO, Film, and Education: Mediating Postwar Paradigms of Communication," in *Useful Cinema,* ed. Charles R. Acland and Heidi Wasson (Durham, NC: Duke University Press, 2011), 95.

5. Quoted in Richard Koszarski, "Subway Commandos: Hollywood Filmmakers at the Signal Corps Photographic Center," *Film History* 14, nos. 3/4 (2002): 302.

6. Joris Ivens, "Making Documentary Films to Meet Today's Needs," *American Cinematographer* 23, no. 7 (July 1942): 299.

7. John Grierson, "First Principles of Documentary," in *The Documentary Film Reader: History, Theory, Criticism,* ed. Jonathan Kahana (Oxford: Oxford University Press, 2016), 217–18.

8. Jonathan Kahana, *Intelligence Work: The Politics of American Documentary* (New York: Columbia University Press, 2008), 114.

9. This was the military's official position on its own films, and it was routinely communicated to the public via the Bureau of Public Relations. See Thomas Doherty, *Projections of War: Hollywood, American Culture, and World War II,* rev. ed. (New York: Columbia University Press, 1999 [1993]), 58.

10. For more on the United Auto Workers and the organization's use of the army documentary *The Negro Soldier,* see Thomas Cripps, *Making Movies Black: The Hollywood Message Movie from World War II to the Civil Rights Era* (Oxford: Oxford University Press, 1993), 113, 158. For more on the use of military documentaries in and by Dallas Rotary clubs, see the published edition of Susan D. Bachrach's U.S. Holocaust Memorial Museum exhibition *Liberation, 1945* (Washington, DC: United States Holocaust Memorial Council, 1995), 67.

11. Ibid.

12. For more on the Bureau of Public Relations, see RG 107, NARA.

13. See Colonel Emanuel Cohen to Joseph Pulitzer, May 25, 1945, in RG 111, box 10, folder labeled "Concentration Camp Atrocities," NARA.

14. Willard Johnson to Major Robert Benjamin, July 2, 1945, in RG 111, box 10, folder labeled "Concentration Camp Atrocities," NARA.

15. Writers' War Board Monthly Report for July 1945 (no. 27, p. 1), in RG 111, box 10, folder labeled "Concentration Camp Atrocities," NARA.

16. Writers' War Board Monthly Report for July 1945 (no. 27, p. 1), in RG 111, box 10, folder labeled "Concentration Camp Atrocities," NARA.

17. Johnson to Benjamin, July 2, 1945.

18. "Paper Asks 'Proof' of German War Loss," *Deseret News* (Salt Lake City, UT), June 19, 1945, 3. See also RG 111, box 10, folder labeled "Concentration Camp Atrocities," NARA.

19. Often at the behest of the BPR and the Writers' War Board, local newspapers, trade unions, and various civic organizations regularly organized screenings of military documentaries in all of these venues—and many more—well into the postwar period.

20. In the parlance of the military's film program, "restricted" was one step beyond "classified" in terms of the constraints that it placed upon a film's distribution and exhibition. For more on these constraints and how they applied to *Field Psychiatry for the General Medical Officer,* see Field Manual 21–7 and L. M. Barker to Commanding Officer, Signal Corps Photographic Center, "MB-5266, *Field Psychiatry for the General Medical Officer,*" April 10, 1945, RG 111, box 10, folder labeled "Field Psychiatry for the General Medical Officer," NARA. See also Jonathan Kahana and Noah Tsika, "*Let There Be Light* and the Military Talking Picture," in *Remaking Reality: US Documentary Culture after 1945,* ed. Sara Blair, Joseph Entin, and Franny Nudelman (Chapel Hill: University of North Carolina Press, forthcoming).

21. See the routing and work sheets and "Source of Material Report" in the *G-5 in Action* file in RG 111, box 10, NARA.

22. Major John S. Bardwell to Paramount Pictures, Inc., September 8, 1947, RG 111, box 10, NARA.

23. Major John S. Bardwell to Look-Ampix, September 5, 1947, RG 111, box 10, NARA.

24. For more on the copyright issues plaguing *The Army Nurse* in the immediate postwar period, see the clipping file on the film in RG 111, box 10, NARA.

25. This is Kirsten Ostherr's evocative phrase for describing the expansion of state-sponsored nonfiction film culture in the immediate postwar period. See Kirsten Ostherr, "Health Films, Cold War, and the Production of Patriotic Audiences: *The Body Fights Bacteria* (1948)," in *Useful Cinema,* ed. Charles R. Acland and Haidee Wasson (Durham, NC: Duke University Press, 2011), 118.

26. Cripps, *Making Movies Black,* 113, 158.

27. A signal corps routing and work sheet from late 1944 objects to the "rather stuffy" title of a training film then in preproduction ("Manufacture and Reworking of 60mm and 80mm Mortars"), arguing that even esoteric subjects deserve a palatable presentation, the better to ensure the "appeal" of a documentary beyond military contexts and to facilitate its transition into these new, previously unimagined arenas. If a "dull" title was a turn-off, preventing a film from being embraced or even requested by organizations not required to screen it, then so was rhetoric that suggested a similarity between military documentaries and other forms of nonfiction film such as newsreels. See "Routing & Work Sheet 10931: Project 13,205," RG 111, box 10, folder labeled "Combat Team," NARA.

28. Erik Barnouw, for instance, refers to the film as "routine," particularly in relation to Huston's later documentaries *San Pietro* (1945) and *Let There Be Light* (1946)—a claim that Gary Edgerton echoes in an essay on Huston's wartime work for the government. Erik Barnouw, *Documentary: A History of the Non-Fiction Film* (Oxford: Oxford University Press, 1993), 162; Gary Edgerton, "Revisiting the Recordings of Wars Past: Remembering the Documentary Trilogy of John Huston," in *Reflections in a Male Eye: John Huston and the American Experience,* ed. Gaylyn Studlar and David Desser (Washington, DC: Smithsonian Institution Press, 1999), 33–61.

29. C. C. Keller to War Activities Committee, October 18, 1943, RG 111, box 3, NARA.

30. Two months before Keller wrote to the War Activities Committee to request a print of *Report from the Aleutians,* another private citizen, Albert Gansberg, contacted the signal corps to request excerpts from the film—only those scenes featuring his son, First Lieutenant S. Gansberg. After consulting with the Bureau of Public Relations, which had no objection, the signal corps sent 16mm excerpts (specially processed at Eastman Kodak) to Gansberg for his own use, thus further confirming the flexibility with which the military approached the use-value of its wartime documentaries. See Colonel Curtis Mitchell to Colonel Barrett, August 11, 1943, RG 111, box 3, NARA.

31. US Army Air Forces, "Your Body in Flight: An Illustrated 'Book of Knowledge' for the Flyer," 20 July 1943, box 13, folder 5, John M. Murray Papers, Manuscript Division, Library of Congress, Washington, DC.

32. Richard Griffith, "Films at the Fair," in *The Documentary Film Reader: History, Theory, Criticism,* ed. Jonathan Kahana (Oxford: Oxford University Press, 2016), 312–21.

33. Ronald Walter Greene, "Pastoral Exhibition: The YMCA Motion Picture Bureau and the Transition to 16mm, 1928–1939," in *Useful Cinema,* ed. Charles R. Acland and Haidee Wasson (Durham, NC: Duke University Press, 2011), 224.

34. Mary Simonson, *Body Knowledge: Performance, Intermediality, and American Entertainment at the Turn of the Twentieth Century* (Oxford: Oxford University Press), 18.

35. Advertisement, *Industrial Relations: A Magazine for Employers* 3, no. 6 (October 1945): 28.

36. "How to Use Films," *Industrial Relations: A Magazine for Employers* 2, no. 7 (November 1944): 23.

37. See, for instance, Seerley Reid, Anita Carpenter, and Annie Rose Daugherty, *U.S. Government Films for Public Educational Use* (Washington, DC: Government Printing Office, 1955), 358.

12

FRAMING THE BOMB IN THE WEST

The View from Lookout Mountain

Susan Courtney

The history of nuclear weapons is also, in several crucial respects, a history of moving images. The history of atomic warfare, certainly, is marked *both* by spectacular displays of military power (first with the annihilation of Hiroshima on August 6, 1945, and then, just three days later, with that of Nagasaki) *and* by striking absences of film and photography documenting the ensuing mass death of over 180,000 people.[1] But in the United States, the history of testing nuclear and thermonuclear weapons—with detonations on land and at sea that were utterly real despite the hypothetical ring to the language of "tests"—was always captured in motion pictures. As Kevin Hamilton and Ned O'Gorman have recently put it: in addition to the considerable "technical [and] scientific data" that such images provided to those who developed the bomb, throughout the Cold War the logic of "deterrence made the display of American power central to [the] exercise of power."[2] That is, films of nuclear weapons tests "were means of establishing the credibility of the overwhelming nuclear threat before the adversary" and also "of communicating . . . American competence and control" of its "daunting new atomic arsenal"—to the Soviets, to US allies, and to the American public.[3] Yet while the screen histories that emerged as a result are considerable, they remain mostly unwritten.[4]

Focused on the period of US atmospheric (above-ground) testing on the continent, from 1945 to 1963, this chapter introduces two related concerns.[5] First, it describes some of the basic conditions and infrastructure of film production of nuclear weapons tests, including the government's secret military film studio dedicated to this work in the hills above Los Angeles. Second, it turns to the representational legacy that resulted, which was by no means limited to films made by or for the military. More specifically, it begins to consider how footage of atomic tests in New

Mexico and Nevada helped to shape popular cultural memory of the bomb by framing it in the desert West, arguably *the* screen space of American exceptionalism.[6]

That atomic test films merit attention is suggested perhaps most concretely by the considerable national resources they commanded. The first atomic detonation took place on July 16, 1945, at a (secret) test, code-named Trinity, in a desert near Alamogordo, New Mexico. According to a detailed "technical history" of this phase of the Manhattan Project, "a good photographic record" of a successful detonation could allow scientists to calculate "the temperature of the fireball" and the yield of the detonation "by measuring the intensity and spectral composition of the light from the blast." And such a record "would be even more important if the detonation was imperfect," since it could help determine what went wrong.[7] To this end, professional photographers Berlyn Brixner and Julian Mack were in charge of over fifty cameras (including pinhole cameras to record gamma rays and spectrographic cameras to monitor live wavelengths), using color as well as black-and-white film stock from 8mm to 35mm, utilizing multiple exposures, lenses, filters, and film speeds, with some Fastax cameras operating up to ten thousand frames per second. Those closest to the blast were housed within a "steel and lead glass bunker" specially designed by Brixner, and to increase the odds of getting as much footage as possible, "an ample supply of hand-held movie cameras [were also distributed] to the scientists and military personnel observing the test."[8] But this would be only a relatively modest beginning.

Less than a year later, one source claims, so much film footage was shot at the much-publicized tests at Bikini Atoll, in the Pacific Proving Ground, as to have caused "a worldwide shortage of film stock for months."[9] Whereas the Trinity test had been kept secret until the news broke of the attack on Hiroshima, the next series of atomic detonations, "Operation Crossroads," was an enormous media event and overt display of American military power. Headed by the US Navy in collaboration with the US Army, it was redubbed "Operation Camera" by the *New York Times,* which claimed it to have been more photographed than "any . . . single event in world history."[10] So elaborate was the spectacle that it merited not one but two "full-dress rehearsal[s]" off the coast of Southern California, in March and May of 1946, which included "more than 300 cameras [of] every type known" in the first case, and in the second, "a wide assortment of still and motion picture camera equipment" to "take pictures of the blast, cloud, target and the like from every conceivable angle."[11] Anticipating the main event at Bikini (then recently taken over by the United States from Japan), the *Times* reported that while photographing an atomic bomb was "a gamble," this test would utilize "some 600 cameras of almost every known type": some located in military aircraft "converted into . . . photographic fortress[es], with cameras in every available place"; some fixed on steel towers set up on surrounding islands; and some placed inside "'drones' [to] be dispatched by their mother ships [to fly] directly into the cloud."[12] One of the planes was said to include "probably the world's largest [and "fastest"] aerial camera," with a "forty-eight-inch telephoto lens" recording "on 9-by-18-inch film."[13] Also noteworthy in a rapidly changing broadcast era still dominated by radio (which brought the sound of the blast to listeners on the continent), six television networks sent a motion-picture cameraman, Leroy G. Phelps, to insure footage for their stations, "despite assurance [from the government] that all official motion pictures . . . [would] be available for TV projection."[14] On the day of the first blast, two New York stations broadcast a "series of films" reported to include the "preparation" of cameramen and the press, and a month later one of those stations advertised that it would air "Operation Crossroads" in a fifteen-minute prime-time slot.[15] A government-produced film by that name would premiere in late October and be screened months later at venues that included a women's-club event and an international film festival.[16]

More enduringly, however, in 1947 the US government substantially expanded its infrastructure for producing (and storing) films and photographs of nuclear weapons tests by converting a World War II radar station in Los Angeles's Laurel Canyon into a top-secret military film studio devoted to this purpose. Known as the Lookout Mountain Air Force Station, or Lookout Mountain Laboratory, and in use until 1969, throughout the 1950s the studio was home base to the air force's 1352nd Photographic Group, with cameramen stationed at both the Pacific Proving Grounds and the Nevada Test Site (figure 12.1). According to a fact sheet on the website of the former test site, which is currently operated by a corporate contractor, National Security Technologies, LLC, for the US Department of Energy [DOE], the Lookout Mountain facility had not only a "still photography laboratory" and equipment "to process 16mm and 35mm motion picture film," but also "animation and editorial departments," "optical printing capabilities," and state-of-the art film technology that included "Cinemascope, stereophonic sound, VistaVision, and even 3-[D] photography." And the building for this fully self-contained film studio included "one full stage, two screening rooms," "17 climate-controlled film vaults," a "bomb shelter," a "helicopter pad," and "two underground parking garages." Equally noteworthy, if by no means surprising for a film studio located minutes from the center of Hollywood, Lookout Mountain was "staffed by both military and civilian personnel recruited from nearby motion picture studios such as Metro-Goldwyn-Mayer, Warner Brothers Studio and RKO Pictures": a total of "more than 250 producers, directors, and cameramen [were] cleared to access top secret and restricted data and sworn to secrecy regarding activities at the studio."[17]

These activities included the production not simply of raw footage of nuclear weapons tests, but also of complete, scripted, sometimes scored films made for a range of audiences on a variety of test-related subjects that routinely featured such footage. The DOE fact sheet estimates that Lookout Mountain "produced millions

FIGURE 12.1. Cameramen film the atomic bomb at the Nevada Test Site (1955).

of feet of classified film," and Hamilton and O'Gorman's research suggests that the unit was responsible for "at least 600 films."[18] Only ninety-seven of the films in the collection associated with Lookout Mountain have been declassified.[19]

Even though most of this remarkable filmic record has yet to be seen, the sample that is available, combined with other related titles accessible elsewhere, makes clear that in addition to producing "secret" films for military and government use, Lookout Mountain was central to generating the mass moving-image culture of the bomb.[20] In addition to films speaking to and/or about different branches of the military, and/or implicitly addressing politicians (e.g., arguing for the continued development of atomic weapons), film production at Lookout Mountain and at both test sites was also vital to films made for the public. Hamilton and O'Gorman report that "films stored at L[ookout] M[ountain] circulated through all levels of publicity and secrecy, from elementary school science classes to the Pentagon," through "the Air Force's distribution network."[21] Some Lookout Mountain films were also available to the public through the free film loan program administered by the Atomic Energy Commission (AEC), through ten regional film libraries throughout the country.[22] What's more, government stock footage of atomic tests was used in the widest possible range of fiction and nonfiction films and television.

Such footage was visible, for example, in feature films as varied as the RKO thriller *Split Second* (1953) and Stanley Kubrick's *Dr. Strangelove* (1964), and throughout the troubled atomic deserts of so much science fiction—from *Invasion U.S.A.* (1952) and *Killers from Outer Space* (1954) to *Invisible Invaders* (1959) and *The Beast of Yucca Flats* (1961). Test site footage is also detectable, as we'll consider, across assorted nontheatrical shorts that circulated widely on 16mm. Such films could be purchased directly from dozens of private and public film production and distribution entities, and the AEC loaned hundreds of them to the public, for free.[23] In addition to nearly two hundred "technical films" for "professional scientists, engineers, and technologists," the AEC film catalog of nearly two hundred more "popular titles" addressed itself to "civil, industrial, television, professional, government, education, [and] youth and adult organizations interested in atomic energy." This "popular" film catalog (which includes two of the three films discussed below) reports "heavy patronage" ("some titles are booked solidly in advance for several months"); is organized to help teachers choose films suited to students at all levels (primary, secondary, and higher education); and states in a foreword that "[a]ll films, except those [few] described as 'NOT cleared for television,' may be shown on television programs as a public service."[24] In short, even the incomplete evidence currently available makes clear that the sphere of influence in question was such that anyone in the United States (and beyond) who saw motion pictures of the bomb in the Cold War era would have been hard-pressed not to encounter it.

Before considering how the bomb was represented in atomic test films, it pays to situate their proliferation within the context of the relative void in US visual culture of images of the bombs dropped on Hiroshima and Nagasaki and their effects, and its multiple causes. At one level, as Akira Lippit has argued, "there can be no authentic photography of atomic war" because the bombs not only incinerated and immobilized people who might have taken pictures of them, but so flooded the field of vision with light as to overwhelm the optics of (ordinary) photography.[25] And the aftermath posed other challenges. Unforgettable in this regard is the story of a Hiroshima photojournalist who survived the bomb, Yoshito Matsushige. Decades later he recalled having walked amid the catastrophe on August 6, thinking "that I should try to photograph it and get the pictures to the newspaper or to army headquarters," where he worked. Yet although Matsushige had enough film in his camera to take twenty-four pictures that day, he took only five. When asked about this, he described what he had seen as "too terrible to take a picture of": "people like boiled fish at the bottom of [a swimming] pool"; a streetcar "jammed with people . . . sitting down or standing still, [but] all burned black . . . and stiff"; streets "crowded with dead and suffering victims" such that it was "hard not to walk on the dead bodies." Matsushige continues: "Before I became a professional cameraman I had been just an ordinary person. So when I was faced with [such] terrible scene[s] I found it difficult to push the shutter."[26] In addition, we know, pictures that *were* taken in the days and weeks to follow were heavily censored by the US government, such that "for decades all that most Americans saw of Hiroshima and Nagasaki were the same repeated black and white images: a mushroom cloud, a battered building, . . . a panorama of emptiness."[27]

The resulting absence of the bomb's mass violence in visual culture resonates still more profoundly when we consider how that void can be said to have been dramatically filled, within a year of the war's nuclear end, with the well-orchestrated spectacle of the Bikini tests in the ostensible emptiness of the Pacific Ocean.[28] And the screen history of nuclear weapons entered a still more prolific phase with the opening of a test site on the continent in 1951. For while the Pacific Proving Grounds remained a key location of nuclear and thermonuclear spectacle throughout the fifties—especially after images announcing the arrival of the hydrogen bomb (hundreds of times more powerful than the atom bombs dropped in Japan) went public in 1954—with the opening of the Nevada Test Site and the scores of detonations filmed there throughout the decade, the desert came to appear onscreen not just as the bomb's birthplace in footage of the Trinity test, as we'll consider, but also as a kind of permanent residence, and ongoing showplace, for the nation's atomic arsenal. Whereas transporting personnel and camera equipment to remote locations in the Pacific by sea and air proved exceptionally expensive, difficult, and slow, the far more readily accessible test site outside of Las Vegas, within driving distance of a dedicated military film studio, meant that both filming and televising the bombs dropped in Nevada became significantly easier to pull off.[29] Put otherwise, conditions were ripe for the production of moving images of the bomb in the American West.

Elsewhere I argue that Hollywood conventions for filming the West as an idealized national screen space—one imagined as (if) having been empty before white settlers and US soldiers filled it—were at once central to, and profoundly called into question by, the proliferation of moving images in which the desert also became a primary scene within which Americans were invited to imagine nuclear weapons.[30] The remainder of the current chapter focuses on two related claims within that larger argument: (1) chronologically speaking, test images of the bomb in such ostensibly empty space came quickly and enduringly to fill the effective void in the filmic record of atomic catastrophe in Japan; and (2) in the process, across a wide range of military, educational, and civil defense films (some but by no means all of which were produced at Lookout Mountain), the imagery that resulted—which I call the atomic screen West—functioned aesthetically and ideologically as an ideal filmic setting for the bomb, serving both to glorify and to normalize it by displaying it as a quasi-magical, quasi-natural phenomenon without human costs. Elsewhere, I investigate how this rhetoric also came seriously into question already in the 1950s—not least with growing concerns about the risks of nuclear testing and the futility of civil defense. Nonetheless, the enduring legacies of the atomic screen West, as well as its limits, repay our attention.

Films produced at Lookout Mountain (e.g., *Target Nevada* [1953]) and others using its stock footage quickly demonstrate that to picture the atomic bomb in the desert (and over the ocean) routinely meant, above all, to picture it without people, or much of anything else; to invite viewers to see it as pure energy, pure spectacle, pure demonstration of technology and power. These tendencies, combined with the then thoroughly familiar visual and political rhetoric of the conventional Hollywood Western, suggest what an ideal filmic location the desert was as the scene within which to present the bomb to Americans in the context of Cold War militarism: so many long shots of A-bombs dropped in ostensibly empty landscapes not only visually minimized their obvious risks but also conjured them within a filmic space already coded in the popular imagination as one of national progress, prerogative, triumph, and sentiment.[31] And, I argue, across a range of films that featured footage of atomic tests, moving images of the bomb in the West routinely eclipsed the visual history of mass atomic violence in Japan, utilizing empty desert space to naturalize and glorify atomic weapons. Below we'll first consider how this began with an enduring tradition that imagined the "birth" of nuclear fission unleashed in the desert as a kind of immaculate conception, and then examine evidence of how that tradition continued to shape the filmic record of the bomb.

Far more than just the physical site of the bomb's first detonation (three weeks before the military use for which it was designed), the desert quickly became the mythic scene of its arrival. For despite the enormous military-industrial-scientific collaboration that spanned several years and multiple locations to bring atomic weapons into being, the desert would be envisioned, repeatedly, as their quasi-magical, quasi-mystical primal scene. This becomes perhaps more curious when we reflect on the fact that, due to the secrecy of the Manhattan Project, news of the Trinity test was not shared with the public until *after* the bombing of Hiroshima, when press releases on both were released simultaneously. One of these releases (now attributed to William Laurence) stressed the "beauty" of "[m]ankind's successful transition to a new age, the Atomic Age . . . in the desertlands of New Mexico."[32] While rhetoric of the bomb's untainted birth in the desert thus first appeared in print, a history of moving images deployed and expanded it, I propose, to shape the filmic record of the bomb for decades to come. Three quite different examples—from 1946, 1952, and 1965—will allow us to consider the use of film footage from, and animation inspired by, both the Trinity test in New Mexico and the scores of atmospheric tests that eventually followed in Nevada.

Released in 1946, the short film *Tale of Two Cities* was billed as "a pictorial report" on Hiroshima and Nagasaki "for the armed forces only," but eventually circulated widely through the AEC's film loan program. In keeping with US censorship of the atomic bombings, this "pictorial report" shows not a single dead body, nor anyone visibly wounded or sick. Instead, images of formerly urban space shockingly emptied become the primary signifiers of the bomb's effects—what the narrator calls the

FIGURE 12.2. The "desert of a debris that was Hiroshima," as presented in.*Tale of Two Cities* (1946).

"desert of a debris that was Hiroshima." (See, for example, figure 12.2.) Such imagery, in part, is symptomatic of Lippit's formulation of the impossibility of photograph-ing nuclear war. Yet *Tale of Two Cities* embraces that structuring absence to the point of excluding any afterimages of human suffering. What's more, the film both opens and closes with footage of the Trinity test, begging us to consider how that footage serves not only in a chronological narrative, and as expedient stock footage, but also, literally, to frame the filmic record of Hiroshima and Nagasaki.

This begins with a filmic rendition of the desert birthplace rhetoric, here expanded such that the empty desert functions not only as the original scene of nuclear fission unleashed, but also as the privileged scene of its ethical deliberation. After opening credits end with the film's title atop a map of Japan that labels the "two cities" at issue, a voice-over accompanying a black screen begins their tale "on a desert morning" when "an atomic age is born": cue Trinity footage (figure 12.3, left). Until aerial foot-age of the mushroom cloud over Nagasaki nine minutes into this twelve-minute film, that Trinity footage is our only direct view of the bomb. What is more, in a film that otherwise proceeds chronologically, that footage returns after the filmic reports from the cities laid waste (albeit without signs of human suffering). At the end of the

FIGURE 12.3. (*Left*) *Tale of Two Cities*, a film reporting catastrophe in Hiroshima and Nagasaki, begins "on a desert morning" in New Mexico with footage of the Trinity test, the first detonation of a nuclear weapon." (*Center*) At its end, *Tale of Two Cities* poses the ethical question of what to do with "atomic power" as if it, too, emerges from "the darkness of a desert morning." (*Right*) With a replay of the Trinity footage, *Tale of Two Cities* finally leaves Japan altogether to let the ethical question hover in the comparatively immaculate emptiness of an actual desert.

Nagasaki segment, the narrator offers that "the world's great minds in science, statecraft, and military matters are wrestling with the problems created by the atom," and here we see the film's most literal trace of atomic death: the rough outline, or reverse shadow, of a human figure on a bridge, left where a victim's body absorbed the radiation that also seared the ground around it. But as an American soldier begins to outline with chalk the negative "of an average man, regardless of race or creed," the voice-over shifts focus to ponder if the "path" of the "atomic footprint" on the bridge "leads to unparalleled progress or," and here the screen goes black once more, "unparalleled destruction." Over the black screen, the narrator recalls the film's beginning: "Just as in the darkness of the desert morning, when the atomic age was born . . ." But this time the void is lit up by a white question mark that rapidly grows to fill the screen (before the blast), as "atomic power puts the question squarely to mankind" (figure 12.3, center). The film then cuts immediately to a replay of the Trinity footage (figure 12.3, right). In short, the bomb without victims returns here precisely at the moment when the film asks the viewer to consider what, now, to do with "atomic power"—leaving us to contemplate the bomb's future by relocating it from the "desert" it inflicted in Japan to the even emptier scene in New Mexico.

Multiple explanations—by turns aesthetic, pragmatic, and rhetorical—suggest themselves as to why this war "report" might conclude with footage of the bomb in the American West. And we need not deny any of them to consider the force with which *Tale of Two Cities* finally leaves those cities behind to pose its ethical question in the comparatively immaculate emptiness of an actual desert. After Hiroshima, the contemplation of "atomic power" would no doubt be easier with images of the bomb unleashed in space understood as having been empty from the start.

If the bomb's arrival in the desert was still news in 1946, an animated educational short from 1952 begins to suggest the endurance of such imagery into the

FIGURE 12.4. (*Left*) *A Is for Atom* (1952), an animated film, also begins with the birth of "the atomic age" in otherwise empty space. (*Center*) The scene of the mushroom cloud alone in the desert is *the* (only) visual signifier of nuclear weapons in *A Is for Atom*. (*Right*) In *A Is for Atom* the mushroom cloud in empty space transmogrifies to become a glowing giant representing the "limitless power" of atomic technology.

Cold War—even to the point of blotting out Japan altogether. Made by John Sutherland Productions for General Electric, which sold it to consumers for "about $120 per print" (according to the AEC popular film catalog, which also loaned it for free), *A Is for Atom* promotes atomic technology by distancing it from, or at least expanding it beyond, nuclear war.[33] It becomes "a giant of limitless power at man's command," envisioned as a glowing colossal figure towering over the earth. And then, "not one but many giants": "the warrior, the destroyer," "the engineer," "the farmer," "the healer," and "the researcher, worker . . . of pure science." By no means surprising in a promotional film, even one that immediately acknowledges public fear about the bomb (before answering it with visions of the good giant powering cities and the like), the history of what the bomb had already done readily disappears. But how it does so is telling. For the scene of the bomb alone in the desert becomes *the* visual signifier of nuclear weapons.

The film opens with the by now predictable, and here animated, scene of the birth of "the atomic age" in otherwise empty space: we see nothing but a dark horizon line across the frame, first lit up with the flash (figure 12.4, left) and then a dark stage for a white mushroom cloud, rendered at such a distance as to remain recognizable but relatively small amid a vast expanse of blank space (figure 12.4, center). From this, the film dissolves to an (animated) aerial view of farmland amid clusters of buildings, over which a large shadow begins to move as the camera moves, too, over the rural landscape to a nearby city. Here the voice-over admits: "There is no denying that since that moment [of its birth in the desert] the shadow of the atomic bomb has been across all our lives." The camera stops at a dense peak of skyscrapers, within which the United Nations logo and its (new) headquarters in Manhattan are suddenly featured, as the voice-over attempts to reassure us that "[a]ll men of good will earnestly hope" for the "realistic control of atomic weapons." "Meanwhile," the voice-over quickly continues, "good sense requires" civil defense (we see that agency's logo, too), and "wisdom demands . . . that we take time to under-stand this force." With this call for wisdom, the mushroom cloud in empty space returns (much as it appears in figure 12.4, center), but now transforms into the glowing giant (figure 12.4, right). In this condensed account of nuclear weapons since Trinity, then, not only does Japan drop out completely, but it *can* drop out because the by now iconic image of a mushroom cloud in the desert readily signi-fies the bomb without showing its potential for mass destruction.

Elsewhere I consider how, in addition to perhaps making the contemplation of nuclear war more bearable than it would have been if envisioned in densely popu-lated areas (whether through animation or footage from Japan), the emptiness of western screen space and its popular film history could also further support the reversal presumably at work when the scene of atomic catastrophe in the popular US imagination became, as Joseph Masco has described it, the mass fantasy of "one's own home . . . devastated, on fire, and in ruins."[34] For this nightmare was also staged in the atomic screen West, and, I argue, came routinely to displace the his-torical nightmare of such scenes in Japan, and US responsibility for them. This dynamic thus calls to mind that of the massacre scenario so central to the Holly-wood Western's routine reassignment of historical identities of aggressor and vic-tim: wherein images of white American homes (wagons, cabins, etc.) "on fire and in ruins" in open space were key among the conventions through which that genre perpetually reimagined, as Janet Walker has put it, "the massacre of American Indi-ans *as* the massacre of settlers."[35] In my own research on atomic test films, I was most shocked to discover unexpected material evidence of such routine "revers[als] of the genocidal onus" (as Walker also puts it) at the Nevada Test Site in the form of what were historically referred to as "Japanese houses" erected there for radiation research, and yet almost entirely eclipsed in the visual record of atomic testing by so many images of American-style test houses "on fire and in ruins."

With these multiple contexts in mind, and to help us further reflect on the lon-gevity and implications of the atomic screen West, I want to close with a brief dis-cussion of *Radioactive Fallout and Shelter,* a civil defense film from 1965—by which point (as everyone knew) the Soviets as well as the United States had possessed thermonuclear weapons for over a decade. Credited as having been produced by the US Department of Health, Education, and Welfare, this film uses footage from the Nevada Test Site that would have been produced at Lookout Mountain (as was, possibly, the entire film), as well as animation shaped by it. Focused on the question of how to protect oneself from fallout (wash your hands, peel vegetables, etc.), most remarkable here is the fact that iconic A-bomb detonations in the empty desert so thoroughly dominate, and generate, central imagery of a film devoted to the discus-sion of what it ultimately describes as an urban H-bomb scenario.

The open admission that mass death on a thermonuclear scale is at stake comes at the end of this twenty-seven-minute film. Speaking directly into the camera, the film's

FIGURE 12.5. *Radioactive Fallout and Shelter* (1965), a film promoting civil defense in the face of possible thermonuclear attack on urban targets, also animates the bomb within an otherwise empty desert.

male narrator states that in a "nuclear attack . . . millions of our people would be killed by the initial blast and heat" and "millions more . . . threatened by death from radioactive fallout." And earlier in the film we see imagery that suggests urban targets: bits of live-action footage of an actual city (with high-rises and a large-scale fallout shelter) and an animated sequence of a dense skyline, also revealing a fallout shelter under a representative skyscraper. Such details make all the more incongruous the film's repeated, structuring, and animated images of exploding bombs and mushroom clouds in utterly empty space. But the film's lesson on radiation is structured around animation that locates the mushroom cloud within a brown, flat, otherwise empty expanse surrounded only, eventually, by distant mountains (figure 12.5). In this atomic desert a cloud labeled "residual radiation" forms before it travels through similarly empty shots to finally arrive at the most minimally populated of places—a remote farm with no living creatures in sight. Here we are told of the radiation's rapid dissipation, as hands of an animated clock, floating in empty sky, spin swiftly.

Two points about this film merit emphasis. The first responds to the obvious question: Why animate the H-bomb in the desert, in 1965, in a film that knows it

FIGURE 12.6. Live-action footage of an atomic test in Nevada that (eventually) matches the animated image of the bomb that precedes it in *Radioactive Fallout and Shelter* demonstrates how such footage came to shape even purely imaginary imagery of the bomb.

would target a city, or several? The most pragmatic answer is revealed after the sequence just described is well under way, when the animated blast and clouds are followed by similar stock footage from the Nevada Test Site (figure 12.6). In part, then, the logic of continuity editing is at work insofar as the animation matches (in advance) that live-action footage. Yet this explanation by no means contains the larger implications of such a choice. Indeed, it speaks to the dominance of such imagery by 1965 that even when it doesn't make narrative sense to envision the bomb in the desert (as if "they" would bomb our test site?), and even when the film also knows and at times admits this (with the fleeting images of cities and the final talk of "millions"), the visual relationship between the bomb and this setting is so entrenched as to make it an acceptable model for the animation of a domestic attack. Put otherwise, the fact that the animation imagines the bomb in the desert before the live-action footage puts it there makes literal the point that, after well over a decade's worth of the mass production and dissemination of such footage, it had come to shape even the purely imagined space of the bomb in whatever context.

The second key point is that, even as this film's animated empty space works to mitigate the potentially terrifying knowledge of urban thermonuclear warfare it elsewhere (minimally) conveys—to the point of the animation showing not a single home within the range of "blast and heat," and only one remote farmhouse at risk of radiation—like other civil defense films, *Radioactive Fallout and Shelter* is equally remarkable for the baldness of its contradictions. Certainly, the atomic screen West could by no means thoroughly guard against the clear possibilities of failure, resistance, and attack—rhetorical and otherwise. Equally certain by 1965, having lived with such risk for over a decade, and only three years after the Cuban Missile Crisis, Americans had long since been invited to imagine the atomic destruction of their cities. In that context, the perpetual replay of the bomb in the empty screen West, even when that location did not make sense, seems to have served as a regular mechanism through which such possibilities came to be knowable, albeit with the profound mixtures of denial and dread that routinely marked mass experience of the Cold War.

Here it seems apt to conclude by reflecting on the fact that the iconography in question, and the critical role it came to play in the bomb's mass mediation, began with military test films and profoundly exceeded them. As long as the world has known nuclear weapons, images of them exploding in seemingly empty space have helped to shape how we imagine, remember, and forget them—at the movies and on TV; in the workplace, club meetings, and classrooms; and now on our computer screens.[36] While the ultimate scope and force of this representational legacy is difficult to quantify, and could by no means have been fully anticipated in advance (by even the most well-organized of institutions), its power remains remarkable, for our nuclear present as well as our nuclear past.

ACKNOWLEDGMENTS

This research was supported by the Tanner Humanities Center at the University of Utah. There, co-fellow Rachel Marston not only shared a fascination with atomic testing that was energizing, but helped me actually get to the test site. I am also grateful to Jennifer Fay, Kevin Hamilton, Ned O'Gorman, and Akira Lippit for collaborating on a panel at the Society for Cinema and Media Studies at which I first presented a version of this chapter. And thank you Haidee Wasson and Lee Grieveson for your excellent feedback.

NOTES

1. This is the current estimate of atomic deaths in both cities (combined) in 1945 alone. Since casualty estimates are notoriously difficult, this figure may be too small and does not include injuries (burns and radiation effects) to thousands of survivors. "A Brief Description," Radiation Effects Research Foundation, accessed July 14, 2016, 4, www.rerf.jp/shared/briefdescript/briefdescript_e.pdf.

2. Kevin Hamilton and Ned O'Gorman, "Visualities of Strategic Vision: Lookout Mountain Laboratory and the Deterrent State from Nuclear Tests to Vietnam," *Visual Studies* 30, no. 2 (2015): 197. Film cameras could see what the human eye could not, and record it, and were thus crucial tools for "collect[ing] volumes of data of [any given] 'shot' for later analysis." Kevin Hamilton and Ned O'Gorman, "Filming a Nuclear State: The USAF's Lookout Mountain Laboratory," in *A Companion to the War Film*, ed. Douglas A. Cunningham and John C. Nelson (Chichester, UK: Wiley, 2016), 136.

3. Hamilton and O'Gorman, "Visualities of Strategic Vision," 198.

4. Hamilton and O'Gorman have done the most to correct this, and promise to expose much of the buried history of atomic test filmmaking in *Lookout America! The Secret Hollywood Film Studio at the Heart of the Cold War State.* (Hanover, NH: Dartmouth College Press, forthcoming 2018). My own discussion here derives from a longer chapter on atomic test films in the context of vernacular screen forms of the American West in the long 1950s. See Susan Courtney, *Split Screen Nation: Moving Images of the American West and South* (New York: Oxford University Press, 2017).

5. From 1945 to 1992 the United States exploded over a thousand nuclear weapons. Of these, 928 were detonated on, above, or under the deserts of the Nevada Test Site, including 100 atmospheric tests. An additional 106 tests occurred in the Pacific. "United States Nuclear Tests: July 1945 through September 1992," US Department of Energy, National Nuclear Security Administration, DOE/NV-209-REV 16, September 2015, xvi, www.nnss.gov/docs/docs_LibraryPublications/DOE_NV-209_Rev16.pdf.

6. Focused on images of nuclear tests in the desert, this chapter does not address those of thermonuclear tests in the Pacific, although the two are often linked, not least by the fantasy that they occurred in "empty" space (cf. n31). I address additional dynamics linking the mediation of these different sites in *Split Screen Nation.* On the Pacific tests, their "Edenic" imagery, and how it was used to mediate the displacement of Pacific Islanders, see Peter B. Hales, "The Atomic Sublime," *American Studies* 32, no. 1 (1991): 17–20.

7. Lillian Hoddeson, Paul W. Henriksen, Roger A. Meade, and Catherine L. Westfall, *Critical Assembly: A Technical History of Los Alamos during the Oppenheimer Years, 1943–1945* (Cambridge: Cambridge University Press, 2004), 354–55.

8. Ibid., 354. Brixner claimed he "did the whole job . . . [setting up] all fifty-some cameras" and was responsible for "almost all the photographs that have been distributed" of the Trinity test. At least one high-quality color image has been attributed to an amateur, Jack Aeby. Berlyn Brixner, as interviewed by Robert Del Tredici in *At Work in the Fields of the Bomb* (New York: Perennial, 1987), 187.

9. Michael Light, *100 Suns* (New York: Knopf, 2003), caption (n.p.) for photo, numbered "058," of the Baker test from Operation Crossroads, held on July 25, 1946.

10. Ray Mackland, "Operation Camera," *New York Times*, June 23, 1946, SM27.

11. "Photo Work Good in Atom Bomb Rehearsal," *New York Times*, March 8, 1946, 3; William L. Laurence, "Bikini Rehearsal Staged by Robots," *New York Times*, May 19, 1946, 8.

12. Mackland, "Operation Camera"; Sidney Shallet, "Test Atomic Bombs to Blast 100 Ships at Marshalls Atoll," *New York Times*, January 25, 1946, 1.

13. Mackland, "Operation Camera."

14. "Television Will Be Used in Atom Bomb Test Films," *New York Times*, March 20, 1946, 11; Sidney Lohman, "Radio Row: One Thing and Another," *New York Times*, June 9, 1946, 49. The air force also later reported "extensive use of drone planes in the two tests . . . with television equipment in the nose." Hanson W. Baldwin, "Lessons Learned in Bikini Tests," *New York Times*, August 1, 1946, 8.

15. T. R. Kennedy Jr., "Radio Sets Big Day for Bikini Details," *New York Times*, June 30, 1946, 4; television schedule, *New York Times*, August 8, 1946, 27.

16. "Douglas Will Open Forum Tomorrow," *New York Times*, October 27, 1946, 53; "Memorial Program Held," *New York Times*, January 7, 1947, 31; "Calendar of Women's Clubs for the Coming Week," *New York Times*, January 9, 1947, 50; "Plans for 'Mrs. Mike'—Festival—Addenda," *New York Times*, May 25, 1947, X5.

17. "Secret Film Studio: Lookout Mountain," National Nuclear Security Administration for the US Department of Energy, DOE/NV-1142, August 2013. www.nnss.gov/docs/fact_sheets/DOENV_1142. pdf. In 2010 the National Nuclear Security Administration (NNSA) renamed the test site in Nevada the Nevada National Security Site (NNSS). In addition to the storage and research of the national nuclear stockpile, this site is currently used by corporate entities for various high-risk activities, including the burial of radioactive waste and counterterrorism training. "NNSA Announces New Name for Test Site," National Nuclear Security Administration, August 23, 2010, https://nnsa.energy.gov/mediaroom /pressreleases/ntsrenaming082310; "Nevada National Security Site: Mission," National Security Technologies LLC, http://www2.nstec.com/pages/NNSS-Mission.aspx.

18. Hamilton and O'Gorman, "Filming a Nuclear State," 130. While the DOE fact sheet estimates that Lookout Mountain produced "more than 6,500 films," Hamilton and O'Gorman's research suggests that that estimate was perhaps derived from the number of cans of film (not films themselves) in the collection. Kevin Hamilton, e-mail to author, May 10 and 11, 2016.

19. A project to declassify the collection ceased after the terrorist attacks of September 11, 2001. "DOE Continues the Declassification and Release of Historical Nuclear Weapons Test Films." "Film Declassification Project, Video Tape Fact Sheets," US Department of Energy, Albuquerque Operations Office, released by Nevada Operations Office, Operated by Bechtel Nevada, September 2000. http:// www.nnsa.energy.gov/albuquerque-operations-office-film-declassification-project-video-tape-facts-sheets-pdf-883.-kb; https://nnsa.energy.gov/sites/default/files/nnsa/foiareadingroom/RR00556.pdf. Martha DeMarre, conversation with author, Nuclear Testing Archive, Las Vegas, April 22, 2011.

20. Cf. Hamilton and O'Gorman, "Filming a Nuclear State," 132.

21. Ibid., 134.

22. About a dozen Lookout Mountain titles appear in the AEC lending catalog, including *Target Nevada, Atomic Tests in Nevada*, and *Operation Ivy*, which I discuss in the longer version of this chapter in *Split Screen Nation*. US Atomic Energy Commission, *16mm Film Catalog*, Popular Level (1966–67), xii, 11, 22–24, 32–34, 43, 47–48.

23. The AEC (lending) catalog notes that "organizations [with ongoing need] for repeated screenings of the same film" may find it easier and cheaper "to own a print than to borrow it," and hence provides names and addresses of thirty-three different distributors. These include well-known private producers and distributors of educational and industrial films (e.g., Calvin, Coronet, Encyclopædia Britannica) and many, assorted public organizations (e.g., educational, governmental, military), as well as multiple offices of the AEC. Ibid., x, iv, xiv, ii.

24. Ibid., i–xiv.

25. "The bombings were themselves a form of total photography that exceeded the economies of representation, testing the very visibility of the visual." Akira Mizuta Lippit, *Atomic Light (Shadow Optics)* (Minneapolis and London: University of Minnesota Press, 2005), 95.

26. Yoshito Matsushige, interviewed in Del Tredici, *Fields of the Bomb*, 187–89; cited in Bryan Taylor, "Nuclear Pictures and Metapictures," *American Literary History* 9, no. 3 (1997): 578.

27. This comes from a voice-over by journalist Greg Mitchell accompanying a short clip (accessible via his blog post "The Great Hiroshima Cover-Up") of some of the twenty hours of long-"suppressed" color film footage. Elsewhere he and coauthor Robert Lifton discuss how "from the start, Americans were not shown the human effects of the bomb," and trace "the same impulses" at play in the Smithsonian's controversial removal of "nearly every photograph of dead or badly injured Japanese civilians" from its Enola Gay exhibit on the bombings' fiftieth anniversary. Robert J. Lifton and Greg Mitchell, *Hiroshima in America: Fifty Years of Denial* (New York: Putnam, 1995), xv. See also George Weller, *First into Nagasaki: The Censored Eyewitness Dispatches on Post-Atomic Japan and Its Prisoners of War*, ed. Anthony Weller (New York: Crown Publishers, 2006).

28. The excessive quantities of footage "exposed . . . at Bikini in 1946" have also been read as "compensat[ion] for the jerky hand-held work done during the atomic bombings" of Japan. Bob

Mielke, "Rhetoric and Ideology in the Nuclear Test Documentary," *Film Quarterly* 58, no. 3 (2005): 29.

29. On the live broadcasting of atomic tests in Nevada via early television, see Mark J. Williams, "History in a Flash: Notes on the Myth of TV 'Liveness,'" in *Collecting Visible Evidence*, ed. Jane Gaines and Michael Renov, Visible Evidence Series 6 (Minneapolis: University of Minnesota Press, 1999), 292–312.

30. Drawing on Scott Simmon's work, in *Split Screen Nation* I discuss how a history of empty screen space in the Hollywood Western routinely facilities conquest logic.

31. Peter Hales first registered the centrality to atomic testing of an aesthetic he coined "the atomic sublime," and with it "ideas that had developed in nineteenth century America around the notions of blessed nature, landscape, religion, personal psychology and manifest destiny." Hales, "The Atomic Sublime," 13. And in a book that appeared after this chapter was written, Hales similarly writes that testing "required an empty landscape," which "in America signifies promise, a vacuum drawing new and renewed people and institutions." Peter B. Hales, *Outside the Gates of Eden: The Dream of America from Hiroshima to Now* (Chicago: University of Chicago Press, 2014), 17.

32. "War Department Release on New Mexico Test, July 16, 1945," published as appendix 6 of H. D. Smyth [for the US War Department], "Atomic Energy for Military Purposes" (1945), 254, 247. A reporter for the *New York Times* and the sole journalist at Trinity and in the plane that bombed Nagasaki, William Laurence was later exposed as having been paid by the War Department. On Laurence's centrality to the US government's narrative of Hiroshima, and of the bomb more generally, see Lifton and Mitchell, *Hiroshima in America*, 12–22.

33. Atomic Energy Commission, *16mm Film Catalog*, 7.

34. Joseph Masco, "'Survival Is Your Business': Engineering Ruins and Affect in Nuclear America," *Cultural Anthropology* 23, no. 2 (2008): 361–62.

35. Janet Walker, "Captive Images in the Traumatic Western: *The Searchers, Pursued, Once upon a Time in the West* and *Lone Star*," in *Westerns: Films through History*, ed. Janet Walker (New York: Routledge, 2001), 227; Walker's italics.

36. A Google image or video search for "nuclear weapons" quickly suggests how central the history of atomic testing photography remains to these weapons' visual representation.

13

OCCUPATION, DIPLOMACY, AND THE MOVING IMAGE

The US Army as Cultural Interlocutor
in Korea, 1945–1948

Sueyoung Park-Primiano

In his evocative essay "Asian Cinema and the American Cultural Imaginary," Wimal Dissanayake examines the profound and paradoxical impact of Hollywood cinema in Japan "as new identities are enforced and new subjectivities conscripted" in response to the uneven and shifting nexus of East–West global relations.[1] His argument that Hollywood promoted "a voracious scopic consumption of images and insert[ed] American-created visualities into circuits of multiple discourse" in Japan and other Asian societies since the Second World War may be further buttressed by the inclusion of American films from the noncommercial sector—specifically, the informational and educational films produced or distributed by the US military in the postwar era.[2] This "parallel industry" of "useful cinema," which more emphatically sought "to instruct, to sell, and to make or remake citizens" than entertain, was a constant companion to film audiences in former Axis territories occupied by the US military.[3] In this chapter I will exclusively examine noncommercial films approved and exhibited in service of the myriad roles of the US military in its effort to "develop wide understanding and acceptance of American foreign policy and the American system of life" on the Korean Peninsula as a bulwark against communism.[4]

On August 15, 1945, Emperor Hirohito made his radio announcement of Japan's defeat, but the official surrender of the colonial governor-general, Abe Nobuyuki, did not take place until September 9, 1945, when seventy-seven US military officers seized control of the government below the thirty-eighth parallel and Korea experienced a de facto liberation after over thirty-five years of Japanese rule.[5] Upon the transfer of power, the US Army Forces in Korea (USAFIK) and the American Military Government (USAMGIK), both under the command of

Lieutenant General John R. Hodge and his superior in Tokyo, General Douglas MacArthur, immediately sought to suppress leftist activities and any unrest deemed as communist and a threat to American interests. The oppressive response is unsurprising given the proximity of the Soviet Red Army occupying Korea north of the thirty-eighth parallel and the resultant visceral fear of its ideological encroachment on the entire indigenous population. The distrust of leftist Koreans, however, was not relegated solely to the American occupation authorities. Postwar planners at the US State Department had also expressed concern that "the economic and political situation in Korea would be conducive to the adoption of communist ideology," and that the "policy and activities of a Russian-sponsored socialist regime in Korea might easily receive popular support" even if the average Korean wasn't favorably disposed toward Soviet Russia.[6] Hence, all Korean media were mobilized by the US military "to carry on an informational and educational campaign to sell to the Koreans our form of democracy" and to contain local revolutionary forces in concordance with the escalating Cold War.[7] This anticipated Truman's Smith-Mundt Act, also known as the "United States Information and Educational Exchange Act of 1948," which for the first time committed the US government in time of peace to conducting international information and educational exchange activities on a global, long-term scale. Thus, the US occupation period (1945–48) represents the first direct involvement of American cultural industries in Korean culture, and motion pictures served as the ideal carrier of information and propaganda in a country where only the very wealthy few owned radios and the high illiteracy rate limited the effectiveness of newspapers.[8]

Foreign control of local media was far from new to the Korean public. Prior to the arrival of the US military, the Korean film industry was on its last legs, being forced to nearly shut down its operation with wartime regulations that demanded it service the needs of the Japanese military. At the time, the colonial Office of Information in the Secretariat of the Government-General was solely responsible for regulating the media. Its duties included the precensoring of the press, radio, and photographs, as well as publishing a weekly digest and a weekly pictorial for propaganda purposes. Upon the establishment of the American Military Government in mid-September 1945, the Office of Information was succeeded by the Korean Relations and Information Section (KRAI), which was made responsible for the entire relationship between the US occupation forces and the Korean population. According to official history, policies and practices of the KRAI and its successors were different from those of the colonial Office of Information. Official history claimed that, whereas the Office of Information had been mainly a censoring organization that suppressed freedom of speech and the press, the KRAI was a releasing organization that protected said freedoms. Yet the reality was that the KRAI and its subsequent bureaus also controlled and censored all Korean media, in addition to executing propaganda. Indeed, the confiscation of all essential media and communication facilities was among the first tasks in which the KRAI was involved, including the joint takeover, with the Communications Bureau of the Military Government, on September 16, 1945, of all ten of the Korean Broad casting Corporation's radio stations operating south of the thirty-eighth parallel.[9]

The chief aim of the KRAI and its successors was to justify American occupation and "to slowly and carefully correct" the general impression that Korea was to receive complete independence immediately.[10] With increasing anti-American demonstrations and leftist demands for immediate independence, however, the KRAI grew in intention, scope, and intensity to suppress both the rising local disaffection with the US occupation and the increasingly revolutionary situation.[11] After multiple augmentations, the KRAI finally reemerged as the Department of Public Information (DPI) in March 1946. Its overall objective was to sell American forms of democracy and "to give the benefit of American training and experience to Koreans, so that when the American forces withdraw they will possess at least basic understanding of the techniques and methods of democratic publicity procedures in the fields of motion pictures, radio, press relations, etc. . . . To supervise the production, distribution, and exhibition of all motion pictures in Korea."[12]

Responding to the need, the DPI's increased agency specialization and expanded propaganda activities relied more on motion pictures as a "fast" medium to accelerate the dissemination of information and propaganda to the Korean masses.[13] As described below, educational documentaries and newsreels were shown free of charge at commercial theaters and, in the rural regions, where there were no commercial theaters or proper venues, in a specially outfitted train or the outdoors.[14]

Reaching remote locations was the responsibility of the Mobile Education Unit of the DPI, which were established to redress the majority of unrest and insurrection that were concentrated in the countryside. On May 6, 1946, the original Mobile Education Unit—composed of sixteen members, including actors, speakers, and technicians—left Seoul by a special train to visit Ch'ungch'ŏng-namdo (a western province in southern Korea), where twenty-one shows, including the American motion pictures *Fury in the Pacific* (1945) and *Freedom of Education*, were presented in twenty days.[15] The train was made up of six distinctively painted cars, and fitted with a recording studio, portable stage equipment, a public-address system, and motion-picture projectors. Prior to this time, the propaganda activities of the US occupation had been more or less centered in Seoul, with indirect communication with the wider population restricted to the distribution of official leaflets and regular mobile public-address broadcasts of news by using city police boxes, which proved ineffective against the rising tide of opposition among Koreans. Paradoxically, the rural-outreach plan was also a continuation of Japan's colonial propaganda program to reach remote areas for total war effort that deployed thirteen provincial mobile movie-projection units established by the centralized Chosŏn Motion Picture Distribution Company in December 1942.[16]

On the Mobile Education Unit's second trip, the American motion picture *The Battle of Iwo Jima* (1945; released commercially as *To the Shores of Iwo Jima*) was one of the feature attractions.[17] Obviously, as with *Fury in the Pacific*, the exhibition of this "spectacularly beautiful and terrible film, by far the best and fullest record of a combined operation," was a strategic move to showcase American superiority over the Japanese and to diminish heightened local unrest by affirming that the United States shared a common enemy with Korea.[18] Shot in glorious Technicolor, *To the Shores of Iwo Jima* closes with the following excerpt from the recording of President Roosevelt's speech to Congress asking for a declaration of war against Japan the day after the attack on Pearl Harbor: "With confidence in our armed forces, with the unbounding determination of our people, we will gain the inevitable triumph. So help us God." For greater emotional effect, this abbreviated "Day of Infamy" speech is scored with "The Battle Hymn of the Republic" and combined with an image of dozens of American jet planes flying high in the sky in perfect chevron formation. Although these films were originally produced for the American audience, with *Fury in the Pacific* specifically produced for the War Finance Division to exhort the purchase of war bonds and to enlist new recruits, the images of wounded American soldiers and the scorched bodies of Japanese soldiers sought to communicate American valor and victory in the Pacific War and thereby impress Korean audiences with the prestige of the US military.

As an indication of its success with the Korean public, the Mobile Education Unit was subsequently dispatched on three-week tours each month with varying education programs, which included illustrated lectures on various subjects: "Need for Good Government," "Democratic Justice," "Meaning of Democratic Freedom," "Korea Must Be United," and "Art of Self-Government."[19] These political lectures on liberal democracy were led by Korean teams trained by the Political Education Section of the DPI using preexisting filmstrips made available for use overseas by the US State Department's Office of International Information and Cultural Affairs (OIC), successor to the Office of War Information. In April 1946, the DPI also created an office in Seoul for the Central Motion Picture Exchange (CMPE, or Chungang Yŏnghwasa), a subsidiary of the Motion Picture Export Association (i.e., Hollywood's export cartel), to be the centralized distribution branch of American films both commercial and noncommercial.[20] Thus began the flooding of Hollywood features into the Korean market, among them Hollywood documentaries and newsreels carefully selected and approved by the US Army Civil Affairs Division (CAD).[21] Hence, feature titles such as Metro-Goldwyn-Mayer's *Boys Town* (Norman Taurog, 1938) and RKO Pictures' *Abe Lincoln in Illinois* (John Cromwell, 1940) were imported along with CAD-chosen educational films—such as RKO Pictures' *Our American Heritage,* a film about the origin of America's basic freedoms, and *Democracy's Diary,* a film about the *New York Times*—to show how "a free and honest newspaper operates in a democracy," to further illustrate American forms of democracy.[22]

The DPI also commenced sending films to the CMPE for distribution once it began locally producing documentaries and newsreels about the American Military Government's activities and significant Korean activities related to the occupation in cooperation with the Signal Service Department of the United States Army Forces in Korea. These films were intended to stimulate interest among the Korean people in military governmental affairs and to mold them into an "enlightened public" suitable for a democratic political system.[23] However, not all films produced by the DPI were political in nature. For example, *The Korean White Angel*, produced in collaboration with the American Military Government's Department of Public Health and Welfare, was a training film featuring the latest modern techniques of nursing.[24] As such, the role of the US military was equally invested in modernizing health services and improving health education, as well as nurturing American democracy—all for the greater goal of improving US-Korea relations. The westward modernizing effort was, of course, more expansive in South Korea than simply improving public health, as indicated in the following press release:

> In a program to orient the staff of the Training Division of the Korean Civil Service in modern and democratic training techniques, five non-military training films have been obtained from the US Army and are being shown as training aids, Kim Sang Pil, division chief reported today. Two of the films now being studied are of an orientation character and three are of a more technical nature. Although produced by the US Army, they are non-military and deal with such subjects as proper use of the telephone, driver's instruction [e.g., driving on the right side as opposed to the left as the Japanese did] and special techniques in carpentry.[25]

Between April 6and June 25, 1946, the DPI licensed 328 motion pictures to be exhibited throughout the occupied south.[26] And by late 1946, noncommercial venues for motion-picture exhibition grew with the development of provincial information centers, whose duties were officially transferred to the Office of Civil Information (OCI) of the USAFIK in June 1948 in anticipation of the dissolution of the American Military Government and the establishment of South Korea's First Republic in August 1948. These "Democracy Information Centers" were to "represent an encouraging and important development in Korean community life" as "instruments of education—not politics or propaganda," whose primary purpose was "to supplement existing opportunities for Korean citizens, young and old, to learn about the rest of the world through pictures, readings materials and radio."[27] Contrary to these pronouncements, however, the information centers were the propaganda arm of the US military, and political education became even more aggressive and pronounced in the spring of 1948. In April 1948 the OCI produced the feature film *The People Vote*, which fictionalized the experiences of a family living in a small town during the prospective election.[28] Another short feature, titled *How to Vote*, instructed the local population on the democratic election process. It also hired the famed Korean filmmaker Ch'oe In-gyu to produce the educational film *Gukmin t'up'yo* (A national referendum) for the information centers. The film, which sought to bring awareness of the significance and the process of a democratic election to the Korean public, was released just ten days before the election on May 10, 1948.[29] These educational films were distributed by OCI branch offices to the Mobile Education Unit and provincial information centers for exhibition in order to promote maximum participation by the Korean population in the general election that would establish the First Republic of Korea and allow the United States to make a graceful exit from the disadvantages and "liabilities" attached to "the continued American military occupation and government of South Korea."[30] In this way, the "Democracy Information Centers" were mobilized for the US occupation's short-term political campaign, which went beyond its inaugural purpose of transmitting American culture "as an instrument of education," as touted by General Hodge earlier.[31]

To further promote the coming election in May, the Speakers Section of the OCI hired 150 special speakers on a temporary basis. The speakers usually operated in their locales to encourage the people there to participate in the election. They were briefed in the field and given printed directives for the campaign. In this effort, the Mobile Education Unit was also utilized to its maximum capacity. The unit distributed printed materials and presented a play, *Father's Native Village*, as well as exhibiting a dubbed American film, *Tuesday in November* (1945), and the aforementioned OCI feature film *The People Vote*.[32] Directed by John Berry and assisted by Nicholas Ray at Paramount, *Tuesday in November* details the process of voting in a small California town during the 1944 presidential election, when President Roosevelt was challenged by Governor Tom Dewey of New York. This film was produced in the United States for the general public overseas, and it was specifically used to inform and interest Koreans, both women and men, in the upcoming election and to encourage their participation. In this effort, the OCI received additional assistance from the United Nations Film Board, which produced the 16mm film *The People's Charter* to promote the very same election—a film that was to be overseen by the United Nations Temporary Commission on Korea.

Having taken over the responsibility of the soon to be defunct DPI in June 1948, the OCI of the US Army Forces in Korea continued to perform distinctively American propaganda functions, such as disseminating information concerning American aid to Korea and information about American life and culture to the indigenous population. Prior to the takeover, the USAFIK had also established its own public-relations office on August 22, 1945. Its chief mission was to inform the American public of its activities and administration, which was also expanded in response to the revolutionary circumstances in Korea to become equally responsible for monitoring US military personnel's conduct and working to improve

US-Korea relations. However, as early as December 1945, the US military and Korean agents cooperated on their first motion-picture production—a timely cultural film, titled *Chayu ŭi chong ŭl ullyŏra* (Ring the freedom bell), in celebration of Korea's liberation from Japan—to shore up local approval of the US occupation of Korea, which was in decline.[33] In advance of the American Military Government's DPI, the joint production marked the start of local filmmaking by the USAFIK as part of its expanded role in civil-affairs relations with Korea.

Locally produced films were also directed at US military and civilian personnel in Korea to "contribute to a better understanding between [the] forces and the Korean people and to avoid friction and undesirable incidents."[34] American soldiers and civilians were encouraged to make "special efforts to treat the Korean population in such a manner as to develop confidence in and increase the prestige of the United States and the United Nations."[35] Educational publications, public performances, and motion pictures on Korean customs and history and the US military's mission and world news were made available and presented at USAFIK libraries and theaters as "one of the best means of furnishing education through recreation to the soldiers in Korea."[36] Sample motion pictures included *The Historic Remains of Shilla*, an ancient Korean dynasty,[37] and *FEC MPS Newsreel no. 1*, the first pictorial news coverage by the Far East Motion Picture Services, introduced by Lieutenant General Robert Eichelberger, the Eighth Army commander, and dealing with the recent earthquake disasters in Japan. These educational and topical programs for American military and civilian personnel were produced in cooperation with the troop information and education officer of the US Army responsible for troop orientation "to help our occupation forces understand what we are trying to accomplish."[38] For this purpose, and to move beyond its diplomatic role as American representatives, the US military sought cooperation from Korean filmmakers to acculturate American soldiers to the East, much as it sought to Americanize Koreans.

Indeed, selling Korea to the American public was equally important to the US military. In May 1946, General Hodge approved the production of a series of Korean newsreels, under the title *Korean Newsreel*, for the dual purpose of informing and educating his troops and photographically documenting US Army activities in Korea for the home front, as required by the War Department.[39] The newsreels were produced on a monthly basis on 35mm film, each running approximately ten minutes. The signal officer of the USAFIK was in charge, with production handled by the 123rd Signal Service Department, and processing was handled in Tokyo. The distribution of these newsreels was controlled by the signal service, and they were intended to be shown together with commercial entertainment films.[40] As for content, the scope of *Korean Newsreel* was promotional (between the Military Government and the US armed forces troops, as well as between the US military and Korea and the American public) and included special military activities, information on Korean life and customs (particularly activity that showed what Koreans were doing to help Americans), points of scenic and historical activity in Korea, and sports and social activities. As the need for improving US-Korea relations heightened, *Korean Newsreel* was succeeded by *Progress of Korea* on January 19, 1947, to become a biweekly series.[41] A letter from Hodge to William M. Carty (representing Paramount News, Fox Movietone, News of the Day, Universal, and March of Time) dated June 28, 1948, further describes the ongoing public-relations problem for the US military with the American public:

> Although I have not yet had the opportunity to see the newsreel of our Korean election, the comments from your office regarding its excellence make me very happy, in that it appears that at least one successful American effort got decent coverage. It was a pleasure to be of assistance to you a representative of the pool of the major newsreel companies of the United States, and I am confident your coverage will do much to present to our fellow Americans at home at least a partial picture of our efforts to aid the Korean people in joining the world family of free nations.[42]

Such concerns were justified: the American public vested little importance in Korea, while tensions continued to mount in Korea that would eventually erupt into the Korean Civil War. Indeed, Hodge's control over Korea was tenuous, with the occupation regime being the "principal source of Korean discontent and instability."[43] Aware of these conditions, both the US Army and the State Department were eager to withdraw all troops from Korea, but not without a guarantee against Soviet control over the entire country, which was why the UN intervention was advocated and the general election in the south was held without North Korea's participation. Once again, Korean filmmakers were enlisted to aid the US military, and among those recruited to ameliorate these conditions was the aforementioned Ch'oe In-gyu, who directed two more films for the US military. These films were made after the establishment of Korea's First Republic, and the audience they addressed was the Americans overseas and at home.[44] As newsreels that sought to bring cultural awareness of Korea and improve Korea-US relations, *Chang Ch'u-hwa muyong* (The dance of Chang Ch'u-hwa; released August 20, 1948) introduced Chang's modern Korean ballet, while *Hŭimang ŭi maul* (The town of Hope; released November 15, 1948) showcased Korea's rural landscape to presumably promote Korea as a modern nation to the cultural elite and attract the mainstream audience with Korea's exotic scenery.

Ch'oe was not the only significant Korean filmmaker recruited by the US military for the purpose of educating the American public. Director An Chŏr-yŏng also sought to bridge the differences between Korea and the United States with his documentary *Mugunghwa* (The rose of Sharon, 1948), named after the national flower of South Korea. The film depicts the Korean diaspora in Hawaii, which represents the first wave of Korean labor migrants.[45] Produced by South Korea's

Ministry of Education, this film was shot in Kodacolor, exhibiting its greater budget and significance, and in 16mm. The nearly thirty-five minutes of the film's content serves to illustrate the voice-over narrator's introduction to the Korean-Hawaiian community (i.e., in its capacity as Americans), its contribution to Korea's liberation from abroad, and its efforts to preserve and celebrate Korean culture (i.e., being Korean). Sequences include a display of different Korean-Hawaiian laborers at work, including women—at the sugar and pineapple fields and factories, the dairy farm, the harbor, and the markets where Korean specialty foods are distributed and sold—as well as different classes of the Korean-Hawaiian social structure, including a Korean doctor whose daily life involves examining sick children followed by a lavish dinner with his family on his large estate. In addition to the work life, sequences depicting the cultural and leisure life include students in classrooms and on campus at the University of Hawaii, a high school graduation, children at Bible study at a Christian academy (*kidok hagwŏn*) founded by the newly elected Korean president, Syngman Rhee, surfers and beachcombers at Waikiki Beach, a college football game, hula dancing, Korean traditional dancing, a procession of Hawaiian culture during Aloha Week, with Chinese, Japanese, Philippine, and Nordic women participating in their traditional dress, and a family gathered together in a sitting room listening to the *Korean National Herald*'s radio news and culture program, which featured such events as the live broadcast of an aria from *La Bohème* sung by a Korean soprano.

As Christina Klein observes, Hawaii was "an important location from which to wage the struggle for the hearts and minds of Asia."[46] In this case, however, An's cheerful images of ethnic Koreans fully immersed in the diverse customs of multiracial, multiethnic Hawaii reciprocate to the American audience the image of America as a pluralist and multicultural society that the US military so forcefully promoted to Korean audiences. In this way, the US military's efforts to secure support for having its mission in Korea include promoting Korea and Korean culture to American civilians at the home front, as well as to American troops in Korea, thus reflecting the gaze and expanding American cinema's domain—or its "semiotic empire," as described by Dissanayake—into which the Korean cultural imaginary, however small, seeped to muddle any straightforward interpretation.[47]

In these manifold ways, the US military's information and propaganda apparatus was pulled and stretched to address a diverse audience, both in Korea and in the United States. To wit, the apparatus went beyond promoting American ideas and ideals of democracy, to include educating the American public about Korean customs and history, and sometimes even the international audience—by sending a Korean delegate to England, for example, to show members of the World Council of Sunday Schools (i.e., the World Council of Christian Education and the Sunday School Association) a picture of Korean life.[48] Although it is difficult to know if these films actually succeeded in Americanizing the Korean population or Koreanizing the American population in Korea or elsewhere, especially since they are clearly marked as government films, given the method of distribution and conspicuous subject matter, it is important to note the knotty positions held by the US military as it sought to justify its actions and policies and legitimize its occupation of the Korean territory to a much larger audience. Certainly, recognition of the diverse types of films distributed by the US military makes it difficult to posit any one-sided interpretation of their exchange and impact, particularly from the United States to Korea—especially since local filmmakers were involved in some of the US military productions. What is clear is that motion pictures played a central role in the dissemination of information and propaganda during the US occupation, and the large quantity and high quality of these films accelerated the growth of a moviegoing audience among southern Koreans, particularly those in the remote rural regions where there were no commercial theaters and where souped-up jeeps and trains brought news from the city and around the world. Such outreach efforts, of course, were far from unique or exclusive to the US military, and they hark back to the work of Soviet revolutionary filmmakers of the 1920s. Even North Korea practiced this tradition of bringing "cinema to the masses" by using "Mobile Film Groups" (*idong yŏngsaban*) throughout the country.[49]

More important, these early networks and methods of disseminating information and propaganda, particularly by using motion pictures, were effectively continued by the State Department's US Information Service (USIS) in 1949 and during the Korean War (1950–53), to be succeeded by the USIS-Korea after 1953. Also continued were the local production of vivid informational films for the purpose of enthralling Americans with striking images of Korea and its culture, but this time by the United Nations. On November 25, 1953, Theodore R. Conant, an American member of the United Nations Korean Reconstruction Agency (UNKRA) Film Unit, wrote rousingly about a "new kind of lecture on Korea, illustrated with 16mm color film, for presentation to the American public during the 1954–55 season." The one-hour screening was promoted as "new" because it presented "Korea *as it is* LIVE!" with ample "motion picture illustration of the background" to support a "well-rounded story of Korea Today," and "not just Korea at war," but "Korean culture, Korean history, Korean children, Korean urban and rural scenes."[50] To be accompanied by an in-person introduction by Conant and Dr. Wilson Gaddis, a Swiss-trained political consultant to the Office of President Syngman Rhee and attached to the Office of Public Information of the Republic of Korea, another legacy of the US occupation years, the lecture intended to "show in an interesting, highly colorful yet authentic way what Korea means to the world. And especially what its future holds for Americans and our free way of life."[51] As such, the lecture was designed to legitimize the South Korean government vis-à-vis the communists in the north as much as it was a rally in support of the United Nations and its humanitarian relief work, which was in desperate need of broad approval, especially with British and European support on the wane.[52]

Thus, US dominance of the visual terrain in South Korea continued unabated beyond the postwar era and throughout the Cold War, first forged by the US military, which wrested control of all media to promote American democracy without irony. Also continued were the US military's role as cultural interlocutor and the enlisting of Korean filmmakers to help promote American democracy and America's way of life. In doing so, the military abetted the newly formed South Korean government in adopting motion pictures and exploiting their use to further its own legitimacy and Cold War agenda abroad. Hence, while there is compelling evidence of slippage within the American semiotic empire that is laid open to multiple interpretations, contradictions, and challenges, compounded by the direction of film traffic originating from multiple vectors and intentions, there is also the undeniable legacy of motion picture's centrality in bolstering sovereignty in South Korea, its years of military rule writ large.

NOTES

All Korean names, words, and titles have been romanized according to the McCune-Reischauer system, with the exception of those names (e.g., Syngman Rhee) and titles (of both publications and films) that already have common English usage. Both Korean and Japanese names have been presented in the Asian style, with last name first and given name last, unless there is a well-known or preferred form. Unless otherwise noted, translations into English are by the author. Moreover, all references to "Korea" are to predivision Korea (pre-1945), "southern Korea" are to US-occupied present-day South Korea (1945–1948), and "South Korea" are to the Republic of Korea, proclaimed on August 15, 1948.

1. Wimal Dissanayake, "Asian Cinema and the American Cultural Imaginary," *Theory, Culture & Society* 13, no. 4 (1996): 120.

2. Ibid., 109.

3. Haidee Wasson and Charles R. Acland, "Introduction: Utility and Cinema," in *Useful Cinema*, ed. Charles R. Acland and Haidee Wasson (Durham, NC: Duke University Press, 2011), 2–3.

4. "Report on the History and Growth of the Office of Civil Information," US Army Forces in Korea (USAFIK), November 10, 1947, Headquarters, USAFIK, signed by James L. Stewart, box 32, record group (RG) 554, National Archives and Records Administration, College Park, MD (hereafter cited as NARA).

5. September 8, 1945, is more commonly given as the date marking the transfer of power, but it is more accurately the day the US military landed on the shore of Inchon, a major city located in the midwestern coast of the Korean Peninsula, approximately seventeen miles from Seoul, and currently home to South Korea's international airport. "Diary of Military Government, 8 September to Date," General Hodge Official Files, USAFIK, box 1, RG 554, NARA.

6. "Policy Paper Prepared in the Department of State," June 22, 1945, *FRUS, 1945* VI: 563, http://digicoll.library.wisc.edu/cgi-bin/FRUS/FRUS-idx?type=goto&id=FRUS.FRUS1945v06&isize=M&submit=Go+to+page&page=563.

7. "President Truman to Ambassador Edwin W. Pauley, at Paris," July 16, 1946, *FRUS, 1946* VIII: 713, http://digital.library.wisc.edu/1711.dl/FRUS.FRUS1946v08; and General Hodge Official File, 1946, box 1, RG 554, NARA.

8. Tae-Jin Yoon, "Mass Media and the Reproduction of the International Order: Presentation of American Culture by American Television Programs Aired in Korea, 1970 to 1989" (PhD diss., University of Minnesota, 1997), 134.

9. "History of the Department of Public Information," August 1948, box 39, RG 554, NARA.

10. Ibid.

11. Sueyoung Park-Primiano, "South Korean Cinema between the Wars: Screening Resistance and Containment under US Intervention and Influence, 1945–60" (PhD diss., New York University, 2015).

12. "History of the Department of Public Information," August 1948, box 39, RG 554, NARA.

13. "Appendix VI, A Statement Policy," [1948], MPAA General Correspondence, reel no. 13, Margaret Herrick Library, Academy of Motion Picture Arts and Science (hereafter cited as MHL).

14. "History of the Department of Public Information," August 1948, box 39, RG 554, NARA.

15. *Fury in the Pacific* is available online at www.youtube.com/watch?v=i7KsOfVm8Bs. This nearly twenty-minute-long black-and-white film "was the first film produced jointly by the American Army, Navy and Marine Corps for public showings. Nine photographers were wounded and one killed in the crew of 39 which took the footage for this story of the landings on Pelelieu and Anguar in the Palaus." The commentary was written by Captain Charles Grayson of the army, and it was distributed by Warner Bros. for the Office of War Information (OWI) in March 1945. See Richard Dyer MacCann, *The People's Films: A Political History of US Government Motion Pictures* (New York: Hastings House, 1973), 167.

16. Takashi Fujitani, "Nation, Blood, and Self-Determination," in *Race for Empire: Koreans as Japanese and Japanese as Americans during World War II* (Berkeley: University of California Press, 2011), 303.

17. Press releases, May 6, 1946, and June 19 and 25, 1946, box 23, RG 554, NARA. *The Battle of Iwo Jima*, also known as *To the Shores of Iwo Jima*, is available online at www.youtube.com/watch?v=KBuXgQRz3II. This Oscar-nominated film "was the first American military picture made according to a carefully worked out battle-plan script," and it was the work of 106 navy, marine corps, and coast guard cameramen, edited at Warner Bros., and released by United Artists for the OWI. See MacCann, *People's Films*, 167.

18. Ibid.

19. Jae Young Cha, "Media Control and Propaganda in Occupied Korea, 1945–1948: Toward an Origin of Cultural Imperialism" (PhD diss., University of Illinois at Urbana-Champaign, 1994), 206.

20. The CMPE had its headquarters in Tokyo, which was also occupied by the US military.

21. Press release, April 8, 1946, box 23, RG 554, NARA.

22. Press releases, April 4–5, 23, 1946, box 23, RG 554, NARA; "Appendix VI, A Statement of Policy," [1948], MPAA, General Correspondence, reel no. 13, MHL.

23. Press release, April 8, 1946, Box 23, RG 554, NARA.

24. Press release, August 23, 1946, Box 23, RG 544, NARA.

25. Press release, September 9, 1947, Box 24, RG 554, NARA.

26. Press release, June 25, 1946, Box 23, RG 554, NARA.

27. Press release April 30, 1948, Box 33, RG 554, NARA.

28. Cha, "Media Control and Propaganda," 226.

29. One of the few Korean filmmakers to bridge the colonial to postcolonial eras, Ch'oe In-gyu is a controversial figure most famously known for his patriotic liberation film *Hurrah! for Freedom* (1946), as well as for several pro-Japanese films, among them *Chip ŭmnŭn chŏnsa* (Angels on the streets, 1941) and *Sarang ŭi maeng-sŏ* (Vow of love, 1945).

30. Leland M. Goodrich. *Korea: A Study of US Policy in the United Nations,* reprint ed. (New York: Council on Foreign Relations, Krause Reprint Co.,1972 [1956]), 28.

31. Press release, May 6, 1948, box 32, RG 554, NARA.

32. According to Richard Dyer MacCann, *Tuesday in November* is "an oversimplification of the electoral system," produced for the Overseas Branch of the OWI in 1945. See MacCann, *People's Films,* 143–44. This seventeen-minute-long black-and-white film is available online at www.youtube.com /watch?v=wZW1DQ8Sd6g.

33. This 16mm film was shot by Han Ch'ang-sŏp, under the direction [of Mason Davy?] of the American Military Government, and edited by Pang Han-jun. "Kunjŏngbu munhwa yŏnghwa kŭnil p'yonjip wansŏng," *Chungang Sinmum* [Central daily news], December 11, 1945, ed. Han'guk Yŏngsang Charyowŏn [Korean Film Archive], *Sinmun kisa ro pon Chosŏn yŏnghwa, 1945–1957* [Korean cinema seen from the news reports], Han'guk yŏnghwa charyo ch'ongso: Ch'op'an (Seoul: Konggan kwa Saramdŭl, 2004), 9.

34. Adjutant General, 091.Countries, November 5–December 23, 1946, box 21, RG 554, NARA.

35. Ibid.

36. Press releases, July 16, 1948, Hist. & Growth of Civil Information Office, box 33, RG 554, NARA; press releases, August 23, 1946, box 24, RG 554, NARA.

37. Shilla, also known as "Silla," was one of the Three Kingdoms of Korea and one of the world's longest sustained dynasties, lasting from 57 BCE to 935 CE.

38. Press releases, July 16, 1948, Hist. & Growth of Civil Information Office, box 33, RG 554, NARA; press releases, August 23, 1946, box 24, RG 554, NARA.

39. Letter dated May 23, 1946, from the War Department to occupation commanding generals related to departmental policy on overseas photography, "Photographs, etc. (1946)," box19, RG 554, NARA.

40. Letter dated June 30, 1947, from Bill Buerkle, Major, Sig C, Photo Officer, to Commanding General Hodge, "Motion Pictures (1947)," box 19, RG 554, NARA.

41. See "Public Relations: Relations with Korea," in "History of the Office of Civil Information," May 30, 1947, through June 30, 1948, box 39, RG 554, NARA.

42. John R. Hodge to William M. Caty, June 28, 1948, box 3, RG 554, NARA.

43. Melvyn P. Leffler, *A Preponderance of Power: National Security, the Truman Administration, and the Cold War* (Stanford, CA: Stanford University Press, 1992), 251.

44. These films are also identified by the Korean Film Archive film database as US Information Service films, but they predate US Information Agency (known overseas as the USIS). And since these films were produced after the founding of Korea's First Republic and for the American audience, they were more than likely produced for the Office of Civil Information or the Public Relations or Signal Office of the USAFIK.

45. From January 1903 to July 1905, approximately seventy-two hundred Koreans responded to the demand for cheap labor, as well as for strikebreakers against Japanese laborers, to work on the sugar plantations in Hawaii. See Pyong Gap Min, *Koreans' Immigration to the US: History and Contemporary Trends,* Research Report no. 3 (New York: Research Center for Korean Community, Queens College of CUNY, January 27, 2011), accessed May 31, 2012, www.qc.cuny.edu/Academics/Centers/RCKC /Documents/Koreans%20Immigration%20to%20the%20US.pdf.

46. Christina Klein, *Cold War Orientalism: Asia in the Middlebrow Imagination, 1945–1961* (Berkeley: University of California Press, 2003), 244.

47. Dissanayake, "Asian Cinema," 119.

48. "Korean Minister to Display Sample of Korean Culture," press releases, July 24, 1947, for American Press, box 24, RG 554, NARA. The Reverend Whang Jai Kyung took with him color slides of Korea, replicas of ancient Korean court instruments, and Korean dolls. The color films showed the Korean

countryside, folk dances, festival celebrations, and customs, which were to be screened for the representatives attending the conference. The reverend was also a skilled musician, and he was scheduled to demonstrate ancient court instruments.

49. Charles K. Armstrong, "The Origins of North Korean Cinema: Art and Propaganda in the Democratic People's Republic," *Acta Koreana* 5, no. 1 (January 2002): 13–14.

50. Conant to US military base in San Francisco, November 25, 1953, Theodore Richard Conant Collection, C. V. Starr East Asian Library, Columbia University.

51. Ibid.

52. Ibid. A letter from Conant to Gordon Hessler dated April 15, 1954, states, "The deal is that UNKRA is allmost [*sic*] on the rocks because the U.K. and other European countries are not very interested in Korea and don't want to put any money into Korean reconstruction. My assignment is [to] whip together whatever publicity material I can, and bring it over to Europe just after the Geneva conference begins. . . . If UNKRA ignomineously [*sic*] folds up it will not only be very bad for Korea but will also harm the whole United Nations as it will mean that in effect from now on Korea will only be a US show . . . [and] that the other nations of the world have ceased to honor the responsibilities taken on by the UN in Korea."

14

SHOTS MADE AROUND THE WORLD

DASPO's Documentation of the Vietnam War

James Paasche

The viewfinder of the camera, one could say, has the opposite function of the gunsight that a soldier levels at his enemy. The latter frames an image for annihilation; the former frames an image for preservation.
—DAVID MACDOUGALL

The Department of the Army Special Photographic Office (DASPO) was a group of specialized filmmaking and still-photography units formed by the US Army in 1962 with the mandate to document the army's efforts during the Cold War. In a bit of interservice competition, the success of the US Air Force's First Motion Picture Unit (FMPU) had a direct influence on the formation of DASPO.[1] Upon leaving a White House briefing with President John F. Kennedy in 1962, General George Decker, chief of staff of the US Army, proclaimed he was tired of looking at "documentary films showing how great the Air Force is."[2] Decker commanded Colonel Arthur Jones, plans officer of the Army Pictorial Center, to form a documentary unit for the army's purposes.

DASPO had three detachments: Pacific (the largest part of DASPO, responsible for almost all of Southeast Asia, with a base of operations in Hawaii), Panama (documenting Cold War activities in Central and South America), and CONUS, or the continental United States. In the first three years of operations of the Pacific detachment alone, over 750,000 feet of color film footage had been given to the army. By 1968, three permanent DASPO units were operating in Southeast Asia: Team Alpha (South Korea), Team Bravo (Thailand), and Team Charlie, headquartered in Saigon.[3] Keeping this network running required extensive coordination, which necessitated a number of rationalized organizational practices. The army envisioned DASPO as part of a worldwide network that provided footage for army producers to use, established a pictorial and moving-image record of the Vietnam War and other Cold War activities, and allowed officials back home to experience the global reach of US military activities firsthand via frontline footage.

DASPO, like many other contemporaneous military film and photo units, could easily be regarded as producers of propaganda, as the media arm of a capitalist, imperialist worldwide mission. As such, DASPO's activities helped document the ways in which the United States spread its political messages through military means. Yet here my aim is not to analyze the films and photos DASPO produced as some sort of form of pure ideology. Rather, in spelling out the procedures and cultural values of the DASPO media workers, I interrogate how their particular form of labor can be seen as indicative of the ways in which military and political ideas are practiced and produced on the ground, in the hands of grunt workers who are significant nodes in a worldwide media network.

This essay focuses on the activities of the Pacific detachment—the largest and most prolific of DASPO detachments—and, more specifically, on DASPO's work in Vietnam from 1962 to 1974. By narrowing in on Team Charlie, this essay engages with three contemporary concerns regarding the Vietnam War and media studies: (1) demythologizing the experience of American soldiers in the war;[4] (2) detailing the production of institutional films;[5] and (3) situating DASPO as a production culture in which film production functioned "to gain and reinforce identity, to forge consensus and order, to perpetuate [DASPO and its] interests."[6] These concerns allow a different picture of the Vietnam War to emerge, one in which heroic myths of deprivation and devastation in the jungle—the subjects of many fictionalized accounts of the war—fade in relief to a vision of the Vietnam War as part of a larger effort to extend American military dominance throughout the world, with film as a key cog of the technological and ideological engine employed to accomplish these goals. By fixing our sights on the practices of a production culture working for an institution like the US Army, we gain a more finely tuned account of the experiences of a particular group of media makers during wartime. Likewise, by following the processes of film production employed by DASPO and analyzing the films themselves, we gain a more inclusive, and realistic, portrait of both the labor of media production and the business of soldiering during the Vietnam War.

DASPO's films and photos traveled from Vietnam through the Army Pictorial Center in New York to arrive at the Pentagon, where they were sometimes screened for officials or sometimes cobbled together to help produce films or be used as sources for television and newspaper reports. This worldwide documentary network, heavily managed by the army, allowed its personnel a certain level of creativity and freedom of movement. As such, DASPO demonstrates just how vital *film* remained, both ideologically and practically, during the years of America's first "living room war."[7]

The first portion of this chapter documents the formation of the unit and explores the hopes the army had for a mobile documentary crew in Vietnam. The second portion details the training of DASPO cameramen at Fort Monmouth, New Jersey. To situate the DASPO filmmakers in Vietnam, the third section examines the complicated production practices of DASCO personnel as media laborers in a specialized unit. Finally, I examine the filmic work of DASPO, including films and raw footage, from a major collection of DASPO photographers at the Vietnam Center and Archive at Texas Tech University (VCA). The films are the end result of a tremendous institutional effort and testify to how seriously the army took the business of filmmaking. They also stand as remarkable documents that enable new glimpses into the historic record of this war. In detailing the processes of making institutional films while examining the products of that labor, this chapter articulates DASPO's history as an example of the complicated negotiations of freedom and control in the institutional management of images.

. . .

The Panama detachment's operations in Central and South America were as ambiguous as the Cold War itself. Though the army was not technically fighting, the nebulous peacekeeping distinction belied the extent to which DASPO Panama participated in gathering information for US purposes through its coverage of "riots, military coups, and natural disasters."[8] For example, in 1964 DASPO cameraman Mike Griffey captured footage of riots in the Panama Canal Zone involving a dispute over US sovereignty of the area.[9] The unedited footage depicts a crazed situation of tear gas, tanks, riot police, cars on fire—visceral reportage of the on-the-ground stakes of the US military's worldwide spread. And while the CONUS detachment usually filmed activities at or near bases across the United States, they were on the ground for Cold War activities in the Dominican Republic. These detachments helped visualize the covert military activities of the United States during the Cold War in an empirical and precise manner.

Narrowing in on Team Charlie's activities in Vietnam during the war allows for a more detailed focus on a unit's operations in a declared war zone, rather than the more ambiguous worldwide stretch enabled by a Cold War perspective. DASPO detachments enjoyed a unique operational designation that distinguished them from the many military photography units working in Vietnam. They reported directly to superiors at the Department of the Army level, which meant that commanders in the theaters in which they operated did not control them. This gave DASPO a high level of autonomy in carrying out orders, much like their professional counterparts in broadcast news or newspapers. Given the territorial structure of the army, it did not sit well with field commanders when DASPO photographers showed up. As Lieutenant Colonel Claude Bache, a DASPO member, noted, local commanders "were obligated to house, feed, transport and pay us, but couldn't tell us what to do."[10]

DASPO interpreted its orders to cover the US Army activities as operational ones, meaning it did not want to cover the political grandstanding of army officials shaking hands with local dignitaries at cocktail parties. Instead, it focused on subjects that mattered to carrying out military activities, which, admittedly, is a broad purview.[11] These activities included documenting army programs helping South Vietnamese citizens and military; depicting army life in Vietnam; acknowledging the specialized labor of forces such as medical and canine-training units; and delineating the vast amounts of technology and equipment employed in the war. Usually, DASPO crews were briefed on assignments by a public information officer, who supplied "the who, what, where, when, how and why of the combat operation," effectively managing the assignments, but not necessarily the soldiers, on the ground.[12] Armed with explicit orders detailing the desired coverage, DASPO photographers worked within the contingencies of wartime media production and the chaotic nature of the American involvement in the Vietnam War. The experiences of DASPO photographers in the field demonstrate how the control over media production in an institutionalized context is fraught with the tension between desired outcomes and the actual experiences of war. These experiences for DASPO photographers usually began at Fort Monmouth, New Jersey.

BASIC (MEDIA) TRAINING

DASPO emerged in a highly developed context for military image making and use. The army, and its communications command, the signal corps, had already created a structure to service filmmaking and photography duties. The Army Pictorial Center (APC), established in 1942 two months after the Japanese attack on Pearl Harbor, and initially known as the Signal Corps Photographic Center, set up shop in the former studio of Famous Players–Lasky, and later Paramount, in Astoria, New York.[13] The APC, according to its own promotional materials, was "a full service motion picture and still photographic production, distribution and storage facility with all the capabilities of any movie studio in the world."[14] The army bought the studio from Paramount, which was in the midst of consolidating its production practices on the West Coast. Thus the army was able to retain some studio talent ("editors, cameramen, producers, directors, photo lab personnel and script-writers") who did not want to abandon their lives on the East Coast.[15] Initially, under the command of Colonel Arthur Jones, the DASPO offices were housed at the APC.[16] Until its closing in 1970, the APC was the place where DASPO photographers sent their photographic and film work for processing, establishing a network in which materials made their way around the world to the APC in Astoria.

DASPO photographers came to the unit with a variety of photographic experience. While initially stocked with soldiers from previous photographic units from World War II and the Korean War, DASPO soon began to take on soldiers trained at the Army Signal School, in Fort Monmouth, New Jersey. The Signal School was, according to a training pamphlet, "a large-scale technical institution that trains students in the techniques required to maintain complex communications, photographic, automatic data processing, and radar equipment utilized by the US Army Signal Corps in worldwide combat support and command operations of the US Army."[17] In placing film training alongside other technical training in communications and computing, the army demonstrated its view of film as a part of the larger technological superiority that was supposed to give the United States a definitive advantage over the North Vietnamese. Films and photos were weapons, useful both tactically and ideologically.

Soldiers who came to Fort Monmouth were chosen because of their interest in communications and photography, but those interests were often born of different motivations. Some, such as Howard Breedlove, were already enlisted men who wanted to try something else: "I went to photo school to get into photography. I had to get out of tanks," he told an interviewer.[18] Others were enlistees who had previous photographic experience, such as Ted Acheson, who had taken photography classes at Marquette University.[19] Some were straight out of high school, with little to no photographic experience. The variety of experience levels speaks to the army's belief that it could make these soldiers filmmakers—that this skill, like learning how to wield weaponry or fix equipment, was something perfected by the military machine and could be passed on through training.

Training at Fort Monmouth usually lasted a few months and combined technical training with more-vague instruction in storytelling. The Signal School's pedagogical style reflected a desire to prepare the students with useful skills through "the practical application method of instruction," which, in its own words, was "learning by doing."[20] Soldiers were taught the technical skills of their given interest, which, for DASPO members, meant taking apart equipment, troubleshooting problems, and repairing cameras, projectors, and sound equipment in order to gain knowledge of how their chosen "weaponry" worked. The Signal School itself framed the training as preparation for a "definite, useful, and interesting military career, which can be the beginning of a fruitful civilian career."[21] This foregrounding of the promise of military labor to pay off in civilian life continues to be one of the chief lures of military recruitment to this day.

The development of skills in telling stories visually occurred in a more haphazard manner than the more regimented technical training. Film crews were often sent off base to practice real-world applications of the classroom skills they had learned. Acheson recounts a circus coming to town and being assigned to "do a story on that just to learn how to put a story together and how to shoot something like that correctly."[22] These kinds of off-the-cuff, learn-by-doing methods offered soldiers experience in constructing stories while dealing with the contingencies of shooting on location. The back-and-forth between technical-skill training and learning by doing also served as a preview of the negotiation between the control the army exerted over their creative activity and the freedom they had in approaching the contingencies of shooting film in Vietnam during wartime.

Greg Adams's training footage, completed during his time at Fort Monmouth, demonstrates the ways in which soldiers were conditioned to think about story.[23] Adams's footage exists in the VCA as separate reels, usually around two minutes long, shot on 8mm, though most of the unit production footage in Vietnam was shot on 16mm. Filled with in-camera edits, establishing shots, canted angles, and other signs of a beginning filmmaker's attempts to construct a simple story in a brief amount of time, the reels reveal how the attention to developing stories became ingrained in the cameramen's work. *Reel 6* stands out for the way in which Adams's attempts to construct a story are made evident in the footage.[24] It depicts a group of children playing war in their classroom, complete with props and a story in which one child soldier is injured. The action moves to an army "hospital" where kid doctors operate on the kid soldier. Needless to say, it is a strange film, especially given the complete lack of information about this exercise. The development of a forward-moving narrative is part and parcel of the game the children were playing; it is not constructed purely by Adams's camera. However, given the in-camera edits, and the variety of shots and angles used in the coverage of the event, the reel shows us Adams thinking cinematically, aware of the need for continuity and the establishment of space as key components of presenting a story in the tradition of classic Hollywood's organization of space and narrative.

More explicit in its depiction of media training, the short reel *Training on the Auricon* depicts a group of soldiers at Fort Monmouth as they take turns training on the Auricon, a sound-on-film–brand camera popular for location shooting.[25] The color footage, shot on a Bolex 16mm camera by one of the instructors at the photo school, depicts the camaraderie among DASPO soldiers and instructors. Along with shots of the men loading cameras while being instructed, the soldiers take turns fake-interviewing each other, with smiles on their faces. These sorts of artifacts demonstrate a reflexivity that is key to John Caldwell's conceptualization of production cultures, one in which the products/films of production cultures act as documents of labor and as the self-realization of that culture through their shared labor.[26] In a sense, a film like *Training on the Auricon* is a simple exercise to test equipment, part of the work assigned to DASPO. In another sense, the goofing around and faux interviews show the sort of camaraderie that is key for small units like DASPO, both as professional media makers and as soldiers within a small unit. Using this distinction to describe DASPO allows us to see how the particularities of the contexts in which they worked helped DASPO members forge a group identity that remains strong years after their service—an identity made clear not only by recollections in the archives, but also through the films and images they produced.

A PRODUCTION CULTURE IN COUNTRY

It is not until DASPO photographers reached Vietnam that we can truly understand the uniqueness of this unit and how its adherence to the imperatives of institutional desires necessitated both a strict attention to orders and the ability to adapt to the contingencies of filmmaking in a war zone. DASPO was just one component of an intense media environment in Vietnam, partly designed by the US government—one in which the media-production arms of the other military services, such as the navy's Pacific Fleet Combat Camera Group, not to mention the United States Information Agency (USIA), professionals of US network television, worldwide print journalists, and film units from both North and South Vietnam, were documenting the war on film as well. DASPO's command designation, which, as previously mentioned, necessitated that it report directly to the Department of the Army commanders back in Washington rather than to in-country leaders on the ground, allowed freedoms not enjoyed by other photographic units in Vietnam. Groups such as the 221st Signal Company, who provided the manpower for the Southeast Asia Pictorial Center (SEAPC), an extensive "lab complex for still photo processing and printing, and six permanent detachments from the DMZ to the delta," were handled by a different level of military command.[27] DASPO, because of its special designation, never processed its materials at SEAPC, instead sending them back to the United States. Again, because its orders were delivered from the States, DASPO was not subject to similar rules (for example, its members were often allowed to wear civilian clothing) or local commanders' whims.

DASPO crews usually had two to three members, made up of a still photographer, a motion-picture cameraman, and a soundman. Small teams allowed a great deal of flexibility and mobility—an important consideration given the material burden (of space, transportation, food, etc.) any extra soldiers placed on units who hosted them. Travel was easier, since a small team was able to hop on helicopters, planes, or jeeps, with minimal equipment, at a moment's notice. Larger photo teams with more equipment would have had to "book reservation on passenger flights around the country."[28] Howard Breedlove described his experience of this mobility as "bouncing," while William Foulke felt he and his fellow DASPO mates were "scavengers" who "imposed upon whoever and wherever the opportunity knocked."[29] Ted Acheson thought that this was an intentional move on the part of the army, since DASPO units were "supposed to be like that so we were not biased by anybody there"[30]—an idea reflecting the discourse surrounding the supposed objectivity or bias of documentary filmmakers and television news coverage at this time.

While the ideal of mobility often invokes a sense of freedom of movement, it is important to keep in mind that DASPO units moved where their orders took them, thus differentiating them from the romantic image of professional media combat reporters, like Michael Herr, during the Vietnam War. Herr, as a reporter for *Esquire,* enjoyed an almost unlimited mobility that many members of the professional press and network news organizations shared during the war, able to hop on helicopters almost unannounced or to follow units or battles on a whim.[31] The large amount of writing and filming done by these sorts of professionals is a material and psychic legacy of the war, with Herr's book *Dispatches* being one of the foremost examples of a particular style of visceral reporting that helped define the Vietnam War as a spectacular media event. However, even though DASPO and other military units had much in common with the professional news and TV reporters made famous during the war, the differences in mobility and institutional contexts of production help differentiate the functions of these various types of media laborers.

Smaller production units and the contingencies of filmmaking during war necessitated the use of filmmaking equipment that was portable and easy to use. Most of the servicemen filming in the early period of the war used Bell & Howell cameras: the Eyemo for 35mm work and the Filmo for 16mm, with the Filmo getting the majority of field work during the Vietnam War. Both cameras were developed with the issue of portability in mind, and they were preferred for their compact design and durability. They were also hand-cranked cameras, which did not require the carrying of a battery—a key consideration in keeping the weight of equipment down. While DASPO commanders often commented on their preference for the use of a tripod to get quality pictures, the portability of these cameras allowed for hand-held shooting—an important factor that enabled DASPO cameramen to respond quickly to the contingencies of a war zone or to move through jungles and swamps.

The arrival of the Arriflex 16BL 16mm camera in 1965 was an important technological moment for filmmakers worldwide who yearned for the mobility of smaller cameras coupled with the ability to record synchronous sound. The preferred camera of many of the filmmakers tied to the Direct Cinema movement in the United States,[32] the Arriflex 16BL was the workhorse of sound-film production for DASPO. It involved the tethering of a soundman, usually using a Nagra audio recorder, to the Arriflex. This equipment required a battery, thus making these units heavier—a consideration that often left DASPO members shedding flak jackets because of the weight. Despite their possible need of them, DASPO members did not often carry guns. They felt that if they needed a gun or flak jacket, it meant they were probably in a situation in which they could pick these items up from bodies on the ground.

The Department of the Army command at the Pentagon assigned the crews to document compelling events or the day-to-day operations of specific detachments. Sometimes they were assigned to cover seemingly important operational activities (e.g., the aftermath of a certain skirmish). At other times, they were used for what amounted to promotional exercises. For example, on October 1, 1968, Colonel Lorenz Beuschel, deputy assistant for Veterinary Services in the army,

FIGURE 14.1. Frame from *Army Combat Photographer* (1970). The film can be found in the Howard Breedlove Collection at the Vietnam Center and Archive at Texas Tech University.

wrote the acting chief of DASPO, First Lieutenant Darrell Winn, to request "that a film be made depicting the various functions of the US Army Veterinary Service in the Republic of Vietnam."[33] The film would be used for training veterinarians in the States and recruiting personnel for Veterinary Services. About three weeks later, Winn sent orders to Team Charlie outlining what was needed for the film:

> Photography should be oriented towards basic survey type documentary coverage and not towards detailed factual medical photography of step-by-step veterinary medicine procedures. The main idea: To photographically depict the various functions of the U.S. Army Veterinary service. . . . Background sound is required, sync or wildtrack, whichever is appropriate. Narration will be prepared by the requestor after filming is complete.[34]

The letter makes clear the chief functions of DASPO photographers: they were *documenters, not documentarians*—footage takers, not filmmakers. Very rarely did they have the opportunity to edit the material they shot. They were assigned to capture footage that would be used later, by the army and a variety of agencies, to be formed into something more meaningful—a process that Phil Rosen has called a "distinction between actuality and meaning, document and documentary."[35] This is an example of the power relations between these DASPO cameramen and the documentary makers, TV producers, and military officials—many of whom worked at far remove from the cameramen in the field—who used their images. DASPO members had but one subordinate role—making images—in this global, bureaucratic process. There is no clear authority to point to for the construction of meanings achieved through these images. The complex relationships among various authorities and subordinates, as realized in the in-depth procedures and minutiae of the DASPO photographers' particular form of media labor, complicates questions about creative agency and institutional modes of making movies.

Key to DASPO's mission was its mandate to document military activities using film and still photography. Caption writing was one integral, and time-consuming, element of this mandate that took up DASPO crews' time after principal photography, since they had to attempt to note every name, rank, detachment, and, often, hometown of the people they photographed. For instance, when filming a general while he shook hands with numerous soldiers, this became a burdensome task. DASPO sent its raw footage directly to the Army Pictorial Center for processing; images and captions then went to the Pentagon. "[D]ecisions about what to keep and what to throw away were made there. After processing, images became available to military publications, the press, and the public at a photographic library in the Pentagon."[36] In essence, they "were creating a visual record of operations, equipment, and personnel for the Pentagon archives."[37] Often, the screening of DASPO material at the Pentagon was the only time some of this footage was viewed. Thus, DASPO often represented the army to itself, but not to the outside world as much as the soldiers' brethren in other photo detachments or in the professional media.

Occasionally, the footage was used to make documentaries aired on television, even though "the film DASPO shot was not intended for civilian consumption"[38]— a key difference between DASPO and almost every other military unit or professional photographic crew working in Vietnam, who imagined the American public and media as their audience, not just their military superiors. So, while they enjoyed some freedoms during operations in Vietnam, DASPO photographers were often beholden to commanding officers in Washington for the use, archiving, and availability of their photographic record during and after the war. These sorts of restrictions ultimately point to the lack of control DASPO photographers had over their materials and, consequently, the particular form of alienated labor they performed.[39]

Communication with superiors back home also took the form of photographic critiques—a requirement for the jobs DASPO photographed, whether still or motion picture. These critiques were part of the quality-control efforts institutionalized by the army, attempts at rationalizing the processing of information provided by these cinematic records as visual data. Critique sheets, sent back to the soldiers following the processing and viewing of footage by superiors, listed pertinent information about the job (location, photographer, date, etc.) along with a review of twelve basic camera techniques such as focus, exposure, composition, and framing. Although one might assume that this sort of attention to detail served as a teaching moment for DASPO photographers, many of the critiques contained a one-word response: "good" or "fair." There was a space for general remarks, which often took the form of advice to correct problems along with some simple affirmation of what was good about the project. The brevity of answers suggests that the completion of these sheets was more a perfunctory task, a way to prove that some action was being taken, however meaningless, the hallmark of busy work in a bureaucracy.

My desire in chronicling the minutiae of DASPO's work is to point to the ways in which the crews' everyday experiences were structured by the army, to counter any sense of romanticism that creeps into the reports about the freewheeling adventures of network news or newspaper reporters during the Vietnam War. The proliferation of critique sheets, film orders, and other paperwork helps make real the tasks considered important in service to the photographic duties of the DASPO units. However minor these tasks might seem in the scheme of things, they were one of the ways the army attempted to control the time and labor of these media workers in adapting the work of filmmaking to institutional imperatives and the bureaucracy that comes with them.

THE FILMIC RECORD

While much of this essay has relied on *documents* from the Vietnam Center and Archive, it is important to examine some of the *films* produced using DASPO's footage, because they stand as historical images of a major war and allow a more inclusive view of the process of institutional filmmaking during a time of heightened attention to the role media plays during war. As I made clear earlier, DASPO's footage traveled worldwide circuits and eventually came to be viewed by larger audiences both during and after the war, often without any direct reference to its provenance. Despite this lack of direct citation, DASPO's members have actively detailed their own stories, through written reports and oral histories, and archived some of their private footage that they kept or snuck away—footage shot using their own cameras rather than army cameras. Thus, the images archived in the DASPO collection at the VCA include private reels, but also video copies of army films in which their work appeared, demonstrating the twisted paths, through multiple countries, formats, and categories (institutional or amateur), that their footage often took. The DASPO cameramen's status as footage accumulators, documenters of private and military history, makes clear that the material abundance and technological superiority with which the army conducted the Vietnam War continues to influence the ways in which we interpret the history of the war.

The Hidden War in Vietnam (1963), a twenty-nine-minute film, contains footage shot by DASPO cameramen a full year before the Gulf of Tonkin incident and the United States' official entry into this already long war. The film's tone connotes objective reportage, establishing the need for American intervention at a time when it was becoming a large part of international and national debate. It was shown as part of *The Big Picture*, an ABC weekly television series (1951–64) that reported world affairs involving the US Army and other military services, long before the war's recognition as a TV war.[40] Narrated by James Arness, famous for his role in the TV Western *Gunsmoke* and an army rifleman himself during World War II, it is a straightforward piece of army propaganda. Arness posits that the reason American forces are in Vietnam is to "bring to this area some tangible proof that the way of life we propose is a good life, worth fighting for." The words and images throughout the film support Claudia Springer's assertion that early army propaganda films produced during the war "shifted attention from the enemy to Vietnam's need for American assistance, as if military service in Vietnam were comparable to joining the Peace Corps."[41] Thus, we have an example of how actuality footage shot by DASPO crews was reused in a semifictional, and highly ideological, manner to present a view of the good work of the army, all of which was presented on a major television network. Were it not shot in color or set in Vietnam, there would be little to distinguish this film in its formal, narrative, and ideological qualities from its World War II predecessors like the *Why We Fight* series of films.

As part of the same ABC series, DASPO footage was also used in *The Soldier's Christmas* (1968), a film that documented soldiers worldwide as they celebrated Christmas.[42] The film begins with a close-up of a branded *The Big Picture* ornament hanging from a Christmas tree amid images of soldiers decorating and soon journeys on to a globe-spanning travelogue demonstrating the reach of the army: Berlin, Korea, Panama, "ice-locked Alaska"; really, there is nowhere the army and its soldiers are not. The film arrives in "the humid heat of Vietnam . . . because even in the combat zone, it is Christmas." Breezy in its depiction of the worldwide scope of US and military power, *The Soldier's Christmas* contains scenes of soldiers helping children in foreign countries learn the rituals of Christmas. However, in one sequence, the lure of the American way is made more explicit. Shots of Christmastime in New York City, ice-skating and the huge tree at Rockefeller Plaza, shop windows with toys—all conjure a fantasy world of American wealth that creates a stark contrast to the scenes involving soldiers standing guard in snowy Berlin. This sequence demonstrates that the spread of American forces worldwide is a key component of maintaining the possibilities of American consumerism back home.

Army Combat Photographer gives an idea of the type of work DASPO photographers performed in Vietnam.[43] It begins, like any number of films made during the early years of the war, with an onscreen narrator—in this case, Sergeant Ray God-dard, DASPO's noncommissioned officer in charge of the Pacific Detachment.[44] Goddard directly addresses the audience, spinning scripted comments about the DASPO man: "a man among men, dedicated to his profession. When the history of the Vietnam conflict is written, it will be his sights and his sounds that will provide a large portion of that history." After this conventional, but reflexive, beginning, the film takes a turn for the experimental—an example of how, even in the military, as with the changes noted by Dave Saunders in examining the Direct Cinema move-ment at the time, "the documentary form was transcending its roots in didacticism and finding new purpose in a world of change, disorder, and unclear horizons."[45] Goddard states: "The following film has no beginning, no middle, and no ending. It is meant to be an impression only. A message not hindered by the traditional struc-ture. It is a combination of motion picture, sound, and still photography obtained in combat by army combat photographers." Trying to give an impression of the DASPO experience, *Army Combat Photographer* displays a self-reflexivity about its produc-tion that points to the restrictions often placed upon DASPO crews by their superi-ors at the command level. The inclusion of whipping and panning, usually judged amateurish techniques by DASPO commanders, makes clear that the contingency of warfare necessitated techniques appropriate to the extreme conditions in which DASPO photographers sometimes found themselves. By switching between still and motion-picture footage, the film demonstrates the ways in which DASPO members worked together. The stills are exclusively of DASPO motion-picture photographers, pointing to the fact there was only one still photographer and one motion-picture photographer on each job; thus, any footage of the filmmakers must have been taken by the still photographer, and vice versa. It also includes one of the more famous sequences taken by a DASPO photographer: Harry Breedlove's footage of a Shell gas station burning, with the letter *S* on the sign destroyed so that it only reads "hell"—a succinct visual metaphor for the Vietnam War writ large. Somehow, this particular piece of footage made its way onto ABC's *That's Incredible!* in a report on the war and media in the 1980s.[46]

DASPO footage, and the films constructed from it, changed styles as the war progressed, matching changing attitudes toward the war while acknowledging shifts in documentary style at the time. The two films I will discuss here, *Drug Edu-cational Field Teams* (1972)[47] and *Peace, Togetherness, and Sammy* (1973),[48] showcase a military worn down by this prolonged war. Turning the camera inward toward soldiers' issues, with little talk of the progress, or lack thereof, of the war, these films could be dismissed as symptomatic of the media's refusal to examine the larger causes of the war. However, as I have argued in this essay, this focus on soldiers' experiences can help make clear how ideology is lived on the ground. Ostensibly made to be screened for new soldiers, even at this very late juncture in the war, these films depict how the contingencies of this particular war (the duration, the changed attitudes about it *within* the army, the development of severe personal problems for its soldiers) could not be accounted for or controlled by the army.

Drug Educational Field Teams details the efforts of the titular group, DEFT, which, according to the film, comprised "unique, highly mobile, preventative education teams composed of carefully selected and trained military and civilian members." "Voice of God"—type narration typical of earlier DASPO films gives way to a polyphonic capturing of sync-sound live footage. The film walks us through a typical DEFT presentation, with prepared lectures by the team followed by intense conversations between DEFT spokespeople and soldiers in which open questioning of army rules takes place. DASPO's camera and sound operators are able to get up close to the soldiers as they ask questions and argue with the DEFT group about marijuana usage and its effects. The cameras' proximity to the crowd of soldiers, some of whom appear to be high or drunk during the presentation, gives the images what David E. James calls "a more than ordinary authority."[49] This authority, based on the cameraman's ability to be there, to capture the reality of war, was a key component of the army's desire for a mobile documentary crew like DASPO. However, this authority cannot deny that the war had changed, and the impact of impromptu recordings of the problems faced by the army could not be foreseen when DASPO was formed. Despite controls at nearly every phase of production, unofficial glimpses of everyday soldier life emerged.

Peace, Togetherness, and Sammy would initially appear to be a trifle, like a Bob Hope USO show. However, just in the tone of the title alone, shorn of the sort of benevolent didacticism typical of earlier military films from this conflict, we can note changes in military attitudes. The film followed Sammy Davis Jr.'s 1972 tour of Vietnam, personally commissioned by President Richard Nixon. Sammy performed for the soldiers' entertainment, while also talking to them about race relations and unavoidable drug-abuse problems. Sammy himself, who served in the army in the 1940s, acknowledges that "the army, being an establishment of its own, it is very hard to make a step forward, change things, because it is a system. But I see the changes in the army between the '40s and '70s."

These changes were visible on a number of levels—most notably, in the form and images the DASPO photographers deliver of an army no longer united. While we do get some narration, mostly of the setting-the-scene type, the film makes extensive use of sync sound in order to help audience members feel like they are there. The film does not move forward in the rhetorical manner in which *The Hidden War in Vietnam* did, with its perpetual proving of its argument through linear progression. Instead, *Peace, Togetherness, and Sammy* jumps between scenes of Sammy interacting with soldiers, Sammy performing before soldiers, Sammy reflecting on his experiences, and on-the-scenes accounts of meetings between drug-addicted soldiers and their counselors—subject matters the army seemingly would want to keep to itself but no longer could.

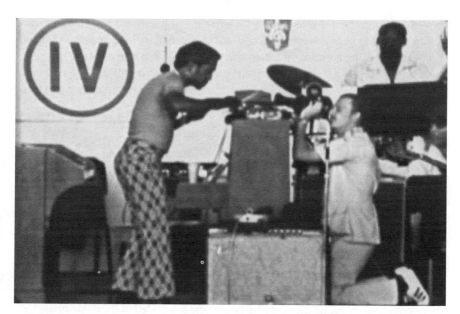

FIGURE 14.2. Frame from *Peace, Togetherness, and Sammy* (1973). Sammy Davis Jr. performs onstage while a DASPO cameraman gets close to film him. The film can be found in the Howard Breedlove Collection at the Vietnam Center and Archive at Texas Tech University.

During Sammy's rap sessions concerning race relations within the army, we get the sort of honest evaluation of the problems that the army, and the United States, faced at this juncture in their history. This sort of confrontational honesty regarding race was not possible in the earlier films discussed here, since the heavily racialized paternalism defining US–Vietnamese relations at the onset of the war could no longer bear up to the realities the army had constructed and filmed during the conflict. Ultimately this film, and the DASPO photographers who shot it, demonstrate the ways in which looking at institutional filmmaking instructs us in how the self-image of an institution changes and adapts to the context in which its images are made, even an institution like the US Army, which had the power and reach to control its own image.

Marita Sturken, writing long after the war, warned scholars, and the US media more broadly, of the lure of "nostalgia for the intensity of the time."[50] Our national memory of this contentious war can be overwrought with the sort of nostalgia with which Sturken is concerned. The recent History Channel documentary series *Vietnam in HD* (2011) stands as only one example of the ways in which our current technologies allow us to manipulate the records of this war, re-forming opinions and memories that have aged. This is what time, and change, do. But as David MacDougall's epigraph that began this chapter indicates, the images that units like DASPO created are "preserved" for us to do with what we will; they are, after all, historical objects. It is up to us to preserve the experiences attached to these images as well—to situate them on the grounds on which they were filmed in order to help us understand how a powerful institution like the US Army could ultimately lose control of both the Vietnam War and the images the institution itself created during that war.

ACKNOWLEDGMENTS

Much of the primary research for this essay was conducted at the Vietnam Center and Archive (henceforth referred to as VCA) at Texas Tech University, June 24–28, 2013. The VCA has vast holdings on many topics related to the Vietnam War, with an emphasis on materials donated by veterans. Their DASPO collection is extensive. The VCA's Reference Archivist, Sheon Montgomery, whose diligence and help made this article possible, assisted me. Most of the materials from this article, including some of the films discussed, can be accessed through the VCA's "Virtual Vietnam Archive," an online search engine located at www.vietnam.ttu.edu /virtualarchive/. In the listings for each item included in the notes I have included the reference number, which should give anyone interested in these materials help in finding them. I would also like to thank Haidee Wasson and Lee Grieveson for their diligent editorial work in rounding this chapter into shape, and to acknowledge Joan Hawkins and our dissertation group for their many readings, in various forms, of this material.

NOTES

Epigraph: David MacDougall, "Beyond Observational Cinema," in *Principles of Visual Anthropology,* 3rd ed., ed. Paul Hockings (Berlin: Mouton de Gruyter, 2003), 123.

1. For an excellent history of this unit, see Douglas Cunningham, "Imaging/Imagining Air Force Identity: 'Hap' Arnold, Warner Bros., and the Formation of the USAAF First Motion Picture Unit," *Moving Image* 5, no. 1 (Spring 2005): 95–124.

2. "The Story of DASPO," Ted Acheson Collection, no. 250105006 (n.d.), 1, Vietnam Center and Archive, Texas Tech University, Lubbock, TX (hereafter cited as VCA). This anecdote has found its way, in many different forms, into almost all of the documents about the beginning of the unit that I found at the VCA. While the wording is different in each one, the general gist of Decker's ire remains constant.

3. Brian Grigsby and Susan Van Dongen, "DASPO Introduction," Bryan Grigsby Collection, no. 10480104001 (n.d.), 1, VCA.

4. See Jennifer Good, Brigitte Lardinois, Paul Lowe, and Val Williams, eds., *Mythologizing the Vietnam War: Visual Culture and Mediated Memory* (Cambridge: Cambridge Scholars Publishing, 2014); Meredith H. Lair, *Armed with Abundance: Consumerism & Soldiering in the Vietnam War* (Chapel Hill: University of North Carolina Press, 2011).

5. See Charles Acland and Haidee Wasson, eds., *Useful Cinema* (Durham, NC: Duke University Press, 2011); and Vinzenz Hediger and Patrick Vonderau, eds., *Films That Work: Industrial Film and the Productivity of Media* (Amsterdam: Amsterdam University Press, 2009).

6. John T. Caldwell, *Production Culture* (Durham, NC: Duke University Press, 2008), 2.

7. Michael Arlen, *Living Room War* (New York: Syracuse University Press, 1997), xi.

8. Grigsby and Van Dongen, "DASPO Introduction," 1.

9. *Panama Riots*, Mike Griffey Collection, no. 1853vi2290 (1964), VCA.

10. Lt. Col. Claude Bache, "The Early DASPO," Ted Acheson Collection, no. 7250105005 (1994), 3, VCA.

11. Ibid.

12. William Foulke, "DASPO/MACV Photo Team Size and Equipment," William Foulke Collection, no. 10400115001 (2004), 3, VCA.

13. Richard Koszarski, "Subway Commandos: Hollywood Filmmakers at the Signal Corps Photographic Center," *Film History* 14, nos. 3/4 (2002): 296–315.

14. This history of the Army Pictorial Center comes from one of the many thorough military websites located on the web. The site offers a view of the importance of history to many of the veterans involved with documenting American engagements in war. www.armypictorialcenter.com/what_was_apc_scpc.htm.

15. William Foulke, "James O. MacIntosh," William Foulke Collection, no. 10400211001 (2006), VCA.

16. Bache, "Early DASPO," 2.

17. *US Army Signal School* (Fort Monmouth, NJ: Army Signal Center and School, 1974), 2, http://files.eric.ed.gov/fulltext/ED090396.pdf.

18. Howard Breedlove, "Interview with Owen Andrews for Time-Life Book," no. 10450102007 (1965), 2, VCA.

19. Ted Acheson, "Oral History," no. OH0291, pt. 1 (n.d.), 5, VCA.

20. "Fort Monmouth Training Pamphlet," 3–4.

21. Ibid., 4.

22. Acheson, "Oral History," 11.

23. The Greg Adams Collection at the VCA is one of the more interesting collections in the archive. It has almost no identifying information about the reels, except for where the footage was taken. Seven of the over thirty reels in this collection were shot at Fort Monmouth during Adams's time in training.

24. *Reel 6*, Greg Adams Collection, no. 1389vi1582 (n.d.), VCA.

25. *Training on the Aurican*, Chuck Abbott Collection, no. 1390vi1649 (dated between November 1966 and April 1967), VCA. Please note that the title is slightly off, spelling the name of the sound-on-film camera as "Aurican" when it was actually "Auricon." I have corrected the spelling in the text; this sort of small error is not uncommon in some of the records in the various veteran-led collections at the VCA.

26. Caldwell, *Production Culture.*

27. Nick Mills, *Combat Photographer* (Boston: Boston Publishing Company, 1983), 9.

28. William Foulke, "DASPO/MACV Photo Team Size and Equipment," William Foulke Collection, no. 10400115001 (2004), 3, VCA.

29. Breedlove, "Interview with Owen Andrews," 4; Foulke, "DASPO/MACV Photo Team Size," 1.

30. Acheson, "Oral History," 35.

31. Michael Herr, *Dispatches* (New York: Alfred A. Knopf, 1977). Herr was one of a number of American print journalists, including figures such as David Halberstam and Gloria Emerson, who were celebrated for their unflinching work during the Vietnam War. Herr passed away on June 23, 2016, as this chapter was being edited.

32. The relationship between the development of sync-sound cameras and the abilities of Direct Cinema practitioners like the Maysles brothers, Richard Leacock, D. A. Pennebaker, and others to supposedly capture a more natural reality have formed the backbone of too many discussions of documentary film since the late 1950s. Many proponents of the Direct Cinema movement slip into a sort of

technologically deterministic argument in which the cameras allowed a freedom of movement that revolutionized this sort of filmmaking and gave control to the subjects being filmed, with the filmmakers now the proverbial fly on the wall. Unfortunately, much of the disdain for this style of filmmaking relies on challenging the rhetoric around these filmmakers rather than the films themselves, which are obviously full of authorial intervention. For a good takedown of these precepts, see Brian Winston, *Claiming the Real II: Documentary; Grierson and Beyond* (London: Palgrave Macmillan, 2008). For a concise history of the movement in its initial context, see Dave Saunders, *Direct Cinema: Observational Documentary and the Politics of the Sixties* (New York: Wallflower Press, 2007).

33. "Letter from Darrell F. Winn Acting Chief, DASPO," Chuck Abbott Collection, no. 13900106013 (1968), VCA.

34. Ibid.

35. Phil Rosen, *Change Mummified: Cinema, Historicity, Theory* (Minneapolis: University of Minnesota Press, 2001), 233.

36. Owen Andrews, C. Douglas Elliott, and Laurence L. Levin, *Vietnam: Images from Combat Photographers* (Washington, DC: Starwood Publishing, 1991), 8.

37. Ibid.

38. William Foulke, "Accredited vs. Non-Accredited Press," no. 10400215001 (2008), 7, VCA.

39. This point was clearly elucidated to me by Haidee Wasson in comments on an earlier version of this essay.

40. *The Big Picture* continued its run in syndication, and on local television channels around the country, until 1970. Given the war's accepted image as the first television war, the lack of attention to this program, which was providing scenes of military-related issues to the homes of American citizens for a long time before the TV war officially started, speaks to how powerful the TV-war paradigm has become.

41. Claudia Springer, "Military Propaganda: Defense Department Films from WWII and Vietnam," *Cultural Critique*, no. 3 (Spring 1986): 159.

42. *The Soldier's Christmas* is available online through the Internet Archive's "Fedflix" collection. https://archive.org/details/gov.dod.dimoc.30225.

43. I have been unable to pin down the exact date of this film's production. It is in a number of the DASPO photographers' collections at the VCA. The copy I saw was in the Howard Breedlove Collection, #1048vi0987. Given that Sgt. Goddard is the on-screen narrator, and that Goddard was the noncommissioned officer in charge of DASPO's Pacific detachment from 1969 to 1972, I would hazard a guess that it was produced in 1970.

44. "DASPO Family Tree," Ted Acheson Collection, no. 7250117002 (n.d.), 4, VCA.

45. Saunders, *Direct Cinema*.

46. Breedlove, "Interview with Owen Andrews," 15. *That's Incredible!* was an ABC TV weekly magazine type of show. Breedlove recalls hearing the soundtrack to the report while he was in another room and running in to see his footage on television—an excellent example of the often-haphazard nature in which this footage was used and viewed.

47. *Drug Educational Field Teams,* Chuck Abbott Collection, no. 1390vi1625 (1973), VCA.

48. *Peace, Togetherness, and Sammy* is available online through the Internet Archive's collection of Department of the Army films: https://archive.org/details/PeaceTogethernessAndSammy. I viewed it at the VCA, as part of the Howard Breedlove Collection, no. 1045VI0876.

49. David E. James, *Allegories of Cinema* (Princeton, NJ: Princeton University Press), 197.

50. Marita Sturken, *Tangled Memories: The Vietnam War, the AIDS Epidemic, and the Politics of Remembering* (Berkeley: University of California Press, 1997), 12.

PART FOUR

THE MILITARY AND ITS COLLABORATORS

15

WAR, MEDIA, AND THE SECURITY OF
STATE AND CAPITAL

Lee Grieveson

The beginnings of US imperialism in the late nineteenth century as marked first by the Spanish-American war, and subsequently by the annexation of territory including Hawaii, Guam, and the Philippines to fashion global trade routes and access to materials in the Caribbean and the Pacific was driven by the twin logics of geopolitical ambition and economic expansion.[1] Practices of "accumulation by dispossession" were accompanied by the professionalization of military forces, beginning in 1898, which would thereafter operate as the *avant garde* for the globalization of US state and capital power.[2] Parts of this newly professionalized and technologically advanced military were utilized in the US intervention in Colombia, in 1904, that created the state of Panama to enable the building of an isthmian canal (completed in 1914) that would radically reshape global trade flows.[3] The protection of those flows, particularly of trade and capital between Britain and the United States, eventually drew the United States, in 1917, into the intra-European imperial conflict of 1914–18. In the same period the US state worked closely with globalizing corporations, and finance capitalists, to support foreign investment and property rights. Examples abound, but the situation in Colombia, again, can be quickly instructive: the country reformed its subsoil laws in 1919 to nationalize crucial resources, but the US state worked together with the Gulf Oil Corporation and significant banks to withhold essential credit to the country until guarantees were given to "safeguard" US investment and "property" in oil production.[4] Countless other examples of what came to be called "dollar imperialism"—or, later, "economic imperialism"—can be cited from this period onward.[5] Over time the process consolidated ties between the US state and corporate/financial elites, as well as mandating the assumption of extraordinary and "exceptional" powers by the state.

The latter process began most notably during the conflict that came to be called World War I, when new practices were innovated to "secure" the continuity of state and prevailing political and economic order. In the early 1920s, and more fully in the face of the collapse of European democracies in the 1930s, jurists and political theorists began to explore the proposed importance of these exceptional state practices to the very maintenance of constitutional security.[6] By this now rather familiar logic, the state might need to act in ways outside of the legal system in order to sustain security and the fusion of geopolitical and economic interests that began most clearly with the compact between state, transnational corporations, and globalizing capital forged in the latter parts of the nineteenth century and manifested acutely in the practices of economic imperialism and warfare throughout the twentieth century.

In this chapter I am interested in exploring the emergence and functioning of one significant, indeed necessarily formative, aspect of these exceptional state practices: the production, management, and control of communication and media. Under the cover of the military exigencies of war, new "exceptional" practices of using and regulating media to foster expansive conceptions of "security" were innovated at a significant moment in the entrenchment of forms of globalizing liberal capitalism. What follows examines the twinned innovation, across the years 1917–19, of new propaganda practices and forms of information and media management that policed a dissidence largely understood in economic terms. I will focus first on the state's innovation of new practices of governance and media management during wartime. The institutions and practices I explore were not directly military ones, though they were established by the state to foster objectives that were militaristic and were indeed directly integrated into practices of warfare. But the phenomena mapped here were also clearly political and economic, and exceeded the immediate exigencies of warfare. I am interested here, that is, in how the state used media for expansive objectives that spanned its domains, linking military, political, and economic imperatives to secure state and capital power. Cinema in commercial and nontheatrical iterations will come in and out of focus in this exploration, but ultimately I am interested in the broader framing of a media system to be useful to state and capital interests. Regulation crossed modes and mechanisms of expression, and other media technologies and forms—like radio—were innovated to be useful in this conjuncture.[7] The state use and regulation of media to foster its security did not recognize the borders later set around the study of separate components of that media system.

Our interest in this volume is to explicate the specific practices and broad logics of the military use of cinema in order principally to contribute to an understanding of how this uniquely powerful institution has deployed the technology, form, and space that came to be called cinema to further its interests. I attend here to thinking further about the goals of the state that wielded military and media power, because it is imperative that the military be connected back to the cognate, collaborating, and constitutive entities that have created the conditions of its existence and directed its actions. Doing so enables me to explore the larger dynamics of power in which the military is implicated, for which it fights, and in whose name its powers are marshaled. I argue that at their broadest these dynamics were driven by the economic and political *logics* of imperialism, and that this process was enacted in specific *contingent* historical circumstances. My interest is in both of those dynamics—that is, in the logics of capital in its corporate US variant, beginning most clearly in the latter years of the nineteenth century and expanding to become globally significant first after the conflict of World War I and then more fully hegemonic after World War II, when the United States became the world's exceptional state.[8] Because this process was driven by the expanding, exceptional logics of state and economic power, it continued beyond wartime, becoming part of a host of new practices to deploy media to be useful to the intertwined interests of the state and large economic actors. New ideas about managing media to (in Walter Lippmann's [in]famous phrase) "manufacture consent" to the prevailing political and economic order became readily manifest in the 1920s, building on the success of wartime propaganda and media management.[9] Wartime praxis (and indeed technology, like radio) was retooled to serve the expansion of a consumer economy and the management of mass democracy. But the fuller realization of exceptional state practices as what Giorgio Agamben calls a lasting "technique of government" awaited the era of permanent war, beginning most clearly with the post–World War II Cold War to secure and expand the liberal capitalist world system, and further intensified with the "War on Terror" from 2001 onward.[10] Direct lines of continuity can be discerned, and I attend briefly to some examples toward the end of this chapter. I explore the beginning of these forms of "exceptional" governance elaborated during wartime and the expansion of economic imperialism in the early twentieth century, then, as one part of a genealogy of the political and economic use of media to sustain the "security" of state and capital.

"THE WAR IS ESTABLISHING THE SCREEN AS PART OF GOVERNMENT WORK"

But first, to the historical detail about the production and use of cinema/media during wartime. President Woodrow Wilson established the Committee on Public Information (CPI) immediately after the United States entered the ongoing conflict between European states, in April 1917, to shape public opinion about the far-flung conflict and to communicate strategic state goals.[11] The new institution was created by executive order, based on the expansion of powers delegated to the president during wartime, and was established without congressional approval. Wilson had previously corresponded with the influential journalist and political commentator Walter Lippmann on the subject of mobilizing public opinion.[12] Lippmann had proposed a clearinghouse for information on government activities, the monitoring of the foreign press, and the need to rally a wide range of communications specialists including people working in the motion-picture industry.[13] George Creel was appointed to head the CPI and quickly created divisions relating to film, news, and "pictorial publicity." Creel argued at the outset that the CPI should principally avoid censorial actions and instead work to disseminate publicity and media, not least because censorship would inflame the troublesome socialist critique of the war that argued that it was driven by the needs of business and finance capital.[14] "Better to have the desired compulsions proceed from within than apply them from without," Creel wrote, in a pithy summary of the logics of what Michel Foucault would later call liberal governmentality.[15] Wilson, Lippmann, and Creel thus innovated a new governmental media agency as a concrete ideological state apparatus that worked to shape perception and allegiance in accord with state policy and to protect the forms of exchange and circulation integral to the liberal capitalist world system.

Cinema became increasingly central to this "public relations" state endeavor. Creel orchestrated an extensive architecture of information, publicity, and persuasive argument that was directed particularly at the migrant working-class audiences drawn to the cheap mass visual media that was cinema and who had complex allegiances to Europe and/or its empires. Vast numbers of public speakers drawn from "bankers, professional or business men" were organized to facilitate this work and sent to cinemas to speak on topics relating to the war.[16] The Four Minute Men, as they were called, got their name both from the "minute men" militia of the Revolutionary War, who had reputedly stood ready to fight at a moment's notice, *and* from the amount of time it typically took for movie theaters to change reels.[17] Creel's naming of them connected ideas about national birth, anticolonial struggle, and the defense of nation (propelled, ironically, by a conflict caused in large part by European colonial expansion and interstate rivalry), with the space and time accorded their sustenance by the relatively new space of cinema.

Brief gaps between filmic entertainment were filled by legions of Four Minute Men delivering short talks on topics such as the reasons for the United States entering the war, the draft, the necessity of buying Liberty Bonds to finance the war, rationing food to support the war, "the Meaning of America," and so on.[18] The state's agenda was sutured into cinema. Speakers worked from scripts and guides circulated by the CPI, many of which were written by advertising executives and which carefully supplemented publicity and information with emotional rhetoric that drew sharp distinctions between the political and moral positions of the combatants. Wilson and Creel's army of citizen–business speakers connected the seat of federal governance in Washington to peripheral regions via the space of cinemas. Occasionally the speeches addressed the perception that the war was "a capitalists' war"—an argument that was, it was claimed, "constantly whispered by German sympathizers."[19] Creel also encouraged the creation of a special propaganda arm within the Department of Labor that flooded factories with posters and speakers designed to defuse the radical charge that the conflict was fueled by the demands of industrialists and finance capitalists.[20] In a rhetorical move that later administrations and other regimes would learn well from, democratic questions about the economic motivations for war were repositioned as undemocratic, disloyal, and dangerous to the state.[21]

Quickly thereafter the CPI began to produce and distribute film material at no charge. Beginning in September 1917, it launched what media historian Stuart Ewen has described as "an unprecedented effort to deploy movies as implements of war."[22] The CPI's Division of Films had an Educational Department that initially distributed films made by the US Army Signal Corps, circulating this military film material through movie theaters and nontheatrical networks made up of patriotic organizations, educational institutions, chambers of commerce, political and social clubs, training camps, and hospitals.[23] Various films produced by industrial corporations were also utilized and widely disseminated by the CPI.[24] Crucial alliances between state and significant economic institutions were fostered to "advertise" the technological strength of the state. The "screen carried the story of America," Creel wrote, "flashing the power of our army and navy, showing our natural resources, our industrial processes, our war spirit, our national life."[25] By the summer of 1918 the CPI had created a Scenario Department that worked closely with commercial film producers, working on the "theory," as Creel framed it, that "propaganda pictures had never been properly made, and that if skill and care were employed in the preparation of the scenarios the resultant pictures could secure a place in regular motion-picture programs."[26] CPI officials sought in this way to draw on the expertise of Hollywood, blending the nonfictional and didactic with the emotional and immersive registers of commercial film. By *learning* from Hollywood to supplement its own persuasive powers, the state became increasingly film-like.

Domestically the CPI's films reached many of the nation's theatrical film screens, and the committee also disseminated film material, principally from the signal corps, to major newsreels.[27] Creel began also to elaborate what he called a "world machinery" to enable "the story of America" to circulate across the globe.[28] Essential to this was the control of export licenses, through the War Trade Office, such that Creel was able to ensure that every shipment of commercial film included 20 percent "educational matter" and that foreign exhibitors would not be able to show US films without also showing the films produced and/or circulated by the CPI.[29] The films created and approved by the CPI thus circulated internationally because of the state's control of export licenses during wartime. Because "exhibitors simply had to have our comedies and dramas," Creel later wrote, "we soon had sole possession of the field. Much as they may have disliked our propaganda features, Douglas Fairbanks, Mary Pickford, and the Keystone Cops were a necessity."[30] Creel was innovating here a practice that shortly thereafter came to be called "block booking": the use of popular, usually star-led films to dominate distribution networks and exhibition spaces—a practice that effectively marginalized the exhibition of other films. But note that Creel is orchestrating this as a political and ideological project just before it becomes standard commercial practice in the film industry, in 1919. From that year the film company that came to be called Paramount used the capital from newly expanded securities markets to fully control production, distribution, and exhibition networks in one corporate form. Creel's practices innovated a controlled global system of circulation and exhibition that used the popularity of industrialized commercial cinema to further successfully merge the emotionally persuasive registers of fiction cinema with the "pedagogical" material produced by the state (and its industrial collaborators) to explicate policy and (in Creel's words) "advertise America."

Executives in Hollywood grasped the opportunity to ally with the federal government as a concrete way of ensuring business during wartime and to uplift the cultural status of the hitherto rather beleaguered industry. Creel had cannily sweetened the pill of the control of export licenses with a promise "to expedite film shipments," making sure there was space on boats for commercial film.[31] Protecting the material infrastructure of circulation was crucial during wartime. (It was, after all, largely the reason the United States entered the conflict.) Creel's innovation was simultaneously beneficial to the commercial interests of the film industry and the ideological interests of the state. From this point the global center for film distribution shifted from London to New York, and Hollywood became the world's dominant film industry.[32] Following in the wake of the ties established between state and film industry, in the summer of 1917 the mainstream film industry's trade organization, the National Association of the Motion Picture Industry (NAMPI), was elected to membership in the US Chamber of Commerce—a key sign of stability and recognition within the wider business and financial community. By the winter of 1917 the film industry was granted the status of "essential industry" from the War Industries Board, despite the fact that the nitric acid in celluloid was a crucial component of high explosives.[33] The ties forged between state and media industry were thus directly beneficial to that industry in two concrete ways: by bringing it into the orbit of the established industries in the Chamber of Commerce, a factor that would be useful to the industry shortly thereafter when sourcing pools of capital to become fully corporate; and by enabling it to stay open during wartime when other businesses were forced to close to conserve resources.

Close ties between the government and the cinema industry were forged around the Liberty Bond campaigns that began in 1917 with the immediate goal of generating debt securities to help finance the conflict. Treasury Secretary William Gibbs McAdoo wrote to the president of NAMPI in mid-1917 to enlist the film industry's support in the first campaign.[34] Responding to the Treasury's request, the film industry produced slides and short films about the campaign and distributed them widely. Wilson's speech about the importance of "liberty loans," for example, was filmed, and eight thousand copies appeared repeatedly in cinemas and other, nontheatrical spaces.[35] Creel's army of Four Minute Men was equipped with speeches about the importance of the bonds. NAMPI organized to attach Liberty Bond trailers to the start of film programs.[36] Private organizations sponsored open-air showings of films to support Liberty Bond drives, and some of the films produced through the cooperation between state and film industry were screened in the rotunda of the Capitol Building—a fitting image of the enmeshing of media and state.[37]

Movie stars were also enlisted to give speeches and then appear in short films that urged people to buy bonds. (Sue Collins explores some of this history in her chapter in this volume.) Mary Pickford toured widely, attended rallies for liberty loans, and met with wealthy investors, lending her persona as "America's sweetheart" and celebrity to the goals of the state. Pickford and Charlie Chaplin made short comic films to support the bond drives. The film *100% American* showed Pickford learning to eschew consumer pleasures for the greater need to buy bonds. Chaplin's *The Bond: A Liberty Loan Appeal* dramatized the ways bonds functioned. Chaplin stands between figures representing Uncle Sam and Industry, and when he buys a bond from Uncle Sam, Industry sets to work to provide military materials to soldiers. By the close of the film Chaplin hits the Kaiser over the head with a large mallet bearing the words "Liberty Bonds." It is a film that comically sketched out the economic model of government debt that supported US military intervention. The media celebrity was put to work to sustain the warfare state.

Partly the Liberty Bond campaigns were driven by the necessity to innovate new state financial practices to sustain the military. Sixty percent of the cost of the conflict was raised in this way—about $21.5 billion, purchased by about one-third of the population.[38] But the loan drives also put into practice new ideas about securities ownership that surfaced first around the turn of the century to foster new forms of "investor democracy" designed to bind citizen to state and to expand and "deepen" the resources necessary to the growth of corporate and financial capital.[39] Bond campaigns during wartime followed these political and economic logics, and were a part of the larger dynamic in which the state worked to expand securities ownership and innovate a new investor-centered theory of political economy as one way of updating older notions of proprietary democracy to bind the heterogeneous population to the state through the matrix of the market. Policy makers argued that "[u]niversal ownership of federal securities would stabilize society by forestalling radicalism and curbing inflation," historian Julia Ott writes. "By extending the opportunity to acquire property in a new form, the wartime state aimed to nudge those prone to radicalism into a classic liberal social contract, in which individuals submitted to the rule of law in order to preserve their property."[40] Bonds bound together state interests to finance the military and warfare, and/therefore to foster its own security, as well as that of the economic institutions, like investment banks, that relied on that expansion of securities. By the 1920s, following the success of the wartime bond drives, an expanded securities market buttressed by new cognate ideas about investor democracy was firmly established. Over the decade and thereafter, these ideals and practices formed the "basic economic precepts of modern conservatism"—principally, that laissez-faire financial markets best allocate capital and risk and that the maximization of shareholder value is the proper goal of state and corporate policy.[41] Capital in the form here principally of bonds (but mutating also into new forms of equity financing in terms of stock) expanded through the process both established by the state in compact with financial elites and innovated initially to finance military expansion and warfare.

I contend here that this extremely significant transformation of political economy was innovated by the state during the exceptional crisis of wartime, to foster expansive political and economic ends. This process made use of media as space and form, and included the new phenomenon of persuasive celebrity essential to the growth of corporate media and its operations thereafter. It is a central tenet of my argument that the state utilized media during the exigencies of wartime to help establish forms of governmental rationality that exceeded the immediate requirements of combat, and expanded thereafter. The process further established significant ties between political and financial elites, including for the first time those who controlled the new media that was cinema. For those media entrepreneurs, the expansion of finance capital in the wake of these developments during the war would enable them to attract the pools of capital necessary to create new national networks of distribution and exhibition and connect these together with production in one corporate entity.[42] Corporate cinema/media settled thereafter into an oligopolistic market that marginalized alternative forms of media culture and so radically limited the public sphere.

Wilson declared himself very satisfied with the results, and with the contribution of cinema to the bond campaigns and war effort. In a letter sent in the summer of 1918 to the head of the film industry's central trade body, he wrote:

> It is my mind not only to bring the motion picture into fullest and most effective contact with the nation's needs, but to give some measure of official recognition to an increasingly important factor in the development of our national life. The film has come to rank as a very high medium for the dissemination of public intelligence and since it speaks a universal language it lends itself importantly to the presentation of America's plans and purposes.[43]

Wilson's letter indicated the importance attached to cinema as a form of mass media at the highest level of state. The president's conception of cinema as a form of communication that crossed linguistic barriers made cinema especially important for the project, both to shape the attitudes and conduct of the diverse populations drawn to the United States from the late nineteenth century *and* to facilitate the globalizing agendas of the state and the large corporations that had flourished since the turn of the century. In the wake of this, offices in the Departments of State and Commerce would in the 1920s work to aid the global circulation of corporate Hollywood as one strand of the new forms of economic imperialism led by the United States—forms that repositioned it as the world's exceptional state thereafter.[44] Quite clearly the use and deployment of media became integral to expansive political and economic objectives in a process that began most concretely during wartime but then expanded. Media as "soft power" supplemented the hard power enabled by the growth of the professionalized military; both were integrated into the security of state and capital.

"SUCH A NATURE AS TO CREATE A CLEAR AND PRESENT DANGER"

The production of propaganda to facilitate military and state goals was twinned with the significant expansion of state censorship and political policing most clearly in the years 1917–19. New policies and practices were innovated and sustained by the judiciary in significant and far-reaching decisions on free speech. Like the activities mapped above, the establishment of new exceptional practices to police political and economic opposition began under the cover of wartime and expanded in the immediate aftermath, becoming central to the agenda of the federal police force in the "Red Scare" of 1919–20. Union members and socialists received the most scrutiny in a process that radically limited dissident speech to further cement the primacy of liberal capitalism. The innovation of this militantly liberal praxis, including broadly the framing of a media system synced to advertising, was a crucial, *formative* episode in the entrenchment of state power and corporate liberal political economy.[45]

Wilson's administration passed first the Espionage Act, in June 1917, which made it a crime to convey information or false statements that could interfere with military operations or promote the success of enemies. Particularly significant to the act was the outlawing of speech—broadly conceived—that could "willfully cause or attempt to cause insubordination, disloyalty, mutiny, or refusal of duty in the military or naval forces of the United States, or . . . willfully obstruct the recruiting or enlistment service of the United States."[46] The clause specifically targeted socialist and pacifist groups' opposition to the war, members of which had argued that the conflict was a consequence of the globalizing expansion of capital, and had at times urged men to resist the draft. Eugene Debs, who was the leader of the Socialist Party, which had polled around one million votes in the election of

1912, had given an antiwar speech in Ohio in 1918 that noted (among other things) that the "ruling class" had "always taught and trained you to believe it to be your patriotic duty to go to war and have yourselves slaughtered at their command."[47] By the next day the speech was scrutinized, first by the US attorney in Cleveland and then by the attorney general, and Debs was arrested, indicted, and ultimately imprisoned with a ten-year sentence under the terms of the Espionage Act.[48] Debs had begun his speech with the prescient observation that "it is extremely dangerous to exercise the constitutional right of free speech in a country fighting to make democracy safe in the world."[49] But truth and irony did not keep him out of prison.

Expanded restrictions on speech and media to protect state and economic interests and to sustain military action were elaborated thereafter, most notably in a revision to the Espionage Act commonly known as the Sedition Act. Passed in May 1918, this revision prohibited "any disloyal, scurrilous, or abusive language about the form of government of the United States, or the Constitution of the United States, or the military and naval forces of the United States."[50] By this expanded definition "sedition" included criticism of the liberal capitalist state, *and* its military, such that indeed the two were positioned as essentially intertwined. Particularly significant were clauses regulating speech about economic practices. Banned speech included that which manifested "intent to obstruct the sale by the United States of bonds or other securities of the United States or the making of loans by or to the United States," or that advocated "any curtailment of production in this country of any thing or things, product or products, necessary or essential to the prosecution of the war."[51] Questioning the economic motivation for war, the expansion of the securities markets to finance warfare, and the nascent form of what would later be called (by the five-star general, and president, Dwight Eisenhower) "the military-industrial complex" were outlawed. But the act did more than enable the post-facto regulation of speech because it gave the postmaster general enlarged powers to police the circulation of materials "in violation of any of the provisions of this Act" through the mail system.[52] By this clause the act specifically targeted the circulation of ideas, information, and media through the federal state's control of mail networks and interstate commerce.

Both acts were specifically used to target socialist opposition to the war as one part of the broader imperative to entrench what economist historian Martin Sklar has called "the corporate reconstruction of American capitalism."[53] By September 1917 the Espionage Act was invoked by the Justice Department to raid the offices of the Industrial Workers of the World union (IWW) around the country, arresting 166 union officials and simultaneously destroying printing presses and private correspondence.[54] Postmaster General Albert Burleson used the Sedition revision to quickly ban socialist publications from the mails, including the journals *American Socialist* and *The Masses* as well as *Solidarity,* the publication of the IWW.[55] Regulation to sustain the militarized state was simultaneously targeted at the socialist and unionist challenge to liberal political economy. Over nineteen hundred prosecutions were carried out under the terms of Espionage-Sedition legislation during the short time the country participated in the war.[56] Debs was but one high-profile example of this extraordinary policing of peaceful dissidence. The radical economist Scott Nearing was also indicted, for scholarship that explored the connections among capitalism, imperialism, and war[57]—connections that I, too, have been exploring (indeed, using some of his scholarship in the process). By early 1918 the mass targeting of IWW members led to a series of political trials that handed out heavy sentences of as much as ten years' imprisonment for circulating material that was often simply pacifist and antiwar.[58] Simultaneously the director of a film about the Revolutionary War of 1776 was jailed, in 1918, under the terms of the Espionage Act because the film showed scenes of British brutality and so, it was claimed, undermined support for the alliance with the imperial British state.[59]

Quite clearly the state's intensified and exceptional surveillance targeted "speech" broadly conceived—stretching across speech, publications, film—that questioned the motivations for war, or otherwise undermined support for it, and in particular that which challenged the ascendancy of the forms of corporate liberalism that led to what Nearing labeled "dollar imperialism" and that underpinned the militant and militarized foreign policy of the United States beginning in the latter years of the nineteenth century. It marked what must be understood as a deformation of the principles of liberal democracy to foster free speech as a necessary and crucial component of any conception of liberty. By radically limiting the possibility of speech that challenged the primacy of the prevailing political and economic order, and its militarized sustenance, the legislation and its policing were consistent with the broader winnowing down of the progressive components of liberalism by the logics of capitalism and its mutation into the "national security liberalism" established in incipient form here and more fully and expansively in the aftermath of World War II.[60]

Debs and other convicted socialists challenged the legality and constitutionality of the state's extraordinary policing of speech. But when the cases reached the US Supreme Court in early 1919, they were dismissed in rulings that upheld the constitutionality of the Espionage and Sedition Acts and delegated authority to the government and the courts to police speech that could present "a clear and present danger" to the "nation" during wartime.[61] New practices of policing, internment, denaturalization, and deportation were simultaneously initiated that specifically targeted migrant workers and those suspected of harboring socialist tendencies.[62] In 1919 Attorney General A. Mitchell Palmer created a new division of the Bureau of Investigation to target suspected radical groups. Palmer organized a series of raids on meetings held by the Union of Russian Workers that were timed to coincide with the second anniversary of the Bolshevik regime in Russia. In January 1920 Palmer's Department of Justice collaborated with local police forces to round up members of the communist party.[63] The bureau became a political police force that targeted radicalism of various types. Chaplin, for example, was investigated by the bureau in the early 1920s, after his progressive political views became apparent—quite a comedown from his role as heroic exemplar of state debt in 1917–18.[64]

Policing media dovetailed again with its deployment. Right at the beginning of 1919, in the immediate aftermath of the war, Wilson authorized the creation of a "Visual Instruction" section of the Bureau of Education to be a "clearing house" through which films produced by the government during the war would be widely circulated so they could have continued—and what one bureaucrat called "greater"—"usefulness."[65] Following this the secretary of the interior asked the secretary of war for cooperation in passing the films produced for the war effort over to the Bureau of Education, from where these films would be distributed to schools and colleges to foster "Americanization."[66] Over one million feet of film were salvaged from the military and CPI and circulated through these emergent nontheatrical networks created by the government in partnership with educational institutions in particular.[67] Simultaneously motion-picture exhibition equipment used abroad by the government during the war was also dispersed at cheap prices to a wider nontheatrical network after the end of the conflict.[68] Both the propaganda films produced by the CPI and the material means for their projection were thus put into circulation as a concrete—material—example both of the extension of the state of exception in the interwar years and of the twinned dynamic of media production and regulation that I have been exploring thus far.

"WE ARE HERE FOR YOUR FUCKING FREEDOM, SO BACK UP, RIGHT NOW"

By 1919 the state had innovated a new exceptional policing of speech and media under the cover of wartime that specifically targeted dissident opposition to the war and to the prevailing political and economic order, and that also granted the military the same protection from criticism as the state. Quite clearly this was a doubled praxis, carried through the production and regulation of speech and media, which began in 1917 but expanded thereafter with the support of legal statutes even after the Sedition Act was revoked in 1920. (The Espionage Act remained, and remains, on the statute book.) I shall in this concluding section take leave of the focus thus far on the years 1917–19 to briefly *sketch* out some of the genealogical lines of descent of this militarized media praxis. I shall briefly explicate three subsequent moments, and make some remarks on the continuity between them: one, the practices (and reflections) that grew directly from the CPI and the militarized control of media in the 1920s; two, the early Cold War period and the use of media to foster the security of a globalizing liberal capitalism; and three, the post-2001 "War on Terror" era.[69]

Creel echoed Wilson's satisfaction with the work of the CPI, as might be expected. In his book about his time at the CPI, eloquently titled *How We Advertised America,* he described his job as "a plain publicity proposition, a vast enterprise in salesmanship, the world's greatest adventure in advertising," and proclaimed that propaganda worked very effectively.[70] Many others concurred. Lippmann's trilogy of books on media, public opinion, and democracy, in particular the 1922 *Public Opinion,* framed the terms of much of this debate in the United States in the 1920s[71] (and indeed, thereafter: James Carey, for example, has called *Public Opinion* "the founding book in American media studies").[72] Lippmann, you will recall, had advised Wilson on setting up the CPI, and he worked to produce and disseminate propaganda in Europe with the military branch of the War Department, from which point he became convinced, his biographer observes, that "public opinion could be molded."[73] The realization that mass media shaped public opinion led directly to the argument that media should therefore be fashioned by experts and elites. Public opinions "must be organized *for the press* if they are to be sound," Lippmann argued, "not *by the press* as is the case today."[74] Once again this pivoted on the idea that media needed to be censored and simultaneously shaped as propaganda. "Without some form of censorship," Lippmann wrote, "propaganda in the strict sense of the word is impossible. In order to conduct a propaganda there must be some barrier between the public and the event. Access to the real environment must be limited, before anyone can create a pseudo-environment that he thinks is wise or desirable."[75] Obviously this meshing of propaganda and censorship mirrored that innovated during the crisis of wartime, when the policing of speech and media dovetailed with the propaganda of the CPI. But now it was proposed as a regular practice for the elite control of media.

Indeed, Lippmann's complex and influential reflection on media and "democratic" order contained remarkable material on cinema as a working model for how political elites could shape and frame perception. *Public Opinion* included a chapter, called "The Enlisting of Interest," that took the fictional film of Hollywood as a way of understanding how "identification" is orchestrated. "Pictures have always been the surest way of conveying an idea. . . . But the idea conveyed is not fully our own until we have identified ourselves with some aspect of the picture . . . the handles for identification are almost always marked. You know who the hero is at once."[76] Politics needed to become more cinematic in marshaling patterns of identification to "manufacture consent" to the prevailing order of things. The entertaining narrative form of corporate media could be retooled to sustain identification with the goals of elites. But those goals should be exempt from democratic management, and needed to be "manufactured," because the mass population was too easily swayed and, frankly, not very smart. Noam Chomsky, in particular, has illuminated the elitist logic of this position.[77] It stretched beyond rhetoric: Lippmann was charged by Wilson and his enigmatic political adviser Colonel

Edward House with drawing up plans for the postwar order that framed Wilson's famous Fourteen Points declaration preceding the Paris peace conference that called for the reestablishment of a global liberal capitalist order.[78]

But the lessons learned from the state's management of media during wartime extended outward also to the commercial sector and shaped the emergent practices of "public relations" to use media to the benefit of first corporate and later political "clients." Propaganda techniques innovated during wartime mutated directly into PR. The clearest example is in the practice of Edward Bernays, who worked for the CPI during wartime and who is now commonly regarded as the "father" of PR in the United States.[79] During 1917, working for the CPI, Bernays "planned and carried out a campaign directed at Latin American businessmen" that both countered German propaganda and connected to the goals of the US state and corporations to establish economic hegemony in the region.[80] To do so he allied with significant corporations, like Ford and International Harvester, and with the American Manufacturers' Export Association, further illustrating the close ties between the interests of state and globalizing corporations. "We sold them American war aims," Bernays later wrote, "and concomitantly they learned to be enthusiastic about American manufacturers and were won over to a desire to deal further with American business men."[81] I take that to be a pretty good summary of the principles that both connected state and corporate interests, imagining them as essentially isomorphic, and utilized military conflict to expand commercial spheres of influence.

PR expanded massively in the 1920s, after the "astounding success of propaganda" during the war had "opened the eyes of the intelligent few in all departments of life to the possibilities of regimenting the public mind."[82] Corporations in particular made use of the framing of media to serve their interests, frequently indeed by suggesting that those interests were the same as the national interest. One brief example of this process in action will have to suffice, and it is one that brings me to the early years of the Cold War. The large corporation United Fruit employed Bernays to help counter the land reforms and proposed nationalization of resources that followed the Guatemalan revolution of 1944. Bernays proposed that the reforms were evidence of the spread of communism, and his savvy media and PR campaign helped prepare the grounds for a CIA-sponsored coup in the country in 1954 that installed a new regime that "rescinded the nationalization, liberalized conditions for foreign investment, curtailed democracy, and severely repressed its opponents."[83] The idea that land might be socially useful and not simply property was to be resisted with militarized force.

PR as the management of perception and media would be central to the conflict of economic systems that was the Cold War across the history of the latter half of the twentieth century. The federal government deployed film and other media, and indeed developed media technologies, as PR for liberal capitalism and to enable its global expansion. One can see this consistently through, for example, the creation of films to supplement the Marshall Plan to rebuild capitalist Europe (explored by Katerina Loukopoulou in her chapter in this volume); the use of film and media—in particular, Hollywood—to help establish "democratic" character structures and institutions in Germany and Japan;[84] the deployment of film, projectors, and radio by the United States Information Agency (USIA), particularly in the crucial region of Southeast Asia beginning in the late 1940s;[85] the financing of film by the CIA and the agency's plans to insert the theme of "freedom" into Hollywood movies in the wonderfully named "Militant Liberty" program;[86] the development of satellite technology as one part of a battle over the control of global communications;[87] and so on. But this deployment of media was twinned with intensified practices of regulation in a way consistent with the dynamics emerging in World War I that I have been exploring here. In 1940, for example, Congress passed another sedition law, commonly known as the Smith Act, which led again directly to the imprisonment of socialists and communists.[88] On the eve of the United States' entrance into World War II, in 1942, the FBI began an intense surveillance of Hollywood because it had become convinced that leftist and communist supporters were using film to influence audiences.[89] FBI agents became film scholars. The efforts mutated into the well-known House Un-American Activities Committee (HUAC) investigations of the film industry beginning in 1947, which culminated with ten writers and filmmakers being imprisoned for refusing to answer questions about their political beliefs or to name others who were active in the progressive "cultural front" of the 1930s. Quite clearly the FBI and HUAC investigations must be understood in the context of a longer history, some of it sketched here, of a militant national policing organization that overtly targeted radicalism and media as part of a state project to support the continued functioning of liberal capitalism.

But that policing extends forward, too, becoming significant to the continued functioning of the military-industrial complex in our current era of digital media and endless war. The FBI and the National Security Agency (NSA) and CIA have massively expanded their surveillance of new forms of social media just as the "War on Terror" has expanded to become a global war. Whistle-blowers alerting us to the expanded surveillance of communication and media (notably Edward Snowden) and the global expansion of war (notably Chelsea Manning) have been targeted (and, in Manning's case, imprisoned under the terms of the Espionage Act first passed in 1917).[90] Censorship, "suppressing dissent and mandating compliance," dovetails, still, with media production and propaganda, albeit now mostly devolved to a deregulated corporate media system and "cyber intelligence complex" fully synced with the sustenance of state power and global liberal capitalism.[91] Recent accounts of this development occasionally note that Manning, for example, was imprisoned under such dated legislation. But it is a mistake to read this as a curious hangover from a bygone era. Rather, it was established as a component of the broader effort to entrench a political economy of benefit to state and financial elites that has been carried out thereafter with the assistance of the *production* and *regulation* of media innovated during the wars of imperial expansion beginning in the latter years of the nineteenth century, expanded during the years 1917–19, and ongoing in the current era of permanent, global, war.

NOTES

1. See, for example, Philip S. Foner, *The Spanish-Cuban-American War and the Birth of American Imperialism, 1895–1902*, 2 vols. (New York: Monthly Review Press, 1972); Paul A. Kramer, *The Blood of Government: Race, Empire, the United States, and the Philippines* (Chapel Hill: University of North Carolina Press, 2006); and Thomas Schoonover, *Uncle Sam's War of 1898 and the Origins of Globalization* (Lexington: University Press of Kentucky, 2013).

2. David Harvey, *Spaces of Global Capitalism: Towards a Theory of Uneven Capitalist Development* (London: Verso, 2006), esp. 69–116; Robert P. Saldin, *War, the American State, and Politics since 1898* (Cambridge: Cambridge University Press, 2011), 12–13, 32–33; Leo Panitch and Sam Gindin, *The Making of Global Capitalism: The Political Economy of American Empire* (London: Verso, 2013), esp. 35–43.

3. John Major, *Prize Possession: The United States and the Panama Canal, 1903–1979* (Cambridge: Cambridge University Press, 1993), 34–63.

4. Greg Grandin, "The Liberal Traditions in the Americas: Rights, Sovereignty, and the Origins of Liberal Multilateralism," *American Historical Review* 117, no. 1 (February 2012): 87–88.

5. Scott Nearing and Joseph Freeman, *Dollar Diplomacy: A Study in American Imperialism* (New York: Allen and Unwin, 1925); Cyrus Veeser, *A World Safe for Capitalism: Dollar Diplomacy and America's Rise to Global Power* (New York: Columbia University Press, 2002). For an exploration of some of those interventions in Latin America in the first half of the century see, for example, Emily S. Rosenberg, *Spreading the American Dream: American Economic and Cultural Expansion, 1890–1945* (New York: Hill and Wang, 1982), 130–49. For the broad sweep of US economic imperialism in the post–World War II period, see David Harvey, *The New Imperialism* (Oxford: Oxford University Press, 2003); Perry Anderson, "Imperium," *New Left Review* 81 (May–June 2013), 5–111; and Panitch and Gindin, *Making of Global Capitalism*, 67–220.

6. Giorgio Agamben, *State of Exception*, trans. Kevin Attell (Chicago: University of Chicago Press, 2005), esp. 6–9, 32–36.

7. Daniel R. Headrick, *The Invisible Weapon: Telecommunications and International Politics 1851–1945* (New York: Oxford University Press, 1991), esp. 139–48; Susan J. Douglas, *Inventing American Broadcasting, 1899–1922* (Baltimore: John Hopkins University Press, 1987), esp. 102–43.

8. On the broad sweep of the political and economic ascent of the United States, see Giovanni Arrighi, *The Long Twentieth Century: Money, Power, and the Origins of Our Times* (London: Verso, 1994).

9. Walter Lippman, *Public Opinion* (Harcourt Brace and Co., 1922; New York: Free Press, 1997), 158.

10. Agamben, *State of Exception*, 6.

11. The most complete history of the Committee on Public Information is Stephen Vaughn, *Holding Fast the Inner Lines: Democracy, Nationalism, and the Committee on Public information* (Chapel Hill: University of North Carolina Press, 1980). The CPI's import for new practices of state propaganda is suggestively sketched by Noam Chomsky in, for example, *Media Control: The Spectacular Achievements of Propaganda* (New York: Seven Stories, 2002), notably 11–21; and explored in Stuart Ewen, *PR! A Social History of Spin* (New York: Basic Books, 1996), 108–25; and Gary S. Messinger, *The Battle for*

the Mind: War and Peace in the Era of Mass Communication (Amherst: University of Massachusetts Press, 2011), esp. 15–37. The subtitle that precedes this paragraph is from page 8 of the July 1918 issue of *Reel and Slide*.

12. Vaughn, *Holding Fast the Inner Lines*, 5–7.

13. Ibid., 6.

14. Ewen, *PR!*, 104–10.

15. George Creel, *How We Advertised America: The First Telling of the Amazing Story of the Committee on Public Information That Carried the Gospel of Americanism to Every Corner of the Globe* (New York: Harper and Brothers, 1920), 17.

16. Ibid., 89. See also Ewen, *PR!*, 103–4.

17. Lisa Mastrangelo, "World War I, Public Intellectuals, And the Four Minute Men: Convergent Ideals of Public Speaking and Civic Participation," *Rhetoric and Public Affairs* 12, no. 4 (2009): 609.

18. The list of bulletins produced for the Four Minute Men is reproduced in Creel, *How We Advertised America*, 86–87.

19. US Committee on Public Information, "Where Did You Get Your Facts?" *Four Minute Man Bulletin* 35 (August 26, 1918), cited in Ewen *PR!*, 103.

20. David M. Kennedy, *Over Here: The First World War and American Society* (New York: Oxford University Press, 1980), 72.

21. Ewen, *PR!*, 3; Christopher Sharrett, "9/11, the Useful Incident, and the Legacy of the Creel Committee," *Cinema Journal* 43, no. 4 (Summer 2004): 125–31.

22. Ewen, *PR!*, 115.

23. Creel, *How We Advertised America*, 119–23.

24. Ibid., 274.

25. Ibid., 273.

26. Ibid., 126.

27. Vaughn, *Holding Fast the Inner Lines*, 205; Creel, *How We Advertised America*, 123.

28. Creel, *How We Advertised America*, 273.

29. Ibid., 276.

30. George Creel, *Rebel at Large: Recollections of Fifty Crowded Years* (New York: G. P. Putnam's Sons, 1947), 169.

31. Creel, *How We Advertised America*, 276.

32. Ruth Vasey, *The World According to Hollywood, 1918–1939* (Madison: University of Wisconsin Press, 1997), 14.

33. Arthur Edwin Krows, "Motion Pictures—Not for Theatres: Part Six," *Educational Screen*, February 1939, 52.

34. *Exhibitor's Trade Review*, June 23, 1917, 173. On the bond campaigns, see James J. Kimble, *Mobilizing the Home Front: War Bonds and Domestic Propaganda* (College Station: Texas A&M University Press, 2006).

35. Leslie Midkiff DeBauche, *Reel Patriotism* (Wisconsin: University of Wisconsin Press, 1997), 118–19.

36. *Motography*, June 16, 1917, 1247.

37. Liberty Loans Committee to Charles F. Horner, Treasury Department, October 21, 1918, record group (RG) 16, box 693, National Archives and Records Administration II, Washington D.C. (hereafter NARA); NAMPI advertisement, *Variety*, October 12, 1917, 36–37; *Moving Picture World*, October 19, 1918, 351–52.

38. Charles Gilbert, *American Financing of World War I* (Westport, CT: Greenwood Press, 1970), 140; Julia C. Ott, *When Wall Street Met Main Street: The Quest for an Investor's Democracy* (Cambridge, MA: Harvard University Press, 2011), 2, 34, 55, 57.

39. Ott, *When Wall Street Met Main Street*, 9–35.

40. Ibid., 59, 60.

41. Julia Cathleen Ott, "When Wall Street Met Main Street: The Quest for an Investors' Democracy and the Emergence of the Retail Investor in the United States, 1890–1930," *Enterprise and Society* 9, no. 4 (December 2008): 625.

42. I explore the ties formed between investment banks and Hollywood, beginning in 1919, in Lee Grieveson, *Cinema and the Wealth of Nations: Media, Capital, and the Liberal World System* (Berkeley: University of California Press, 2018).

43. Woodrow Wilson, *Exhibitor's Trade Review,* July 1918, cited in DeBauche, *Reel Patriotism,* 109.

44. Ulf Jonas Bjork, "The US Commerce Department Aids Hollywood Exports, 1921–1933," *Historian* 62, no. 3 (March 2000): 575–88.

45. I borrow the term "corporate liberal" here principally from the economic historian Martin Sklar, who has influentially argued that corporate liberalism emerged as a prevalent praxis in the United States around the turn of the century among government, judicial, and industrial and financial organizations "to transact the corporate reconstruction of the political-economic order on the basis of the mutual adaptation of corporate capitalism and the American liberal tradition." Martin J. Sklar, *The Corporate Reconstruction of American Capitalism, 1890–1916: The Market, the Law, and Politics* (Cambridge: Cambridge University Press, 1988), 34. The subtitle that precedes this paragraph is from *Schenck v. United States* 249 US 47 (1919).

46. Espionage Act, June 15 1917, Pub. L. 65–24, 40 Stat. 217. On the passage of the Espionage and Sedition Acts, and legal response, see David M. Rabban, *Free Speech in Its Forgotten Years* (Cambridge: Cambridge University Press, 1997), esp. 248–98.

47. Eugene V. Debs, "The Canton, Ohio, Speech," June 16, 1918, accessed July 23, 2017, www.marxists.org/archive/debs/works/1918/canton.htm.

48. David L. Sterling, "In Defense of Debs: The Lawyers and the Espionage Act Case," *Indiana Magazine of History* 83, no. 1 (March 1987): 20–22.

49. Debs, "The Canton, Ohio, Speech." Debs referred here to Wilson's spurious claim that the war was fought to "make democracy safe for the world."

50. Sedition Act, May 16, 1918, Pub. L. 65–150, 40 Stat. 553.

51. Ibid.

52. Ibid.

53. Sklar, *Corporate Reconstruction of American Capitalism.*

54. Joseph A. McCartin, *Labor's Great War: The Struggle for Industrial Democracy and the Origins of Modern American Labor Relations, 1912–1921* (Chapel Hill: University of North Carolina Press, 1997), 68–69.

55. Alan Dawley, *Struggles for Justice: Social Responsibility and the Liberal State* (Cambridge, MA: Harvard University Press, 1991), 188.

56. Brett Gary, *The Nervous Liberals: Propaganda Anxieties from World War I to the Cold War* (New York: Columbia University Press, 1999), 22.

57. Emily S. Rosenberg, "Economic Interest and United States Foreign Policy," in *American Foreign Relations Reconsidered, 1890–1993,* ed. Gordon Martel (London: Routledge, 1994), 38–39.

58. Stephen M. Kohn, *American Political Prisoners: Prosecutions under the Espionage and Sedition Acts* (Westport, CT: Praeger, 1994), 14–19.

59. *Moving Picture World,* December 22, 1917, 1786; *Moving Picture World,* December 29, 1917, 1947; Richard Wood, ed., *Film and Propaganda in America: A Documentary History,* vol. 1, *World War I* (Westport, CT: Greenwood Press, 1990), 296.

60. I summarize, and necessarily simplify, a more complex argument here about the relationship among liberalism, democracy, and capitalism, as explicated in particular by the political sociologist C. B. Macpherson. See in particular *The Life and Times of Liberal Democracy* (Oxford: Oxford University Press, 1977). Perry Anderson argues that a form of national security liberalism began in the period

around the turn of the century but was fully established with the National Security Act of 1947. Anderson, "Imperium," 30.

61. *Schenck v. United States* 249 US 47. See also *Debs v. United States* 249 US 211 (1919).

62. For material on the 1917 Immigration Act, the 1918 Alien Anarchist Act, Americanization campaigns, and the corporate counteroffensive in 1919 against union membership, see, for example, John Higham, *Strangers in the Land: Patterns of American Nativism, 1860–1925,* 2nd ed. (New Brunswick, NJ: Rutgers University Press, 1992), 200–203; and Christopher Capozzola, *Uncle Sam Wants You: World War I and the Making of the Modern American Citizen* (Oxford: Oxford University Press, 2008), 202–4.

63. Higham, *Strangers in the Land,* 230–32.

64. In 1922 the deputy head of the bureau, J. Edgar Hoover, ordered that Chaplin be watched closely as a suspected communist sympathizer. Bureau agents reported that Chaplin was part of a communist plot to use movies to make a "propagandist appeal for the cause of the labor movement and the revolution." "Report of Special Agent A. A. Hopkins," August 15, 1922, Los Angeles, cited in Steven J. Ross, *Hollywood Left and Right: How Movie Stars Shaped American Politics* (New York: Oxford University Press, 2011), 11.

65. Franklin K. Lane to Secretary of War, January 23, 1919, RG 12, box 42, Records of the Bureau of Education, Records of the Office of the Commission, Historical Files, 1870–1950, NARA; J. J. Cotter, Administrative Assistant, Department of the Interior, memorandum for Dr. Pettijohn, June 6, 1919, Visual Instruction Section, Division of Educational Extension, "Purpose of Section: Re-stated from Various Reports Submitted to the Director since January 1, 1919," RG 12, box 16, 1, NARA; "Memorandum from Mr. Pettijohn to Dr. Claxton," n.d., RG 12, box 16, 1, NARA.

66. "In Charge of the Work of Visual Instruction," Division of Educational Extension, to Mr. J. F. Abel, February 3, 1919, RG 12, box 42, 1, NARA.

67. C. H. Moore, "Future of the Screen in Education and Industrials," *Reel and Slide,* August 1919, 10.

68. Arthur Edwin Krows, "Motion Pictures—Not for Theatres: Part 8," *Educational Screen,* April 1939, 123.

69. The subtitle preceding this paragraph consists of words spoken by an exasperated American marine in Baghdad after the fall of Iraq in 2003; they are heard in the documentary miniseries *The Trap: What Happened to Our Dream of Freedom,* directed by Adam Curtis (UK: BBC, 2007).

70. Creel, *How We Advertised America,* 4.

71. Walter Lippmann, *Liberty and the News* (New York: Harcourt, Brace and Howe, 1920); Lippmann, *Public Opinion;* Walter Lippmann, *The Phantom Public* (New York: Harcourt, Brace and Co., 1925).

72. James W. Carey, *Communication as Culture: Essays on Media and Society* (Winchester, MA: Unwin Hyman, 1989), 75.

73. Ronald Steel, *Walter Lippmann and the American Century* (Boston: Little, Brown, 1980), 172.

74. Lippmann, *Public Opinion,* 24.

75. Ibid., 29.

76. Ibid., 97.

77. For example, Noam Chomsky, *Necessary Illusions: Thought Control in Democratic Societies* (London: Pluto Press, 1999), 30–32.

78. Steel, *Lippmann and the American Century,* 128–40.

79. Ewen begins the brilliant *PR!* with account of the work of Bernays (3–19), and discusses him in further detail (159–73). Adam Curtis, too, begins with Bernays in his remarkable documentary series *The Century of Self* (UK: BBC, 2002).

80. Edward L. Bernays, *Biography of an Idea: Memoirs of Public Relations Counsel Edward L. Bernays* (New York: Simon and Schuster, 1965), 157.

81. Edward Bernays, "Publicity in International Trade: How Public Opinion Abroad Was Influenced by the United States Government during the War," *Association News* 1, no. 24 (1920): 3.

82. Edward L. Bernays, *Propaganda* (New York: H. Liveright, 1928), 27.

83. Neil Smith, *The Endgame of Globalization* (London: Routledge, 2005), 120. The history of these endeavors is explicated in Brendan Fischer, "A Banana Republic Once Again?" *Center for Media and Democracy's PR Watch*, December 27, 2010, accessed July 24, 2017, www.prwatch.org/news/2010/12/9834 /banana-republic-once-again; and Nicholas Cullather, *Operation PBSUCCESS: The United States and Guatemala, 1952–1954* (Washington DC: Center for the Study of Intelligence, 1994).

84. Jennifer Fay, *Theaters of Occupation: Hollywood and the Reeducation of Postwar Germany* (Minneapolis: University of Minnesota Press, 2008); Hiroshi Kitamura, *Screening Enlightenment: Hollywood and the Cultural Reconstruction of Defeated Japan* (Ithaca, NY: Cornell University Press, 2010).

85. Nicholas Cull, *The Cold War and the United States Information Agency: American Propaganda and Public Diplomacy, 1945–1989* (Cambridge: Cambridge University Press, 2008); Marc Frey, "Tools of Empire: Persuasion and the United States Modernizing Mission in Southeast Asia," *Diplomatic History* 27, no. 4 (September 2003).

86. Daniel Leab, *Orwell Subverted: The CIA and the Filming of Animal Farm* (Philadelphia: Penn State University Press, 2007); Frances Stonor Saunders, *Who Paid the Piper? The CIA and the Cultural Cold War* (London: Granta, 1999), 1–6, 279–301; Hugh Wilford, *The Mighty Wurlitzer: How the CIA Played America* (Cambridge, MA: Harvard University Press, 2008), 117–21.

87. James Schwoch, *Global TV: New Media and the Cold War, 1946–69* (Chicago: University of Illinois Press, 2009).

88. Kohn, *American Political Prisoners*, 21.

89. John Sbardellati, *J. Edgar Hoover Goes to the Movies: The FBI and the Origins of Hollywood's Cold War* (Ithaca, NY: Cornell University Press, 2012).

90. The Espionage Act is now 18 USC ch. 37, and was the legislation invoked in 2013 to prosecute Chelsea Manning for leaking materials relating to the wars in Afghanistan and Iraq. Manning served seven years of a thirty-five-year prison sentence. Edward Snowden was charged in the same year with violating the Espionage Act for leaking information from the National Security Agency that revealed the extent of the massive global surveillance programs run by the NSA in alliance with other security agencies across the globe. Snowden currently lives in exile in Russia.

91. Glen Greenwald, *No Place to Hide: Edward Snowden, the NSA and the Surveillance State* (London: Hamish Hamilton, 2015), 4; Barrett Brown, "The Cyber-Intelligence Complex and Its Useful Idiots," *Guardian*, July 1, 2013. Brown is currently serving sixty-three months in prison on charges relating principally to the dissemination of information.

16

STAR TESTIMONIES

World War and the Cultural Politics of Authority

Sue Collins

In the aftermath of World War I (1914–18), when Walter Lippmann decried the abuses of propaganda in a democratic state and Harold Lasswell published his influential study on war propaganda, film stardom's role in the Great War's domestic mobilization escaped critique.[1] In fact, during the interwar years when scholars, public intellectuals, and practitioners debated the virtues and detriments of propaganda, the influence of Hollywood stars on political matters went unnoticed— with the exception, perhaps, of Edward Bernays, who while writing in the 1920s recognized that politicians might capitalize from their association with popular actors.[2] What Paul Lazarsfeld and his colleagues described as a "'two-step flow of communication," developed in the early 1940s, neglected the possibility of film stars serving as "opinion leaders" because the researchers focused on the interpersonal context of everyday life.[3] It would seem that film stars, whose aura is produced and maintained at a distance, required separate consideration, if any at all. It was not until 1943, after an eighteen-hour radio bond drive conducted by popular singer and radio personality Kate Smith, that sociologists began to take seriously the entertainment celebrity's political import in moments of crisis such as world war. Robert Merton and his research team studied the audience's reception of this proto–media event, prefiguring Richard Dyer's work on the star image by thirty years when they noted the "congruity" between Smith's "public image" and her on-air persona as the marathon's host. Building on this early work, three years after the war's end, Merton and Lazarsfeld argued that mass media confer legitimation and prestige on individuals by virtue of their exposure to the public.[4] This was hardly news to Hollywood, whose stars had lent their names, images, and bodies to the War Department for almost a quarter of a century.

This chapter historicizes Hollywood stardom's legitimation as a source of political authority expedient to wartime and a postwar militarized state. It shows, in the first place, how film stars' access to the public sphere grew out of a cultural precedent owed, in part, to the legitimate stage, where the terms for actors' political activities were initially inscribed. Second, I argue that the conferral of political authority onto film stars was necessarily preceded by the early industry's struggle for economic and cultural legitimacy as motion-picture professionals tried to reshape cinema in the public imaginary. Situating cinema during World War I within a complex discursive struggle over its cultural value and political legitimacy, I suggest that Wilsonian officials distinguished between commercial Hollywood-style film and other extant uses of the motion picture as a medium, and they valued the different sectors of the business differently. More specifically, government officials preferred to control film production processes through their own film division, but they needed the industry's distribution network and, above all, access to commercial spaces of exhibition. Wilson's administration employed film for bureaucratic functions prior to the war, but officials held uneven if not ambiguous opinions on the value of *commercial Hollywood film* even as they recognized its popularity. Third, I argue that the earliest recruitment of film stars into wartime propaganda on the national stage was also slow to materialize because the stars' rhetorical value competed with traditional modes of authority such as the written word and oratory by renowned elites. Wilson's Committee on Public Information (CPI) and the Treasury Department relied on these established rhetorical modes before federal bureaucrats were convinced to tap into the popular appeal of screen stars. Film stars were recruited into war mobilization at the local level from the start, but their inclusion at the national level did not occur until the third bond drive of April 1918, a full year after the United States first intervened in the world conflict. Once the cultural power of film stardom to galvanize the public's attention was established, the logic of star recruitment as a crucial personification of state discourse in wartime seemed indispensable and inevitable. Last, I examine stardom's configuration during World War II, when war work under Hollywood's auspices expanded to incorporate theatrical entertainers crossing over to the new medium of radio and the musical film genre. Here, too, stardom's cultural function merged with its political one, generating a well-rehearsed ancillary of liberal governance to serve war mobilization, military financing, and soldier relief. Notable at this moment was the institutionalization of the United Service Organizations (USO), and with it the normalizing apolitical role granted to Hollywood as a permanent military relief agency serving the militarized state during and beyond World War II, and throughout the Cold War as well.

In the course of tracing Hollywood's role as adjunct to the War Department from its inception during the Great War to its expansive service during World War II (1939–45), this chapter frames stardom's endorsement of the state's wartime objectives as a component of cultural policy. It is useful to see negotiation over stardom's political authority during war mobilization as, to borrow from Tony Bennett, both an "object" and "instrument" of cultural policy underpinning the governmentalization of social life in everyday contexts. For Bennett, culture is both an aesthetic and intellectual enterprise and, following Raymond Williams, "whole ways of life," constituting a field upon which governmental regulation may act. Cultural policy, as I use the term in the world war context, involved the state's strategies to promote the population's self-governance (its behavior during wartime, if you will) through cultural practices (e.g., signifying practices, communications systems, "morals, manners, and codes of conduct, etc.").[5] Notable at this historical moment is the US government's valorization of entertainment stardom as a newfound mode of authority exploitable for propaganda, for soldier training, and for war relief domestically and on the overseas front. This chapter charts the convergence of film stardom with political authority, documenting a period when entertainment stars, already loved by a vast public, first worked for the government to model ideal citizenship. It shows how the government's use of stardom's power to promote its policies signified the state's recognition of the popular film star as *celebrity*—that is, as a modern metaphor for the celebrated person in the public sphere. With this, celebrities, including cultural elites and now film stars, became more central to state security. Lee Grieveson, in his chapter in this volume, shows how cinema and "persuasive celebrity" during the bond drives of World War I articulate to the beginnings of what he calls "'exceptional' governance," imbricating state interests with militarization, finance capital, and a new "investor democracy," outlasting the exigencies of wartime.

Film stardom's endorsement of dominant political ideology during the Great War disciplined national consciousness through the consumption of popular culture. Stars' wartime feature filmographies, their participation in promotional film shorts and trailers, and their live appearances to promote enlistment, conservation, and bond sales worked to exhort American movie fans to voluntarily follow the stars' lead as citizen exemplars. The star image embodied at once the extraordinary performer on the big screen, the ordinary individual as a part of the collective, and the charismatic (patriotic) leader whose influence could channel the collective toward self-governed behavior. At the same time, the stars' patriotic activities provided a counterpoint to the repressive consequences of the CPI campaign, and thus helped stabilize the sociopolitical climate in a moment of intense national crisis. Amid violent antiwar dissent and abuses toward so-called slackers pervading the country, the spectacle of star appearances negated such realities. Twenty years later, President Roosevelt's favorable opinion on motion pictures as a means to reach the public meant that Hollywood was regarded as an "essential industry" during World War II, facilitating its considerable contributions to wartime activity. Roosevelt's Office of War Information (OWI) did not hesitate to embrace the film industry in the mobilization and relief effort. Upon American entry into that war, the Treasury Department immediately recruited stars from cinema, radio, and the stage to inspire Americans to finance the war through bond purchases. In the same way that stardom's political import exceeded the boundaries of the World War I propaganda campaign by normalizing stardom's testimonial power, the already established articulation of patriotic star appearances and wartime relief with celebrity authority during World War II recapitulated the significance of American cinema and moviegoing habits in everyday life.

AUTHORIZING STARS

In the years prior to the First World War, entertainment professionals in the United States inspired no special authority bearing on politics or governance. The idea or logic developed during wartime that professional actors' opinions and practices should be accorded legitimacy with respect to politics—an area outside their field of training—was predicated on stage actors' struggle for cultural recognition in the late nineteenth century, during which time their political subjectivity was largely circumscribed. The infrastructures of publicity and celebrity journalism had much to do with elevating the profession of acting, particularly as actors' unconventional lifestyles began to stand in desirable contrast to the constraints and routinization of modernity.[6] But at the same time, public performance mapped onto an emerging "culture of personality" that instructed people through prevalent personality and self-help literature on modes of self-presentation in response to a burgeoning consumer culture.[7] For Richard Sennett, the turn to personality consequently elevated the performing artist with extraordinary talent and public expressiveness to charismatic celebrity whose authority rested on inviting "audience fantasy about what he was 'really' like."[8] Having won a certain visibility in the cultural sphere, a few stage stars negotiated the earliest conversions of "capital," in Pierre Bourdieu's terms, from their field of theatrical performance into the political field as activists addressing progressive social reform, political corruption, and women's rights, among other issues.[9] However, as a marginalized social group that fought for respectability, actors generally avoided controversy and were aware of the risks involved in managing their star image and commodity value. According to Benjamin McArthur, despite a few exceptions, political apathy characterized the theatrical profession as a whole in the pre–World War I period.[10] Film actors, many of whom had been lured from Broadway, continued this trend.

The arrival of the motion picture and its feature players provoked the legitimate theater to consolidate its hold on highbrow culture in sharp distinction to the new medium, which would have the ironic effect of rendering stage stardom less relevant to war mobilization. Stage producers fought off the menace of film's growing popularity by emphasizing the dichotomy between the "serious" live stage and

motion pictures. Condemning the latter as artistically substandard, theatrical producers contributed to the growing hierarchy of cultural tastes, or what Lawrence
Levine calls the "sacralization of culture."[11] Efforts to differentiate the legitimate
stage by reproving motion pictures prompted film professionals to overturn perceptions of its inferiority, in part, by appropriating some of the means by which
stage stardom was valorized.[12] By mid-1914, screen stardom's evolving cultural
cachet began to merge with the film industry's concentrated efforts to uplift perceptions of motion pictures in order to abate persistent criticisms of the medium
as cheap or lowbrow. The larger struggle over Hollywood's cultural legitimacy in
the early teens was a critical precursor to the industry's prospective value to the
government as a component of its propaganda campaign. Theatrical stardom initiated the terms for the professional entertainer to stay within the acceptable boundaries of sociopolitical activity, while film stardom's visibility and political import
quickly eclipsed what Broadway could offer when it came time to mobilize for war.
Stage stars asserted their value in localized ways—most notably, through war relief
domestically and overseas during the Great War, and without much recognition
compared to the publicity afforded film stars for their role in helping to finance the
war. Even the more private and intimate activities constituting soldier care and
soldier entertainment consigned to stage stardom during World War I would be
overwhelmed by film stardom and the consolidation of entertainment talent by
Hollywood studios during World War II.

"SLAP THE KAISER IN THE FACE WITH EVERY DOLLAR YOU CAN RAISE"

Despite the emergence in the teens of a dominant mode of production—what
would be referred to as "Hollywood" in the postwar period—cinema was not
monolithic. During the neutrality years and First World War period, commercial
cinema competed with other possibilities for the medium's development. There
existed, for instance, numerous examples of what Charles Acland and Haidee Wasson denote as "useful cinema" and what Steven Ross calls "worker filmmaking."[13]
For some progressives, the motion picture's promise was noncommercial, as a
form for edification at the very least, and for social and cultural uplift at its best. At
the same time, in 1915 the US Supreme Court downgraded film's cultural value
when it rendered it a business "pure and simple," conducted to earn profit like
other "spectacles." The denial of First Amendment rights to the motion picture in
Mutual v. Ohio was both an outcome of censorship battles over persistent critiques
of cinema's perceived moral hazards and an impetus for the industry to better
control its public image. It also obscured and ultimately failed to account for a
growing range of film activity that was expanding the use of film in noncommercial manners.

In 1917, the motion picture's utility to war mobilization was certainly not lost on the Wilson administration, but some bureaucrats were more reticent than others about assigning dominion to Hollywood over the production of government films. As Thomas Doherty puts it, "[G]overnment policy blended an instinctive awareness that cinema and war were natural mates with a suspicion that the new medium was combustible and liable to misfire."[14] CPI head George Creel claimed that he wanted to rely upon commercial producers to organize CPI's use of film, but the War Department thought differently. When the industry offered to organize for war mobilization, Wilson's officials accepted insofar as exhibitors' screens were critical in helping the government convey its messages whether by way of its own slides, trailers, propaganda films, or Four Minute Men speeches.[15] Theater lobbies were also ideal locations for enlistment and bond-drive campaigns. Concerning the production of government films, however, the industry found its efforts thwarted from the start. The CPI oversaw the production of its own films, had distribution authority over military footage, and controlled the terms for export of all films. As far as the War Department was concerned, only military personnel were allowed to film in the theaters of war for documentation purposes.

Nonetheless, for film-industry leaders, the war provided an opportune moment for securing long-term economic advantages, or what Leslie DeBauche refers to as "practical patriotism."[16] Upon US intervention, the industry strategized, in the first place, to minimize the adverse effects of wartime austerity measures and taxation, and second, to secure from political elites the recognition it claimed to deserve by calling itself (erroneously) the nation's "fifth industry." At stake was the reimagining of commercial film as a cultural form that was as good as, if not superior to, traditional modes of persuasion, expressions of national identity, and tools for political and cultural policy. Key to industry leaders' strategy was proving that they could aid the government's campaign for war mobilization. Such assistance would prove that the film industry deserved essential-industry status during wartime.[17] In support of this aim, the industry's trade association—the National Association of the Motion Picture Industry (NAMPI)—formed a War Co-operation Committee (WCC) in anticipation of working with the CPI for the duration of the war.

Among the first obstacles the industry faced concerned the army's training camps, where NAMPI found its initial efforts to supply motion pictures for soldier recreation blocked by camp policy.[18] Determined to avoid the military delinquency occurring during the Mexican-American border war in 1916, Secretary of War Newton Baker staffed the Commission on Training Camp Activities (CTCA) with social reformers whose idea of wholesome recreation was antithetical to commercial amusements thought to be corrupting urban youth, one of which were "cheap motion-picture shows."[19] CTCA officials privileged the legitimate stage for the grand Liberty theaters they had built in the camps and cantonments, imagining that such programming would cultivate intellectual development while also guarding against vulgar and licentious entertainment lurking outside the camps.[20] Motion-picture exhibition was relegated to YMCA huts, administered under arrangement with the Community Motion Picture Bureau (CMPB), a film-distribution service run by former journalist and editor of *Youth's Companion* Warren Dunham Foster. At the start of intervention, Foster offered his services to the army at cost. By 1917, at least two months before NAMPI's efforts to win government contracts, the CMPB was awarded sole authority to oversee motion-picture screening in the army camps under the auspices of the YMCA's War Work Council; subsequently, it supplied films to other welfare organizations, including the Knights of Columbus, the Jewish Welfare Board, the Salvation Army, and the Red Cross. Two years later, it was managing an estimated 97 percent of the films seen by army and navy personnel, both domestically and overseas.[21]

Given Baker's orientation toward social engineering, the CMPB's censoring service and guarantee that its films would be in keeping with the wholesome camp mandate was ideal. In effect, CMPB "editors" screened every film in possession, rejecting outright films that contained drinking scenes, gambling, or sexually suggestive narratives—particularly ones intimating infidelity, noted as (love) "triangles."[22] Consequently, several films with enormous box-office appeal were denied soldiers. For example, William S. Hart's "bad man" role and the settings in which he interacted with shady others were off-limits, as was Theda Bara's popular "vamp" portrayals, even though both actors contributed heartily to war mobilization. Conversely, Douglas Fairbanks's persona modeled precisely the clean, healthy, and moral example the military sought to inscribe in its trainees. As a spokesperson for self-made success, Fairbanks gave advice on modern living in two authored books and a motion-picture magazine column, and in numerous articles and interviews he "extolled the virtues of training one's body to win the battles of life."[23] Indeed, what Gaylyn Studlar calls the "intertextual chain" of Fairbanks's on- and off-screen texts was focused around the perfection of manhood, ideals of character building, and the physical antics of the masculine American hero.[24] In February 1918, the War Department requested that Fairbanks make a "propaganda" film that would convey to soldiers in training that "clean living and physical fitness are, after loyalty and obedience, the prime requisites for a soldier."[25] Following the mandate, Fairbanks aimed his scenario at slackerism, or "the soldier who deliberately sets out to do himself an injury that will prevent him from taking part in military activities." Such a man's cowardice, Fairbanks indicted, was due to an "unhealthy" mind.[26] Fairbanks's film short for the fourth Liberty Loan drive, *Sic 'Em Sam* (1918), in which Fairbanks as Democracy physically beats up Prussianism and flushes him down the sewer, was also awarded special exhibition in the training and overseas camps.

Before Fairbanks's successes, however, NAMPI leaders were unable for various reasons to build anything like the comprehensive government film program that operated during World War II. NAMPI's president, William Brady, could not overcome objections by others who had a stake in the government's policy toward film. Some members of the American industry objected to the role played by the YMCA—but also by the Red Cross, which had its own motion-picture bureau, and the US Army Signal Corps—in making or showing films. The signal corps was designated by Baker to produce a visual documentation of the war's history, which resulted in the constitution of the CPI's Division of Film six months after intervention. Creel had sole authority to distribute its films and photographs. Because of the sensitive nature of field and combat cinematography and because the signal corps's mandate included using film for training purposes, its personnel were limited to military staff who were trained in-house. For its official propaganda films, the CPI used signal corps footage, but it also established its own production unit within the Division of Film. During the last six months of the war, the CPI produced feature-length series, two- and one-reel films, and newsreels under the directorship of Charles S. Hart, a former advertising manager for *Heart's Magazine*. Hart had no prior experience in the motion-picture business, taking over the Division of Film a full year after the United States declared war on the Central Powers. Only after complaints from industry representatives that the government had ignored offers of assistance by the industry—as well as Hart's takeover—did the division endeavor to recruit experienced industry professionals for its production staff and to invite assistance from private companies to produce documentaries through its Scenario Department.[27] For the first year of the war, however, the studio heads who made up the executive and general membership of the WCC nonetheless effectively promoted their studio brands when they eagerly lent their stars to the Liberty Loan and War Savings campaigns.

Eventually the Treasury Department used every available form of publicity to promote its five bond drives and single protracted savings campaign, but in the beginning Secretary McAdoo resisted the employment of outside publicity apparatuses, including the Hollywood film industry.[28] Initially, the War Loan Organization relied on well-established modes of rhetorical address to craft the appeals—namely, through print, visual art, and oratory—produced or delivered by prestigious or renowned individuals. Because the organization's Speakers' Bureau was only loosely organized for the first loan drive, it was largely unable to procure prominent speakers for the start of the campaign. Once McAdoo issued a call for "speakers of national reputation" to deliver addresses across the country, fifty-seven spokespersons were recruited for the second bond drive, including current and former high-level politicians and congressional representatives, civil servants, business and labor leaders, military officers, diplomats, evangelists, authors, professors, attorneys, and prominent association representatives. For the third loan, the bureau's list of some forty "prominent persons" grew to include individuals in fields of cultural production such as artists, cartoonists, singers, vaudeville performers, and actors—both stage and motion picture.[29]

Well before this point, however, film and stage stars had been making personal appearances to sell war bonds in theaters, department stores, and hotel lobbies; on busy sidewalks; and at private receptions and local bond rallies. Local organizers tasked with making enormous quotas were the first to seek the assistance of film-star capital. For example, when Mary Pickford accepted an invitation by the chairman of the Twelfth Federal District to appear at the "big Civic Auditorium" in San Francisco during the first Liberty Loan drive, her scheduled appearance, according to *Motography,* was publicized on the front page of the dailies. The featured speaker, Pickford reportedly stimulated some $2 million in bond subscriptions that night.[30] At the request of Cincinnati's mayor, Marguerite Clark's two-day appearance during the second loan drive was associated with an amount in excess of $14.4 million in bond sales. Personally selling $1 million in bonds in twelve hours, Clark used an application printed with her photograph, which had been sent to thousands of potential bond buyers in advance of her arrival. Those who bought directly from Clark received a tag reading, "I am helping Marguerite Clark Sell Liberty Bonds."[31]

Douglas Fairbanks Sr. was the first star to tour for the Liberty Loan. For the second drive, his press agent, Pete Smith, arranged a cross-country trip, stopping in big cities for special engagements and in small towns for five minutes at a time so that Fairbanks could speak to the large crowds that gathered at the rail stations. By the time he returned to California, Fairbanks had personally sold in excess of $1 million in bond subscriptions, which no doubt convinced McAdoo to solicit stars to serve the government for the next loan. The Third Liberty Loan (March 2–April 6, 1918) marked the official recruitment of Hollywood's biggest stars to tour nationally for the bond drive. The "Big Three" (Pickford, Fairbanks, and Charlie Chaplin), William Hart, and Marie Dressler (who represented Broadway) lent their marquee value and live bodies to the campaign by touring assigned regions of the country for up to three weeks.

Preaching the virtues of Liberty Bond investments, thrift, and Americanism in their speeches, the stars endured the nervous tension of huge crowds that poured out to witness the "real" person behind the screen image. In recurring narratives reported in popular and trade presses throughout the stars' bond tours, the writers described, on the one hand, surging masses of spectators requiring police forces to maintain order, and on the other, accounts of how the stars' playful interactions with the crowds worked to reposition them as well-intentioned fans who deserved a closer look at their screen idols.[32] Such scenes accord with David Marshall's supposition on celebrity's discursive emergence at the turn of the century.[33] Marshall theorizes celebrity as a means of representing and celebrating conceptions of individualism in democratic capitalism, and as a site to house the affective power of the audience—an entity imagined, at that time, to require strategies for its containment and governance. Drawing from crowd, mass society, and Freudian theory,

Marshall traces celebrity's relation to its audience in modern culture to show how celebrity functions as a new form of public leadership able to harness the perceived strains of irrationality emerging from the crowd or modern "mass."[34] Consigned by the state to the center of political spectacle, stars were charismatic leaders addressing the childlike (fan-like) mass; in city after city, the stars channeled affective crowd sentiment toward virtuous, patriotic, and self-governing conduct in service to the state's wartime needs.

Press discourses on public reactions to the stars' live appearances also worked to eclipse stubborn perceptions of commercial motion pictures as lowbrow, and moviegoing as morally suspect. The industry's burgeoning star system, more generally, had been working to abate regulatory attacks on cinema through its star personae, whose constructed roles corresponded to normative American values and common cultural experiences, as is clearly exemplified by Fairbanks's perceived contribution to military training. Stars were screen idols not only to the working and immigrant classes, but also to middle-class America, for whom they served as enduring models of personality and consumerism in daily life.[35] But by this point in the industry's growth, star popularity, in fact, was not confined to lower- and middle-class boundaries. To be sure, the staggering sums of bond sales attributed to the movie stars during huge public rallies functioned to bridge the gap between popular and high culture, but these scenes were misleading indicators. At the same time that they attracted mammoth crowds, star appearances more fruitfully focused on the wealthy and institutional buyers who could actually afford the bonds' large denominations, and who capitalized on their tax benefits.[36] Upon their arrival in a city or town, stars sold bonds publicly and with much fanfare for all to see, and then later in the afternoon or throughout the evening, they personally approached wealthy investors who wished to meet them in private settings. Everywhere Pickford went, for instance, she was greeted by hordes of adoring fans, but then soon after was wrestled away from surging crowds to refined tea lounges and elaborate dining rooms where she met millionaires, wealthy representatives from women's societies, and institutional buyers, the aggregate of whom bought bonds in the tens of thousands and made up over 80 percent of total bond subscriptions.[37]

In addition to touring and giving speeches at bond rallies and other sites, dozens of stars from major studios participated in the making of Liberty Loan propaganda films. Created explicitly to boost the drives, these short films were developed out of exhibitors' practice of using trailers to make short announcements, which by 1917 was a standard way to advertise forthcoming productions.[38] For the second loan, the industry's trade association, NAMPI, oversaw the production of the series *Three Billion Dollars in Three Weeks*. Publicized as an "all-star feature production" bringing together "for the first time" screen and stage stars with government officials under the same billing, the series comprised five distinct episodes of

FIGURE 16.1. Douglas Fairbanks as Democracy boxing Prussianism in his short film for the third Liberty Loan drive, *Swat the Kaiser* (1918). On the right, also shown are "Bull" Montana as Prussianism, Gustav von Seifferitz as Uncle Sam, Tully Marshall as Death, and Sara Mason as Liberty from the same film. Fairbanks used the same characters for his Liberty Loan short *Sic 'Em Sam* (1918). *Moving Picture World*, April 27, 1918, 521. (Courtesy of the Media History Digital Library.)

about five hundred feet each, to be run in any order. One hundred prints of each of the episodes were produced without charge, and ten companies belonging to NAMPI were assigned to handle their distribution, along with sending seventeen thousand slides to exhibitors nationwide free of charge.[39] At his own expense, Fairbanks produced an allegorical short, *Swat the Kaiser,* for the third loan, starring Fairbanks as Democracy defeating Prussianism in a boxing match. (See figure 16.1.) These entertaining, rent-free propaganda shorts featuring popular stars were no doubt preferred by exhibitors over more slides or patriotic speakers between reels. More important, the film shorts, along with a few produced for Hoover's Food Administration starting in fall 1917, inspired the strategy for the Fourth Liberty Loan.

By mid-August 1918, NAMPI representatives announced an industry-wide project involving the production of "miniature features" by select companies and their stars in scenarios written expressly for the fourth loan.[40] In cooperation with the Treasury Department's Liberty Loan director of publicity, Frank Wilson, fourteen studios overseen by producer Adolph Zukor produced thirty-seven distinct film shorts featuring over forty film stars and ranging in length from three hundred to one thousand feet, each with a trailer in which McAdoo appealed directly to the public: "Buy Liberty Bonds and help put Pershing's headquarters somewhere in Germany instead of somewhere in France." Such unprecedented coordination paid off. Two days prior to the films' delivery date to the Treasury Department, the industry trades announced that the War Industries Board had awarded the film industry "essential industry" status.[41]

Despite their ill timing with the influenza pandemic, the Liberty Loan film project nonetheless signified the Wilson administration's official inclusion of Hollywood's mode of production in government cultural policy. Frank Wilson's communication with Zukor indicating his specifications for the films' tone clearly demonstrates the government's shift in attitude toward employing commercial cinema. Wilson requested that Zukor steer the process so that scenario writers would create a certain type of film compatible with the "national spirit" the government was "inculcating" across other media—an affective appeal emphasizing sacrifice and determination, but also one not above inciting fear of atrocities and hatred against Germany. Frank Wilson suggested that it was "necessary to show some atrocity stuff," which was remarkable given President Wilson's noted distaste for "the medieval bloodlust" of "[h]ate-the-Hun" films and his initial efforts at neutrality.[42] About a quarter of the film shorts targeted American outrage over alleged German atrocities. These productions roused audiences' recollections of the "rape of Belgium" by depicting German soldiers as *Huns,* an "iconographic shorthand," as Nicoletta Gullace suggests, that evoked "themes of racial 'otherness' and primitive atavism," which had been made familiar to Americans in cartoon and poster propaganda.[43] On the heels of war-preparedness films, and more blatantly after US intervention, scenario writers adopted melodramatic atrocity narratives that at once simplified war's complexity and visually heightened its drama.

In a sense, the Liberty Bond films represented the industry's larger purview on US intervention as the nation proceeded from war preparation to national chauvinism.[44] As evident by the *Exhibitor's Press Book*'s scenario descriptions, the narrative formula relied primarily on simplistic allegory and parable to "whop" the kaiser, depict atrocities, represent the virtues of self-sacrifice and bond investing, and admonish slackerism.[45] The loan shorts also constructed national jingoism by using individual stars. The writer for the *Chicago Post* designated each film as "an expression of the personality of the star who offers it"—for example, Pickford's childlike character, Chaplin's tramp, Fairbanks's agile athlete, and Hart's "bad man,"—the "Big Four"—among others.[46] But it was not merely the pleasurable intertextual recognition of one's favorite screen idol that afforded the film project's political import. Punctuated with first-person narrative title cards testifying to the imperative of bond subscriptions, stars performances interpolated audiences with direct appeals to the camera. Based on the shorts' descriptions and the surviving footage, it is possible that many of the stars broke the narrative frame to address audiences eye-to-eye, which was both novel and what in part overdetermined the films' status *as propaganda,* as opposed to mere entertainment. As a protoform of para-social interaction, the patriotic star testimonial signified something new in the film industry's development.[47] The Liberty Bond films demonstrated the entertainment's industry's organizing potential and sociocultural import, and the Big Four's heavily publicized official recognition of their testimonial authority as national spokespersons was synecdoche for a wider logic normalizing the authority of entertainment celebrities in the public sphere beyond wartime.

"THE DEADLY SERIOUS PURPOSE BEHIND THE FUN OF ALL THESE STARS"

If some Wilsonian bureaucrats had been reticent about adopting the Hollywood style for the government's film program during the Great War, such reservations were overcome in the Roosevelt administration on the eve of another international conflict. Hollywood had shown its utility to war mobilization in the previous war and now stood to significantly impact this next one. This is not to say, however, that Hollywood had no adversaries. While Roosevelt encouraged Hollywood's anti-Nazi activities during the interwar years, Senator Gerald Nye and his cohort charged the film industry and the government with mutual collusion for flooding motion-picture screens with propaganda designed to "rouse" the country into "a state of hysteria."[48] But after the bombing of Pearl Harbor, the need for Hollywood's assistance in war mobilization was incontrovertible. Even though collaboration between the Office of War Information's (OWI) Bureau of Motion Pictures and Hollywood's War Activities Committee (WAC) was not without its controversies during Roosevelt's administration, as Gregory Black and Clayton Koppes show, the film industry enjoyed a resurgence of institutional recognition and respect.[49] Like before, this, too, would be temporary.

For Hollywood after 1941, US intervention meant total war insofar as every sector of the business was enlisted for war mobilization, and each accommodated the government to an unprecedented extent. Studio production personnel who won deferments from Selective Service when designated as "indispensable individuals" (actors, writers, directors, producers, camera technicians, and sound engineers) cooperated with the OWI and War Department officials to produce newsreels, "pedagogical" and propaganda films, bond shorts, and government-sanctioned entertaining movies in 35mm and 16mm for domestic and international audiences, as well as for the troops in the camps and at the front. The partnership between the Motion Picture Industry's WAC and the War Department, in fact, constituted an unparalleled distribution and exhibition circuit encompassing the globe.[50] Hollywood's capacity to influence public opinion was understood by Roosevelt as key to efficient mobilization, even though his political adversaries and the general public eyed propaganda with suspicion. Wartime collaboration across a multitude of government branches afforded Hollywood new ways to imbricate entertainment into state power as patriotic expressions of the American Way. WAC's comprehensive tally of Hollywood's war work equipped industry leaders to stave off hostile antitrust legislation and to engage the familiar debate that resurfaced in the press over whether actors were more valuable in the armed forces or as agents of war mobilization and relief.

Because many entertainment professionals had participated in the Popular Front and were active against anti-Semitism in the 1930s, support for intervention against Nazi Germany's aggression had grounding in Hollywood well before Pearl Harbor turned public opinion toward war. Hollywood's full transition to anti-Fascist wartime served the cause of national unity, but it also rewrote World War I's postwar discontent, "re-mythologizing" the conflict as "a national crusade worthy of admiration," while also refocusing democracy in support of consumer ideology and away from class conflict.[51] Filmmakers fell in line with the new consensus through the promotion of their films, which provided meaning and purpose for US intervention, often in grandiose terms. For their part, Hollywood stars sprang forth to personally endorse US Defense Bonds and to support war relief for soldiers' comfort—namely, through USO tours, benefit performances, and hospital visits. But this time, the stars worked under the auspices of the Hollywood Victory Committee (HVC), a centralized clearinghouse committee.[52] The War Activities Committee created the HVC immediately after Pearl Harbor to coordinate screen and radio talent appearances.[53] Chaired by the vice-president of the Association of Motion Picture Producers, the HVC was dominated by film-industry personnel, but it also included representatives from the broadcast networks, the stage, and actors' unions.

The HVC's management of a broad spectrum of stars was a logical outcome of stars' effective appearances during World War I and in the subsequent interwar years. In the immediate postwar context, Broadway and Hollywood continued to support the American Red Cross and other war-relief funds aiding Hoover's food initiative, disabled veterans, war widows and orphans, and starving or displaced European children and adults. Providing benefit plays and screenings gratis were a common way of raising money for charity, sometimes with the added feature of stars giving talks or conducting auctions after the show.[54] Charity events became increasingly common throughout the late 1920s and '30s to support community needs (poverty, illness, victims of catastrophe, memorial funds, hospitals, schools, etc.) and civic groups at local and national levels (American Legion, Salvation Army, Scouts, Lions Club, sheriffs' associations, Community Chest, etc.). During the Great Depression, Hollywood's philanthropic activities helped develop and promote its civic image in response to the economic crisis, since such efforts helped stave off criticism questioning the wealth and lavish lifestyles of Hollywood's privileged during national hard times, as well as ongoing censorship threats and residual skepticism brought on by Hollywood scandals.[55]

During the interwar period, the studio system consolidated and secured its dominance over filmmaking, while it rationalized the "star-making process," poaching from radio and stage talent to build individual studio brands and star images.[56] It was not unusual for a studio contract to include dominion over stars' public appearances, which were commonly linked to publicizing films; but studios also pressured their highest earners to make appearances in support of charity organizations. As Kathryn Brownell points out, studio publicity departments projected their stars' off-screen images as "dedicated community activists, concerned about the social problems of hunger, sickness, and homeless," which helped to improve Hollywood's civic image while it also provided individual entertainment professionals with valuable experience in fund-raising and publicity that could be deployed later in electoral politics.[57] Requests for film- and radio-star appearances for benefit performances during the Depression became so common that both networks and studios strategized to put a stop to such free performances, particularly as network sponsors became interested in acquiring big-name stars on their shows. Studios went so far as to arrange for the Hays office to handle all requests for charity appearances in order to institute some control over the process and to avoid an individual studio from having to directly refuse requests.[58]

If exhibitors, broadcasters, and regulators prevented studios from penetrating the business of radio to the extent they wanted, nothing stopped them from taking the lead in consolidating entertainment-labor power for war mobilization. Such efforts to combine all talent under the jurisdiction of powerful film-industry leaders during the war helped to mitigate exhibitors' discontent over film-star crossover into radio.[59] Studios also promoted the idea of "Hollywood" as a stand-in for the entertainment industry more broadly. Whereas Broadway actors and musical performers provided live entertainment for the soldiers and sailors in the camps and at the front during World War I, the Hollywood musical's appropriation of Broadway and vaudeville catapulted the most popular performers and comedians who had become stars of radio in their own right into serving the USO tours and doing *Command Performance* radio broadcasts.[60] Headlining its performers as "Hollywood personalities," the motion-picture industry took credit for an aggregate of over 55,000 star appearances, including USO tours involving 176 personalities on 122 overseas tours, and over 400 actors and actresses who toured 406 hospitals and training camps.[61] In handling what it called "an avalanche of requests for 'free talent,'" the HVC claimed that it allocated "available personalities where they would do the most overall good," but the committee likely managed stars' schedules like scarce resources in order to control the circulation and economic value of the star commodity, which favored the biggest names from the film industry.[62]

To be sure, actors coordinated with the government and civic organizations' wartime needs during World War II to an extent unimaginable during the Great War, across eight bond drives from 1941 to 1945. For the most part, the same activities involving live appearances and patriotic personae were repeated during World War II but on a much greater scale, with radio performances adding a significant new dimension, and with charity and war-relief work greatly expanded. As for selling war bonds, the HVC worked with Treasury's war-bond staff to arrange tours of individual stars, but also groups of stars, to American and Canadian cities.

FIGURE 16.2. First Lady Eleanor Roosevelt hosted more than twenty Hollywood stars who were part of the *Hollywood Victory Caravan* musical revue at the White House on April 30, 1942, before the show's opening. It played in fourteen cities over two weeks and netted $800,000 for army and navy relief funds. Shown here are (*seated, from left*) Oliver Hardy, Joan Blondell, Charlotte Greenwood, Charles Boyer, Risë Stevens, Desi Arnaz, Frank McHugh, writer Matt Brooks, James Cagney, Pat O'Brien, Juanita Stark, Alma Carroll; (*standing, from left*) Merle Oberon, Eleanor Powell, Arleen Whelan, Marie McDonald, Fay McKenzie, Katharine Booth, Mrs. Roosevelt, Frances Gifford, Frances Langford, Elyse Knox, Cary Grant, Claudette Colbert, Bob Hope, Ray Middleton, Joan Bennett, Bert Lahr, director Mark Sandrich, writer Jack Rose, Stan Laurel, Jerry Colonna, and Groucho Marx. (Courtesy of the Bob Hope Collection, Motion Picture, Broadcasting and Recording Sound Division, Library of Congress, Washington, DC.)

In its 1942 report, the HVC listed 2,773 appearances by 270 actors for the Treasury Department alone.[63] There were star extravaganzas such as *Stars over America*, *Hollywood Bond Cavalcade*, and *Hollywood Victory Caravan*, involving groups of stars on tour for weeks at a time (see figure 16.2), and there were hundreds of individual tours and appearances. Most involved large public gatherings, but stars also visited smaller venues such as factories and industrial plants to promote bond subscriptions through the payroll-deduction program. While the former were heavily publicized through print and radio to help bring in billions in bond sales, the latter indicated the Treasury Department's intention to reach, through more intimate appeals, a much greater percentage of wage earners than it could during the Liberty Bond drives.[64]

Hundreds of bond shorts and newsreel trailers were made by or in cooperation with the film industry for the Treasury Department.[65] WAC produced thirty-eight entertainment feature shorts involving "top stars" using formats that reflected the imbrication of filmed and broadcast musical performances into entertainment structures. Moving from simplistic allegory and parable that characterized the Liberty Loans, filmic bond appeals in the 1940s borrowed from newsreels, the motion-picture musical genre, and live and broadcast variety-show performances. Stars performing war work in live settings such as bond rallies and USO performances, and in over two hundred broadcast recordings, were often filmed, and such clips were inserted along with other footage into newsreel-like trailers, such as *Movies for Millions* (1942), which combined such footage with upcoming feature-film announcements. The narrative musical bond short borrowed from the film genre's reliance on "backstage" show-business plots about characters working to put on a show; however, the "'improvisation' in a rehearsal atmosphere," as Jane Feuer puts it, was performed by the stars as themselves.[66] For example, Paramount's two-reel *Hollywood Victory Caravan* (1945) tells the story of a young woman desperate for train travel to Washington, DC, to meet her wounded GI brother. Apparently, she can get there only if Bing Crosby gives her permission to ride with the *Victory War Bonds* show, which entails her sneaking onto the studio lot to meet Crosby and other stars, to witness musical rehearsals, and to see the final performance in which Bob Hope emcees song-and-dance numbers and Humphrey Bogart makes a personal appeal to buy bonds. Similarly, 20th Century-Fox's two-reel *All-Star Bond Rally* (1945) wrapped its star-studded live variety show in a narrative involving popular radio-character comedians Fibber and Molly McGee attending the show, then buying bonds after, as instructed. (See figures 16.3 and 16.4.) Many bond shorts distributed in 35mm for theatrical release were also made available in 16mm (including *All-Star Bond Rally*) to substantially extend their reach in community, school, factory, and other workplace venues. The *All-Star Bond Rally* live performance at the Roxy Theater in New York City was broadcast and transcribed for radio rebroadcast, as well as shown on the television station WRGB to a live audience.[67] Television networks would soon eclipse the film industry's consolidation of stars' authority when TV variety shows, sitcoms, and dramas become the dominant platform for stars to promote the postwar US savings-bond program.[68]

If World War II transformed the stars, as Brownell suggests, "from consumer icons and civic role models into patriotic leaders and government spokespersons," it did so not for the first time but the second.[69] During the Great War, film stars inhabited the public sphere of political wartime discourse not to engage the conflict as a matter of debate but to wholly endorse it ideologically, effecting a new

FIGURE 16.3. Still from *All-Star War Bonds Rally* (20th Century-Fox, 1945) showing Fibber McGee and Molly in the lobby of a theater featuring the film *All-Star Bond Rally* (1945), inviting viewers to buy a bond. (Courtesy of Internet Archive.)

barometer of celebrity authority. World War I's inclusion of star testimonials on behalf of state and military power was predicated on an acceptance of the film industry's cultural legitimation, which gave meaning to its stars' authority in the wartime public sphere. This prepared the ground for the mobilization of stardom in the next international conflict. Starting in the 1920s, Hollywood worked with the State Department to facilitate the export of movies showcasing American ideology and consumer goods, normalizing relations with the government in noncrisis conditions, despite some department opposition. More important, not only did the industry's vigilance with respect to self-regulation during the interwar years help abate persistent criticism of cinema's negative societal effects, but its centralized mechanisms of control minimized disruptions in film output caused by censorship or consumer opposition in domestic and international markets, thus affording Hollywood stars the exposure to dominate audience preferences globally.[70] That Hollywood films and their stars could influence public opinion did not escape Roosevelt, who in taking the stars' cultural significance seriously enough, appointed Douglas Fairbanks Jr. in 1941 as cultural ambassador to Latin America to promote the president's foreign policy on the eve of the US declaration of war.[71] Hollywood's full enlistment in the Second World War crystalized its alliance with Washington, achieving, as Thomas Doherty suggests, "an ascendancy in American culture it was never again to recapture."[72]

FIGURE 16.4. *All-Star Bond Rally* (1945). (*Top row, from left to right*) Frank Sinatra, Bing Crosby, Bob Hope, Harpo Marx, Betty Grable. (*Middle row, from left*) Linda Darnell, Vivian Blaine. (*Bottom row, from left*) Carmen Miranda, Marian and Jim Jordan ("Fibber McGee and Molly"). Canadian Motion Picture War Services Committee, 1945. Reproduction. (Courtesy of the Bob Hope Collection, Motion Picture, Broadcasting and Recorded Sound Division, Motion Picture, Library of Congress, Washington, DC.)

The HVC's consolidation of talent also had noteworthy consequences concerning the eventual shift in focus on the film star from being the economic heart of Hollywood to being a celebrity in the broader category of entertainer; however, at this moment film stars and other professional performers were subsumed under Hollywood's dominant configuration as "personalities" when the word "star" was not or could not be used. More significantly, the HVC's discursive accounting of talent in the aggregate elided distinctions in the public imaginary between two ways for stars to participate in a militarized state: as advocates with a standpoint, and as relief workers requiring no standpoint. In a sense, the HVC moderated the stars' political subjectivities by collapsing, on the one hand, the authority of their overt and active testimony on behalf of belligerent state power, and on the other, the respite of their entertaining presence when serving the US military in combat. In effect, the HVC's management of stars dispensed for war relief—particularly the extensive soldier-entertainment function of the USO—instituted an apolitical association between Hollywood and the militarized state that would remain prevalent during war and peace.

NOTES

1. Walter Lippmann, *Public Opinion* (New York: Harcourt Brace and Co., 1922); Harold D. Lasswell, *Propaganda Technique in the World War* (New York: Alfred A. Knopf, 1927).

2. Edward Bernays, *Propaganda* (New York: H. Liveright, 1928), 59–60, 117.

3. Paul F. Lazarsfeld, Hazel Gaudet, and Bernard Berelson, *The People's Choice: How the Voter Makes Up His Mind in a Presidential Campaign* (New York: Duell Sloan and Pearce, 1944). Lazarsfeld and his colleagues found that during election seasons people tended to form opinions by relying on individuals in their social networks who were better informed through their media consumption. In the introduction to Lazarsfeld and Elihu Katz's *Personal Influence: The Part Played by the People in the Flow of Mass Communications* (New York: Free Press, 1955), Elmer Rober neglected reference to entertainment celebrities in his discussion of what he termed "Great Disseminators" whose reach extended to large numbers of people who regularly "listened" to them, such as famous political figures, journalists, writers, and business leaders.

4. Robert Merton, Marjorie Fiske, and Alberta Curtis, *Mass Persuasion: The Social Psychology of a War Bond Drive* (New York: Harper & Brothers, 1946), 96; Richard Dyer, *Stars* (London: British Film Institute, 1986); Paul Lazarsfeld and Robert K. Merton, "Mass Communication, Popular Taste, and Organized Social Action," in *The Communication of Ideas*, ed. L. Bryson (New York: Harper, 1948), 95–118.

5. Tony Bennett, "Putting Policy into Cultural Studies," in *Cultural Studies*, ed. Lawrence Grossberg, Gary Nelson, and Paula Treichler (New York: Routledge, 1992), 26; Raymond Williams, *Marxism and Literature* (New York: Oxford University Press, 1977), 17.

6. Charles Ponce de Leon, *Self-Exposure: Human-Interest Journalism and the Emergence of Celebrity in America, 1890–1940* (Chapel Hill: University of North Carolina Press, 2002); Benjamin McArthur, *Actors and American Culture, 1880–1920* (Iowa City: University of Iowa Press, 2000); Richard Sennett, *The Fall of Public Man: On the Social Psychology of Capitalism* (New York: Random House, 1974).

7. Warren W. Susman, *Culture as History: The Transformation of American Society in the Twentieth Century* (New York: Pantheon, 1984).

8. Sennett, *Fall of Public Man*, 210.

9. For examples of actors' activism in the late nineteenth century, see Edward Earl, "The Political Image of American Actors, 1865–1920" (PhD diss., University of Missouri, 1974).

10. McArthur, *Actors and American Culture*, 154.

11. Lawrence Lavine, *Highbrow/Lowbrow: The Emergence of Cultural Hierarchy in America* (Cambridge, MA: Harvard University Press, 1988).

12. See, for example, Richard deCordova, *Picture Personalities: The Emergence of the Star System in America* (Urbana: University of Illinois Press, 1990); and Richard Abel, *Americanizing the Movies and "Movie-Mad" Audiences, 1910–1914* (Berkeley: University of California Press, 2006).

13. Charles R. Acland and Haidee Wasson, *Useful Cinema* (Durham, NC: Duke University Press, 2011); Steven J. Ross, *Working-Class Hollywood: Silent Film and the Shaping of Class in America* (Princeton, NJ: Princeton University Press, 1998).

The subheading that precedes this paragraph is from Enid Bennett in a Liberty Loan Appeal, 1918, Exhibitors Press Book, 39, Scrapbooks, v. 18, Guy Emerson Records, 1919–20, Widener Depository, Harvard University.

14. Thomas Doherty, *Projections of War: Hollywood, American Culture, and World War II* (New York: Columbia University Press, 1993), 88.

15. Four Minute Men were citizen volunteer speakers organized to promote war mobilization by making four-minute speeches in public locations nationwide. For more information about the Four Minute Men, see Lee Grieveson's chapter in this volume.

16. Leslie Midkiff DeBauche, *Reel Patriotism: The Movies and World War I* (Madison: University of Wisconsin Press, 1997). Also see Larry Wayne Ward, *The Motion Picture Goes to War: The US Government Film Effort during World War I* (Ann Arbor, MI: UMI Research Press, 1985), 14.

17. The strategy of the National Association of the Motion Picture Industry (NAMPI) to protect its production levels is evident in the industry's trade discourse, particularly prior to winning essential status in August 1918. The first industry-wide move was to support the Liberty Loans. "To the Men and Women of the Motion Picture Industry," *Motion Picture News*, June 23, 1917, 3892. Common was the refrain that war mobilization was an opportunity to assert the value of the industry, which the president of NAMPI, William Brady, suggested would be seen as "a great national institution on the same basis with the newspapers." "Industry Aids Liberty Loan," *Motography*, June 2, 1917, 1137. Throughout the trades, industry leaders repeated to their constituency the case that motion pictures were being recognized as "the greatest vehicle of thought transmission so far known to man," with which the government could communicate critical information during wartime. See "Industry Honored by Government," *Motography*, August 4, 1917, 265.

18. Sue Collins, "Film, Cultural Policy, and the World War I Training Camps: Send Your Soldier to the Show with Smileage," *Film History* 26, no. 1 (April 2014): 1–49.

19. Daniel Beaver, *Newton D. Baker and the American War Effort, 1917–1919* (Lincoln: University of Nebraska Press, 1966), 220; also see Weldon B. Durham, *Liberty Theatres of the United States Army, 1917–1919* (Jefferson, NC: McFarland & Company, 2006), 34–35.

20. Due to poor management, by mid-1918 vaudeville and motion pictures—two attractions not originally part of the Liberty theaters' imagined program—made up 60 percent of the theaters' programming. Collins, "World War I Training Camps." On the film industry's failure to win government contracts for film distribution, see Henry MacMahon, "'Uplifters' Boss War Films," *Moving Picture World*, January 26, 1918, 492.

21. Warren Dunham Foster, "History of Community Motion Picture Bureau," February 25, 1959, 3, Subject File: Community Motion Picture Bureau, Motion Picture, Broadcasting, and Recorded Sound Division, Library of Congress, Washington, DC.

22. CMPB censors kept notations on index cards for every film screened. An examination of Artcraft Pictures shows that out of 149 identifiably reviewed titles produced between 1916 and 1920, 66 (44 percent) were accredited, 3 (2 percent) were acceptable with cuts, 21 (14 percent) were earmarked for military stations only, 1 (.06 percent) was marked for special screening, and 58 (39 percent) were rejected. Collins, "World War I Training Camps," 25.

23. Lary May, *Screening Out the Past: The Birth of Mass Culture and the Motion Picture Industry* (Oxford: Oxford University Press, 1980), 112.

24. Gaylyn Studlar, *This Mad Masquerade: Stardom and Masculinity in the Jazz Age* (New York: Columbia University Press, 1996).

25. "Propaganda Film for Fairbanks," *Motion Picture News*, February 10, 1918. The title of this scenario is uncertain, but the October 1918 issue of the *Social Hygiene Bulletin* reported that Fairbanks was

likely to appear in and help produce an army film entitled *Come Clean* ("Notes from the War Department Commission on Training Camps," 5). However, my research has not yet found evidence that such a film was actually made.

26. "Fairbanks to Make a 'Pep' Film," *Moving Picture World*, July 27, 1918, 561.

27. As Larry Wayne Ward notes, Creel had indicated that he did not want the CPI to "compete" with the commercial industry, but after Hart was brought on board that directive was abandoned. Hart created an "Advisory Board of Motion Picture Directors" to recommend screenplays for the Division of Film, but there is no evidence that the directors participated in any CPI productions. The reworking of the Scenario Department under Hart allowed the film division to control its scripts while circumventing production costs by contracting private producers to make the films and then giving them full commercial rights to the pictures. Shortly before the war's end, the Scenario Department began to make films without the assistance of commercial producers for reasons unexplained. Ward, *Motion Picture Goes to War*, 94–105.

28. In part, this may have had to do with the fact that CPI strategy deviated from precedence in that no publicity agents had been employed directly by the federal government. See Donald Fishman, "George Creel: Freedom of Speech, the Film Industry, and Censorship during World War I," *Free Speech Yearbook* 39 (2001): 35. After a dispute with Creel over the benefits of coordinating the services of civic agencies, Creel defended his organizational motives to McAdoo by pointing out that initially McAdoo had not been in favor of organizing outside agents, including the motion-picture industry. Creel to McAdoo, January 11, 1918, record group (RG) 63, E-1, box 6, National Archives and Records Administration, College Park, Maryland (hereafter cited as NACP).

29. Report, "Speaker Proposed for the Third Liberty Loan," RG 53, E-622, box 8, NACP.

30. "Mary Pickford Doing 'Bit,'" *Motography*, July 7, 1917, 33.

31. "Marguerite Clark Sells Liberty Bonds," *Moving Picture World*, November 10, 1917, 898.

32. Sue Collins, "Bonding with the Crowd: Silent Film, Liveness, and the Public Sphere," in *Convergence Media History*, ed. Janet Staiger and Sabine Hake (New York: Routledge, 2009), 117–26.

33. P. David Marshall, *Celebrity and Power: Fame in Contemporary Culture* (Minneapolis: University of Minnesota Press, 1997).

34. Marshall's objective is not to defend crowd and mass society theories as a model for the social; rather, he is interested in showing how celebrity's emergence and commodification ties to certain schools of American thought (i.e., social psychology, behaviorism, mass communication research) that sought to rationalize the crowd or mass as a configuration of audience. Marshall, *Celebrity and Power*, 27–49. On cinema's perceived effects on its audience and the problem of its governance in the early twentieth century, see Lee Grieveson, "Cinema Studies and the Conduct of Conduct," in *Inventing Film Studies*, ed. Lee Grieveson and Haidee Wasson (Durham, NC: Duke University Press, 2008), 3–37.

35. See Susman, *Culture as History;* May, *Screening Out the Past;* and Lee Grieveson, "Stars and Audiences in Early American Cinema," *Screening the Past*, no. 14 (November 6, 2002).

36. The lowest bond denomination was $50. In 1918, a clerical worker or federal employee earning from $1,400 to $1,700 a year would have found the full cash outlay for a $50 bond prohibitive, which is why bonds were also sold through installment plans.

37. Sung Won Kang and Hugh Rockoff, "Capitalizing Patriotism: The Liberty Loans of World War I," *Financial History Review* 22, no. 1 (2015): 45–78.

38. Janet Staiger, "Announcing Wares, Winning Patrons, Voicing Ideals: Thinking about the History and Theory of Film Advertising," *Cinema Journal* 29, no. 3 (Spring 1990): 26.

39. "Five Hundred Prints for Liberty Film," *Moving Picture World*, October 13, 1917, 209; "How to Get Liberty Loan Picture," *Moving Picture World*, October 20, 1917, 363; "Imposing Array of Stage and Screen Stars in Film Which Will Advertise Second Liberty Loan," *Exhibitor's Trade Review*, September 29, 1917, 1313.

40. "Industry Mobilizes to Aid the Fourth Liberty Loan," *Exhibitors Herald & Motography*, August 10, 1918, 33.

41. "Entire Industry Is Declared Essential," *Wids Daily*, August 26, 1918, 1.

42. "Producers Eager to Make Features for Liberty Loan," *Exhibitors Herald & Motography*, August 17, 1918, 29. On Woodrow Wilson and film, see Kevin Brownlow, *The War, the West, and the Wilderness* (New York: Alfred Knopf, 1978), 130; and Michael T. Isenberg, *War on Film: The American Cinema and World War I, 1914–1941* (London: Associated University Press, 1981), 151–52.

43. Nicoletta F. Gullace, "Barbaric Anti-Modernism: Representations of the 'Hun' in Britain, North America, Australia, and Beyond," in *Picture This: World War I and Visual Culture*, ed. Pearl James (Lincoln: University of Nebraska Press, 2009), 61–62.

44. Sue Collins, "Star Testimonials and Trailers: Mobilizing during World War I," *Cinema Journal* 57, no. 1 (2017): 46–70.

45. *Exhibitor's Press Book*, Scrapbooks, v. 18, Guy Emerson Records, 1919–20, Widener Depository, Harvard University.

46. Genevieve Harris, "Stars Set Out to Aid Fourth Loan," *Chicago Post*, September 21, 1918, Mary Pickford Scrapbook no. 31, 25, Margaret Herrick Library, Academy of Motion Picture Arts and Sciences, Beverly Hills, CA.

47. Donald Horton and Richard R. Wohl use the term "para-social interaction" to describe a "simulacrum of conversation" that occurs when a mass medium is treated as if it is a mode of interpersonal communication, such as a talk show host's use of camera and props to effect a sense of intimacy that blurs the line between formal performance and informal conversation with audiences. This type of address works to deny itself as performance so that audiences feel they "know" a media figure as they do a friend. Donald Horton and Richard R. Wohl, "Mass Communication and Para-Social Interaction," *Psychiatry* 19 (1956): 215–29.

48. Kathryn Cramer Brownell, *Showbiz Politics: Hollywood in American Political Life* (Chapel Hill: University of North Carolina Press, 2014), 42. The subheading that precedes this paragraph is a quote from Bob Hope in 20th Century-Fox's *All-Star Bond Rally* (1945). Internet Archive, accessed May 20, 2015, https://archive.org/details/AllStarBondRally. See also Clayton R. Koppes and Gregory D. Black, *Hollywood Goes to War: How Politics, Profits, and Propaganda Shaped World War II Movies* (Berkeley: University of California Press, 1990).

49. Clayton R. Koppes and Gregory D. Black, *Hollywood Goes to War: How Politics, Profits, and Propaganda Shaped World War II Movies* (Berkeley: University of California Press, 1990).

50. Thomas Schatz, *Boom and Bust: The American Cinema in the 1940s* (Berkeley: University of California Press, 1999), 144–47; "Industry Is Essential, Says Selective Service Official," *Showmen's Trade Review*, February 14, 1942, 5. On Hollywood's relation to Roosevelt, see Brownell, *Showbiz Politics*, 52–64.

51. Doherty, *Projections of War*, 100; Lary May, *The Big Tomorrow: Hollywood and the Politics of the American Way* (Chicago: University of Chicago Press, 2000).

52. War Activities Committee, Motion Picture Industry, *Movies at War, 1942–1945*.

53. "Free Talent Plan Is Approved by AMPP," *Motion Picture Daily*, December 31, 1941, 6. The committee changed its name from the Hollywood Coordinating Committee for Stage, Screen, and Radio to the Hollywood Victory Committee in early January, 1942, and then again, after the war, to the Hollywood Coordinating Committee, under which it conducted its work until January 1956, when it disbanded.

54. Theatrical professionals were well accustomed to donating their labor on behalf of the "benefit matinee" performance, a fund-raising mechanism dating back at least to late eighteenth-century England, intended to care for stage workers suffering poverty. Catherine Hindson, *London's West End Actresses and the Origins of Celebrity Charity, 1880–1920* (Iowa City: University of Iowa Press, 2016). In 1921 the Motion Picture Relief Fund was founded as a charity organization dedicated to motion-picture professionals.

55. See, for example, Leslie Paris, "Small Mercies: Colleen Moore's Doll House and National Charity Tour," in *Acts of Possession: Collecting in America*, ed. Leah Dilworth (New Brunswick, NJ: Rutgers University Press, 2003), 119–220.

56. Tino Balio, *Grand Design: Hollywood as a Modern Business Enterprise, 1930–1939* (Berkeley: University of California Press, 1993).

57. Brownell, *Showbiz Politics*, 26–28. Brownell's examination of Hollywood's involvement with President Roosevelt's "Birthday Balls" and Warm Springs Foundation for Infantile Paralysis (1934–45), which actor Eddie Cantor dubbed the "March of Dimes" in 1938, demonstrates a critical passage for Hollywood's testimonial power—that is, from philanthropy to political activism influencing electoral and policy outcomes (29–41).

58. Michelle Hilmes, *Hollywood and Broadcasting: From Radio to Cable* (Urbana: University of Illinois Press, 1990), 57.

59. In *Hollywood and Broadcasting*, Hilmes explains that Hollywood producers' forays, first into network ownership and operation, and later into radio programming in the 1930s, resulted in the temporary 1932 ban on Hollywood stars performing on radio. The ban was intended to appease exhibitors who objected to the frequency of free film-star appearances on radio because they saw it as competition for audiences who might stay home in lieu of moviegoing.

60. Pickford, Fairbanks, and Chaplin were asked by the Overseas Theatrical League to entertain troops at the front, reportedly because the soldiers requested their presence, but they declined. "Yankee Soldiers Aboard Ask for Screen Stars," *Motion Picture World*, September 21, 1918, 1699.

61. Motion Picture Industry Western Division, "Final Report of the Hollywood Victory Committee," 1946, Margaret Herrick Library, Academy of Motion Picture Arts and Sciences, Beverly Hills, CA.

62. Industry Service Bureau of Motion Pictures, "First Yearly Report of the Hollywood Victory Committee," 1942, Margaret Herrick Library, Academy of Motion Picture Arts and Sciences, Beverly Hills, CA.

63. Ibid., 9.

64. The Defense Bonds campaign was modeled after the "baby bond" program instituted in 1935 to normalize savings bonds in everyday habits of thrift and investment. The $25 Series E bond was created to target wage earners and small investors who could not be reached with higher denominations. Laurence M. Olney, *The War Bond Story* (Washington, DC: US Savings Bonds Division, 1971), 1–2.

65. Ibid., 25.

66. Jane Feuer, *The Hollywood Musical* (Bloomington: Indiana University Press, 1993), 12.

67. "Regional Newsreel," *Showman's Trade Review*, May 19, 1945, 22.

68. Numerous stars participated in several early postwar and Cold War campaigns, including Mary Pickford's 1952 national tour. In the mid-1960s, the Advertising Council coordinated special TV commercials involving Hollywood and Broadway stars to "support America's servicemen" through the Treasury Department's Payroll Savings Plan campaign. US Department of the Treasury, *A History of the United States Savings Bond Program* (Washington, DC: US Savings Bonds Division, Department of the Treasury, 1984), 25.

69. Brownell, *Showbiz Politics*, 44.

70. See Ruth Vasey, *The World according to Hollywood, 1918–1939* (Madison: University of Wisconsin Press, 1997); and John Trumpbour, *Selling Hollywood to the World: US and European Struggles for Mastery of the Global Film Industry, 1920–1950* (New York: Cambridge University Press, 2002).

71. Brownell, *Showbiz Politics*, 49.

72. Doherty, *Projections of War*, 13–14.

17

"A TREACHEROUS TIGHTROPE"

The Office of War Information, Psychological Warfare,
and Film Distribution in Liberated Europe

Alice Lovejoy

In an April 1944 funding appeal to the House Appropriations Committee, Elmer Davis, director of the US Office of War Information (hereafter, OWI), characterized the agency—which managed the country's World War II "information" (as propaganda was commonly termed in this period)—as "in effect a specialized branch of the military forces." The OWI was, he argued, "comparable to parachute troops or anti-tank battalions—a special branch which attacks the enemy's will to victory and confidence in victory, and counteracts his attacks on the mind and will of the populations of the occupied countries."[1] Davis's lofty metaphor was apt, for in the same month as his appeal, OWI officers joined the newly founded Psychological Warfare Division of the Supreme Headquarters Allied Expeditionary Force (PWD/SHAEF). Although military in nature and command, PWD was staffed largely with civilian personnel from four Allied propaganda agencies: the OWI, the US Office of Strategic Services (OSS), and the British Political Warfare Executive (PWE) and Ministry of Information (MOI).[2] During the liberation of Europe, OWI officers assigned to PWD carried out SHAEF's psychological-warfare activities, charged with disseminating media friendly to the United States, Britain, and their allies, and temporarily managing local media infrastructure.

A centerpiece of the OWI's contribution to SHAEF's psychological-warfare program was a package of forty Hollywood features. Ranging from *Our Town* to *It Started with Eve,* and accompanied by industry shorts, these films were intended, in the words of the OWI, to "express the American way of life."[3] Yet their presence alongside the government-produced documentaries and newsreels that made up the remainder of the United States' contribution also spoke to a defining characteristic of the OWI's Bureau of Motion Pictures: its close links with the American film industry. The bureau was not only, as Davis put it, the industry's central government contact, but also an advocate for Hollywood's interests, particularly abroad.[4]

This chapter examines the economic, ideological, and military questions that intersected in these forty films' selection and distribution. It does so from the viewpoints of, on the one hand, the OWI (and its officers assigned to PWD/ SHAEF), and on the other, Allied countries for which the films were destined: Belgium, the Netherlands, Norway, and the chapter's central case study, Czechoslovakia. While as Ian Jarvie has demonstrated in his important studies of the American film industry's twentieth-century foreign policy, the PWD/SHAEF program encapsulates the synergy between film-industry and government interests that characterized US commercial film exports from the interwar to postwar periods, the program's history also makes clear that, during and after World War II, this synergy was undergirded by military institutions and logistics.[5] Viewed, moreover, from the perspectives of the United States' foreign interlocutors, the forty films' trajectory from wartime negotiations to postwar distribution also offers a valuable perspective on Europe's fraught political, cultural, and diplomatic relationship with American cinema on the cusp of the Cold War, calling into question the common understanding of media distribution in that period as governed by the hardening ideological binaries of the late 1940s. Media, as the OWI films make clear, also circulated according to complex political and pragmatic logics that were at times markedly similar East and West.[6]

THE OWI AND THE AMERICAN FILM INDUSTRY

The Office of War Information was established by Franklin Roosevelt in June 1942, and, as Allan M. Winkler writes, charged with "communicat[ing] American aims in the struggle at hand and at the same time tr[ying] to convey to audiences at home and abroad the ideals that could give rise to a peaceful, democratic world."[7] The agency's activities spanned multiple media—among them radio, print, and cinema, with the latter managed both by its Bureau of Motion Pictures, whose purview was primarily domestic, and its Overseas Bureau.

Both departments' involvement with the American film industry has been documented in detail elsewhere. These histories show that the OWI's two film branches were involved in establishing thematic and generic guidelines for Hollywood productions; approving commercially produced films for the Overseas Bureau's psychological-warfare and informational programs; recruiting industry talent to produce the OWI's own films; and managing the distribution of these and other government-produced films.[8] Many of the agency's officials, indeed, had previously worked in Hollywood, prominently among them screenwriter and producer Robert Riskin, the Overseas Bureau's chief. It was under Riskin's leadership that the Overseas Bureau assembled the list of films that would be distributed in the

PWD program. The forty films chosen by the OWI represented eight major studios, and included, among others, war pictures such as *Action in the North Atlantic*, films on patriotic American themes (*Young Tom Edison*), comedies (*I Married a Witch*), and musicals (*No, No, Nanette*).[9]

If the thematic links were tenuous between certain films on this list and the informational purposes for which they were intended, this was evidently of little concern to the OWI: for the agency, the films' status as products of the American film industry was as important as their content.[10] A 1945 article in the Montana daily *Missoulian* made this blurring of boundaries explicit, describing PWD/SHAEF's film program as an advance "into the cultural vacuum left behind the retreating Germans," in which "the American motion picture is bringing reminders of a way of life where freedom of speech and of religion is taken for granted, along with such trivia as chocolate bars, coffee, electric refrigerators and central heating."[11]

Indeed, the OWI's Hollywood films did not merely picture a "way of life" to which consumer goods and freedom of speech were equally central, but themselves functioned as chips in a larger economic game: in exchange for the film industry releasing foreign-language versions of its titles to the OWI—involving "an outlay," as Riskin wrote, "of almost a million dollars"—the OWI agreed to make "every effort . . . to protect [the studios'] interests as far as it was possible to do under war conditions."[12] On a practical level, this required OWI officers assigned to PWD to manage the films' distribution during liberation and, under SHAEF governance, to collect returns, and also, as Jarvie describes, physically repossess "the firms, premises, and films of American [Hollywood] subsidiary companies" located in liberated countries.[13] These military activities, in turn, were intended to ensure the American film industry an advantageous position in postwar Europe "no later than the return to indigenous government," in order to preempt the kinds of protectionist measures (e.g., quotas and tariffs) that many European governments had imposed on American exports before the war.[14]

EXILE GOVERNMENTS, PROPAGANDA, AND LEGITIMACY

The OWI's relationship to the American film industry proved the thorniest dimension of its plans for film distribution in liberated Europe. In its own words, the agency walked a "treacherous tightrope" between "ensur[ing] the execution of [its] informational responsibility through the film medium, and at the same time . . . safeguard[ing] the legitimate interests of the American film industry in the face of strong government sentiments for official monopoly controls in these areas."[15] These tensions played out with particular force in the OWI's negotiations with the countries in which films were to be distributed.

The nerve center for these plans and negotiations was the Overseas Bureau's London Outpost and its Films Division. London was not only the headquarters of the OWI's European activities (as well as, after April 1944, of SHAEF), but, for much of the war, home to the exile governments of numerous occupied European countries—among them Belgium, Czechoslovakia, Free France, the Netherlands, Norway, and Poland.[16] Although they were allies, a fundamental imbalance of power underlay the OWI's negotiations with these governments, which had abandoned territory, infrastructure, and armies in fleeing to Britain. Accordingly, propaganda was one of the few tools with which the exile governments could advocate for their own return to power, and they devoted considerable energy to producing and distributing films, radio programs, newspapers, books, magazines, gramophone records, and photographs that aimed to foster public sympathy with their countries' plight, and cultivate consensus about their leadership.[17] Yet most of the London governments were also poor, and depended on countries such as the United States and the United Kingdom in order to produce the very propaganda that could demonstrate their sovereignty and legitimacy. Exile-government film units, for instance, relied heavily on Britain's Ministry of Information (MOI), and collaborated with the MOI and the OWI on productions such as the *Free World* newsreel series.[18]

This double bind of sovereignty and dependency complicated negotiations about the OWI's distribution plans. Since early in the war, postwar film exhibition had been a source of concern for the exile governments. Uncertain about the state in which they would find their home countries' cinematic infrastructure and stock of films, as well as about the mood of populations emerging from years of occupation, the governments were anxious to ensure both that they had sufficient films to show after liberation, and that these films would support their claims to legitimacy. German and Italian films, for instance, could not be shown, nor could wartime films made by collaborationist domestic film industries, while there were not enough European films produced during the war or "domestic" films produced in exile to fill cinema programs. Thus, despite their longstanding, shared mistrust of the US film industry, the governments were compelled to collaborate with the OWI—as a paradoxical expression of the same national concerns that drove interwar quotas, tariffs, and the like. The following section of this chapter traces the OWI's negotiations with the exile governments through the case of Czechoslovakia, with additional reference to Belgium, the Netherlands, and Norway. Taken together, these examples reveal the simultaneous apprehension, frustration, and resignation that characterized the exile governments' interactions with the US agency.

OWI NEGOTIATIONS WITH ALLIED GOVERNMENTS

Czechoslovakia's relationship with the American film industry had historically been warm. As Jindřiška Bláhová notes, before the war, the country had been

"America's biggest and most lucrative market in Eastern Europe," although, like other European countries, it imposed limits on American film imports between 1932 and 1935.[19] During the war, plans for its postwar film industry were made simultaneously by two groups: domestically, by the underground National Assembly of Czech Film Workers; and in London, by the exile government's Ministry of Foreign Affairs and Ministry of Industry, Trade, and Business.

The exiled ministries began discussions with the OWI in summer 1943, following a brief, disorganized period during which each ministry independently approached American and British commercial film producers about distributing their productions after the war. Although these overtures were unsuccessful—in each case, the relevant information agency (MOI, OWI) intervened and steered the Czechoslovak government toward its own foreign distribution efforts (which, after SHAEF was established, were folded into PWD's plans)[20]—they nevertheless highlight the cultural and economic factors underpinning Czechoslovakia's negotiations with the OWI. First, like its interwar predecessor, the exile government was wary of the American film industry, which it expected to attempt to "flood" the Czechoslovak market after the war—an eventuality it tried to preempt by negotiating advantageous import agreements with other countries.[21] Second, the government wanted to exercise maximum choice over what was screened in Czechoslovakia, selecting only high-quality films with culturally or nationally suitable subjects. Indeed, even after it had been informed that the OWI was the sole channel through which European governments would receive American features, the Ministry of Foreign Affairs continued to pursue other avenues: in June 1943, the ministry's film officer, Viktor Fischl, requested that the New York–based Czechoslovak Information Service hold discussions with the American studios, "in case the OWI Film Division's plan should not suit our ideas about the film program for Czechoslovak cinemas in the first months after the war."[22] And in a telegram at the end of July, Foreign Minister Jan Masaryk asked Czechoslovakia's San Francisco consulate to request lists of films from "interested Hollywood firms." "We would like," Masaryk said, "to choose the most suitable pictures."[23]

Also evident from these negotiations, however, is the fact that Czechoslovak government officials were above all anxious to ensure that the country's cinemas would remain open immediately after the war.[24] Other exile governments shared this concern. In winter 1944, for instance, Belgian representatives in London worried about finding themselves "with a Belgian network that belongs entirely to the American market," a situation they characterized as "a matter of national autonomy." Yet the fact remained that it was "impossible to produce films in Belgium," requiring them to negotiate with the OWI.[25]

Czechoslovakia's exile government, too, continued discussions with the OWI. Throughout, the ministries pressed the agency to allow the exile government to select titles, and the OWI continually suggested that it would be allowed to do so.

On August 25, 1943, Fischl wrote to Samuel Spewack, of the London Outpost's Films Division, that "as soon as a list of these films . . . is available, I should very much like to see it and I trust that you will then give me an opportunity to judge which of the suggested films we regard as most suitable for Czechoslovakia."[26] Spewack, in reply, assured him "that we will not only consult with you on the question of films suitable for Czechoslovakia, but will be very grateful for any advice you may give us."[27] When Fischl received an initial list in October, and complained about "the selection, on which we unfortunately did not have an influence and which I personally do not consider the most advantageous," OWI official Lacy Kastner agreed to "attempt to amend the list of films for Czechoslovakia."[28]

Czechoslovakia was not the only country with reservations about the films selected by the OWI. At a November 16, 1943, meeting in New York of the Inter-Allied Information Committee's Film Sub-Committee, discussion turned to recent trade-press reports that OWI films for the liberation period had been selected without "cooperation between OWI and representatives of Allied governments." Riskin, it was reported, disputed this claim, but had nonetheless agreed to submit a list of films selected for each country to the committee, to whose recommendations it would give "full consideration," even though he "could offer no assurance of adoption of the suggestions."[29]

The list duly followed, with a request for comments on their appropriateness.[30] The Czechoslovak Information Service in New York made no objection, but requested that Hollywood films about Czechoslovakia—notably Fritz Lang's *Hangmen Also Die,* a dramatization of the 1942 assassination of Reichsprotektor Reinhard Heydrich by British-trained Czechoslovak paratroopers—be added to its list.[31] Yet when a revised slate of films, "especially selected for Czechoslovakian audiences," arrived in January 1944, Lang's film was nowhere to be found, and the list closely resembled the one sent previously.[32] The possibility of its alteration, moreover, seemed foreclosed, since most of the films had already been translated into Czech and Slovak.[33]

The OWI's inflexibility about the Hollywood features was echoed in its negotiations with the Norwegian Government Film Unit (NGFU), which took issue with both the program's contents and the patronizing rhetoric that accompanied it. The NFGU described the voiceover commentary for Frank Capra's *Why We Fight* series, for instance, as "childishly naïve, somewhat hollow and bombastic, and often with a historical perspective on subjects that will . . . be poorly received. Even worse, there are also considerable falsehoods—e.g., the section on the war in Norway is inaccurate." The OWI, the NGFU explained, "stated that they wished to prepare these films in Norwegian because [Norwegians] needed a lesson in democracy. This led to an even harsher reply from our side."[34] In February 1944 correspondence with William Patterson, OWI London Outpost Film Division chief, Lieutenant Eiliv Odde Hauge, the NGFU's chief, took a more diplomatic tone, forwarding comments by the Norwegian Board of Censors about Howard Hawks's *Sergeant York,* and suggesting changes to the voiceover for the Norwegian section of Capra's *Divide and Conquer.*[35] While the edits to the Capra film were accepted, the comments on *Sergeant York* were not: the Hollywood features, with their industry backing, were untouchable. "While in the case of the Hollywood features and shorts," Patterson wrote, "most of which have superimposed titles, we welcome criticisms and suggestions, it is not in order to correct these particular films, but to avoid similar mistakes in future superimposing."[36]

Nevertheless, this "treacherous tightrope" between information and industry was a matter of debate within the Overseas Bureau, pitting Patterson and Riskin against Louis Lober, then deputy chief of the bureau. In a March 1944 letter to Lober, Patterson acknowledged the latter's claim that "it would cause an embarrassing situation if the representatives of the exiled governments were to object to certain films at this stage of the operation." Yet Patterson and Riskin saw "no other alternative than submitting these films for approval to the officials of what are in fact sovereign allied nations," and held that if the governments "do not want any film or films distributed in their countries, the film or films will not be distributed over their protest by the OWI, which is the agency of their ally, the United States of America."[37] Even refusal, however, apparently had its limits: after the Netherlands Information Bureau rejected certain titles—deeming them "only suitable for adults"—American and British agencies reserved the right to recensor the films.[38] In the end, the lists of films slated for distribution in each European country were nearly identical.[39]

LIBERATION: WESTERN EUROPE

Lober's industry-friendly standpoint prevailed in an agreement that the OWI signed with the Czechoslovak exile government on October 10, 1944.[40] The text specified that the OWI "welcome[d] the collaboration of the Czechoslovak Government in the choice of suitable material, but reserve[d] for itself the right to decide which film or films" would be distributed. "After the return of the Czechoslovak Government to Czechoslovakia and the establishment of an American Mission in that country," the OWI could "terminate this agreement and arrange for the distribution of its films in Czechoslovakia through commercial or other channels."[41] None of this came to pass, however, because the US Army liberated only a small part of western Bohemia in April 1945. (The Red Army liberated the majority of the country a month later.) In PWD/SHAEF's absence, the OWI's Czechoslovak program was suspended.

In the parts of Western Europe that SHAEF did liberate, cinema's role in the psychological-warfare campaigns was planned with military precision. PWD assembled detailed film programs and distribution schedules, and stockpiled prints in Allied locations near the territory to be liberated.[42] During liberation,

OWI and MOI film officers assigned to PWD were among SHAEF's front-line forces.[43] Plans for this, too, proved a flash point for conflict between the exile governments' national concerns and the OWI's responsibility to the American film industry. In a June 1944 meeting between Norway and British and American members of PWD/SHAEF, for instance, Hauge stated that the exile government preferred "to have a Norwegian in charge of all matters relating to films, right from the beginning." Patterson refused, explaining "that the OWI desired to have an experienced British or American films man named *Films Officer to Norway* [italics in the original] primarily to insure an efficient distribution of Allied films in consonance with Allied policies and also to discharge its secondary responsibility as trustee for the films turned over voluntarily for this purpose by the American film companies." Reiterating the OWI's language of industry stewardship, he explained that the "OWI, in a sense, holds these films in trust and is responsible for seeing that they are distributed in the most effective manner possible."[44] Reporting on a similar meeting held a month earlier, a Belgian exile-government representative noted with concern that the OWI films officer assigned to Belgium as part of PWD, a Captain Elliot, "appears to be one of the ex-representatives of United Artists in Belgium."[45]

On the ground, indeed, OWI officers in PWD kept a close watch on industry interests, as Kastner, another veteran of Hollywood's European branches, reported from France in October 1944. By this point, two months after the liberation of Paris, PWD had taken over film exchanges in major cities, and distribution was running smoothly. Matters would not be so simple when the French government returned to power, however: Kastner warned that the French were "planning all kinds of restrictions on the importation of ... American films, and I am very much afraid that unless someone from the Hays organization as well as a Film Attaché for the American embassy is sent over rapidly that they will try to rush through their nefarious plans and beat us to it. ... Being in PWD," he added, "I cannot fight with them as my job is to keep on good terms with them."[46]

If OWI officers in PWD could not intervene, they nonetheless monitored such developments in all countries, with the aim of turning over distribution to commercial companies only when policies toward American cinema seemed favorable. In Belgium and Luxembourg, PWD film operations ended on July 6, 1945, at which point Patterson reported that no new quota or import restrictions had been instated by the countries' governments. In the Netherlands, operations would continue "until we know ... the final result of discussions ... between Dutch government officials and the Hays office."[47] Ultimately, however, all of the countries discussed in this chapter adopted restrictive measures against American cinema, including import duties, taxes, quotas, and government monopolies on film trade.[48] If in this sense the forty films failed, to quote Jarvie, to "enhance the position of [the American] export film industry" in Western Europe, they proved to be to the industry's benefit in Czechoslovakia—a country in which the OWI's distribution plans had been abandoned.[49]

POSTWAR CZECHOSLOVAKIA

American film distribution was a politically volatile subject in Czechoslovakia in the months after the country's liberation, when the largely communist National Assembly of Czech Film Workers became Czechoslovakia's official film organization, sidelining many of the figures who had negotiated distribution agreements in London. In June and July 1945, the assembly signed agreements with the Soviet Union's foreign film-distribution organ, Soyuzintorgkino, guaranteeing Soviet films 60 percent of the exhibition time in Czechoslovak cinemas.[50] As the Czechoslovak film industry's relationship with the Soviet Union's warmed, its relationship with the United States' cooled. And when, in August, President Edvard Beneš announced the nationalization of the industry, the American film industry—which refused to deal with government monopolies, considering them incompatible with the principle of free trade—ceased relations with Czechoslovakia entirely.[51]

In this stalemate, the OWI films proved a saving grace. This emerged within a course of events involving the Motion Picture Export Association (MPEA) and the US Department of State that are beyond the scope of this chapter, and have been chronicled in detail by Petr Mareš and Jindřiška Bláhová.[52] At their core, however, was the United States' dual interest in cinema as an economic force and as a tool for propaganda. The former conception drove the MPEA, which was founded in September 1945 to combat foreign restrictions on American film trade; the latter was held by the State Department, which maintained that American cinema could help shift Czechoslovak politics—strategically poised, at this moment, between East and West—in its favor.[53]

The Czechoslovak film industry was apprehensive about both conceptions of American cinema, yet it found itself in an untenable position in fall 1945, when Soyuzintorgkino proved unable to provide all of the films it had promised.[54] Complicating matters further, as Bláhová describes, the British and French films for which Czechoslovakia had signed agreements in September 1945 were facing problems in transit to the country; thus, she writes, "without Hollywood product, [the Czechoslovak film industry] would most likely be unable to keep . . . theatres supplied with enough new films to keep attracting audiences."[55] The OWI films offered a way out of this impasse that was acceptable to Czechoslovakia, the State Department, and the MPEA, serving as an interim means of filling Czechoslovak screens while the country negotiated a new agreement with the United States. On the one hand, the package of films satisfied the State Department's vision of American cinema's "informational" role in the evolving geopolitical situation. On the other, it was tolerable to the MPEA, which would not be required to negotiate a new agreement with a state monopoly, yet would be granted entry into the Czechoslovak market.[56] On May 10, 1946, an agreement was signed allowing certain films from the OWI package to be distributed in Czechoslovakia—the precursor to a formal agreement between the country and the MPEA signed on September 17, 1946. Among the 140 titles in this agreement were the majority of the OWI films.[57]

CONCLUSION

As Elmer Davis suggested in the speech with which this chapter begins, the foreign film-distribution activities that OWI officers carried out in PWD/SHAEF were practical, material—and not merely ideological—processes. Like "parachute troops or anti-tank battalions," these officers considered the logistics of storage and freight; of schedules and staff assignments. Lacy Kastner's report from France emphasizes the inextricability of these material and ideological concerns: it was only through SHAEF's military provisions of fuel, insignia, and papers that Hollywood films, and with them images of the "American way of life," were able to traverse France, where there was "no proper means of communication except by car and . . . no gas whatsoever . . . except that . . . supplied by the Army."[58]

Viewing the OWI/PWD program through a material lens, however, also calls its effectiveness into question. In Czechoslovakia, for instance, while viewers were certainly eager to see the Hollywood productions, it was primarily such material, not ideological, factors that led to the films' distribution in the country. With the Soviet Union unable to fulfill its agreement, and an insufficient number of other available films, Czechoslovak cinemas required American films simply to stay open in the first, fragile year after the film industry's nationalization. To borrow Bláhová's phrasing, the decision to import Hollywood films had to do, most fundamentally, with the nationalized film industry's "need to secure its own survival."[59]

These forty films thus illuminate the multiple and shifting forces that underpinned Europe's relationship with American cinema from World War II through the early Cold War. On the one hand, they highlight the importance of pragmatic concerns to film import and export policies, which are frequently interpreted through the often-strident political rhetoric of the period, particularly in Eastern Europe.[60] On the other hand, comparison between Western and Eastern Europe demonstrates the uniformity in European approaches to the American film industry in these years. During the war, all of the governments discussed in this chapter regarded Hollywood with mistrust, although due to the uncomfortable confluence of nationalism and economic exigency—and, at the war's end, military dependency—all were forced to accept the OWI's one-size-fits-all distribution proposals. These sentiments remained the same after the war, despite the Continent's increasing division. As the Czechoslovak case demonstrates, that country's agreement with the MPEA in fact reflected the increasing influence, on Eastern Europe, of the Soviet Union, which promised more films than its beleaguered industry could deliver.

The American officials involved in brokering this agreement did not interpret matters in this way: as Mareš writes, the Czechoslovak agreement was hailed as a success by both the State Department and the MPEA, representatives of the dual forces—information and industry—that drove the OWI films' history.[61] A final lesson from these forty films, then, is the consistent and relatively uncontroversial nature of this pairing, throughout the institutional and political shifts of the period 1943–46. From wartime information and psychological warfare to Cold War propaganda, US government and film-industry aims intertwined in the OWI films, which—whether as cargo in military jeeps and transport planes or the subject of diplomatic agreements—functioned, as the *Missoulian* described, as bearers of the message of liberal capitalism, and cogs in this system themselves.

APPENDIX: AMERICAN FEATURE FILMS PREPARED BY THE OFFICE OF WAR INFORMATION FOR DISTRIBUTION IN LIBERATED EUROPE

This list is provisional and incomplete, representing films selected as of March 6, 1944. Information regarding languages of translation for films provided by Twentieth Century-Fox is not available.[62]

Languages of Translation

Bulgarian, Czech, Danish, Dutch, Flemish, French, German, Greek, Hungarian, Italian, Norwegian, Polish, Romanian, Serbo-Croatian

Columbia

The More the Merrier (1943, all languages)
Here Comes Mr. Jordan (1941, all languages)
You Were Never Lovelier (1942, all languages)
Our Wife (1941, all languages)
My Sister Eileen (1942, all languages except Greek)

MGM

Joe Smith, American (1942, all languages)
The Human Comedy (1943, all languages)
Pride and Prejudice (1940, all languages except Bulgarian, Hungarian, and Serbo-Croatian)
Seven Sweethearts (1942, all languages except Dutch)
Young Tom Edison (1940, all languages except Bulgarian, Hungarian, and Serbo-Croatian

Paramount

Christmas in July (1940, all languages)
Hold Back the Dawn (1941, all languages)
There's Magic in Music (1941, all languages)
So Proudly We Hail (1941, all languages)
The Great Man's Lady (1942, all languages)

RKO

Mr. and Mrs. Smith (1941, all languages)
No, No, Nanette (1940, all languages)
Tom, Dick, and Harry (1941, all languages)
The Navy Comes Through (1942, all languages)
Abe Lincoln in Illinois (1940, all languages)
The Story of Vernon and Irene Castle (1939, Italian only)

United Artists

The Gold Rush (1925, all languages)
I Married a Witch (1942, all languages)
Our Town (1940, all languages)
Pot o' Gold (1941, all languages)
Long Voyage Home (1940, Danish, Dutch, Flemish, French, Greek, Italian, and Norwegian only)

Universal

Appointment for Love (1941, all languages)
It Started with Eve (1941, all languages)
Shadow of a Doubt (1943, all languages)
If I Had My Way (1940, Danish, Dutch, Flemish, French, Greek, Italian, Norwegian only)
It's a Date (1942, all languages)
Corvette K-225 (1943, Bulgarian, Czech, German, Hungarian, Polish, Romanian, Serbo-Croatian only)
Phantom of the Opera (1943, Bulgarian, Czech, German, Hungarian, Polish, Romanian, Serbo-Croatian only)

Warner Bros.

Air Force (1943, all languages)
Sergeant York (1941, all languages except German)
Across the Pacific (1942, all languages)

Twentieth Century-Fox

Moontide (1942)
The Sullivans (1942)
Tales of Manhattan (1942)
Remember the Day (1941)

NOTES

1. Statement of Elmer Davis to House Appropriations Committee, April 19, 1944, record group (RG) 208, Records of the Historian Relating to the Overseas Branch, box 3, Reports—II, National Archives and Records Administration, College Park, Maryland (hereafter cited as NARA).

2. Clayton D. Laurie, *The Propaganda Warriors: America's Crusade against Nazi Germany* (Lawrence: University Press of Kansas, 1996), 188–89.

3. Czechoslovak Information Service, New York to MZV London, Příprava filmů v čs. versi pro dobu poválečnou, 2 August 1943, fond LA 1939–1945, k. 252, sl. Filmy pro poválečnou potřebu—Filmy americké, Archive of the Ministry of Foreign Affairs, Prague (hereafter cited as A MZV). All translations from Czech and French in this essay are the author's own.

4. Elmer Davis to House, April 19, 1944, RG 208, Records of the Historian Relating to the Overseas Branch, box 3, Reports—II, NARA. In keeping with SHAEF's dual American-British command, PWD's film program also included British features and documentaries, and a handful of Soviet films.

5. Ian Jarvie, "The Postwar Economic Foreign Policy of the American Film Industry," *Film History* 4, no. 4 (1990); Ian Jarvie, *Hollywood's Overseas Campaign* (New York: Cambridge University Press, 1992).

6. Studies of the OWI's interaction with foreign governments have typically been written from the perspectives of single nations. See, for example, Bénédicte Rochet, "Les actualités filmées," *Revue Belge d'Histoire Contemporaine* 34, nos. 1–2 (2009); Jindřiška Bláhová, "A Tough Job for Donald Duck: Hollywood, Czechoslovakia, and Selling Films behind the Iron Curtain, 1944–1951" (PhD diss., University of East Anglia, UK, 2010); and Petr Mareš, "Politika a 'pohyblivé obrázky': Spor o dovoz amerických filmů do Československa po druhé světové válce," *Iluminace* 6, no. 1 (1994): 77–96. On OWI publications in the Netherlands, see Marja Roholl, "Preparing for Victory: The U.S. Office of War Information Overseas Branch's Illustrated Magazines in the Netherlands and the Foundations for the American Century, 1944–1945," *European Journal of American Studies* 7, no. 2 (2012): 2–18.

7. Allan M. Winkler, *The Politics of Propaganda: The Office of War Information, 1942–1945* (New Haven, CT: Yale University Press, 1978), 1.

8. Minutes New York Review Board, March 24, 1945, RG 208, Records of the Historian Relating to the Overseas Branch, box 2, Overseas Branch—Motion Picture Bureau March 1945, NARA; Draft Motion Picture Guidance, August 24, 1944, RG 208, Records of the Historian Relating to the Overseas Branch, box 2, Overseas Branch—Motion Picture Bureau Aug.–Sept. 1944, NARA. For more on the OWI's film activities, see, for example, Winkler, *Politics of Propaganda;* Richard Dyer MacCann, *The People's Films: A Political History of US Government Motion Pictures* (New York: Hastings House Publishers, 1973); Ian Scott, "From Toscanini to Tennessee: Robert Riskin, the OWI and the Construction of American Propaganda in World War II," *Journal of American Studies* 40, no. 2 (2006): 347–66; and Charles Alexander Holmes Thomson, *Overseas Information Service of the United States Government* (Washington, DC: Brookings Institution, 1948; reprint, New York: Arno Press, 1972); and Clayton R. Koppes and Gregory D. Black, "What to Show the World: The Office of War Information and Hollywood, 1942–1945," *Journal of American History* 64, no. 1 (1977): 87–105.

9. Report—Motion Picture Bureau, June 15, 1943–July 15, 1943, RG 208, Records of the Historian Relating to the Overseas Branch, box 2, Motion Pictures (OB), NARA.

10. These tenuous links did not go unnoticed: As Jennifer Fay writes of PWD/SHAEF's "reeducation" program for Germany, of which the OWI films were a part, test audiences of German POWs reported learning from films such as *Christmas in July* "that America was money-mad and that greed and business dominate American thinking." The films nevertheless remained in PWD/SHAEF's film programs for Germany. Jennifer Fay, *Theaters of Occupation: Hollywood and the Reeducation of Postwar Germany*, 2nd ed. (Minneapolis: University of Minnesota Press, 2008), 51.

11. "A Better Influence," *Missoulian*, March 13, 1945.

12. Memorandum to Edward Barrett, Executive Director, OB, from Robert Riskin, Motion Picture Bureau, OBNY, August 12, 1944, RG 208, Records of the Historian Relating to the Overseas Branch, box 2, Bureau of Overseas Motion Pictures 1942–45, NARA.

13. Jarvie, "Postwar Economic Foreign Policy," 281. For more on the OWI's activities within PWD, see Thomson, *Overseas Information Service*, 7.

14. Ibid. On interwar European restrictive measures on American film exports, see Andrew Higson and Richard Maltby, eds., *"Film Europe" and "Film America": Cinema, Commerce and Cultural Exchange, 1920–1939* (Exeter, UK: University of Exeter Press, 1999).

15. Budget Justification First Six Months—Operating Plan for Films Division, July 1, 1945–December 31, 1945, RG 208, Records of the Historian Relating to the Overseas Branch, box 3, London Office: Film Division, NARA.

16. On PWD/SHAEF's institutional history and its relationship to the OWI's London Outpost, see Winkler, *Politics of Propaganda*.

17. On legitimacy and the exile governments, see Martin Conway, "Legacies of Exile: The Exile Governments in London during the Second World War and the Politics of Post-War Europe," in *Europe in Exile*, ed. Martin Conway and José Gotovitch (New York: Berghahn, 2001), 255–74.

18. Budget Justification First Six Months, NARA.

19. "American Films Reach Accords with Holland, Czecho, Denmark," *Variety*, September 18, 1946, 13, quoted in Bláhová, "Tough Job for Donald Duck," 49.

20. Fischl to Kraus, June 10, 1943, fond LA 1939–1945, k. 252, Osvěta—filmy, sl. Filmy pro poválečnou potřebu—Filmy anglické, A MZV. For more on MOI plans for distribution in liberated Europe, see Jarvie, *Hollywood's Overseas Campaign*, 206.

21. A. Fried to Mrs. Cornell, May 18, 1943, fond LA 1939–1945, k. 252, Osvěta—filmy, sl. Filmy pro poválečnou potřebu—Filmy anglické, A MZV.

22. Fischl to Informační služba, New York, Filmy pro Československo, June 12, 1943, fond LA 1939–1945, k. 252, Osvěta—filmy, sl. Filmy pro poválečnou potřebu—Filmy americké, A MZV.

23. Telegram from Masaryk to San Francisco Consulate, July 31, 1943, fond LA 1939–1945, k. 252, Osvěta—filmy, sl. Filmy pro poválečnou potřebu—Filmy americké, A MZV.

24. MPOŽ to Předseda vlády, Nákup a příprava filmů pro domov, July 19, 1944, fond LA 1939–1945, k. 252, Osvěta—filmy, sl. Filmy pro poválečnou potřebu—Filmy sovětské, A MZV.

25. Réunion des membres de la Commission d'Examen des Films, February 24, 1944, AA763/1–12/8/Lévy, Centre for Historical Research and Documentation on War and Contemporary Society, Brussels (hereafter cited as CEGES).

26. Fischl to Spewack, August 24, 1943, fond LA 1939–1945, k. 252, Osvěta—filmy, sl. Filmy pro poválečnou potřebu—Filmy americké, A MZV.

27. Spewack to Fischl, August 30, 1943, fond LA 1939–1945, k. 252, Osvěta—filmy, sl. Filmy pro poválečnou potřebu—Filmy americké, A MZV.

28. Filmy pro poválečnou Evropu, October 12, 1943, fond LA 1939–1945, k. 252, Osvěta—filmy, sl. Filmy pro poválečnou potřebu—Filmy americké, A MZV.

29. Minutes of Inter-Allied Information Office Film Committee, November 16, 1943, fond LA 1939–1945, k. 252, Osvěta—filmy, sl. Filmy pro poválečnou potřebu—Filmy americké, A MZV. The OWI, like the exile governments, was a member of the Inter-Allied Information Committee.

30. Janeček to members of the UNIO Film Committee and others, December 3, 1943, fond LA-O, Diplomatický sbor ZÚ Čsl. New York, k. 148, sl. New York—Filmy a filmová pásma, A MZV.

31. Czechoslovak Information Service to Janeček, December 9, 1943, LA-O, Diplomatický sbor ZÚ Čsl. New York, k. 148, sl. New York—Filmy a filmová pásma, A MZV. The assassination was a major propaganda point for the Czechoslovak exile government. See Chad Bryant, *Prague in Black: Czech Nationalism and Nazi Rule* (Cambridge, MA: Harvard University Press, 2007).

32. Letter from William Patterson, January 7, 1944, fond LA 1939–1945, k. 252, Osvěta—filmy, sl. Filmy pro poválečnou potřebu—Filmy americké, A MZV.

33. Czechoslovak Information Service to MZV London, February 4, 1944, fond LA 1939–1945, k. 252, Osvěta—filmy, sl. Filmy pro poválečnou potřebu—Filmy anglické, A MZV. The same was true of the list of films submitted to the Belgian government in the same month. Réunion des membres de la Commission d'Examen des Films, February 24, 1944, AA763/1–12/8/Lévy, CEGES.

34. Amerikanske film, Arkiv S-2057, Regjeringens informasjonskontor London, EB-L0002, Kortfilmer (1944), National Archives of Norway (Riksarkivet), Oslo (hereafter cited as Riksarkivet). Translation by Adam Oberlin.

35. Hauge to Patterson, February 17, 1944, and Patterson to Hauge, February 14, 1944, Arkiv S-2057, Regjeringens informasjonskontor London, EB-L0001, Film: Divide and Conquer, 1944, Riksarkivet.

36. Ibid.

37. Copy of a letter to Mr. Lober from Mr. Patterson in London, March 13, 1944, RG 208, Records of the Office of War Information, box 131, London—Motion Pictures, NARA.

38. Report on Keurings Commissies, June 1, 1944, Londens Archief 2.05/80, Inv. no. 5845, National Archives of the Netherlands (Nationaal Archief), The Hague.

39. Of the thirty-seven films selected for translation into Norwegian as of March 6, 1944, for instance, all but *Abe Lincoln in Illinois* were included in the package sent to the country. *Action in the North Atlantic* (Warner Bros., 1943) and *The Men in Her Life* (Columbia, 1941) were added, for a total of thirty-eight American features. Arkiv S-2057, Regjeringens informasjonskontor London, EB-L0004, SHAEF—1945, Riksarkivet. A small number of films were slated for distribution only in Eastern or Western Europe; certain other titles had minor geographic exclusions. See the appendix to this chapter for more information.

40. Czechoslovak Government Information Service, NY, to MZV London, Poválečná filmová distribuce v ČSR—zaslání zprávy, November 21, 1944, fond LA-O, Diplomatický sbor ZÚ Čsl. New York, k. 148, sl. New York—Filmy a filmová pásma, A MZV.

41. Mareš, "Politika a 'pohyblivé obrázky,'" 83; Czechoslovak Government Information Service, NY to MZV London, Poválečná filmová distribuce v ČSR—zaslání zprávy, November 21, 1944, fond LA-O, Diplomatický sbor ZÚ Čsl. New York, k. 148, sl. New York—Filmy a filmová pásma, A MZV.

42. The stockpile location for Norway, for instance, was Aberdeen, Scotland; for France, it was "MGM premises in Algiers." Copy of memorandum from Alberts to Barnes, October 14, 1944, RG 208, Records of the Historian Relating to the Overseas Branch, box 3, Report on French Stockpile Operations July–November 1944, NARA.

43. Millar to Hauge, March 29, 1945, and Plan for PWD Film Operations in Norway, Arkiv S-2057, Regjeringens informasjonskontor London, EB—L0004, SHAEF—1945, Riksarkivet. On the significance of the American and British films distributed in liberated Norway by PWD/SHAEF, see Sara Brinch and Gunnar Iversen, *Virkelighetsbilder: Norsk dokumentarfilm gjennom hundre år* (Oslo: Universitetsforlaget, 2001).

44. Report on a meeting held on June 29, 1944, at 3 p.m. at P.W.D. Headquarters, Arkiv S-2057, Regjeringens informasjonskontor London, EB—L0004, SHAEF—1945, Riksarkivet.

45. Cinéma—Libération, May 25, 1944, AA763/1–12/8/Lévy, CEGES.

46. Copy of a letter from Kastner to Riskin, October 28, 1944, RG 208, Records of the Historian Relating to the Overseas Branch, box 2, Overseas Branch—Motion Picture Bureau, Oct.–Dec. 1944, NARA.

47. Patterson and Silverstein to Riskin, 29 June 1945, RG 208, Records of the Historian Relating to the Overseas Branch, box 2, OB Motion Picture Bureau June 1945, NARA.

48. See Jarvie's informative table, "Trade Barriers Confronting the American Motion Picture Industry in 1947," in "Postwar Economic Foreign Policy," 282.

49. Jarvie, *Hollywood's Overseas Campaign*, 205.

50. Mareš, "Politika a 'pohyblivé obrázky,'" 78. See also Jindřich Elbl, "Pravda o našich filmových smlouvách," *Filmová Práce* 1, no. 23 (October 26, 1945): 5–7.

51. Mareš, "Politika a 'pohyblivé obrázky,'" 80.

52. Mareš, "Politika a 'pohyblivé obrázky'"; Bláhová, "A Tough Job for Donald Duck."

53. On this situation, see also Pavel Skopal, "Filmy pana velvyslance: Československé filmové publikum a americký Státní department (1945–1960)," *Iluminace* 20, no. 3 (2008): 175–88. These geopolitics defined Czechoslovakia between 1945 and 1948, when the country was governed by a National Front coalition of six left or left-leaning parties. Although the Soviet Union played an important role in determining the shape of postwar Czechoslovak politics, and the Communist Party freely won 38 percent of the vote in the country's 1946 elections, the events of February 1948—in which the resignation of non-Communist ministers led to the formation of a Communist-controlled government—were not preordained. Rather, as historian Bradley Abrams has argued, they emerged from Czechoslovak communist intellectuals' success in framing a Soviet-oriented form of communism as a natural, *national* response to Czechoslovakia's wartime experience. Bradley F. Abrams, *The Struggle for the Soul of the Nation* (Lanham, MD: Rowman and Littlefield, 2004), 181. On American-Czechoslovak diplomatic relations in this period, see Igor Lukes, *On the Edge of the Cold War: American Diplomats and Spies in Postwar Prague* (New York: Oxford University Press, 2012).

54. Mareš, "Politika a 'pohyblivé obrázky,'" 83–84.

55. Bláhová, "Tough Job for Donald Duck," 75. On the agreements with England and France, see Elbl, "Pravda," 5.

56. As Bláhová describes, the MPAA saw Czechoslovakia as a "testing ground for Eastern Europe," and hoped that "dealing successfully with the Czechoslovak Film Monopoly would increase significantly its chances of expanding across Eastern Europe." Bláhová, "Tough Job for Donald Duck," 67–68.

57. Mareš, "Politika a 'pohyblivé obrázky,'" 91; Motion Picture Export Association—Seznam 140 filmů, fond MI, k. 233, sl. USA—filmový dovoz, National Archives of the Czech Republic, Prague.

58. Copy of a letter from Kastner to Riskin, October 28, 1944, RG 208, Records of the Historian Relating to the Overseas Branch, box 2, Overseas Branch—Motion Picture Bureau, Oct.–Dec. 1944, NARA.

59. Bláhová, "Tough Job for Donald Duck," 75.

60. As Mareš writes, some early postwar Czechoslovak film officials called for breaking ties with America, and for a "clear orientation to the East." Mareš, "Politika a 'pohyblivé obrázky,'" 84.

61. Ibid., 95.

62. Sources: List of Industry's Stockpile Features & Shorts, fond LA-D, k. 40, sl. Filmy pro poválečnou distribuci, A MZV; Arkiv S-2057, Regjeringens informasjonskontor London, EB-L0004, SHAEF—1945, Riksarkivet.

18

"A CAMPAIGN OF TRUTH"

Marshall Plan Films in Greece

Katerina Loukopoulou

*[A] highly skillful and substantial campaign of truth is as indispensable as an
air force.*
—EDWARD BARRETT, *TRUTH IS OUR WEAPON*, 1953

To what extent can a "campaign of truth" be likened to the power of an air force?
For Edward Barrett, a highly influential officer of the State Department in the early
1950s, such an aphorism was more than a matter of metaphorical excess. Its rationale derived from the powerful fusion of the United States' military might (its hard
power) with a concentrated deployment of propaganda campaigns (its soft power)
in the aftermath of World War II and the start of the so-called Cold War.[1] An
exemplar of this new state of affairs was the public campaign of the European
Recovery Program (ERP, 1948–52), widely known then and now as the "Marshall
Plan" (MP), named after its driving force General George Marshall, who engineered the plan's parameters.[2] Hailed for his decisive leadership of the Allied
Forces' victory in World War II as chief of staff of the US Army, later, as Secretary
of State, Marshall exercised both a postwar influence and strategic planning that
were expansive.

The MP consisted of $12.5 billion of predominantly material aid for the recon-
struction of the Western European economies devastated by World War II. Its
implementation was overseen by the State Department and the Department of
Commerce and executed through a newly established agency, the Economic
Cooperation Administration (ECA), which had offices in Washington and in each
of the eighteen Western European countries that received the aid. The nature of
this aid was multifaceted and adjusted to each country's circumstances. But in all
cases, the economic recovery program was supplemented by what Barrett called "a
campaign of truth"—that is, "friendly persuasion" publicity about the MP's necessity. Cinema was a crucial part of this campaign to the extent that the MP films

have been retrospectively described as "celluloid weapons."[3] This chapter will discuss the relevance of this idea to the unique situation of Greece, where World War II morphed into a civil war that lasted up to 1949 and came to an end after the forceful intervention of the US Air Force.

This civil war quickly acquired international dimensions, as had been the case with the Spanish Civil War in the 1930s. The Greek Civil War was fought between the right-wing Greek Government Army (backed by the United Kingdom and the United States) and the left-wing Democratic Army of Greece (backed by Yugoslavia and the USSR). Greece, therefore, became the first hot spot of the Cold War, with the US military playing a decisive role in the final outcome of suppressing the Democratic Army, whose forces included a large part of the wartime Greek resistance that had previously fought next to the Allied Forces against the Nazi occupation.[4] Owing to this swift change of alliances, the Greeks' perception of the US military intervention during the civil war, and of the MP aid that followed suit, was divided.

When trying to disentangle the complexities pertaining to the multifarious uses of the MP and its cultural propaganda, challenging questions emerge: Can films be as effective as weapons? Against whom and to win what kind of battle? And moreover, within what kind of "war" context? The MP's cinematic campaign operated within a new state of geopolitics in which the boundaries between militaristic and economic intervention were becoming increasingly blurred. For example, a 1948 *New Yorker* cartoon shows US military strategists deliberating in front of a map of Western Europe. The caption reads: "The guerrilla activities near Nestorion [a village in northern Greece where the decisive battles of the civil war took place] have been suppressed with thirty million dollars in Greek aid, including tractors, other farm machinery, and a large shipment of road-building equipment. The Communist inspired agitation in central Italy is being countered vigorously by the distribution of machine tools and twenty thousand long tons of cereals, mostly wheat."[5] By mocking the duality of the MP's military-cum-humanitarian aid, this cartoon indicates how the MP was openly criticized in the United States itself for crudely conflating military with economic intervention, especially in countries like Greece and Italy, where the successful campaigns of the left-wing parties could have potentially led to an alliance with the communist Eastern Bloc. The cartoon's underlying subtext related to the contemporaneous efforts of US foreign policymakers to contain communism by gradually replacing the US military presence in Europe with US material aid and by shaping the European economic systems as compatible with the US one. And to achieve this, the Marshall Planners recruited cinema as well as tractors to the cause.

Thanks to the ECA's well-funded communications network across Europe, approximately three hundred documentary and informational films were produced, widely distributed, and exhibited in both theatrical and nontheatrical venues.[6] Their aim was not only to propagate the MP's necessity, but most crucially to project the vision of a united Western Europe. To this end, US staff with in-depth knowledge of the European context were recruited to oversee the MP's European Film Unit based in Paris. This was the case of Stuart Schulberg, who during the war had been making training films for the Office of Strategic Services (OSS) and who, prior to taking charge of the MP Film Unit, had been chief of the US Military Government's Documentary Film Unit in Berlin. The overall strategy, though, was to confer a European identity on the MP film campaign by recruiting European filmmakers and production companies to shoot on location; producing multilingual versions of the films and organizing an effective operational system for their trans-European circulation; and above all commissioning films that promoted European unity and cooperation, such as the 1951 series *The Changing Face of Europe*. As a result, critics of the time viewed these films as "a promising European Documentary Movement," as influential film critic Arthur Knight noted in 1951.[7]

But from a more recent perspective, these European MP films resemble a cinematic time capsule. Because of the US Education Exchange Act of 1948, which did not allow the United States' foreign information activities to be used domestically, these films had received little attention until 1990, when this ban was lifted.[8] It is mainly since 2004, with the *Selling Democracy* program of MP films circulating at international Festivals and online archives, that this hitherto uncharted territory of moving images has emerged. The scholarship on the MP films has since grown steadily, focusing either on case studies of country-specific films, such as the ones about Ireland, Austria, Germany, Norway, and Italy, or on comparative perspectives.[9] If there is a common conclusion emerging from the existing scholarship, it is that the MP propaganda mechanisms spread the US government's underlying anticommunist ideology through the projection of a vision of liberal democracy driven by rapid economic recovery and cooperation between the eighteen countries that received the MP aid.

The MP films about Greece have not been researched so far, and their case is as exceptional as the state of a country during and after a fierce civil war. A striking example of the "Greek exception," as historian Stelios Zachariou has noted, was that by October 1949, when the civil war ended, approximately 80 percent of the MP aid to Greece had been channeled to fund the Greek government's military operations against the Democratic Army.[10] The MP thus ensured that Greece "more than any other European country" retained "its Western orientation by playing an integral role in the termination of the Civil War."[11]

By contextualizing the MP films about Greece and their recurrent themes, this chapter aims to investigate how the geopolitical dimension became intertwined with the cultural one. It will do so by exploring how the films constructed an audiovisual narrative to represent Greece as a case of exceptional geopolitical significance, and how this rhetoric would have resonated with the audiences (Greek and

European) that these films were addressing. By viewing all the extant MP films about Greece as a group, what emerges as a trope is the mapping of the national-reconstruction discourse onto emotive references to classical antiquity as a universal value. Most of the films strive to create links between ancient and modern Greece, offering a narrative of transhistorical continuity and common European heritage. Such is the case with *Victory at Thermopylae* (David Kurland, 1950) and *Island Odyssey* (1950), this chapter's main case studies; as well as with *Marshall Plan at Work in Greece* (James Hill, 1950), *The Corinth Canal* (John Ferno, 1950), *A Doctor for Ardaknos* (John Ferno, 1951), and *The Good Life* (Humphrey Jennings and Graham Wallace, 1951). While direct references to classical heritage are less prevalent in the other three extant MP films about Greece—*Return from the Valley* (John Ferno, 1950), *Mill Town* (David Kurland, 1950), and *Story of Koula* (Vittorio Gallo, 1951)—there is still a particular emphasis on tradition, history, and village life.[12]

My aim is to position these MP films within some of the historical contexts that will help us understand what this cinematographic offensive stood for in the aftermath of the first post–World War II civil war in Europe. Through textual and contextual analysis of the narratives of two films, where classical antiquity stands for the larger cause of liberal democracy, my intention is to reconstruct what film historian Tom Gunning calls "the original horizon of expectation in which films were produced and received".[13] The chapter thus contributes to the growing literature on the "cultural dynamics" of the Cold War—part of a historiographical revision that advocates the "cultural turn" of the "new" Cold War history, where artistic production is conceived as a constitutive force of power formations rather than a mere reflection.[14] And by extension, this cultural turn applies to histories of the relationship between the US military and the formation of Cold War cinematic propaganda during a period when media "campaigns of truth" often exercised as powerful an influence as actual military aggressions. In the case of Greece, the MP publicity campaign was engineered with the aim of perpetuating the geopolitical status quo that the US Army and Air Force had first enforced during the civil war.

NAPALM, GIFTS, AND FILMS

The rhetorical excesses of film and cultural propaganda used during World War II have been understood, and even justified, with reference to the wartime state of urgency.[15] But what about the specificity of film propaganda from one ally toward another within a state of peace and reconstruction? As David Ellwood, historian of postwar reconstruction in Europe, has put it, "[T]he United States . . . invented with the ERP a new method for projecting its power into Europe," which he described as "the greatest international propaganda operation ever seen in peacetime."[16] What this "new method" was and how it operated have been the subject of debates and new scholarship, which no longer approach the MP solely on military, economic, and political terms, but pay equal attention to the publicity campaign and "cultural diplomacy" aspects.[17]

This new historiographical emphasis revisits and contextualizes anew the "international persuasion" campaigns led by the foreign-policy strategists of the United States after the Second World War. Among the various manifestations of the United States' new foreign policy of "friendly persuasion" is Barrett's 1953 memoir, *Truth Is Our Weapon*. Barrett wrote it after having served as assistant secretary of state for international information for President Harry Truman from 1950 to 1952 and previously for the Office of War Information, as well as having been involved in Voice of America and the first United Nations radio effort. In his memoir, Barrett summed up what had become official US policy by 1953, embraced both by Truman and by Dwight Eisenhower: "We cannot hope to win the cold war unless we win the minds of men. . . . The great, prolonged war of ideas must be waged with as much skill, professional competence, and steadfastness as are needed in any military conflict." And he conceded: "Simply transplanting the highly developed American techniques of advertising and public relations to foreign lands can produce gross blunders. What sells soap in Indiana can unsell democracy in India."[18] The MP's publicity campaign is an example of this culture-specific approach.

Barrett's above manifesto chimes with the description offered by Lothar Wolff, the first chief of the MP Film Unit headquarters in Paris and former long-time editor of *The March of Time* (1935–51) series of newsreels: "All of them [the MP films] were prepared by Europeans exclusively *for* Europeans. European producers were allowed by their American supervisors in ECA's motion-picture section to tell the MP story in the style most appreciated by their fellow Europeans . . . if the propaganda content seems perhaps too subtle, it should be remembered that these techniques are considered most effective for transatlantic audiences."[19] Research on the country-specific MP films has highlighted how an engagement with national-identity politics permeated their narratives either to suggest a break with tradition and the disturbing past (Germany, Austria) or to capitalize on the specific country's cinematic strengths (Italy's neorealist movement).[20]

The implementation of the MP in Greece is replete with the paradoxes of the beginnings of the Cold War, when alliances were in a state of flux. Greece was at the central stage of the "war or peace" scenarios written at the time and in the historiography of the Cold War since.[21] In June 1947, in his capacity as secretary of state, General Marshall persuaded President Truman of the need for the United States to boost European economies with immediate financial aid—a strategy now widely regarded as a screen for the US containment strategy against communism, known as the Truman Doctrine. Truman's foreign-policy priorities were officially launched in March 1947, when he addressed Congress to make a case for the United States to step in and to cover for Britain's withdrawal of its economic and military support to Greece and Turkey—two countries whose geopolitical alliances with Western Europe and the United States were being threatened by the Soviet Union's increasing influence on southeastern Europe.

The unexpected ferocity of the Greek Civil War precipitated this, as alluded to in Truman's famous exhortation: "[I]t must be the policy of the United States to support free people who are resisting attempted subjugation by armed minorities or by outside pressure."[22] General Marshall tapped into the preeminent fear of the Truman administration—that the Mediterranean Sea would be transformed into a "Soviet lake," accentuated because of the prospect of a communist electoral victory in Italy in 1948 and, even more urgently, the ongoing civil war in Greece. As influential US strategist John Foster Dulles put it in his 1950 foreign policy directive *War or Peace:* "If Greece had fallen, much would have fallen with it. Control of Greece and of the Greek islands would have carried a dominance in the eastern Mediterranean even greater than Molotov sought when he asked for Tripolitania. Turkey would have been virtually surrounded and cut off from the West, and made an easy prey."[23] Barrett's analogy between a campaign and an air force is particularly relevant to Greece, because it was the only European country that experienced the post–World War II "campaign of truth" in *all* its forms: military intervention, economic aid, and cultural propaganda.

Stark contradictions characterized the chain of events that unfolded. In August 1949, the US Air Force, with the collaboration of the Greek Government Army, dropped large amounts of napalm in the northern regions of Greece to wipe out the Democratic Army and to bring the civil war to an end by October.[24] And on December 21, 1949, the millionth ton of MP aid arrived at the port of Piraeus and was paraded in central Athens with formal ceremonies.[25] An apparent divergence of purpose thus emerged between uses of MP funding for destruction (of the political enemy) and for reconstruction (of the economy). But the ultimate objective of these strategies and their propaganda mechanisms was the same: to ensure that the Greek polity and economic system met the ideological exigencies of the United States.

To this end, the MP films about Greece followed the predominant patterns of the overall MP publicity campaign across Western Europe. Its main characteristic was the conflation of US foreign policy with discourses of liberal humanism, productivity, and individual freedom. The rhetoric of most MP films aimed to transpose war traumas into concrete visualizations of material and ideological reconstruction. For example, an MP film about Italy, *A Village without Words* (1950), dramatizes the overnight transformation of a small deserted town into a thriving hub of productivity upon the arrival of MP aid. Other films offered dramatized reconstructions of the personal stories by individuals whose lives were affected by the US economic aid, such as *Me and Mr. Marshall* (1950), a German miner's first-person narration about his finding employment. In a similar vein, a film about Greece, *The Story of*

Koula, narrates the persistent efforts of a Greek boy and his grandfather to acquire an MP-shipped US mule in order to transform the rate of productivity of their small farm. But in the case of Greece, such a narrative had additional militaristic connotations. US mules (originally aimed for economic reconstruction as part of the MP aid) had been extensively used by the Greek government during the civil war to fight the Democratic Army, which had retreated to the mountainous and difficult-to-reach provinces of mainland and northern Greece.[26]

The ways that the target audience experienced these screen narratives needs thus to be related to Sandra Schulberg's point that the MP's "genius lay not in sending money but in shipping tangible goods—fuel, fertilizer, food, farm animals, machinery—that were essential for life and for economic recovery."[27] These products bore the MP's logo (which resembled the American flag), and their delivery was often accompanied by formal ceremonies and nontheatrical screenings of MP films, as I will discuss later in this chapter with the case of *Island Odyssey.*

This material and visual barrage of MP aid arriving in European countries prompted the French intellectual Georges Bataille to include the MP in his long-gestated anthropological and philosophical diatribe on the notions of "the accursed share" and "gift economy" [1949]: "[I]f war is necessary to the American economy, it does not follow that war has to hold to the traditional form. . . . The Marshall Plan succeeds in giving a clear focus to the current conflict. It is not essentially the struggle of two military powers for hegemony; it is the struggle of two economic methods. The Marshall Plan offers an organization of surplus against the accumulation of the Stalin plans."[28] Bataille's macroeconomic analysis of the MP "gift" aimed to deconstruct the way in which US militarism was aligned with the plan's aim to create a material surplus that would drive both European and US economies. His critique echoed the skepticism toward the MP in countries with strong Communist parties (France, Greece, Italy), where the American aid was often perceived as part and parcel of geopolitical domination.

GEOPOLITICAL SCREENS AND NARRATIVES

In the case of Greece, prominent among the MP's tangible goods were films, mainly viewed in nontheatrical contexts. As Albert Hemsing put it in his memoir about his work for the European Film Unit in Paris: "Non-theatrical distribution . . . was the primary vehicle for the Marshall Plan films," singling out Greece (alongside Italy and Turkey) as the countries where mobile film units were more widely and frequently used.[29] This was especially important for the nonurban areas of Greece (such as the islands and the remote villages), where no cinemas existed within traveling distance. As noted in a 1950 ECA report about the progress of the MP's Overseas Information Program in the section "Reaching the Hard-to-Reach": "Greece and Turkey are at the bottom of the list [range of commercial cinemas as per population] with one theatre for every 50,000 and one for every 100,000 persons respectively," while Sweden is at the top "with one for every 3,000 persons." The report goes on to describe how "mobile units carrying projectors and sound equipment travel the back country whenever weather permits to put on 'Village Square Shows.' . . . People come from miles around on foot and the event makes a deep impression on the whole locality."[30] In Greece, therefore, MP films would have been the first encounter with the medium for a large part of the population, especially for the young generations. As in other European countries, Greek audiences watched a range of MP films, dubbed into their national language—not only films about how their own country was recovering from the war thanks to the American aid, but also (and mainly) films about other countries and about European cooperation.

The notion of the MP films as "celluloid weapons" is particularly apt here, because Greek audiences of the time experienced the foreign military intervention, the economic aid, and the propaganda campaigns in quick succession. Since Greece at the time was a country with scarcely any tradition and actual infrastructure of documentary production and distribution, the MP films about Greece had to be produced by non-Greek filmmakers from the ECA units of London (e.g., *The Good Life*, by Humphrey Jennings), Paris (e.g., John Ferno's films), and Rome (e.g., *Story of Koula*, by Vittorio Gallo). This was another facet of the Greek exception, considering that the majority of MP films about a specific country would conventionally be directed by local filmmakers, sometimes building on the specific country's cinematic tradition, as in the cases of Italy (neorealism) and the United Kingdom (the British Documentary Movement).

Apart from newsreels, hardly any documentaries about Greece during this crucial historical conjuncture exist. In general, up to the late 1950s nonfiction cinema about Greece was sparse, mainly taking the form of travelogues.[31] Moreover, Greece's own film production was meager in comparison with that of other European countries. Even more disadvantaged was the exhibition sector, for two reasons: first, it was disproportionally concentrated in the urban areas of Athens and Thessaloniki; and second, in 1949 film exhibition suffered from the introduction of new taxation on "public spectacles" to be charged in urban cinemas at a time when the income of the average Greek citizen was at its lowest.[32] In contrast, the nontheatrical circulation of the MP films was well organized and no entrance fee was charged, so the films reached a large part of the population in both urban and nonurban areas.

To approach the contingent meanings and resonances of the MP films about Greece, a good starting point is to juxtapose the documentary *Victory at Thermopylae* (1950) with one of the newsreels circulating in theatrical and nontheatrical venues at around the same time, not only in Greece but all over Western Europe. A fragment from a 1951 US newsreel covers the celebration of the third anniversary of the MP in Greece, reporting on a ceremony held at Thermopylae, a historical location with symbolic resonance, widely associated with the resistance of ancient Greeks against the Persian invaders. The newsreel shows American and Greek dignitaries surrounded by an infantry guard of honor, and it concludes with a girl, representing Greece, offering flowers to the controversial US ambassador to Greece, John Peurifoy, who is heading a group of forty-eight girls representing each of the US states. He proceeds to plant an olive tree in memory of the three hundred Spartans who fought the Persian invaders.[33] The organization of such a ritualized event to celebrate the MP aid had an additional historical relevance: it was at Thermopylae that in 1941 a decisive battle against the Nazi invasion had been fought by British Commonwealth forces, which eventually had to retreat. But defense of the passage had helped to allow the evacuation of British forces from southern Greece. By the time this newsreel and the MP documentary *Victory at Thermopylae* were shown to audiences in the early 1950s, the location had accreted multiple meanings and connotations in terms of resistance to foreign aggression.

Considering that this location was still a strategic passage along the eastern seacoast of Greece for any form of military operation, the ceremony's deeply symbolic character indicated the new geopolitical alliances: the United States acted as a guarantor of safety from any invasion by Greece's communist northern neighbors. But the United States' new "weapon" to defend this significant location was the boost to agricultural productivity: this tool would win the new ideological and economic battle over an area where the ancient Greeks and more recently the British had been defeated. And the MP would consolidate this new state of affairs with the economic prosperity it promised to the area.

While the above newsreel reported on the MP's actuality, the documentary film *Victory at Thermopylae* offered a more structured narrative about the MP-supported boost of agriculture in the area. If the title created the expectation of an educational film about ancient military history, its subject matter is actually the modernization of Greek agriculture—an MP-funded experiment in soil reclamation that had started in the nearby village of Anthele in 1949. The title and one of the first lines of the voice-over commentary set the tone of a transhistorical narrative: "Anthele is a small village on the delta of [the] Sperchios River near Thermopylae, where the ancient Greeks suffered one of the classic defeats in history." After an introduction to the village's traditional setting and views of arid land, American engineers arrive and negotiate with the villagers a plan of collaboration to drain the land of its sea salts so that, by the end of the film's ten minutes, the plain yields its first harvest of rice, and the name of the American engineer leading the project (Walter Packard) adorns the village's central street (Fig. 18.1).

This MP documentary thus bears the word "victory" in its title in a self-congratulatory way. The implication is that Greek agriculture has "won the battle" thanks to American engineering ingenuity. Unlike the Persians and the Germans,

FIGURE 18.1. The last shot of *Victory at Thermopylae* features a road sign at the central square of Anthele inscribed with the name of the lead US engineer, Walter Packard, in both Greek and English.

the United States is represented not as invader but as ally-engineer, helping to boost the local and national economy. Considering that Walter Packard was a real agricultural engineer, and a former director of the New Deal's Resettlement Administration with a reputation as a "New Dealer" committed to "cooperative commonwealth," the film acquires undertones of a New Deal view of reconstruction, especially in the scenes depicting communal efforts.[34] But in *Victory at Thermopylae* the political agenda is dictated by the need for post-civil-war reeducation about the benefits of reconciliation for the good of productivity and the national economy, which ultimately will guarantee Greece's strength.

Very little is known about the filmmaker, David Kurland, but his style seems to follow in the steps of Pare Lorentz and the 1930s New Deal documentaries as well as the British Documentary Movement's post–World War II foray into international politics with films like *The World Is Rich* (1947). In all cases, the audiovisual rhetoric mobilizes scientific knowledge to propose solutions and to visualize change through a dynamic mode of editing and optimistic voice-over commentary. *Victory at Thermopylae* evidences Kurland's ambition to shape his material creatively, as in his earlier MP documentary about Italy, *Village without Words*. Historian and curator of MP films Rainer Rother has called this latter film a "model Marshall Plan film . . . which takes on the form of a hymn . . . of the aid program," since it is one of the very few MP films without voice-over narration: the editing and Alberico Vitalini's lyrical music carry the message of reconstruction.[35]

Similarly, Vitalini's composition for *Victory at Thermopylae* aims for an emotional response, to stir exhilarating feelings that the MP aid would lift the village of Anthele out of poverty and into productivity and prosperity. Hence Walter Packard's engineering work is presented as the first real *victory* taking place at the historic location of Thermopylae. At the place where both the three hundred Spartans in ancient times and British Commonwealth troops in recent historical memory fought but were ultimately defeated, the MP aid brings a victorious change to the landscape and the agricultural economy—developments that will guarantee Greece's geopolitical alliance with the so-called free world.

With economic editing and narration, the film conflates three temporalities: the present tense of the MP-aided reconstruction process; the very recent history (German occupation and civil war); and the country's ancient history. The evocation of the ancient battle of Thermopylae is the film's ideological *punctum*. Within the context of the early stages of the Cold War, classical antiquity was perceived through a dual perspective: as an apolitical cultural terrain, potent enough to conjure up sentiments of national and trans-European unity; and as what political scientist Alexander Kazamias has called "a Greek version of anti-communism" exploited by the royalist, right-wing government to promote a new discourse of "national mindedness."[36] *Victory at Thermopylae*'s evocation of the classical past to promote the unity of a rural community had a topical resonance: the civil war had been fought more intensely in small towns, remote areas, and mountainous villages (where the Democratic Army had its strongholds) than in the urban centers. References to the classical heritage of Greece in relation to an agricultural community's regeneration function as a kind of rhetorical glue, binding together visions of the country's past, present, and future to form a grand narrative that chimed with the official Greek propaganda for "national mindedness."

Most of the MP films about Greece (*The Marshall Plan at Work in Greece, Corinth Canal,* and *The Good Life*) reference classical antiquity's iconography, with views of the Acropolis, the Temple of Apollo at Corinth, and the archaeological sites of Dodoni and Knossos. Sequences of ancient Greece's heritage frame the narratives of each film's account of MP's beneficial impact on the Greek economy and health system and on Greek agriculture, while the voice-over commentaries are replete with exaltations of the universality of this heritage as the basis for the future of European cooperation.

Another MP film about Greece, *Island Odyssey,* expands this rhetoric even further. The film features the itinerary of a US boat carrying MP material aid and publicity exhibits as it visits the Greek islands and sets up open-air exhibitions and film screenings. Its narrative is punctuated by maps that highlight the country's crucial geopolitical position between the Eastern and Western Blocs: for example, an animated map-diagram traces the boat's trajectory, linking all the islands that received the MP aid and thus demonstrating the geo-spatial expansion of the United States influence in the area.

Island Odyssey is also a rare case of a reflexive film about the ways propaganda is localized and experienced by its target audience. The film is a publicity stunt, showing how positively the Greeks welcome the MP aid. It evidences the ideological uses of film exhibition strategies, and the promotion of cinema as one of the MP's most important vehicles for reconstruction. One of the film's key sequences features crowds gathering to watch the MP films, and the voice-over commentary narrates: "Of all the showboat offerings, the one most looked forward to is the outdoor movie."

It is striking that films feature prominently among the material aid arriving at the island—as necessities rather than entertainment. *Island Odyssey* includes a rather long sequence that documents how the MP boat's crew sets up an open-air screening during which crowds gather to watch a film narrated in Greek about the MP-aided reconstruction in France (Fig. 18.2). With this *mise-en-abyme* (a film within a film) sequence, *Island Odyssey* presents the illusion of a mirror by seeking to intensify the process through which actual audiences would identify with the ones that the film depicts. In doing so, it frames the eventhood of the screening of an MP film as a catalyst to the country's post-civil-war recovery from division.

The very title *Island Odyssey* invites comparisons with the Homeric epic. The voice-over explicitly states this: "[F]rom island to island renowned in legend and history, from port to port that once knew the tiny barges of Phoenician traders and the war galleys of the Athenian Republic, the showboat carries its cargo, a portable open-air exhibit telling the story of Marshall aid." It was no coincidence that the MP mission used a vessel named after the American philhellene Samuel Gridley Howe, who, inspired by Lord Byron, had supported the war for Greek independence and had sailed for Greece in 1824.

While close-ups of the boat's Greek and US flags waving next to each other accentuate the post–World War II American-Hellenic alliance, the film's rhetoric promotes an illusion of teleological continuity between the ancient past (the Athenian Republic) and contemporary occurrences (the United States as leader of the so-called free world). This echoes an established strategy of nineteenth-century Western European historians and ethnographers, who had laid the foundations of this myth—Greece as the historical and cultural fulcrum of European civilization—that popularized a Eurocentric perspective on the Mediterranean Sea by largely excluding from their European histories the neighboring Asian and North African cultures.[37] With uplifting tunes and commentary, *Island Odyssey* celebrates the efforts of the United States and Greece to collaborate for the protection of the geopolitical status quo of the area. The maps of Greece and diagrams that frame

FIGURE 18.2. A film within a film: *Island Odyssey* represents the open-air screening of MP films as a means by which the island's community is united.

the film's narrative become powerful reminders of the US strategy of containment—to preserve the Aegean Sea as part of the Western alliances that the MP aid helps to establish.

Island Odyssey is emblematic of the historical conjuncture within which the MP films were produced. Its reflexive emphasis on film's role in the reconstruction of Europe emphasizes how important the medium became during and after World War II to inter- and transnational propaganda. When the MP films were touring Europe's theatrical and nontheatrical screens, cinema effectively had a monopoly on audiovisual communication, before television's predominance from the mid-1950s onward. And in Greece, the MP films (as *Island Odyssey* emphatically shows) *did* "reach the hard-to-reach," becoming part and parcel of the MP economic aid, which had almost overnight replaced the US military intervention.

The MP films projected a vision of European history in the making by triggering narratives of an imagined future. When this is accomplished by means of nonfiction codes and conventions, such as the use of real locations, peoples, and national languages, the illusion of a tangible futurity becomes more poignant by comparison to fiction cinema. The MP documentaries' rhetoric projected the futurity of Europe's reconstruction, which was still full of both potentialities and instabilities. Even more than "a campaign of truth," the MP films could be likened to a campaign of imagined futures.

These films in a way complement the US *March of Time* newsreels also circulating on Western European screens at the time. If *March of Time* reported on the now and the immediate, the MP documentaries were imbued with the sense of the march of modern history, in which the MP aid was envisioned as a perpetuator of a Pax Americana, guaranteed by the powerful US military, whose presence continued to be visible in many European countries after World War II (Greece, Austria, Germany) and expanded across Western Europe with the 1949 North Atlantic Treaty Organization. In the case of the films about Greece, the country's classical heritage was projected as the semantic referent by which both its own future and "free" Europe's were measured. The films' audiovisual rhetoric articulated a self-conscious historical point of view, which propagated the MP aid as a teleological necessity that linked the country's distant past with the new future for the whole of Western Europe visualized on-screen.

ACKNOWLEDGMENTS

Research for this chapter was funded by the "Supporting Postdoctoral Researchers" action of the "Education and Lifelong Learning" program, financed by the European Union's National Strategic Research Framework (2007–13; http://www.espa.gr/en), administered in Greece by the Secretariat of Research and Technology and by the Research Office of Panteion University, which hosted the Fellowship. For advice and support, I thank the project's scientific adviser, Professor Yannis Skarpelos. For help with the archival research and viewing MP films, I thank Linda R. Christenson, the MP filmographer; and the staffs at the Imperial War Museum Film Archive, London; the EYE Film Archives, Amsterdam; and the Historical Archives of the Piraeus Bank Group Cultural Foundation, Athens.

NOTES

Epigraph: Edward Barrett, *Truth Is Our Weapon* (New York: Funk & Wagnalls, 1953), x.

1. Joseph Nye, *Soft Power: The Means to Success in World Politics* (New York: Public Affairs, 2004).

2. Throughout the essay, I use the abbreviation MP (Marshall Plan) to refer to the European Recovery Program (ERP).

3. Thomas Doherty, "A Symposium on the Marshall Plan Films," *Historical Journal of Film, Radio and Television* 25, no.1 (2005): 151. For the history of the MP films' "rediscovery," the process of compiling a filmography, and the films' exhibition since 1990, see Albert Hemsing, "The Marshall Plan's European Film Unit, 1948–55: A Memoir and Filmography," *Historical Journal of Film, Radio and Television* 14, no. 3 (1994): 269–97; Linda R. Christenson, *Marshall Plan Filmography,* accessed July 20, 2015, www .marshallfilms.org/mpfdetail.asp#acknowledgments; and Sandra Schulberg's website *Selling Democracy,* accessed July 20, 2015, www.sellingdemocracy.org/acknowledgements.html.

4. Key references about the complex origins of this civil war and its international dimensions are, respectively, David Close, *The Origins of the Greek Civil War* (London: Longman, 1995); and Amikam Nachmani, *International Intervention in the Greek Civil War* (New York: Praeger, 1990).

5. Sandra Schulberg, *Selling Democracy: Films of the Marshall Plan, 1948–53,* Touring Program, 2005–2010, Fourth Edition (New York: Schulberg Productions, 2008), 19.

6. The most comprehensive source of information for these films is the MP Filmography, compiled by Linda R. Christenson, accessed March 25, 2015, www.marshallfilms.org/mpf.asp. The main scholarly source on the MP Campaign of Information and Propaganda is Günter Bischof and Dieter Stiefel, eds. *Images of the Marshall Plan in Europe: Films, Photographs, Exhibits, Posters* (Innsbruck: StudienVerlag, 2009), and the book's companion website, accessed March 25, 2015, www.marshallplanimages.org.

7. For the high expectations of the MP films as the beginning of a European film movement, see Arthur Knight, "Documentary—Rallying Point for Europe," *Saturday Review,* February 17, 1951, 42; and the view of a British filmmaker who made films for the MP, quoted in James Piers Taylor, "Less Film Society—More Fleet Street: Peter Hopkinson," in *Shadows of Progress: Documentary Film in Post-War Britain,* ed. Patrick Russell and James Piers Taylor (London: BFI/Palgrave, 2010), 220.

8. For more details about the lift of the ban, see Hemsing, "Marshall Plan's European Film Unit," 276.

9. Bernadette Whelan, "Marshall Plan Publicity and Propaganda in Italy and Ireland, 1947–1951," *Historical Journal of Film, Radio and Television* 23, no. 4 (2003): 311–28; Regina M. Longo, "Between Documentary and Neorealism: Marshall Plan Films in Italy (1948–1955)," *California Italian Studies* 3, no. 2 (2012), accessed February 10, 2014, http://escholarship.org/uc/item/0dq0394d. On Germany, Austria, and Norway, see the respective chapters in Bischof and Stiefel, *Images of the Marshall Plan.* For a comparative study of four MP films (United Kingdom, France, Austria, and Germany), see Frank Mehring, "The Promises of 'Young Europe': Cultural Diplomacy, Cosmopolitanism, and Youth Culture in the Films of the Marshall Plan," *European Journal of American Studies* 7, no. 2 (2012), accessed April 10, 2015, http://ejas.revues.org/9701.

10. Stelios Zachariou, "The Dichotomy of Projecting the Marshall Plan in Greece: The Ideological Battle vs. the Rehabilitation Effort," in Bischof and Stiefel, *Images of the Marshall Plan,* 108.

11. Stelios Zachariou, "Struggle for Survival: American Aid and Greek Reconstruction," in *The Marshall Plan: Fifty Years After*, ed. Martin A. Schain (New York: Palgrave, 2001), 160.

12. The main source for identifying these films is the MP Filmography, accessed March 25, 2015, www.marshallfilms.org/mpf.asp. No director is credited for *Island Odyssey;* the only existing information is that it was produced by the ECA Paris for ECA Greece. Viewing copies for all nine documentaries about Greece are available in English at the US National Archives and Records Administration (NARA), and information about them is included on the aforementioned MP Filmography website. This is a comprehensive list of the extant MP films about Greece as far as the following criteria are met: viewing copies available; confirmed MP sponsorship; documentary mode of production. However, it is possible that more MP films about Greece and other European countries could be identified in the future. No copies have been located so far in Greek or with Greek subtitles. Digital files of a selection of MP films (including a few about Greece) dubbed in German and French can be viewed at the following online collections, accessed July 20, 2015: Deutsches Historisches Museum (DHM), www.dhm.de /filmarchiv/die-filme; Institut National de l'Audiovisuel (INA), www.ina.fr.

13. Tom Gunning, "Before Documentary: Early Nonfiction Films and the 'View' Aesthetic," in *Uncharted Territory: Essays on Early Nonfiction Film*, ed. Daan Hertogs and Nico De Klerk (Amsterdam: Stichting Nederlands Filmmuseum, 1997), 9.

14. For a succinct summary of this "cultural turn," see the introduction to Tony Shaw and Denise J. Youngblood, *Cinematic Cold War: The American and Soviet Struggle for Hearts and Minds* (Lawrence: University Press of Kansas, 2010).

15. For example, see, K. R. M. Short, ed., *Film and Radio Propaganda in World War II* (Knoxville: University of Tennessee Press, 1983).

16. David Ellwood, "'You Too Can Be Like Us: Selling the Marshall Plan," *History Today* 48 (October 1998): 33; David Ellwood, *Rebuilding Europe: Western Europe, American and Postwar Reconstruction* (London: Longman, 1992).

17. For a historiography of the MP propaganda campaign, see David Ellwood, "Film and the Marshall Plan," in Bischof and Stiefel, *Images of the Marshall Plan*, 61–68.

18. Edward Barrett, *Truth Is Our Weapon* (New York: Funk & Wagnalls Co., 1953), ix–x.

19. Lothar Wolff, quoted in Hemsing, "Marshall Plan's European Film Unit," 273.

20. For example, see Ramon Reichert, "Culture and Identity Politics: Narrative Strategies in Austrian Marshall Plan Films," in Bischof and Stiefel, *Images of the Marshall Plan*, 129–38; and on Italy, see Longo, "Between Documentary and Neorealism."

21. See, for example, John Foster Dulles, *War or Peace* (London: George G. Harrap & Co., 1950); and for examples of histories of the Cold War, which highlight the Greek Civil War as one of its defining moments, see the references in notes 22 and 24.

22. Robert J. McMahon, *The Cold War: A Very Short Introduction* (Oxford: Oxford University Press, 2003), 29.

23. Dulles, *War or Peace*, 161.

24. On the uses of napalm during the Greek Civil War, see Howard Jones, *A New Kind of War: America's Global Strategy and the Truman Doctrine in Greece* (New York: Oxford University Press, 1997), 127, 170, 187, 217–18.

25. A photograph of this parade is available at the online archive of the George C. Marshall Foundation, accessed May 10, 2015, http://marshallfoundation.org/library/photographs/millionth-ton-of-margcmo0174.

26. Emmett M. Essin, *Shavetails and Bell Sharps: The History of the U.S. Army Mule* (Lincoln: University of Nebraska Press, 1997), 194–95.

27. Schulberg, *Selling Democracy*, 10.

28. Georges Bataille, *The Accursed Share: An Essay on General Economy*, vol. 1, *Consumption* [1949], trans. Robert Hurley (New York: Zone Books, 1988), 172–73. France was the European country with the

most widespread anti-American sentiment in relation to the ERP. Brian Angus McKenzie explores how the pro-ERP campaign was deployed and received in France in his study *Remaking France: Americanization, Public Diplomacy, and the Marshall Plan* (New York: Bergham, 2005). McKenzie, however, makes no reference to Bataille's 1949 critique, which must have been widely read, considering that at the time he was as prominent an intellectual figure as Jean-Paul Sartre.

29. Hemsing, "Marshall Plan's European Film Unit," 274.

30. Economic Cooperation Administration 2nd Year, "Overseas Information Program," pamphlet of material presented to Congress, July 1950, 12. I thank the MP filmographer Linda R. Christenson for lending me a copy of this publication, which is available in a good range of libraries, according to www .worldcat.org.

31. Andreas Pagoulatos and Nikos Stabakis, "Greece," in *The Concise Routledge Encyclopedia of the Documentary Film,* ed. Ian Aitken (New York: Routledge, 2013), 325. This is the only account in English about the history of documentary film in Greece. For a more detailed exploration of the particular trends and Greek documentarians, see the journal article in Greek by Andreas Pagoulatos and Vassilis Spiliopoulos, "Astiko kai ypaithrio topio sto elliniko documentaire" (Urban and rural landscape in Greek documentary), *Outopia,* no. 47 (2001): 45–53, accessed December 20, 2014, http://pandemos .panteion.gr/index.php?lang=en&op=record&type=&page=0&match=&pid=iid:3540&q=&scope=&s ort=title&asc=.

32. Vrasidas Karalis, *A History of Greek Cinema* (New York: Continuum, 2012), 44–50. This tax was imposed with the personal intervention of Queen Frederica of Greece to fund her charity work setting up orphanages and school camps for the children of the civil war.

33. This newsreel features as part of the MP filmography, held at the NARA archives, accessed March 25, 2015, www.marshallfilms.org/filminfo.asp?id=NEWS/CTAG-1. On Peurifoy's interventionist politics, see James Edward Miller, *The United States and the Making of Modern Greece: History and Power, 1950–1974* (Chapel Hill: University of North Carolina Press, 2009), 35, 38, 41.

34. Rosemary Feuer, *Radical Unionism in the Midwest* (Urbana: University of Illinois Press, 2006), 165.

35. Rainer Rother, Synopsis of *Village without Words,* MP Films online collection of the Deutsches Historisches Museum, accessed May 10, 2015, www.dhm.de/filmarchiv/die-filme/village-without-words.

36. Alexander Kazamias, "Antiquity as Cold War Propaganda: The Political Uses of the Classical Past in Post-Civil War Greece," in *Re-Imagining the Past: Antiquity and Modern Greek Culture,* ed. Dimitris Tziovas (Oxford: Oxford University Press, 2014), 128.

37. Michael Herzfeld, *Ours Once More: Folklore, Ideology and the Making of Modern Greece* (Austin: University of Texas Press, 1982).

BIBLIOGRAPHY

Abel, Richard. *Americanizing the Movies and "Movie-Mad" Audiences, 1910–1914*. Berkeley: University of California Press, 2006.

Abrams, Bradley F. *The Struggle for the Soul of the Nation: Czech Culture and the Rise of Communism*. Lanham, MD: Rowman and Littlefield, 2004.

Ackerly, Spafford. "Trends in Mental Hygiene: An Interpretation." *Review of Educational Research* 13, no. 5 (1943): 416–21.

Acland, Charles. "Curtains, Carts and the Mobile Screen." *Screen* 50, no. 1 (2009): 148–66.

———. *Swift Viewing: The Popular Life of Subliminal Influence*. Durham, NC: Duke University Press, 2012.

Acland, Charles R., and Haidee Wasson. "Introduction: Utility and Cinema." In *Useful Cinema*, edited by Charles R. Acland and Haidee Wasson, 1–14. Durham, NC: Duke University Press, 2011.

———, eds. *Useful Cinema*. Durham, NC: Duke University Press, 2011.

Agamben, Giorgio. *State of Exception*. Translated by Kevin Attell. Chicago: University of Chicago Press, 2005.

Albarino, Richard. "How Many Film Sites Are There?" *Variety*, January 8, 1975, 7.

Alford, Matthew. "The Political Impact of the Department of Defense on Hollywood Cinema." *Quarterly Review of Film and Video* 33, no. 4 (2016): 332–47.

Alicoate, Jack, ed. "US Army Post Theaters." In *The 1945 Film Daily Year Book of Motion Pictures*. New York: Film Daily, 1945.

Anderson, Perry. "Imperium." *New Left Review* 81 (May–June 2013): 5–111.

Andrews, Owen C., Douglas Elliott, and Laurence L. Levin. *Vietnam: Images from Combat Photographers*. Washington, DC: Starwood Publishing, 1991.

Ansorge, Joseph Teboho. "Orientalism in the Machine." In *Orientalism and War*, edited by Tarak Barkawi and Keith Stanski, 129–50. London: Hurst and Company, 2012.

Appel, Kenneth, and Edward Strecker. *Psychiatry and Modern Warfare.* New York: Macmillan Company, 1945.

Arlen, Michael. *Living Room War.* New York: Syracuse University Press, 1997.

Armstrong, Charles K. "The Origins of North Korean Cinema: Art and Propaganda in the Democratic People's Republic." *Acta Koreana* 5, no. 1 (January 2002): 1–19.

Aron, Raymond. *Guerre et paix entre les nations.* Paris: Calman-Lévy, 1962.

Arrighi, Giovanni. *The Long Twentieth Century: Money, Power, and the Origins of Our Times.* London: Verso, 1994.

Arrigo, Jean Maria, and Richard V. Wagner. "Psychologists and Military Interrogators Rethink the Psychology of Torture." *Peace and Conflict* 13, no. 4 (2007): 393–98.

Atwan, Abdel Bari. *Islamic State: The Digital Caliphate.* London: Saqi, 2015.

Aussaresses, Paul. *The Battle of the Casbah: Terrorism and Counterterrorism in Algeria, 1955–1957.* New York: Enigma Books, 2002.

Bacevich, Andrew. *America's War for the Greater Middle East.* New York: Random House, 2016.

Bachrach. Susan D. *Liberation, 1945.* Edited by Stephen Goodell and Susan B. Bachrach. Washington, DC: United States Holocaust Memorial Museum, 1995. Exhibition catalog.

Balio, Tino. *Grand Design: Hollywood as a Modern Business Enterprise, 1930–1939.* Berkeley: University of California Press, 1993.

Barnouw, Erik. *Documentary: A History of the Non-Fiction Film.* Oxford: Oxford University Press, 1993.

Barrett, Edward. *Truth Is Our Weapon.* New York: Funk & Wagnalls Co., 1953.

Basinger, Jeanine. *The World War II Combat Film: Anatomy of a Genre.* Middletown, CT: Wesleyan University Press, 2003.

Bataille, Georges. *The Accursed Share: An Essay on General Economy.* Vol. 1, *Consumption.* 1949. Translated by Robert Hurley. New York: Zone Books, 1988.

Bateson, Gregory. "Cultural and Thematic Analysis of Fictional Films." *Transactions of the New York Academy of Sciences,* 2nd ser., 5, no. 4 (February 1943): 72–78.

———. "Some Systematic Approaches to the Study of Culture and Personality." *Character and Personality* 11, no. 1 (1942): 76–82.

Baudry, Jean-Louis. "Ideological Effects of the Basic Cinematographic Apparatus." In *Narrative, Apparatus, Ideology,* edited by Phil Rosen, 286–98. New York: Columbia University Press, 1986.

Baun, Capt. Richard A. "Soldiers with Cameras." *Army Digest,* March 1964, 51–53.

Beaver, Daniel. *Newton D. Baker and the American War Effort, 1917–1919.* Lincoln: University of Nebraska Press, 1966.

Beck, L. F. "Program of Films." *American Psychologist* 1, no. 10 (October 1946): 448–58.

———. "A Second Review of 16-Millimeter Films in Psychology and Allied Sciences." *Psychological Bulletin* 39, no. 1 (January 1942): 48–67.

Belmonte, Laura. *Selling the American Way: US Propaganda and the Cold War.* Philadelphia: University of Pennsylvania Press, 2008.

Belton, John. *Widescreen Cinema.* Cambridge, MA: Harvard University Press, 1992.

Benjamin, Medea. *Drone Warfare: Killing by Remote Control.* New York: OR Books, 2012.

Bennett, Tony. "Putting Policy into Cultural Studies." In *Cultural Studies,* edited by Lawrence Grossberg, Gary Nelson, and Paula Treichler, 23–34. New York: Routledge, 1992.

Bernays, Edward L. *Biography of an Idea: Memoirs of Public Relations Counsel Edward L. Bernays.* New York: Simon and Schuster, 1965.

———. *Propaganda.* New York: H. Liveright, 1928.

Bettis, Moody C., Daniel I. Malamud, and Rachel F. Malamud. "Deepening a Group's Insight into Human Relations: A Compilation of Aids." *Journal of Clinical Psychology* 5 (1949): 114–22.

Bignardi, Irene. "The Making of the *Battle of Algiers.*" *Cineaste* 25, no. 2 (2000): 14–22.

———. *Memorie estorte a uno smemorato: Vita di Gillo Pontecorvo.* Milan: Feltrinelli, 1999.

Binder, Werner. *Abu Ghraib und die Folgen: Ein Skandal als ikonische Wende im Krieg gegen den Terror.* Bielefeld: transcript, 2014.

Bischof, Günter, and Dieter Stiefel, eds. *Images of the Marshall Plan in Europe: Films, Photographs, Exhibits, Posters.* Innsbruck: StudienVerlag, 2009. Accessed March 25, 2015. www.marshallplanimages.org.

Bishop, Robert Lee. "The Overseas Branch of the Office of War Information." PhD diss., University of Wisconsin, 1966.

Bjork, Ulf Jonas. "The US Commerce Department Aids Hollywood Exports, 1921–1933." *Historian* 62, no. 3 (March 2000): 575–88.

Black, Gregory D., and Clayton R. Koppes. "OWI Goes to the Movies: The Bureau of Intelligence's Criticism of Hollywood, 1942–43." *Prologue* 6, no. 1 (1974): 44–59.

Bláhová, Jindřiška. "A Tough Job for Donald Duck: Hollywood, Czechoslovakia, and Selling Films behind the Iron Curtain, 1944–1951." Ph.D. diss., University of East Anglia, UK, 2010.

Blum, William. *Killing Hope: US Military and CIA Interventions since WWII.* New York: Zed Books, 2003.

Boorstin, Daniel. *The Image: A Guide to Pseudo-Events in America.* New York: Atheneum, 1971.

Braceland, Francis J. "Psychiatric Lessons from World War II." *American Journal of Psychiatry* 103, no. 5 (1947): 587–593.

Braun, Marta. *Picturing Time: The Work of Etienne-Jules Marey (1830–1904).* Chicago: University of Chicago Press, 1992.

Braverman, Harry. *Labor and Monopoly Capital: The Degradation of Work in the Twentieth Century.* New York: Monthly Review Press, 1974.

Brinch, Sara, and Gunnar Iversen. *Virkelighetsbilder: Norsk dokumentarfilm gjennom hundre år.* Oslo: Universitetsforlaget, 2001.

Brinkley, Alan. "World War II and American Liberalism." In *The War in American Culture: Society and Consciousness during World War II,* edited by Lewis A. Erenberg and Susan E. Hirsch, 313–30. Chicago: University of Chicago Press, 1996.

Brownell, Kathryn Cramer. *Showbiz Politics: Hollywood in American Political Life.* Chapel Hill: University of North Carolina Press, 2014.

Brownlow, Kevin. *The War, the West, and the Wilderness.* New York: Alfred Knopf, 1978.

Bryant, Chad. *Prague in Black: Czech Nationalism and Nazi Rule.* Cambridge, MA: Harvard University Press, 2007.

Bush, Vannevar. "As We May Think." *Atlantic Monthly,* July 1945, 101–8.

Caillé, Patricia. "The Illegitimate Legitimacy of *The Battle of Algiers* in French Film Culture." *Interventions: International Journal of Postcolonial Studies* 9, no. 3 (2007): 371–88.

Cairns, John C. "Algeria: The Last Ordeal." *International Journal* 17, no. 2 (1962): 87–97.

Calder, Kent E. *Embattled Garrisons: Comparative Base Politics and American Globalism.* Princeton, NJ: Princeton University Press, 2007.

Caldwell, John T. *Production Culture.* Durham, NC: Duke University Press, 2008.

Capozzola, Christopher. *Uncle Sam Wants You: World War I and the Making of the Modern American Citizen.* Oxford: Oxford University Press, 2008.

Carey, James W. *Communication as Culture: Essays on Media and Society.* Winchester, MA: Unwin Hyman, 1989.

Carruthers, Susan L. *The Media at War.* London: Palgrave Macmillan, 1999.

Castells, Manuel. *The Rise of Network Society.* 2nd ed. Oxford: Blackwell, 2000.

Ceplair, Larry. *Anti-Communism in Twentieth Century America: A Critical History.* Santa Barbara, CA: Prager, 2011.

Cha, Jae Young. "Media Control and Propaganda in Occupied Korea, 1945–1948: Toward an Origin of Cultural Imperialism." PhD diss., University of Illinois at Urbana-Champaign, 1994.

Chomsky, Noam. *Media Control: The Spectacular Achievements of Propaganda.* New York: Seven Stories, 2002.

———. *Necessary Illusions: Thought Control in Democratic Societies.* London: Pluto Press, 1999.

Christenson, Linda R. *Marshall Plan Filmography.* Accessed July 20, 2015. www.marshallfilms .org/mpfdetail.asp#acknowledgments.

Clausewitz, Carl von. *On War.* Princeton, NJ: Princeton University Press, 1976.

———. *Vom Kriege: Hinterlassenes Werk des Generals Carl von Clausewitz.* 1832. 18th ed. Bonn: Dümmler, 1973.

Close, David. *The Origins of the Greek Civil War.* London: Longman, 1995.

Coatsworth, John. "The Cold War in Central America, 1975–1991." In *Cambridge History of the Cold War,* vol. 3, edited by Melvyn P. Leffler and Odd Arne Westad, 220–21. Cambridge: Cambridge University Press, 2012.

Cohen, Lizabeth. *A Consumer's Republic.* New York: Vintage Books, 2003.

Coles, Harry L., and Albert K. Weinberg. *Civil Affairs: Soldiers Become Governors.* United States Army in World War II. Washington, DC: Office of the Chief of Military History, Department of the Army, 1964.

Collins, Sue. "Bonding with the Crowd: Silent Film, Liveness, and the Public Sphere." In *Convergence Media History,* edited by Janet Staiger and Sabine Hake, 117–26. New York: Routledge, 2009.

———. "Film, Cultural Policy, and World War I Training Camps: Send Your Soldier to the Show with Smileage." *Film History: An International Journal* 26, no. 1 (2014): 1–49.

———. "Star Testimonials and Trailers: Mobilizing during World War I," *Cinema Journal* 57, no. 1 (2017): 46–70.

"Combat Psychiatry." Supplement, *Bulletin of the U.S. Army Medical Department* 9 (1949). Prepared under the direction of R. W. Bliss, Surgeon General. Washington, DC: Government Printing Office, 1949.

Conway, Martin. "Legacies of Exile: The Exile Governments in London during the Second World War and the Politics of Post-War Europe." In *Europe in Exile: European Exile Communities in Britain, 1940–1945,* edited by Martin Conway and José Gotovitch, 255–74. New York: Berghahn, 2001.

Cornish, Paul. "Machine Gun." In *International Encyclopedia of the First World War,* edited by Ute Daniel, Peter Gatrell, Oliver Janz, Heather Jones, Jennifer Keene, Alan Kramer, and Bill Nasson. Berlin: Freie Universität Berlin, 2014. Accessed October 22, 2016. doi: 10.15463/ie1418.10779.

Courtney, Susan. *Hollywood Fantasies of Miscegenation: Spectacular Narratives of Gender and Race.* Princeton, NJ: Princeton University Press, 2005.

———. *Split Screen Nation: Moving Images of American West and South.* New York: Oxford University Press, 2017.

Cowan, Michael. "From the Astonished Spectator to the Spectator in Movement: Exhibition Advertisements in 1920s Germany and Austria." *Canadian Journal of Film Studies* 23, no. 1 (2014): 2–29.

———. *Walter Ruttman and the Cinema of Multiplicity: Avant Garde, Advertising, Modernity.* Amsterdam: Amsterdam University Press, 2014.

Cowen, Deborah. *The Deadly Life of Logistics: Mapping Violence in Global Trade.* Minneapolis: University of Minnesota Press, 2014.

Crafton, Donald. *Before Mickey: The Animated Film, 1898–1928.* Cambridge, MA: MIT Press, 1982.

Creel, George. *How We Advertised America: The First Telling of the Amazing Story of the Committee on Public Information That Carried the Gospel of Americanism to Every Corner of the Globe.* New York: Harper and Brothers, 1920.

———. *Rebel at Large: Recollections of Fifty Crowded Years.* New York: G. P. Putnam's Sons, 1947.

Cripps, Thomas. *Making Movies Black: The Hollywood Message Movie from World War II to the Civil Rights Era.* Oxford: Oxford University Press, 1993.

Culbert, David, ed. *Film and Propaganda: A Documentary History.* 4 vols. Westport, CT: Greenwood Press, 1990.

Cull, Nicholas. *The Cold War and the United States Information Agency: American Propaganda and Public Diplomacy, 1945–1989.* New York and London: Cambridge University Press, 2008.

Cullather, Nicholas. *Operation PBSUCCESS: The United States and Guatemala, 1952–1954.* Washington DC: Center for the Study of Intelligence, 1994.

Cumings, Bruce. *The Origins of the Korean War: Liberation and the Emergence of Separate Regimes, 1945–1947.* Princeton, NJ: Princeton University Press, 1981.

Cunningham, Douglas. "Imaging/Imagining Air Force Identity: 'Hap' Arnold, Warner Bros., and the Formation of the USAAF First Motion Picture Unit." *Moving Image* 5, no.1 (Spring 2005): 95–124.

———. "Imagining Air Force Identity: Masculinity, Aeriality, and the Films of the US Army Air Forces First Motion Picture Unit." PhD diss., University of California, Berkeley, 2009.

Cunningham, Douglas A., and John C. Nelson, eds. *A Companion to the War Film.* Chichester, UK: John Wiley & Sons, 2016.

Curtis, Scott. "Images of Efficiency: The Films of Frank B. Gilbreth." In *Films That Work: Industrial Film and the Productivity of Media,* edited by Vinzenz Hediger and Patrick Vonderau, 85–99. Amsterdam: Amsterdam University Press, 2009.

———. *The Shape of Spectatorship: Art, Science, and Early Cinema in Germany.* New York: Columbia University Press, 2015.

Dawley, Alan. *Struggles for Justice: Social Responsibility and the Liberal State.* Cambridge, MA: Harvard University Press, 1991.

de Maistre, Joseph. *Lettres à un gentilhomme russe sur l'inquisition espagnole.* Lyon: J. B. Pélagaud, 1871.

DeBauche, Leslie Midkiff. *Reel Patriotism: The Movies and World War I.* Madison: University of Wisconsin Press, 1997.

Decherney, Peter. *Hollywood and the Culture Elite: How the Movies Became American.* New York: Columbia University Press, 2005.

deCordova, Richard. *Picture Personalities: The Emergence of the Star System in America.* Urbana: University of Illinois Press, 1990.

Del Tredici, Robert. *At Work in the Fields of the Bomb.* New York: Perennial, 1987.

DeMasters, Karen. "On the Map: New Life for a Theater Where War-Bound Officers Caught a Movie." *New York Times,* January 30, 2000, NJ3.

Der Derian, James. *Virtuous War: Mapping the Military-Industrial-Media-Entertainment Network.* Boulder, CO: Westview Press, 2001.

Dissanayake, Wimal. "Asian Cinema and the American Cultural Imaginary," *Theory, Culture & Society* 13, no. 4 (1996): 109–22.

Dmytryk, Edward. *Odd Man Out: A Memoir of the Hollywood Ten.* Carbondale: Southern Illinois University Press, 1996.

Doherty, Thomas. *Projections of War: Hollywood, American Culture, and World War II.* 1993. Rev. ed. New York: Columbia University Press, 1999.

———. "A Symposium on the Marshall Plan Films." *Historical Journal of Film, Radio and Television* 25, no. 1 (March 2005): 151–54.

Douglas, Susan J. *Inventing American Broadcasting, 1899–1922.* Baltimore: John Hopkins University Press, 1987.

Druick, Zoë. "UNESCO, Film, and Education: Mediating Postwar Paradigms of Communication." In *Useful Cinema,* edited by Charles R. Acland and Haidee Wasson, 81–102. Durham, NC: Duke University Press, 2011.

Drury, Horace B. *Scientific Management: A History and Criticism.* 1915. 3rd ed. New York: Longmans, Green & Co., 1922.

Dulles, John Foster. *War or Peace.* London: George G. Harrap & Co., 1950.

Durham, Weldon. *Liberty Theatres of the United States Army, 1917–1919.* Jefferson, NC: McFarland & Company, 2006.

Dyer, Richard. *Stars.* London: British Film Institute, 1986.

Earl, Edward, "The Political Image of American Actors, 1865–1920" PhD diss., University of Missouri, 1974.

Edgerton, Gary. "Revisiting the Recordings of Wars Past: Remembering the Documentary Trilogy of John Huston." In *Reflections in a Male Eye: John Huston and the American Experience,* edited by Gaylyn Studlar and David Desser, 33–62. Washington, DC: Smithsonian Institution Press, 1999.

Edwards, Richard. *Contested Terrain: The Transformation of the Workplace in the Twentieth Century.* New York: Basic Books, 1979.

Eggertsen, Lt. Claude A. "Education Home from the Wars." *Educational Administration & Supervision* 31 (1945): 483–94.

Elbl, Jindřich. "Pravda o našich filmových smlouvách." *Filmová Práce* 1, no. 23 (October 26, 1945): 5–7.

Elias, Norbert. *Studien über die Deutschen: Machtkämpfe und Habitusentwicklung im 19. und 20. Jahrhundert.* Frankfurt am Main: Suhrkamp, 1989.

Elkins, James. "Harold Edgerton's Rapatronic Photographs of Atomic Tests." *History of Photography* 28, no. 1 (Spring 2004): 74–81.

Ellwood, David. "Film and the Marshall Plan." In *Images of the Marshall Plan in Europe: Films, Photographs, Exhibits, Posters,* edited by Günter Bischof and Dieter Stiefel, 61–68. Innsbruck: StudienVerlag, 2009.

———. *Rebuilding Europe: Western Europe, American and Postwar Reconstruction.* London: Longman, 1992.

———. "'You Too Can Be Like Us': Selling the Marshall Plan." *History Today* 48, no. 10 (October 1998): 33–54.

Essin, Emmett M. *Shavetails and Bell Sharps: The History of the U.S. Army Mule.* Lincoln: University of Nebraska Press, 1997.

Etzkowitz, Henry. "The Making of an Entrepreneurial University: The Traffic among MIT, Industry and the Military, 1860–1960." In *Science, Technology and the Military,* edited by Everett Mendelsohn, Merritt Roe Smith, and Peter Weingart, 515–40. Boston: Kulwer Academic Publishers, 1988.

Ewen, Stuart. *PR! A Social History of Spin.* New York: Basic Books, 1996.

Fagelson, William Friedman. "Fighting Films: The Everyday Tactics of World War II Soldiers." *Cinema Journal* 40, no. 3 (Spring 2001): 94–112.

Fallows, James. *Blind into Baghdad: America's War in Iraq.* New York: Vintage, 2006.

Fanon, Frantz. *Œuvres.* Paris: La Découverte, 2011.

Fay, Jennifer. *Theaters of Occupation: Hollywood and the Reeducation of Postwar Germany.* 2nd ed. Minneapolis: University of Minnesota Press, 2008.

Ferenczi, Sándor, Karl Abraham, Ernst Simmel, and Ernest Jones. *Psychoanalysis and the War Neuroses.* Introduction by Sigmund Freud. London: International Psycho-Analytical Press, 1921.

Feuer, Jane. *The Hollywood Musical.* Bloomington: Indiana University Press, 1993.

Feuer, Rosemary. *Radical Unionism in the Midwest.* Urbana: University of Illinois Press, 2006.

Fieni, David. "Cinematic Checkpoints and Sovereign Time." *Journal of Post-Colonial Writing* 50, no.1 (2014): 6–18.

Finkel, David. *The Good Soldiers.* New York: Picador, 2009.

Fishman, Donald. "George Creel: Freedom of Speech, the Film Industry, and Censorship during World War I." *Free Speech Yearbook* 39 (2001): 34–56.

Foner, Philip S. *The Spanish-Cuban-American War and the Birth of American Imperialism, 1895–1902.* 2 vols. New York: Monthly Review Press, 1972.

Forsberg, Walter. "God Must Have Painted Those Pictures: Illuminating Auroratone's Lost History." *Incite!* no. 4 (Fall 2013). Accessed July 23, 2015. www.incite-online.net /forsberg4.html.

Fousek, John. *To Lead the Free World: American Nationalism and the Cultural Roots of the Cold War.* Chapel Hill: University of North Carolina Press, 2000.

Freedman, Des, and Daya Kishan Thussu. *Media and Terrorism: Global Perspectives.* London: Sage, 2012.

Frey, Marc. "Tools of Empire: Persuasion and the United States Modernizing Mission in Southeast Asia." *Diplomatic History* 27, no. 4 (September 2003): 543–68.

Fujitani, Takashi. "Nation, Blood, and Self-Determination." In *Race for Empire: Koreans as Japanese and Japanese as Americans during World War II,* 299–334. Berkeley: University of California Press, 2011. doi:10.1525/california/9780520262232.003.0008.

Galula, David. *Counterinsurgency Warfare: Theory and Practice.* Westport, CT: Praeger, 1964.

———. *Pacification in Algeria, 1956–1958.* Santa Monica, CA, and Arlington, VA: Rand, 2006.

Gary, Brett. *The Nervous Liberals: Propaganda Anxieties from World War I to the Cold War.* New York: Columbia University Press, 1999.

Gaycken, Oliver. *Devices of Curiosity: Early Cinema and Popular Science.* New York: Oxford University Press, 2015.

Gelb, Leslie H. "The Defense Budget: More, More, More." *New York Times,* June 15, 1975, E2.

Gerstle, Gary. "A State Both Strong and Weak." *American Historical Review* 115, no. 3 (June 2010): 779–85.

Gibson, James J., ed. *Motion Picture Testing and Research, Report.* Army Air Forces Aviation Psychology Program Research Reports 7. Washington, DC: Government Printing Office, 1947.

Gilbert, Charles. *American Financing of World War I.* Westport, CT: Greenwood Press, 1970.

Gilbreth, Frank B. "Applications of Motion Study: Its Use in Developing Best Methods of Work." *Management and Administration* 7, no. 9 (1924): 295–97.

Gilbreth, Frank B., and Lillian M. Gilbreth. *Applied Motion Study: A Collection of Papers on the Efficient Method to Industrial Preparedness.* New York: Sturgis & Walton Company, 1917.

———. "Motion Study for the Crippled Soldier." In *Applied Motion Study: A Collection of Papers on the Efficient Method to Industrial Preparedness,* 131–37. New York: Sturgis & Walton Company, 1917.

Gonzalez, Roberto J. "Towards Mercenary Anthropology? The New US Army Counterinsurgency Manual FM 3–24 and the Military-Anthropology Complex." *Anthropology Today* 23, no. 3 (2007): 14–19.

Good, Jennifer, Brigitte Lardinois, Paul Lowe, and Val Williams, eds. *Mythologizing the Vietnam War: Visual Culture and Mediated Memory.* Cambridge: Cambridge Scholars Publishing, 2014.

Goodman, Amy, and David Goodman. "The Hiroshima Cover-Up." *Baltimore Sun,* August 5, 2005. http://articles.baltimoresun.com/2005-08-05/news/0508050019_1_atomic-bombings-bomb-on-hiroshima-george-weller.

Goodrich, Leland M. *Korea: A Study of US Policy in the United Nations.* 1956. Reprint. New York: Council on Foreign Relations, Krause Reprint Co., 1972.

Graham, Laurel. "Lillian Gilbreth and the Mental Revolution at Macy's, 1925–1928." *Journal of Management History* 6, no. 7 (2000): 285–305.

Grandin, Greg. "The Liberal Traditions in the Americas: Rights, Sovereignty, and the Origins of Liberal Multilateralism." *American Historical Review* 117, no. 1 (February 2012): 68–91.

Greene, Ronald Walter. "Pastoral Exhibition: The YMCA Motion Picture Bureau and the Transition to 16mm, 1928–1939." In *Useful Cinema*, edited by Charles R. Acland and Haidee Wasson, 205–29. Durham, NC: Duke University Press, 2011.

Greenwald, Glen. *No Place to Hide: Edward Snowden, the NSA and the Surveillance State.* London: Hamish Hamilton, 2015.

Grierson, John. "First Principles of Documentary." In *The Documentary Film Reader: History, Theory, Criticism,* edited by Jonathan Kahana, 217–25. Oxford: Oxford University Press, 2016.

Grieveson, Lee. "The Cinema and the (Common) Wealth of Nations." In *Empire and Film,* edited by Lee Grieveson and Colin MacCabe, 73–114. London: British Film Institute, 2011.

———. *Cinema and the Wealth of Nations: Media, Capital, and the Liberal World System.* Berkeley: University of California Press, 2017.

———. "Cinema Studies and the Conduct of Conduct." In *Inventing Film Studies,* edited by Lee Grieveson and Haidee Wasson, 3–37. Durham, NC: Duke University Press, 2008.

———. "Stars and Audiences in Early American Cinema." *Screening the Past,* no. 14 (2002).

———. "The Work of Film in the Age of Fordist Mechanization." *Cinema Journal* 51, no. 3 (Spring 2012): 25–51.

Grieveson, Lee, and Colin MacCabe, eds. *Empire and Film.* London: Palgrave Macmillan, 2011.

———, eds. *Film and the End of Empire.* London: Palgrave Macmillan, 2011.

Griffin, John D. M., and William Line. "Trends in Mental Hygiene." *Review of Educational Research* 16, no. 5 (1946): 394–400.

Griffin, Michael. "Media Images of War." *Media, War, and Conflict* 3, no. 1 (2010): 7–41.

Griffith, Paddy. *Battle Tactics of the Western Front: The British Army's Art of Attack, 1916–18.* New Haven, CT: Yale University Press, 1994.

Griffith, Richard. "Films at the Fair." In *The Documentary Film Reader: History, Theory, Criticism,* edited by Jonathan Kahana, 312–21. Oxford: Oxford University Press, 2016.

Grob, Gerald N. *From Asylum to Community: Mental Health Policy in Modern America.* Princeton, NJ: Princeton University Press, 2014.

———. *The Mad among Us: A History of the Care of America's Mentally Ill.* New York: Free Press, 1994.

———. *Mental Illness and American Society, 1875–1940.* Princeton, NJ: Princeton University Press, 1983.

Gronke, Paul, and Darjus Rejali. "US Public Opinion on Torture, 2001–2009." *Political Science and Politics* 43, no. 3 (2010): 437–44.

Grotelueschen, Mark E. "Warfare 1917–1918 (USA)." In *International Encyclopedia of the First World War,* edited by Ute Daniel, Peter Gatrell, Oliver Janz, Heather Jones, Jennifer Keene, Alan Kramer, and Bill Nasson. Berlin: Freie Universität Berlin, 2014. Accessed October 22, 2016. doi: 10.15463/ie1418.10021.

Gullace, Nicoletta F. "Barbaric Anti-Modernism: Representations of the 'Hun' in Britain, North America, Australia, and Beyond." In *Picture This: World War I and Visual Culture,* edited by Pearl James, 61–78. Lincoln: University of Nebraska Press, 2009.

Gunning, Tom. "Before Documentary: Early Nonfiction Films and the 'View' Aesthetic." In *Uncharted Territory: Essays on Early Nonfiction Film*, edited by Daan Hertogs and Nico De Klerk. Amsterdam: Stichting Nederlands Filmmuseum, 1997.

Habgood, Carol A., and Marcia Skaer. *One Hundred Years of Service: A History of the Army and Air Force Exchange Service, 1895 to 1995*. Dallas: Army & Air Force Exchange Service, 1994.

Haddow, Robert H. *Pavilions of Plenty: Exhibiting American Culture Abroad in the 1950s*. Washington, DC: Smithsonian Institution Press, 1997.

Hafsteinsson, Sigurjón Baldur, and Tinna Grétarsdóttir. "Screening Propaganda: The Reception of Soviet and American Film Screenings in Rural Iceland, 1950–1975." *Film History* 23, no. 4 (2011): 361–75.

Hales, Peter B. "The Atomic Sublime." *American Studies* 32, no. 1 (1991): 6–31.

———. *Outside the Gates of Eden: The Dream of America from Hiroshima to Now*. Chicago: University of Chicago Press, 2014.

Hallin, Daniel C. *The Uncensored War: The Media and Vietnam*. Oxford: Oxford University Press, 1986. Reprint, Berkeley: University of California Press, 1989.

Halpern, Sue. "Virtual Iraq: Using Simulation to Treat a New Generation of Traumatized Veterans." *New Yorker*, May 19, 2008. Accessed August 10, 2015. www.newyorker.com /magazine/2008/05/19/virtual-iraq.

Hamilton, Kevin, and Ned O'Gorman. "At the Interface: The Loaded Rhetorical Gestures of Nuclear Legitimacy and Illegitimacy." *Communication and Critical/Cultural Studies* 8, no. 1 (2011): 41–66.

———. "Filming a Nuclear State: The USAF's Lookout Mountain Laboratory." In *A Companion to the War Film*, edited by Douglas A. Cunningham and John C. Nelson, 129–49. Chichester, UK: John Wiley & Sons, 2016.

———. "Visualities of Strategic Vision: Lookout Mountain Laboratory and the Deterrent State from Nuclear Tests to Vietnam." *Visual Studies* 30, no. 2 (2015): 195–208.

Han'guk Yŏngsang Charyowŏn [Korean Film Archive], ed. *Sinmun kisa ro pon Chosŏn yŏnghwa, 1945–1957* [Korean cinema seen from the news reports]. Han'guk yŏnghwa charyo ch'ongso. Ch'op'an. Seoul: Konggan kwa Saramdŭl, 2004.

Harvey, David. *The New Imperialism*. Oxford: Oxford University Press, 2003.

———. *Spaces of Global Capitalism: Towards a Theory of Uneven Capitalist Development*. London: Verso, 2006.

Headrick, Daniel R. *The Invisible Weapon: Telecommunications and International Politics, 1851–1945*. New York: Oxford University Press, 1991.

Hediger, Vinzenz. "Von Hollywood lernen heißt führen lernen." *Montage AV* 15, no. 2 (2006): 139–52.

Hediger, Vinzenz, and Patrick Vonderau, eds. *Films That Work: Industrial Film and the Productivity of Media*. Amsterdam: Amsterdam University Press, 2009.

Hemsing, Albert. "The Marshall Plan's European Film Unit, 1948–55: A Memoir and Filmography." *Historical Journal of Film, Radio and Television* 14, no. 3 (1994): 269–97.

Herman, Ellen. *The Romance of American Psychology: Political Culture in the Age of Experts*. Berkeley: University of California Press, 1995.

Herr, Michael. *Dispatches*. New York: Alfred A. Knopf, 1977.

Herzfeld, Michael. *Ours Once More: Folklore, Ideology and the Making of Modern Greece.* Austin: University of Texas Press, 1982.

Higham, John. *Strangers in the Land: Patterns of American Nativism, 1860–1925.* 2nd ed. New Brunswick, NJ: Rutgers University Press, 1992.

Higson, Andrew, and Richard Maltby, eds. *"Film Europe" and "Film America": Cinema, Commerce and Cultural Exchange, 1920–1939.* Exeter, UK: University of Exeter Press, 1999.

Hilmes, Michelle. *Hollywood and Broadcasting: From Radio to Cable.* Urbana: University of Illinois Press, 1990.

Hindson, Catherine. *London's West End Actresses and the Origins of Celebrity Charity, 1880–1920.* Iowa City: University of Iowa Press, 2016.

Hoberman, J. *The Dreamlife: Movies, Media, and the Mythology of the Sixties.* New York: New Press, 2003.

Hoddeson, Lillian, Paul W. Henriksen, Roger A. Meade, and Catherine Westfall. *Critical Assembly: A Technical History of Los Alamos during the Oppenheimer Years, 1943–1945.* Cambridge: Cambridge University Press, 2004.

Hogan, Michael. *A Cross of Iron: Harry S. Truman and the Origins of the National Security State, 1945–1954.* Cambridge: Cambridge University Press, 1998.

Hoof, Florian. *Angels of Efficiency: A Media History of Consulting.* New York: Oxford University Press, forthcoming.

———. *Engel der Effizienz: Eine Mediengeschichte der Unternehmensberatung, 1880–1930.* Konstanz, Germany: Konstanz University Press, 2015.

——— "'The One Best Way': Bildgebende Verfahren der Ökonomie als strukturverändernder Innovationsschub der Managementtheorie ab 1860." *Montage AV* 15, no. 1 (2006): 123–38.

———. "'The Useful, the Bad and the Ugly': An Epistemological Perspective on Media-Based Education." In *Cultural Studies Meets TEFL in Graphic Novels, Film and Visual Culture,* edited by Daniela Elsner and Sissy Helff, 201–17. Berlin: LIT Verlag, 2013.

Horten, Gerd. *Radio Goes to War: The Cultural Politics of Propaganda during World War II.* Berkeley: University of California Press, 2003.

Horton, Donald, and Richard R. Wohl. "Mass Communication and Para-Social Interaction." *Psychiatry* 19 (1956): 215–29.

Hose, Wally. *Soundies.* St. Louis, MO: Wally's Multimedia LLC, 2007.

Hounshell, David. "The Evolution of Industrial Research in the United States." In *Engines of Innovation: U.S. Industrial Research at the End of an Era,* edited by Richard S. Rosenbloom and William J. Spencer, 13–85. Boston: Harvard Business School Press, 1996.

Isenberg, Michael T. *War on Film: The American Cinema and World War I, 1914–1941.* London: Associated University Press, 1981.

Ivens, Joris. "Making Documentary Films to Meet Today's Needs." *American Cinematographer* 23, no. 7 (July 1942): 298–333.

James, David E. *Allegories of Cinema.* Princeton, NJ: Princeton University Press, 1989.

———, ed. *To Free the Cinema: Jonas Mekas and the New York Underground.* Princeton, NJ: Princeton University Press, 1992.

Jarvie, Ian. *Hollywood's Overseas Campaign: The North Atlantic Movie Trade, 1920–1950.* New York: Cambridge University Press, 1992.

————. "The Postwar Economic Foreign Policy of the American Film Industry: Europe, 1945–1950." *Film History* 4, no. 4 (1990): 277–88.

Jenkins, Tricia. *The CIA in Hollywood: How the Agency Shapes Film and Television*. Austin: University of Texas Press, 2012.

————. "How the Central intelligence Agency Works with Hollywood: An Interview with Paul Barry, the CIA's New Entertainment Industry Liaison." *Media, Culture, and Society* 31, no. 3 (2009): 489–95.

Jones, Edgar, and Simon Wessely. *Shell Shock to PTSD: Military Psychiatry from 1900 to the Gulf War*. Maudsley Monographs 47. New York: Psychology Press, 2005.

Jones, Howard. *A New Kind of War: America's Global Strategy and the Truman Doctrine in Greece*. New York: Oxford University Press, 1997.

Jones, Maxwell, and J. M. Tanner. "The Clinical Characteristics, Treatments, and Rehabilitation of Repatriated Prisoners of War with Neurosis." *Journal of Neurology, Neurosurgery, and Psychiatry* 11, no. 1 (1948): 53–60.

Jowett, Garth. *Film, the Democratic Art: A Social History of American Film*. Boston: Little, Brown and Company, 1976.

Kahana, Jonathan. *Intelligence Work: The Politics of American Documentary*. New York: Columbia University Press, 2008.

Kahana, Jonathan, and Noah Tsika. "*Let There Be Light* and the Military Talking Picture." In *Remaking Reality: US Documentary Culture after 1945*, edited by Sara Blair, Joseph Entin, and Franny Nudelman. Chapel Hill: University of North Carolina Press, forthcoming.

Kahn, Herman. *On Thermonuclear War*. Princeton, NJ: Princeton University Press, 1960.

Kalyvas, Stathis N. *The Logic of Violence in Civil War*. Cambridge and New York: Cambridge University Press, 2006.

Kang, Sung Won, and Hugh Rockoff. "Capitalizing Patriotism: The Liberty Loans of World War I." *Financial History Review* 22, no. 1 (2015): 45–78.

Kaplan, Caren. "Precision Targets: GPS and the Militarization of US Consumer Identity." *American Quarterly* 58, no. 3 (2006): 693–713.

Kaplan, Fred. *The Insurgents: David Petraeus and the Plot to Change the American Way of War*. New York: Simon and Schuster, 2013.

————. "Vietnam! Vietnam! An Exclusive Report on John Ford's Propaganda Documentary for the USIA." *Cineaste* 7, no. 3 (Fall 1976): 20–23.

Karalis, Vrasidas. *A History of Greek Cinema*. New York: Continuum, 2012.

Kartchner, Fred D., and Ija N. Korner. "Use of Hypnosis in Treatment of Acute Combat Reactions." *American Journal of Psychiatry* 103, no. 5 (1947): 630–36.

Katz, Barry. "'Visual Presentation' and National Intelligence." *Design Issues* 12, no. 2 (Summer 1996): 3–21.

Katz, Elias. "Audio-Visual Aids for Mental Hygiene and Psychiatry." *Journal of Clinical Psychology* 3 (1947): 43–46.

————. "A Brief Survey of the Use of Motion Pictures for the Treatment of Neuropsychiatric Patients." *Psychiatric Quarterly* 20, no. 1 (March 1946): 204–16.

Katz, Elias, and H. E. Rubin. "Auroratone Films for the Treatment of Psychotic Depressions in an Army General Hospital." *Journal of Clinical Psychology* 2 (1946): 333–40.

Kaufman, Michael T. "What Does the Pentagon See in *Battle of Algiers*?" *New York Times*, September 7, 2003.

Kazamias, Alexander. "Antiquity as Cold War Propaganda: The Political Uses of the Classical Past in Post-Civil War Greece." In *Re-Imagining the Past: Antiquity and Modern Greek Culture,* edited by Dimitris Tziovas, 128–46. Oxford: Oxford University Press, 2014.

Kelley, Andrea. "'A Revolution in the Atmosphere': The Dynamics of Site and Screen in 1940s Soundies." *Cinema Journal* 54 no. 2 (Winter 2015): 72–93.

Kennedy, David M. *Over Here: The First World War and American Society.* New York: Oxford University Press, 1980.

Kilcullen, David. *The Accidental Guerilla: Fighting Small Wars in the Midst of a Big One.* New York: Oxford University Press, 2009.

———. *Blood Year: Islamic State and the Failures of the War on Terror.* London: Hurst, 2016.

——— *Counterinsurgency.* New York: Oxford University Press, 2010.

———. *Out of the Mountains: The Coming Age of the Urban Guerilla.* New York: Oxford University Press, 2013.

———. "Twenty-Eight Articles: Fundamentals of Company-Level Counterinsurgency." *Military Review* 83, no. 3 (May–June 2006): 103–8.

Kimble, James J. *Mobilizing the Home Front: War Bonds and Domestic Propaganda.* College Station: Texas A&M University Press, 2006.

Kinzer, Stephen. *All the Shah's Men: An American Coup and the Roots of Middle East Terror.* Hoboken, NJ: John Wiley, 2008.

Kitamura, Hiroshi. *Screening Enlightenment: Hollywood and the Cultural Reconstruction of Defeated Japan.* Ithaca, NY: Cornell University Press, 2010.

Kittler, Friedrich A. *Gramophone, Film, Typewriter.* Translated by Geoffrey Winthrop-Young and Michael Wutz. Stanford, CA: Stanford University Press, 1999.

Klein, Christina. *Cold War Orientalism: Asia in the Middlebrow Imagination, 1945–1961.* Berkeley: University of California Press, 2003.

Kohn, Stephen M. *American Political Prisoners: Prosecutions under the Espionage and Sedition Acts.* Westport, CT: Praeger, 1994.

Koistinen, Paul A. C. *Mobilizing for Modern War: The Political Economy of American Warfare, 1865–1919.* Lawrence: University Press of Kansas, 1997.

———. *State of War: The Political Economy of American Warfare, 1945–2011.* Lawrence: University Press of Kansas, 2012.

Koppes, Clayton R. "Regulating the Screen: The Office of War Information and the Production Code Administration." In *Boom and Bust: The American Cinema in the 1940s,* by Thomas Schatz, 262–81. Berkeley: University of California Press, 1999.

Koppes, Clayton R., and Gregory D. Black. *Hollywood Goes to War: How Politics, Profits and Propaganda Shaped World War II Movies.* New York: Free Press, 1987. Paperback printing, Berkeley: University of California Press, 1990.

———. "What to Show the World: The Office of War Information and Hollywood, 1942–1945." *Journal of American History* 64, no. 1 (1977): 87–105.

Koszarski, Richard. "Subway Commandos: Hollywood Filmmakers at the Signal Corps Photographic Center." *Film History* 14, nos. 3/4 (2002): 296–315.

Kozloff, Max, William Johnson, and Richard Corliss. "Shooting at Wars: Three Views." *Film Quarterly* 21, no. 2 (1967–68): 27–36.

Kraines, Samuel. "Psychiatric Orientation of Military Nonmedical Personnel." In *Manual of Military Neuropsychiatry,* edited by Harry C. Solomon and Paul I. Yakolev, 481–505. Philadelphia: W. B. Saunders Company, 1944.

Kramer, Paul A. *The Blood of Government: Race, Empire, the United States, and the Philippines.* Chapel Hill: University of North Carolina Press, 2006.

Krukones, James H. "Peacefully Coexisting on a Wide Screen: Kinopanorama vs. Cinerama, 1952–1966." *Studies in Russian and Soviet Cinema* 4, no. 3 (2010): 283–305.

Kryder, Daniel. *Divided Arsenal: Race and the American State during World War II.* New York: Cambridge University Press, 2000.

Kurth, James. "Military-Industrial Complex." In *The Oxford Companion to American Military History,* edited by John Whiteclay Chambers II, 440–42. Oxford: Oxford University Press, 1999.

Lair, Meredith H. *Armed with Abundance: Consumerism & Soldiering in the Vietnam War.* Chapel Hill: University of North Carolina Press, 2011.

Lammers, Dirk. "Digital Age Prompting Closing of Base Theaters." *Military Times,* January 20, 2013. http://archive.militarytimes.com/article/20130120/BENEFITS07/301200308 /Digital-age-prompting-closure-base-theaters.

LaMonica, Jeffrey. "Infantry." In *International Encyclopedia of the First World War,* edited by Ute Daniel, Peter Gatrell, Oliver Janz, Heather Jones, Jennifer Keene, Alan Kramer, and Bill Nasson. Berlin: Freie Universität Berlin, 2014. Accessed October 22, 2016. doi: 10.15463/ie1418.10773.

Lancaster, Jane. *Making Time: Lillian Moller Gilbreth—A Life beyond "Cheaper by the Dozen."* Lebanon, NH: Northeastern University Press, 2004.

Lasswell, Harold D. *Propaganda Technique in the World War.* New York: Alfred A. Knopf, 1927.

Laurie, Clayton D. *The Propaganda Warriors: America's Crusade against Nazi Germany.* Lawrence: University Press of Kansas, 1996.

Lavine, Lawrence. *Highbrow/Lowbrow: The Emergence of Cultural Hierarchy in America.* Cambridge, MA: Harvard University Press, 1988.

Lawrence, T. E. "Twenty-Seven Articles." *Arab Bulletin* 60, August 20, 1917.

Lazarsfeld, Paul F., Hazel Gaudet, and Bernard Berelson. *The People's Choice: How the Voter Makes Up His Mind in a Presidential Campaign.* New York: Duell, Sloan and Pearce, 1944.

Lazarsfeld, Paul F., and Elihu Katz. *Personal Influence: The Part Played by the People in the Flow of Mass Communications.* New York: Free Press, 1955.

Lazarsfeld, Paul F., and Robert K. Merton. "Mass Communication, Popular Taste, and Organized Social Action." In *The Communication of Ideas,* edited by L. Bryson, 95–118. New York: Harper, 1948.

Lazreg, Marnia. *Torture and the Twilight of Empire: From Algiers to Baghdad.* Princeton, NJ: Princeton University Press, 2007.

Leab, Daniel. *Orwell Subverted: The CIA and the Filming of "Animal Farm."* Philadelphia: Penn State University Press, 2007.

Ledbetter, James. *Unwarranted Influence: Dwight D. Eisenhower and the Military-Industrial Complex.* New Haven, CT: Yale University Press, 2011.

LeFeber, Walter. *The American Search for Opportunity, 1865–1913.* Vol. 2 of *The Cambridge History of American Foreign Relations.* Cambridge: Cambridge University Press, 1993.

Leffler, Melvin P. *A Preponderance of Power: National Security, the Truman Administration, and the Cold War.* Stanford, CA: Stanford University Press, 1992.

Leslie, Stuart W. *The Cold War and American Science: The Military-Industrial-Academic Complex at MIT and Stanford.* New York: Columbia University Press, 1994.

Lester, Peter. "'Four Cents to Sea': 16mm, the Royal Canadian Naval Film Society and the Mobilization of Entertainment." *Film History* 25, no. 4 (2013): 62–81.

———. "'Sweet Sixteen' Goes to War: Hollywood, the NAAF and 16mm Film Exhibition in Canada during World War II." *Canadian Journal of Film Studies* 19, no. 1 (Spring 2010): 2–19.

Lev, Peter. *The Fifties: Transforming the Screen, 1950–1959.* Berkeley: University of California Press, 2003.

Lewis, Adrian R. *The American Culture of War: The History of US Military Force from World II to Operation Iraqi Freedom.* London: Routledge, 2007.

Lewis, Jon. *Hollywood v. Hard Core: How the Struggle over Censorship Saved the Modern Film Industry.* New York: New York University Press, 2000.

Lifton, Robert J., and Greg Mitchell. *Hiroshima in America: Fifty Years of Denial.* New York: Putnam, 1995.

Light, Michael. *100 Suns.* New York: Knopf, 2003.

Lindstrom, Richard. "Science and Management: Popular Knowledge, Work, and Authority in the Twentieth-Century United States." PhD diss., Purdue University, 2000.

Lippit, Akira Mizuta. *Atomic Light (Shadow Optics).* Minneapolis: University of Minnesota Press, 2005.

Lippmann, Walter. *Liberty and the News.* New York: Harcourt, Brace and Howe, 1920.

———. *The Phantom Public.* New York: Harcourt, Brace and Co., 1925.

———. *Public Opinion.* New York: Free Press, 1997 [Harcourt Brace and Co., 1922].

Longo, Regina M. "Between Documentary and Neorealism: Marshall Plan Films in Italy (1948–1955)." *California Italian Studies* 3, no. 2 (2012). Accessed February 10, 2014. http://escholarship.org/uc/item/0dq0394d.

Loss, Christopher P. "Reading between Enemy Lines: Armed Services Editions and World War II." *Journal of Military History* 67, no. 3 (July 2003): 811–34.

Lovejoy, Alice. *Army Film and the Avant Garde: Cinema and Experimental Film in the Czechoslovak Military.* Bloomington: Indiana University Press, 2015.

Lukes, Igor. *On the Edge of the Cold War: American Diplomats and Spies in Postwar Prague.* New York: Oxford University Press, 2012.

MacCann, Richard Dyer. *The People's Films: A Political History of US Government Motion Pictures.* New York: Hasting House, 1973.

MacDougall, David. "Beyond Observational Cinema." In *Principles of Visual Anthropology,* 3rd ed., edited by Paul Hockings, 115–32. Berlin: Mouton de Gruyter, 2003.

MacGillivary, Scott, and Ted Okuda. *The Soundies Book: A Revised and Expanded Guide to the "Music Videos" of the 1940s.* New York: iUniverse, 2007.

Macpherson, C. B. *The Life and Times of Liberal Democracy.* Oxford: Oxford University Press, 1977.

Major, John. *Prize Possession: The United States and the Panama Canal, 1903–1979.* Cambridge: Cambridge University Press, 1993.

Malaparte, Curzio. *Tecnica del colpo di stato.* Milan: Adelphi, 2011.

Mandler, Peter. *Return from the Natives: How Margaret Mead Won the Second World War and Lost the Cold War*. New Haven, CT: Yale University Press, 2013.

Mann, Michael. *Incoherent Empire*. London: Verso, 2005.

Marchand, Roland. *Advertising the American Dream: Making Way for Modernity, 1920–1940*. Berkeley: University of California Press, 1985.

Mareš, Petr. "Politika a 'pohyblivé obrázky': Spor o dovoz amerických filmů do Československa po druhé světové válce." *Iluminace* 6, no. 1 (1994): 77–96.

Marker, Chris. "And Now This Is Cinerama." In *Cinéma 53 à travers le monde*, edited by Andre Bazin, Jacques Doniol-Valcroze, Gavin Lambert, Chris Marker, Jean Queval, and Jean-Louis Tallenay, 18–23. Paris: Les Editions du Cerf, 1954.

Marshall, P. David. *Celebrity and Power: Fame in Contemporary Culture*. Minneapolis: University of Minnesota Press, 1997.

Masco, Joseph. "'Survival Is Your Business': Engineering Ruins and Affect in Nuclear America." *Cultural Anthropology* 23, no. 2 (2008): 361–98.

Mastrangelo, Lisa. "World War I, Public Intellectuals, and the Four Minute Men: Convergent Ideals of Public Speaking and Civic Participation." *Rhetoric & Public Affairs* 12, no. 4 (2009): 607–33.

May, Lary. *The Big Tomorrow: Hollywood and the Politics of the American Way*. Chicago: University of Chicago Press, 2000.

———. *Screening Out the Past: The Birth of Mass Culture and the Motion Picture Industry*. Oxford: Oxford University Press, 1980.

Mayer, Jane. *The Dark Side: The Inside Story of How the War on Terror Turned into a War on American Ideals*. New York: Anchor Books, 2009.

McArthur, Benjamin. *Actors and American Culture, 1880–1920*. Iowa City: University of Iowa Press, 2000.

McCarthy, Anna. *Ambient Television*. Durham, NC: Duke University Press, 2001.

McCartin, Joseph A. *Labor's Great War: The Struggle for Industrial Democracy and the Origins of Modern American Labor Relations, 1912–1921*. Chapel Hill: University of North Carolina Press, 1997.

McCormick, Thomas J. *China Market: America's Quest for Informal Empire, 1893–1901*. Chicago: Quadrangle Books, 1967.

McKenzie, Brian Angus. *Remaking France: Americanization, Public Diplomacy, and the Marshall Plan*. New York: Bergham, 2005.

McLay, Robert N. *At War with PTSD: Battling Post Traumatic Stress Disorder with Virtual Reality*. Baltimore, MD: Johns Hopkins University Press, 2012.

McMahon, Robert J. *The Cold War: A Very Short Introduction*. Oxford: Oxford University Press, 2003.

Mead, Margaret, and Rhoda Métraux, eds. *The Study of Culture at a Distance*. Chicago: University of Chicago Press, 1953.

Medical Department of the United States Army in the World War. *Official History*. Vol. 10, *Neuropsychiatry*. Prepared under the direction of M. W. Ireland. Washington, DC: Government Printing Office, 1929.

Medical Department of the United States Army in World War II. *Neuropsychiatry in World War II*. Vol. 1, *Zone of the Interior*. Prepared under the direction of Leonard D. Heaton.

Edited by Robert J. Bernucci and Albert J. Glass. Washington, DC: Office of the Surgeon General Department US Army, 1966.

Medlin, Mary Jane. "A Community Project in Service Men's Recreation." *Journal of Health and Physical Education* 14 (1943): 362–402.

Mehring, Frank. "The Promises of 'Young Europe': Cultural Diplomacy, Cosmopolitanism, and Youth Culture in the Films of the Marshall Plan." *European Journal of American Studies* 7, no. 2 (2012). Accessed April 10, 2015. http://ejas.revues.org/9701.

Mendelsohn, Everett, Merritt Roe Smith, and Peter Weingart, eds. *Science, Technology and the Military.* Boston: Kulwer Academic Publishers, 1988.

Menninger, William. "Psychiatric Objectives in the Army." *American Journal of Psychiatry* 102, no. 1 (July 1945): 101–7.

Merton, Robert, Marjorie Fiske, and Alberta Curtis. *Mass Persuasion: The Social Psychology of a War Bond Drive.* New York: Harper & Brothers, 1946.

Messinger, Gary S. *The Battle for the Mind: War and Peace in the Era of Mass Communication.* Amherst: University of Massachusetts Press, 2011.

Mielke, Bob. "Rhetoric and Ideology in the Nuclear Test Documentary." *Film Quarterly* 58, no. 3 (2005): 28–37.

Miller, James Edward. *The United States and the Making of Modern Greece: History and Power, 1950–1974.* Chapel Hill: University of North Carolina Press, 2009.

Miller, Toby. "The Media-Military Industrial Complex." In *The Global Industrial Complex: Systems of Domination,* edited by Steven Best, Richard Kahn, Anthony J. Nocella II, and Peter McLaren, 97–116. Lanham, MD: Lexington Books, 2011.

Mills, Nick. *Combat Photographer.* Boston: Boston Publishing Company, 1983.

Min, Pyong Gap. *Koreans' Immigration to the U.S.: History and Contemporary Trends.* Research Report no. 3. New York: Research Center for Korean Community, Queens College of CUNY, January 27, 2011. Accessed May 31, 2012. www.qc.cuny.edu/Academics/Centers/RCKC/Documents/Koreans%20Immigration%20to%20the%20US.pdf.

Mitchell, Greg. "The Great Hiroshima Cover-up." Blog, *Nation.* August 3, 2011. www.thenation.com/blog/162543/great-hiroshima-cover.

Montessori, Maria. *The Montessori Method.* New York: Frederick A. Stokes Company, 1912.

Moreno, Jacob L. "Psychodrama and Therapeutic Motion Pictures." *Sociometry* 7 (1944): 230–44.

Morey, Anne. *Hollywood Outsiders: The Adaptation of the Film Industry, 1913–1934.* Minneapolis: University of Minnesota Press, 2003.

Morgan, C. A., III. "From *Let There Be Light* to *Shades of Grey:* The Construction of Authoritative Knowledge about Combat Fatigue (1945–48)." In *Signs of Life: Medicine and Cinema,* edited by Graeme Harper and Andrew Moor, 132–52. London: Wallflower Press, 2005.

Mowitt, John. "Fanon's 'guerre des ondes': Resisting the Call of Orientalism." In *Orientalism and War,* edited by Tarak Barkawi, and Keith Stanski, 223–44. London: Hurst and Company, 2012.

Munson, Edward L. *The Management of Men: A Handbook on the Systematic Development of Morale and the Control of Human Behavior.* New York: Henry Holt and Co., 1921.

Musser, Charles. *The Emergence of Cinema: The American Screen to 1907.* New York: Scribner's, 1990.

Nachmani, Amikam. *International Intervention in the Greek Civil War.* New York: Praeger, 1990.

Nagl, John A. *Learning to Eat Soup with a Knife: Counterinsurgency Lessons from Malaya and Vietnam.* Chicago: University of Chicago Press, 2002.

Nearing, Scott, and Joseph Freeman. *Dollar Diplomacy: A Study in American Imperialism.* New York: Allen and Unwin, 1925.

Nieland, Justus. *Happiness by Design: Modernism, Film, and Media in the Eames Era.* Minneapolis: University of Minnesota Press, forthcoming.

Nilsen, Sarah. *Projecting America, 1958: Film and Cultural Diplomacy at the Brussels World's Fair.* Jefferson, NC: McFarland & Company, 2011.

North, Edmund. "The Secondary or Psychological Phase of Training Films." *Journal of the Society for Motion Picture Engineers* 42, no. 2 (February 1944): 119.

Nye, Joseph. *Soft Power: The Means to Success in World Politics.* New York: Public Affairs, 2004.

O'Gorman, Ned, and Kevin Hamilton. "EG&G and the Deep Media of Timing, Firing, and Exposing." *Journal of War and Culture Studies* 9, no. 2 (May 2016): 182–201.

Olney, Laurence M. *The War Bond Story.* Washington, DC: U.S. Savings Bonds Division, 1971.

Orgeron, Devin, Marsha Orgeron, and Dan Streible, eds. *Learning with the Lights Off: Educational Film in the United States.* New York: Oxford University Press, 2012.

Ostherr, Kirsten. "Health Films, Cold War, and the Production of Patriotic Audiences: *The Body Fights Bacteria* (1948)." In *Useful Cinema,* edited by Charles R. Acland and Haidee Wasson, 103–24. Durham, NC: Duke University Press, 2011.

Ott, Julia C. *When Wall Street Met Main Street: The Quest for an Investor's Democracy.* Cambridge, MA: Harvard University Press, 2011.

———. "When Wall Street Met Main Street: The Quest for an Investors' Democracy and the Emergence of the Retail Investor in the United States, 1890–1930." *Enterprise & Society* 9, no. 4 (December 2008): 619–30.

Pagoulatos, Andreas, and Vassilis Spiliopoulos. "Astiko kai ypaithrio topio sto elliniko documentaire" [Urban and rural landscape in Greek documentary]. *Outopia,* no. 47 (2001): 45–53. Accessed December 20, 2014. http://pandemos.panteion.gr/index.php?lang=en&op=record&type=&page=0&match=&pid=iid:3540&q=&scope=&sort=title&asc=.

Pagoulatos, Andreas, and Nikos Stabakis. "Greece." In *The Concise Routledge Encyclopedia of the Documentary Film,* edited by Ian Aitken, 324–32. New York: Routledge, 2013.

Panitch, Leo, and Sam Gindin. *The Making of Global Capitalism: The Political Economy of American Empire.* London: Verso, 2013.

Paris, Leslie. "Small Mercies: Colleen Moore's Doll House and National Charity Tour." In *Acts of Possession: Collecting in America,* edited by Leah Dilworth, 190–220. New Brunswick, NJ: Rutgers University Press, 2003.

Park-Primiano, Sueyoung. "South Korean Cinema between the Wars: Screening Resistance and Containment under US Intervention and Influence, 1945–60." PhD diss., New York University, 2015.

Parks, Lisa, and Caren Kaplan, eds. *Life in the Age of Drones.* Durham, NC: Duke University Press, forthcoming.

Pierson, Michelle, David E. James, and Paul Arthur, eds. *Optic Antics: The Cinema of Ken Jacobs.* Oxford and New York: Oxford University Press, 2011.

Pizzitola, Louis. *Hearst over Hollywood: Power, Passion and Propaganda in the Movies.* New York: Columbia University Press, 2013.

Pols, Hans. "War Neurosis, Adjustment Problems in Veterans, and an Ill Nation: The Disciplinary Project of Military Psychiatry during and after World War II." In *The Self as Project: Politics and the Human Sciences,* edited by Greg Eghigian, Andreas Killen, and Christine Lauenberger, 72–92. Chicago: University of Chicago Press, 2007.

Ponce de Leon, Charles. *Self-Exposure: Human-Interest Journalism and the Emergence of Celebrity in America, 1890–1940.* Chapel Hill: University of North Carolina Press, 2002.

Price, Brian. "One Best Way: Frank and Lillian Gilbreth's Transformation of Scientific Management, 1885–1940." PhD diss., Purdue University, 1987.

Price, David H. "Gregory Bateson and the OSS: World War II and Bateson's Assessment of Applied Anthropology." *Human Organization* 57, no. 4 (Winter 1998): 379–84.

Quarles, Benjamin, and Bernard Nally, eds. *Taps for a Jim Crow Army.* Lexington: University Press of Kentucky, 1993.

Rabban, David M. *Free Speech in Its Forgotten Years.* Cambridge: Cambridge University Press, 1997.

Rabinbach, Anson. *The Human Motor: Energy, Fatigue, and the Origins of Modernity.* Berkeley: University of California Press, 1992.

Rabinowitz, Paula. "Wreckage upon Wreckage: History, Documentary and the Ruins of Memory." *History and Theory* 32, no. 2 (May 1993): 119–37.

Raimondo-Souto, H. Mario. *Motion Picture Photography: A History, 1891–1960.* Jefferson, NC: McFarland and Company, 2007.

Reeves, Nicholas. "Official British Film Propaganda." In *The First World War and Popular Cinema: 1914 to the Present,* edited by Michael Paris, 27–50. New Brunswick, NJ: Rutgers University Press, 2000.

Reichert, Ramon. "Culture and Identity Politics: Narrative Strategies in Austrian Marshall Plan Films." In *Images of the Marshall Plan in Europe: Films, Photographs, Exhibits, Posters,* edited by Günter Bischof and Dieter Stiefel, 129–38. Innsbruck: StudienVerlag, 2009.

Reid, Seerley, Anita Carpenter, and Annie Rose Daugherty. *U.S. Government Films for Public Educational Use.* Washington, DC: Government Printing Office, 1955.

Rice, Tom. *White Robes, Silver Screens: Movies and the Making of the Ku Klux Klan.* Bloomington: Indiana University Press, 2015.

Rich, Paul B. "Rossellini, Pontecorvo, and the Neorealist Cinema of Insurgency." *Small Wars and Insurgencies* 26, no. 4 (2015): 640–67.

Riegler, Thomas. "Gillo Pontecorvo's 'Dictatorship of the Truth'—A Legacy." *Studies in European Cinema* 6, no. 1 (2009): 47–62.

Robb, David L. *Operation Hollywood: How the Pentagon Shapes and Censors the Movies.* New York: Prometheus Books, 2004.

Rochet, Bénédicte. "Les actualités filmées, une arme de propagande opérante? Les initiatives du gouvernement belge entre 1940 et 1945." *Revue Belge d'Histoire Contemporaine* 34, nos. 1–2 (2009): 177–97.

Rogers, Ariel. "'Smothered in Baked Alaska': The Anxious Appeal of Widescreen Cinema." *Cinema Journal* 51, no. 3 (Spring 2012): 74–96.

Roholl, Marja. "Preparing for Victory: The U.S. Office of War Information Overseas Branch's Illustrated Magazines in the Netherlands and the Foundations for the American Century, 1944–1945." *European Journal of American Studies* 7, no. 2 (2012): 2–18.

Rojek, Chris. *Celebrity.* London: Reaktion Books, 2001.

Rollins, Peter C. "Frank Capra's *Why We Fight* Film Series and Our American Dream." *Journal of American Culture* 19, no. 4 (1996): 81–86.

Rome, Howard P. "Military Group Psychotherapy." *American Journal of Psychiatry* 101, no. 4 (1945): 494–97.

———. "Therapeutic Films and Group Psychotherapy." *Sociometry* 8, nos. 3/4 (1945): 247–54.

Rose, Nikolas. *Inventing Ourselves.* Cambridge: Cambridge University Press, 1998.

Rosen, Phil. *Change Mummified: Cinema, Historicity, Theory.* Minneapolis: University of Minnesota Press, 2001.

Rosenberg, Emily S. "Economic Interest and United States Foreign Policy." In *American Foreign Relations Reconsidered, 1890–1993*, edited by Gordon Martel, 37–49. London: Routledge, 1994.

———. *Financial Missionaries to the World: The Politics and Culture of Dollar Diplomacy, 1900–1930.* Cambridge, MA: Harvard University Press, 1999.

———. *Spreading the American Dream: American Economic and Cultural Expansion, 1890–1945.* New York: Hill and Wang, 1982.

Ross, Steven J. *Hollywood Left and Right: How Movie Stars Shaped American Politics.* New York: Oxford University Press, 2011.

———. *Working-Class Hollywood: Silent Film and the Shaping of Class in America.* Princeton, NJ: Princeton University Press, 1998.

Rumer, Thomas A. *The American Legion: An Official History, 1919–1989.* New York: M. Evans & Company, 1990.

Saldin, Robert P. *War, the American State, and Politics since 1898.* Cambridge: Cambridge University Press, 2011.

Salt, Barry. *Film Style and Technology.* London: Starword, 1992.

Sammond, Nicholas. "Picture This: Lillian Gilbreth's Industrial Cinema for the Home." *Camera Obscura* 21, no. 3 (2006): 103–32.

Sarasin, Philipp. "Der öffentlich sichtbare Körper: Vom Spektakel der Anatomie zu den 'Curiosités physiologiques.'" In *Physiologie und industrielle Gesellschaft*, edited by Philipp Sarasin and Jakob Tanner, 419–52. Frankfurt am Main: Suhrkamp, 1998.

Saul, Leon J., Howard Rome, and Edwin Leuser. "Desensitization in Combat Fatigue Patients." *American Journal of Psychiatry* 102, no. 4 (1946): 476–78.

Saunders, Dave. *Direct Cinema: Observational Documentary and the Politics of the Sixties.* New York: Wallflower Press, 2007.

Saunders, Frances Stonor. *The Cultural Cold War: the CIA and the World of Arts and Letters.* New York: New Press, 1999.

———. *Who Paid the Piper? The CIA and the Cultural Cold War.* London: Granta, 1999.

Sbardellati, John. *J. Edgar Hoover Goes to the Movies: The FBI and the Origins of Hollywood's Cold War.* Ithaca, NY: Cornell University Press, 2012.

Schatz, Thomas. *Boom and Bust: American Cinema in the 1940s.* Berkeley: University of California Press, 1999.

——. "The Motion Picture Industry during World War II." In *Boom and Bust,* 131–68. Berkeley: University of California Press, 1999.

——. "Wartime Stars, Genres, and Production Trends." In *Boom and Bust,* 203–61. Berkeley: University of California Press, 1999.

Schmitt, Carl. *Der Nomos der Erde im Völkerrecht des Jus Publicum Europaeum.* Berlin: Duncker & Humblot, 1950.

——. *Theorie des Partisanen: Zwischenbemerkung zum Begriff des Politischen.* Berlin: Duncker & Humblot, 1963.

Schoonover, Thomas D. *Uncle Sam's War of 1898 and the Origins of Globalization.* Lexington: University Press of Kentucky, 2013.

——. *The United States in Central America, 1860–1911: Episodes of Social Imperialism and Imperial Rivalry in the World System.* Durham, NC: Duke University Press, 1991.

Schulberg, Sandra. *Selling Democracy: Films of the Marshall Plan, 1948–1953.* Accessed July 20, 2015. www.sellingdemocracy.org/acknowledgements.html.

——. *Selling Democracy: Films of the Marshall Plan, 1948–53.* Touring Program, 2005–2010. 4th ed. New York: Schulberg Productions, 2008.

Schwartz, Louis A. "Group Psychotherapy in the War Neuroses." *American Journal of Psychiatry* 101, no. 4 (1945): 489–500.

Schwoch, James. *Global TV: New Media and the Cold War, 1946–69.* Chicago: University of Illinois Press, 2009.

Scott, Ian. "From Toscanini to Tennessee: Robert Riskin, the OWI and the Construction of American Propaganda in World War II." *Journal of American Studies* 40, no. 2 (2006): 347–66.

Segrave, Kerry. *Foreign Films in America: A History.* Jefferson, NC: McFarland and Company, 2004.

Sell, Mary Ann, and Wolfgang Sell. "View-Master in WWII: Military Training Reels." In *View-Master Memories,* edited by Mary Ann Sell, Wolfgang Sell, and Charley van Pelt, 229–31. 2000. 2nd printing. Maineville, OH: Mary Ann Sell and Wolfgang Sell, 2007.

Sennett, Richard. *The Fall of Public Man: On the Social Psychology of Capitalism.* New York: Random House, 1974.

Sharrett, Christopher. "9/11, the Useful Incident, and the Legacy of the Creel Committee." *Cinema Journal* 43, no. 4 (Summer 2004): 125–31.

Shaw, Tony, and Denise J. Youngblood. Introduction to *Cinematic Cold War: The American and Soviet Struggle for Hearts and Minds,* edited by Tony Shaw and Denise J. Youngblood. Lawrence: University Press of Kansas, 2010.

Shephard, Ben. *A War of Nerves: Soldiers and Psychiatrists in the Twentieth Century.* Cambridge, MA: Harvard University Press, 2001.

Short, K. R. M., ed. *Film and Radio Propaganda in World War II.* Knoxville: University of Tennessee Press, 1983.

Silbey, David J. *A War of Frontier and Empire: The Philippine-American War, 1898–1902.* New York: Hill and Wang, 2008.

Simmon, Scott. *The Invention of the Western Film: A Cultural History of the Genre's First Half Century.* Cambridge: Cambridge University Press, 2003.

Simonson, Mary. *Body Knowledge: Performance, Intermediality, and American Entertainment at the Turn of the Twentieth Century.* Oxford: Oxford University Press, 2013.

Sitney, P. Adams. *Visionary Film.* New York: Oxford University Press, 1974.

Sklar, Martin J. *The Corporate Reconstruction of American Capitalism, 1890–1916: The Market, the Law, and Politics.* Cambridge: Cambridge University Press, 1988.

Sklar, Robert. *Movie-Made America: A Cultural History of American Movies.* New York: Vintage Books, 1994.

Skopal, Pavel. "Filmy pana velvyslance: Československé filmové publikum a americký Státní department (1945–1960)." *Iluminace* 20, no. 3 (2008): 175–88.

Smith, John Kenly, Jr. "World War II and the Transformation of the American Chemical Industry." In *Science, Technology and the Military,* edited by Everett Mendelsohn, Merritt Roe Smith, and Peter Weingart, 307–22. Dordrecht, Netherlands: Kulwer Academic Publishers, 1988.

Smith, Murray. "*The Battle of Algiers:* Colonial Struggle and Collective Allegiance." In *Terrorism, Media, Liberation,* edited by John Slocum, 94–110. New Brunswick, NJ: Rutgers University Press, 2005.

Smith, Neil. *The Endgame of Globalization.* London: Routledge, 2005.

Smoodin, Eric. "Introduction: The History of Film History." In *Looking past the Screen,* edited by Jon Lewis and Eric Smoodin, 1–33. Durham, NC: Duke University Press, 2007.

Smyth, H. D. *Atomic Energy for Military Purposes; The Official Report on the Development of the Atomic Bomb under the Auspices of the United States Government, 1940–1945.* Princeton, NJ: Princeton University Press, 1945.

Sobchack, Vivian. "'Surge and Splendor': A Phenomenology of the Hollywood Historical Epic." *Representations,* no. 29 (Winter 1990): 24–49.

Spottiswoode, Raymond. *Film and Its Techniques.* Berkeley: University of California Press, 1951.

Spring, Joel. *Educating the Consumer Citizen: A History of the Marriage of Schools, Advertising and Media.* Mahwah, NJ: Lawrence Erlbaum Associates, 2003.

Springer, Claudia. "Military Propaganda: Defense Department Films from WWII and Vietnam." *Cultural Critique,* no. 3 (Spring 1986): 151–67.

Sproule, J. Michael. *Propaganda and Democracy: The American Experience of Media and Mass Persuasion.* New York: Cambridge University Press, 1997.

Sragow, Michael. *Victor Fleming: An American Movie Master.* New York: Pantheon Books, 2008.

Staiger, Janet. "Announcing Wares, Winning Patrons, Voicing Ideals: Thinking about the History and Theory of Film Advertising." *Cinema Journal* 29, no. 3 (Spring 1990): 3–31.

Steel, Ronald. *Walter Lippmann and the American Century.* Boston: Little, Brown, 1980.

Steimatsky, Noa. *Italian Locations: Reinhabiting the Past in Postwar Cinema.* Minneapolis: University of Minnesota Press, 2008.

Sterling, David L. "In Defense of Debs: The Lawyers and the Espionage Act Case." *Indiana Magazine of History* 83, no. 1 (March 1987): 17–42.

Studlar, Gaylyn. *This Mad Masquerade: Stardom and Masculinity in the Jazz Age.* New York: Columbia University Press, 1996.

Sturken, Marita. *Tangled Memories: The Vietnam War, the AIDS Epidemic, and the Politics of Remembering.* Berkeley: University of California Press, 1997.

Sullivan, Gerald. *Margaret Mead, Gregory Bateson, and Highland Bali: Fieldwork Photographs of Bayung Gedé, 1936–1939.* Chicago: University of Chicago Press, 1999.

Susman, Warren W. *Culture as History: The Transformation of American Society in the Twentieth Century.* New York: Pantheon, 1984.

Sutherland, Jonathan B. *African Americans at War: An Encyclopedia.* 2 vols. Santa Barbara, CA: ABC-CLIO, 2004.

Svan, Jennifer H. "Some AAFES Theaters Going Digital, but Others Shuttering." *Stars and Stripes,* February 14, 2013. www.stripes.com/military-life/some-aafes-theaters-going-digital-but-others-shuttering-1.207965.

Takahashi, Tess. "Experimental Screens in the 1960s and 1970s: The Site of Community." *Cinema Journal* 51, no. 2 (Winter 2012): 162–67.

Taylor, Bryan C. "Nuclear Pictures and Metapictures." *American Literary History* 9, no. 3 (1997): 567–97.

Taylor, Dwyn. "Military Architecture Goes Modern." *Military Engineer,* n.d. http://themilitaryengineer.com/index.php/item/184-military-architecture-goes-modern.

Taylor, Frederick W. *The Principles of Scientific Management.* Norwood, MA: Plimpton Press, 1911.

Taylor, Giles. "A Military Use for Widescreen Cinema: Training the Body through Immersive Media." *Velvet Light Trap* 72 (Fall 2013): 17–32.

Taylor, James Piers. "Less Film Society—More Fleet Street: Peter Hopkinson." In *Shadows of Progress: Documentary Film in Post-War Britain,* edited by Patrick Russell and James Piers Taylor. London: BFI/Palgrave, 2010.

Thompson, Kristin, and David Bordwell. *Film History: An Introduction.* 3rd ed. New York: McGraw-Hill, 2010.

Thomson, Charles Alexander Holmes. *Overseas Information Service of the United States Government.* International Propaganda and Communication. Washington, DC: Brookings Institution, 1948. Reprint, New York: Arno Press, 1972.

Thorpe, Rebecca. *The American Warfare State: The Domestic Politics of Military Spending.* Chicago: University of Chicago Press, 2014.

Trumpbour, John. *Selling Hollywood to the World: U.S. and European Struggles for Mastery of the Global Film Industry, 1920–1950.* New York: Cambridge University Press, 2002.

Tsika, Noah. "The Soldier's Circle: The Social Documentary and the American Military, 1940–1945." PhD diss., New York University, 2012.

Tureen, Louis L., and Martin Stein. "The Base Section Psychiatric Hospital." In "Combat Psychiatry," suppl., *Bulletin of the U.S. Army Medical Department* 9 (1949): 105–34.

Turner, Fred. *The Democratic Surround: Multimedia and American Liberalism from World War II to the Psychedelic Sixties.* Chicago: University of Chicago Press, 2013.

US Army and US Marine Corps. *Counterinsurgency Field Manual.* Chicago and London: University of Chicago Press, 2007.

US Bureau of Foreign and Domestic Commerce, Office of Industrial Trade. *World Trade in Commodities.* Vol. 9, pts. 9–24. Washington, DC: Government Printing Office, 1949.

US Senate, Special Committee Investigating the National Defense Program. *Investigation of the National Defense Program: Part 17, Army Commissions and Military Activity of Motion Picture Personnel.* 78th Cong., 1st sess., 1943. Washington, DC: Government Printing Office, 1943.

US Temporary National Economic Committee. "The Motion Picture Industry—A Pattern of Control." In *Investigation of Concentration of Economic Power.* Washington, DC: Government Printing Office, 1941.

US Treasury Department. *A History of the United States Savings Bond Program*. Washington, DC: Department of the Treasury, 1984.

Väliaho, Pasi. "Affectivity, Biopolitics and the Virtual Reality of War." *Theory, Culture & Society* 29, no. 2 (2012): 63–83.

Vasey, Ruth. *The World according to Hollywood, 1918–1939*. Madison: University of Wisconsin Press, 1997.

Vaughn, Stephen. *Holding Fast the Inner Lines: Democracy, Nationalism, and the Committee on Public Information*. Chapel Hill: University of North Carolina Press, 1980.

Veeser, Cyrus. *A World Safe for Capitalism: Dollar Diplomacy and America's Rise to Global Power*. New York: Columbia University Press, 2002.

Virilio, Paul. *War and Cinema: The Logistics of Perception*. Translated by Patrick Camiller. London and New York: Verso, 1989.

Wachtel, Nathan. *La logique des bûchers*. Paris: Editions du Seuil, 2009.

Waddis, Emma. "'One Foot in the Air?' Landscape in the Soviet and Russian Road Movie." In *Cinema and Landscape*, edited by Graeme Harper and Jonathan Rayner, 73–88. Bristol, UK, and Chicago: Intellect, 2010.

Walker, Janet. "Captive Images in the Traumatic Western: *The Searchers, Pursued, Once upon a Time in the West* and *Lone Star*." In *Westerns: Films through History*, edited by Janet Walker, New York: Routledge, 2001.

Waller, Fred. "The Archaeology of Cinerama." *Film History: An International Journal* 5, no. 3 (September 1993): 289–97.

———. "Cinerama Goes to War." In *New Screen Techniques*, edited by Martin Quigley, 119–26. Groton, MA: Quigley Publishing Company, 1953.

Waller, Gregory A. "Projecting the Promise of 16mm, 1935–45." In *Useful Cinema*, edited by Charles R. Acland and Haidee Wasson, 125–48. Durham, NC: Duke University Press, 2011.

War Activities Committee, Motion Picture Industry. *Movies at War*. Washington, DC: Government Printing Office, 1942–45.

Ward, Larry Wayne. *The Motion Picture Goes to War: The U.S. Government Film Effort during the World War I*. Ann Arbor, MI: UMI Research Press, 1985.

Wasson, Haidee. *Museum Movies: The Museum of Modern Art and the Birth of Art Cinema*. Berkeley: University of California Press, 2005.

———. "The Other Small Screen: Moving Images at New York's World Fair, 1939." *Canadian Journal of Film Studies* 21 no. 1 (Spring 2012): 81–103.

———. "Protocols of Portability." *Film History: An International Journal* 25, nos. 1–2 (2013): 236–47.

Weiner, Tim. *Legacy of Ashes: The History of the CIA*. London: Penguin, 2008.

Weller, George. *First into Nagasaki: The Censored Eyewitness Dispatches on Post-Atomic Japan and Its Prisoners of War*. Edited by Anthony Weller. New York: Crown Publishers, 2006.

Westad, Odd Arne. *The Global Cold War: Third World Interventions and the Making of Our Times*. New York: Cambridge University Press, 2005.

Weyeneth, Raymond R. "The Architecture of Racial Segregation: The Challenges of Preserving the Problematical Past." *Public Historian* 27, no. 4 (Fall 2005): 11–44.

Whelan, Bernadette. "Marshall Plan Publicity and Propaganda in Italy and Ireland, 1947–1951." *Historical Journal of Film, Radio and Television* 23, no. 4 (2003): 311–28.

Whissel, Kristen. *Picturing American Modernity: Traffic, Technology, and the Silent Cinema.* Durham, NC: Duke University Press, 2008.

Whitfield, Stephen J. "*Cine Qua Non:* The Political Import and Impact of *The Battle of Algiers.*" *Révue Lisa* 10, no. 1 (2012): 249–70.

Wilford, Hugh. *The Mighty Wurlitzer: How the CIA Played America.* Cambridge, MA: Harvard University Press, 2008.

Williams, Mark J. "History in a Flash: Notes on the Myth of TV 'Liveness.'" In *Collecting Visible Evidence,* edited by Jane Gaines and Michael Renov, Visible Evidence Series 6. Minneapolis: University of Minnesota Press, 1999.

Williams, Raymond. *Marxism and Literature.* New York: Oxford University Press, 1977.

———. *Television: Technology and Cultural Form.* London and New York: Routledge, 1974.

Williams, William Appleman. *The Tragedy of American Diplomacy.* New York: W. W. Norton, 2009.

Winkler, Allan M. *The Politics of Propaganda: The Office of War Information, 1942–1945.* New Haven, CT: Yale University Press, 1978.

Winston, Brian. *Claiming the Real II: Documentary; Grierson and Beyond.* London: Palgrave Macmillan, 2008.

Winter, Alison. "Film and the Construction of Memory in Psychoanalysis, 1940–1960." *Science in Context* 19, no. 1 (2006): 111–36.

———. *Memory: Fragments of a Modern History.* Chicago: University of Chicago Press, 2012.

Wood, Richard, ed. *Film and Propaganda in America: A Documentary History.* Vol. 1, *World War I.* Westport, CT: Greenwood Press, 1990.

Yecies, Brian, and Ae-Gyung Shim. *Korea's Occupied Cinemas, 1893–1948.* New York: Routledge, 2011.

Yoon, Tae-Jin. "Mass Media and the Reproduction of the International Order: Presentation of American Culture by American Television Programs Aired in Korea, 1970 to 1989." PhD diss., University of Minnesota, 1997.

Youngblood, Gene. *Expanded Cinema.* New York: E. P. Dutton & Co., 1970.

Zachariou, Stelios. "The Dichotomy of Projecting the Marshall Plan in Greece: The Ideological Battle vs. the Rehabilitation Effort." In *Images of the Marshall Plan in Europe: Films, Photographs, Exhibits, Posters,* edited by Günter Bischof and Dieter Stiefel, 107–13. Innsbruck: StudienVerlag, 2009.

———. "Struggle for Survival: American Aid and Greek Reconstruction." In *The Marshall Plan: Fifty Years After,* edited by Martin A. Schain, 153–163. New York: Palgrave, 2001.

Zdriluk, Beth. "Mary Pickford and Questions of National Identity during World War I." *Kinema,* Spring 2005. Accessed June 1, 2012. www.kinema.uwaterloo.ca/article.php?id=62&feature.

CONTRIBUTORS

NATHANIEL BRENNAN is a doctoral candidate in Cinema Studies at New York University, completing a dissertation on collaborations between the Museum of Modern Art Film Library and the federal government during World War II. His work has appeared in *Film History*, the *Journal of Chinese Cinemas* and the volumes *Global Neorealism: The Transnational History of a Film Style* and *American and Chinese-Language Cinemas: Examining Cultural Flows*.

SUE COLLINS is an associate professor in the Department of Humanities at Michigan Technological University. Her work on film history, war and propaganda, and celebrity has appeared in *Film History*, *Cinema Journal*, *Television & New Media*, and several edited volumes. She is currently working on the manuscript of a book to be titled *Calling All Stars: Hollywood, Cultural Labor, and the Politics of Authority during World War I*.

SUSAN COURTNEY is Professor of Film and Media Studies and English at the University of South Carolina, where she cofounded the Orphan Film Symposium. She is the author of *Split Screen Nation: Moving Images of the American West and South* and *Hollywood Fantasies of Miscegenation: Spectacular Narratives of Gender and Race, 1903-1967*.

LEE GRIEVESON is Professor of Media History at University College London. He is the author of *Policing Cinema: Movies and Censorship in Early Twentieth Century America* and *Cinema and the Wealth of Nations: Media, Capital, and the Liberal World System*. Grieveson has coedited several books, including most recently *Inventing Film Studies*, *Empire and Film*, and *Film and the End of Empire*.

VINZENZ HEDIGER is professor of cinema studies at Goethe-Universität Frankfurt am Main, where he directs the Research Training Program (Graduiertenkolleg) "Configurations of Film." His publications include *Films That Work: Industrial Cinema and the Productivity of Media* (with Patrick Vonderau) and *Nostalgia for the Coming Attraction: American*

Movie Trailers and the Culture of Film Consumption (forthcoming). He is a cofounder of NECS, the European Network for Cinema and Media Studies (www.necs.org), and was the founding editor of the *Zeitschrift für Medienwissenschaft* (www.zfmedienwissenschaft.de). He also served in the Swiss army in the summer of 1989, preparing for the hot phase of the Cold War. His last day of service was November 9, 1989.

FLORIAN HOOF is a postdoctoral researcher at the Institute for Advanced Study Media Cultures of Computer Simulation at Leuphana University Lüneburg. He is the author of *Engel der Effizienz: Eine Mediengeschichte der Unternehmensberatung*, a translation of which is forthcoming from Oxford University Press under the title *Angels of Efficiency: A Media History of Consulting*. Hoof is currently working on research focusing on a project to be called "Uncertainty in Digital Film Culture." Furthermore, he has initiated a project on film, media, and organizations (www.sociomateriality.de).

ANDREA KELLEY is Assistant Professor of Media Studies at Auburn University's School of Communication and Journalism. Her research examines American film history and screen technologies. She is the author of *Soundies Jukebox Films and the Shift to Small Screen Culture* (forthcoming). Her articles have appeared in *Cinema Journal, Continuum,* and *Spectator.*

KATERINA LOUKOPOULOU is Associate Lecturer at the London College of Communication of the University of the Arts London (UAL). Her publications include an essay in the collection *Learning with the Lights Off: Educational Film in the US* and journal articles in *Film History, Visual Culture in Britain,* and the *International Journal of Media and Cultural Politics.* Her current project, supported by a British Academy/Leverhulme Small Research Grant, investigates the relationship between pacifism and documentary cinema.

ALICE LOVEJOY is Associate Professor in the Department of Cultural Studies and Comparative Literature and the Moving Image Studies Program at the University of Minnesota. She is the author of *Army Film and the Avant Garde: Cinema and Experiment in the Czechoslovak Military,* which was awarded the MLA's Aldo and Jeanne Scaglione Prize for Studies in Slavic Languages and Literatures, and her writing has appeared in journals, including *Screen, The Moving Image,* and *Film Comment,* where she has also worked as an editor. Her current research examines cinema and the war economy during World War II, and the intertwined histories of a series of postwar children's film and media institutions.

ROSS MELNICK is Associate Professor of Film and Media Studies at University of California, Santa Barbara. His most recent book, *American Showman: Samuel "Roxy" Rothafel and the Birth of the Entertainment Industry,* received the Theatre Historical Society's Book of the Year award. His research focuses on film exhibition, historical media industries, radio history, global cinema, moving image journalism, and transnational Hollywood. His articles have been published in *Cinema Journal, Film History, Historical Journal of Film, Radio and Television,* and the *Moving Image,* and in several edited collections. For his research on Hollywood's global exhibition operations from 1923 to 2013, he was a National Endowment for the Humanities fellow in 2015-16 and an Academy Film Scholar in 2017.

JAMES PAASCHE is a Visiting Assistant Professor of Film and Media Studies in the Department of Communication and Theatre at DePauw University. He is a PhD candidate in the Department of Communication and Culture at Indiana University. His dissertation, "Point and Shoot: Military Filmmaking during the Vietnam War," examines institutional, amateur, and documentary films shot by US soldiers and other American citizens during the war. He is the former managing editor of the international journal *Film History.*

SUEYOUNG PARK-PRIMIANO is a Postdoctoral Teaching Fellow in Screen Studies at Ithaca College. She specializes in East Asian and American film history, postwar international cinema, and Cold War visual culture. She is a contributing author to *American Militarism on the Small Screen; Popular Culture in Asia: Memory, City, Celebrity; Directory of World Cinema: South Korea;* and the *Routledge Encyclopedia of Modernism.*

REBECCA PRIME is a writer, arts educator, and film historian whose publications include *Cinematic Homecomings: Exile and Return in Transnational Cinema* and *Hollywood Exiles in Europe: The Blacklist and Cold War Film Culture,* the latter of which received the Best First Book Award from the Society of Cinema and Media Studies.

TOM RICE is a Senior Lecturer in Film Studies at the University of St. Andrews. He is the author of *White Robes, Silver Screens: Movies and the Making of the Ku Klux Klan.* He previously worked as the senior researcher on a major project on British colonial film (www .colonialfilm.org.uk) and has written extensively on colonial, government, and educational film, as well as nontheatrical film in America. His articles have appeared in a number of journals, including *Film History, Journal of British Cinema and Television, Historical Journal of Film, Radio and Television,* and *Journal of American Studies.*

KAIA SCOTT is a PhD candidate in Film and Moving Image Studies at Concordia University in Montreal, where she has taught courses on visual culture in modern public spaces. She is currently working on her dissertation: "Cultures of the Damaged Mind: Military Psychiatric Cinema in the Second World War."

NOAH TSIKA is Assistant Professor of Media Studies at Queens College, CUNY. Among his books are *Nollywood Stars: Media and Migration in West Africa and the Diaspora; Pink 2.0: Encoding Queer Cinema on the Internet;* and *Traumatic Imprints: Cinema, Military Psychiatry, and the Aftermath of War* (forthcoming from the University of California Press).

HAIDEE WASSON is Professor of Film and Media at the School of Cinema, Concordia University, Montreal. She has taught also at the University of Minnesota and at Harvard University. She is author of the award-winning *Museum Movies: The Museum of Modern Art and the Birth of Art Cinema* and a coeditor of *Inventing Film Studies* (with Lee Grieveson) and of *Useful Cinema* (with Charles Acland). She edits the "Cultural Histories of Cinema" book series for the British Film Institute with Lee Grieveson-a series dedicated to analyzing cinema's expansive role in the complex social, economic, and political dynamics of the twentieth and twenty-first centuries. She serves on multiple editorial boards and has published and lectured widely on American film history, museums, and more recently film technology. She is currently completing a book on portable media, with a focus on film projectors.